Attitudes towards Sexuality in Judaism and Christianity in the Hellenistic Greco-Roman Era

Enoch, Levi, and Jubilees on Sexuality

The Dead Sea Scrolls on Sexuality

The Pseudepigrapha on Sexuality

THE PSEUDEPIGRAPHA
on
SEXUALITY

Attitudes towards Sexuality
in Apocalypses, Testaments, Legends,
Wisdom, and Related Literature

William Loader

with a contribution by
Ibolya Balla
on
Ben Sira / Sirach

WILLIAM B. EERDMANS PUBLISHING COMPANY
GRAND RAPIDS, MICHIGAN / CAMBRIDGE, U.K.

Published 2011 by
Wm. B. Eerdmans Publishing Co.
2140 Oak Industrial Drive N.E., Grand Rapids, Michigan 49505 /
P.O. Box 163, Cambridge CB3 9PU U.K.

Printed in the United States of America

16 15 14 13 12 11   7 6 5 4 3 2 1

ISBN 978-0-8028-6666-0

www.eerdmans.com

Contents

Acknowledgments   x

Introduction   1

PART ONE

ATTITUDES TOWARDS SEXUALITY IN
APOCALYPSES, TESTAMENTS, AND RELATED WRITINGS   4

1.1   Later Enoch Literature   4
       1.1.1   The Parables of Enoch (1 Enoch 37 – 71)   4
       1.1.2   2 Enoch   37
1.2   The Sibylline Oracles   56
       1.2.1   Sibylline Oracles Book 3   56
              1.2.1.1 Sib. Or. 3:97-349, 489-829   56
              1.2.1.2 Sib. Or. 3:350-488   62
              1.2.1.3 Sib. Or. 3:1-96   64
       1.2.2   Sibylline Oracles Book 4   64
       1.2.3   Sibylline Oracles Book 5   65
       1.2.4   Sibylline Oracles Books 1-2   68
       1.2.5   Sibylline Oracles Books 7 and 11   78
              1.2.5.1 Sibylline Oracles Book 7   78
              1.2.5.2 Sibylline Oracles Book 11   78
1.3   Jeremiah, Baruch, and Ezra Literature   79

1.3.1   Letter of Jeremiah   79
1.3.2   Baruch   81
1.3.3   4 Ezra   85
1.3.4   2 Baruch   98
1.4   Other Apocalypses and Testaments   106
1.4.1   Apocalypse of Abraham   106
1.4.2   Testament of Moses   111
1.4.3   Testament of Job   115
1.4.4   Testament of Abraham   133
1.4.5   Testament of Solomon   136

PART TWO

ATTITUDES TOWARDS SEXUALITY IN
HISTORIES, LEGENDS, AND RELATED WRITINGS   142

2.1   Septuagintal Literature   142
2.1.1   "The Tale of the Three Youths" (1 Esdras 3:1 – 5:6) 142
2.1.2   Tobit   147
2.1.3   Judith   185
2.1.4   Susanna   214
2.1.5   Additions to Esther   236
2.1.6   1 and 2 Maccabees   243
   2.1.6.1   1 Maccabees   244
   2.1.6.2   2 Maccabees   253
2.2   Beyond the Septuagint   258
2.2.1   The Book of Biblical Antiquities Liber Antiquitatum Biblicarum
         (LAB)/Pseudo-Philo   258
2.2.2   Joseph and Aseneth   300
2.3   Later Works of Disputed Provenance   334
2.3.1   The Lives of the Prophets and the Martyrdom of Isaiah   334
2.3.2   The History of the Rechabites or the Story of Zosimus   334
2.3.3   The Life of Adam and Eve and the Apocalypse of Moses   336

PART THREE

ATTITUDES TOWARDS SEXUALITY IN PSALMS,
WISDOM WRITINGS, AND FRAGMENTARY WORKS   342

3.1   Psalms   342
    3.1.1   The Psalms of Solomon   342
3.2   Wisdom Writings   362
    3.2.1   Ben Sira / Sirach (by Ibolya Balla)   362
    3.2.2   Wisdom of Solomon   398
    3.2.3   Pseudo-Aristeas   426
    3.2.4   4 Maccabees   440
    3.2.5   Pseudo-Phocylides   457
3.3   Fragmentary Judeo-Hellenistic Works   476
    3.3.1   Theodotus   476
    3.3.2   Ezekiel the Tragedian   484
    3.3.3   Pseudo-Eupolemus   485
    3.3.4   Other Fragmentary Remains   487
        3.3.4.1   Demetrius   487
        3.3.4.2   Pseudo-Sophocles   488
        3.3.4.3   Pseudo-Menander / Pseudo-Philemon   488

Conclusion   490

Bibliography   514

Index of Modern Authors   552

Index of Ancient Sources   559

Acknowledgments

This book is the third volume to emerge from my ongoing research on attitudes towards sexuality in Judaism and Christianity of the Hellenistic Greco-Roman era, a five year project funded through an Australian Professorial Fellowship from the Australian Research Council, which I commenced mid 2005. Murdoch University has provided invaluable infrastructure support, not least through inter-library loans scheme which has found obscure literature for me from all over the world.

Parts of the work have been read by colleagues abroad whose comments I have greatly appreciated: Kenneth Atkinson (*Psalms of Solomon*); John J. Collins (Wisdom of Solomon and the *Sibylline Oracles*); George Nickelsburg (*Parables of Enoch*); Andrei Orlov (*2 Enoch* and the *Apocalypse of Abraham*), and Angela Standhartinger (*Joseph and Aseneth*). In addition, I had opportunity to present some of this material to a staff-postgraduate research seminar and a conference on the Septuagint at Stellenbosch University, South Africa, in August, 2008 (*Joseph and Aseneth* and the Additions to Esther). Though primarily through printed page and computer screen, I feel I have nevertheless been greatly enriched by meeting and engaging with so many scholars who have wrestled with the very wide range of texts discussed in this volume.

I am especially grateful to Mary J. Marshall who not only proof reads, but brings to her pencilled comments a high level of observant expertise in biblical languages and exegesis. It is a privilege to be able to include a section on Ben Sira/Sirach by Ibolya Balla, based on her very fine dissertation, completed in English as a second language far from her native Hungary.

I also express my appreciation again to William B. Eerdmans Jr for his support and encouragement, and for his willingness to publish the results of this research.

Introduction

This investigation forms part of a larger project of research on attitudes towards sexuality in Judaism and Christianity in the Hellenistic Greco-Roman era. As in the previous volumes, sexuality is understood in the broad sense of matters pertaining to sexuality rather than in the more defined sense which we find in discussion of sexual orientation and sexual theory. The first volume dealt with the early Enoch literature, *Aramaic Levi Document*, and *Jubilees*,[1] the second, with the Dead Sea Scrolls.[2] This volume contains mostly pseudepigraphic writings, hence the overall title, but not exclusively so. Thus it contains works such as Ben Sira and Theodotus. The material of the first volume would also have fallen into the category of pseudepigraphy as would some from the second. The selection in this volume, the third, is, therefore, an endeavour to include all pertinent Jewish literature beyond that covered in the first two volumes, on the one side, and Philo, Josephus, and the *Testaments of the Twelve Patriarchs*, on the other, which will be the focus of the fourth volume.

We have before us, therefore, a large and diverse collection of writings and fragments. As in previous volumes I have given priority to discussing each in its own integrity. This is all the more relevant here, given the range of dates, settings, and styles. The sequence and arrangement of the material follows broad categories. It is not based on date and only loosely on genre. Most of the material falls clearly within the parameters of the period of research, from the 3rd century B.C.E. to the end of the first century C.E. The dating of some works is a matter of

---

[1] William Loader, *Enoch, Levi, and Jubilees on Sexuality: Attitudes towards Sexuality in the Early Enoch Literature, the Aramaic Levi Document, and the Book of Jubilees* (Grand Rapids: Eerdmans, 2007).

[2] William Loader, *The Dead Sea Scrolls on Sexuality: Attitudes towards Sexuality in Sectarian and Related Literature at Qumran* (Grand Rapids: Eerdmans, 2009).

1

debate or uncertainty. All discussions deal briefly with these issues. Identifying what is Jewish within what comes to us as a Christian edition, for instance, in *Sibylline Oracles* 1 – 2 or the *Testament of Abraham*, is fraught with difficulty, so that any conclusions about times and settings of attitudes must in such instances be tentative.

While in some cases matters pertaining to sexuality are incidental at most, in others they famously take centre stage, such as in the exploits of Judith, and Susanna's brave resistance against her sexual predators. There is romance, such as in the seriously entertaining *Joseph and Aseneth*, and reversal, such as in the translation of Esther and its additions which depict her not as elevated to high favour as queen, but as dragooned into sexual service against her will. There are various retellings of the garden of Eden, including some which appear to see sexual desire as a curse, or which defy the story to declare the earth not cursed at all but the events of the garden as effecting the divine plan. The Watchers, so central in *1 Enoch* and *Jubilees*, continue to be the focus of reflection in some writings, their story sometimes combined with the garden story and with Satan. The Watchers' fate in a lake of burning fire may well have inspired the author of the *Parables of Enoch* to connect Herod's visit to hot springs as a basis for warning rulers they face the same fate when what once warmed them will burn them up for their sexual profligacy. The Watcher myth also forms the backdrop of the bizarre demons and their fateful sexual aberrations in the *Testament of Solomon*.

Ideals of marriage inform the depictions in Tobit and the *Testament of Job*, tinged with marital realities far from ideal. Similarly both Ben Sira in his advice and the retellings in *LAB* (*Pseudo-Philo*) take us into the complex dynamics of rivalry within polygynous marriage. Some authors have clearly found inspiration in observing the processes of conception, pregnancy and childbirth. Overarching, and sometimes overbearing, structures of household norms dominate, even where women are seen to break the pattern temporarily – only to be reaccommodated to male perceptions of good order. Some authors know their contemporary "pop-psychology" well and rail against the passions, but in almost all instances this is about control and moderation not denial. A number of authors hide behind a Gentile mask, while espousing their Jewish values in such terms, *Pseudo-Phocylides* carrying off a deception which lasted successfully for centuries. In others, such as the Sibylline authors, or *Pseudo-Aristeas*, for all the careful imitations of archaic language and style, the bent is obvious and surprisingly conservative. For one of the former, Adam's *libido* in the garden is reduced to wanting conversation – which he gets; but elsewhere authors show no reluctance to recognise beauty and sexual attraction, often at the expense of depicting many men as rather stupid when they don't know what to do with their sexual responses or as downright evil when they plan and engage in abuse. Sex is surpisingly virulent in many of these writings. Ben Sira engages the erotic in very full measure to extrapolate the image of Wisdom from Proverbs, though seems more comfortable with its metaphors than its reality. We even find some authors rebuking the punitive moralisers, a lesson which Abraham had to learn according to the testament bearing his name, and one, taught by subtle subversion in the story of Aseneth the Gentile proselyte, where, of all people, Levi, for some the hero of anti-Gentile zeal, especially against intermarriage, becomes her champion.

Concern with intermarriage plays itself out in various ways. For *LAB* it is much more serious than incest (so: Tamar) and even than the vicious rape of the Levite's concubine, a fate which those sleeping with Gentiles apparently deserve. Most attacks on same-sex relations are about male exploitation of minors, though there are condemnations of adult relations, even one on female-female relations, and usually based on arguments about the divine order of nature. These are just some of the gems, or sometimes sharp and rugged stones, embedded in this rich quarry of material.

This investigation is not about gathering stones, let alone, then assembling them into a contrived pattern, but about analysing each writing which has it own story to tell. In the concluding observations, however, there is a thematic review, which identifies a range of responses to various aspects of sexuality and offers some comment on what appears to lie behind these responses.

The discussion of each writing begins with questions of a broader nature, including the extant text, and possible settings and purpose. Unless otherwise indicated, the translations cited in this work are from the *New Revised Standard Version (NRSV)* (Hebrew Bible), *NETS* (Septuagint),[3] *OTP*,[4] and in particular instances other recent translations. Where I have produced my own or modified a translation I indicate that with an asterisk.

I am pleased to include in this volume a chapter on Ben Sira / Sirach by Ibolya Balla, based on her recently completed PhD dissertation, "Attitudes towards Sexuality in Ben Sira" (Murdoch University, 2008).

---

[3] Albert Pietersma and Benjamin G. Wright, ed. *A New English Translation of the Septuagint* (Oxford: Oxford University Press, 2007).

[4] James H. Charlesworth, ed. *The Old Testament Pseudepigrapha: Volume One: Apocalyptic Literature and Testaments; Volume 2: Expansions of the "Old Testament" and Legends, Wisdom and Philosophical Literature, Prayers, Psalms, and Odes, Fragments of Lost Judeo-Hellenistic Works* (Garden City: Doubleday, 1983, 1985).

PART ONE

Attitudes towards Sexuality in Apocalypses, Testaments, and Related Writings

1.1 Later Enoch Literature

1.1.1 The Parables of Enoch (1 Enoch 37 – 71)

The Parables of Enoch (*1 Enoch* 37 – 71) form part of the collection known to us as *1 Enoch*.[1] Some parts of the collection had been associated together very early and that association is evident in the surviving Aramaic fragments found at Qumran. Thus 4Q205 and 4Q206 contain parts of both the *Book of the Watchers* and the *Dream Visions* and 4Q203 + 204 contains parts of the *Book of the Watchers*, the *Book of Giants*, the *Dream Visions*, and the *Epistle of Enoch*. The chapters known as the *Parables* or *Similitudes of Enoch* have left no trace there. They survive only in the Ethiopic translation. There they are the second of five main parts, mirroring the Pentateuch, with two appendices. [2] While the five-fold

---

[1] Unless otherwise indicated, all quotations derive from George W. E. Nickelsburg, and James C. VanderKam, *1 Enoch: A New Translation* (Minneapolis: Fortress, 2004) (hereafter abbreviated "NV"). The text is that of Michael A. Knibb, *The Ethiopic Book of Enoch: A New Edition in the Light of the Aramaic Dead Sea Fragments* (2 vols: Oxford: Clarendon, 1978).

[2] J. T. Milik, "Problèmes de la littérature Hénochique à la lumière des fragments araméens de Qumrân, *HTR* 64 (1971) 333-78; J. T. Milik, *The Books of Enoch: Aramaic Fragments of Qumran Cave 4* (Oxford: Clarendon, 1976), conjectured that their original place was filled by the *Book of the Giants* (or the *Book of Noah*?) (4).

pattern may explain the present form of the collection, there is insufficient evidence to support that it had an earlier five-fold form or even that the component works were always configured into the sequence in which we now find them.[3] It makes better sense to see in the *Parables* a work composed in Aramaic,[4] under the influence of especially the *Book of the Watchers*[5] and possibly early Noachic traditions,[6] but having had an independent existence and then later been incorporated into the *1 Enoch* collection.

Its absence from among the fragments at Qumran may, but need not, indicate that it was not then in existence.[7] It was indeed most likely to have been in existence before the settlement at Qumran was destroyed by the Romans in 69 C.E. Its probable influence on the Gospel according to Matthew and the Book of Revelation excludes a date after around 85 C.E. One of the few internal indicators

---

[3] So Eibert I. C. Tigchelaar, "Remarks on Transmission and Traditions in the Parables of Enoch: Response to James VanderKam," in *Enoch and the Messiah Son of Man: Revisiting the Book of Parables* (ed. Gabriele Boccaccini; Grand Rapids: Eerdmans, 2007) 100-109, 102-104. See also Michael Knibb, "The Book of Enoch or Books of Enoch? The Textual Evidence for 1 Enoch," in *The Early Enoch Literature* (ed. Gabriele Boccaccini and John J. Collins; JSJSup 121; Leiden: Brill, 2007) 21-40.

[4] See also George W. E. Nickelsburg, *Jewish Literature Between the Bible and the Mishnah: A Literary and Historical Introduction* (2d ed.; Minneapolis: Fortress Press, 2005) 256.

[5] On the relation between the *Book of Parables* and the *Book of the Watchers* and the *Book of the Luminaries*, see the discussion of James C. VanderKam, "The Book of Parables within the Enoch Tradition," in *Enoch and the Messiah Son of Man: Revisiting the Book of Parables* (ed. Gabriele Boccaccini; Grand Rapids: Eerdmans, 2007) 81-99.

[6] See Tigchelaar, "Remarks," who, while noting possible influence from the *Book of the Watchers*, also argues for a differentiated approach which takes into account different levels of influence at the various stages of development which the *Book of Parables* reflects (104-106).

[7] For the discussion of date which follows see the review of research in David W. Suter, "Enoch in Sheol: Updating the Dating of the Book of Parables," in *Enoch and the Messiah Son of Man: Revisiting the Book of Parables* (ed. Gabriele Boccaccini; Grand Rapids: Eerdmans, 2007) 415-43; and the response in the same volume by Michael Stone, "Enoch's Date in Limbo: or, Some Considerations on David Suter's Analysis of the Book of the Parables," 444-49. In the editorial introduction Gabriele Boccaccini, "The Enoch Seminar at Camaldoli," 3-16, writes of the dating of the Parables to around the turn of the era: "It can now be confidently said that the position … is confirmed and supported by the overwhelming majority of specialists in the Enoch literature and Second Temple Judaism" (15), reflecting somewhat more confidence than the conclusions of Suter's survey would allow. See also in the same volume George W. E. Nickelsburg, "Discerning the Structure(s) of the Enochic Book of Parables," 23-47, 47; Nickelsburg, *Jewish Literature*, 254; and James R. Davila, *The Provenance of the Pseudepigrapha* (JSJSup 105; Leiden: Brill, 2005) 135-37.

(56:7) suggests that the author is unaware of the fall of Jerusalem in 70 C.E. Another may allude to the threat of the Parthians in the mid first century B.C.E. (56:5-8).[8] There may also be a reference to Herod's seeking healing in the hot pools of Callirhoe (67:8-13; cf. Josephus *A.J.* 17.169-172; *B.J.* 1.656-58).[9] Charlesworth suggests that the focus on evil landowners reflects confiscations in the reign of Herod.[10] It is difficult to be more precise. It does, however, enable us to see how an author worked with the Enoch tradition, probably some time around the turn of the era, and, in particular, to observe what the document preserves of attitudes towards sexuality.

After the title given in the words of the author in 37:1, "The second vision which he saw"[11] (cf. the title, "The Book of Parables", is based on the designation in 82:1), we immediately hear the words of Enoch, who, following a common pattern in the document of sudden switches of speaking voices, introduces himself as imparting wisdom given him by God to give to dwellers on earth. This is in itself interesting, since it connects with wisdom literature and uses a common expression, "beginning of wisdom" (37:3; cf. 37:2), but like *1/4QInstruction* lays claim to wisdom which also includes information about a final judgement.

The document stands above all under the influence of the *Book of the Watchers*, whose sequence it follows, especially in the first parable, as

---

[8] Most recently defended by Luca Arcari, "A Symbolic Transfiguration of a Historical Event: The Parthian Invasion in Josephus and the Parables of Enoch," in *Enoch and the Messiah Son of Man: Revisiting the Book of Parables* (ed. Gabriele Boccaccini; Grand Rapids: Eerdmans, 2007) 478-86; and in the same volume see also Hanan Eshel, "An Allusion in the Parables of Enoch to the Acts of Matthias Antigonus in 40 B.C.E.?" 487-91, who suggests an allusion to the mutilation of Hyrcanus II; and Pierluigi Piovanelli, "'A Testimony for the Kings and the Mighty Who Possess the Earth': The Thirst for Justice and Peace in the Parables of Enoch," 363-79, 275.

[9] Most recently defended by Darrell D. Hannah, "The Book of Noah, the Death of Herod the Great, and the Date of the Parables of Enoch," in *Enoch and the Messiah Son of Man: Revisiting the Book of Parables* (ed. Gabriele Boccaccini; Grand Rapids: Eerdmans, 2007) 469-77; as also Piovanelli, "Testimony," 376; but see also the critical assessment in the same volume by Lester L. Grabbe, "The Parables of Enoch in Second Temple Jewish Society," 386-402, 393-94.

[10] James H. Charlesworth, "Can We Discern the Composition Date of the Parables of Enoch?" in *Enoch and the Messiah Son of Man: Revisiting the Book of Parables* (ed. Gabriele Boccaccini; Grand Rapids: Eerdmans, 2007) 450-68.

[11] NV read: "The vision of wisdom that Enoch saw" with a footnote explaining: "All Eth MSS begin with *The second vision that he saw*" then explained as "almost certainly a gloss that postdates the section's incorporation into the corpus" (50 n. a). Cf. Michael A. Knibb, "The Structure and Composition of the Parables of Enoch," in *Enoch and the Messiah Son of Man: Revisiting the Book of Parables* (ed. Gabriele Boccaccini; Grand Rapids: Eerdmans, 2007) 48-64, who argues that these words indicate that the work was composed directly to be a continuation of the *Book of the Watchers* (48).

Nickelsburg demonstrates.[12] This Enoch then provides a structural overview of the work, as he reports: "Three parables were (imparted) to me" (37:5). These are then marked in 38:1 as "the First Parable", reaching to 44:1; "the second parable", 45:1, reaching to 57:3; and "the third parable", 58:1, reaching to 69:29. In the final section, 70 – 71, we then hear the author directly reporting Enoch's ascension to heaven. This seemingly neat structure is disturbed however by what appear to be extraneous traditions woven into the document. Thus, for instance, 65:1 – 68:4 present words of Noah which are only loosely integrated into the document. There are other such unevennesses, possibly reflecting the author's use of sources or his combining different materials loosely and sometimes without providing any transition.[13] We shall take the detailed discussion of these into account where they have significance for our investigation.

The First Parable (38:1 – 44:1)

The theme of all three parables is the coming judgement, in which the figure variously designated as the Righteous One, the Chosen, and Son of Man, acts as God's agent. The work has for this reason received much attention from scholars seeking a background for christology. Already the opening account, 38:1-5, which envisages a time when "the congregation of the righteous appears" (38:1) and "the Righteous One appears in the presence of the righteous" (38:2), enables us to see a vision of judgement which entails the righteous and their leader engaged in annihilating the wicked and their leaders (cf. 1:3c-9). The wicked will be driven off from the righteous and chosen (38:3) and cease to exist (38:6). It gives particular attention to the kings and the mighty who now control the land, and who will be given into the hands of the righteous (38:5; cf. 1:8-9). The author will doubtless identify himself as belonging to the congregation of the righteous. They appear regularly as a group and at one point are joined by others who see their success over against the kings (50:2). We are probably dealing with hearers who

---

[12] So Nickelsburg, "Discerning the Structure(s)," 26-34.

[13] For most recent discussion of the structure and indications of redaction and additions, see Nickelsburg, "Discerning the Structure(s)"; and related discussions in *Enoch and the Messiah Son of Man: Revisiting the Book of Parables* (ed. Gabriele Boccaccini; Grand Rapids: Eerdmans, 2007): Knibb, "Structure," 48-64; Loren T. Stuckenbruck, "The Parables of Enoch according to George Nickelsburg and Michael Knibb: A Summary and Discussion of Some Remaining Questions," 65-71; and Benjamin G. Wright, "The Structure of the Parables of Enoch: A Response to George Nickelsburg and Michael Knibb," 72-78.

understand themselves to be a group within Israel, hopeful that the rest of Israel will ultimately join them.[14]

Somewhat unmediated, the author then interrupts Enoch's account in 39:1 to address the hearers,[15] giving a brief account of the Watcher myth based on 6 – 16: "in those days, sons of the chosen and holy were descending from the highest heaven and their seed was becoming one with the sons of men".[16] "Those days" (39:1, 2, 3) refer to Enoch's time. While the verb *yewarredu* could be read with Black as a future, "will descend", and so refer to "fresh assaults of angelic 'watchers' on mankind",[17] the context, which reports events of Enoch's time, repeating "in those days" and including his ascent (39:3), suggests that reading it as past imperfect is preferable. The words, "and there will be no mercy for them" (omitted by NV), refer to future judgement of the Watchers for their deed before the flood, a firm element in the tradition (10:12-14).

The summary of the myth in 39:1 describes the Watchers as "sons of the chosen and holy". "Sons of" will reflect semitic usage of speaking of members belonging to a group, here, the angels, as in the common expression "sons of Israel", rather than to literal sonship. Behind it is the expression "sons of heaven" in 6:2 and "sons of God" in Gen 6:2. VanderKam notes that "many manuscripts, including those of the β family, read *daqiq* rather than *daqiqa*, yielding the meaning 'chosen and holy children'".[18]

To speak of "their seed" as "becoming one with the sons of man" is also somewhat ambiguous. "Their seed" will refer here not to their offspring, nor to their semen, but to themselves as a kind or category, namely, holy angels. It refers to their having engaged in sexual relations with "sons of men", meaning not males,

---

[14] Cf. Daniel C. Olson, in consultation with Melkesedek Workeneh, *Enoch: A New Translation; The Ethiopic Book of Enoch, or 1 Enoch, Translated with Annotations and Cross-References* (North Richland Hills: BIBAL, 2004), who takes "the others" as a reference to Gentiles (94). I consider this unlikely since Gentiles do not feature elsewhere in the writing.

[15] On the likelihood that 39:1-2 is not an addition, but functions as an address by the author to the hearers serving to explain "how Enoch, himself, the recipient of the vision, came to be in the position in which he found himself", see VanderKam, "Book of Parables," 86 n. 13.

[16] On this see also VanderKam, "Book of Parables," who shows that "virtually every word in 39:1 can be located in 1 En 6-16" (86). See, however, Tigchelaar, "Remarks," who also notes significant differences, including "the chosen and holy children" or "the sons of the chosen and holy"; and "their seed will become (or was becoming) one with the sons of men", continuing also in 39:2-3 (107).

[17] Matthew Black, *The Book of Enoch or 1 Enoch: A New English Edition* (SVTP 7; Leiden: Brill, 1985) 196; Olson, *Enoch*, 76.

[18] VanderKam, "Book of Parables," 86 n. 14.

but humankind, and in particular, women.[19] This brief statement focuses solely on the act of illicit intercourse.[20] It says nothing of their progeny, the giants and the evil spirits, an element also not taken up elsewhere in the work, nor does it mention impartation of forbidden knowledge, an aspect which is, however, the main focus of attention in other allusions to the Watchers' deed in the work.[21]

The summary in 39:1 could be heard as almost as neutral as the Genesis account. The author does not pause to dwell on the nature of the deed as sexual wrongdoing, but his next comments, in 39:2, clearly show that this is far from neutral. For he reminds the hearers of the earlier writings: "In those days Enoch received books of jealous wrath and rage", revealing what he sees as their main concern and reaction to the angels' deed, and implicitly invites comparison between their own day and the times of Enoch, but without further elucidation. He then moves to describe Enoch's ascent (cf. 12:1) as being taken up in a whirlwind, reminiscent of Elijah: "In those days a whirlwind snatched me up from the face of the earth" (39:3).

Enoch then reports what he sees in the heavenly world, including the resting places of the holy ones and of the righteous (39:4-8). They are with the angels in God's presence. Enoch goes on to speak of "that place" (39:10) (though some MSS have "in those days"). It is in effect the heavenly temple, full of worshipping angels, and including the four different figures, reminiscent of Rev 4:6-11, but identified as Michael, Raphael, Gabriel and Phanuel (40:1-10). It is important to see that this describes the situation before the judgement, since thereafter the document envisages everlasting life for the righteous and chosen ones on a renewed earth. Had the document indicated that the temple was to be their permanent abode, then one certain implication would be that there would be no room for sexual relations, for marrying or being given in marriage, in such a context.

He then reports seeing the "secrets of heaven", explained as referring to the judgement and the driving off of the wicked and their destruction, 41:1-2, matching the account in 38:1-5. This passage speaks of "the dwelling places of the chosen and the dwelling places of the holy ones", from which the wicked are expelled. This is probably not the same as their resting places in the heavenly temple, as in 39:4, but presumably refers to dwelling places on earth, though this is not made explicit. The penultimate verse of the parable speaks of "the holy ones

---

[19] VanderKam, "Book of Parables," notes that the expression that their seed became one with the sons of men does not appear in the *Book of the Watchers*, but approximates to 7:1 (87).

[20] So VanderKam, "Book of Parables," who notes that only here does this strand of tradition associated with Shemihazah appear (87).

[21] Nickelsburg, *Jewish Literature*, 249.

who dwell on the earth and believe in the name of the Lord of Spirit forever and ever" (43:4), probably suggesting permanent dwelling on (a renewed) earth.

Between 41:1-2 and the conclusion of the parable, we find at first an extensive section about other secrets which Enoch saw, relating, in particular to lightning and thunder, meteorological phenomena, the sun and moon (41:3-8), and concluding in 41:9 with a statement about the judge seeing all and judging them. In the preserved sequence this merges together the divine order of creation with the divine order of judgement, which underlies the sense of order in much apocalyptic literature. As in *1 Enoch* 1 – 5, the passage emphasises that the heavenly bodies "do not leave the course and they neither extend nor diminish their course", but keep to the oath they have sworn (41:5), an image developed extensively in 69:13-25. Both the sense of fixed order and the contrast between light and darkness (41:8) serve to reinforce the distinction between sinners and the righteous, as those who flout God's order and those who follow it. The word, Law, does not appear in the document, but it clearly assumes a divine order.[22]

We find the same juxtaposition of heavenly bodies (lightning and stars) and their order and judgement continuing in 43:1-3, but preceded in 42:1-3, somewhat unmediated, by accounts of Wisdom and its opposite, here, Iniquity. Both are pictured as women seeking a dwelling place, the former finding none among "the sons of men", echoing a tradition found already in the *Epistle of Enoch*, "I know that sinners will tempt people to do harm to wisdom; and no place will be found for her, and none of the temptation will diminish" (94:5). The latter, Iniquity, finds "those whom she did not seek" and dwells among them as "rain in a desert and dew in a thirsty land".[23] While both are pictured as women, the focus is not on sexual relations nor on seductiveness on the part of either, as in Proverbs and elsewhere, but is more generic in emphasis and depiction. At most one might observe that the story of the descents of the women stand in parallel to the reference to the descent of the Watchers in 39:1. The imagery for Iniquity derives from another aspect of reality altogether, speaking of rain for the dry land and water for the thirsty. The passage has, therefore, little to say in relation to attitudes to sexuality. The nature of Iniquity will be informed by the sense of divine order reflected in the context and so represent its transgression.

The role of the passage may be polemical against the temple establishment and its interpreters, especially if written in contrast to the claims of Sirach 24 and Baruch 4 about wisdom finding its dwelling in Israel and its temple (cf. also John

---

[22] Davila, *Provenance*, writes: "The Similitudes of Enoch shows no interest in Torah observance, makes no mention of the temple cult or priesthood, and gives no indication of any sense of Jewish national or ethnic identity" (133).

[23] Nickelsburg, "Discerning the Structure(s)," relocates 42:1-3 to between 42:2 and 3 (29), the order reproduced in NV 56; but see Wright, "Structure," who notes that with the relocation the text "still sits uncomfortably" in its context (73).

1:9-11), and perhaps even employing the image of water subversively, normally used of the positive offering of wisdom and Law (e.g. Sir 24:25-31). In its present context it appears to supplement the reference in 41:1-9 to the wicked "who deny the name of the Lord of Spirits" and their judgement, explaining how their wickedness was nourished. The passage seems sharply polemical against such people (who may also be the sinners in the presence of the righteous who must be expelled according to 38:3). Nothing, however, suggests particular disputes, for instance, over interpretation of the Law with another group, if, for instance, one is the butt here of irony.[24]

The Second Parable (45:1 – 57:3)

The second parable also focuses on judgement. It begins with the author declaring that "those who deny the name of the dwelling of the holy ones and of the Lord of Spirits" (similarly 45:2, "who have denied the name of the Lord of Spirits"; cf. 45:3 "appeal to my glorious name") will have no dwelling place in heaven or earth, but will be kept "for the day of affliction and tribulation" (45:1-2). This may simply refer generically to all sinners. It may refer specifically to enemies close to the author's community. From 45:3 we find God speaking directly. 45:3 introduces the figure of "the Chosen One" (see already 39:6; 40:5), to be identified with "the Righteous One" of 38:2. He "will sit on the throne of glory" and test their works (45:3). In this context we read that both heaven and earth will be transformed (reflecting Isa 65:17) and more importantly that the chosen ones will dwell on earth in God's presence (45:5) and sinners will be annihilated (45:5-6). Assuming some coherence with the first parable, this suggests that the heavenly dwelling places in the first vision (39:4-8; 41:2) refer to the time before the judgement and that subsequent to the judgement the righteous will dwell again on earth (perhaps already 43:4), elsewhere described as resurrected life. We hear nothing about the nature of that life, for instance, whether it includes family life, marriage, and sexual relations.

The second parable also expands our understanding of the way the author sees the exercise of judgement. The human-like figure, identified as the Chosen and Righteous One, will be God's agent in tipping the mighty from their couches (a probable allusion to their indulgent feasts) and dethroning them (46:4-5). Hearers who are aware of the content of 67:8-13, which speaks of the lust of the flesh among the kings, might also associate this with sexual wrongdoing. We then hear that their offences include failure to acknowledge God as the source of their

---

[24] Davila, *Provenance*, notes that "it is possible that a debate over calendrical matters, perhaps in relation to the solar or lunisolar calendar, is reflected in *1 En.* 41:3-9, although, if so, the issues involved are not laid out clearly" (133).

kingdom (46:5) and to "exalt the name of the Lord of Spirits" (46:6). They practice idolatry and rest on their wealth and "persecute the houses of his congregation and the faithful who depend on the name of the Lord of Spirits" (46:8).[25] Again nothing suggests a sexual theme, although it might be envisaged as belonging to the depiction of the mighty on their couches.

Thus focus turns in 47:1-4 to the righteous, including the prayers of the righteous in heaven for those on earth. In an echo of the imagery used negatively of Iniquity and her recipients in 42:3, 48:1 speaks of abounding springs of wisdom for the righteous (similarly 49:1-4 which identifies the Chosen One as the bearer of wisdom). In what follows, the persecution of the righteous receives elaboration, the cry of "the blood of the righteous" appealing for divine action (47:1-4), recalling 9:2-3. In 48:1-10 Enoch then hails the hidden pre-existent Son of Man (similarly 62:7), who is to overcome the kings. As in 38:1-5, we read again that they will fall into the hands of the chosen ones, and face annihilation (48:9). The theme of wisdom returns in 49:1-4 where it is hailed as an attribute of the Chosen One.

In 50:1-3 we have the interesting comment that there are some who will repent when they see that "in those days a change will occur for the holy and chosen, and the light of days will dwell upon them" (50:1). "Evil will be stirred up against the sinners; but the righteous will conquer in the name of the Lord" (50:2a). "He will show (this) to the others, so that they repent and abandon the works of their hands" (50:2b). This may well reflect the author's situation and be a further indication that he and his group stand over against "the others", whoever they may be and whatever "the work of their hands" might mean. In 51:1-5 Enoch returns to the promise of a future dwelling on the earth, but, again, without detail which would allow us to identify what form of life that may take.

In 52:1-9 we have an indirect reflection of the detail of the Watcher myth which portrays Asael bringing the skills of metallurgy.[26] Here only the theme of metal features. The mountains of iron, copper, silver, gold, soft metal, and lead will be melted into non existence (cf. also 65:7-8). The passage appears therefore to be taking up from the *Book of the Watchers* not only the Asael tradition of 8:1, but also the report in 18:6-9; 24:2-4 of Enoch seeing seven mountains, the seventh of which is Zion.[27] Here only six are mentioned and the focus is entirely on the

---

[25] The reference in 46:7 apparently to kings judging the stars of heaven, alludes not to the Watchers as stars as in 86:1, 3, but to Isa 14:13-14. See the discussion in David Suter, *Tradition and Composition in the Parables of Enoch* (SBLDS 47; Missoula: Scholars, 1979) 107-10.

[26] On this see Ida Fröhlich, "The Parables of Enoch and Qumran Literature," in *Enoch and the Messiah Son of Man: Revisiting the Book of Parables* (ed. Gabriele Boccaccini; Grand Rapids: Eerdmans, 2007) 343-51, 346-47.

[27] On this see Nickelsburg, "Discerning the Structure(s)," 31.

metals. Thus the passage addresses warfare, declaring that before the coming Chosen One these mountains will melt like wax (52:6; cf. also 53:7) and there will "not be iron for war, nor a garment for a breastplate, bronze will be of no use, and tin will not be reckoned, and lead will not be desired" (52:8). Knibb notes the transformation of the vision of the mountains by "association with the traditions, familiar from theophanic passages, of the melting of the mountains at the coming of God (Mic 1:4; Ps 97:5; cf. Nah 1:5; Judg 5:4)" and further by the imagery of world empires as in Dan 2:31-45.[28] Nothing is said of use of metals for ornamentation and cosmetics, equipping women for seduction as in 8:1-2.[29]

In 53:1-6, 54:2 Enoch reports seeing a deep valley prepared for the destruction of sinners, especially for the kings and the mighty. Then 54:1, 3-6 reports another valley, where chains are being prepared for "the host of Azazel" whose jaws will be covered with jagged stones. Azazel is named as their leader also in 55:4, as the passage continues after the digression in 54:7 – 55:2 about the flood. This reflects a development of the myth in which Asael has become the chief figure, rather than Shemihazah, as already in 10:4-8 ("over him write all sins" 10:8), and has been identified with Azazel.[30] The motif of jagged stones covering their jaws appears also to derive from the myth (10:5). The passage goes on in 54:6 to depict Michael, Raphael, Gabriel, and Phanuel, casting the host of Azazel into the burning furnace. The charge against them is their "becoming servants of Satan, and leading astray those who dwell on the earth" (54:6). Here the Watcher myth has been subsumed within a wider frame of reference in which the chief source of sin is Satan.[31] Nothing indicates how they lead people astray (an image repeated in 56:4). The wider context suggests it might include false teaching, but equally, hearers aware of 39:1 and especially 69:4-5 might see this in sexual terms. Again, however, there is no specific mention of sexual themes. The focus appears to be not the act of sexual wrongdoing, but the corruption of humankind through

---

[28] Knibb, "Structure," 56.

[29] Similarly Tigchelaar, "Remarks," who notes that whereas the focus in the *Book of the Watchers* is on production of weapons of war and adornments for seduction, here "the stress is on metallurgy per se, and the fashioning of idols" (108). He continues: "The mantic arts, as a special kind of secret described in detail in the Book of the Watchers, are absent from this section. Here the interpolation from a Noachic source runs parallel to the account in chaps. 6-11, but there are no signs of a dependence on the Book of the Watchers" (108).

[30] See also VanderKam, "Book of Parables," who writes that the reference to Azazel's host is "a sign that the writer knows a composite of stories regarding the angels and that he is not alluding simply to the Asael sections that modern scholars have isolated in the Book of the Watchers" (88; similarly 89).

[31] VanderKam, "Book of Parables," writes: "Satan is imported by the writer (see also 65:6), but the sin of misleading comes from the Book of the Watchers (cf. 8:1-2; 9:8; 13:2; 16:3)" (89).

teaching metallurgy, and even then, primarily concerned with instruments of warfare, not female instruments of seduction.

In 54:7 – 55:2 we find a description of the flood. While it has been designated a digression (so: NV), it belongs with the events of 54:5 which describe the incarceration of the hosts of Azazel, which according to the *Book of the Watchers* took place before the flood (10:4-8, 11-15), and reflects the responses to earth's plight described in 10:1-3. Its relevance to the context is therefore explained by the reference to the Watchers and to God's judgement of humankind ("all who dwell on the earth and who dwell beneath the ends of heaven"; 54:9), corrupted by their deeds.[32] The account is replete with God's promise of the rainbow as a sign that he will not repeat the flood. Nothing indicates a concern with sexual wrongdoing. Incidental to the description is an interesting description of the waters above and below as representing male and female (54:8). This probably draws on some reworking of the ancient cosmogony myth of male and female. The author uses such gender images also in 60:7-8, 16, but without any indication of a particular attitude towards the difference.

In 55:3 the author continues to have God speaking, but as now returning to the theme of the Watchers' eschatological punishment and destruction (55:3 – 56:4), the motif introduced already in 54:6 by the author in his own words. It is interesting that God then addresses the "mighty kings who dwell on the earth" and asks them to watch the judgement of "Azazel and all his associates and all his host" by the Chosen One (55:3). This will belong to the theme of warfare for which the Watchers equipped the kings, not least in teaching them the skills of metallurgy. Nothing suggests that sexual sins or seduction are in mind. It may well reflect a creative reworking of the tradition according to which the Watchers were made to watch the mutual self-destruction of their offspring, the giants (10:9, 12; 12:6). As Suter demonstrates, it also reflects the influence of Isa 24:21-22, which sets the punishment of the heavenly host and the punishment of the kings and the mighty in parallel ("On that day the LORD will punish the host of heaven in heaven, and on earth the kings of the earth. They will be gathered together like prisoners in a pit; they will be shut up in a prison, and after many days they will be punished").[33]

In 56:1-4 we return to the voice of Enoch who tells us that he saw "hosts of angels of punishment" holding chains of iron and bronze, thus producing a subtle reversal: the metals of warfare now serve the punishment for warfare. In response to Enoch's asking for whom these are intended, the angel of peace explains that they are for "their chosen and beloved ones" a description repeated twice (56:3, 4).

---

[32] See also VanderKam, "Book of Parables," who writes of the section about the flood, that "it makes some sense in this section about punishments since in chap. 10 the flood serves to destroy the earth" (88).

[33] Suter, *Tradition and Composition*, 52.

They are to be annihilated and "the days of their leading astray will henceforth not be reckoned" (56:4). The latter statement could simply mean that they will no longer lead people astray, but this is unlikely since they have been bound in the valley since their incarceration long ago. It must mean something like: their impact is over and significance can be forgotten.

More complicated is the meaning of "their chosen and beloved ones". What is the reference of the suffix "their"? To whom are these the "chosen and beloved ones"? The immediate referent could be the angels of punishment. One possibility would be that it refers therefore to the status which the "chosen and beloved ones" once held before they sinned, when they were part of the company of the angels and as such, "chosen" and "beloved" to each other. Alternatively, we should see the angels of punishment within a theistic framework in which they are among those, like the satans, commissioned to afflict. Then the angels of punishment would have the task to punish those who had in a sense been their allies and friends.

More probably we should read "their" in relation not to the angels of punishment, but to "Azazel and all his associates" (55:4). Then "their chosen and beloved ones" would refer to their offspring, alluded to in the expression, "all his host" (55:4). In support of this interpretation, when the same act of judgement is described in 54:5, those being punished are, indeed, described as "the host of Azazel". This implies that the judgement relates to the demons, as already Charles suggested, who pointed out the use of "beloved" in 10:12; 14:6, referring to the Watchers' offspring.[34] This gains further support from the motif of shackles of iron and bronze, which, as Olson observes, "are frequently invoked in later Jewish magical and exorcistic texts in order to bind demons".[35]

A further alternative would be to see the "chosen" and "beloved" as a reference not to demons, but to human agents, such as false teachers (56:4) or kings. Thus David Suter argues that the reference is not to demons but to kings, as already Schodde had suggested.[36] He notes the parallel between the judgement of the two in Isa 24:21-22, cited above, and that the terms "chosen" and "beloved" probably belong not to the discourse of family affection, but to the relationship with God, so that "chosen" and "beloved" are used here in much the same way as we find them in Mark 1:11; 9:7; and 2 Peter 1:17. By analogy then, this language is employed to describe Azazel and his "chosen" and "beloved" agents, namely the

---

[34] So R. H. Charles, "Book of Enoch," *APOT*, 2.163-281, 221; similarly Black, *Book of Enoch*, 221; Knibb, "Structure," 57.

[35] Olson, *Enoch*, 102.

[36] Suter, *Tradition and Composition*, 52-54; G. H. Schodde, *The Book of Enoch* (Andover: Draper, 1882), cited in Black, *Book of Enoch*, 221, who also draws attention to Gustav Dillmann, *Das Buch Henoch* (Leipzig: F.C.W. Vogel, 1853), who in the light of the similar scene of judgement in 90:26-27 sees an allusion to "the blinded sheep".

kings and the mighty. Certainly the punishment of the kings is a feature of the *Book of Parables*. Nevertheless the parallel with 54:5 makes it more likely that the reference here is to demons, not teachers or kings. The discourse of agency fits as description of them just as well as it would kings. Furthermore kings are called in 55:4 to observe this act of judgement, which excludes the possibility that it is their own judgement.

Thus 56:3-4 seems best taken closely with 54:5 as a reference to the final punishment of Azazel and his host. The notion that the offspring included demons is already implied in 10:15. The passage reflects a reworking of the tradition found in the *Book of the Watchers*. No mention is made of the giants, but only of the demonic offspring. There could be reference to the wives of the Watchers and among the "beloved", who might be seen as agents of leading people astray, but this is uncertain (but see the discussion of 60:24b-25 below). The motif of the Watchers' having to observe the demise of their giant offspring (10:12) has metamorphosed into a statement that the kings must observe the judgement of the Watchers and their host (55:4).[37] This is to serve as a warning to them. Again nothing intimates that sexual wrongdoing is a concern, neither in the activities of Azazel's host, nor in the possible reference to women, nor in the activities of the kings, although the intratextual link with 39:1 would preserve this in the background for any hearer listening to the work in sequence. Only in 67:8-13 do we find a connection between the sins of the kings and "the lusts of the flesh".

The notion of God's judgement being expressed also through a victory over the kings (cf. 38:5-6; 46:4-8; 53:5; 54:2) reappears in 56:5-8, this time, with participation by angels, who stir them up to warfare, reminiscent of the angels' setting the giants on a course of mutual self-destruction in the myth (10:9). They fail to conquer Jerusalem (56:7). This is scarcely likely to have been written in the aftermath of the fall of Jerusalem in 70 C.E.[38] As noted in the introduction above, it may allude to Parthian invasions from the east in the mid first century B.C.E. In 57:1-5 Enoch then reports the appearance of a host of chariots and men, from east and west coming towards the south, who are then finally brought to submission: "they all fell down and worshipped the Lord of Spirits" (57:2), possibly an allusion

---

[37] Cf. Black, *Book of Enoch*, who notes that " in the oldest form of the legend, the 'beloved ones' of the watchers destroyed themselves in the presence of their parents (9.9,12)" (221).

[38] Olson, *Enoch*, comments: "It is hard to see how these words could have been written after the destruction of 70CE. Only a walled city could be described as an obstacle to cavalry" (102).

to the Roman armies and their ultimate submission[39] or perhaps to the return of the dispersion.[40]

The Third Parable (58:1 – 69:25)

The Third Parable begins with Enoch speaking, telling us that the righteous and chosen "will be in the light of the sun" permanently with no night (58:3, 5-6) and "the days of their life will have no end, and the days of the holy will be innumerable" (58:3). Their future hope is clearly on earth (58:5), as in 45:4-5. This image, with parallels in Revelation and elsewhere (e.g. *2 Enoch* 65:7-11) still does not tell us the nature of that life on earth, including what role marriage and sexual relations might play. Living forever need not mean no sexual intercourse, unless the author believes that no need of progeny and so of procreation excludes it, as in *1 Enoch* 15:6-7. One wonders what implications the author might have drawn from the notion of endless day in relation to the Sabbath and sexual relations, but the text preserves no such reflection.

There follows in 59:1-3 a description of meteorological secrets, recalling similar astronomical information in chapters 41 – 44 in the first parable. Here as there, there may have been dislocations of text. Thus NV make 59:1-3 and 60:11-22 a single sequence, followed by 60:23; 60:1-10; and 60:24-25. In the transmitted order we find the order of meteorology juxtaposed to information about the coming heavenly judgement.

Within the meteorological information it is interesting that in 60:16 we find a description of the wind of the sea as "masculine and strong, and according to the power of its strength, it draws it back with a rein; and thus it is driven and scattered among all the mountains of the earth". It reflects an understanding of "masculine" as strong and controlled. It also reflects experience of sea breezes and thus a location where they were in effect.

In 60:23 the narrative locates the vision "toward the Garden of the Righteous in the year 500, in the seventh month, on the fourteenth of the month, in the life of <Noah> (corrected from "Enoch" read in all mss)" (60:23). The incidental reference to "the garden where the chosen righteous dwell" alludes to paradise, which presumably is understood to belong in the heavenly realms to which Enoch has been taken up (see also 60:8; 61:12), but more likely is to be located on earth, so that 60:23 would refer to the place from which Enoch was taken up and in that sense where he saw the heavenly visions. An earthly location appears to assumed in 60:8 (see below).

---

[39] So Schodde, *Book of Enoch*; NV 6.

[40] So Charles, *APOT*, 2.222; Suter, *Tradition and Composition*, 197 n. 30; Olson, *Enoch*, who refers to Deut 30:4 (104); Knibb, "Structure," referring to Ezekiel 38 – 39 (58).

In the material pertaining to judgement we have in 60:1-6 another reference to "thousands of thousands and ten thousand times ten thousand" (cf. 40:1; 71:8, 13). Enoch reports Michael's explanation: "Until today has been the day of his mercy" (60:5). Enoch is to see the day of judgement. In 60:7-10, 24-25, we then hear of Leviathan and Behemoth:

> on that day two monsters were separated – the female monster whose name is Leviathan, to dwell in the depth of the ocean, above the fountain of the waters. But the name of the male is Behemoth, who occupies with his breast the trackless desert named Dundayn east of the garden where the chosen and righteous dwell, where my great-grandfather was taken up, the seventh from Adam, the first man whom the Lord of Spirits created. (60:7-8)

This draws on ancient mythology. There is no commentary in the text enabling us to see their particular role and no symbolism as with the beasts of Revelation. The reference to gender may well reflect a form of the creation myth which assumes separation of male and female, sometimes as earth and heaven, but here in a form which explains two monsters. A form of the myth appears also behind the description of the waters above and below as representing male and female in 54:8.

Clearly we now have Noah speaking, because there is reference to the speaker's great-grandfather who was taken up, an allusion to Enoch. In 65:1 – 69:25 we have a block of material which similarly assumes Noah is speaking. Perhaps the author assumes Noah's persona.[41]

In 60:24b-25 Enoch speaks of punishment and of children being killed with their mothers and fathers. The text appears to be defective and NV speak of "a snarl of duplications and omissions" in the these lines.[42] This could refer to persecution, but more likely refers to those being punished. It might reflect the myth and refer to the killing of the Watchers who descended and became fathers, and so the human women as mothers, and their offspring as the children. If so, it might support seeing in the "beloved" also a reference to the women.

The next scene portrays the angels being given long ropes to draw back into existence those who had been killed by desert, beasts, and fish (61:1-5). It appears

---

[41] See Nickelsburg, "Discerning the Structure(s)," who tentatively identifies the sequence 60:7-10 + 60:23(?) + 60:24a as belonging to an interpolation within an interpolation from a Noachic source (36-37). On the Noachic tradition see also Knibb, "Structure," 59.

[42] NV 76 n. m. See also Knibb, *Ethiopic Book of Enoch*, 1.170 and 2.148. See also Knibb, "Structure," where he suggests that the text reflects a tradition present in 4 Ezra 6:52, according to which the monsters become food for the righteous, as attested in MSTana 9 (59).

to be a form of resurrection of those who have died and a gathering of the chosen. In 61:6-13 we are then presented with a scene of worship, but which also includes a description of judgement of the holy ones in heaven (61:8), however without further specification of their crime. In 61:12 we then hear that among those blessing God are "all the chosen who dwell in the garden of life". The "garden", an allusion to Eden, had already been mentioned in 60:8, 23, where it is described as the "garden of the righteous". Nothing indicates that this garden is seen as a sanctuary or temple as in *Jubilees*, which would have implications for sexual relations. The juxtaposition of "all the holy ones who are in heaven" to "all the chosen who dwell in the garden of life" may reflect that the garden is, itself, not located in heaven. *2 Enoch* assumes a connection between the heavenly and earthly garden, as though at that point heaven and earth meet (8:1; 32:2; 42:3).

In 62:1 – 63:12 we then have another depiction of the judgement, especially of the kings and "those who possess the earth" (62:1).[43] Again the judgement is for annihilation (62:20; as already 39:5-6). The author uses the common image of birth pains to describe what will befall them when they see the Son of Man, but with greater elaboration than is usually the case: "And pain will come upon them as (upon) a woman in labor, when the child enters the mouth of the womb, and she has difficulty in giving birth" (62:4). In 62:9-12 the author draws on the Watcher myth, as elaborated in *1 Enoch* 12 – 16, where the Watchers ask Enoch to intercede on their behalf. Here Enoch plays no such role. The kings worship and seek mercy, but receive none, being delivered to the angels of punishment "for the iniquity they did to his children and his chosen ones" (62:11). The author then indulges in the hope that the righteous will be able to watch their punishment as a spectacle as the Lord of Spirits is drunk with rage (62:11-12). One wonders if this may reflect fondness of engagement in viewing such spectacles in real life in the Greco-Roman world.

By contrast the righteous and chosen will eat forever with that Son of Man and "they will lie down and rise up forever" (62:14), another reference to everlasting life. Their receiving a garment of glory that will not wear out is a form of resurrection to everlasting life (62:16). Nothing enables us to see what implications there might be for the author's attitude towards sexual relations in the embodied life to come. In 63:1-12 the author elaborates the confession of the kings. They describe their sinfulness, saying, "Our lives are full of ill-gotten wealth" (62:10). The theme of wealth met us earlier in 46:7, "their power (rests) on their wealth". Nothing indicates sexual wrongdoing belongs to their misdeeds.

In 64:1-2, almost as an appendix (as already in 54:1, 4-6), we then find reference also to "other figures" beside the kings: "These are the angels who

---

[43] See Nickelsburg, *Jewish Literature*, who sees here "a reworked form of the tradition that occurs also in Wisdom 2,4-5" (254).

descended upon the earth. And what was secret they revealed to human beings, and they led the human beings astray so that they committed sin" (64:2). While Charles saw this section as out of place,[44] Nickelsburg has argued more recently that "its presence here should not surprise us", since the theme of the angels has featured already in 39:1-2, is found juxtaposed to the kings and mighty in 53:1 – 56:4, their judgement announced in 61:8-9 isw not otherwise described in 62 – 63, and they feature again in the conclusion to the section in 69:27-28.[45] It is interesting that the focus here falls on the giving of secrets, not on the illicit sexual intercourse. Read intratextually the focus is almost certainly knowledge about metallurgy leading to warfare and making of idols, but also sorcery and spells (cf. 52: 1 – 54:6; 65:6b).[46]

The sequel to the judgement scene in chaps. 62 – 63; 64:1-2 is widely recognised as coming in 69:26-29. It reaffirms that sinners will be annihilated from the earth (69:27). In 69:28 it picks up the allusion in 64:2 to the angels "who led human beings astray": "And those who led the world astray will be bound in chains, in the assembly of the place of their destruction they will be confined; and their works will vanish from the face of the earth". The image of chains appeared already in 54:4 and 56:1-2 in relation to those leading people astray who are to be understood as referring to Azazel and his demons (54:6 and 56:4). The vanishing of their works recalls the declaration in 56:4 that their days will "not be reckoned". Thus "nothing that is corruptible" (69:29) will survive. The enemies, namely rulers and the wicked, and Azazel and the demons, have been removed. The leading astray by the angels will relate primarily to the passing on of illicit knowledge, as in 64:2. Again there is no indication that issues of sexual wrongdoing formed a significant component of the wickedness of either group, if we consider the text simply as a continuation of 62 – 64:2. People listening to the transmitted text, however, would doubtless hear these words differently, since the intervening material does, indeed, include sexual themes.

The author or editor has included material after 64:2 which speaks of Noah approaching his great-grandfather, Enoch, about "the quaking of the earth" (65:4, 9) and reporting Enoch's reply and what he showed Noah (65:1 – 66:1). The motif of someone seeking Enoch's advice is known to us from both *1 Enoch* 106-107 and *Genesis Apocryphon*, where Methuselah seeks out Enoch after hearing from

---

[44] Charles, *APOT*, 2.230.

[45] Nickelsburg, "Discerning the Structure(s)," 39; similarly Knibb, "Structure," 60.

[46] VanderKam, "Book of Parables," notes "a blending of traditions: the descending angels (said only of Shemihazah and his associates in 1 En 6-11) revealed secrets to humans and thus led them astray (traditions supposedly not associated with Shemihazah and company in 6-11)" (89). VanderKam's "supposedly" is appropriate, because in fact as it stands 6 – 11 does depict Shemihazah and his associates as bearing secret information about potions and spells (7:1b; 8:3b; cf. 65:6b).

Lamech about the extraordinary child, Noah. Here Noah seeks out Enoch at "the ends of the earth" and issues a cry: "hear me, hear me, hear me!" (65:2). While parallelling the story of Methuselah, it also recalls the cry of earth's inhabitants in 9:2, and earlier in the *Parables*, in 47:1-4. "The earth had tilted and its destruction was near" (65:1), as Enoch explains, because of its corruption through the Watchers. It is a fitting addition following the reference in 64:1-2 to the Watchers and to human sin. The focus is again on forbidden knowledge, not sexual wrongdoing. Thus Enoch explains: "for they have learned the secrets of the angels, and all the violence of the satans, and all their powers, the hidden secrets and all the powers of those who practice sorcery and the powers of spells, and the powers of those who cast molten images in all the earth" (65:6).[47] Apart from the making of idols, the list matches the concerns expressed in 8:1 about Asael's teaching, but also the teaching or sorcery and spells by the 200 who came down with Shemihazah (7:1; 8:3) and by Gadre'el and Kasdeya in 69:6-7, 12. The concern with metallurgy, already an issue in 52:2-9, comes to further expression in 65:7-8, which mentions silver, soft metal, lead and tin. The explanation continues in 65:10-11 with mention of sorceries (reconstructed) and hidden knowledge.

In 66:1-2 then we read of the flood unleashed "for the judgement and destruction of all who reside and dwell on the earth". The flood had already been depicted in 54:7 – 55:2. As in 10:1-15, it belonged within the complex events of judgement which included, beside the flood, the binding of Asael and imprisonment of the Watchers until the day of their judgement and the mutual self-destruction of the giants. Thus 67:1-3, like 10:1-3, describe the instruction by God to Noah to build the ark and the promise that his seed will be forever and that "they will be blessed and be multiplied on the earth". Similarly Enoch had told Noah in 65:12: his descendants "will be without number forever", but again without further elaboration. This does, of course, refer to the normal processes of progeny and procreation and fits the many generations after Noah. It is not a reference to the eschaton or the age to come.

In 67:4-12 we find Noah reporting, as expected, the judgement on "those angels who showed iniquity" (67:4) and "led astray" (67:6, 7). As elsewhere in the document there is nothing corresponding to the concern in 10:9-10 with the giants.

---

[47] But see Pierluigi Piovanelli, "A Theology of the Supernatural in the Book of Watchers? An African Perspective," in *The Origins of Enochic Judaism: Proceedings of the First Enoch Seminar, University of Michigan, Sesto Fiorentino, Italy, June 19-23, 2001* (ed. G. Boccaccini; Torino: Silvio Zamorani Editore, 2002) = *Henoch* 24 (2002) 87-98, who argues that "*xaylomu lä-xebrat* is not 'the power of the ropes ... neither 'the power of magical spells' ... but 'the power of (cosmetic) colours' revealed by Azazel to the women in *1 Enoch 8:1*". He notes that "the guttural consonants *x / h* alternate quite freely in the spelling of the Ethiopic manuscripts" and that the word represented here is *hebr*, "colour" (88).

In 67:4 we find a cross reference to the passage earlier in the document, where the author had Enoch see the valley prepared for the Watchers (54:1, 4-6; 55:3 – 56:4). "And he will confine those angels who showed iniquity in that burning valley that my great-grandfather Enoch had shown me previously in the West by the mountains of gold and silver and iron and soft metal and tin" (67:4; cf. 52:2-6; 53:6). This shows some editorial awareness in relating the Noah material to the rest of the work (see also 68:1, in which Noah reports that Enoch gave him the *Book of the Parables*).

It is interesting that we find in this depiction of the burning valley[48] some further description of the wrongdoing of the angels, but also of the means of punishment. With regard to the latter we read of "a great disturbance and troubling of the waters" (67:5), which together with "fiery molten metal" produced a smell of sulphur mixed with the waters (67:6). There was a valley under which there was burning (67:6) and "through the valleys of that (area) rivers of fire issue" (67:7). This reflects the common assumption (not at all unscientific!) that hot pools and springs are connected to underground fire, frequently seen as related to the fires of hell.[49] With regard to those being punished, they include the angels who "led astray those who dwell on earth" (67:7; similarly 67:6), an accusation repeated elsewhere (54:6; 56:4; 64:2; 69:28), but also "the kings and the mighty and the exalted and those who dwell on the earth" (67:8).

The passage is rather complicated in the way it depicts the effects of the fire and water. With regard to the kings and the mighty the passage envisages two stages. In 67:8 it describes how the waters will (serve) them "for the healing of their flesh and the judgement of their spirits" (67:8). Here we read that "their spirits are full of lust, so that their flesh will be judged, because they denied the Lord of Spirits" (67:8). We return below to the theme of lust, but at this point note that this judgement appears to be something occurring during their lives on earth. Thus the statement continues: "And they see their judgment every day and do not believe in his name" (67:8). While one can imagine that waters bring healing, it is not clear how waters bring judgement to the spirit, unless as Olson suggests, the hot waters should have reminded them of the fires of judgement below, but they took no notice.[50] The following lines may indicate how this is so: "And the more

---

[48] Suter, *Tradition and Composition*, rightly points out that "valley" must mean more than indentation in the earth's surface. Rather it envisages connection with the fires of Sheol and so should be seen as a euphemism for Gehenna. He also notes that it corresponds to pit or cistern in Isa 24:22 as an aspect of what he sees as midrashic interpretation of Isa 24:17-23 in the *Parables* (56-57).

[49] See Olson, *Enoch*, who cites *b. Shab.* 39a (122). See also Black, *Book of Enoch*, 242. Suter, *Tradition and Composition*, speaks of folktale which connects the thermal spring with the punishment of demons (55).

[50] Olson, *Enoch*, 124; similarly Black, *Book of Enoch*, 242.

their flesh is burnt, the more a change takes place in their spirits, forever and ever, because before the Lord of Spirits no lying word is spoken" (67:9). The burning of their flesh might refer to fever or the symptoms of sexually transmitted diseases from which they seek relief in the waters[51] or, less likely, it could possibly refer to burning in the waters through sulphur. The process appears to be understood as something positive since it deals with lying (or alternatively, "idle words"). Metallurgical practices possibly underlie the image, so that the heating is seen as leading to purification. Here, however, the process envisaged is one which leads not to moral renewal, leading to escape from judgement, but to acknowledgement of sin. This appears to be the meaning of what follows: "For judgment will come upon them because they believe in the lust of their flesh, but they deny the spirit of the Lord" (67:10). In 67:13 Michael explains: "For these waters of judgment (serve) for the healing of the flesh of the <kings>[52] and for the lust of their flesh, and they do not see and do not believe that those waters will be changed and become a fire that burns forever". Clearly this envisages the end of the process intimated in 67:9, which speaks of the burning of their flesh, where the waters effectively become a lake of fire (as in Rev 20:10). An author appears here to be playing with the image of hot pools and imagining that one day those who use them will be burnt up in them.[53]

The passage interrupts the account of the judgement of the kings to report the judgement of the angels through the waters, but this time, by contrast, envisaging a change in the opposite direction: "For when the angels are judged in those waters, those springs of water will change their temperature, and when the angels come up, the waters of those springs will be changed and become cold" (67:11). The assumption could be that cold water inflicts judgement on the angels. Perhaps the sense is that this reverses their natural state as fiery and shining, effectively destroying them. Alternatively, the waters become cold after the angels have come up out of and left the waters which were used for their interim punishment, and

---

[51] Olson, *Enoch*, 124. Cf. Black, *Book of Enoch*, who suggests burning with lust, referring to Hos 7:4; Sir 23:17; 1 Cor 7:9 (242-43). See also Prov 6:27.

[52] All MSS use the word for angel, *mal'ak*, which most interpreters see as resulting from the confusion of מלכיא "king" and מלאכיא "angel". So Charles, *APOT*, 2.232; Knibb, *Enoch*, 158. Olson, *Enoch*, however argues that no emendation is required since Ethiopic *mal'ak* can also mean ruler and regularly translates ἄρχων ("ruler") in the Ethiopic Bible (124).

[53] Suter, *Tradition and Composition*, suggests that the warm waters comfort the senses, but "dull the spirit through the incitation of lust", rendering the kings "insensitive to the demands of the Lord of Spirits" so that their future punishment of both flesh and spirit is assured when the fire of the eschaton comes, recalling the hardening of Pharaoh's heart in Exod 14:17-18 (55-56).

now are taken off to their final judgement.[54] They would need to be heated up again to punish the kings. The words of Michael, which follow, certainly depict this as the judgment on the angels which serves then as "a testimony for the kings and the mighty who possess the earth" (67:12). Apparently the author wants the report of the judgement of the angels in the waters to be a sign to the kings about the judgement they will face in the water.

The fault with the spirits of the kings and the mighty is that they "are full of lust" and "denied the Lord of Spirits" (67:8); "they believe in the lust of their flesh, but they deny the spirit of the Lord" (67:10; similarly 13). The word, *tawnet*, has a range of meaning including "game, entertainment, music, orgy, lust", so could indicate illicit sexual desire, but need not. The author may have in mind also the sexual lust of the Watchers, but nothing indicates this, although the message of their judgement carries the implication: do as they did and you will suffer the same fate.

The author has creatively (even if confusedly) worked with the image of hot springs used for healing to depict judgement of both the angels and the kings. In doing so he appears also to have drawn upon imagery from the processes of metallurgy and possibly from the metaphor of burning in relation to sexual desire, and the sensations of burning related to the symptoms of sexually transmitted diseases, such as gonorrhoea and syphilis.

Heated bath houses and hot springs did indeed feature as one of the luxuries of the wealthy ruling classes and normally people bathed naked, which might lead to various sexual activities. This was the case whether bathing was single sex, in which case activity was homosexual, or mixed. At least at this level the author probably has the practices of his day in mind. The contemporary reference may however be more specific if, as many have suggested, we have an allusion here to Herod the Great's retreat to the hot pools of Callirhoe to seek relief from his ailments, as reported in Jos *A.J.* 17.168-172; *B.J.* 1.656-658,[55] which might have included symptoms of sexually transmitted disease.[56]

Darrell Hannah has recently defended the proposal.[57] His argument is based partly on demonstrating that Callirhoe would have been well known at the time

---

[54] So Black, *Book of Enoch*, 242.

[55] Gillian Bampfylde, "The Similitudes of Enoch: Historical Allusions," *JSJ* 15 (1984) 9-31, 28-30; Jonas C. Greenfield and Michael E. Stone, "The Enochic Pentateuch and the Date of the Similitudes," *HTR* 71 (1977) 51–65, 60; Black, *Book of Enoch*, 242; Nickelsburg, "Discerning the Structure(s)," 47.

[56] G. A. Williamson, ed. *Josephus: The Jewish War* (London: Penguin, rev. ed.; 1981) notes: "Of the various diagnoses suggested for Herod's complaint, arteriosclerosis seems the most convincing" (424 n. 30).

[57] Hannah, "Book of Noah," 469-77. In agreement: Paolo Sacchi, "The 2005 Camaldoli Seminar on the Parables of Enoch: Summary and Prospects for Future

and that archaeological evidence confirms its usage during Herod's reign. "Herod's ill-fated visit to the famous thermal baths on the eastern shore of the Dead Sea could not but have been well-known in both Jewish and pagan circles".[58] More significantly he notes that the material in question belongs to what is widely acknowledged as Noachic material which has been interpolated by a redactor into the text. This passage has peculiarities, however, since it contains some anomalies suggesting that these verses are the work of the redactor, not part of the Noachic source. This explains why we suddenly have reference to "the kings, the mighty ones and nobles who possess the earth", a common theme in the *Parables*, and the occurrence here of "the Lord of the Spirits" (8-9).[59] It also explains why the focus here is suddenly not warfare and violence (as 46:4-5, 7-8; 48:10; 62:11; 63:1-4, 7, 10), but sexual lust, which, he argues, was widely alleged against Herod (Josephus *A.J.* 15.319-322; *B.J.* 1.477), and for which his demise was seen as punishment (Josephus *A.J.* 17.168-171).[60] Accordingly, Hannah concludes: "Thus, the second half of 1 En 67 can easily be understood as an allusion to Herod the Great's visit to the waters of Callirrhoe in the latter half of March 4 B.C.E".[61] He sees the expansion by the redactor as standing in some tension to the Noachic material being interpolated, but as reflecting a concrete situation. He also deals with possible objections,[62] including that Josephus described the waters as sweet, whereas 67:6 suggests they were sulphurous (apparently some pools were; some were not), the location in "the west" (which can be justified from the perspective of Noah's location), and the widespread use of warm baths at the time.

While Hannah's concern is to apply these observations to the issue of dating, for our investigation they are significant in explaining the concern here with sexual lust, not otherwise a significant feature in the *Parables*. As we have noted, it appears here primarily in relation to rulers, but may not be absent in the depiction of the judgement of the angels. Their sexual wrongdoing received attention in 39:1. It also becomes the focus again in what follows.

In 68:1 we have words of Noah explaining that Enoch gave the speaker "the explanation of all these secrets in a book, and in the parables that were given to him". We then return to a report of Michael's words, as in 67:12-13, but now in conversation with Raphael, in which he reports unrest at the severity of the judgement meted out to the angels (68:2 – 69:1). This "humane" perspective might

---

Research," in *Enoch and the Messiah Son of Man: Revisiting the Book of Parables* (ed. Gabriele Boccaccini; Grand Rapids: Eerdmans, 2007) 499-512, 510.

[58] Hannah, "Book of Noah," 470-71.

[59] Hannah, "Book of Noah," 473.

[60] Hannah, "Book of Noah," 474.

[61] Hannah, "Book of Noah," 475.

[62] Hannah, "Book of Noah," 476-77.

perhaps reflect some unease in the author or his community about such theology, but Michael then relents. It also parallels the account in *1 Enoch* 12 – 16 where Enoch agrees to intercede for the angels. No such intervention happens here. Michael designates their offence as being that "they act as if they were like the Lord" (68:5) and they have shown secrets "to those who dwell on the earth" (69:1). Here we find not illicit lusting but giving of information as the major concern.

The focus on the fallen Watchers continues with the list of the names of the twenty angels who were leaders of the 200 who descended (based on 6:6), beginning with Shemihazah, and with Asael coming tenth but a conjectured Asael also as twenty-first (69:2-3). It matches the list in 6:7-8 with some minor exceptions. Here as there, Shemihazah is the first, though otherwise in the document Azazel is the leading figure. More significant is the second list, which like the second list in 8:3, gives not only names but functions. It brings five different names together with the charge brought against them.

Each of these is then identified with a different name in a second list and their charge detailed. As Nickelsburg notes, "two of the major issues are illicit sex and violence".[63] Shemihazah is called Yeqon and described as "the one who led all the children of the angels astray and brought them down upon the earth, and led them astray through the daughters of men" (69:4). "Children" refers here not literally to offspring, but to those who belonged to the angelic host. This appears to describe what we find in 6:3, which portrays Shemihazah as needing to persuade the other Watchers to join him on his sexual escapade. It is expressed in a form which seems to inculcate the women, since it portrays him as using the women to lead them astray. This would lay some blame on the women and is consistent with what we find in *1 Enoch* 6 – 11. Nothing, however, is said of any initiatives on their part, such as is implied in their use of cosmetics and adornments in 8:1.

The second angel, who is called Asbe'el, also led the children of the holy angels astray "so that they ruined their bodies through the daughters of men" (69:5). Ruining their bodies probably refers here to defilement through their act of sexual intercourse with women as humankind, as in *1 Enoch* 6 – 16, rather any temporary impurity such as through seminal emission or contact with a menstruant or virginal blood. Nothing connects this ruination to their potential status as priests. Both of these first two angels instigate sexual wrongdoing. The second is an adviser, an element not evident elsewhere in the tradition. Black suggests that this angel is to be identified with Kasbe'el in 69:13, but the context there suggests otherwise.[64]

---

[63] Nickelsburg, "Discerning the Structure(s)," 40. He also notes the possibility that with 64:1-2, 69:4-12 may have been part of the original form of the last part of the Parables, being reflected in 69:28 (41).

[64] Black, *Book of Enoch*, 247.

The third figure, called Gadre'el, "showed all the blows of death to the sons of men" (69:6).[65] This is about magic and sorcery. It corresponds to the secrets of sorcery and charms revealed by the Watchers according to 7:1 (cf. also 9:8) and by Hermani according to 8:3. It adds, however, that "he led Eve astray", but does not enable us to know how or in what sense. It also adds that he taught about armour and weapons, leading to warfare. This is traditionally a feature associated with Asael (Azazel) (8:1). His leading Eve astray is an activity which long precedes the descent, perhaps reflecting the possibility that the list originally had nothing to do with the myth of the Watchers' fall or that this figure has been assimilated into it secondarily. Azazel is linked to the deception of Eve in *Apoc. Abr.* 22:5 – 23:12, esp. 23:10-11.[66] While leading Eve astray is juxtaposed to the preceding two angels' deed of sexual wrongdoing, a sexual reference need not be implied in the leading astray of Eve here, although this should not be excluded as a possibility especially in contexts where the ambiguity of the LXX translation might have played a role.[67] Coblentz Bautch notes that Eve alone is mentioned here as misled, and without any reference to Adam.[68] This too may reflect the focus in the preceding two accounts on angels in relation to women. There is no indication that her deception was the origin or cause of sin. The angels have the blame for that. Nor is there reference to obtaining wisdom as in 32:6 nor any hints of messianic prefiguring as in 85:3.[69]

The fourth, Penemue, is blamed as the one who "showed the sons of men the bitter and the sweet", probably an allusion to magic potions, and "all the secrets of wisdom" (69:8-11). The bitter and sweet potions correspond to the secrets about the cutting of roots and plants, revealed to the women by the Watchers according to 7:1 and by Shemihazah according to 8:3. Curiously Penemue also "gave humans knowledge about writing with ink and papyrus, and therefore many went astray from of old and forever and until this day. For humans were not born for this purpose, to confirm their trustworthiness through pen and ink" (69:10). It

---

[65] On the name, see the discussion in Kelley Coblentz Bautch, "Adamic Traditions in the Parables? A Query on 1 Enoch 69:6," in *Enoch and the Messiah Son of Man: Revisiting the Book of Parables* (ed. Gabriele Boccaccini; Grand Rapids: Eerdmans, 2007) 352-60, 356-57, who notes that in Zohar *Vayaqhel* 202a the figure is associated with war as here.

[66] Coblentz Bautch, "Adamic Traditions," 356; and see our discussion below.

[67] On this see William Loader, *The Septuagint, Sexuality, and the New Testament: Case Studies on the Impact of the LXX in Philo and the New Testament* (Grand Rapids: Eerdmans, 2004) 45-46.

[68] Coblentz Bautch, "Adamic Traditions," 355.

[69] So Coblentz Bautch, "Adamic Traditions," 352-53. She also notes that the *Animal Apocalypse* passes over their sin altogether, presenting Eve as a heifer and Adam as a white bull, apparently prefiguring the Messiah, having therefore "no tree, forbidden or otherwise, no illicit gain of knowledge, no expulsion from Eden, and no recapitulation of any part of Gen 3" (354).

stands in some tension with other statements in the Enoch tradition which see Enoch as a scribe. The author is surely not objecting to his own activity as author, but probably to legal use of documents and possibly also the passing on of forbidden teachings. That writings can be said to "lead astray" alerts us to the possibility that other references to leading astray may have false or forbidden teaching in mind. Death comes here not through Eve's and Adam's sin and tasting of the tree of knowledge of good and evil, but through illicit knowledge passed on by books: "And death, which ruins everything, would not have laid its hand on them. But through this, their knowledge, they are perishing, and through this power it devours" (69:11) (a reworking of the Genesis tradition?). The statement that "humans were not created to be different from the angels, so that they should remain pure and righteous" also has illicit knowledge as its focus.

The next figure, Kasdeya, seems also related to sorcery.[70] He "showed the sons of men all the evil blows of spirits and demons, and the blows of the foetus in the womb, so that it aborts, the bite of the serpent, and the blow that comes in the noon day heat (cf. Ps 91:5-6), the son of the serpent, whose name (is) Taba'et" (69:12). These will reflect knowledge and practices of primitive medicine, probably including inducing abortions, possibly through physical blows or through spells and incantations.[71]

Knibb remarks that this list of five angels "provides a tradition about the fall of the Watchers quite different from that in chaps. 6-8".[72] Certainly this applies to the names, but much of the content is similar (sexual wrongdoing, imparting of forbidden knowledge and skills, including sorcery and magic potions)[73] with the exception of the reference to Eve and the focus on particular demonic activities revealed by Kasdeya. That element may well be understood, nevertheless, as belonging to the activity of seduction of women which was part of the myth in its original setting. Tigchelaar notes that the list "shows an awareness of different stories of falls of angels".[74] It is interesting that, as elsewhere in the *Parables*, no

---

[70] Olson, *Enoch*, notes that it reflects the Aramaic for Chaldean, a term used often for magicians, as already Dan 12:2 (128)

[71] Olson, *Enoch*, notes that "demons that cause miscarriages, abortions, and death for newborns are among the most durable types in demonic lore" (128).

[72] Knibb, "Structure," 61.

[73] VanderKam, "Parables," writes of the second list that it "clearly echoes the story of the angels who sinned" (96; similarly 90). See also the cautionary comments of Tigchelaar, "Remarks," noting that here and elsewhere we cannot necessarily conclude that parallels between the *Book of Parables* and the *Book of the Watchers* mean dependence on the latter and not on other sources (106-109). On the other hand, a strong case can be made that it should be seen as a possible source – indeed the only surviving one for which we could make such a claim.

[74] So Tigchelaar, "Remarks," 108.

mention is made of the giants. The theme associated with them in 7:3, namely warfare and violence, belongs to Asael/Azazel, and is associated here with the second figure. The strong presence here of the angels' sexual wrongdoing, already noted in 39:1, makes it likely that hearers familiar with the whole would see it implied elsewhere when the sin of the angels is identified generically and might also see it as characteristic of the rulers.

In 69:13-22 the document appears to bring relief from what could have been seen as hopeless, namely the impact of the five evil angels. It reports the basis for countering their influence: the name and the oath, and provides an explanation of how the oath became available. There are also different ways of understanding the sequence of events.[75] I read it as follows: Kasbe'el showed the oath to holy ones after Michael acceded to his request to reveal to him the secret name, and so Michael allowed him to become head of the oath, though Michael remained its keeper. The holy ones could then use it against the fallen comrades. It is the same oath and name which established and maintains creation and which through the good angels is accessible to the hearers of the *Parable* in their having to cope with the impact of the fallen angels.

Thus a certain Kasbe'el[76] "the head of the oath", "showed it to the holy ones when he was dwelling on high in glory" and apparently persuaded Michael that he should show him "the secret name, so that they might make mention of it in the oath" (69:14).[77] Making mention of the name in the oath is in order "that those

---

[75] Knibb, *Enoch*, for instance, sees reference to two different oaths, the one alluded to in 6:3-6 and a divine oath entrusted to Michael which was used in the act of creation (162), following A. Caquot and P. Geoltrain, "Notes sur le texte éthiopien des 'Paraboles' d'Hénoch," *Sem* 13 (1963) 39-54, 52-54. Olson, *Enoch*, sees Kasbe'el as a former good angel who tried to bribe Michael and the holy ones by revealing the Beqa oath to them, hoping Michael would reciprocate; or alternatively he revealed the oath to the fallen angels, realized the mistake and then tried to win Michael's support to counter them (271). Black, *Book of Enoch*, identifies Kasbe'el with the second angel, 'Asbe'el (246-47) and contemplates an attempt to trick Michael (248).

[76] Suter, *Tradition and Composition*, notes that Charles, *APOT*, understands Kasbe'el to be one of the fallen angels and suggests that "it is a understandable that the fallen angels would want to obtain the powers of such an oath" (21). Similarly, Black, *Book of Enoch*, 247-48; Olson, *Enoch*, 271. Against this, Suter writes, Kasabel, "'Ram of God,' does not seem to be thought of elsewhere as a fallen angel, but rather as an angel of good will" (21). Rather "the correct interpretation seems to be that Kasabel and Michael are joining forces to use the oath to restore the cosmic order disturbed by the fall of the angels" (21). He also argues the independence of this tradition from the fallen angels, pointing to the presence of oath in association with an angelic list in 41:3 – 44:1 (21).

[77] Jonathan Ben-Dov, "Exegetical Notes on Cosmology in the Parables of Enoch," in *Enoch and the Messiah Son of Man: Revisiting the Book of Parables* (ed. Gabriele Boccaccini; Grand Rapids: Eerdmans, 2007) 143-49, notes the reference to a mutual oath

who showed the sons of men everything that was in secret might quake at the name of the oath" (69:14).[78] The primary focus here appears then to be exorcism or at least exercise of power over the disobedient angels. In 69:15 we read that this initiative succeeded and the oath was put into Michael's hands and that its power was to control the sinful angels.[79] Accordingly 69:16 reports, apparently of Michael and Kasbe'el, that "they are strong through this oath", presumably to combat these opposing forces (69:16). Alternatively the "they" might already refer to the elements of creation to be listed below. There follows then a reinforcement of the power of the oath, to reassure hearers that it can achieve what is claimed. It was used in the creation of the waters, the deeps, the sun and moon and the stars. This coheres with the focus on such matters earlier in the *Parables*, where their mention relates to the divine ordering of the universe. Here the oath with the secret name, almost certainly the divine name, functions as elsewhere God's wisdom and the Logos do. Like them it is not only the agent of creation, but also sustains it (so 69:25).[80]

While the above interpretation, I suggest, makes good sense of the role of the passage in its context, there are a number of points where the MSS vary and the

---

among the angels in 41:5 which he contrasts with the imposed oath here. He writes: "The origin for the idea of a divine fiat imposed on the luminaries lies in Jeremiah's prophecy", citing Jer 33:20, 25 (149).

[78] The name referred to in the oath is given in 69:13 as Biqa, which appears to be a transliteration of the Hebrew, בְּךָ "by you", for instance, as referring to God in Isa 26:13 and elsewhere. It is later known to have been treated as a number (as already here), designating 22, which was also associated with the divine name by other obscure means of gematria. On this see Olson, *Enoch*, who draws attention to the tradition in Zohar *Shemoth* 9a-9b from the late 13th century (271-72). There it is treated as a name which came into possession of evil powers, but that is not apparent here unless one sees Kasbe'el as a fallen angel (see the discussion of this option below). For an alternative gematria explanation see Black, *Book of Enoch*, 247-48.

[79] There are variants among the MSS concerning the word associated with "this oath" in 69:15, some of which read *'aka'e* , whose meaning is obscure but may have been a mystical name; one MS, Tana, reads *'ekuy* "evil".

[80] Suter, *Tradition and Composition*, draws attention to parallels in the later Helakoth literature which speaks of God writing on Metatron's forehead the letters by which things were created and of a divine spell which binds the cosmos in order (22-23). He notes also the use of similar tradition in incantation in the magical text, *Logos Ebraikos* (22-23), to which Moses Gaster drew attention (Moses Gaster, "The Logos Ebraikos in the Magical Papyrus of Paris, and the Book of Enoch," *JRAS*, 3d series, 33 [1901] 109-17), but argues that "in the literature it functions at the cosmic level" (23). The immediately preceding context suggests rather that both levels are in operation. The function of 69:13-25 is to indicate a basis of hope for the afflicted to enable them to counter what the angels unleashed and to ground it by using evidence of the power of the oath in creation.

meaning is obscure, which might result in a quite opposite interpretation, namely that Kasbe'el belongs on the side of the evil angels. This appears to me to make much less sense in the context. The primary focus seems rather to be dealing with the angelic powers as agents of harm and especially the dangers let loose by the last of the five angels, Kasdeya, and to affirm hope based on using the oath and the name against these powers. Issues pertaining to sexuality seem confined to countering the effects of demons in the processes of pregnancy and childbirth alluded to there.

We noted above that 69:26-29 is widely seen as the sequel to 62 – 63, but is now separated by material linked to Noah which the author or editor has included. In its current form the reference to the "name" of the Son of Man is to be read closely with the "name" of the oath. This is seen clearly by Gieschen, who writes: "The significance of the revealing of the name of the Son of Man becomes readily apparent when one sees the relationship between the Divine Name, the oath used in creation, and the name of the Son of Man in 1 En 69".[81] The function of the name in relation to the Son of Man is eschatological, whereas its function in association with the oath relates to the creation and its maintenance, but there is a sense in which the Son of Man is now to exercise the same kind of authority, and is seen, therefore, as doing so as a bearer of the divine name (cf. the giving of the divine name in Phil 2:2-10).[82] The joy of the elect is that the enthroned Son of Man will banish sinners forever and destroy the Watchers and their works forever and prevail by his word (recalling the power of the oath in 13-25). No mention is made of specific wickedness, including sexual wrongdoing.

The final two chapters return to the ascension of Enoch, again, as in 39:3, using imagery from the ascent of Elijah, and, as there, leading into an account of his vision of the heavenly world, including the temple, which echoes *1 Enoch* 13. He is also shown "the place of the chosen and the righteous", where he saw "the first fathers and the righteous, who were dwelling in that place from of old" (70:3-4). This is clearly on earth, since he saw it before completing his ascent to heaven (71:1). The allusion is to Eden. The final identification of Enoch as the Son of

---

[81] Charles A. Gieschen, "The Name of the Son of Man in the Parables of Enoch," in *Enoch and the Messiah Son of Man: Revisiting the Book of Parables* (ed. Gabriele Boccaccini; Grand Rapids: Eerdmans, 2007) 238-49, 241. He notes the importance of the divine name in the Parables.

[82] See also Gieschen, "Name," who notes the idea of imparting divine power by putting the name on the angel in Exod 23:20-22, or in the temple, or seeing it as subject of actions (Isa 30:27; Prov 18:10). Similar authorizations using the divine occur in *3 Enoch* 12:5 and *Apoc. Abr.* 10:3, 8 (243-45), to which I would add the giving of the name which is above every name to Jesus at his exaltation in Phil 2:9-11. He notes also the association of name and oath in *Jub.* 36:7, and of name and word in Philo *Conf.* 146; Wis 18:14-16; and John 12:23; 17:6a, 11b-12a, 26; Rev 19:11-16 (245-47).

Man (71:14) is the focus of major discussions, but like the rest of the material in these chapters has no particular relevance to issues of sexuality.

Conclusion

Overall the document does not exhibit a major concern with matters pertaining to sexuality or with sexual wrongdoing, although the latter is a minor concern. It knows and uses the myth of the Watchers as depicted in *1 Enoch* 6 – 11 and 12 – 16, whether directly or indirectly, and reflects a form of the myth which has undergone further development. The Watchers appear in 39:1 as belonging to ("sons of") "the chosen and holy", and in 54:4-6 both as the "host of Azazel", reflecting the development in which Asael, who has become Azazel, is portrayed as their leader, and as "servants of Satan", reflecting a wider frame of reference in which the chief source of sin is Satan. Similarly 55:3 speaks of "Azazel and all his associates and all his host" and 56:3, 4 of that host as "their chosen and beloved ones". The reference to children killed with their fathers and mothers (60:24-25) might also be to the Watchers and their offspring (as demons, not as giants), and possibly to the Watchers' wives. In 64:2 the author speaks simply of "the angels who descended" and in 65:6-7 simply of "angels", here in association with "satans". Similarly we read of "those angels who showed iniquity" (67:4) and "led astray" (67:6, 7) and in 67:11 simply of "the angels". By contrast, 69:2-3 and 4-12 contain two lists of names, the second also describing specific functions.

The most common charge against the angels is that they lead astray (54:6; 56:4; 64:2; 67:6, 7; 69:4, 5; 6, 9: 69:28). Sometimes the accusation stands without specific indication of how this was done, as in 54:6 and 56:4. The preceding reference to metallurgy and the probable irony of having Azazel and his host shackled with chains of iron and bronze, makes it likely that the accusation relates to their teaching about metallurgy, which provided humans with the means to make war, a charge levelled at Asael in 8:1. In 64:2 leading astray is specifically linked to their passing on of what was secret, most likely also related to metallurgy, but, as the following context suggests, also other secrets of angels and satans, including sorcery, spells and the making of idols (65:6). As in 54:6 and 56:4, the references in 67:6, 7 do specify the charge, but by now a hearer would already be clear that it relates to forbidden knowledge previously mentioned.

In the second list of angels we have the fullest account of their crimes. They include leading astray through teaching the skills of making weaponry (Gadreel 69:6) and various kinds of sorcery and spells and potions (Kasdeya 69:12; Penemue 69:8). The list goes beyond that, however, in two significant ways. First, it depicts the skill of writing with pen and ink as corrupting (Penemue 69:9-10), indicating that the concern is not only what angels taught but also those who have passed on such knowledge in writing, thus, false teaching (69:11). Second, the list gives prominence to the leading astray not of humans but of angels by Yeqon and Asbeel. This addresses the angels' sexual wrongdoing by having intercourse with women, but, unlike Genesis 6 and, to some degree, *1 Enoch* 6 – 8, the emphasis falls on these two angels as instigators. There is some basis for this development in 6:3 where Shemihazah has to ensure the others join him, but according to 6:2 they hardly needed convincing and were at most in danger of getting cold feet. The depiction of Yeqon and Asbeel goes far beyond that. Within each description we find further aspects which reflect the myth. Yeqon leads the angels astray through the daughters of men. This may implicate them in some of the blame, as appears to be the case in 8:1, but it is noteworthy that we find no reference to the role of metallurgy in this as providing for cosmetics and ornaments. Similarly in response to Asbeel's advice the angels are said to ruin their bodies, an echo of the tradition about defilement through mixing of kinds, but no connection is made with their possible status as priests as in the *Book of the Watchers*. The use of the motif of leading astray in relation to Eve is striking and probably reflects the diverse origins of the traditions in the second list, since it goes beyond the framework of the myth of a descent of Watchers in the time of Jared.[83] It may indicate that this was sexual seduction, but that is uncertain.

The presence of sexual themes in relation to the angels would not come as a surprise for someone listening to the transmitted text, since it featured in the first reference to the angels in 39:1, which reports that "the sons of the chosen and holy were descending from the highest heaven , and their seed was becoming one with the sons of men". The "books of jealous wrath and rage and books of trepidation and consternation" which Enoch is said in 39:2 to have received would have called to mind for hearers books of Enoch with which they were familiar, presumably at least the *Book of the Watchers*. While 39:1 refers to the sexual wrongdoing, however, its function in the context appears to be more generally to alert the reader to the problems to which Enoch would see solutions in the visions which follow. Except for the latter parts of the third parable, the focus in relation to the angels' wrongdoing lies on the imparting of secrets and the way it has created a problem on earth, namely, the actions of the kings and the wealthy. These are depicted primarily in terms of warfare, exploitation of the poor, and idolatry.[84]

---

[83] Annette Yoshiko Reed, *Fallen Angels and the History of Judaism and Christianity: The Reception of Enochic Literature* (New York: Cambridge University Press, 2005), notes that here "angelic descent floats free from its moorings in the period directly preceding the Flood, and hence, Gen 6:1-4", seeing it as a possible intermediate stage in "the gradual transference of traditions about the antediluvian descent of the angels onto the figure of the Serpent/Satan" (115). She writes of the *Parables* conflating "the corrupting teachings of the Watchers with the Serpent's seduction of Eve" (115).

[84] Reed, *Fallen Angels*, writes of the author's treatment of the Watchers as "downplaying their sexual dalliances with the daughters of men", rightly pointing to the

A sexual component to the woes facing humanity is not, however, entirely absent. It may be implied already in the reference to God's agent tipping the mighty from their couches (a probable allusion to their indulgent feasts) (46:4-5). It is not, however, until we reach the section which exploits the imagery of hot pools and the subterranean fires of judgement that we find what is most likely to be an allusion to sexual wrongdoing on the part of kings and the dreadful irony that where they seek comfort they will one day find a lake of fire. One might have expected specific allusion to the punishment of the angels also for sexual wrongdoing, but this is at most implied. The emphasis on the sin of sexual wrongdoing appears nowhere else in relation to the kings. It may appear here because of specific accusations being made against Herod, if the scene alludes to his visit to Callirhoe.

Not all charges against the angels have an equivalent in the actions of the kings. This is true of sorcery, spells, and potions. The wiles taught by Kasdeya include a focus on harm brought to women, foetuses, and newborns (69:12), reflecting issues at all levels of human life. Chains are associated with exorcism in later tradition and so probably reflect the perception that for the hearers a primary manifestation of the outcome of the angels' activity is in the works of demons. Such demonic activities seem to be a concern for the author. Against them he offers the assurance of countering such powers with the oath of the name.

While the *Book of Parables* seems beholden to the myth of the Watchers, probably in the form known to us in the *Book of the Watchers*, it reflects some interesting reworkings of that myth.[85] We noted above the shift from Asael to Azazel and the prominence of this figure, and the setting of the myth within a wider framework of understanding evil where Satan is the chief figure. The second list of names also reflects the impact of other traditions. Both there and in what follows in the obscure 69:13-14 we encounter a level of activity above the angels who sinned, so that we hear of Yeqon's initiative, Asbe'el's advice, Kasbe'el's negotiation, all new elements in the tradition. Similarly 68:2 – 69:1 may well reflect the need to deal with critical assessment of the myth, transposed into such a high level exchange. It stands in contrast to the account in *1 Enoch* 12 – 16 where

---

emphasis on communication of illicit knowledge (113), but incorrectly states that "the only reference to the Watchers' sexual sins occurs in 1 En 69" (114), since that ignores 39:1.

[85] See Fröhlich, "Parables," who concludes: "The Book of Parables seems to know of a larger tradition on the Watchers than what we find in the Book of the Watchers" (350). Cf. Grabbe, "Parables of Enoch," who understates the importance of the myth when he writes of the "centrality of the angelic world, including both good and bad angels, but no special preoccupation with the myth of the fallen angels (unlike the Book of the Watchers)" (397) and speaks of a de-emphasising of the myth of the fallen angels (402).

Enoch does agree to intercede for the angels. Its allegation, in 68:4, that "they act as if they were like the Lord", is an innovative assessment of their sin.

Other interesting twists and turns include the omission of all references to the giants and to the association of the skills of metallurgy with the production of cosmetics and ornaments for women. It is not clear to what extent the Watchers' women have a place in the document. They could be included among the "beloved" of Azazel and his associates (56:3-4) and there is a possible allusion to their destruction along with their husbands and their children, the demons. While no mention is made of binding the Watchers, as in 10:4,[86] the motif of placing them in iron and bronze chains appears to reflect a reworking of the emphasis on metallurgy linked to Asael, which is greatly expanded in association with a reworking of the mountain tradition in 18:6-9; 24:2-4, and to function ironically: they are chained by their own devices.

We find a creative re-use of the motif in 9:2-3 of earth's people crying: the cry of "the blood of the righteous" (47:1-4), recalling also the blood of Abel (Gen 4:10); and Noah's cry: "hear me, hear me, hear me!" (65:2). The latter is a reworking of the tradition reflected in *1 Enoch* 106-107 and *Genesis Apocryphon* where not Noah, but his grandfather, Methuselah, seeks out Enoch. The motif of punishing the Watchers by forcing them to observe the mutual self-destruction of the giants in 10:12; 12:6 has metamorphosed into the kings being asked to observe the judgement of "Azazel and all his associates and all his host" by the Chosen One (55:3; cf. 62:11-12 which has the righteous enjoy the spectacle of observing the punishment of the kings). Similarly in 56:5-8 we read that the angels stir kings up to warfare (and so defeat), reminiscent of Gabriel setting the giants on a course of mutual self-destruction in 10:9-10. In a sense the scene at the hot springs reflects a very creative development of the myth, by building on the motif of the fires of punishment and combining it with the hot pools, the beliefs that their heat is generated from subterranean fire, the reputation for such bath houses to be places of debauchery, and a likely allusion to Herod.

Two further sets of mythical material contain sexual associations although these are not developed as such. The first is the use of Wisdom and Wickedness as two female figures, serving now as a parody on the claims, such as we see reflected in Sirach 24 and Baruch 4, that Israel possesses Wisdom through possessing Torah. Unlike in the development of these figures elsewhere, sexual imagery is absent. There is an interesting twist in the fact that Iniquity is portrayed as the bearer of rain for the dry earth, a reversal of the tradition which sees Wisdom as water for the thirsty, though the author also knows that tradition (48:1; 49:1-4). The second is the use of the male and female monster figures, Leviathan and Behemoth, and their separation, perhaps reflecting an ancient myth of sexual

---

[86] So Fröhlich, "Parables," 347.

union between heaven and earth, but now not fulfilling sexual role in the *Parables*. The myth of the separation of male and female, above and below, also appears in 54:8. The sea wind is also specifically gendered (60:16), but has no mate and seems to be no more than elaborated imagery, as is the more than usually descriptive reference to the sudden onset of the pains of contractions before birth (62:14).

Aside from specific references to sexual themes, it is interesting to note that the *Parables* assume everlasting life is the reward of the righteous. It also appears to envisage future life as one on a transformed earth (43:4; 45:4-5; 51:1-5; 58:3-6), not in heaven, though that is seen as the dwelling place of spirits before the judgement (39:4-8; 41:2). The garden which Enoch sees in his vision is best understood as located on earth (60:8; 61:12; 60:23; 61:12). In 61:1-5 the document depicts a resurrection of the righteous and similarly 62:14-16 envisages a future for the righteous of eating with that Son of Man and lying down and rising up forever, clad in garments of glory which will not wear out. This future state is one of eternal day. Unlike the promise to Noah that his seed would multiply, the document says nothing to indicate whether or not family, procreation, or sexual relations will form part of that future. Nothing suggests a state of being nor a location (such as a temple or the garden of Eden understood as a temple) nor an understanding of time (including eternal day as sabbath) which would necessarily exclude sexual relations (such as we find in 15:6; Mark 12:25; and *Jubilees*). On the other hand, nowhere is the issue of future sexual relations addressed.

The discussion above deals with the text as we have received it. It is interesting to pursue what would be different if we take into account what might have been an earlier form of the text, such as in the most recent reconstruction, as tentatively proposed by Nickelsburg: 37 – 54:6; 56:1-4; 58:1 – 59:3; 60:11-22; 61:1 – 64:2; 69:2-12, 26-29; 70:1-2. To the proposed secondary additions belong: 54:7 – 55:4—mainly about the flood and repeating the judging of Azazel; 57:1-3, the sequel to Parthians; 60:1-10, 24a-25, primarily about the Leviathan/Behemoth myth and the killing of children with their parents; 65:1 – 69:1, the Noah material about Enoch's prediction of the punishment of the angels, God's depiction of the hot pool/lake of fire of judgement, and Michael's misgivings; 69:13-25, the name and the oath; and most of the concluding two chapters. The major implication for the depiction of attitudes towards sexuality would be that the proposed document would lack reference to the sexual wrongdoing by kings. In addition the possible reference to the Watchers with their wives and children would go. Apart from that the conclusions above would stand.

Overall the document appears designed to offer hope in face of violence and oppression. While it may warn against false teaching and certainly attacks illicit knowledge, it is otherwise not concerned with ethical instruction, though ethical perspectives dictate its negative depiction of both the angels and the kings and wealthy. These will have their roots in the document's religious tradition, presumably the biblical law, though this nowhere receives attention, nor do, for instance, the ethical instructions contained in the *Epistle of Enoch*, although it, too, is concerned with violence and exploitation of the poor. There also seems to be little interest in matters of cult, although cultic notions inform its depiction of the heavenly world. Given the absence of ethical teaching, it is difficult to assess the absence of reference to Torah. The document does reflect interaction with a range of biblical and extra-biblical writings (including Genesis; Psalms; Isaiah; Ezekiel; Zechariah; Daniel; *1 Enoch* 1-36). Its preoccupation with offering hope within the framework of the Enoch pseudepigraphy, focused on what needs to change about others, not how his own community may change, means that references to issues of sexuality and anything like ethical instruction are incidental. Nevertheless the author clearly sees sexual wrongdoing as an element in what indirectly caused the current chaos and in the preserved text also an aspect of that chaos reflected in the profligate lives of the rich.

1.1.2   2 Enoch

In his introduction to *2 Enoch* Francis Andersen emphasises caution in relation to conclusions about most of the key issues concerning the document, including reconstructing textual history, date, and provenance.[87] His tentative assessment is that it represents a Jewish work from the turn of the era, reflecting a form of Judaism which stands in the Enoch tradition and "knows nothing of developments between the Flood and the end of the world, so there is no place for Abraham, Moses, and the rest; there is no reference to the Torah".[88] Nickelsburg and Böttrich independently conclude that the dating is probably first century C.E. before 70 and, on grounds of parallels with Egyptian mythological traditions also present in Philo, written in Alexandria.[89] Unlike the *Parables*, it contains ethical instruction in the teaching given by Enoch to his family, but also at various points throughout the account of Enoch's heavenly travels. This reflects the purpose of the work, which appears to be to advocate a life of faith in one God and observance of God's laws, reinforced by promise of reward and threat of judgement, and by the positive example of Enoch and the negative example of the Watchers.

---

[87] Francis I. Andersen, "2 (Slavonic Apocalypse of) Enoch," *OTP*, 1.91–100.

[88] Andersen, *OTP*, 1.96.

[89] Nickelsburg, *Jewish Literature*, 221-25; Christfried Böttrich, *Das slavische Henochbuch* (JSHRZ 5.7; Gütersloh: Gütersloher Verlagshaus, 1995) 807-13; see also Andrei A. Orlov, "Noah's Younger Brother Revisited: Anti-Noachic Polemics and the Date of 2 (Slavonic) Enoch," *Henoch* 26 (2004) 172-87, esp. 176-87.

Any discussion of the work must take into account the diverse textual tradition, in which one may speak of a longer and a shorter recension, although this is already an oversimplification. Because some of the references pertinent to matters of sexuality occur only in the longer recension, our discussion needs to take into account whether this reflects expansion, as was commonly thought, or abbreviation, as more recently argued by Böttrich, who assembles evidence to suggest that the demands of fitting the work into collections and the predispositions of Christian editors led to a trimming of the texts.[90] These circumstances will accordingly inform our analysis.

The instruction begins, indeed, even before Enoch ascends, when the two angels tell him to speak to his sons about what they should do in his absence (1:9 – 2:4). That instruction reflects concern with cult and sacrifice, but also with idolatry. In his ascent Enoch first sees the "the elders, the rulers of the stellar orders" (4:1)[91] and the treasuries of snow and elements related to weather. This is an element in the emphasis on divine ordering, which serves as an example for the need of divine order among human beings.

In 7:1-2 in the 2nd heaven we then encounter the negative example of the condemned angels awaiting judgement because "they are evil rebels against the Lord" (7:3), a probable allusion to the myth of the Watchers, but the account does not specify their crime and is thus without reference to their sexual wrongdoing.[92] Unlike in *1 Enoch* 13:4-7, here Enoch refuses their request to intercede on their behalf (7:4-5). Here, too, the cosmology is different, since they are kept not below (cf. *1 Enoch* 10:13), but above in the second heaven.

---

[90] Böttrich, *Henochbuch*, 788-95. See also his detailed discussion, which forms the basis of this treatment here, in Christfried Böttrich, *Weltweisheit-Menschheitsethik-Urkult: Studien zum slavischen Henochbuch* (WUNT 2.50; Tübingen: Mohr Siebeck, 1992).

[91] The translation throughout is that of Andersen, *OTP*, 1.102-213, unless otherwise indicated by an asterisk. I have been dependent on secondary literature for discussion of the Slavonic text.

[92] Cf. Andrei A. Orlov, "On the Polemical Nature of 2 (Slavonic) Enoch: A Reply to C. Böttrich," *JSJ* 34 (2003) 274-303, who argues that the disobedience may reflect the Adamic tradition being adapted in *1 Enoch* 21 – 22, which includes the notion that some angels refused to venerate Adam (287-89). The primary allusion seems, however, to be to the Watchers as in 18:1-9, but Orlov suggests that the presence there of Sataneil as their leader may reflect a close connection between the Watcher myth and the Adamic myth of Satan's refusal to venerate Adam (288 n. 34). Orlov's perceptive delineation of differences in relation both to Adamic and later to Noachic traditions is the basis for his confident hypothesis that such changes are an expression of polemical intent, though we find no explicit evidence of such intent elsewhere in the writing. See his extended discussion in Andrei A. Orlov, *The Enoch-Metatron Tradition* (TSAJ 107; Tübingen: Mohr Siebeck, 2005), where he argues implicit evidence of polemic intent in relation to Adam (211-53), Moses (254-303), and Noah (304-33).

In the 3rd heaven he sees paradise, indescribably pleasant, with trees in full bloom and bearing fruit, and in their midst the tree of life (8:1-8). The longer recension locates paradise "between corruptible and incorruptible" and in MSS J and P records that Enoch saw paradise when he looked downward (8:1). The assumption appears to be that paradise is connected to the earth at Eden. Thus 31:2 assumes heaven is open to view from Eden (similarly 42:3).[93] This probably explains the reference in 8:4 to the root of paradise at the exit that leads to the earth.[94]

In 9:1 the angel emphasises that paradise is the reward of the righteous, maintaining the ethical focus. Accordingly the righteous turn from injustice, give right judgment, feed the hungry, clothe the naked, lift up the fallen, help the injured and orphans, and worship God alone. By contrast, but serving the same function, 10:1-6 depicts a frightful place of judgement for the unrighteous. Their deeds include witchcraft, boastfulness, stealing souls secretly (probably referring to witchcraft),[95] acting in contrast to the righteous in relation to the hungry and naked, and idolatry. One ms (P) adds a reference to sexual wrongdoing, referring to those "who practice on the earth the sin which is against nature, which is child corruption in the anus in the manner of Sodom". It gives particular prominence to this concern by setting it at the head of the list of sins. Similar additional material appears in this MS in 34:2b. Böttrich explains its absence in other MSS as the work of church censors, pointing out that concern with pederasty is reflected also in *Ps.-Phoc.* 213; *Sib. Or.* 5:166, 430; *T. Levi* 17:11.[96] In addition, only P has the list of vices in 10:4: "stealing, lying, insulting, coveting, resentment, fornication, murder". Accordingly, in its text fornication and male-male sex are prominent concerns.[97]

The theme of divine order continues in the 4th heaven, where Enoch sees the movements of the sun and moon which shape the calendar (11 – 17). Then in 18:1-9 Enoch sees in the fifth heaven the "Grigori" (a transliteration of the Greek word

---

[93] Cf. 71:28 where the longer recension has Adam in paradise for 7 years with "heaven open to him all the time up until he sinned". By contrast 32:1 has him in paradise for a mere five and a half hours.

[94] On this distinctive understanding of paradise and its influence see Böttrich, *Henochbuch*, 846-47.

[95] See Böttrich, *Henochbuch*, who, while noting that in *T. Jos.* 13:1 it refers to enslavement, points to Ezek 13:17 LXX, where it is an allegation against female mantics (857).

[96] Böttrich, *Henochbuch*, 857; Böttrich, *Weltweisheit-Menschheitsethik-Urkult*, 187.

[97] So Karl-Wilhelm Niebuhr, *Gesetz und Paränese: Katechismusartige Weisungsreihen in der frühjüdischen Literatur* (WUNT 2.28; Tübingen: Mohr Siebeck, 1987), though without noting its singular attestation (189). He points to the depiction of idolatry as the source of all ethical evil in Wis 14:22-31 (189). There, too, same-sex relations feature as also, possibly under its influence, in Rom 1:18-27.

for Watchers, γρήγοροι), dejected and silent, so that there was no liturgy in the fifth heaven (18:1-2). The angel explains that 200 of their number had descended to Mt Hermon, "to defile themselves with human wives" (18:5 [A]). The longer recension, which alone in 18:3 mentions 200, reads: "And they saw the daughters of men, how beautiful they were; and they took wives for themselves, and the earth was defiled by their deeds. Who in the entire time of this age acted lawlessly and practiced miscegenation and gave birth to giants and great monsters and great enmity" (18:4 [J]). This appears to be directly dependent on *1 Enoch* 6:1 – 7:6.[98] According to Böttrich the reference to Satanail as their leader in 18:3 is a later Christian interpolation, as also in 31:4.[99] It is noteworthy that only the act of sexual wrongdoing receives mention, not the imparting of illicit knowledge and skills. The reference to liturgy reflects the tradition in *1 Enoch* 12 – 16 that they were priests. In contrast to Enoch's response to the wicked in the third heaven, here Enoch reports that, as in *1 Enoch* 13:4-7, he had prayed for the brothers of the Grigori who had sinned, that God had assigned them to a place beneath the earth, and that the Grigori should recommence their liturgical duties of praise. The dependence on *1 Enoch* may account for the cosmological anomaly that has the fallen Watchers confined beneath the earth (18:7; cf. *1 Enoch* 10:12), where *2 Enoch* had located them in the second heaven (7:1-2). More significant is the question what role the depiction of the Watchers' sexual wrongdoing plays here. Is the judgement on the Watchers functioning as a warning to the hearers not to commit acts of sexual wrongdoing, or more generically not to commit any kind of sin?

The image of the sixth heaven (19:1-7), like those of the first and fourth, reinforces the sense of divine order, a model for what is asked also of human beings. The seventh heaven (20:1 – 21:6) depicts "from a distance the Lord, sitting on his throne" (20:3), but again surrounded by worshipping hosts of angels, who again are portrayed as "carrying out his will" (21:1). Enoch is rewarded by being brought face to face with the Lord and being transformed into the likeness of an angel (22:1-10), which both underlines his uniqueness, but at the same time assures the righteous that they, too, will be rewarded. Enoch is instructed to write 360 (or 366) books based on records of the Lord's deeds (22:11 – 23:6) and then given direct instruction from the Lord, himself (24:1-2a), beginning with an account of creation (24:2b – 33:2), much of which is missing in the shorter recension. Material unique to the longer recension incudes an account of an archangel's rebellion and attempt to become equal to God's power, as a result of which he was hurled down from the height and "he was flying around in the air,

---

[98] Andersen, *OTP*, sees the passage as evidence that at least here the longer recension is to be seen as more original (1.131).

[99] Böttrich, *Henochbuch*, 876, who notes the same expression occurs in 7:3 without the name.

ceaselessly, above the Bottomless" (29:4-6), identified in the MS P as "Satanail". The account, which reproduces a tradition known also from *Adam and Eve* 12 – 14, has its roots in Isa 14:12-14.[100]

The longer recension, which follows the scheme of days of creation, reports the creation of paradise on the third day (30:1). Its account of the creation of fish, birds, and reptiles, mentions that they were male and female (30:7; similarly *Jub.* 3:3). Where the shorter recension simply reports: "When I had finished this, I commanded my wisdom to create man" (30:8 [A]) and has no further material before 33:3, the longer recension depicts human creation from seven components (earth, sun, sea, stone, clouds, earth, wind) with seven properties, including the five senses.[101] It then cites a poem:

> From invisible and visible substances I created man.
> From both his natures come both death and life.
> And (as my) image he knows the word like (no) other creature.
> But even at his greatest he is small,
> And again at his smallest he is great. (30:10)

The focus on the creation of the human being continues as God declares him to be a second angel, to be a king on the earth, and to have wisdom (30:11-12), and explains his name, Adam, on the basis of an anagram (based on Greek) (30:13).[102] In 30:14-15 we then read that God "gave him free will" and "pointed out to him the two ways – light and darkness", which are good and bad. Then God adds: "Whereas I have come to know his nature,[103] he does not know his own nature. That is why ignorance is more lamentable than the sin such as it is in him to sin" (30:16).[104] He then also reports the creation of woman from the man's rib.[105]

---

[100] Böttrich, *Henochbuch*, 910.

[101] On this see Christfried Böttrich, *Adam als Mikrokosmos: Eine Untersuchung zum slavische Henochbuch* (Frankfurt: Peter Lang, 1995) 35-53.

[102] On this see Böttrich, *Adam als Mikrokosmos*, 17-34.

[103] Behind the word translated "nature" lies the Greek word, οὐσία, "being" (Böttrich, *Henochbuch*, 921).

[104] On the importance of understanding and insight in *2 Enoch* see also Böttrich, *Weltweisheit-Menschheitsethik-Urkult*, 162-63.

[105] Orlov, "Polemical Nature," points out that references to Adam are extensive in the work in contrast to their sparseness in earlier Enoch literature, where it also never elevates Adam's status as here (276-77). He goes on to argue that the author deliberately depicts the elevated qualities associated with Adam before he sinned, such as his kingship (30:12), as transferred to Enoch (39:8; 46:1-2) (280-85). Thus he sees in *1 Enoch* 21 – 22 the depiction of Enoch standing before God's face, a deliberate reuse of tradition elsewhere associated with Adam's creation in God's image (286-87) as identified by Michael E. Stone, "The Fall of Satan and Adam's Penance: Three Notes on *The Books of Adam and Eve*," in *Literature*

The depiction of human beings as having by their substance a vulnerability to sin, unless they obtain true self-understanding and so choose the path of good, is a striking anthropology. While there is some emphasis on self-knowledge, as in 30:16, the major emphasis is on knowledge or wisdom generally. We see this in the detail that wisdom was already an agent in human creation. We see it also in the image of Enoch as one who teaches both about the structure of reality under God as proper and orderly and about what is good and bad behaviour among human beings with the consequences of reward and judgement. It is interesting not only because this depiction shows no sign that issues of sexuality are problematic, but also in that we find no echo of humans being made "male and female" from Gen 1:27, though it features in the descriptions of the animals in 30:7, nor of partnership, including sexual union, from Gen 2:20-25.

The statement, "I created for him a wife, so that death might come by his wife" (30:17; cf. Sir 25:24; *Sib. Or.* 1:42-45), seems entirely negative. It matches 31:6, which reports that the devil contacted only Eve, not Adam. The final comment, "I took his last word, and I called her name Mother, that is to say, Euva, Adam-Mother; earthly and life", represents a Hebrew play on the last letter of Adam (מ and אם = "mother").[106]

The concern with human obedience comes to expression in the depiction of the garden of Eden: "And I created a garden in Edem, in the east, so that he might keep the agreement and preserve the commandment. And I created for him an open heaven, so that he might look upon the angels, singing the triumphal song" (31:1-2). This coheres with the understanding expressed earlier in the depiction of the third heaven, which assumes a connection between Eden and the heavenly world (8:1 J P; similarly 42:3; 71:28). This sets the context for describing the role of the devil Satanael. Already 29:4-5 had reported his rebellion and expulsion from the heavens. We learn incidentally that God "wished to create another world, so that everything could be subject to Adam on the earth, to rule and to reign over it" (31:3). This is interesting because it implies that Adam's departure from paradise was part of the divine plan, not punishment. Even the reference in 32:1, "I will send you away to what I took you from", need not be seen as punishment.

The author offers a brief analysis of Satanael's psychology: "In this way he became different from the angels. His nature did not change, <but> his thought did, since his consciousness of righteous and sinful things changed." (31:5).

---

on Adam and Eve (SVTP 15; ed. Gary Anderson, Michael Stone, and Johannes Tromp; Leiden: Brill, 2000) 43-56, 47-48. Orlov makes similar claims for the Adamic origins of the designation of Enoch as "youth" (10:4) (289-92), the rejection of earthly food by Enoch in 56:2 (293-94), his anointing with oil from the tree of life in 22:9 (297-99); and his having carried away the sin of humankind (Adam) in 65:5 (299-302).

[106] Andersen, *OTP*, 1.153.

Böttrich notes that 31:4-5 belong together, with 31:4 employing a play on words possible only in Slavonic to explain his name, and 31:5, a description found almost word for word in Ps.-Athanasius, and so concludes that these verses are a later Christian interpolation.[107] In 31:6 we then read that the devil "became aware of his condemnation and of the sin which he sinned previously. And that is why he thought up the scheme against Adam". Such self-knowledge had already been valued in connection with the creation of human beings and in relation to discussion of their nature (30:16). It ought to lead to righteous action. Here it leads to the opposite. The explanation in 31:5 seems closely related to this issue, and may be warding off alternative anthropologies which explain evil by an ontological change of some kind. Thus the devil remained an angel by nature, but made wrong choices. Human beings are the same.

This probably also explains the care with which the author depicts what went wrong with humans. Thus he depicts the devil as scheming against Adam by approaching Eve. He corrupted Eve (31:6). The Slavonic word translated "corrupt", like the verb ἀπατάω, which it will have translated, and which, in turn, is based on its use in Gen 3:13 LXX (ἠπάτησέν "deceived, seduced"), has a range of meaning, including sexually seduce.[108] There is, however, no evidence that the author used it in a sexual sense. Instead the issue is depicted as a failure of knowledge or wisdom. Thus in 31:7 we read of God's curse: "But in account of <her> nescience I cursed them". The pronoun rendered "her" could alternatively read "his" or "their". There immediately follows a qualification:

> But those whom I had blessed previously, them I did not curse; <and those whom I had not blessed previously, even them I did not curse>—neither mankind I cursed, nor the earth, nor any other creature, but only mankind's evil fruit-bearing. This is why the fruit of doing good is sweat and exertion. (31:7)

Read in the light of what follows, the opening statement, "but in account of <her/his their> nescience I cursed them", will probably refer then to the woman's ignorance. As in 30:16 the emphasis lies on ignorance rather than sin, but the ignorance is clearly blameworthy. As in 30:17 the curse which comes upon both Eve and Adam is death. 31:7 explains the curse as relating to "mankind's evil fruit-bearing" in contrast to "the fruit of doing good" which entails "sweat and exertion". The broader allusion to fruit-bearing is probably to be taken in a metaphorical sense as referring to deeds.[109] One might have expected here a reference to the processes of birth, so that we would have here a juxtaposition of

---

[107] Böttrich, *Henochbuch*, 925.

[108] So Böttrich, *Henochbuch*, 927. For evidence of use of the LXX by the author of *2 Enoch* see his discussion on p. 809.

[109] So Böttrich, *Henochbuch*, 928.

the curses which fall on the woman and the man according to Gen 3:16-20, pain in childbirth and hardship in toil. "Evil fruit-bearing" would then refer to the hardship entailed in bearing children, but would in no way impugn conception of children and so sexual relations.

The account does not allude to the woman's desire or returning to her husband and his ruling over her (cf. Gen 3:16) and seems deliberately to contradict the report in Gen 3:17-18 that the ground, itself, is cursed. Thus the author seems intent on differentiating these negative effects from the quality of human being, but also the being of creatures and the earth itself, which are not to be seen as cursed. Again, we appear to be dealing with the warding off of an ontological dualism which might see these as cursed and evil. Nor does the author appear to blame human sexuality for Eve's sin.

The merging of the two creation stories into one, set within the framework of the seven days, has led the author to place the events of the second creation, the corruption of Eve, the subsequent curses, and the reassurance to Adam of a new future on earth, all within a short period on day six, a mere "five and a half hours" (32:1).[110] Again we appear to have a revision of Gen 3:19, "You are dust and to dust you shall return", which in Gen 3:19 LXX reads: γῆ εἶ καὶ εἰς γῆν ἀπελεύσῃ "You are earth and to earth you will return". Accordingly, 32:1a reads: "You are earth and into the earth once again you will go, out of which I took you". This may refer to death, as in Gen 3:19, but just as likely belongs closely with what follows, according to which God declares: "I will not destroy you, but will send you away to what I took you from" (32:1b).[111] The assumption here is that Adam was created outside paradise, as assumed in *Jubilees* 3, and was then introduced into it. This is a possible interpretation of Gen 2:8. In other words, God is now sending Adam into the earth to rule and reign over it, just as he had planned (cf. 31:3).[112]

In its depiction of the human condition *2 Enoch* has no notion of original sin, nor of deterministic dualism set by God-given portions of light and darkness as in the *Treatise on the Two Spirits*, nor of a suprahistorical origin of evil brought into being by the Watchers' sin. Here their deed has no permanent consequences,

---

[110] Böttrich, *Henochbuch*, assesses this as a Christian interpolation, noting the discrepancy between this detail preserved in MSS J and P and 71:28d which speaks of 7 years and the later Christian reckoning of 5500 before the messiah appears (929; 804). It may however be the result of the author's merging the two creation stories.

[111] It continues: "Then I can take you once again at my second coming", which Andersen, *OTP*, argues should not be seen as a Christian interpolation, but as expressing the kind of eschatological return of God depicted in *Jub.* 1:26 (1. 155). See also Paolo Sacchi, *Jewish Apocalyptic and its History* (JSPSup 20; Sheffield: Sheffield Academic Press, 1990) 247; and Böttrich, *Henochbuch*, who points to *Apoc. Mos.* 39 and *Adam and Eve* 47 (928).

[112] On this see Böttrich, *Henochbuch*, 928.

except for them, and serves only paradigmatically, as a warning against rebellion. As Sacchi observes, *2 Enoch* is closer to the *Epistle of Enoch*, which makes human beings and their choices responsible for sin, and *2 Enoch's* rejection of intercession belongs to this insistence on human accountability.[113] On the other hand, as 41:1-2 shows, the work is not optimistic: Enoch weeps at the depravity of humankind.[114]

Both recensions then report God's commissioning of Enoch to return to earth with his handwritten books, to give them to his children and, through them, to subsequent generations (33:3-12), so that they may know that, as he puts it, "there is no one who opposes me or is insubordinate; and all submit themselves to my sole rule and work my sole dominion" and that "they will understand this also how there is no other Creator except myself" (anti-gnostic?) (33:7). He assures Enoch that Michail will intercede for him, interestingly because of not only his writings, but also those of Adam and Seth (33:10-12; the longer recension adding Enos, Kainan, Maleleil, and Ared).

The commissioning functions as another opportunity to identify major concerns which the author sees as needing to be addressed, since it explicitly addresses "the wickedness of mankind" (34:1). The shorter recension continues:

> They will not carry the yoke which I have placed on them. Nor do they sow the seed which I have given them, but they have renounced my yoke, and they will take on another yoke; and they will sow worthless seed, and do obeisance to vain gods. And they will reject my sole rule. And all the world will sin by injustices and crimes and adulteries and idolatries. (34:1-2a)

The images of yoke and seed, which appear also in the longer recension, are probably to be understood in the context of marriage as a common metaphor, used to depict a breakdown in the relationship between God and people because the latter will go after other gods. At the same time "yoke" is being used as a way of describing the law of God.[115] The focus on idolatry also fits the emphasis on God alone as creator in 33:7. Sowing seed is probably an allusion to sexual intercourse and so describes the adulterous relationship of idolatry. It is not clear to what

---

[113] Sacchi, *Jewish Apocalyptic*, 242-44.

[114] See Charles A. Gieschen, "The different functions of a similar Melchizedek tradition in 2 Enoch and the Epistle to the Hebrews," in *Early Christian Interpretation of the Scriptures of Israel: Investigations and Proposals* (ed. Craig A. Evans and James A. Sanders; Sheffield: Sheffield Academic Press, 1997) 364-79, 367.

[115] Böttrich, *Henochbuch*, notes that MS P makes specific mention of the commandments in the preceding words (936).

degree the passage goes beyond metaphor to describe adultery in a literal sense.[116] The longer recension elaborates the accusation of wickedness by listing "fornications" (34:2) and MS P makes particular reference to sodomy: "abominable fornications that is, friend with friend in the anus, and every other kind of wicked uncleanness which it is disgusting to report", recalling its additional material in 10:4 concerning the same theme, though in 34:2 the focus is not limited to pederasty but extends to all anal intercourse between males. Here as there, Böttrich sees P preserving what is likely to have been original and which later orthodox Christian editors deleted.[117]

Enoch is given 30 days in which to pass on instructions and the books to his family (36:1). Accordingly Enoch begins his instructions, emphasising that he is just a human being like his addressees (perhaps to counter undue elevation of his person which some may been advocating?) (39:5). It matches the focus of the writer's anthropology that he has Enoch declare: "I know everything" (40:2), so that Enoch's teaching is the true antidote to the ignorance which he made the central concern about humanity. The knowledge which Enoch proceeds to impart reiterates what the hearer has already learned in earlier chapters, although differently expressed. The repetition serves to reinforce the learning. Accordingly, he begins by emphasising the divine ordering of creation (40:2-12). There is also mention of the place of condemnation and that he "wrote down all the judgments of the judged, and … knew all their accusations" (40:12-13). No specific link is made to the Watchers. Instead Enoch speaks of "the impious", referring to human beings and their sin. In the longer recension these are identified as "all those from the age of his ancestors, with Adam and Eve" (41:1), possibly a Christian interpolation.[118]

The report on paradise serves as the occasion for a series of beatitudes, for which entry into paradise is the promised reward. The commended behaviours include true worship, right judgement, clothing the naked, feeding the hungry, ensuring justice for the widow, orphan, and those treated unjustly, sowing right seed, speaking the truth, being compassionate, understanding the Lord's works and knowing the Creator (42:6-14).[119] "Sowing right seed" (42:11) may well refer to right sexual relations. It is the only blessing with an appended promise of its own: "for he shall harvest it sevenfold", which may be a metaphor or could envisage

---

[116] Böttrich, *Henochbuch*, mentions the angels' sexual wrongdoing and Onan's spilling seed (Gen 38:9) (937), but this misses the primary focus, which belongs to the familiar image of idolatry and adultery.

[117] Böttrich, *Henochbuch*, 789; Böttrich, *Weltweisheit-Menschheitsethik-Urkult*, 187.

[118] Andersen, *OTP*, 1.166.

[119] See Niebuhr, *Gesetz und Paränese*, for the distinctive emphasis here on response to the needy (192).

abundant offspring. Alternatively, the image functions as a description of the ethical life.[120]

Enoch continues his discourse by reporting his understanding about differences among people on the basis of property, wisdom, intelligence, craftiness and "silence of the lips" (43:2), categories greatly expanded in the longer recension, but then concludes that "no one is better than he who fears the Lord; for those who fear the Lord will be glorious forever" (43:3). He then makes the extraordinary claim that God created humankind "in a facsimile of his own face", so that all, great and small are to be respected (44:1-2). This coheres with the ethical emphasis on compassion which comes to expression in further beatitudes emphasising support for the broken, generosity to the needy, and just scales (44:3-5), expressed also as something greater than lighting many lamps and offering many sacrifices (45:1-3). In these and the exhortations which follow, issues pertaining to sexuality play no evident role. To respond positively to Enoch's instruction is to bear one's yoke (48:9; 51:3). This includes being prepared to suffer loss, leaving vengeance to God, but also living generously towards orphans, widows, and the foreigner (50:4-6).[121] In 52:1-15 we find alternating beatitudes and curses which focus on praising God and respecting God's creatures and fellow human beings, but without addressing sexual themes.

Enoch then announces that his time is up, that he had in any case lost appetite for earthly food and pleasure (55:1 – 56:2). Again, nothing suggests such pleasure, including sexual pleasure, should it be envisaged here, is evil in itself. In his parting words Enoch speaks of human management of animals and their souls, including that they will testify against human beings at the judgement. He speaks of appropriate procedures of sacrifice (59:3)[122] and warns: "Whoever does harm to any animal in secret, it is an evil custom; he acts lawlessly with his own soul" (59:5). This may address the practice of bestiality. In the shorter recension 58:6 reads: "He who grazes the souls <of the beasts> badly commits iniquity against his

---

[120] Böttrich, *Henochbuch*, refers to the image of sowing righteousness in Job 4:9; Prov 11:18; 22:8; Hos 10:12; Gal 6:7; and similar texts in Philo (956).

[121] Nickelsburg, *Jewish Literature*, notes that the themes of vengeance and putting up with loss here in 50:4-5 match concerns in *1 Enoch* 95:5 and 94:8 (396).

[122] Whereas some have taken the requirement of tying animals' legs as indicative of a sectarian stance since it conflicts with rabbinic provisions, it appears likely that this simply reflected common practice in Egypt and may have been assumed "in ignorance rather than repudiation of the custom in Jerusalem". So John J. Collins, *The Apocalyptic Imagination: An Introduction to Jewish Apocalyptic Literature* (2d ed.; Grand Rapids: Eerdmans, 1998) 247, and see Böttrich, *Henochbuch*, 987. On the possible sectarian nature of the document, see Sacchi, *Jewish Apocalyptic*, who as well as citing this issue of sacrifice, notes the solar calendar (243).

own soul", whereas the longer recension reads: "And every kind of animal soul will accuse the human beings who have fed them badly".

In 61:2 we find a version of the golden rule in the context of warnings against murder and violence and promises about blessed dwellings in the great age for the righteous (61:2-3). In 63:1-2 we find further encouragement to express that righteousness by clothing the naked and giving bread to the poor. Enoch reminds his children that the age of creation is to be followed by the great age, a single age in which "there will be neither years nor months, nor days and hours", in which the righteous will escape judgment and live with "neither weariness nor suffering nor affliction nor expectation of violence nor the pain of the night nor darkness" but live in eternal light, their faces shining like the sun (65:7-11). The notion of an eternal day occurs also in the *Parables of Enoch* (*1 Enoch* 58:3). The longer recension expands the exhortation to live faithfully in the face of a list of adversities, and to love one another, with the promise they will "shine seven times brighter than the sun" (66:6-7). Nothing indicates what that might mean for sexual relations.

In 67:1-3 we then read of Enoch being taken back up to the highest heaven. Meanwhile on earth his son Methusalam assumed priestly leadership,[123] offered appropriate sacrifice (68:5-7; 69:1-19), corrected "those who had apostasized ... and converted them. And there was not found one person turning himself from the Lord during all the days that Methusalam lived" (70:1-2). He is then instructed to commission Noah's younger brother Nir with the priesthood (70:4) and told of impending judgment.[124] The wrong consists of envy, people sinning against people, and nation waging war against nation, bloodshed and confusion (70:5). Beyond that, to the delight of the adversary, people would abandon their Creator, treat fixed elements of sky and living things on land and sea as gods and "all the earth will change its order" to anticipate the time of destruction (70:6-7). The description of sin focuses on violence, rather than injustice and neglect of the poor

---

[123] For the prediction of Methusalam's radiance as a counter to traditions depicting the radiance of the child Noah, as reflected in the *Genesis Apocryphon*, *1 Enoch* 106 and 1Q19, see Orlov, "Noah's Younger Brother Revisited," 182-84, who sees behind such polemics priestly disputes about priestly succession (185-87).

[124] For the proposal that the choice of Nir reflects a deliberate downplaying of Noah as a means of countering the influence of Noachic tradition such as we find in the *Genesis Apocryphon* and the *Parables of Enoch*, see Andrei A Orlov, "'Noah's Younger Brother': Anti-Noachic Polemics in 2 Enoch," *Henoch* 22 (2003) 259-73; Orlov, "Noah's Younger Brother Revisited," 172-87.

as elsewhere. It also makes no mention of sexual wrongdoing. In 70:23 we read that these predictions came true.[125]

The final two chapters relate to the birth to Nir's wife, Sopanim, of Melkisedek, who was to be "the head of the priests in another generation" (71:34 [A]). The account describes Sopanim as "sterile and never having given birth to a child by Nir" (and presumably not to anyone else) and being "in the time of her old age, and in the day of death" (71:1-2a). The motif of sterility before birth of a significant figure features in various ways in the accounts of Sarah, Rebecca, Rachel, Hannah, and Elizabeth. One difference here is that "Nir the priest had not slept with her, from the day that the Lord had appointed him" (71:2b). This serves to indicate that either something miraculous or something untoward has happened. The absence of intercourse during the time of Nir's priesthood may reflect a stance which saw celibacy as required by priests, as among some Christian clergy, which would be contrary to normal practice and unexpected, but it may simply be reporting that it did not happen. As in the story of Mary we read that they abstained from intercourse until the child, Jesus, was born, so the aim is probably to remove any explanation that might attribute the pregnancy to subsequent intercourse, the difference, here, however, being that Sopanim was not a virgin (cf. *Prot. Jas.* 4:2 about Mary's parents).

The motif of shame is first and foremost over against Nir and then, when the apparently illicit pregnancy became known, before the people, and would mean disgrace for Nir. The concern is about more than shame. It is also about Nir's defilement on the assumption that his wife had become unclean for him having slept with another man, and so he would be rendered unfit to serve before the Lord and so sin if he did so (71:6). In the story of Mary and Joseph the shame of Mary's pregnancy appears to be related similarly to the implied act of adultery, which required divorce, publicly or privately, but probably also to the assumption that they would have abstained from sexual intercourse before marriage.

Nir's confrontation of Sopanim recalls Lamech's confrontation of Bitenosh in *1 Enoch* 106 and *Genesis Apocryphon*, where he suspects the wondrous baby, Noah, results from intercourse with one of the Watchers. That conflict is resolved by the assurance from Bitenosh that the child is his and was conceived during a highly pleasurable act of intercourse, so memorable that it could be recalled some ten months later. Here Sopanim insists no intercourse has taken place, according to some MSS of the shorter recension: nothing reflecting youthful passion (71:7), and even speaks of her not knowing how "the indecency" of her womb was conceived (71:7). The longer recension has her speak of not knowing how her menopause

---

[125] The longer recension lists this as the third time that the devil became ruler, the first being before paradise, and the second in paradise (70:25). Böttrich, *Henochbuch*, sees this as a late gloss under the influence of dualistic thought (1017).

and barrenness had been reversed.[126] In response to Nir's confrontation Sopanim falls down and dies (71:9).

According to two MSS of the shorter recension the angel Gabriel then intervenes, reassuring the conscience- and grief-stricken Nir, that he is not at fault, and declaring: "this child which is to be born of her is a righteous fruit, and one whom I shall receive into paradise, so that you will not be the father of a gift of God" (71:11). Why a "gift of God" may not have a human father is not clear, but probably the focus is not Nir's disqualification, but the divine origin of the pregnancy. Nor should we assume that human parenthood would render fruit unrighteous. It had not done so for Enoch or Methusalam. In addition, nothing suggests divine impregnation or the like (cf. 71:30, which speaks of creation in the womb). The continuation in 71:12 reads as though no such angelic appearance had taken place. In all likelihood the intervention of Gabriel is a clumsy later interpolation.[127]

Thus 71:12 has Nir not knowing any such insight and running to fetch his elder brother, Noe, who consoles him, declaring: "The Lord today has covered up our scandal, in that nobody from the people knows this" and advises accordingly that they hasten to bury her, which they proceed to do, wrapping her in black garments and secretly digging a grave (71:12-16). Then we read: "They dug a grave in secret. And a child came out from the dead Sopanim" (71:17). The sepulchre (referred to in 71:17a in the shorter recension) served here not as a tomb after which the body would be buried much later, but simply as a place to lay the body in preparation for burial.

"They saw the child sitting beside the dead Sopanim, and wiping his clothing", fully developed physically, blessing the Lord, and wearing the badge of priesthood on his chest (71:17-19). This recalls the wondrous child, Noah, who according to *1 Enoch* 106:3 "stood up from the hands of the midwife, and he opened his mouth and praised the Lord <of eternity>". There, however, and in the parallel in 1QapGen 5.3-13, the focus is on his glowing appearance. Nothing like that is said of this child. The emphasis in *2 Enoch* is on priesthood; hence the badge and then the clothing of the child in the garments of priesthood, giving him holy bread, before naming him Melkisedek (71:21). The identification of Melchisedek and priesthood derives ultimately from Gen 14:18. This discovery, rather than Gabriel's revelation, changes their minds. They honour Sopanim with a public burial in bright garments (71:22-23).

---

[126] On the motif of barrenness as a way of emphasising God's gift of fertility, not to be confused with the image of Jerusalem as desolate mother, see K. Blessing, "Desolate Jerusalem and Barren Matriarch: Two Distinct Figures in the Pseudepigrapha," *JSP* 18 (1998) 47-69, 51-56.

[127] So Böttrich, *Henochbuch*, 1021.

In response to Nir's anxiety about protecting the child, the Lord tells Nir that he will send Michael to transport him to "the paradise of Edem", where Adam had been for seven years before he sinned (71:28), so that he would "not perish along with those who are perishing in this generation", and reassures him: "Melkisedek will be the priest to all holy priests, and I will establish him so that he will be the head of the priests of the future" (71:29). The MSS which interpolate a reference to Gabriel's intervention earlier, replace Michael with Gabriel here, probably under influence of the Lukan birth narratives.[128]

In response Nir blesses God who "has created a great priest in the womb of Sapanim" (71:30).[129] In 71:32-36 or, with Orlov, 7:34-36, the longer recension brings a Christian interpolation which develops a Melchizedek-Christ and Adam-Christ typology.[130] In 71:37 we then read that in the flood all will perish except Noah, who "will be preserved in that generation for procreation," an interesting perspective, which says nothing of his particular merits, perhaps not to reflect on Nir. From Noah "will arise numerous people, and Melkisedek will become the head of priests reigning over a royal people who serve" the Lord (71:37). The longer recension, which here reads "another Melchizedek" reflects the work of the interpolator. Then after some reluctance and confusion on Nir's part (72:1-4) Michael (shorter recension: Gabriel) succeeds in taking the child to "the paradise of Edem" (72:5, 8-11). The work will have closed with a report of the flood, now apparently in a form reworked according to later Christian chronography.[131] Neither here nor in the depictions of wickedness before the flood do sexual themes appear.

---

[128] On this see Böttrich, *Henochbuch*, 1026.

[129] In Andersen's translation both recensions have a different spelling of the name in what appears to be poetic material, from what they use in the narrative: Sopanim (longer), Sothanim (shorter). The different spellings (both of Sothanim and of Nir's ancestors) probably indicates that the author is using tradition. Böttrich, *Henochbuch*, who uses MS R, shows no such discrepancy.

[130] On this see Böttrich, *Henochbuch*, 1027; and Orlov, "Polemical Nature," 275 n. 2. The extra material in 71:34-36 speaks of another Melkisedek and 12 after him, including a last, called "the Word and Power of God" who will be priest at Akhuzan, "the centre of the earth, where Adam was created" and was buried and buried Abel, and where also Melkisedek was buried. Similarly in 72:6-7 we find material identifying "another Melkisedek" who will be "the first priest and king in the city Salim" and setting his appearance within a time scheme. Of these verses Andersen, *OTP*, writes: "In vss. 6f. a Christian scribe has brought in various items from the Gk. Chronographers" (1.211).

[131] See Böttrich, *Henochbuch*, 1036.

Conclusion

2 Enoch clearly has a strong ethical focus.[132] This includes concern about feeding the hungry, clothing the naked, caring about widows, orphans, and foreigners, as well as avoiding all kind of injustice.[133] As Collins notes, there is no mention made of distinctively Jewish laws such as circumcision, food or sabbath laws; the emphasis is ethical combined with rejection of idolatry, as was typical of diaspora Hellenistic Judaism.[134] This focus comes to expression when Enoch is depicted as giving instructions (42:6-14; 44:3-5; 50:5-6; 63:1-2) and when his angelic guide is identifying what it means to be righteous (9:1) and wicked (10:1-6).[135] The author reinforces this emphasis by using the traditional hierarchy of values which puts

---

[132] Böttrich, *Henochbuch*, sees a threefold focus: "Weisheit, Ethik, und Kult" (wisdom, ethics, and liturgy or worship) (815). While noting that *2 Enoch* stands within a developing Enoch tradition, he rightly observes that it employs apocalyptic motifs from that tradition, such as the heavenly journey, not to address a crisis, but to promote ethical teaching and in this sense stands also in the wisdom tradition in which it draws on Sirach in particular (807-808, 816). Accordingly hope is based not on God's history with Israel or on awaiting future divine intervention, but on understanding the different spheres of reality above and below (816). Similarly Collins, *Apocalyptic Imagination*, 246; John J. Collins, *Between Athens and Jerusalem: Jewish Identity in the Hellenistic Diaspora* (2d ed; Grand Rapids: Eerdmans, 2000) 254-55. Böttrich notes that there is no sense of imminent eschatology and special interim ethics (819). He writes of the author's constant concern with building reassurance within and outwardly to depict Jewish faith as sensible and successful (815). I would see the primary aim as one using positive (Enoch, the righteous) and negative (Watchers, the wicked, flood generation) examples and depiction of heavenly order to promote an ethical life of faith in one God, informed by Enochic teaching tradition. The relationship to God assumes also the importance of the temple, engagement in pilgrimage and offering, proper observance of sacrifices, and a special claim to priesthood based on the Melchisedek tradition.

[133] To some degree this parallels the emphasis in the *Epistle of Enoch* with its many woes about injustice and the abuse of wealth (94:6-8; 95:5-7; 96:4-8; 97:8-10), but there the attacks are more intense and appear to have particular situations in mind, whereas here in *2 Enoch* the tone is much less polemical.

[134] So Collins, *Apocalyptic Imagination*, 246.

[135] Niebuhr, *Gesetz und Paränese*, addresses the absence of the word, Law, in *2 Enoch*, noting that "commandment" features rarely, twice in the singular (7:3; 31:1), once of Enoch's commandments (36:1) and once of God's (65:5; which he misreads as human commandments), although he sees the Law alluded to under the image of the yoke (34:1), or as what is "well-pleasing" (55:3) and as the "foundations of the ancient fathers" (52:9-10). These and the instructions of Enoch take over the function of the Law for the time when Torah did not yet exist (193). He sees, therefore no tension between Enochic instruction and the Law. Cf. Nickelsburg, *Jewish Literature*, who sees the work portraying Enoch as superior to Moses (225), although that need not imply conflict between the two.

compassion ahead of performing sacrifices, though without demeaning the latter, which are also clearly of concern (45:1-3; cf. 59:3; 68:5-7; 69:1-19) and by the extraordinary declaration that human faces are facsimiles of the divine and so to be treated with dignity and respect (44:1-2), all the more impressive because it comes after a section which identifies differences and inequalities among people (43:2). To follow Enoch's teaching is to bear one's yoke (48:9; 51:3). The work also employs the traditional topos of marriage, for which it also uses the images of the yoke and sowing seed, to address faithfulness and unfaithfulness in people's relationship with God, thus depicting idolatry as adultery (34:1-2; cf. also 2:2; 10:6).

The primary reinforcement for such teaching, however, comes through the account of Enoch's heavenly journey through the seven heavens. On the one hand, the total submission of all to divine ordering serves as an example to humanity. "Humanity, evidently, should do likewise."[136] On the other hand, the rebellion of some Watchers serves as a warning against disobedience. In addition, depictions of reward and punishment of human beings strengthen the message.[137] The primary myth which serves to illustrate negative behaviour appears to derive from the account in *1 Enoch* 6 – 16 (7:1-5; 18:1-9; cf. 40:12-13). Where their sin is specified it is not that they imparted forbidden knowledge, such as sorcery or metallurgy, but that they engaged in sexual intercourse with women (18:5). This act of sexual wrongdoing appears to function in the narrative not as a warning against sexual wrongdoing in particular, but against wrongdoing in general. Thus we find in the ethical exhortations little indication that sexual wrongdoing was a matter of importance.[138]

There are a few instances where a concern with sexual wrongdoing does, however, appear. The promise that those who sow their seed rightly will reap a rich harvest (42:11) is probably an exhortation to right sexual behaviour, thus avoiding adultery and perhaps other forms of illicit sexual activity. The concern about abominable things done to animals in secret, for which their souls will report the perpetrators at the judgement (59:5; 58:6; cf. 58:6 [J] which speaks of feeding them badly), probably refers to bestiality. These are, however, isolated instances. MS P of the longer recension has material at 10:4 and 34:2 concerned with anal intercourse between males and in relation to children, which it attacks as contrary

---

[136] So Collins, *Between Athens and Jerusalem*, 254.

[137] Niebuhr, *Gesetz und Paränese*, observes that already in the descriptions of Enoch's heavenly journey the contrast between the righteous and sinners functions paranetically (187).

[138] Sacchi, *Jewish Apocalyptic*, assuming the P text not be original, writes: "A prominent characteristic of the morality of *2 Enoch* is the absence of the theme of fornication" (245).

to nature and as after the manner of Sodom. The fact that this concern does not appear elsewhere in ethical exhortations favours seeing it as an expansion.

The longer recension contains additional information about the devil, identified as Satanael. This includes the three times when he sought to assert his rule (70:25): his attempt to claim equality with God, for which he was cast down from heaven (29:4-6); his corruption of Eve (31:6); and his rule before the flood (70:25). Some of this may be interpolated material. While, like the LXX, it uses a word to describe the devil's deception of Eve which could imply seduction, nothing indicates that this is so. Consistent with the findings above, the wickedness before the flood in both recensions is not depicted as including sexual wrongdoing in particular. Its chief characteristic is violence and bloodshed (70:5, 23; cf. also 61:2-3).

More significant is the large block of additional material in the longer recension in which the second event occurred, especially if with Böttrich we explain its absence in the shorter recension as the result of abbreviation. This material reflects a reworking of the narrative of human creation. Significantly it omits detail pertinent to sexuality, such as "male and female" from Gen 1:27 (though mentioned in relation to animals, 30:7), and the union, including sexual union, depicted in Gen 2:20-25. It then retells Genesis 3 in a way that changes its focus. Adam's being sent from the garden into earth's regions was not punishment, but God's plan that he should reign over it (31:3; 32:1).[139] The ground is not cursed, but, together with the creatures, remains good (31:7a). The curse is confined to the processes of childbirth and the man's toil and sweat (31:7b-8). Gone is any reference to the woman's returning in sexual passion to her husband and his rule over her. When the text speaks of cursing "mankind's evil fruit-bearing" (31:7b), the focus is not that the processes, including sexual relations, are evil, but that the process is painful, or, alternatively that evil doing is cursed. The text preserves the reference to death as a consequence (30:17), but has transferred the pun of Adam returning to Adamah, which it knows in its Greek form, as Adam the earthling returning to earth, into a statement not of punishment but of commission as God sent Adam out into the earth (32:1), which had been God's plan for him from the beginning (31:3). The text is careful to have the devil make contact only with Eve, not Adam (31:6b). As noted above, there is no indication that the word used for deception here is meant to carry sexual overtones (seduction).

In this context the longer recension also focuses on human psychology, arguing that human ignorance rather than sin is the core problem (30:16; 31:7), and accordingly the true knowledge provided by Enoch (and 2 Enoch!) can help human beings avoid sin (cf. 40:2). This accounts for human vulnerability to sin

---

[139] In this sense the text is governed primarily by Gen 1:28.

and can be addressed. Nothing suggests that human sexuality, Adam's or Eve's, is problematic. The work also offers a psychology of Satanael according to which through his sin "he became different from the angels", yet "his nature did not change, <but> his thought did, since his consciousness of righteous and sinful things changed. And he became aware of his condemnation and of the sin which he sinned previously. And that is why he thought up the scheme against Adam" (31:5-6). A similar concern with ontology appears to lie behind the emphasis that the sin did not change Adam's and humankind's nature. The revision of the curses may indicate that the author was warding off an ontological dualism. It may also account for the emphasis, found in both recensions, on Enoch remaining human (39:5), and on God's purpose through Enoch's instruction: "they will understand this also how there is no other Creator except myself" (33:7).

The account of the birth of Melchisedek is remarkable, though not without parallel elsewhere. In relation to matters pertaining to sexuality, it may reflect an ideal that priests not engage in sexual intercourse for the period of their service, but this is far from certain. It could indicate a demeaning of sexual intercourse among human beings as unable to produce what is good, but this would stand in contradiction to the origins of Enoch. Rather, it is likely that the focus in Melchizedek's miraculous birth does not imply disparagement of human sexuality, but serves to heighten Melchizedek's status as a special creation of God. The use of direct creation in relation to his conception (71:30) appears to exclude any sense of divine procreation. The beginning of the story reflects values which see pregnancy from another through adultery as abhorrent, indeed portrays Sopanim decrying the indecency of her womb (71:7), and as shameful for Nir before the community and defiling through her uncleanness in a way that would render his exercise of priesthood in that state a sin (71:6). In none of this, not even her denying having had recent experience of youthful passion in some MSS, is sexual expression treated as negative in itself.

Finally the work depicts the future of the righteous as one of living in paradise in perpetual light. Nothing suggests paradise is a temple which would exclude sexual relations. The peculiar location of paradise as both Eden and in the third heaven appears to reflect the notion that the garden of Eden is open to the heavenly world. The experience of Enoch, whose receives new garments, an image of resurrection existence, is also to be assumed for the righteous who therefore live in an embodied state. Asking what shape that life might have had and what it might mean to live in perpetual light is to go beyond the author's range of vision, although he does, at least, attend to one aspect by assuring his hearers that they would not suffer from weariness. Sexual expression seems far from his concerns, as is sexual wrongdoing from his ethics with some few exceptions, despite the centrality of the Watcher myth in a form that portrays their deed primarily in those terms.

1.2   The Sibylline Oracles

The 14 books in the collection known as the *Sibylline Oracles* are poetic works, consisting of loosely connected oracles, written in hexameters and attributed to a woman, the ancient pagan Erithrean sibyl.[140] They are modelled on the much earlier Greek and Roman traditions about sibyls who predicted the future.[141] The works in the collection which are both Jewish and Christian and sometimes indecipherably mixed or impossible to attribute with any certainty, and which also incorporate pagan material, range in date from the second century B.C.E. to the seventh century C.E.. Those which fall within our period are Books 1 – 5, 7, 11.[142] Of these the earliest is the core of material in Book 3.

1.2.1   Sibylline Oracles Book 3

1.2.1.1   Sib. Or. 3:97-349, 489-829

The earliest work preserved in the collection known as the *Sibylline Oracles* comprises *Sib. Or.* 3:97-349, 489-829. It is widely held to have been composed in Egypt during the second century B.C.E. and to include predictions of hope related to the reign of Ptolemy VI Philometor (180-145 B.C.E.) or Ptolemy VIII Physcon (145-116 B.C.E.), which envisaged widespread conversion to Judaism and the

---

[140] While observing that attribution here of female authorship "may attest to women's religious roles in the Greco-Roman world and within the two covenant communities" [Jewish and Christian] (107), Amy-Jill Levine, "The Sibylline Oracles," in *Searching the Scriptures. Volume Two: A Feminist Commentary*, (ed. Elisabeth Schüssler Fiorenza; London: SCM, 1995) 99-108, notes that "the Sibyl can at best represent exceptional women" (107). The proliferation of Sibylline traditions among various communities she sees as indicating that "the form was utilized by authors – sex unknown – who hid behind the Sibyl's pseudepigraphic skirts" (100).

[141] On the various sibyls and their background see Jane Lucy Lightfoot, *The Sibylline Oracles: With Introduction, Translation and Commentary on the First and Second Books* (Oxford: Oxford University Press, 2007) 3-23.

[142] For a general introduction see John J. Collins, "Sibylline Oracles," *OTP*, 1.317-24, whose translation is the one cited in this discussion; Nickelsburg, *Jewish Literature*, 193-94; Collins, *Apocalyptic Imagination*, 116-18; Collins, *ABD*, 6.2–6; Gerbern S. Oegema, *Einführung zu den Jüdischen Schriften aus hellenistisch-römischer Zeit: Apokalypsen* (JSHRZ 6.1.5; Gütersloh: Gütersloher Verlagshaus, 2001) 165-81; and the extensive treatment in Lightfoot, *Sibylline Oracles*, 3-253. For a detailed discussion of the MSS and the history of research see also Rieuwerd Buitenwerf, *Book III of the Sibylline Oracles and its Social Setting: With an Introduction, Translation, and Commentary* (SVTP 17; Leiden: Brill, 2003) 5-123.

establishment of Jewish rule.[143] Its relevance to matters pertaining to sexuality arises because of a few references in which the author includes sexual wrongdoing among the grounds for God's judgement against the wicked.

In 3:110-155 we find ourselves in Greek mythology, with the sibyl recounting the stories of Cronos, Titan, and Iapetus, children of Gaia and Ouranos, but here interpreted euhemeristically as human beings.[144] It includes the Titans' killing of Rhea's male newborns (perhaps implying a parallel with Moses' story)[145] and then the war of the Titans against the sons of Cronos as "the first beginning of war for mortals" (3:155; but cf. also 3:103 where this is said also of the dispersion after the destruction of the tower of Babel).[146] At no point do the sexual misadventures

---

[143] This consensus, identified already by John J. Collins, *The Sibylline Oracles of Egyptian Judaism* (SBLDS 13; Missoula: Scholars Press, 1974) and subsequent works, has been recently challenged by Buitenwerf, *Sibylline Oracles*, who proposes that fragments i and iii (cited in Theophilus' *Ad Autolycum*) and *Sib. Or.* 3:93-829 are to be seen as belonging to a single work, composed in Asia Minor somewhere between 80 and 31 B.C.E. (124-34). Key issues include whether references to a seventh king are literal and apply to Ptolemy VI Philometor (180-145 B.C.E.) or Ptolemy VIII Physcon (145-116 B.C.E.) or whether they are symbolic of the time of eschatological fulfilment and whether events alluded to include not only Rome's conquest of Greece in 146 B.C.E. in 3:171-193, the fall of Carthage in 3:484 and the destruction of Corinth in 3:487-488, but also whether 3:350-362 alludes to the Mithridatic wars which started in 88 B.C.E. This depends on the doubtful assumption that 3:295-488 are integral to the text and not as most assume, on grounds of style and content, a secondary expansion. Here, notably, we find the allusions both to the later events and to Asian interests which Buitenwerf stresses. See the critical assessment in John J. Collins, "The Third Sibyl Revisited," in *Things Revealed: Studies in Honor of Michael E. Stone* (ed. Esther Chazon and David Satran; Leiden: Brill, 2004) 3–19, who also challenges basis for the denial of the temporal meaning of seventh by Erich Gruen, *Heritage and Hellenism: The Reinvention of Jewish Tradition* (Berkeley: University of California Press, 1998) 272-77, and the earlier assertions of Book 3's unity in Valentin Nikiprowetzky, *La Troisième Sibylle* (Ètudes Juives 9; Paris: Mouton, 1970) 206-17. See also Collins, *Between Athens and Jerusalem*, 85, 88-95.

[144] On this see Buitenwerf, *Sibylline Oracles*, 330-31.

[145] So Levine, "Sibylline Oracles," 105.

[146] On the war of the Titans with Zeus, Jan K. Bremmer, "Remember the Titans!" in *The Fall of the Angels* (ed. Christoph Auffarth and Loren T. Stuckenbruck; Themes in Biblical Narrative 6; Leiden: Brill, 2004) 35-61, notes the apparent dependence of *Sib. Or.* 3:105-58 on Euhemerus *Sacred History*, 300 B.C.E. (56-58) and observes: "the wars between the successors of Alexander the Great must have lent Zeus' struggle an unsuspected actuality. Its attraction to Jews is proved not only by the *Third Sibylline Oracle*, but also by the fact that in their rewriting of the division of the earth in *Genesis* 10 the authors of *Jubilees* (*ca.* 150 B.C.: cc. 8-9) and the *Apocryphon of Genesis* (*ca.* 50 B.C.: *1QapGen ar* XVI-XVII) display exactly the same scheme as the *Third Sibylline Oracle*" (57).

surface. This is the beginning of the rise of kingdoms, including, finally, Rome (3:160).

The first pertinent reference to sexual issues comes in the oracle which ensues in 3:162-195, in the attack on a "kingdom, white and many-headed from the western sea" (3:175-176), normally identified with Rome. They will oppress mortals, "but those men will have a great fall when they launch on a course of unjust haughtiness. Immediately compulsion to impiety will come upon these men" (3:182-184). The sibyl then identifies male same-sex acts: "Male will have intercourse with male and they will set up boys in houses of ill-fame (αἰσχροῖς ἐν τεγέεσσι)[147] and in those days there will be a great affliction among men" (3:185-187). The "affliction" belongs not specifically to same-sex acts or their possible consequences but more generically to what the author goes on to describe as great confusion, cutting up everything and filling everything with evil and love of ill-gotten wealth "in many places, but especially in Macedonia" (3:187-190). Collins notes that the cutting up alludes to the division of Macedonia by the Romans after the battle of Pydna in 168 B.C.E.[148]

In the next oracle, 3:196-294, the sibyl returns to the account of evils. The first was God's punishment of the Titans (3:199-202). Then in the second we meet a depiction of the Greeks who "will have tyrannies and proud kings overbearing and impious, adulterous and wicked in all respects" (3:202-204), probably a reference to its ancient kings, since an allusion to Troy follows.[149] Evil falls on many other nations beside Troy, including "upon the pious men who live around the great temple of Solomon, and who are the offspring of righteous men". Thus far the ethical concerns have included warfare, male same-sex relations and illicit wealth. The sibyl's exposition of the Jews includes: rejection of sorcery and astrology, "love of money, which begets innumerable evils for mortal men, war, and limitless famine" (3:235-236), "unjust measurements, night robberies, boundary manipulation, oppression of widows and the poor" (3:238-247). The sibyl declares that this is God's law "common to all" (3:247) and then relates how this Law was given on Sinai (3:248-260). The evils they suffer include that they "will see innocent children and wives in slavery to hostile men" (3:268-70; cf. also 3:525-527), which would have included sexual exploitation and abuse, though this goes unmentioned, and their being scattered across the earth where people would be offended at their customs (3:270-272). The sibyl attributes the destruction of the temple and desolation of the land to the people's idolatry (3:273-281).

---

[147] Buitenwerf, *Sibylline Oracles*, notes that "in Hellenistic Greek τέγος ('roof') can also mean 'brothel'" (186).

[148] Collins, *OTP,* 1.366.

[149] So Buitenwerf, *Sibylline Oracles*, 196; cf. Collins, *OTP,* 1.366, who suggests an allusion to Helen of Troy in the reference to adultery.

The woes against various nations in 3:489-544 describe wickedness only in general terms ("unjust tongue and lawless, unholy life" composing "terrible words, false and unjust" (3:496-498). The exhortation to the Greeks focuses primarily on idols. It includes an image of suffering by the Greeks which might include sexual exploitation: barbarians "will take many slaves to another land by compulsion, children and broad-girdled women, delicate ones from their chambers, falling forward on tender feet. They will see themselves suffering every terrible outrage" (3:525-528).

We find the next specific reference to sexual issues when the sibyl then returns to praise the "sacred race of pious men" (3:573), in 3:573-600. Here the author declares that Jews reject idolatry, honour God and their parents[150] (3:594) and then continues:

> Greatly, surpassing all men, 595 they are mindful of holy wedlock (μέγα δ'ἔξοχα πάντων ἀνθρώπων ὅσιης εὐνῆς μεμνημένοι εἰσίν), 596 and they do not engage in impious (or: impure, immoral) intercourse with male children (κοὐδέ πρὸς ἀρσενικοὺς παῖδας μίγνυνται ἀνάγνως), 597 as do Phoenicians, Egyptians, and Romans, 598, spacious Greece and many nations of others, 599 Persians and Galatians and all Asia, transgressing, 599 the holy law of immortal God, which they transgressed (παραβάντες ἀθανάτοιο θεοῦ ἁγνὸν νόμον, ὅν παρέβησεν. (3:594-600)[151]

Here we find condemnation of adultery[152] and male same-sex relations juxtaposed, as later in 3:764. The "holy law of immortal God" (cf. also 3:276, 284) probably alludes to the Mosaic Law and to the prohibitions in Leviticus 18 and 20. It is understood by the author, however, to be the same law which is "common to all" (3:248), in a broader sense the law of creation (also Mosaic Law) as the law God has set by nature, which assumes sexual intercourse must be confined to relations between men and women. Earlier in the same passage the devotion of the Jews is said to include that "at dawn they lift up holy arms towards heaven, from their beds, always sanctifying their flesh (χρόα so Clement of Alexandria *Protr.* 6.70; the MSS read χέρας "hands")[153] with water" (3:591-593). The section began with a note about their honouring the temple and here we find allusions probably to ritual

---

[150] For the possible allusion to the Decalogue see Buitenwerf, *Sibylline Oracles*, who points out, however, that this was also a shared value with non-Jewish culture (263).

[151] On the final two words where the text is "irreparably corrupt" – so Buitenwerf, *Sibylline Oracles*, 264, see J. Geffcken, *Die Oracula Sibyllina* (GCS 8; Leipzig: Hinrichs, 1902) 79.

[152] For condemnation of adultery elsewhere see Buitenwerf, *Sibylline Oracles*, who alludes to Wisd 14:24, 26; Sir 23:8; *Ps.-Phoc.* 175-217; Philo *Hypoth.* 7.1; Josephus *Ap.* 2.201, 215; *Pss. Sol.* 8:10; Rom 2:22; Heb 13:4 (263 n. 47).

[153] See the discussion of the variants in Buitenwerf, *Sibylline Oracles*, 262.

lustration. While this might have relevance for need for purification after sexual emissions, it will also reflect a wider concern with purity, though the MSS variant may limit it to purification of only the hands.[154] Rising at dawn to worship was apparently common Jewish practice[155] as was engaging in rituals of purification. These practices have parallels in Philo's descriptions of the Therapeutae and seems also to have been a practice of Essenes and perhaps others. The selection of nations divides them into two groups: "Phoenicians, Egyptians, and Romans, spacious Greece", and then "many nations of others, Persians and Galatians and all Asia". It is impressively wide in range.

The prophecy of judgement which follows in 3:601-618 again targets idolatry, which also informs the call to worship the one God in 3:619-634. The depiction of the eschatological climax of history and of hope in the remainder of the work similarly includes few specific references to sin. It includes the theme of greed and exploitation (3:639-642): "Love of gain will be shepherd of evils for cities" (3:642); and assault on the temple. Within the depiction of impending judgement the sibyl addresses the hearer, warning against unlawful worship and then adding: "Avoid adultery and indiscriminate (ἄκριτον; undifferentiated, i.e. not differentiating male from female) intercourse with males" (μοιχείας πεφύλαξο καὶ ἄρσενος ἄκριτον 3:764). That exhortation continues: "rear your own offspring and do not kill it, for the Immortal is angry at whoever commits these sins" (3:765-766). Here the allusion will be to exposure of infants, especially female infants.[156] By contrast the vision of the eschatological kingdom, a rich pastiche of intertextual allusions to the biblical prophets (including Isa 2:3; 11:6-8; 12:6; 60:1; 65:25; Dan 2:44; 7:27; Zech 2:10; 14:16) depicts a safe place for babies, for not even serpents and asps will harm them, and a future on earth in peace with just distribution of wealth (3:767-795). Nothing is said of sexual relations, but these appear to be assumed as part of the normal life of marriage, family and birth of babies (cf. also 3:702-704, which speaks of a peaceful life around the temple; and 3:744-759, which predicts abundant fruit and herds and peace under God's law).

---

[154] On parallels to the washing of hands see Buitenwerf, *Sibylline Oracles*, who notes *Let. Arist.* 305-306; and draws attention to Josephus *A.J.* 12.106; Mark 7:4 and parr. For the practice of bathing before prayer see Josephus *A.J.* 14.258; Acts 16:13; Jdt 12:7; CD 11.21 – 12.1.

[155] So Buitenwerf, *Sibylline Oracles*, who points to Wis 16:28-29; *Pss. Sol.* 6:4; *Let. Arist.* 304-306; 4Q503; Philo *Contempl.* 27, 89; Josephus *B.J.* 2.128; *A.J.* 4.212, noting that it was also not uncommon in other religious communities (262 n. 44).

[156] Buitenwerf, *Sibylline Oracles*, notes that the same juxtaposition of vices occurs in Josephus *Ap.* 2.199-202; *Ps.-Phoc.* 175-205 and on infanticide points to Philo *Spec.* 3.110-119; *Hypoth.* 7.7; Josephus *Ap.* 2.202 (288).

Conclusion

Specific ethical concerns in the work are somewhat limited. Apparently designed both to reassure and encourage Jews and to persuade sympathetic Gentiles also to espouse Jewish values,[157] the work makes common cause in attacking what both would have recognised as evils present within their world:[158] pederasty,[159] male prostitution (and probably male same-sex acts generally), adultery, and infanticide. Grounds for these attacks are to be found primarily in Mosaic Law, but probably also in a shared notion of what is natural and natural law, alluded to in 3:758 as "a common law for men through the whole earth" (κοίνον τε νόμον κατὰ γαῖαν ἀπασαν) (similarly 3:248).[160] Three aspects of male same-sex activity are

---

[157] Cf. John M. G. Barclay, *Jews in the Mediterranean Diaspora from Alexander to Trajan (323 BCE–117 CE)* (Edinburgh: T&T Clark, 1996) 218-25, who writes: "Adopting the scornful Sibylline mask allows these Jewish oracle-mongers to launch a vigorous attack on other nations" (221). He denies positive allusions to a seventh Ptolemaic king (222-23), describing the work as hostile and antagonistic towards Gentiles, at most "a proselytization by fear" (222), though he acknowledges "some degree of acculturation" (224) in the adaptation of the genre. See the refutation in Collins, *Between Athens and Jerusalem*, who argues that despite its "triumphalist and condescending" manner the work envisages positive Gentile responses, including conversion (161). Cf. also Erich S. Gruen, *Diaspora: Jews amidst Greeks and Romans* (Cambridge: Harvard University Press, 2002), who notes that despite its "dire predictions for the Greek" the work can also "display magnanimity and "extends a hand to the Hellenic world" (230).

[158] Buitenwerf, *Sibylline Oracles*, sees the work as ostensibly addressed to Greeks, as convention about the sibyl required, but actually addressed to Jews to urge observance of divine law in a form that also had entertainment value (373-81), and as assuming respect for the figure of the pagan sibyl whom it grants a pedigree by making her Noah's daughter-in-law (3:827) (371-73). But see Collins, *Between Athens and Jerusalem*, who writes: "The reason why a Jewish author put the praise of Judaism in the mouth of a pagan sibyl is clear enough: to put the praise of Judaism in the mouth of a pagan prophetess of hoary antiquity and respected authority" (84). This served to bolster Jewish self-confidence (84). Levine, "Sibylline Oracles," notes that the connection with Noah "is also depicted on third-century C.E. coins from Apamea-Kobotos" (102).

[159] Buitenwerf, *Sibylline Oracles*, sees the author's attack on male same-sex relations as "a Jewish element", but notes that the author may not have been aware that this was so (356), citing Plato, *Leg.* 636C; Mus Ruf, Fr 12; Plutarch, *Brut. an.* 990D-F.

[160] See also Buitenwerf, *Sibylline Oracles*, 339-42, who notes that "for the author, righteousness was the core of the law, both natural law and the Mosaic law" (341) and that the latter "was taken by the author as a specimen or expression of natural law" who "did not see a fundamental difference between Jewish law and natural law" (341), the chief difference being that Jews kept it and others did not. He argues for a similar twofold sense of the law in Sirach and Philo (456-62). Collins, *Between Athens and Jerusalem*, points also to Wisdom 13 and Romans 1 (162).

potentially envisaged: sexual relations between men and boys, viewed from the perspective of condemning men's actions; setting up houses of ill-fame indicates development of male prostitution where the boys function as prostitutes; general condemnation of sexual intercourse between males, probably targeting any such intercourse, including between adult males. The other pertinent references relate primarily to adultery. Although the author notes that some Jewish customs cause offence (3:272), we find no reference to specifics, thus no mention of issues such as diet, sabbath, or circumcision.[161] As Collins notes, "The tension between the universalistic understanding of the law and the particularistic attachment to land and temple is quite typical of Diaspora Judaism in the Hellenistic period, although the sibyl is exceptional in the prominence she gives to the sacrificial cult".[162]

On the positive side the work assumes a place for normal sexual relations in its vision of the eschatological kingdom, thus reflecting no indication of a value system which might call it into question.

1.2.1.2   Sib. Or. 3:350-488

This section, which is usually dated to the first century B.C.E. prior to the battle of Actium 31 B.C.E. and contains nothing specifically Jewish, makes no reference to sexual wrongdoing. It does, however, use sexual imagery in attacking Rome in 3:357-358: "virgin, often drunken with your weddings with many suitors, as a slave will you wed, without decorum". Many see here a response to criticism of Cleopatra's many marriages.[163] It reflects a negative view of having multiple marriages. The passage then continues with what may be a further allusion to Cleopatra: "Often the mistress (δέσποινα) will cut your delicate hair and, dispensing justice, will cast you from heaven to earth, but from earth will again raise you up to heaven, because mortals are involved in a wretched and unjust life" (3:359-362).[164] Then the ups and downs of Rome's status appear to be related to the vicissitudes of Cleopatra's relations with Roman leaders and aspirants to leadership. Alternatively the focus is the war with Mithridates.[165]

Sexual imagery also underlies the depiction of Alexander's Macedonia in 3:381-387, where he is referred to as "progeny of bastards and slaves" (a probable

---

[161] Similarly Collins, *Between Athens and Jerusalem*, 164, who notes, nevertheless, that its attack on astrology and divination would not have been shared by most (including the Stoics) in the world of the time, though certainly by some (163-64).

[162] Collins, *Between Athens and Jerusalem*, 165.

[163] Collins, *OTP*, 1.370.

[164] So Collins, *Sibylline Oracles of Egyptian Judaism*, 58-62.

[165] So Buitenwerf, *Sibylline Oracles*, who reads the allusions as relating to Rome's relations with Asia (223), following Gruen, *Heritage and Hellenism*, 281.

allusion to his claim to be son of Zeus Ammon)[166] and as "having been called mistress (δεσπότις) of every land which the sun beholds". Sexual imagery also informs the depiction of Troy: "You will be a prey to men who are lovers (ἕλωρ ἔση ἀνθρωποισιν ἐρασταῖς)", alluding to the debacle over Helen (3:413).[167] Rhodes, which will be "daughter for a day", is to suffer a similar fate: "Afterward you will be a prey to lovers (ἕλωρ ἔση ἀνθρωποισιν ἐρασταῖς) in beauty and wealth. You will place a terrible yoke on your neck" (3:445-447), probably alluding to its capture by Rome in 167 B.C.E.[168] The destruction of Samos is to be mourned by "wives with splendidly robed maidens" (3:454-55; cf. 3:525-527). Italy's fate is to suffer at the hand of civil war:[169] "native blood, much bemoaned, inexhaustible, notorious, will ravage you, shameless one (ἀναιδέα σε κεραΐξει)". It will "not be mother of good people, but nurse of wild beasts" (3:465-69), a subtle reversal of the myth of Romulus and Remus. Though the verb is not used specifically in a sexual sense of "ravage", the image will include sexual violation. The sexual imagery reappears in 3:480 where in speaking of drownings related to Sardinia the sibyl cries: "Alas for all the virgins whom Hades will wed".

Unlike in 3:97-349, 489-829, we find here no attacks on sexual wrongdoing. Conversely, unlike there, we find frequent use of sexual imagery to describe devastation and suffering. The depiction of cities as female is widely attested in both pagan and Jewish literature.[170] The sexual imagery also reveals systems of value, including disapproval of having many marriages and the shame of having one's hair cut off, as in the charge and threat against Rome.[171] We do find a wide range of ethical issues in the image of the blessings of a future life of peace in 3:367-380, but nothing pertaining to sexuality.

---

[166] Collins, *OTP*, 1.370. See also Buitenwerf, *Sibylline Oracles*, who notes the claim of divine sonship also in relation to his successors (227). The *Book of the Watchers* may also reflect a disparagement of this claim, though differently from here, since it suggests they are like the monsters born from the Watchers.

[167] So Buitenwerf, *Sibylline Oracles*, 231.

[168] Collins, *OTP*, 1.372; Jörg-Dieter Gauger, *Sybillinische Weissagungen: Griechisch Deutsch: Auf der Grundlage der Ausgabe von Alfons Kurfeiss* (2d ed.; Düsseldorf: Artemis & Winkler, 2002), 498.

[169] Collins, *OTP*, notes that "this might refer to the Slave Wars, Social War, or the civil war of Marius and Sulla, from the late end cent./early 1st cent. B.C." (1.372). See also Buitenwerf, *Sibylline Oracles*, 234.

[170] See, for instance, the parallels collated in Gauger, *Sybillinische Weissagungen*, 429; see also Buitenwerf, *Sibylline Oracles*, 223.

[171] Buitenwerf, *Sibylline Oracles*, 223.

1.2.1.3 Sib. Or. 3:1-96

These verses are widely acknowledged to have belonged to the end of the lost Book 2.[172] Some, if not all, of this material dates to after the battle of Actium in 31 B.C.E. since it assumes Rome's control over Egypt. The denunciation of idolatry in 3:8-45 includes what appears to be an attack on the Romans as "a crafty and evil race of impious and false double-tongued men and immoral adulterous (κακοηθῶν λεκτροκλόπων) idol worshippers" (3:36-38). It continues with allegations of greed, then adds: "They will have no fidelity at all. Many widowed women will love other men secretly for gain; and those who have husbands will not keep hold of the rope of life (οὐ σπάρτην κατέχουσι βίου)" (3:43-45). While the charge of adultery in 3:37-38 might apply equally to men, these lines focus on widows engaging in prostitution and wives committing adultery. The charge of infidelity against the former may imply that widows who have not remarried continue to have an obligation of fidelity to their dead husbands. The image of the rope of life represents the marriage relationship.

The following material concerns Rome and its demise and the coming of judgement in the time when "the world will be governed under the hands of a woman", also described as a widow (3:75, 77), and apparently to be identified with Cleopatra.[173] There is no indication that being ruled by a woman, in particular, is seen negatively. Her reign is set in contrast to God's and so she represents God's eschatological adversary (cf. the image of Babylon becoming a widow in Isa 47:8-9; Revelation 17 – 18), a negative depiction reflected also in later books of the *Sibylline Oracles* (cf. 11:243-260, 272-314).[174]

1.2.2   Sibylline Oracles Book 4

Collins describes the fourth book as "a political oracle from the Hellenistic age updated by a Jew in the late first century A.D."[175] after the destruction of the temple to which it refers (4:116), probably shortly after the eruption of Vesuvius in 79 C.E. (4:130-35), and most likely in Syria or the Jordan valley.[176] Material

---

[172] See the most recent discussion in Buitenwerf, *Sibylline Oracles*, 65-91. He sees 3:93-95 however as belonging with fragment 3 of Theophilus to the early part of Book 3. Neither fragment 1 nor fragment 3 contains material pertinent to our theme.

[173] So Collins, *Sibylline Oracles of Egyptian Judaism*, who also discusses proposed alternatives, Rome or the Messiah (67-70).

[174] On this see Collins, *Sibylline Oracles of Egyptian Judaism*, 70-71. He points to the similar image of Babylon in Isa 47:8-9 who becomes a widow.

[175] Collins, *OTP*, 1.381.

[176] Collins, *OTP*, 1.382. See also Oegema, *Einführung*, 168-72.

pertinent to sexuality comes in the Jewish redactional sections. Thus in the praise of the righteous in 4:24-39, which applauds their worship of God and rejection of temples and their idols, we read that they "commit no wicked murder, nor deal in dishonest gain, which are most horrible things. Neither have they disgraceful desire for another's spouse (οὐδ' ἄρ' ἐπ' ἀλλοτρίη κοίτη πόθον αἰσχρὸν ἔχοντες) or for hateful and repulsive abuse of a male (οὐδὲ ἐπ' ἄρσενὸς ὕβριν ἀπεχθέα τε στυγερήν τε)" (4:31-33). As in Book 3 the focus is adultery and male same-sex relations. There follows the claim that "Other men will never imitate their way 36 or piety or customs, because they desire shamelessness (ἀναιδείαν ποθέοντες). 37 On the contrary, they deride them with mockery and laughter. 38 Infantile in their foolishness, they will falsely attribute to those 39 what wicked and evil deeds they themselves commit" (4:35-39). The desire for shamelessness will pick up the sexual reference, that is, it alleges that the unrighteous engage in adultery and male same-sex activity. It is possible that the sexual focus is also present when the text claims that they charge the righteous with such "wicked and evil deeds". Judgement awaits them (4:42-43), whereas "the pious will remain on fertile soil" (4:45), reflecting an earth-based embodied eschatology, which has implication for the place of sexual relations, but that is not addressed here.

In 4:152-158 we find a depiction of evil in the last times, which reports that "untrustworthy men, living for unholy deeds, will commit outrage, wicked and evil deeds" (4:154-155) and speaks of them "rejoicing in outrages and applying their hands to blood" (4:158). The unholy deeds may be heard in the light of the earlier concerns with adultery and male same-sex relations, but here the focus seems rather on violence. The same is true of the call to repentance in 4:162-165, which calls people to "abandon daggers and groanings, murders and outrages" (4:163-164).

1.2.3   Sibylline Oracles Book 5

This work seems likely to have been composed at the end of the period under our review and quite possibly just beyond it, certainly those sections which refer to Hadrian and the Jewish revolts of 115 C.E. It is "an important witness to at least one strand of Egyptian Judaism in the period between the Jewish revolts"[177] (5:66-70 and 132-135 C.E.).[178] Its attack on Egypt 5:52-92 includes indictment for its

---

[177] Collins, *OTP*, 1.391.

[178] See also the discussion in Stephen Felder, "What is The Fifth Sibylline Oracle?" *JSJ* 33 (2002) 363-85, who argues for two levels of Jewish material, the second reusing and

treatment of Jews and its idolatry, in which the sibyl also speaks of "things which it is not even lawful for me to mention (ἄτε μοι θέμις οὐδ' ἀγορεύειν)" (5:79). This appears to relate to some object of veneration (as also in fragment 3:31)[179] rather than to particular actions, which might include sexual wrongdoing.

The depiction of Nero refers to his alleged birth from Zeus and Hera (5:140),[180] and his murder of his mother in 5:142 (cf. also 5:262)[181] and apparently again in 5:145-146, where the sibyl declares that "he destroyed many men and laid hands on the womb.[182] He sinned against spouses, and was sprung from abominable people", thus referring also to his crimes against his wives and their former husbands[183] and reversing the claims about his divine birth. In the oracle against Rome in 5:162-178 we then find the first specific references to sexual wrongdoing: "With you are found adulteries and illicit intercourse with boys (μοιχεία παρὰ σοὶ καὶ παίδων μῖξις ἄθεσμος). 167 Effeminate and unjust (θηλυδενὴς ἄδικός τε), evil city, ill-fated above all. 168 Alas, city of the Latin land, unclean in all things (πάντ' ἀκάθαρτε)" (5:166-168). As in Book 3 the allegations target adultery and male same-sex relations. For males to be θηλυδενής ("effeminate"), taking the female role in male same-sex acts is to deny their maleness and so incur great shame. Rome is also the focus in the allegations in 5:386-396

386 Matricides, desist from boldness and evil daring, 387 you who formerly impiously catered for pederasty (οἳ τὸ πάλαι παίδων κοίτή ἐπορίζετ' ἀναγῶς) 388 and set up in houses prostitutes who were pure before (καὶ τέγεσιν πόρνας ἐστήσατε τὰς πάλαι ἀγνάς), 389 with insults and punishment and toilsome disgrace (ὕβρεσι καὶ κολάσει κἀσχημοσύνη πολυμόχθῳ). 390 For in you mother had intercourse with child unlawfully, 391 and daughter was joined to her begetter as bride (ἐν σοὶ γὰρ μήτηρ τέκνῳ ἐμίγη ἀθεμίστως. καὶ θυγάτηρ γενετῆρι ἐῷ συζεύξατο νύμφη). 392 In you also kings defiled their ill-fated mouths (ἐν σοὶ καὶ βασιλεῖς στόμα

---

supplementing the first and deriving from the latter decades of the first century C.E. (370-85).

[179] Felder, "What is The Fifth Sibylline Oracle?" notes that the attacks on idolatry in what he sees as the older layer of Jewish material are directly specifically against Egyptian worship of animal figures and would win Greek sympathy (378-79).

[180] Collins, OTP, notes its sarcasm, alluding to the kind of claims of mysterious events at his birth as reported by Suetonius, Nero 6 (1.396).

[181] Reported in Suetonius, Nero, 34 and as widely known in 39.

[182] This may refer to his matricide, but might possibly allude to his killing his wife, Poppaea, by kicking her when she was pregnant (Suetonius, Nero, 35). See also Jan W. van Henten, "Nero Redivivus Demolished: The Coherence of the Nero Traditions in the Sibylline Oracles," JSP 21(2000) 3-17, 6-7.

[183] See Suetonius, Nero, 35.

δύσμορον ἐξεμίηναν). 393 In you also evil men practiced bestiality (ἐν σοὶ καὶ κτηνῶν εὗρον κοίτην κακοὶ ἄνδρες). 394 Be silent, most lamentable evil city, which indulges in revelry. 395 For no longer in you will virgin maidens tend the divine fire of sacred nourishing wood. (5:386-96)

We find here a range of what the Sibyl saw as acts of sexual wrongdoing, beginning with pederasty (παὶδων κοὶτή), then moving to setting up brothels. Here, unlike in 3:185, which speaks of boy prostitutes, we have reference to women (πόρνας), who were once pure (ἀγνάς, probably implying that they were virgins) being put into brothels. "Insults and punishment and toilsome disgrace" may be targeting the abuses associated with such exploitation.[184] In addition the charge of incest is laid, of parents with their children, reminiscent of *Pss. Sol.* 8:9. The accusation that "kings defiled their ill-fated mouths" appears to target oral sex, in particular, male same-sex *fellatio*. The list then extends to bestiality. Juxtaposing these activities to the warning that virgin maidens would no longer tend the divine fire seems deliberately to play on the sexual theme. For Rome to lose its vestal virgins is to speak of its defeat and destruction, an allusion to the destruction of the temple of Vesta in 64 C.E. The promise of reversal with the advent of a saviour figure in 5:414-433, includes the declaration: "For terrible things no longer happen to wretched mortals, 430 no adulteries or illicit love of boys (οὐδε γαμοκλοπίη καὶ παίδων Κύπρις ἄθεσμος),[185] 431 no murder, or din of battle, but competition is fair among all" (5:429-431). Again we see as in 5:166-168 an emphasis on adultery and same-sex relations.

Aside from these instances the focus in the depictions of the emperors' misdeeds (5:1-52), and of the wicked Nero (5:93-110, 137-181, 214-227, 361-385) is on violence and in most of the oracles of judgement against nations it is on violence and idolatry, particularly in relation to Egypt and its treatment of God's people. Charges of sexual wrongdoing are directed towards the Romans and consist primarily of adultery and same-sex relations and, in one instance, *fellatio*, incest, and bestiality.

Images of hope in 5:247-270 and 5:414-433 envisage life lived by God's people around the city "made more brilliant than the stars" (5:420-21; a common motif associated with eschatology and resurrection) and the temple (5:422-428) "in the middle of the earth" (5:250), in peace (also 5:384-385), without "the unclean foot of Greeks" (5:264) and with the divine law in their hearts ("they will have a

---

[184] Felder, "What is The Fifth Sibylline Oracle?" argues that we should see in 5:386-396, as in 5:361-385, the work of an anti-Roman author writing in the last decades of the first century C.E., who draws on older material, partly found within the book (e.g. 5:394; cf. 5:317) (370-71). He also sees the related material in 5:162-178 as the work of the same anti-Roman redaction (375).

[185] The word, Κύπρις, a name of Aphrodite, is used for "passion, love".

mind in their breasts that conforms to your laws" 5:265). Being without "the unclean foot of Greeks" (5:264) may imply Jews living in isolation and so rejection of intermarriage, as apparently also in *Pss. Sol.* 17:28. But the images also include the vision of a temple in Egypt (5:493-503). Both sets of images assume an earth-based eschatology of human beings living in community, and presumably therefore sexual relations.

1.2.4   Sibylline Oracles Books 1-2

Noting that Books 1-2 were originally one work, divided by a later copyist, Collins sees that work as consisting of "an original Jewish oracle and an extensive Christian redaction".[186] The latter appears to have taken place beyond our period in the second century C.E., whereas the former may even be earlier than the destruction of the temple in 70 C.E. and seems to have originated in Phrygia. While not questioning the location, Lightfoot's recent analysis gives cause for caution about date and Jewish origin, while not ruling it out.[187] She contemplates the possibility that the whole is a Christian work, adapting diverse but already Christian sources, though agreeing that one can identify a stratification.[188] Absence of Christian motifs from the earliest stage need not exclude its being Christian, but

---

[186] Collins, *OTP*, 1.330. For a general introduction see pp. 330-34 and "Sibylline Oracles," 376-79.

[187] Lightfoot, *Sibylline Oracles*, writes: "The traditional view, that the oracle consists of a Jewish underlay plus Christian additions, may be right, but it cannot be ruled out that the oracle is a unified, necessarily Christian, composition, wrought out of different materials" (104). Discussing the connection with the city of Apamea Kibotos in Phrygia as the supposed site of the landing of the ark (1:261-266), reflected also in coins, she concludes that it is insufficient to give a clear date or to enable one to conclude Jewish or Christian authorship (99) and that "our exiguous evidence cannot be pressed to show that Apamea's Flood-myth is necessarily Jewish rather than Christian" (102). Even the clear break in 1:323 where the christology section begins may mean no more than that one Christian writer was taking over from another (103). The view expressed in Emil Schürer, *The History of the Jewish People in the Age of Jesus Christ (175 B.C. – A.D. 135): Vol. III.1* (3 vols; ed. Geza Vermes; Fergus Millar, and Martin Goodman; Edinburgh: T&T Clark, 1986) is more definite: "the complete lack of attestation of the 'Jewish' sections in the Church Fathers of the first three centuries speaks rather for a late origin, in which case they are likely to be Christian" (645); in agreement: Helmut Merkel, *Sibyllinen* (JSHRZ 5.8; Gütersloh: Gütersloher Verlagshaus, 1998) 1041-1148, 1070.

[188] The outline of its stratification which follows, though not its interpretation, follows Lightfoot, *Sibylline Oracles*, 97-99. See also Collins, *OTP*, 1.332-33. In Lightfoot's assessment an author "assembled it all in imitation of the structure of the Apocalypse of Weeks but wadded with all sorts of other material, Enochic, Petrine, Sibylline" (149).

makes that, in my view, less likely, though we cannot escape the uncertainties. The earlier, probably Jewish, stratum reflects the influence of Hesiod, *Works and Days*, especially in the assumption of two cycles of five generations (1:1-323; 2:6-33, 154-176), but also of the *Apocalypse of Weeks* (*1 Enoch* 93:1-10; 91:11-17), with its ten weeks and similarly two major acts of judgement, the flood and the end.[189] The eighth and ninth generations are missing and appear to have been replaced by Christian material which interrupts the sequence at 1:323, continuing to 1:400, after which we return after a brief transition, 2:1-5, to the tenth generation (2:6-33, 154-176). Into it more Christian material has been interpolated, 2:34-153, including a large chunk cited from *Pseudo-Phocylides*, 2:56-148. Christian material returns from 2:177 to the end, including material from 2:194 on, showing dependence on the mid second century *Apocalypse of Peter*.[190]

This complicates our assessment of the material in relation to sexual issues. We are on reasonably firm ground in material pertaining to the first generation, which is probably Jewish, since it is atypical of later Christian concerns which would have given much greater emphasis to the fall. Its depiction of human creation is distinctive:

> And then later he again fashioned an animate object (lit. a work breathed into) (ἔπλασεν πάλιν ἔμπνοον ἔργον), 23 making a copy from his own image, youthful man (εἰκόνος ἐξ ἰδίης ἀπομαξάμενος νέον ἄνδρα), 24 beautiful, wonderful (καλὸν θεσπέσιον). He bade him live in an 25 ambrosial garden (ἐν παραδείσῳ ἀμβροσίῳ), so that he might be concerned with beautiful (or: good) works (ὡς οἱ καλὰ ἔργα μεμήλῃ). 26 But he being alone in the luxuriant plantation of the garden 27 desired conversation (αὐτὰρ ὁ μοῦνος ἐὼν παραδείσου ἐριθηλέϊ κήπῳ προσλαλίην ποθέεσκε), and prayed to behold another form 28 like his own (καὶ ηὔχετο εἶδος ἀθρῆσαι ἀλλ᾽ οἷον αὐτὸς ἔχεν). God himself indeed took a bone from his 29 flank and made Eve, a wonderful maidenly 30 spouse (ἐποιήσατο Εὔαν ἀγητήν, κουριδίην ἄλοχον), whom he gave to this man to live with him in the garden. 31 And he, when he saw her, was suddenly greatly 32 amazed in spirit, rejoicing, such a corresponding 33 copy did he see. (ὅ δὲ μιν κατιδὼν μέγα θυμῷ

---

[189] Lightfoot, *Sibylline Oracles*, 111, 113. She notes that there, too, we find disruption after the seventh week (113). She sees the link with the Apocalypse as one of a number of indications that the author is familiar with Enochic traditions (114). Others include use of the myth of the Watchers and the prominence given to Noah (126-27). At the same time she notes the possibility that the pagan sibyl used a similar scheme, concluding, "One suspects that various oracles of this general shape were drifting about, and assuredly the situation was more complicated than we can now reconstruct" (118). Thus, she observes, "We miss regularity in the Sibyl's scheme of ages because several forces are exerting an influence on it. The underlying biblical account comes into complicated interplay with Hesiod, on the one hand, and classical, sophistic ideas of cultural advance, on the other" (125).

[190] Lightfoot, *Sibylline Oracles*, 104, 137-43.

θαῦμ' ἔχεν ἐξαίφνης, κεχαρημένος, οἷον ὁρατο ἀντίτυπον μίμημα). They (lit. she) conversed with wise words 34 which flowed spontaneously (σοφοῖς δ'ἠμείβετο μύθοις αὐτομάτοις ῥείουσι), for God had taken care of everything (θεῷ γὰρ πάντ' ἐμεμήλει). 35 For they neither covered their minds with licentiousness 36 nor felt shame (οὔτε γὰρ ἀκρασίη νόον ἔσκεπον οὔτε αἰδῷ ἄμφεχον), but were far removed from evil heart (ἀλλ' ἦσαν κραδίης ἀπάνευθε κακοῖο); 37 and they walked like wild beasts with uncovered limbs (χὼς θῆρες βαίνεσκον ἀποσκεπέεσσι μέλεσσιν)". (1:22-37)

This re-writing of the Genesis story trims it of all dialogue and merges the two Genesis accounts into one, based on the second.[191] It portrays the man as beautiful and wonderful, since he reflects the image of God,[192] and possibly "young". In 1:22-24 it combines the allusion in Gen 1:26 and 27 to creation after the divine image (κατ' εἰκόνα) with an allusion to Gen 2:7 (καὶ ἔπλασεν ὁ θεὸς τὸν ἄνθρωπον χοῦν ἀπὸ τῆς γῆς καὶ ἐνεφύσησεν εἰς τὸ πρόσωπον αὐτοῦ πνοὴν ζωῆς καὶ ἐγένετο ὁ ἄνθρωπος εἰς ψυχὴν ζῶσαν). But it passes over Gen 1:27 about making male and female and Gen 1:28, the command to multiply, which it postpones until they are outside the garden.[193] Nothing suggests this relates to seeing the garden as a temple as in *Jubilees*. Instead, it portrays the man as commanded to live in the garden "so that he might be concerned with beautiful (or: good) works" (ὡς οἱ καλὰ ἔργα μεμήλη).[194] This may well be a spiritualisation of what Gen 2:15 describes as God's commission to the man to work and watch over the garden (ἔθετο αὐτὸν ἐν τῷ παραδείσῳ ἐργάζεσθαι αὐτὸν καὶ φυλάσσειν "put him in the orchard to till and keep it" [*NETS*]).

The author then portrays the (young) man as "lonely" (μοῦνος) and desiring "conversation" (προσλαλίην) and praying to see a face like his own (ηὔχετο εἶδος ἀθρῆσαι ἀλλ' οἷον αὐτὸς ἔχεν) (1:27-28). As in *Gen. Rab.* 17:5, the Sibyl reports God as responding to the man's initiative and assumes the hearers' knowledge of the creation of animals and their being brought to the man. We read then that God took a rib from his side "and made Eve, a wonderful maidenly spouse" (ἐποιήσατο Εὔαν ἀγητὴν, κουριδίην ἄλοχον) (1:29-30), here directly named from the beginning. The Homeric phrase, κουριδίην ἄλοχον, "maidenly spouse" reflects the marriage theme of Gen 2:20-25, but without its aetiology of

---

[191] Lightfoot, *Sibylline Oracles*, who notes this is the reverse of *Jubilees* which makes the first account the basis for its story (332).

[192] Lightfoot, *Sibylline Oracles*, 340.

[193] So Lightfoot, *Sibylline Oracles*, who observes: "God's blessing on his creatures is reserved for their entry into the real world" (335).

[194] As Lightfoot, *Sibylline Oracles*, notes, the beginning of agriculture must wait till after the expulsion (340).

marriage and sexual intercourse.[195] The man does rejoice at catching sight of the woman, but nothing suggests this is sexual. Instead, in contrast to *Jubilees* where sexual intercourse becomes central, he has wanted "conversation" (προσλαλίην) and that is what he gets. Thus the sibyl reports: "She conversed with wise words 34 which flowed spontaneously"* (σοφοῖς δ'ἠμείβετο μύθοις αὐτομάτοις ῥείουσι) (1:33-34). This is now an aetiology of language.[196]

There is a striking absence of sexual motifs. Their nakedness is not suppressed (1:37), but mentioned only after the author assures the hearers: "For they neither covered their minds with licentiousness 36 nor felt shame (οὔτε γὰρ ἀκρασίη νόον ἔσκεπον οὔτε αἰδῶ ἄμφεχον), but were far removed from evil heart (ἀλλ' ἦσαν καρδίης ἀπάνευθε κακοῖο)" (1:35-36).[197] The reference to going about like the animals with uncovered μέλεσσιν, i.e., genitalia (1:37), reflects not unbridled sexual activity, but a "pre-civilised" state.[198] In other words, having suppressed all positive sexual allusions, the author's only allusion to sexuality is to depict the absence of licentiousness and of an evil heart. This appears to reflect a mindset which saw sex as something dangerous and certainly not worthy of mention as something positive.[199]

The continuation rewrites the account of sin. Like *Jubilees*, the work portrays the prohibition about touching the tree as having been directed not just to the man, as in Gen 2:13-14, but also to the woman. Unlike *Jubilees*, the purpose of the change appears to be to render more credible its depiction which states: "But the woman first became a betrayer to him. 43 She gave, and persuaded him to sin in his ignorance" (ἀλλὰ γυνὴ πρώτη προδότις < > γίνετ' ἐκείνῳ, ἡ δῶκεν, τοῦτον δ' ἀδαῆ πείθεσκεν ἁμαρτεῖν) (1:42-43). As in *2 Enoch* the focus falls

---

[195] Lightfoot, *Sibylline Oracles*, writes: "Whether or not it has any emotive content here, it reflects Genesis' presentation of the relationship as the origin and pattern of human marriage. ... Yet the Sibyl does not directly broach the much-discussed topic of Adam and Eve's sexual relations in Eden. ... On the one hand, she emphasises Adam's appreciation of Eve; on the other, she places the commandment to be fruitful and multiply on their expulsion from the garden" (341).

[196] So Lightfoot, *Sibylline Oracles*: "The story, is, in fact, shot through with aetiology" (335).

[197] Lightfoot, *Sibylline Oracles* notes that the Sibyl does not take "a position on whether the first humans were chaste within Eden" (342); similarly p. 333.

[198] So Lightfoot, *Sibylline Oracles*, 343.

[199] J. Edward Ellis, *Paul and Ancient Views of Sexual Desire: Paul's Sexual Ethics in 1 Thessalonians 4, 1 Corinthians 7 and Romans 1* (LNTS 354; London: T&T Clark, 2007), reads the reference to ἀκρασία and the evil heart in 1:35-36 as implying that this was why they did not engage in sexual intercourse (1:33), concluding, "then, any inclination towards sex, even within marriage in the garden, is evil and constitutes ἀκρασία (19). This certainly reflects "a low view of sex and sexual desire" (20).

on ignorance, though there it is Eve's ignorance, whereas here it is Adam's (*2 Enoch* 31:7; cf. 30:16).[200] While the Sibyl lays blame also on the man, "He was persuaded by the woman's words, forgot 45 about his immortal creator, and neglected clear commands" (ὃς δὲ γυναικὸς ἔπεσσι πεπεισμένος ἐκλελάθεσκεν ἀθανάτου κτίστου, σαφέων δ' ἀμέλησεν ἐφετμῶν) (1:44-45), the account makes the woman primarily responsible, an emphasis present already in Sir 25:24 (similarly *2 Enoch* 30:17).[201]

The description of the consequences omits all reference to God's words of judgment to the woman, and the man. As Lightfoot notes, we have here "little sense that this is a fall, into sinfulness".[202] There is but a faint echo in the report that "the Immortal became angry with them and expelled them 51 from the place of immortals. For it had been decreed 52 that they remain in a mortal place, since they had not kept 53 the command of the great Immortal God, and attended to it" (1:51-53). As in *2 Enoch* 30 - 32, gone, therefore, is any reference to the woman's subservience to the man, her sexual passion which has her constantly returning to him, her pain in childbirth, and to both returning to their place of origin, the woman to the man, the man to the ground (cf. Gen 3:16-19).

Far from cursed, the ground is "fruitful" (ζείδωρον 1:54), and as in *2 Enoch* 31:7 not therefore cursed. The author then retrieves the command to increase and multiply from Gen 1:28 and has it serve as their commission as they leave the garden: "Increase, multiply, and work on earth 58 with skill, so that by sweat you may have your fill of food" (1:57-58), an aetiology of agriculture.[203] Increasing and multiplying necessarily entailed sexual relations and may have been seen by the author as their primary function. In 1:65-67 we read that they fulfilled their commission: they "multiplied as the universal ruler 66 himself commanded" (1:65-66).[204]

---

[200] Lightfoot, *Sibylline Oracles*, draws attention to traditions of Adam's not knowing in Adam and Eve literature (345). Other parallels she notes are the transfer immediately to the mortal from the immortal place without an intervening trial, reduction of judgements to the pronouncement against the snake, which is transferred to the end of the episode, and the blessing and positive agricultural commission (336).

[201] Levine, "Sibylline Oracles," notes the irony that here Adam is disapproved of for listening to a woman's word "given that the genre itself insists the reader be persuaded by a woman's words" (104).

[202] So Lightfoot, *Sibylline Oracles*, 335.

[203] So Lightfoot, *Sibylline Oracles*, 347.

[204] Ellis, *Sexual Desire*, points out that in this work "sex and procreation are results of the fall", and the command to multiply a forced necessity because they had to leave the paradise for a mortal place (19-20). He rightly cautions against reading too much that is positive from this commandment. On the other hand, it makes it hard to sustain the view he is arguing that "sexual intercourse is viewed as evil" (20).

The work then uses a framework of thought based on Hesiod in describing the appearances of a series of races. A first race of human beings (1:65-86), who became innumerable peoples, lived in idyllic conditions "a very lovely life" (εἰς ζωὴν πολυήρατον 1:70). There are no sexual motifs in the description beyond what multiplying implies. This is also true of their sins, which are primarily sins of violence (including towards parents, with allusions to Greek mythology and the intergenerational conflict played out there).

Without any basis in Genesis the work assumes the annihilation of most of the first race and the fashioning by God of a second from their righteous remnant (1:87-104). Their chief characteristic is invention and discovery in response to need across a broad range of areas, agriculture, carpentry, seafaring, astronomy, divination, medicine, magic (1:93-96). In 1:98-100 we then read that these were "enterprising Watchers, who received this appellation 99 because they had a sleepless mind in their hearts and an insatiable personality" (γρήγοροι ἀλφηστῆρες, ἐπωνυμίης μετέχοντες ταύτης, ὅττι μετὰ φρέσιν ἀκοίμητον νόον εἶχον ἄπλητόν τε δέμας)". This is an interesting reworking of elements of the myth. The explanation of the name, "Watchers", demythologises its origin. It is not evident that the author differentiates among the inventions and discoveries nor that they are depicted as illicit. This may reflect knowledge of a version of the myth such as we find in *Jubilees* where the Watchers on earth taught such skills under divine commission (4:15; 5:6; 7:21), but here they are human not heavenly beings. This matches the euhemeristic approach attested also in 3:110-155. They were "not bringers of evil, as in some other sources, but culture heroes, inventors of technology".[205] Nothing is said of sexual wrongdoing, including their intercourse with human women,[206] nor of inventions such as of ornaments and cosmetics through Asael's revelations as in *1 Enoch* 8:1-2, although some knowledge of their wickedness is presupposed in the Sibyl's comment that they "went under the dread house of Tartarus 102 guarded by unbreakable bonds, to make retribution, 103 to Gehenna of terrible, raging, undying fire" (1:101-103).[207] It speaks of punishment, but without giving an account of their crime.

The third generation, reported briefly, also stands within the tradition of the myth of the Watchers. It depicts the giants and their violence, as reported in *1 Enoch* 7:2-5. Their behaviour is similar to the fourth generation of young,

---

[205] Lightfoot, *Sibylline Oracles*, 335.

[206] Collins, *OTP*, translates ἄπλητὸν τε δέμας "insatiable personality", but it probably means no more than "great, big frame" and does not suggest "desire" or "passion", as "insatiable" may suggest. Thus it should not be read as an allusion to their sexual lusting.

[207] See also Lightfoot, *Sibylline Oracles*, who writes: "Thus it comes as a surprise when the Watchers come to the bad end that they do, although their fate – to be bound in Tartarus against the final judgement, when they will be cast into the fire – derives from Enochic tradition, too" (356).

bloodthirsty men (1:109-119).[208] In the brief depiction of the fifth generation, the author compares with "those Giants" (ἐκεῖνοι γίγαντες probably the third, possibly also the fourth generation) (1:124), as inferior and even more insolent (1:120-124). Here the figure of Noah enters the account, commissioned to preach repentance and prepare "an imperishable 133 wooden house" (1:132-133). Thus far sexual wrongdoing has not featured in the failings of the successive generations. It does however receive brief mention in the account of Noah's preaching:

> O very wretched, evil-hearted fickle men, 175 abandoning modesty (αἰδοίην προλιπόντες), desiring shamelessness 176 (ἀναιδείην ποθέοντες), tyrants in fickleness and violent sinners, 177 liars, sated with faithlessness (ἀπιστοκόροι), evildoers, truthful in nothing, 178 adulterers (λεκτροκλόποι), ingenious at pouring out slander, not fearing the anger of the most high God, 179 you who were preserved till the fifth generation to make retribution. (1:174-180)[209]

Lightfoot notes that the Sibyl makes no mention of the commands of Gen 9:1-7, including the twice repeated command to be fruitful and multiply.

The disjointedness of the text and apparent omissions mean that after the story of Noah and the brief account of the Titans as a seventh generation, we jump across what is a later Christian interpolation in 1:324-400 to an account of the tenth generation, which begins in 2:6. It speaks of the evils of slavery and plundering temples (2:13-14) and self-destruction (2:20-22).[210] Conversely its image of hope portrays "deep peace and understanding, 30 and the fruitful earth will again bear more numerous fruits, 31 being neither divided nor in servitude any longer. 32 Every harbour, every port will be free for men 33 as it was before, and shamelessness (ἀναειδείη) will perish" (2:29-33). This interesting economic analysis may imply changes in relation to sexuality both with regard to servitude (slaves were sexually exploited) and in its reference to shamelessness, but there is nothing explicit.

Some MSS incorporate in 2:56-148 a section from *Pseudo-Phocylides*, which we shall discuss in its original context. The description of depravation and depravity in 2:154-164 includes reference to cannibalism (children eating their

---

[208] Lightfoot, *Sibylline Oracles*, observes that the third race matches Hesiod's, and that there, in *1 Enoch* and here, the giants destroy themselves in battle (362).

[209] Lightfoot, *Sibylline Oracles*, notes that the list of sins is paralleled in 2:254-264 and 3:36-40 (377). The parallel to λεκτροκλόποι "adulterers" (1:178) in 2:258 has κλεψίγαμοι (cf. λεκτροκλόπων 3:38). She notes the parallel material to 1:175-78 in 8:184-187; and to 1:183, 93-97 in 7:7-12, and that it appears more original in this context (391).

[210] This motif may derive from the Watcher myth which has divine initiative set the giants on a course of mutual self-destruction.

parents 2:158-161) and the enigmatic claim that "when the species of females 164 does not give birth, the harvest of articulate men has come" (ἡνίκα φῦλα γυναικῶν μὴ τίκτωσιν, ἔφυ τὸ θέρος μερόπων ἀνθρώπων 2:163-164). It may well be, as Lightfoot suggests, a lift from the *Gospel of the Egyptians* (Clem. Alex. *Strom.* 3.6.45.3; 3.9.64.1; *Exc.* 67.2), where the harvest points to the final coming of Christ and so of judgement and sees Christ as having come to undo the works of the female.[211]

From 2:194 the work reflects extensive use of the *Apocalypse of Peter*.[212] In 2:221-226 we read of a literal resurrection, apparently of all, and 2:227-237 portrays all being brought to judgement, including the Titans and Giants, an allusion to the Watcher myth, although it does not include the Watchers. The "impious" (ἀσεβεῖς 2:254) are "as many as formerly did evil 256 or committed murders, and as many as are accomplices, 257 liars, and crafty thieves, and dread destroyers of houses, 258 parasites, and adulterers (τ' οἰκοφθόροι αἰνοί δειπνολόχοι καὶ κλεψίγαμοι), who pour out slander, 259 terrible violent men, and lawless ones, and idol worshippers" (2:255-59). "Dread destroyers of houses, parasites, and adulterers" (τ' οἰκοφθόροι αἰνοί δειπνολόχοι καὶ κλεψίγαμοι) probably all relate to adultery and adulterous activity. The destruction of households (rather than buildings) features also in the attacks in *Pss. Sol.* 4:9-13, 20 (cf. also Wis 3:16-19; 4:3-5). The word, δειπνολόχοι ("parasites"), has a special meaning and refers to those who sought to make their way into other people's banquets, here in the sense of not only intruding but also using that frequently notorious setting to seduce.[213] The list of offenders continues and includes those who have financially exploited widows and orphans, neglected or abused parents, reneged on promises, and slaves who have turned on their masters (2:267-273), and practised sorcery (2:283). Sexual issues return in the listing of

> those who defiled their flesh by licentiousness (τὴν σάρκα ἀσελγείη ἐμίηναν), 280 or as many as undid the girdle of virginity 281 by secret intercourse (ἠδ' ὁπόσοι ζώνην τὴν παρθενικὴν ἀπέλυσαν λάθρη μισγόμενοι), as many as aborted 282 what they carried in their womb (ὅσσαι δ' ἐνὶ γαστέρι φόρτους ἐκτρώσκουσιν), as many as cast forth their offspring unlawfully (ὅσοι τε τόκους ῥίπτουσιν ἀθέσμως). (2:279-282)

---

[211] Lightfoot, *Sibylline Oracles*, 470-71.

[212] On this see Lightfoot, *Sibylline Oracles*, 137-43.

[213] On these see Mary J. Marshall, *Jesus and the Banquets: An Investigation of the Early Christian Tradition concerning Jesus' Presence at Banquets with Toll Collectors and Sinners* (PhD Thesis; Murdoch University, 2002) 154-57.

This second list appears to be derived from the *Apocalypse of Peter*.[214] The focus is moral defilement, beginning with a general statement, but then specifying pre-marital intercourse by or with virgins, abortion, and exposure. Lightfoot notes the formal differences between the first, shorter list and the second, suggesting that the former is based on the Decalogue and is typical of similar lists found in Hellenistic Judaism and early Christianity.[215] She notes that within these, "sexual ethics also play quite a large role. Adultery is the *sine qua non* of tour-of-hell literature".[216]

The image of hope already sketched in 2:29-34 in terms of freedom and peace, comes to more detailed expression in 2:312-338. As there, it clearly assumes embodied life on earth, characterised by abundance. There is a major emphasis on equality: "For there will be no poor man there, no rich, and no tyrant, no slave". There will be no day and night or seasons but one long day. Then the author adds: "no marriage, no death, no sales, no purchases"* (οὐ γάμον, οὐ θάνατον, οὐ πράσεις, οὐδ' ἀγορασμούς) (2:328).[217] Juxtaposition of marriage and commerce occurs elsewhere and reflects that fact that marriage includes financial transactions (cf. CD 13.16b-19). The statement that there will be no marriage is a significant parallel to Mark 12:25. Its likely rationale here appears not to be the sacredness of this new space and new day, as one might deduce from *Jubilees* which forbids sexual intercourse in paradise and on the Sabbath (50:8), but a notion of everlasting life, which, for an author who apparently sees sexual relations as only for procreation, makes sexual relations and so marriage redundant, as assumed also in *1 Enoch* 15:5-7 and also Luke 20:34-36. One might wonder whether its presence here reflects that Christian tradition, though the passage as a whole about what is absent in the world to come, 2:322-329, displays otherwise no distinctively Christian traits, and the attitude towards sexuality coheres with the revision of the creation stories.[218]

The work ends with a confession of the sibyl (2:339-347) who rues her fate on the day of judgement for among other things "caring neither for marriage nor for

---

[214] Lightfoot, *Sibylline Oracles*, 507.

[215] Lightfoot, *Sibylline Oracles*, 506.

[216] Lightfoot, *Sibylline Oracles*, 507.

[217] Lightfoot, *Sibylline Oracles*, observes that 2:322-329 "largely correspond to blocks elsewhere in the corpus, where they occur in different contexts" (529). It is "a specialised example of the description of another world (Paradise, a Golden Age) in terms of harmful or incommodious things that it lacks" (529). She notes parallels but not in relation to marriage (529). J. Geffcken, *Komposition und Entstehungszeit der Oracula Sibyllina* (TU 23, N.F. 8.1; Leipzig: Hinrichs, 1902), argued that 2:325-327, 329 derive from 8.424-427 (51). A. Kurfess, "Oracula Sibyllina I/II," *ZNW* 40 (1941) 151-65, argued the reverse (165); similarly Collins, *OTP*, 1.332.

[218] Lightfoot, *Sibylline Oracles*, puts it among instances where the Sibyl supplements the *Apocalypse of Peter* with "traditional material from her eschatological repertoire" (140).

reasons" (οὔτε γάμῳ μεμελημένη οὔτε λογισμοῖς) (2:341). This enigmatic comment has a parallel in 7:152-154, where the charge she lays against herself is sexual promiscuity. That may be intended also here. Both probably reflect Christian redactional work which seeks to put the pagan sibyl in her place.

Conclusion

The work now designated *Sibylline Oracles* 1-2, may well be important evidence for what appears to be a form of pre-70 C.E. diaspora Judaism in which an author, well versed in both Jewish and Greek tradition (especially Hesiod), enables us to see some significant developments in attitudes towards sexuality. The first is the remarkable omission of sexual dimensions from the Genesis creation story and probably reflects a negative stance towards sexual relations except for purposes of procreation. The omission was noted also in relation to the so-called curses of the man and woman in Gen 3:16-19. As in *2 Enoch*, Eve is primarily to blame, Adam's primary sin is ignorance, and the story has been reworked, so that life on earth beyond the garden is seen not as punishment, but as something positive.

The second major change occurs in the author's demythologising of the Watchers. They cease to be heavenly figures, but rather now appear as tireless inventors and discoverers who belong to the ancient past of humanity and who stay awake with their inventiveness. Nothing remains of their sexual wrongdoing. Sexual wrongdoing does, however, feature in descriptions of human sin and includes adultery and related activity, licentiousness in general (also noted as absent from the first couple), engagement in secret pre-marital sex (depicted in relation to female virginity), as well as abortion and exposure of infants, but these may well derive from later Christian tradition.

The third remarkable feature is in the author's eschatology which envisages an embodied human community characterised by radical equality and freedom, living in an eternal day, but, negatively, by absence of commerce and marriage. Absence of marriage most likely also implies absence of sexual relations. This may have Jewish origins and so may provide evidence of similar developments to what underlies Christian tradition when it, too, envisages a future without sexual engagement. It coheres with what appears to be the author's suppression of sexual aspects of the creation story and probably reflects the view that sex has no place for purposes other than for procreation, so no place in the timeless age without death, envisaged for the eschaton.

1.2.5 Sibylline Oracles Books 7 and 11

1.2.5.1 Sibylline Oracles Book 7

This work is widely held to be a product of the second century C.E.[219] It has no discernibly Jewish substratum, though it may draw on earlier pagan oracles. In an oracle against the Parthians we read of "terrible weddings of brides because of lawless tribes. For mother will have her own son also as husband. Son will have intercourse with mother. Daughter reclining on father, will sleep according to this savage custom" (7:42-45). The following context appears to refer to their defeat of the Romans at Carrhae in 53 B.C.E.[220] At most it preserves an instance of the allegation of incest against Parthians (cf. Philo *Spec.* 3.13), though such incest is alleged against Rome in 5:390-91. The works ends as did Book 2 with a confession by the sibyl, which, as there, includes sexual promiscuity: "For what evils I formerly did knowingly! And I performed many other things badly through neglect. I have known innumerable beds, but no marriage concerned me (μυρία μέν μοι λέκτρα, γάμος δ᾽ οὐδεὶς ἐμελήθη). Utterly faithless, I imposed a savage oath on all" (7:151-154) – probably to secrecy (cf. the probably similar oaths to secrecy about sexual wrongdoing in *Pss. Sol.* 8:10). As noted above, this is probably Christian redaction designed to ward off taking the sibyl as more than a convenient mouthpiece of oracles. She is certainly not to be taken as an example.

1.2.5.2 Sibylline Oracles Book 11

This is the only other work which may belong to our period[221] and has some pertinent references. They are however few. The sibyl uses marital imagery. Thus "Egypt will be a ruling bride" (11:232) in connection with Alexander's founding of Alexandria. Such imagery serves then to allude to Cleopatra and her relations with Mark Antony and then Octavian: "later you will come to bed 284 with the terrible one himself. The conclusion is the joining marriage" (11:283-284). For her it then predicts a fate worse than widowhood (11:285-297).

---

[219] So Collins, *OTP*, 1.408-409.

[220] So Collins, *OTP*, 1.411.

[221] On its likely date to the turn of the era and its relation to Books 12-14 see Collins, *OTP*, 1.430-33.

1.3 Jeremiah, Baruch, and Ezra Literature

1.3.1 Letter of Jeremiah

This alleged letter of Jeremiah (cf. Jeremiah 29) to those going into exile (1:1) is primarily an attack on idols, based on Jer 10:1-16[222] (cf. also Wisdom 13 –15) and a plea to remain faithful to God alone ("Say in your heart, 'It is you, O Lord, whom we must worship'") (6). Idols are "like a scarecrow in a cucumber bed" (70).[223] Its date and place of origin are unknown, but could have been written for any diaspora situation where such practices were prominent,[224] probably between the late fourth and the second century B.C.E.[225]

Its attack includes some incidental references relevant to sexuality, including prostitution: "Sometimes the priests secretly take gold and silver from their gods and spend it on themselves, or even give some of it to the prostitutes on the terrace (ταῖς ἐπὶ τοῦ τέγους πόρναις)" (10-11). The word τέγους (lit. "roof")[226] might also mean "house" or "brothel" (as in *Sib. Or.* 3:185-187; 5:388). The

---

[222] On the author's dependence on Jer 10:2-25 and 29:1-23, see Reinhard Gregor Kratz, "Die Rezeption von Jer 10 und 29 im pseudepigraphischen Brief des Jeremia," in *Das Judentum im Zeitalter des Zweiten Tempels* (FAT 42; Tübingen: Mohr Siebeck, 2004) 316-39.

[223] Cited from Jer 10:5, though absent from the Septuagint. On this see Kratz, "Rezeption," 312-23.

[224] On this see Lutz Doering, "Jeremiah and the 'Diaspora Letters' in Ancient Judaism: Epistolary Communication with the Golah as Medium for Dealing with the Present," in *Reading the Present in the Qumran Library: The Perception of the Contemporary by Means of Scriptural Interpretation*s (ed. Kristin de Troyer and Armin Lange; SBLSym 30; Atlanta: SBL, 2005) 43-72, who argues that the state support for Babylonian cults under Alexander and the Seleucids indicates that we should locate the addressees in the eastern Diaspora (51).

[225] On the allusion to the work in 2 Macc 2:1-3 and its possible presence among fragments from Qumran Cave 7, which suggests an origin prior to 100 B.C.E., see Nickelsburg, *Jewish Writings*, 35; and Daniel J. Harrington, *Invitation to the Apocrypha* (Grand Rapids: Eerdmans, 1999) 103. Moore, *Daniel, Esther and Jeremiah: The Additions* (AB 44; New York: Doubleday, 1977) argues that the allusion to seven generations in v. 3 should be taken seriously as indicated a date in the late fourth century (327-28). On the original language as Hebrew see the persuasive arguments in C. J. Ball, "Epistle of Jeremy," *APOT*, 1.596-611; Moore, *Additions*, 326-27; Kratz, "Rezeption," 320.

[226] Moore, *Additions*, understands it literally to mean that the women sat on the roof as "either the place where they slept on summer nights, or it was where they performed their ritual acts" (338). He notes also Torrey's argument for an Aramaic original on the basis "that the Greek translator misread *'al agrā*, "for (their) hire," as *'al iggārā*, "on the roof" (338). So Charles C. Torrey, *The Apocryphal Literature* (New Haven: Yale University Press, 1945) 66.

second reference to prostitutes suggests that they are seated outside, perhaps in an accessible roofed enclosure. Thus we read:

αἱ δὲ γυναῖκες περιθέμεναι σχοινία ἐν ταῖς ὁδοῖς ἐγκάθηνται θυμιῶσαι τὰ πίτυρα 43 ὅταν δέ τις αὐτῶν ἐφελκυσθεῖσα ὑπό τινος τῶν παραπορευομένων κοιμηθῇ τὴν πλησίον ὀνειδίζει ὅτι οὐκ ἠξίωται ὥσπερ καὶ αὐτὴ οὔτε τὸ σχοινίον αὐτῆς διερράγη.

And the women, with cords around them, sit along the passageways, burning bran for incense. 43 When one of them is led off by one of the passers-by and is taken to bed by him, she derides the woman next to her, because she was not as attractive as herself and her cord was not broken. (42-43)

These women may simply be performing acts of devotion like others, but are more likely to have belonged to the cult (cf. 30, which mentions women preparing meals for the idols), and so have been understood to be cult prostitutes, an institution condemned in Deut 23:17-18. The allusion to Bel (42-43) may indicate the cult of Marduk (cf. Isa 46:1; Jer 50:2; 51:44).[227] The breaking of the cord would indicate acceptance of a client. It would reflect a practice according to which the man untied or tore the cord as part of the ritual of gaining access to the prostitute. As Buden, however, has shown,[228] this interpretation depends largely on the account in Herodotus *Hist.* 1.199, where he reports a custom according to which Babylonians require every woman to serve once as a temple prostitute (to have intercourse with a foreigner) for Aphrodite (to be equated with Tammuz). He describes how accordingly women sit with headbands and behind ropes while men survey them and choose one by tossing a silver coin onto her lap to which she must respond as a sacred obligation to the deity.[229] One could then understand that this might lead to derision of the unchosen. Our passage would reflect some such practice, and is perhaps dependent directly or indirectly on Herodotus, though some details do not match. Thus Herodotus makes no mention of burning cakes of bran,[230] the details about cords and strings differ, and our passage makes no

[227] See the extended discussion in Weigand Naumann, *Untersuchungen über den apokryphen Jeremiasbrief* (BZAW 25; Giessen: Töpelmann, 1913) 1-53, which shows that the details fit the Babylonian cult of Marduk (3-31). See also Moore, *Additions*, 329.

[228] Stephanie Lynn Budin, *The Myth of Sacred Prostitution in Antiquity* (Cambridge: Cambridge University Press, 2008) 105-11.

[229] *Testament of Judah* appears to know at least the practice of exposing girls to prostitution at the gate: "For it was a law of the Amorites that she who was about to marry should sit in prostitution by the gate for seven days" (12:2).

[230] Moore, *Additions*, notes that some have taken this as a reference not to sacrifice but to producing a magic aphrodisiac (348).

mention of a universal obligation or a one-off act.[231] There is serious doubt about the reality of what Herodotus describes.[232] In any case, here the detail serves denigration. The derisory tone of the writing here attacks not only idolatry, but also the mean spirited behaviour of its devotees and personnel.

The attacks on personnel are elsewhere mainly directed towards the priests who are depicted as exploiting the system to their own ends, selling the sacrifices, having their wives keep some of the meat for themselves, not giving a thought for the poor and helpless (28; similarly 36-38), and using temple clothes to dress their wives and children (33). Jewish purity laws are reflected in the report that "sacrifices to them [idols] may even be touched by women in their menstrual periods or at childbirth" (μεταδιδόασιν τῶν θυσιῶν αὐτῶν ἀποκαθημένη καὶ λεχὼ ἅπτονται) (29).

While the work is primarily an unrelenting attack on idolatry, fuelled probably as much by biblical precedents as by actual experience,[233] and intolerant of understandings which might see idols functioning as symbols, its allegations of moral corruption of various kinds include sexual wrongdoing. The association between idolatry and sexual wrongdoing reappears in Wisdom 13 – 15, Romans 1, and elsewhere. Here the focus is apparently sacral prostitution (real or otherwise).

1.3.2 Baruch

The book of Baruch is a composite work comprising four main sections.[234] The first two sections are in prose and comprise an introduction, composed by the compiler of the whole (1:1-14), and two prayers of confession (1:15 – 2:5; 2:6 – 3:8), allegedly sent by Baruch from Babylon to the remnant in Jerusalem after the destruction of 586 B.C.E. urging them to pray for themselves and for the exiles. Both prayers have close parallels in Daniel 9, especially the second, and may, like it, be drawn from older sources.[235] This material, heavily dependent on Jeremiah,

---

[231] See the discussion in Moore, *Additions*, 348-49, who cites Herodotus in full and alludes to a similar account in Strabo *Geogr.* 16.1, writing later than both and apparently dependent on Herodotus; and more recently Budin, *Sacred Prostitution*, 110-11.

[232] Budin, *Sacred Prostitution*, 58-90.

[233] So Harrington, *Apocrypha*, 107. Moore, *Additions*, writes: "It is as though the author of the Epistle were criticizing a Mesopotamian religion and its gods *from afar*" (329).

[234] See the introduction in Moore, *Additions*, 257-63; Nickelsburg, *Jewish Writings*, 94-97.

[235] See the discussion in Moore, *Additions*, 291-93 and Rodney Alan Werline, *Penitential Prayer in Second Temple Judaism: The Development of a Religious Institution* (SBLEJL 13; Atlanta: Scholars, 1998) 65-108 .

was apparently written in Hebrew and translated into the Greek in which it survives by the same translator who translated or revised Jeremiah 29 – 52.[236] The initial composition probably dates to the early second century B.C.E.,[237] though some have argued very specifically for a date in the 160s, understanding the work as a plea for submission to the Seleucids.[238] The final two sections comprise a wisdom poem and a hymn of encouragement, both probably originally written in Hebrew in Palestine,[239] and incorporated into the present work some time before the early first century B.C.E.

There is little in the first three sections which pertains to our theme. The second prayer includes reference to those in Hades "whose spirit has been taken from their bodies, will not ascribe glory and justice to the Lord" (2:17), but more significantly, depicts God's threat of desolation against those who refuse to accept Babylon's rule. Its images, drawn from Jeremiah (7:34; 16:9; 33:10-11), include the joy of the wedding: gone will be "the voice of mirth and the voice of gladness, the voice of the bridegroom and the voice of the bride, and the whole land will be desolate without inhabitants" (2:23). It then holds to the prospect that those in exile will "come to themselves" (2:30) and depicts God's promise: "I will bring them again into the land that I swore to give to their ancestors, to Abraham, Isaac, and Jacob, and they will rule over it; and I will increase them, and they will not be diminished (καὶ πληθυνῶ αὐτούς καὶ οὐ μὴ σμικρυνθῶσιν)" (2:34). Such future hope thus entails a return to the joy of marriage, including sexual relations and fruitfulness. Beyond these positive intimations there are no particular references pertaining to sexuality.

The second half of the work, which changes from prose to poetry, comprises two parts, which have diverse origins, and both of which employ gendered images, first in depicting God's wisdom and then in depicting Jerusalem. Thus in the poem in 3:9-37; 4:1 the author hails "the commandments of life" (3:9) as God's wisdom. This is something more than an abstract allusion to the commandments. For

---

[236] Emanuel Tov, *The Septuagint Translation of Jeremiah and Baruch* (HSM 8; Missoula: Scholars, 1976) 111-33, 165; Moore, *Additions*, 258. The Greek translation was known to Ben Sira's grandson writing before 116 B.C.E.

[237] Moore, *Additions*, contemplates that 5:5-9 may have been written in Greek and been added in the late first century B.C.E., possibly inspired by the *Psalms of Solomon* 11 (316).

[238] So Jonathan A. Goldstein, "The Apocryphal Book of 1 Baruch," *PAAJR* 46-47 (1979-1980) 179-99; Odil Hannes Steck, *Das apokryphe Baruchbuch: Studien zu Rezeption und Konzentration "kanonischer" Überlieferung* (FRLANT 160; Göttingen: Vandenhoeck & Ruprecht, 1993) 294-303; André Kabaselle Mukenge, *L'unité littéraire du livre de Baruch* (EBib 38; Paris: Gabalda, 1998) 412-26; Nickelsburg, *Jewish Writings*, 97.

[239] See David G. Burke, *The Poetry of Baruch: A Reconstruction and Analysis of the Original Hebrew Text of Baruch 3:9–5:9* (SBLSCS 10; Chico: Scholars, 1982).

wisdom is a "fountain" (3:12; cf. Jer 2:13; Sir 1:1, 5; 4 Ezra 14:47); is to be found in a place (3:14-15a; cf. Job 28:12, 20); and, as a woman managing a household, has storehouses (3:15b); and has her commended paths (3:20-23), which the giants did not tread and so perished (3:24-28). Later generations "have not learned the way to knowledge, nor understood her paths, nor laid hold of her (οὐδὲ ἀντελάβοντο αὐτῆς)" (3:20). She cannot be purchased or discovered except through God: "the one who knows all things knows her (ὁ εἰδὼς τὰ πάντα γινώσκει αὐτήν), he found her by his understanding" (3:29-36a; cf. the less personal image in Job 28:23 "God understands the way to it, and he knows its place"). God made her known to Israel as "the book of the commandments", so that "all who hold her fast will live (πάντες οἱ κρατοῦντες αὐτῆς εἰς ζωήν)" (3:36b – 4:1).[240] Thus Israel is to "take her (ἐπιλαβοῦ αὐτῆς); walk towards the shining of her light" (4:2). The author employs the image of wisdom as a woman to reinforce his message that life comes through keeping the commandments, opening and closing his poem with reference to the commandments as the way to life (3:9; 4:1).

The female image of wisdom includes household management (storehouses) and direction (paths), but also relationship (knowing her), which may also include a sense of intimacy which is sexual (know, take), though this is not explicitly developed. It at least assumes that such intimacy is something good and appropriate to use as an image for both the people's and God's relation to the wisdom of the commandments. Unlike in Job 28:12-27 which lies behind much of the passage, wisdom, here, is portrayed as a woman and identified with the Law, as in Sir 24:1-34 (esp. 24:23). As Nickelsburg notes, "the personification of Wisdom in Baruch 3:8 – 4:4 is less clear than it is in Sirach 24. ... Only in Baruch 4:1 is she the subject of a verb of action".[241] Nevertheless, the element of personification remains and may include sexual references.[242]

The reference to the giants in 3:26-28 warrants further attention. Speaking of God's vast territory the author writes:

26 ἐκεῖ ἐγεννήθησαν οἱ γίγαντες οἱ ὀνομαστοὶ οἱ ἀπ' ἀρχῆς γενόμενοι
εὐμεγέθεις ἐπιστάμενοι πόλεμον 27 οὐ τούτους ἐξελέξατο ὁ θεὸς οὐδὲ ὁδὸν

---

[240] While it would be easy to read "Afterward she appeared on earth and lived with humankind" in 3:37 as a Christian interpolation, it more likely reproduces the notion present in Sir 24:10-12 (and reflected on negatively in the *Epistle of Enoch, 1 Enoch* 94:5 and the *Parables of Enoch, 1 Enoch* 42:1-3) that wisdom came to dwell with Israel.

[241] Nickelsburg, *Jewish Writings*, 96.

[242] See elsewhere on the notion of God knowing wisdom and especially of human beings relating intimately to her (Prov 9:1-6; Sir 6:18-31; 14:20 - 15:10 and in 51:13-30; Wis 8:1-9, 16-18).

ἐπιστήμης ἔδωκεν αὐτοῖς 28 καὶ ἀπώλοντο παρὰ τὸ μὴ ἔχειν φρόνησιν
ἀπώλοντο διὰ τὴν ἀβουλίαν αὐτῶν.

26 The giants were born there, who were famous of old, great in stature, expert in war.
27 God did not choose them, or give them the way to knowledge; 28 so they perished
because they had no wisdom, they perished through their folly. (3:26-28)

This stands in contrast to the Watcher myth, as preserved in the *Book of the
Watchers* and in *Jubilees*, because it makes no reference to the event which led to
the birth of the giants, nor does it depict them as horrendous monsters of violence.
Instead, they are granted recognition as having been famous, great in stature, and
expert in war. The latter may derive from the account in *1 Enoch* 6 – 11, but it
could be simply an elaboration of Gen 6:4, which speaks of them as "warriors".
These are not, apparently, in themselves the grounds for their demise, let alone,
judgement by divinely induced self-destruction, as in the *Book of the Watchers*.
Rather, they perished because they were foolish and lacked wisdom, something
left unspecified.[243] Sexual issues which belong to the myth make no appearance
here.

The second instance of using female imagery comes in the depiction of
Jerusalem as a woman, drawing inspiration especially from Isaiah 40 – 55. While
in 4:5-9a the hymn addresses the people, Israel, in 4:9b-29 it reports words spoken
by Jerusalem as a bereft mother to her children ("you grieved Jerusalem, who
reared you" 4:8). She then speaks to her neighbours, portraying the loss of her sons
and daughters, recalling her joy in nurturing them, and asking that they not rejoice
over her plight, which she describes not only as being bereft of children, but also
as a widow (4:9-12a). She goes on to explain that failure to keep God's
commandments was the reason why God "brought a distant nation against them"
and so deprived her, "the widow", "the lonely woman" of her children (4:12b-16).
From that point she turns to address her children, first telling them to go to their
fate, but also promising them that if they cry to God, God will bring them back
(4:17-29). Unlike the image of wisdom as a woman, here the role is more
confined. Jerusalem is mother. Only her designation as widow might raise
questions of marriage, but that is not addressed nor are any issues pertaining to
sexuality.

The image continues in 4:30 – 5:9 within an address to Jerusalem again cast in
the role of the bereft mother. Here the words of comfort include reference to other
cities and especially to the one that received her offspring, also spoken of as a
woman (4:32-35). In words rich with intertextual allusions (Isa 43:5; 60:4; Zech

---

[243] Moore, *Additions*, notes that they are "viewed in an unfavorable light" (300). Cf.
Wis 14:6, which depicts them as arrogant, and Sir 16:7, as rebellious.

8:7-8; Isa 52:1; 61:10),[244] it tells mother, Jerusalem, to deck herself with clothes of celebration as she sees her returning children (4:36 – 5:9). There are close parallels between 5:5-9 and *Pss. Sol.* 11:3-8 (5:2-7) in substance and sequence, either reflecting dependence of the former on the latter, use of a common source, or, more probably dependence of the latter on the former.[245] The image remains consistently one of the bereft and now comforted mother.

Apart from affirming a future which assumes marriage, sexual relations, and childbearing as normal, this work is significant for its use of female imagery for wisdom and for Jerusalem. In the latter reference the role is solely maternal;[246] in the former the role is more broadly conceived and includes possible references to sexual intimacy in a way that by implication values sexual relations.

1.3.3   4 Ezra

The apocalypse of Ezra, preserved in a sevenfold structure as chapters 3 – 14 of 2 Esdras, was written originally in Hebrew in the late first century C.E. in response to theological issues raised by the destruction of the temple in 70 C.E. It is a remarkable instance of critical theodicy, a rich resource for investigating eschatological ideas and a challenge to the interpreter to give account of continuities and discontinuities in its development.[247] These issues are not to be rehearsed here, but to be borne in mind as we approach the text with a question not usually asked of it, namely, what it might tell us about attitudes towards sexuality, and for which it offers at most only indirect information.

In the first of the work's seven sections Ezra's brief review of human history in his prayer begins with reference to the Genesis account of the creation of humankind and of human sin (3:4-7). It makes no mention of Eve or of the first pair coming together, including in sexual union, nor of sexual components in

---

[244] Isa 61:10, which lies behind 5:2, includes imagery of rejoicing as a bridegroom and as a bride, but that finds no place here.

[245] See the discussion in Moore, *Additions*, 258, 314-16; and Wilhelm Pesch, "Die Abhängigkeit des 11 salomonischen Psalms vom letzten Kapitel des Buches Baruch," *ZAW* 67(1955) 251-63, who make a strong case for the priority of Baruch.

[246] On use of maternal imagery to depict Zion, see: Isa 49:14-23; 54:1-13; 60:4-9; cf. Isa 47:1-9 which uses it negatively of an enemy city as a mother with her children.

[247] For a brief introduction of the issues see Nickelsburg, *Jewish Literature*, 270-77; Collins, *Apocalyptic Imagination*, 195-212; Oegema, *Einführung*, 97-98; and the extended discussion in Bruce W. Longenecker, *2 Esdras* (GAP; Sheffield: Sheffield Academic Press, 1995) and his earlier discussion in Bruce W. Longenecker, *Eschatology and the Covenant: A Comparison of 4 Ezra and Romans 1–11* (JSNTSup 57; Sheffield: JSOT, 1991).

God's judgement because of their sin.[248] It differs from Genesis in its understanding of sequence: "you led him into the garden (*induxisti eum in paradisum*) which your right hand had planted before the earth appeared (*antequam terra adventaret*)" (3:6)[249] not after it, as in Gen 2:4-8.[250] This may reflect the sequence in *Jubilees* which also has the creation of human beings taking place outside the garden and then their being led into the garden (3:8-14), though *Jubilees* does not postpone the creation of earth till after that event as here. It appears to imply a non-terrestrial paradise and traditions of a pre-existent immortal Adam.[251] It also depicts creation using Gen 2:7 to indicate that God made Adam a "lifeless body" (*corpus mortuum*), and then "breathed into him the breath of life" (3:5), an act of vivification not the imparting of a soul or mind.[252] Nothing suggests faulty or divided substance, let alone anything suspect about sexuality.

In relation to Adam's sin we read simply: "immediately you appointed death for him and his descendants" (3:7). Yet, as the account of Noah's generation shows, *their* death is also *their* own doing (3:12-14). As Levison notes, "Ezra draws only a correspondence, not a causal connection, between the death of Adam and the sinful nations: *sicut Ade mors, sic et his diluuium*".[253] There is also no indication here that the ground is cursed (a view present also in *2 Enoch* 31:7 and *Sib. Or.* 1:54). Even in 7:12 which recalls the so-called curse of Gen 3:14-19, only the elements of sorrow and hardship appear; and also nothing related to sexuality. The account of human sin before the flood (3:7b-11) makes no mention of the Watchers, nor of sexual sin among human beings. The same is true of the account of sin after the flood (3:12-14)[254] and down to the giving of the Law at Sinai (3:15-19). Then Ezra bemoans human sin:

---

[248] On the function of the pessimistic review of history as introducing key motifs (Jerusalem, the evil heart, Israel) and paradoxically hope based on the notion of history as preordained by God, see Pieter G. R. De Villiers, "Understanding the Way of God: Form, Function and Message of the Historical Review in 4 Ezra 3:4-27," *SBLSP* 20 1981 (ed. Kent Harold Richards; Chico: Scholars, 1981) 357-78, 366-67.

[249] The translation is *NRSV*, except where I produce a modified translation, which I indicate with an asterisk.

[250] Michael Edward Stone, *4 Ezra: A Commentary on the Book of Fourth Ezra* (Hermeneia; Minneapolis: Augsburg Fortress, 1990) notes that this is the oldest attestation of this sequence (68).

[251] So John R. Levison, *Portraits of Adam in Early Judaism* (JSPSup 1; Sheffield: JSOT, 1988), which he sees the author then suppressing as he depicts Adam in negative terms (117). Not Adam but the righteous elect will one day enter this paradise (127).

[252] So Levison, *Portraits of Adam*, who points in contrast to Wisd 15:10-11; Philo *Opif* 134-135; and *LAB* 1.31-34 (115).

[253] Levison, *Portraits of Adam*, 116, but notes that he can affirm both (117).

[254] Nothing suggests that the detail in 3:12a that they multiplied, with its obvious sexual implications is something negative.

Yet you did not take away their evil heart from them, so that your law might produce fruit in them. 21 For the first Adam, burdened with an evil heart, transgressed and was overcome, as were also all who were descended from him. 22 Thus the disease became permanent; the law was in the hearts of the people along with the evil root; but what was good departed, and the evil remained. (3:20-22)

"Evil heart" probably reflects Gen 6:5 (וכל יצר מחשבת לבו רק רע כל היום "all the inclination of the thoughts of his heart was only bad continually"). A similar ambiguity exists here as in depicting death, but the focus lies primarily on human responsibility: "As Adam was burdened by the evil heart, transgressed, and was overcome, so all his descendants were burdened, transgressed, and were overcome".[255] The author nowhere explains the origin of "the evil heart" nor how it came to be present in all Adam's descendants.[256] Nothing suggests that "evil heart" here nor its perpetuation relates in particular to sexual wrongdoing[257] nor does it do so in the depiction of sin arising from the evil heart in Jerusalem in and after the time of David (3:25-26). This is also true when Ezra points to the sins of Babylon (3:28-30, 36).

The angel's response also returns to Adam: "For a grain of evil seed was sown in Adam's heart from the beginning, and how much ungodliness it has produced until now—and will produce until the time of threshing comes!" (4:30; see also 4:28-29 and 8:6; 6:26). Nothing suggests God sowed the seed.[258] Uriel's view appears to be that despite the impact of the evil heart some can remain righteous, and is thus less pessimistic than Ezra.[259] Nothing, not even the image of seed, connects this with sexuality.

In 4:35-43 we have the first of a number of instances where the work employs images of childbirth in addressing the issue of the timing of the harvest: "Did not the souls of the righteous in their chambers ask about these matters, saying, 'How long are we to remain here?'" (4:35). Uriel's second reply then includes the words: "Go and ask a pregnant woman whether, when her nine months have been

---

[255] Levison, *Portraits of Adam*, 118. He notes Ezra's ambiguity also in 7:116-126 and that "despite the intensity of his desire to defend Israel by attributing sin to Adam's transgression and the evil heart, Ezra never successfully attributes physical death, sin, and eschatological damnation to Adam" (126).

[256] Levison, *Portraits of Adam*, writes that Ezra "attributes sin to the evil heart, as does Uriel, without exploring precisely how Adam transmitted it to his descendants" (126).

[257] Collins, *Apocalyptic Imagination*, notes Ezra's "pessimistic attitude to the judgment, which sees most of humanity as helpless before the evil inclination and allows little if any space for atonement or divine mercy" (211). See also Michael Desjardins, "Law in 2 Baruch and 4 Ezra," *ScRel/StRel* 14 (1985) 25-37, 33-34.

[258] So Stone, *4 Ezra*, who contrasts this with what is found in rabbinic sources (64). See also Collins, *Apocalyptic Imagination*, 211.

[259] So Levison, *Portraits of Adam*, 118.

completed, her womb can keep the fetus within her any longer" (4:40), continuing on to declare: "In Hades the chambers of the souls are like the womb. For just as a woman who is in labor makes haste to escape the pangs of birth, so also do these places hasten to give back those things that were committed to them from the beginning" (4:41b-42). The point appears to be that when the requisite number of souls have gathered in the heavenly chambers, then the birth, the resurrection, will take place.[260] Such natal imagery plays a strikingly prominent role in the work, as we shall see below.

Among the portents of the end time 5:8 mentions that "menstruous women shall bring forth monsters". Similar portents appear in 6:21, indicative of disorder,[261] to which we shall return. The imagery of normal childbirth returns in Ezra's second conversation where he asks about successive generations. The angel replies: "Ask a woman's womb, and say to it, 'If you bear ten children, why one after another?' Request it therefore to produce ten at one time." (5:46). Using the same imagery the angel explains how the end will come: "Even so I have given the womb of the earth to those who from time to time are sown in it. For as an infant does not bring forth, and a woman who has become old does not bring forth any longer, so I have made the same rule for the world that I created" (5:48-49).[262] In the same way God's ordering of the time before the end is to be trusted. Ezra, too, plays with the image in his response: "Is our mother, of whom you have told me, still young? Or is she now approaching old age?" (5:50), to which the angel replies: "Ask a woman who bears children, and she will tell you. Say to her, 'Why are those whom you have borne recently not like those whom you bore before, but smaller in stature?'" (5:51b-52) and goes on to explain that Ezra's generation belong to the latter and so can expect the end soon, since the earth (mother) will soon cease bearing children. Behind this notion may lie a popular fallacious belief that children born later are less strong,[263] but also the notion that the first human generations were gargantuan (in both size and longevity).[264]

---

[260] See Stone, *4 Ezra*, 99.

[261] Jacob Myers, *I and II Esdras* (AB 42; Garden City: Doubleday, 1974) 177, notes that "the idea of women bearing monsters occurs also in the Oath of Plataea said to have been sworn by the Greeks before the battle (479 B.C.)," pointing to Peter Green, *The Year of Salamis, 480-479 B.C.* (London: Weidenfeld & Nicolson, 1970) 240, and observes that birth irregularities also feature in predictions of the future in *Jub.* 23:25; Matt 24:19; and Mark 13:17 (177); similarly Stone, *4 Ezra*, 112.

[262] On the earth as womb or mother see Stone, *4 Ezra*, 98-99, who notes that it also lies behind the notion of earth bringing forth: "Adam (7:116), the mind (7:62), humans (6:54), and cattle (6:53)" (99 n. 47).

[263] For the opposite view in Babylonian wisdom literature see W. G. Lambert, *Babylonian Wisdom Literature* (Oxford: Oxford University Press, 1960) 86-87. Neither view has substance in reality, although a combination of factors such as size of family and

The imagery of childbirth returns yet again in the account of the day of God's visitation. Then "children a year old shall speak with their voices, and pregnant women shall give birth to premature children at three and four months, and these shall live and leap about" (6:21). This could reflect notions of enhanced fertility and fruitfulness, but it stands juxtaposed to other phenomena which are clearly negative: "Sown places shall suddenly appear unsown, and full storehouses shall suddenly be found to be empty; the trumpet shall sound aloud, and when all hear it, they shall suddenly be terrified" (6:22-23; similarly negative: 6:24), so that the irregular births must also be seen as negative signs as already in 5:8, discussed above.[265] The depiction of hope, which follows, includes the changing of "the heart of earth's inhabitants" and the removal of evil (6:26-28), but includes no references, positive or negative, to sexuality.[266]

In recounting creation after the pattern of the six days of Genesis 1 in the third section of the work the author has Ezra return to the creation of humankind (cf. 3:4-7), but mentions only Adam's rule over the animals (6:54),[267] nothing about being male and female[268] nor about being in God's image (the latter passed over also in *Jubilees*; though it appears in 4 Ezra 8:44) nor about the seventh day and the sabbath. When the author speaks of other nations which descended from Adam, using disparaging images drawn from Isa 40:15-17 (6:56),[269] he appears to

---

increased poverty and malnourishment would affect the health of mothers and influence the size and health of babies.

[264] So also Myers, *I and II Esdras*, 195; Stone, *4 Ezra*, 153-54, who notes the idea of degeneration of generations in Philo, *Opif.* 141-142 and as a commonplace in Greek thought reaching back to Hesiod (154).

[265] Stone, *4 Ezra*, notes the parallel in *Jub.* 23:25 (170), but there we read of gray haired offspring, the result of shortening of life; similarly *Sib. Or.* 2:155. That is not the case here where we have something closer to the phenomenon depicted positively of Noah in *1 Enoch* 106 and *Genesis Apocryphon* and Melchisedek in *2 Enoch*, only here as negative and associated with a shortened pregnancy, underlining the chaotic.

[266] On the possible use of oracular poetic sources here and in 5:1-11 see Stone, *4 Ezra*, 167.

[267] Levison, *Portraits of Adam*, suggests that the words "as ruler over all the works that you had made" (6:54) indicate dominion over heavenly bodies who according to 6:45-46 were commanded to obey him and may reflect a notion of a celestial Adam (119-20, 125-26).

[268] Noted but without further comment by Joan E. Cook, "Creation in 4 Ezra: the Biblical Theme in Support of Theodicy," in *Creation in the Biblical Traditions* (ed. Richard J. Clifford and John J. Collins; CBQMS 24; Washington: CBAA, 1992) 129-39, 133-34.

[269] Cook, "Creation in 4 Ezra," notes: "By juxtaposing the themes of creation and election Ezra sets the stage for his explicit complaint about the situation of the Jews" (135). She also notes that 4 Ezra does not refer to the idea that creation is good (138).

share with *Jubilees* the notion that Israel existed from the beginning. It enables him to claim that only Israel was chosen to be heir of the dominion with which Adam was endowed.[270]

Uriel's response to Ezra's claim that Israel had fared badly as the chosen people is to point to present hardship and the promise of future fulfilment for the obedient. In doing so the author has Uriel pick up elements of the so-called curses of Gen 3:16-20, but only selectively. Thus 7:12 indicates toilsomeness of the world as the fruit of Adam's sin,[271] but nothing is made here or elsewhere of those aspects pertinent to sexuality, such as women's passion and husband's rule, and pain in pregnancy and childbirth, an area with which the author otherwise shows familiarity and interest. In responding to Ezra's next complaint that the righteous suffer whereas "the ungodly" who "have done wickedly" (again without sexual allusions) do not (7:17-18), the angel explains the giving of divine commandments and their wilful transgression by human beings (also without sexual allusions) (7:20-25).

The angel's response also includes another depiction of the day of judgement, including resurrection for judgement and a picture of endless day for the righteous without

> sun or moon or stars, 40 or cloud or thunder or lightning, or wind or water or air, or darkness or evening or morning, 41 or summer or spring or heat or winter or frost or cold, or hail or rain or dew, 42 or noon or night, or dawn or shining or brightness or light, but only the splendor of the glory of the Most High. (7:39-42)

This recalls the image of the endless day (but 7:43 says: "It will last as though for a week of years"; cf. Dan 9:24, 26; *2 Bar.* 28:2) in *2 Enoch* 65:7-11; *1 Enoch* (*Parables of Enoch*) 58:3, 5-6, and as there does not address the implications for sexual relations, for instance, that might see them as redundant since no procreation is required. It reflects the image of hope in Isa 60:19-20, which declares that God will be the only light necessary.

Ezra's objection that the almost universal sinfulness makes the situation hopeless, again has no particularly sexual allusions:

---

[270] So Levison, *Portraits of Adam*, 120-21.

[271] So Michael A. Knibb, "The Second Book of Esdras," in R. J. Coggins and M. A. Knibb, *The First and Second Books of Esdras* (CBC; Cambridge: Cambridge University Press, 1979) 162. Levison, *Portraits of Adam*, notes: "The list of difficulties differs from Gen 3.14-19, yet the words, 'sorrowful' and 'toilsome', the second and third words employed, recall the curses of Genesis. The word, *dolentes*, recalls בעצב in Gen 3:16. the word, *laborioisi*, recalls בעצבון in Gen 3:17" (121).

> For an evil heart has grown up in us, which has alienated us from God, and has brought us into corruption and the ways of death, and has shown us the paths of perdition and removed us far from life—and that not merely for a few but for almost all who have been created. (7:48)

In pressing his case that humans are in a hopeless situation Ezra returns again to the Genesis account creation of human beings (and especially their corrupt minds) from dust, but again without sexual references (7:62-69), though, as Stone notes, the allusion to earth bringing forth in 7:62, returns to the notion of earth as mother or womb.[272] This is true also of the angel's retort that the mind should have enabled them to understand and obey (7:70-74) and of the explanation of the fate of disobedient souls after death (7:75-87). References to sin remain generic also in the account of the destiny after death of the souls of the righteous, who can look forward in future to a resurrection body which shines like the stars (7:88-99; cf. Dan 12:3).

In explaining the exclusion of the possibility of intercession and in Ezra's counter arguments, which include allusion to Sodom, there is also no sexual reference (7:100-115). Ezra's bemoaning of the human condition in 7:110-126 returns once more to the primal sin, but, again, mentioning only Adam: "O Adam, what have you done? For though it was you who sinned, the fall (*casus*)[273] was not yours alone, but ours also who are your descendants" 7:118 (cf. *2 Bar.* 54:19; 48:42). Again we find no mention of Eve nor of any sexual issues. It speaks of the reward of those few who exercised self-control: "the faces of those who practiced self-control (*qui abstinentiam habuerunt*) shall shine more than the stars" (7:125; cf. 7:97), but nothing suggests an allusion to self-control in the area of sexuality in particular, though this is certainly possible. The textual reference to "self-control" (*abstinentiam*) is present only in Latin and Ethiopic, not Syriac and Armenian.[274]

The motif of childbirth, which featured in 4:35, 40-42; 5:46-52; and 6:21, reappears in 8:4-19 where Ezra introduces his prayer. The author shows Ezra imparting wisdom to his own soul: "Not of your own will did you come into the world, and against your will you depart" (8:5; cf. *2 Bar.* 48:15). The prayer includes the image of seed: "Give us a seed for our heart and cultivation of our understanding so that fruit may be produced, by which every mortal who bears the likeness of a human being may be able to live" (8:6).[275] This is an agricultural

---

[272] Stone, *4 Ezra*, 232.

[273] Levison, *Portraits of Adam*, notes that *casus* need not mean moral fall, but that this is probably its meaning here (123).

[274] See Stone, *4 Ezra*, 253. Syriac reads, "the saints" and Armenian "the just".

[275] On the close connection between life and keeping the Law in 4 Ezra see Shannon Burkes, "'Life' Redefined: Wisdom and Law in Fourth Ezra and Second Baruch," *CBQ* 63 (2001) 55-71, 57-63; also Shannon Burkes, *God, Self, and Death: The Shape of Religious*

rather than a sexual metaphor and derives from the image of the tree of life as in 3:20 and may echo the promise of a new heart in Ezek 36:26-27.[276] The words "every mortal who bears the likeness of a human being" appear to allude to Gen 1:26-27. The appeal to creation appears also in the following verse: "we are a work of your hands, as you have declared". Then the focus shifts back to pregnancy and childbirth: "And because you give life to the body that is now fashioned in the womb, and furnish it with members, what you have created is preserved amid fire and water, and for nine months the womb endures your creature that has been created in it" (8:8). God's involvement is then emphasised: "But that which keeps and that which is kept shall both be kept by your keeping" (8:9a).[277] That emphasis then continues:

> And when the womb gives up again what has been created in it, 10 you have commanded that from the members themselves (that is, from the breasts) milk, the fruit of the breasts, should be supplied, 11 so that what has been fashioned may be nourished for a time; and afterwards you will still guide it in your mercy. (8:9b-11)

This is part of Ezra's argument that human beings should then not be so lightly discarded by God, but its interest for us is that it shows the extent to which the author employs natal imagery.

Ezra's plea for God's clemency towards sinful humanity in 8:19-36 remains typically generic in relation to sin. To God's response that as with a farmer's sowing of seeds only some succeed (8:41), Ezra protests by returning again to Gen 1:26-27:

> But people, who have been formed by your hands and are called your own image because they are made like you, and for whose sake you have formed all things – have you also made them like the farmer's seed? (8:44)

God's response is to remind Ezra of his reward:

Transformation in the Second Temple Period (JSJSup 79; Leiden: Brill, 2003) 211-12. See also Philip Francis Esler, "The Social Function of *4 Ezra*," *JSNT* 53 (1994) 99-123, on the function of the Law as providing "a mode of behaviour which will ensure the continuing existence of a Jewish people and a Jewish identity at a time when the Temple, the other institution, once central to that identity, lies in ruins" (120).

[276] So Knibb, "2 Esdras," 200.

[277] Stone, *4 Ezra*, notes that "it is a common place for God to be credited with the wonder of conception" (266). He notes also the diverse medical models in Job 10:10-11 and Wis 7:1-2 and that no parallels are known to the link here with just fire and water (266). Cf. Philo *Opif.* 146, who speaks of the body consisting of earth, water, air and fire.

51 But think of your own case, and inquire concerning the glory of those who are like yourself, 52 because it is for you that paradise is opened, the tree of life is planted, the age to come is prepared, plenty is provided, a city is built, rest is appointed, goodness is established and wisdom perfected beforehand. 53 The root of evil is sealed up from you, illness is banished from you, and death is hidden; Hades has fled and corruption has been forgotten; 54 sorrows have passed away, and in the end the treasure of immortality is made manifest. (8:51-54)

The future hope depicted here, which recalls 7:117-126, includes paradise and its tree of life, a city (presumably a renewed Jerusalem), and freedom from sickness and death. It recalls the image of the future in *1 Enoch* which envisages paradise and the tree, but also a temple.[278] Again, it is difficult to discern what the author envisages in relation to sexual relations. The elaboration of future hope in 9:8 assumes Israel's land: the righteous "will see my salvation in my land and within my borders, which I have sanctified for myself from the beginning." Depiction of the wicked and wickedness remains generic ("abused my ways ... rejected them with contempt" 9:9; "did not acknowledge me" 9:10; "scorned my law" 9:11). The root (53) has no sexual sense here.

Within the fourth and middle section, 9:27 – 10:60, the author returns to images relating to childbirth and parenthood as he depicts Ezra encountering a distressed woman who explains her predicament (9:38 – 10:24). Having been sterile for 30 years[279] she gave birth to a son, whom she brought up to marriageable age. Then she reports: "But it happened that when my son entered his wedding chamber, he fell down and died" (10:1). This motif appears also in Tob 7:11; 8:10 and may be a topos of folklore. The author then has Ezra apply the image to Zion, by comparing the woman's grief to the grief of Zion. "For Zion, the mother of us all, is in deep grief and great distress" (10:7; cf. also 6:19).[280]

The woman remains in the picture, is even rebuked for the persistence of her lament, but serves as a prop for the author's assertion of the much greater grief of what he describes as mother Israel. Reflecting the transformation of Ezra's stance in this pivotal section, he is shown here acting as Uriel did in the first three visions and espousing his theology.[281] As Longenecker puts it, "Here the patient has

---

[278] Stone, *4 Ezra*, notes the juxtaposition of rest, paradise and fruit in *T. Levi* 18:9-10 (286).

[279] Stone, *4 Ezra*, notes the common motif of sterility, as in Gen 11:30; Judg 13:2; 1 Sam 1:16) (313). On the 30 years cf. 3:1.

[280] On Zion as mother see Isa 50:1; Jer 50:12; Hos 2:4; 4:5; Bar 4:16, 19-23, 36-37; 5:5-6.

[281] On this see Longenecker, *2 Esdras*, 59-66, who writes: "If the woman embodies the kind of attitudes and behaviour evidenced by Ezra in episodes I to III, Ezra here does not join her in her disgruntlement but now takes the place held by Uriel in the earlier episodes" (61). See also Stone, *4 Ezra*, 318-20; and the critical discussion in Edith M. Humphrey, *The*

become the doctor, and the medicine he prescribes is that which he himself has earlier refused".[282] In 10:9 there is a transition from Zion to earth. While most see it as a general reference to the earth as in 6:53; 7:62, 116,[283] it might also be understood as land, namely the land of Israel.[284] Here the natal imagery returns: "Now ask the earth (*terram*), and she will tell you that it is she who ought to mourn over so many who have come into being upon her" (10:9). Ezra continues the image in rebuking the woman for asserting that hers is a special case: "Just as you brought forth in sorrow, so the earth also has from the beginning given her fruit, that is, humankind, to him who made her" (10:14). He seeks to persuade her to return to her husband in the city (10:15-20), but then turns attention to the extent of Zion's woes (10:21-23). Among these are acts of sexual wrongdoing perpetrated against her inhabitants: "our virgins have been defiled, and our wives have been ravished" (10:22).[285]

Then suddenly the images merge as the woman begins to shine: "her face suddenly began to shine exceedingly; her countenance flashed like lightning" (10:25; cf. the similar eschatological imagery in 9:97, 125) and she disappears. Instead Ezra sees a city being rebuilt (10:27). Collins notes that it recalls the literary function of Nathan's parable to David.[286] The woman has become a symbol of the renewed city (cf. 7:26; 8:52; 13:36). Uriel's interpretation makes this explicit: "The woman whom you saw is Zion, which you now behold as a city being built" (10:44). That interpretation explains the allegory. The thirty years are

---

Ladies and the Cities: Transformation and Apocalyptic Identity in Joseph and Aseneth, 4 Ezra, the Apocalypse and the Shepherd of Hermas (JSPSup 17; Sheffield: Sheffield Academic Press, 1995), 59-73, who argues that at no point does Ezra show regret for his earlier questions, but that true understanding comes through seeing identity between lamenting Jerusalem and the heavenly Jerusalem (73-81). See also the discussion in Collins, *Apocalyptic Imagination*, who argues that finding himself in the role of the comforter, Ezra sees his own lamenting from a new perspective (206, 211), so that "If our problems cannot be solved, we must look away from them, and contemplate what is positive" (211).

[282] Longenecker, *2 Esdras*, 66.

[283] Stone, *4 Ezra*, 322; Humphrey, *The Ladies and the Cities*, who sees a possible allusion to here to universal humanity (78-79). "Ask the earth" appears also in 7:54 of the earth in general.

[284] On the importance of land in 4 Ezra see Daniel J. Harrington, "The 'Holy Land' in Pseudo-Philo, 4 Ezra, and 2 Baruch," in *Emanuel: Studies in Hebrew Bible, Septuagint, and Dead Sea Scrolls in Honor of Emanuel Tov* (ed. Shalom M. Paul, Robert A. Kraft, Lawrence H. Schiffman, and Weston W. Fields, with the assistance of Eva Ben-David; VTSup 94; Leiden: Brill, 2003) 661-72, who however passes over 10:9.

[285] Taking wives as booty was a common practice in war. See Jdt 4:12; and 1 Macc 1:32; 3:20; 2 Macc 5:24.

[286] Collins, *Apocalyptic Imagination*, 206.

3000 years before the temple of Solomon (10:45-46). The bringing up is the period of the temple (10:47). Dying in the wedding chamber means the destruction of the city (10:48). Ezra is then encouraged to see the splendour of the heavenly city (10:49-55).

In the fifth section the images of the eagle, representing Rome and its emperors Vespasian, Titus, and Domitian (11:1-35), and then of the lion, the Messiah (11:36 – 12:39), continue to speak of wickedness without reference to sexual issues, though in a manner that is more specific:

> You have judged the earth, but not with truth, 42 for you have oppressed the meek and injured the peaceable; you have hated those who tell the truth, and have loved liars; you have destroyed the homes of those who brought forth fruit, and have laid low the walls of those who did you no harm. (11:41-42)

Ezra's instruction to Jerusalem's inhabitants who come out to meet him, "Now go to your homes, every one of you, and after these days I will come to you" (12:49), echoes his instruction to the woman in her grief (10:17). Ezra's vision of the man from the sea and its interpretation (13:1-58), the sixth section, contains no specific comment about wrongdoing.

In the final section the instruction to Ezra about two revelations to Moses on Sinai, including secret revelation, recalls *Jubilees* (14:5-7), apparently equating to the 24 and 70 mentioned in 14:45-46.[287] God then commands Ezra:

> renounce the life that is corruptible, and put away from you mortal thoughts; cast away from you the burdens of humankind, and divest yourself now of your weak nature (*infirmam naturam*); lay to one side the thoughts that are most grievous to you. (14:13-15)

None of this need pertain to sexuality. Recalling its earlier theory that latest born children of many are weaker, the text depicts the weakness of the earth and thus

---

[287] Longenecker, *2 Esdras*, sees "70" as derived from the Hebrew letters for secret סוד (91) and as indicative that the author saw also his own writing not as instruction for the people as a whole but as the revealed wisdom of a learned leader concerning "eschatological secrets" for the wise (92, 100-104) and so as quite different from those eschatologies which encouraged popular or military resistance against Rome (104-107), emphasising, rather, faith that the future lies with God's initiatives and that the people should be encouraged to be observant. See also Daniel J. Harrington, "Wisdom and Apocalyptic in 4QInstruction and 4 Ezra," in *Wisdom and Apocalypticism in the Dead Sea Scrolls and in the Biblical Tradition* (ed. Florentino García Martínez; BETL163; Leuven: Peeters, 2003) 343-55, who writes: "According to 4 Ezra human wisdom has virtually disappeared, and real knowledge is possible only through revelation or apocalyptic" (354-55).

the increase of evils (14:17; cf. 5:46-52). The "weak nature" appears rather to describe the frailty of mortal human life, as in 7:15-16 (cf. also 4:11).[288] In Ezra's last words to the people the depiction of the sins and transgressions of the ancestors (14:30-31) remains generic.

Conclusion

The Ezra apocalypse has only one reference to sexual wrongdoing, its depiction of defiled virgins and ravished wives during the sack of Jerusalem (10:22). Nowhere else in its constant concern with human sin, mostly identified in general terms, including the reference to Sodom, does the work make specific reference to sexual wrongdoing. Possible allusions, such as "evil heart", the need for self-control and "weak nature", are best understood in a general sense. While references to specific acts of wrongdoing are in any case rare, the absence of references to sexual wrongdoing can be taken as evidence that it was not seen as a concern worth mentioning.

A regular element in the concern with sin is the interpretation of the Genesis account of humankind's creation and disobedience. It never mentions Eve, instead attributing the first sin to Adam, nor does it mention male female relations, including sexual relations, which are an important element in the Genesis account. Nor does it take up sexual or sexually related themes from the curses in Genesis, instead focussing only on death and hardship. Its understanding of creation appears to be influenced by *Jubilees* or *Jubilees'* tradition when it has Adam's creation take place outside the garden and Israel apparently created beside the other nations from the beginning, but its lack of interest in matters sexual is in stark contrast to *Jubilees*.

Another particular feature of the writing is its author's use of imagery drawn from the processes of pregnancy and birth.[289] The interest is not in the processes, themselves, but in their use as imagery to support argument (by both Ezra and Uriel). The range and frequency are impressive. It includes the nine month duration of pregnancy, including reference to the foetus and to painful contractions (4:40-42); advanced age in childbearing and the notion that children born later are smaller and weaker (5:46-52); the nine months of pregnancy as a period of

---

[288] So Stone, *4 Ezra*, 66, 422. He notes that "this view of death is not connected with a negative evaluation of the body" (66).

[289] On this see also Luzia Sutter Rehmann, "Das vierte Esrabuch: Vom Ringen um neues Leben, von der sich erfüllenden Zeit und der Verwandlung der Erde," in *Kompendium Feministische Bibelauslegung* (ed. Luise Schottroff, Marie-Theres Wacker, Claudia Janssen, and Beate Wehn; Gütersloh: Gütersloher Verlagshaus, 1999) 450-58, who writes of a theological gynaecology of the author, related to the vision of the earth giving birth (456-58).

fashioning, preserving with fire and water, and birth and breast feeding (8:9-11); the distressed woman who had been sterile, given birth, and whose son had died on the wedding night (9:38 – 10:4); and her giving birth and the land's giving birth (10:14). The image of the land giving birth occurs also in 6:53, 54, 7:62, 116. In addition, among negative portents entailing childbirth we find: menstruating women bearing monsters (5:8) and premature prodigies (6:21).

The largely positive use of these images reflects at least a positive appreciation and arguably particular attention to these matters on the part of the author, who shows himself (presumably male?) as having engaged in reflection on them. This includes the mistaken conclusion that children born later are likely to be less strong. This may indeed have often been the case where the health of a mother had deteriorated as she became older, where perhaps the demands of an increased number of children increased poverty and led to inadequate nutrition during pregnancy, and perhaps also that at least the firstborn received greater attention and favour. Nothing in the use of the images suggests a negative attitude towards such matters. The image of the distressed woman draws on the motif of Jerusalem as a mother mourning for her children and is traditional, but in the author's hands it has been expanded with the motif of a firstborn son who dies on the first night in the bridal chamber. The image is left for the hearer to interpret. We are apparently to assume that he dies before being able to engage in sexual intercourse with the bride or perhaps in the process, probably a known motif. More significantly, the author develops the image into a clever piece of creative writing designed to effect insight by a process of what may be called "defamiliarisation".[290]

The situation with regard to future hope is complicated by the two-staged eschatology, the four hundred year reign of the Messiah, then, after seven days of silence, the renewed creation, and by the nature of the future Jerusalem and the land.[291] More difficult is the question whether the eschatology implies continuance of family life, including sexual relations, or whether the author assumes these cease, for instance on the grounds that where people live forever in eternal day procreation is redundant (assuming that procreation alone is its purpose), or that entry into paradise equates to entering a temple as in *Jubilees* and so necessitates sexual abstinence. While we have noted influence from *Jubilees* in relation to creation, there is insufficient evidence to determine whether its understanding of paradise as a temple underlies the image in 4 Ezra. Similarly the text does not tell us enough to detect a view of sexual relations which saw its sole function as procreation.

---

[290] On this see Esler, "Social Function," 112-13.

[291] Harrington, "Holy Land," notes the importance of both city and land throughout the work (5:24-25; 7:26; 8:52; 9:8; 12:34; 13:48), including that "the place of eschatological refuge will be the holy land" (666).

The primary conclusion is thus to note the absence of the theme of sexual wrongdoing (with a single, incidental exception) in a writing so concerned with sin and its influence. Neither sexual wrongdoing nor myths of sexual wrongdoing by Watchers play a role. The absence or omission of sexual and sexually related themes in its numerous interpretations of Genesis 1 – 3 coheres with these conclusions as does the absence of any indication of the role of sexual relations in the age to come. On the other hand, the writing is remarkable for the extent and range of its use of imagery drawn from the processes of pregnancy and childbirth, reflecting what was both a positive appreciation and probably a special interest, unparalleled in most writings of the period.

1.3.4   2 Baruch

The Jewish Apocalypse of Baruch,[292] composed originally in Greek (probably), probably early second century C.E., so arguably just outside our period, and surviving mainly in Syriac, belongs to the same world as 4 Ezra, has a similar sevenfold structure, though less clearly defined, and also addresses issues raised by the destruction of Jerusalem.[293] References pertinent to sexuality are few.

The first section (1:1 – 9:2) has Baruch speak of the city as his mother (3:1-3; also 10:16).[294] The Lord's response is to reassure him that there is a heavenly city to be revealed, just as there is a paradise, located, as in 4 Ezra, in the heavenly world.(4:2-6). The second section (10:1 – 12:5) includes a lament in which Baruch

---

[292] For the critical edition of the Syriac and Greek and Latin versions see Daniel M. Gurtner, with David M. Miller and Ian W. Scott, ed. "'2 Baruch': Edition 2.0," in *The Online Critical Pseudepigrapha* (ed. Ken M. Penner, David M. Miller, and Ian W. Scott; Atlanta: SBL, 2007) no pages; online: http://www.purl.org/net/ocp/2Bar.html. The translation is that of A. F. J. Klijn, "2 (Syriac Apocalypse of) Baruch," *OTP*, 1.615–52. On the full text preserved in free translation into Arabic see Fred Leemhuis, "The Arabic Version of the Apocalypse of Baruch: A Christian Text?" *JSP* 4 (1989) 19-26.

[293] For a general introduction see Nickelsburg, *Jewish Writings*, 277-85, which includes a discussion of the possible relations with 4 Ezra; Collins, *Apocalyptic Imagination*, 212-25; Oegema, *Einführung*, 59-61. See also A. F. J. Klijn, "Recent Developments in the Study of the Syriac Apocalypse of Baruch," *JSP* 4 (1989) 3-17, including his review of the slightly diverging interpretations of the writing's purpose in response to the destruction of the city in dealing with grief and consolation and the admonition to observe the Law (7-8). On its Jewish origin see Davila, *Provenance*, 126-31, who includes critical discussion of alleged Christian authorship as proposed by Rivka Nir, *The Destruction of Jerusalem and the Idea of Redemption in the Syriac Apocalypse of Baruch* (SBLEJL 20; Leiden: Brill, 2003).

[294] On the image of the city as desolate mother and the hope of restoration in *2 Baruch* see Blessing, "Desolate Jerusalem," 60-65.

calls for signs of grief. These include bridegrooms not entering, nor brides adorning themselves, women not seeking to bear children, and an affirmation that those who are barren or childless will be happy (10:13-16). It stands beside words to farmers that they not sow and to vines not to produce (10:9-10) and virgins not to spin fine clothes (10:19).[295]

Baruch's dialogues in the third section (13:1 – 20:6) raise similar complaints to those of the early sections of 4 Ezra, to which the Lord replies, including reference to Adam's sin and its impact (17 – 18), but nothing pertains to sexual issues. The fourth section (21:1 – 34:1) continues in similar vein, again with God referring to Adam's sin in response (23:4). Mostly sin is handled generically. In 27:1-14, however, God lists twelve periods of history. The tenth is characterised by "rape (ܚܛܘܦܝܐ)[296] and much violence" and the eleventh by "injustice and unchastity (ܙܢܝܘܬܐ)"[297] (27:11, 12), but these are not developed further. The image of hope in 29:1-8 speaks of a future of abundant harvests, but no connection is made to human fertility and offspring.

The fifth section (35:1 – 47:1) includes a symbolic depiction of the wicked nations as trees (36 – 40), but without any sexual references. Of potential relevance is the reference in 41:3-4 to some who have separated themselves from divine statutes and others who have joined the people coming from former disregard of the Law.[298] In the following chapter we learn more. It reads:

> As for those who have first subjected themselves and have withdrawn later and who mingled themselves (ܐܬܚܠܛܘ) with the seed of the mingled nations, their first time will be considered as mountains (ܐܝܟ ܛܘܪܐ).[299] 5 And those who first did not know life and who later knew it exactly and who mingled (ܐܬܚܠܛܘ) with the seed of

---

[295] Cf. Nir, *Destruction of Jerusalem*, who uses the reference to virgins to argue that it reflects a Christian tradition such as is reflected in *Prot. Jas.* 10:1, and so postdates it (107-17).

[296] J. Payne Smith, *A Compendious Syriac Dictionary* (Eugene: Wipf and Stock, 1999) gives the meaning as "seizing by force, rapine, rape" (138). R. H. Charles, rev. L. H. Brockington, "The Syrian Apocalypse of Baruch," *AOT*, 835-96, renders: "havoc" (855); R. H. Charles, "II Baruch," *APOT*, 2.470–526: "rapine" (497); A. F. J. Klijn, "Der syrische Baruch-Apokalypse," in *Apokalypsen* (JSHRZ 5.2; Gütersloh: Gütersloher Verlagshaus, 1976) 103-84: "Vergewaltigung" (140).

[297] Charles, *AOT*: "impurity" (855). Smith, *Syriac*, indicates the notion of licence, intemperance, wantonness (598).

[298] The imagery, "have fled under your wings", occurs in relation to proselytes and occurs also in Ruth 2:12; Pss 36:8; 57:2.

[299] Charles, *AOT*: "their former manner of life will count for nothing" (862).

the people (lit. peoples) who separated themselves,[300] their first time will be considered as mountains (ܣܘܪ̈ܐ ܐܢܘܢ).[301] (42:4-5)

The issue is mingling with non-Jews, which might be general in its reference[302] or, more likely, refers to intermarriage, a theme addressed elsewhere, especially in *Jubilees, Aramaic Levi Document, 4QMMT, LAB*, Additions to Esther; and earlier in Ezra and Nehemiah.[303] The same word is used to describe the angels' engaging in sexual intercourse with women in 56:12 and probably at least includes this meaning here and also in 48:23. Behind it is probably ערב which Ezra 9:2 uses of intermarriage. There appear to be two groups of apostates, observant Jews and those who became observant Jews, i.e., proselytes. The former mingled with non-Jews, probably including intermarriage and the latter mingled with the former after they became apostates, including, probably, by intermarriage. Both stand under disapproval and will face judgment. Klijn translates the enigmatic final two words of each verse as indicating that the apostates "will be considered as mountains".[304] According to 35:5 mountains are to be overthrown.

We appear to have a trace here of interaction relating to three groups. Some of the author's group separate and marry non-Jews. They are joined by some who first joined the author's group and then went to the others. It recalls the divisions reflected in some of the sectarian documents at Qumran which in part also pertained to issues of marriage, especially in *4QMMT*. Nothing here, however, suggests we are dealing with a sectarian group.[305] "The mingled nations" occurs in Jer 25:20, 24 where it refers to some of the subject peoples of Pharaoh. Here it appears to function as a reference to non-Jews in general. The situation presupposed in the passage is that the author sees widespread apostasy from faithful observance of Torah (which it is strongly espousing) and identifies

---

[300] Charles, *AOT*: "joined the people set apart from other peoples" (862).

[301] Charles, *AOT*: "their manner of life will count for nothing either" (862).

[302] So for instance Gwendolyn B. Sayler, *Have the Promises Failed? A Literary Analysis of 2 Baruch* (SBLDS 72; Atlanta: Scholars, 1984), who speaks of "assimilation to the ways of the nations" (51).

[303] Klijn, *OTP*, 1.633 notes the use of "mixing" in relation to the prohibition of intermarriage in *Jub*. 30:7; *T. Levi* 9:10; and Philo *Spec*. 3.29.

[304] Klijn, *OTP*, 1, notes that the expression "is unknown and cannot be satisfactorily emended" (634). In Klijn, *JSHRZ* 5.2, 148, however he notes that Pierre-Maurice Bogaert, *Apocalypse de Baruch: Introduction, Traduction du Syriaque et Commentaire* (2 vols SC 144–45: Paris: Cerf, 1969) 1.490; 2.76) emends the second word to a singular, *rmṭ'* "dust". This might play on a return to the dust of the earth.

[305] Cf. Saylor, *Have the Promises Failed?* who suggests the group may have seen the temple as defiled already before 70 C.E. (115). As John F. Hobbins, "The Summing up of History in 2 Baruch," *JQR* 89 (1998) 45-79, notes, "The book's distinction between the many faithless and few righteous Jews is a nonsectarian one (18:1-19:3; 41:3; 42:4)" (52).

particular instances of it including among those who had become proselytes. Unlike the author of *4QMMT*, he takes his stand over against those who have separated themselves, not as one who has done so, himself. In 44:9, 12 the references to pollution and corruption are probably generic.

The sixth section (47:2 – 77:26) includes a brief reference to humans having no choice in their birth and death (48:15-16), but more significantly a further reference to intermarriage (cf. 43:4-5; 56:12):

> 22 In you we have put our trust, because behold, your Law is with us, and we know that we do not fall as long as we keep your statutes. 23 We shall be blessed; at least, we did not mingle with the nations. For we are a people of the Name 24 we who have received one Law from the One. (48:22-24)

Given the paucity of references to specific sins in the work the repetition of this theme underlines its significance.

Baruch bemoans Adam's sin and also mentions Eve: "O Adam, what did you do to all who were born after you? And what will be said of the first Eve who obeyed the serpent, so that the whole multitude is going to corruption?" (48:42-43). 48:45-46 continues with an allusion to Adam's formation from the dust of the ground, but only to set him beside all others who have sinned. In 51:1-16 we then have a depiction of future life. It includes images of the shining glory of the righteous and the statement that "time will no longer make them older. For they will live in the heights of that world and they will be like the angels and be equal to stars" (51:9-10), their excellence exceeding that of angels (51:13), but we find here no indication of the implications of the new embodiment for sexual relations, except that not growing older (also 51:16) would, one imagines remove the need for procreation.

In 53 – 77 we then find a large section which begins with a vision of clouds pouring rain on the earth twelve times, producing an alternating sequence of black and bright waters until lightning at the top of the cloud brought healing (53:1-12). It becomes the climax of the book with a strong emphasis on keeping the Law.[306] First we hear of Baruch's prayer, in which he gives thanks for his blessings and blesses his mother: "Blessed is my mother among those who bear, and praised among women is she who bore me" (54:10). He also notes Adam's sin and the death it brought while also affirming individual responsibility for the torment which awaits them (54:15, 19). The interpretation (56 – 74) depicts each of the twelve stages as moments of sinfulness and then of hope in history. The first

---

[306] On its role as the highpoint of the writing, see Martin Leuenberger, "Ort und Funktion der Wolkenvision und ihrer Deutung in der syrischen Baruchapokalypse: Eine These zu deren thematischer Entfaltung," *JSJ* 36 (2005) 206-46, 218-31.

moment of sin is predictably Adam's transgression (here, no mention of Eve) (56:5). The effects are described as follows:

> For when he transgressed, untimely death came into being, mourning was mentioned, affliction was prepared, illness was created, labor accomplished, pride began to come into existence, the realm of death began to ask to be renewed with blood, the conception[307] of children came about, the passion of the parents was produced, the loftiness of men was humiliated, and goodness vanished. (56:6)

Gen 3:16-19 lies behind this, but some elements go beyond it. These include premature death (perhaps an allusion to the murder of Abel),[308] mourning (again a possible allusion to Adam and Eve's mourning at Abel's death),[309] affliction, illness, pride, humiliation, and the vanishing of goodness.[310] While the words used for "affliction" and "illness" may have general reference, in the Peshitta the latter, "*k'b*', translates עצב, found twice in Gen 3:16 and once in 3:17"[311] and in 73:7 refers to the pain of childbirth. This makes it likely that the next word, "labour", also refers to the pains of childbirth as in Gen 3:16-17, rather than the curse of having to toil hard on the cursed ground as in Gen 3:19. Levison challenges the basis for translating the next reference as "conception of children", arguing convincingly that "there is hardly any lexical support for that interpretation. The word denotes 'taking away', and refers, once again to death; this time death 'takes away' small children".[312] Should it refer to conception, then it would make not just pain in pregnancy and childbirth but also conception, itself, a fruit of Adam's sin. Levison notes that "'the passion of the parents' … *rtḥ*', literally 'bubbling up', connotes the desire which results in the conception of children".[313] Whether taken on its own or in association with the possible reference to conception in what precedes, the statement appears to indicate that the author sees sexual desire and procreation as the result of Adam's transgression. They are not themselves transgression, but like all the other items in the list, seen negatively. They are necessary evils. Behind this probably lies the notion that Adam, before he sinned, was immortal, so that no progeny would be necessary (similarly *Sib. Or.* 1:57-58).

---

[307] Charles, *APOT*: "begetting" (513).

[308] So Levison, *Portraits of Adam*, who notes that the same word is used of violent death in 73:3-4 where these effects are reversed (139).

[309] So Levison, *Portraits of Adam*, who points to *Apoc. Mos.* 1 – 4 (139). See also *Jub.* 4:7.

[310] Levison, *Portraits of Adam*, notes that this may allude to the wickedness of humanity depicted in Gen 6:5-12, to which the author is about to turn in depicting the myth of the Watchers (141).

[311] So Levison, *Portraits of Adam*, 140.

[312] Levison, *Portraits of Adam*, 140.

[313] Levison, *Portraits of Adam*, 141.

A second aspect of the first black waters is the deed of the Watchers:

10 For he who was a danger to himself was also a danger to the angels. 11 For they possessed freedom in that time in which they were created. 12 And some of them came down and mingled themselves (ܐܬܚܠܛܘ) with women. 13 At that time they who acted like this were tormented in chains. 14 But the rest of the multitude of angels, who have no number, restrained themselves. 15 And those living on earth perished together through the waters of the flood. 16 These are the first black waters. (56:10-16)

This contains a few notable features. Adam, that is humankind, and by implication, women, became a danger to the angels. This implies blame on both women and angels for their deed and so tells of a negative stance towards women's sexuality – an aspect of the necessary evil which Adam's deed brought. Their coming down reflects the form of the myth in Gen 6:1-4 and *1 Enoch* 6 – 16, not that supposed in *Jubilees* where their coming down preceded their wrongdoing and was on divine command. "Mingled themselves with" refers to sexual intercourse, probably also its meaning in 42:4-5 and 48:23. Their being tormented in chains derives not from Genesis but from other versions of the myth, such as we find in *1 Enoch* 6 – 11. "Those living on earth" may refer to angels, but this is unlikely since the author knows the tradition about their being tormented in chains, presumably as elsewhere until the day of judgment. It might refer to their offspring, the giants, who are not mentioned as such, but more probably it simply refers to the sinners of Noah's generation.

The sins of the third black waters were a "mingling of all sins", but also Egypt's oppression of Israel's sons (58:1-2). In the account of the fourth bright waters the angel Ramael reports that Moses saw "the likeness of Zion" (59:4) and "the greatness of Paradise" (59:8), presumably in heaven. The sins of the fifth waters are the invocations of the incantations of the Amorites, "the wickedness of their mysteries, and the mingling (not the same word) of their pollutions" (60:1-2). When it then reports that "even Israel was polluted with sins in these days of the judges", this may refer to forbidden intermarriage (Judg 3:5-6), but may have broader reference. The seventh black waters speaks of the sins of Jeroboam in making the golden calves, and of his successors in idolatry, and subsequent famine leading even to the horrors of cannibalism (62:1-8). The ninth black waters, the time of Manasseh, includes not only "perverted judgment" and bloodshed, but also that he "violently polluted married women" (64:2). The latter goes beyond the accounts in 2 Kings and 2 Chronicles, but recalls the possible allusion to rape in 27:11. Sayler notes some common elements between Baruch's statements and Abraham's in discussing Sodom, which was also filled with wickedness but had one who was righteous (3:1-3; cf. Gen 18:3; and 14:5-8; cf. Gen 18:16-23). She also suggests that "Manasseh is a prototype of the many Jews mentioned in the conversation" in 41 – 43, noting the *Martyrdom of Isaiah*'s depiction of accusations made against Isaiah that he equated Manasseh's transformed Jerusalem with Sodom (3:6-10).[314] One might indeed go further and wonder whether the allegation that Manasseh "violently polluted married women" (64:2) might also derive from this connection, namely, echoing the violent actions of the men of Sodom. The final black waters, the eleventh, relate to the destruction of Jerusalem (67:1-9).

Sexual themes appear in the first, ninth, and possibly the fifth. Otherwise the focus is on wickedness in general and on idolatry. This is also the case in the additional set of final waters in 70:1-10. It speaks of warfare, the rise of despised rulers, the impious, and the foolish, but contains nothing about sexual wrongdoing. The vision of final joy then depicts a time when "nobody will again die untimely" (reversing one of Adam's effects) (73:3), "judgment, condemnations, contentions, revenges, blood, passions, zeal, hate" will be "uprooted" (73:4), but also that "women will no longer have pain when they bear, nor will they be tormented when they yield the fruits of their womb" (73:7). "Passions" here probably includes sexual passion, probably understood as excessive passion.[315] What is being reversed here is not conception, but the curse of Gen 3:16, namely pain in pregnancy and childbirth.[316] It also assumes sexual relations, at least for procreation, as an element of life in the new age.[317]

The final section of *2 Baruch* (78:1 – 87:1) reports Baruch's letter, which includes reference to the nations as a mere vapour, a drop, spittle, smoke, withering grass, a passing wave or passing cloud, who engage in wickedness, impiety, disobedience, cruelty and pride (82:4-9), nothing, however, pertaining to sexual wrongdoing. In 83:5 it warns about looking "upon the delights of the present nations" which might include it, but the reference is probably broader. In 83:14, however, we read of their "splendour" and "delight", which will turn into "ruin of silence" and in 83:18 this has sexual connotations: "And every desire of lust[318] [*AOT*: "spoils of passion"] changes into the judgment of punishment". This comes amid a series of sayings about reversals of qualities into their opposite in 83:10-21, including health, might, power, youthful energy, beauty of gracefulness, infantile pride, glory of haughtiness, joy and delight, clamour of pride, possession

---

[314] Sayler, *Have the Promises Failed?* 92-94.

[315] Ellis, *Sexual Desire*, opts to read it as rejection of all, not just excessive, passion in the light of 56:5 (22).

[316] Sayler, *Have the Promises Failed?* argues however that it might match since in 56:6 the expression "conception of children" which she translates, "generating (*nsb'*) of children" means bearing them in pain (70, 71 n. 58), although the text does not indicate that.

[317] Ellis, *Sexual Desire*, notes that "sex and reproduction are not 'uprooted' along with revenge, hate, and passions (73.4)" (22).

[318] According to Klijn, *OTP* 1, lit. "lusts" (650).

of riches, seizing desire, capability of deceit, sweetness of ointments, and friendship.

Conclusion

2 Baruch is concerned with observance of Torah as the way to live in the aftermath of the destruction of the city and amid the vicissitudes of life under Roman domination while awaiting hope of a new age which lies in God's hands,[319] and so is concerned with sin, often spoken of generically, but sometimes with specific reference, especially in such lists of wrongdoing as we see reversed in 83:10-21. In the depiction of twelve periods of history it mentions "rape and much violence" and "injustice and unchastity" (27:11, 12) and in the interpretation of the twelve waters, that Manasseh "violently polluted married women" (64:2), which may be connected with traditions about Sodom. "Every desire of lust" is one among many behaviours to find its nemesis in judgement (83:18) and may be envisaged when the author speaks of the nations' delights (83:5, 15). Intermarriage appears to receive mention in the context of reporting a group which had separated itself and which proselytes joined (41:3-4; 42:4), providing an interesting parallel to *4QMMT* where in reverse a group separated itself from the majority for the same reason. The concern recurs in 48:22-24, may also feature in the depiction of the sin in the days of the Judges (60:1-2), and in 56:12 the same word describes the Watchers' act of sexual intercourse with women.

There are many references to Adam (and once to Eve) in the context of explaining the origin of sin and death, while emphasising that all since Adam bear responsibility for their plight.[320] Of particular interest is the depiction of Adam's legacy as conception of children and sexual passion between parents (56:6), which while not disparaging either as sinful, depicts them as a necessary evil, consequent upon Adam's losing his immortality and so needing to procreate. The account of the Watchers' sexual mingling with human women also implicates the latter, who are depicted as a danger (56:10), another outcome of Adam's sin, because it created the need for sexual passion and procreation. Interestingly the new age reverses one of the other outcomes, premature death (51:9-10, 16; 73:3), but limits the reversal related to childbirth to the removal of pain in pregnancy and childbirth

---

[319] On the rejection of continuing armed resistance to Rome see Frederick J. Murphy, "2 Baruch and the Romans," *JBL* 104 (1985) 663-69.

[320] On the anthropocentric perspective of *2 Baruch*, see Bogaert, *Apocalypse de Baruch*, who points to 14:18-19, which declares that the world was created for humankind (1.399) and to 51:10-12, according to which the future excellence of the righteous will exceed that of the angels (1.400).

(73:7).[321] While the eschatological visions are not always clear,[322] there is clear indication that the author envisages sexual relations as belonging in the age to come, perhaps only for procreation. The promised abundant harvest (29:1-8) is not applied to human progeny.

Most other references consist of individual motifs, such as Jerusalem as mother (3:1-3; also 10:16), grief expressed as not marrying or giving birth (10:13-16), virgins not weaving fine clothes (10:19), having no choice in being born or dying (48:15-16), and declaring one's mother blessed (54:10).

1.4   Other Apocalypses and Testaments

1.4.1   Apocalypse of Abraham

Like *4 Ezra* and *2 Baruch*, the *Apocalypse of Abraham*, composed originally in Hebrew, then translated in Greek and surviving in Church Slavonic, appears to have been written in the aftermath of the destruction of Jerusalem in 70 C.E.[323] Its allusions to issues of sexuality are minimal. Its first 7 chapters use the story of

---

[321] Mark F. Whitters, "Testament and canon in the Letter of Second Baruch (2 Baruch 78-87)," *JSP* 12 (2001) 149-63, notes the universal perspective of this hope, implying an openness to Gentiles joining, and also cohering with a major difference from 4 Ezra which sees its knowledge as secret and available only for a few (161-62).

[322] See the discussion in Frederick J. Murphy, *The Structure and Meaning of Second Baruch* (SBLDS 78; Atlanta: Scholars, 1985) 31-67, who concludes that the author sees "heaven as the place of the final abode of the righteous" (67); but for a contrary view which sees a restoration on earth see Hobbins, "Summing up of History," 54-76, who argues that the author envisages a future in which heaven and earth co-exist. George W. E. Nickelsburg, "Where Is the Place of Eschatological Blessing?" in *Things Revealed: Studies in Early Jewish and Christian Literature in Honor of Michael E. Stone* (ed. Esther G. Chazon, David Satran, and Ruth A. Clements; JSJSup 89; Leiden: Brill, 2004) 53-71, concludes in perhaps too systematising a manner that the author envisages "a renewed earth, blessed with fertility", but that "it will not be the home of the resurrected righteous" who "will ascend to heaven, ... where they will be transformed into the splendour of the angels and the stars (chapters 49-51" (67). See also his *Jewish Literature*, where he writes: "Probably we are dealing with different traditions that stand in tension with one another", though he notes that Dan 12:1-3 is a precedent (283).

[323] See the general introductions in Nickelsburg, *Jewish Literature*, 285-88; Collins, *Apocalyptic Imagination*, 225-32; Oegema, *Einführung*, 118-20. See also Alexander Kulik, *Retroverting Slavonic Pseudepigrapha: Toward the Original of the Apocalypse of Abraham* (SBLTCS 3; Leiden: Brill, 2005). I am dependent on secondary literature for discussion of the Slavonic. For the translation I use R. Rubinkiewicz, revised and notes added by H. P. Lunt, "Apocalypse of Abraham," *OTP*, 1.689-705.

Abraham's rejection of his father's idolatry to depict idols and their construction as an absurd activity and then to debunk any notion that aspects of creation like fire, water, earth, and sun, can be deemed gods. At no point do we find a connection between idolatry and sexual wrongdoing, as often occurs elsewhere. Similarly in the instructions to Abraham to prepare himself for ascent and revelation through forty days of fasting, abstinence from wine, and from anointing himself with oil (9:7), nothing is said about sexual abstinence. The work designates Abraham as "friend of God"(10:5) and frequently as loved by God, but never in the context, for instance, of rejection of illicit intermarriage, as with that other "friend of God", Phinehas (*Jub.* 30:20; Ps 106:30-31; Num 25:6-13; *4QMMT* C 31-32).

The retelling of Abraham's dividing the animals for sacrifice in Gen 15:9-11 introduces Azazel. He appears in place of the birds of prey as "an unclean bird" (13:3), challenging Abraham about his presence "on the holy heights, where no one eats or drinks, nor is there food upon them for men" (13:4; cf. *Jub.* 11:18-22). Box notes a similar observation made in the *Testament of Abraham* where Michael declares that "all the heavenly beings are incorporeal, and they neither eat nor drink" (A 4:9).[324] A further implication may be that in such places other physical activity also does not take place, like sexual relations, but this is not necessarily so. Abraham's guide, the angel Iaoel, confronts the "disgrace" (13:6b), that is Azazel: "Shame on you, Azazel! For Abraham's portion is in heaven, and yours is on earth, for you have selected here, (and) become enamored of the dwelling place of your blemish" (Kulik: "desired it to be the dwelling place of your impurity";[325] cf. 13:7-8a). As in the *Parables of Enoch* and *4QAges of Creation*, here Asael of the *Book of the Watchers* has become Azazel and assumed primary responsibility for their descent and sexual wrongdoing and its effects. The closest it comes to an allusion to sexual wrongdoing is the word, "enamoured", but even this refers not to women as its object but to earth as dwelling place. There is also no specific reference to sexual wrongdoing in the depiction of the effects of Azazel's action. Instead we hear that through him "the all-evil spirit (is) a liar"(13:9) and that wrath will face those who "live impiously" (13:9). Finally Abraham and presumably his own are to receive the heavenly garment once worn by Azazel in heaven (13:14).[326] Azazel has no right to tempt them and Abraham is instructed not to engage him (13:11-13; 14:14:9-14). He is banished (echoing the ritual of Atonement Day; Lev 16:8, 21) into the untrodden parts of the earth to have as his heritage those who are with him, "with the stars and with the men born by the

---

[324] G. H. Box, *The Apocalypse of Abraham* (London: SPCK, 1919) 52.

[325] Kulik, *Retroverting*, 20.

[326] Box, *Apocalypse of Abraham*, notes that *Asc. Is.* 4:16 mentions heavenly garments stored up in heaven (53).

clouds" (14:6), possibly an allusion to the others who descended, who are depicted as stars in the *Animal Apocalypse*, and to their offspring (*1 Enoch* 86:1-3).

We return to stars allocated to Azazel after Abraham's ascent and elaborate throne vision (15:1 – 18:14; cf. *2 Bar.* 4:4 and 4 Ezra 3:13–14): Abraham is to look at the stars beneath him, who are numbered as are the nations set aside for Azazel (20:5).[327] The assumption is that Azazel is active on earth. This may or may not include the notion that he is on earth at the head of the host of evil spirits or a proportion of them (cf. *Jub.* 10:5-11; *1 Enoch* 15:8-12). Abraham's request for information about how this came about elicits a depiction of creation, including the garden of Eden (21:1-6), and humanity divided in two, some on the right, some on the left (21:7; cf. 4QInstr^c/4Q417 1 i.16b-18a). Of the people on earth with Azazel, those on the right are God's people; the others are destined for perdition (22:5). Again, nothing is said of sexual wrongdoing nor of issues of intermarriage.

The following depiction of sin in the garden speaks of one who "seduced Eve" (23:1), but gives no indication that this is sexual in nature. If the Greek reflects the LXX, then "seduce" was a possible meaning of ἀπατάω, but not its only meaning. It could still mean "deceive". The passage depicts Adam and Eve as entwined together, probably an elaboration of their becoming one flesh, which includes sexual union. "And I saw there a man very great in height and terrible in breadth, incomparable in aspect, entwined with a woman who was also equal to the man in aspect and size" (23:5). While the super-proportioned primordial couple stand beneath a tree, "(something) like a dragon" with six wings on either side stood behind it feeding them with grapes, the tree understood as a grapevine (23:6-8). An explicit identification of the dragon with Azazel comes only in God's response to Abraham's request for an explanation and occurs in the context of a symbolic interpretation of the scene where Adam represents humanity and Eve represents its thought/desire: "This is the world of men, this is Adam and this is their thought on earth, this is Eve. And he who is between them is the impiety of their behaviour unto perdition, Azazel himself"(23:10-11). Slavonic *"pomyšlenie* is 'thought' in any possible sense, including 'intention, plan', or negative 'plot, evil design,' and

---

[327] The text is corrupt and unclear. "So shall I place for your seed the nations and men set apart for me in my lot with Azazel" might imply that this is a foreign intrusion which equates the God of Abraham with an evil deity aligned with Azazel, and stem from Bogomil sectarian influence, as Lunt in Rubinkiewicz, *OTP*, 1.684 suggests. One would have expected "set apart for me" to belong to "your seed", but perhaps the whole refers to the seed as those nations and men set apart as God's lot among all the people on earth who are now in the realm of Azazel. Lunt detects Bogomil influence also in 20:7 and 22:5 (684), but there, too, its seems to me that the assumption is that God has a chosen people out of those now in the realm of Azazel, namely human beings on earth.

'desire'".[328] Given the allusion to "desire" in 24:9, this is probably the connotation of the word here. We appear therefore to have before us a depiction of human sin as occasioned by humankind's failure to control desire, expressed in gendered form, as failure of the man to control woman's desire. This would have its roots in the curse in Genesis according to which the woman has desire which is to be controlled, but projected back into the very nature of woman from the beginning, a notion present also in Philo, for instance. The account does not disparage the entwining itself, which probably includes an allusion also to sexual union.[329] Perhaps the motif of entwining plays on the image of the vine from which the grapes derive, but this need not imply anything negative. The passage depicts desire in feminine terms and probably includes in this female sexual desire in particular, even though the allegory now uses Eve as a symbol of "thought/desire" in a manner which is presumably applicable to all human beings. It is interesting that Azazel is here reduced to being a symbol of sin, impiety, itself.

In 24:1-4 we return to the account of the peoples and hear God's announcement that he is to explain what is to come. He then instructs Abraham to look at the picture and begins with Adam and Eve (24:5). 24:1-4 follows well directly after 22:5 and both the repetition of reference to Adam and Eve and the distinctive account in 23, including its anthropological allegory, might suggest that this was a secondary expansion by the author or a reviser. It certainly stands out thus far over against what precedes inasmuch as it brings issues of sexuality into focus.

In 24:5-8 we have a brief account of Adam and Eve, Cain and Abel, the Watchers, and Sodom and Gomorrah, though in the case of the latter two not explicitly identified as such. Of Adam and Eve it simply notes that with them was "the crafty adversary". In the work as it now stands this recalls the preceding chapter. "The adversary", described also as "the lawless one" then accounts for Cain's breaking the law by murdering Abel (24:5). In 24:6 we have an allusion to the myth of the Watchers: "And I saw there fornication and those who desired it and its defilement and their zeal; and the fire of their corruption in the lower depths of the earth" (24:6). Here the focus is not the single figure Azazel, but the plural Watchers. "Fornication", here, alludes to their act of sexual intercourse with women. That this was "defilement" and resulted in their binding in the fiery depths of the earth derives not from Genesis 6, but is detail given in the *Book of the Watchers* (*1 Enoch* 9:8; 10:12-13) and probably derives from that tradition. We

---

[328] Lunt, *OTP* 1.700. Kulik, *Retroverting*, suggests behind it lies either "Gk ἐπιθυμία – Heb מחמד, or Gr διάνοια – Heb יצר" (27) and see his discussion on p. 84.

[329] Cf. Lunt, *OTP* 1, who writes of 23:4-10 that it "claims that the sin of Adam and Eve consisted in the conjugal relation" (684), which he sees as reflecting Bogomil rejection of marriage, but see the critical assessment in Kulik, *Retroverting*, 3.

noted above the possible allusion to the sexual lust of Azazel in 13:8. In 24:7 we read of "theft and those who hasten after it". Its particular reference is unclear.

We then read in 24:8 what appears to be a reference to Sodom and Gomorrah: "I saw there naked men, forehead to forehead, and their shame and the harm (they wrought) against their friends and their retribution". The allusion seems best understood as depicting homoerotic behaviour (though the physical position does not suggest anal intercourse, commonly described as sodomy)[330] and, given the attempt at male rape in the story of Sodom and Gomorrah against Lot's guests and the subsequent destruction, it appears that the author concludes that not only male rape but also male same-sex relations characterised these people who were therefore punished. We have then an instance here both of assuming that same-sex relations characterised the cities but also of concluding that they warranted their destruction.

The sexual theme continues in what immediately follows where we read: "And I saw their desire (*epithumia*), and in her hand (was) the head of every kind of lawlessness; and her torment and her dispersal destined for destruction" (24:9). Lunt notes that "desire" (*želanie*) is a neuter followed by possessives which are feminine, "surely reflecting mechanical translation of pronouns referring to Gk. *epithumia*".[331] The reference to "desire" in this context includes a significant emphasis on sexual lust. It also recalls the allegory of Eve as representing "thought/desire" in 23:10. The notion that desire ἐπιθυμία is "the head of every kind of lawlessness" finds a parallel in *T. Sim.* 5:3 (ἡ πορνεία μήτηρ ἐστὶ πάντων τῶν κακῶν "sexual immorality is the mother of all evils").

In 25:1 – 27:12 we find a discussion of the destruction of the temple which attributes this act to corruption, represented as idolatry, thus recalling Abraham's encounter with his father.[332] God tells Abraham: "the people who will come to me out of you will make me angry" (25:5). But nowhere here do we find the theme of sexual wrongdoing. The same is true of God's response to Abraham's questions about the future of the people, elaborated in the final chapters, including the Christian interpolation in 29:3-13.[333]

---

[330] Similarly A. Pennington, "The Apocalypse of Abraham," *AOT*, 363–91, 386; Belkis Philonenko-Sayar and Marc Philonenko, *Die Apokalypse Abrahams* (JSHRZ 5.5; Gütersloh: Gütersloher Verlagshaus, 1982) 447. Cf. Kulik, *Retroverting*, "I saw there two bare-headed men against me and their shame and the harm against their fellows and their retribution" (29).

[331] Lunt, *OTP*, 1.701.

[332] On this see Collins, *Apocalyptic Imagination*, 231-32.

[333] On the issue of Christian interpolation see the discussion in Robert G. Hall, "The 'Christian interpolation' in the Apocalypse of Abraham," *JBL* 107 (1988) 107-10, who on the basis of tensions in the text argues that only the interpretation derives from Christian interpolation and that the vision refers to the Roman emperor, probably Hadrian.

Conclusion

While the work begins with an elaborate disparagement of idolatry and later applies this to what it sees as inappropriate behaviour in the temple warranting its destruction, it does not associate idolatry and sexual wrongdoing nor link Abraham's being a friend of God with concerns about sexual behaviour. It does however make reference to the sexual wrongdoing of the Watchers. In doing so it uses what appears to be Enochic tradition from the *Book of the Watchers* about their defilement and binding in fiery depth of the earth and from the *Animal Apocalypse*, depicting them as stars, and about Azazel, in particular. It contains an allegorical interpretation of Adam and Eve in the garden, which has Adam represent humanity and Eve, desire, including sexual desire, and Azazel, sin. The "seduction" of Eve is probably her "deception" rather than being seen as a sexual act. On the other hand the document highlights the importance of "desire", which includes "sexual desire", as an impulse for sin both in the allegory and in the evaluation of primeval events. It accounts for Cain's murderous act, and also for the sexual wrongdoing of the Watchers and of Lot's fellow citizens, who are depicted as engaging in male same-sex relations. While inappropriate behaviour expressing sexual desire is clearly condemned, nothing suggests that sexual desire in itself is evil. The entwinedness of the first couple is not disparaged, nor does Abraham's ascent to receive divine revelation warrant sexual abstinence.

1.4.2   Testament of Moses

This important work, extant in a single Latin manuscript, though incomplete, appears to have been written in Greek in the late first century B.C.E. or early first century C.E.[334]   Opinion is divided over whether it is a revision of an earlier composition stemming from the aftermath of Antiochus Epiphanes' action against Jerusalem in 167 B.C.E. and before the successes of Judas,[335] or whether allusions

---

[334] For the Latin text I use David M. Miller, ed. "'Assumption of Moses': Edition 1.0," in *The Online Critical Pseudepigrapha* (ed. Ken M. Penner, David M. Miller, and Ian W. Scott; Atlanta: SBL, 2007) no pages; online: http://www.purl.org/net/ocp/Mois.html. For the English translation I use John Priest, "Testament of Moses," *OTP* 2.927-34.

[335] See the overviews in Nickelsburg, *Jewish Literature*, 74-77, 247-48; Collins, *Apocalyptic Imagination*, 128-33; and their earlier discussions in George W. E. Nickelsburg, ed., *Studies on the Testament of Moses* (SBLSCS 4; Cambridge: SBL, 1973): John J. Collins, "The Date and Provenance of the Testament of Moses," 15-37; George W. E. Nickelsburg, "An Antiochan Date for the Testament of Moses," 33-37; and John J. Collins, "Some Remaining Traditio-Historical Problems in the Testament of Moses," 38-43. See also Oegema, *Einführung*, 34-36.

to that time function much as they do in Mark 13, as an eschatological type, and so cannot be used to posit the existence of an earlier work.[336] It projects itself as an account of Moses' predictions given as parting words to Joshua within the framework of Deuteronomy 31 – 34 and of deuteronomistic theology.[337] The work has little reference to issues pertaining to sexuality.

In its final form chapters 5 – 7 of the work report on the Hasmonean period and the reign of Herod, beginning with a note about punishment meted out by people who also perpetrate the same crimes and about divisions or distancing from the truth.[338] Moses declares (apparently through unknown citations)[339] that they will pollute the temple, but does not say how except that it is *in genationibus*, which Priest construes as "with the customs of the nations" (5:3).[340] This might allude to calendrical disputes, but could cover a range of disapproved practices, including sexual wrongdoing. The prediction also uses the familiar image of prostitution to describe idolatry: *fornicabunt post deos alienos* "they will play the harlot after foreign gods" (5:3; cf. Deut 31:16),[341] speaks of polluting sacrifices (5:4) and says of the perpetrators: *non sunt sacerdotes sed serui de seruis nati* "are not (truly) priests (at all), but slaves, yea sons of slaves" (5:4), the latter, an accusation made against Hyrcanus (Josephus *A.J.* 13.291-292).

In 6:2 it speaks of a *rex petulans qui non erit de genere sacerdotum* "a wanton king, not of a priestly family", an allusion to Herod the Great, identified by his rule of 34 years (6:6). The description of godlessness in 7:1-4 lists all kinds of sin: destructive, godless, deceitful, self-pleasing, false and loving feasts at every hour

---

[336] Cf. Johannes Tromp, *The Assumption of Moses: A Critical Edition with Commentary* (SVTP 10; Leiden: Brill, 1993), who rather sees a future figure modelled on Antiochus Epiphanes (121-23; 215). Similarly, Priest, *OTP*, 2.920-21; Davila, *Provenance*, 153; Kenneth R. Atkinson, "Taxo's Martyrdom and the Role of the *Nuntius* in the *Testament of Moses*: Implications for Understanding the Role of Other Intermediary Figures," *JBL* 125 (2006) 453-76, who writes: "Although these travails are reminiscent of the Antiochan persecution, they are perhaps closer to the eschatological woes found in Mark 13" (463). But see the critique in Nickelsburg, "Antiochan Date," 34-35 (conceded by Collins, "Some Remaining Traditio-Historical Problems," 39) of using the Markan parallel on grounds that the Testament is too specific in its detail.

[337] So Nickelsburg, *Jewish Literature*, 75.

[338] On the sense of *dividere* here as distancing see Tromp, *Assumption*, 189.

[339] See Tromp, *Assumption*, 189-90. He notes the similar accusations in Jer 11:10 (which includes in the Vulgate: *post deos alienos*) and Deut 31:29; cf. also 31:16 (Vulgate: *fornicabitur post deos alienos*).

[340] Priest, *OTP*, 2.929; cf. Tromp, *Assumption*, who conjectures *inquinationibus* and translates "with pollutions" (12-13).

[341] On this see Norbert Johannes Hofmann, *Die Assumptio Mosis: Studien zur Rezeption massgültiger Überlieferung* (JSJSup 67; Leiden: Brill, 2000) 108-109.

of the day, devouring and gluttonous,[342] but nothing about sexual wrongdoing. In 7:8-10 it repeats the reference to feasts, wining and dining, and adds touching unclean things with hand and mind (*et manus eorum et mentes inmunda tractantes*, "they, with hand and mind, will touch impure things; *et super dicent 10 noli ....* *tange ne inquines me locoin quo ...* and they will even say, 'Do not touch me, lest you pollute me in the position I occupy ...'"), but again, nothing pertaining to sexuality, though this might have been included among the concerns with impurity (e.g., after seminal discharge; after childbirth; during menstruation).

In chapter 8 we appear to move back in time from chapters 6 – 7, to the intervention of Antiochus Epiphanes, but this may be no more than typological employment of that event to describe what is to follow Herod and the intervention of Varus in response to the uprisings after his death (6:8-9). Moses predicts of a "king of the kings" that *confitentes circumcisionem in cruce suspendit* "he will crucify those who confess their circumcision" (8:1)[343] and even torture and imprison those who deny (or destroy or conceal)[344] it (8:2). Then 8:3b reports: *Et filii eorum pueri secabantur a medicis pueri inducere acrosisam illis* "and their young sons will be cut by physicians to bring forward their foreskins". This recalls the concern with circumcision in *Jubilees*, perhaps contemporary with the work in its earlier recension, where we read that some either neglect circumcision or leave it incomplete (*Jub.* 15:33-34). A similar concern is reported in 1 Macc 1:14-15, where some seek to remove the marks of circumcision. The allusions in 8:1, 3 may then indicate similar concern with circumcision in the context of relations with non-Jews and most probably in the context of nakedness, such as was expected in the Hellenistic gymnasium and in sports. On the other hand, as Atkinson notes, the measures in 1 Macc 1:14-15 are not the same as what is being described in 8:3. The latter describes epispasm, which while it "existed in the Hellenistic and Roman periods, literary evidence suggests that it reached its greatest popularity during the first century C.E.".[345] One might add that the scenario envisaged in 8:1-3 indicates measures of oppression, rather than the dangers of assimilation reflected in *Jubilees* and 1 Maccabees.[346] On the other hand, whether as historical

---

[342] On the typical list of vices see Tromp, *Assumption*, who notes that its ethics "are the common stock of contemporary moral teaching, pagan and Jewish" but that "the only typically Jewish issue in the list is perhaps the preoccupation with ritual purity" (208).

[343] Tromp, *Assumption*, sees the reference to circumcision here as a metaphor for Judaism (217), but the literal meaning assumed in 8:3b favours taking it literally here in the sense that circumcision was a sign of Jewishness.

[344] Priest, *OTP*, 2.930 emends *necantes* to *negantes*, but notes that it might also mean "conceal".

[345] Atkinson, "Taxo's Martyrdom," 466.

[346] Noted already by Collins, "Date and Provenance," who points to the voluntariness assumed in 1 Macc 1:16 (20).

reference or as prefiguring the future the extent of exact correspondence to what is attested elsewhere is not of major importance, since either way an allusion to Antiochus is implied.[347]

When 8:3a reports, *et uxores eorum diis donabuntur gentibus* "and their wives will be given to the gods of the nations", this could refer to sacral prostitution or might simply refer to wives being taken captive as booty.[348] If behind *uxores* is γυναῖκες, then the allusion could be not to wives, but to women being given in intermarriage, which would be another echo of a major concern in *Jubilees*, but this is uncertain and, given the context of oppression which the passage envisages, might be better understood as describing a common fate of captured women.

The testament appears to identify these events as occurring under duress as a result of oppression (by Antiochus or by the one whom he prefigures). This is different from both *Jubilees* and from *1 Maccabees*, where both seem to allude to the earlier period. On the other hand, one might imagine that Antiochus' intervention intensified the pressure. The testament may have had its origin among those who did not join Mattathias and fight, and differed also from those of *Jubilees* who rejected fighting on the sabbath (50:12; cf. 1 Macc 2:29-38; 2 Macc 6:11),[349] but rather embraced passive resistance, choosing, as those who identified with Taxo and his seven sons, to die rather than contravene these laws, believing that in response to their unjust slaughter the God of vengeance would act (9:6-7; cf. Deut 32:34-43).[350]

Beyond these references the only other allusions pertaining broadly to sexuality are minor and incidental. In 4:3 Moses reports a prayer for the people, including the words, "they, their wives, and their children, have gone as captives into a foreign land, surrounded by the gates of strangers". The elaboration will not have been superfluous, given the norms of war. In 11:12 Joshua protests his incompetence, asking how he can be "as a father to his only son, or as a mother is to her virgin daughter who is being prepared for her husband; a mother who is disquieted guarding (the daughter's) body from the sun and (seeing to it) that (the

---

[347] Similarly Collins, "Date and Provenance," 22.

[348] Tromp, *Assumption*, argues that the manuscript's *diisdonare* is better taken as "a vulgar Latin variant of *didare*, 'to divide' ... a synonym of *dividere*, a word often used in connection with war booty" (218-19). One might note: as in English, "to divide the spoils".

[349] Despite these differences, both works have much in common, including attacks of the priesthood who are polluting the temple and the notion of Israel as chosen from the beginning of time, expressed blatantly in the Testament in the words, "he created the world on behalf of his people" (1:13).

[350] On the other hand, Atkinson, "Taxo's Martyrdom," notes, Taxo is far from a quietest figure, but rather "is a militant individual who seeks his own death as a means to exterminate the wicked for all time" (473).

daughter's) feet are not without shoes when she runs upon the ground". The extensiveness of the female imagery is noteworthy.

Overall, while the review of the Hasmonean and Herodian material contains nothing explicitly sexual, there seems to be a reflection of concern both with circumcision (in the context of demands for nakedness) and possibly intermarriage to foreigners in relation to the earlier period, attested also in *Jubilees* and 1 Maccabees. Beyond that, we have echoes of the allegation that John Hyrcanus was son of a slave, the familiar metaphorical use of prostitution to describe idolatry, details of women and children facing captivity, probably also in 8:3, and use especially of mothering images to describe leadership.

1.4.3   Testament of Job

Job's alleged words to his sons and daughters, a work composed in Greek[351] probably around the turn of the millennia,[352] have little to say which directly concerns sexuality but much to say potentially pertaining to gender. The account of Job's rejection of idolatry and destruction of the idol's temple with which Job begins his speech (2:1 – 5:3) makes no links between idolatry and sexual wrongdoing. The work does, however, exhibit particular interest in women both within Job's family and in the wider community. One of the primary characteristics of Job's goodness is his many initiatives to care for the poor, among whom the author includes widows in particular (9:2, 5; 10:2; 13:4; 14:2; 16:3; 53:3). Care for the poor and destitute, expressed in a range of ways, is a constant theme in the depiction of Job's activities (9:2, 5-6; 10:1-7; 11:5, 9, 11; 12:1; 13:5; 15:5, 17:3; 25:5; 30:5; 32:2-3, 7; 44:2-4; 53:2-4),[353] described as "service" (διακονία 11:1, 2, 3; 15:1; διακονέω 12:1; 15:8), and features also in his exhortations (45:2).

Beyond these general references individual women play a significant role with the work, but opinion is divided about the author's attitude. Collins sees the author

---

[351] The translation is that of Russell P. Spittler, "Testament of Job," *OTP*, 1.829–68, but I have used the name Sitidos rather than Sitis, for Job's wife, following Pieter W. van der Horst, "Images of Women in the Testament of Job," in *Studies on the Testament of Job* (ed. Michael Knibb and Pieter W. van der Horst; SNTSMS 66; Cambridge: Cambridge University Press, 1989) 93-116, who prefers Sitidos as the *lectio difficilior* (96-97). For the Greek text I use: Ian W. Scott, ed. "'Testament of Job': Edition 1.0," in *The Online Critical Pseudepigrapha* (ed. Ken M. Penner, David M. Miller, and Ian W. Scott; Atlanta: SBL, 2006) no pages; online: http://www.purl.org/net/ocp/TJob.html.

[352] See the introduction in Nickelsburg, *Jewish Literature*, 315-22; Collins, *Between Athens and Jerusalem*, 240-48.

[353] Cf. Job 24:3-4, 9-10; 29:12-13; 31:16-22.

depicting women as lacking insight,[354] a situation only changed by Job's intervention for his daughters. "They are not evil"; they "are victims rather than agents of deception".[355] Van der Horst agrees. Of Sitidos he writes:

> Although Job's wife is presented as a more sympathetic personality than the kings, it is in the final analysis also true that, in spite of her good intentions, she does not have awareness of and insight into the invisible background of the things that happen. She has no spiritual intelligence and in spite of her virtues she errs repeatedly.[356]

Thus "she belongs to the category of the ignorant and the foolish whom Satan can easily get into his grip. This is an image of women that is well known to us from many other Jewish writings of the Hellenistic and Roman periods".[357] Van der Horst rejects, however, Collins' generalisation about all women lacking insight, including the daughters as only to be helped by Job's intervention, arguing that "Job's servant and his wife are enlightened only incidentally and momentarily", whereas the daughters "undergo a radical and lasting change; in fact they become virtually heavenly beings".[358] He concludes that "this essential difference makes it impossible, … to speak in a generalising way of women as symbols of ignorance in T. Job".[359] He speculates that the author may draw on a tradition for this depiction which had its origins in a setting where women would have had leadership roles.[360]

Susan Garrett, on the other hand, argues that while modern readers might view the women sympathetically, this would not have been the case in the ancient world where all would be seen negatively as "preoccupied with that which is earthly and corruptible".[361] "Job's wife, Sitidos, epitomizes the feminine preoccupation with the cycle of birth, life, death, and burial".[362] Thus "she errs, not 'in spite of her virtues,' as van der Horst contends, but *because of them*".[363] This has potential implications for the author's attitude also to sexuality. Even more strongly than van der Horst, she identifies the author's stance towards women as informed by the approach typified in Philo "who can speak positively about the

---

[354] Collins, *Between Athens and Jerusalem*, 244.

[355] Collins, *Between Athens and Jerusalem*, 244.

[356] Van der Horst, "Images of Women," (99).

[357] Van der Horst, "Images of Women," 100.

[358] Van der Horst, "Images of Women," 104.

[359] Van der Horst, "Images of Women," 106.

[360] Van der Horst, "Images of Women, 113-14. He even contemplates possible female authorship of the source which lies behind the depiction of the daughters (114).

[361] Susan R. Garrett, "The 'Weaker Sex' in the *Testament of Job*," *JBL* 112 (1993) 55-70, 57.

[362] Garrett, "Weaker Sex," 57.

[363] Garrett, "Weaker Sex," 57, referring to van der Horst, "Images of Women," 99.

women of the Therapeutae because they have abandoned interest in those aspects of their femaleness that would otherwise bind them to the corruptible realm: intercourse, conception, and the bearing of children".[364]

Kugler and Rohrbaugh argue that the work should be read within the framework of an honour–shame culture, within which the author depicts the women as failing because of their concern with earthly honour, Job's and their own, and that the daughters as Jews are shown to escape this by focussing on honour which comes alone from God.[365] They turn Garrett's observations about the degrading role of women away from using it to signal women as a theme of prominence and instead argue that the women serve the larger theme of how to cope with loss of honour which comes about through loss of wealth, and hardship. This is an issue which the author sees playing itself out in Egyptian Jewry of the time, which was suffering the effects of disadvantage through Roman imperial policy.[366]

The various readings also have implications for how the author might have understood sexuality and how potential hearers might have understood his work. I want therefore to review the relevant material sequentially in the light of these overarching constructions in order to test these perceptions within the specific context of each.

Job's opening address to his second set of children places heavy emphasis upon their being "a chosen and honoured race" through their mother, Dinah (1:5), and, to some degree, also through himself as a descendant of Esau, Jacob's brother (1:6). The demarcation from non-Jews then comes to expression in the destruction of the idol's temple, reminiscent of the story of Abraham in *Jubilees* (2:1 – 5:3; cf. *Jub.* 12:12-15). Significantly the temple is designated a "place of Satan" (3:6), who is to feature in the exchanges which follow. For his zeal and piety Job is warned he will face Satan's attacks (4:3), but promised that, if he is patient, he will be restored and will be resurrected, having defeated Satan in the contest and having won the crown (4:4-10). This matches the actual outcome: Job endures, bests Satan in the contest (27:2-5), has his wealth restored (44:1-2; 47:5-9), and looks to the prospect of the heavenly reward to which his soul then ascends (52:6-10).

---

[364] Garrett, "Weaker Sex," 58.

[365] Robert A. Kugler, and Richard L. Rohrbaugh, "On Women and Honor in the Testament of Job," *JSP* 14 (2004) 43-62, 49, 58-62.

[366] Kugler and Rohrbaugh, "On Women and Honor," 49, 53-56. The women of *T. Job* accordingly "revealed to Jews of early Roman-era Egypt the folly of clinging to acquired honor shattered by Roman policies and the wisdom of relying instead on the unassailable honor God ascribes to the faithful children of Israel" (62).

The door maid

The first of Satan's assaults come when as a beggar he knocks on Job's door (6:4-5). The door maid[367] at first follows Job's instructions to tell anyone one looking for him that he had no time to meet with them (6:1-2, 6). Satan returns as a yoked beggar wanting bread, to which on the maid's report, Job gives a burnt loaf of bread, indicating that he should not expect any bread from him (7:1-4). The author then indicates that the maid relented and gave the beggar a good loaf of her own (7:5-6). She does not know that it is Satan and thus shows compassion, although, as Kugler and Rohrbaugh point out, she does so according to the text "because she was ashamed". This need not be blameworthy in itself, as they infer, perhaps anachronistically.[368] They then agree with Satan's rebuke which follows in 7:8-9, in which he declares her an evil servant for not carrying out Job's instructions.[369]

Compassion for the needy receives major emphasis in the work, as we have seen, but in this instance it is inappropriate to act on it, both because it is exercised knowingly against Job's instruction and because unwittingly it helps Satan. Garrett also notes that the ancient hearer would look on this with disapproval,[370] and this is surely correct. By her act of disobedience, she writes, "Job's doormaid opened herself to Satan's attack"[371] but then continues: "No matter that she acted out of compassion and charity; she should have known that the devil is the craftiest of all creatures, using the cleverest of disguises and the smoothest of words", noting that ignorance was also no excuse in the case of Eve and the forbidden fruit and when lured from the river (*Adam and Eve* 6–11; *Apoc. Mos.* 29).[372] The passage should not be seen as impugning compassion itself, for instance as a gendered preoccupation with earthly concerns, which Garrett's overall analysis might suggest. Compassion for the needy is far too prominent in the work for us to dismiss its presence here or to see concern with honour as disqualifying its validity. Part of the dramatic effect of the story is precisely that it brings positive values, compassion for the beggar, honour, knowledge, and obedience into tension. The issue is how these are resolved. If they have not done so already, the hearers (certainly those hearing the work more than one time) would know to

---

[367] Spittler, *OTP*, 1, notes that there are six different words used to describe female slaves (835 n. 26).

[368] Kugler and Rohrbaugh, "On Women and Honor," 58. They take 7:11 as the door maid's words and as concerned with her own honour (59).

[369] Kugler and Rohrbaugh, "On Women and Honor," 59.

[370] Garrett, "Weaker Sex," 60.

[371] Garrett, "Weaker Sex," 60.

[372] Garrett, "Weaker Sex," 61.

value compassion and so view the door maid's virtue sympathetically.[373] She loses that sympathy in the way she resolves the tension: by neglecting what they would have seen as the primary obligation, obedience to the master. One can scarcely blame her failure to see Satan in the beggar, though that failure does represent a failed state of being of those who have not been enlightened, as much among men as among women, as we shall see. Her unwitting ignorance became combined with her disobedience in her failure to control the otherwise laudable response of compassion.

Sitidos

Similar issues arise with Sitidos, but major sections intervene (9:1 – 20:9) which are central to the story and the overriding concerns of the work. These emphasise Job's abundant and practical generosity (whose importance we have already noted in discussing compassion), his wealth, musical skills, and piety (9:1 – 15:9) and then, by contrast his losses of property (16:1-7), the killing of his children (17:1 – 19:4), and the plagues which heap distress on him (20:1-9). This then sets the scene for Job's account of his first wife, Sitidos. Her name may be connected to the word, σίτος, "bread", and reflect her role in seeking bread for her husband.[374] Within the family the work identifies Dinah, daughter of Jacob, as Job's second wife (1:8),[375] mother of the three daughters who feature in the final chapters,[376] but particular attention is given to Sitidos, his first wife.

We approach the account of Sitidos having just learned of the importance of compassion for the needy, Job's primary virtue beside his faith, but also of the reversal of fortunes for Job and his family. We then read that Job is appalled when he sees that his wife has been made a female slave and that she was serving in order to be able to provide food for him (21:1-2). After reporting his outburst at this situation (21:3), Job declares: "After this I regained my senses" (21:4). This might mean that he simply calmed down. It could mean that he saw the situation in

---

[373] So Randall D. Chesnutt, "Revelatory Experiences Attributed to Biblical Women in Early Jewish Literature," in *"Women Like This": New Perspectives on Jewish Women in the Greco-Roman World* (ed. Amy-Jill Levine; SBLEJL 1; Atlanta: Scholars, 1991) 107-25, 117.

[374] So van der Horst, "Images of Women," 97.

[375] For the tradition that Dinah was Job's wife see *LAB* 8:7-8; *Gen. Rab.* 57:4; 76:9; *Tg. Job* 2:9.

[376] Their names derive from Job 42:13-15 and are given according to the LXX. As van der Horst, "Images of Women," notes, the third, Amaltheias Keras, "means 'horn of Amaltheia', who was the goat that nurtured the infant Zeus on Crete and whose horn became a symbol of abundance (*cornucopia*)" (95).

a new light, so that it no longer appalled him. He could live with the shame of being provided for in this way.

There is no indication that he disapproves of her compassion towards him or sees it as weak and womanly. This is also true of his description of her sharing her bread with him and despairing, "Woe is me! Soon he will not even get enough bread!" (22:1-2), although the tone of despair does conflict with his stance of patient endurance (as in the contrast between Tobit and his despairing wife, Anna. Tob 2:11-14). Something is going wrong. The intratextual echoes with the door maid and her compassion might at least cause the hearers to wonder whether this compassion, too, is vulnerable to be misled. On the other hand, unlike with the door maid, there is no act of disobedience in her action. Job's report that she goes to the market to beg for bread (22:3) does not indicate disapproval or disparagement.[377]

This question becomes acute in what Kugler and Rohrbaugh rightly depict as an event bringing great shame on herself and on Job: allowing her hair to be shaved in public (23:7-9).[378] Such exposure, as Garrett notes, belonged to sexual disgrace.[379] Letting down one's hair was a sign of sexual immorality. The hearer thus recognises the extent of the shame which this brings both on herself and her husband, while realising that she has not committed sexual wrongdoing, such as might easily have happened had she strategised to earn money for bread by prostitution. Garrett observes that it was "a tragic and culpable move",[380] yet precisely because it was tragic and well intentioned its culpability is enmeshed in ambiguity which the hearer would surely appreciate. Satan's stealthily accompanying her and leading her astray (23:13) is the result.

The author then has Sitidos speak, bemoaning both Job's and her own plight, using the words of Job 2:8-9, and repeating their gist in her own words (24:1-10). She also rehearses what the author has already reported in Job's account and tells her own story. Importantly the author provides in this second account the clues as to the impact of her actions and to what went wrong. That includes the shamefulness of begging, not identified as such in Job's account but presupposed, but not as an act of wrongdoing. By contrast, in depicting the deal with the seller about her hair, she declares: "Being remiss, I said to him, 'Go ahead, cut my hair'"

---

[377] Cf. Kugler and Rohrbaugh, "On Women and Honor," who see Sitidos' actions as blameworthy rather than virtuous since they are concerned with upholding the honour which she sees as appropriate for Job (59).

[378] Kugler and Rohrbaugh, "On Women and Honor,": "Blinded to his identity by her passion for her husband's honor, she permits Satan to shear from her head her womanly source of honor, her hair, and this in the open market (22.3–23.11), the place of reputation" (59).

[379] Garrett, "Weaker Sex," 62.

[380] Garrett, "Weaker Sex," 63.

(κἀγὼ ἐκκακήσασα εἶπον αὐτῷ ᾿Αναστὰς κεῖρόν με) (24:10) including its consequence as shameful and inappropriate: "So he arose and cut my hair disgracefully in the market, while the crowd stood by and marvelled" (24:10). This was the point where she claims her actions went from what brought shame to what was also sinful. The level of shame receives further emphasis in the lament which follows, with its refrain, "Now she sells her hair for loaves!", in which her riches and generosity are five times set in contrast to her act of selling her hair for loaves (25:1-8). The effect is to emphasise how wretched she has become. It may by implication emphasise the guilt, which she acknowledges, though that is not explicit.

Her concluding words, advising Job to "speak some word against the Lord and die" (καὶ εἰπόν τι ῥῆμα κύριον καὶ τελεύτα), as in Job 2:9e LXX (ומת ברך אלהים), clearly must be understood negatively, however sympathetically the hearer might sense her plight.[381] Following the lead of the Septuagint, though in different words, the author supplements her call with reference to her own plight, both before it: "In the weakness of my heart, my bones are crushed" (ἐπὶ ἀσθενεία τῆς καρδίας μου συνετρίβη μου τὰ ὀστᾶ) and after it: "Then I too shall be freed from weariness that issues from the pain of your body" (καὶ ἐγὼ δὲ ἀπαλλαγήσομαι ἀκηδίας διὰ πόνου σου τοῦ σώματος). It was a counsel of despair and disbelief. The author thus has her couch it not only as concern for Job, but also as concern for herself. She is crushed and seeks relief from having to humiliate herself to keep him alive. As van der Horst notes, her explanation "emphasizes that even her call to speak a word against God arises from good intentions and from sheer despair about Job's misery".[382]

---

[381] See however Luzia Sutter Rehmann, "Das Testament Hiobs: Hiob, Dina und ihre Töchter," in *Kompendium Feministische Bibelauslegung* (ed. Luise Schottroff, Marie-Theres Wacker, Claudia Janssen, and Beate Wehn; Gütersloh: Gütersloher Verlagshaus, 1999) 465-73, who argues that Sitidos is encouraging Job to do something positive: take his case to God (468). This belongs to her very positive reconstruction of Sitidos, whom she argues, the author identifies as Dinah by name change. This fascinating thesis is difficult, however, to sustain, especially since the author appears to support Job's assessment of her plea and, not least, because it flies in the face of 1:7 which differentiates both wives. Otherwise I think she brings out Sitidos' positive traits more clearly than many others have done. She also points to the interesting parallel with the woman in 4 Ezra 9 – 10, including grief, humiliation, imagery of giving birth, and resurrection/transformation and imagery of a city (470).

[382] Van der Horst, "Images of Women," 98. Cf. Kugler and Rohrbaugh, "On Women and Honor," who write: "Notably Sitidos' advice to Job in 25.9-10 does not betray despair, but rather her enduring hope for herself. Her declamation exceeds her biblical admonition that he curse God and die (Job 2.9) with the words, καὶ ἐγὼ δὲ ἀπαλλαγήσομαι ἀκηδίας διὰ πόνου σου τοῦ σώματος ('again I will be free from the tiredness that comes from

Such despair is often replicated in human experience among those severely ill and their carers. It is in that sense understandable, but in view of the author inappropriate. Thus he has Job declare that her advice pains him more than all else (26:1-2). He acknowledges her suffering and his own (26:3), but confronts her with the fact that by cursing the Lord they would alienate themselves from true wealth and reminds her that former blessings are a basis for believing that eventually God will have pity (26:3b-5). As Job goes on to declare, Sitidos had espoused Satan's perspective, who had unsettled her reasoning, adding: "he seeks to make an exhibition of you as one of the senseless women who misguide their husbands' sincerity" (βούλεται γάρ σε δεῖξαι ὥσπερ μίαν τῶν ἀφρόνων γυναικῶν τῶν πλανησάντων τῶν ἑαυτῶν ἀνδρῶν τὴν ἁπλότητα), an adaptation of Job 2:10 ("you have spoken as one of the foolish women" ὥσπερ μία τῶν ἀφρόνων γυναικῶν ἐλάλησας). It reflects an assumption of blame on women for misleading their husbands, but allows that Sitidos need not follow this path. It is important to note here that this is not a statement about all women, but confronts Sitidos with Satan's success in making her look like some particular women, namely those who undermine their husband's integrity. The assumption is that Sitidos need not have fallen for this trap. She fell into it by failing to control her compassion. Job had controlled his by realising he could no longer respond to people coming to his door. Whereas the door maid's fault was allowing such compassion to override Job's instructions, Sitidos' fault is first to allow compassion to override what she admits was wrong (the selling of her hair) and then sliding into despair and disbelief. It is not evident that the author blames either of them for not recognising Satan and, as we shall see, such ignorance is not gender specific. Thus being like one of the foolish women is not to be equated with being woman.

In rejecting Sitidos' proposal Job is depicted as responding to her nevertheless with considerable empathy, further evidence that this would be part of what the author might also expect of his audience. He could have disowned her as an instrument of Satan. Instead he speaks as a caring husband, telling her of the effect of her words, recalling their common suffering, challenging her not to put their (not just his) future hope of true wealth in jeopardy, and urging a common response: "Rather let us be patient till the Lord, in pity, shows us mercy" (26:1-5). This stands in conflict with any reading which sees the author writing Sitidos off as a hopeless instance of wayward womanhood. Even the statement pointing out to her that Satan stands behind her is couched in the context of the possibility that this need not be so.

---

labors for your body'). This sentiment already reveals her turn toward preserving her own interests if Job cares nothing for his honor" (59).

The author continues by depicting an exchange between Job and Satan in which Satan, weeping, acknowledges Job's victory and leaves him for three years (27:1-7). Sitidos had become an agent of Satan by her action, but is not beyond the pale. She will reappear, but first the author reports the return of Satan, this time working not through women but through men. Satan launches his new assault through Job's former colleague kings. It is important to note that here we have males failing in insight, initially to recognise that this was indeed the once glorious Job, perhaps understandable, but then to reject his claims about a heavenly kingdom. As with the two women, so here, the author plays with the hearers' sympathy in depicting Baldad's concern that Job may be "emotionally disturbed" (35:4), though here the appeal is less sympathetic and more in the interests of dramatic irony. Thus the quasi-counselling session that follows confirms that Job has his wits about him, even in the face of Baldad's challenge about the trustworthiness of a God who inflicts such woes. Job then flatly rejects their next initiative to have physicians examine him. Within the drama the kings fail to believe and to see at least as much as does Sitidos, who is scolded by Job for not trusting God's eventual mercy. Their spokesperson will call God's goodness into question.

Near the end of this account Sitidos reappears in poverty (39:1). Job explains that she "arrived in tattered garments, fleeing from the servitude of the official she served, since he had forbidden her to leave lest the fellow kings see her and seize her" (39:1-2). That fear may have related to sexual abduction. She made her own way to the kings, casting herself before them in her wretched state and appealing to them to recognise who she is and the glory she had. Their response, since they had come to recognise that it really was Job who had now met them in poverty and distress, is great lamentation (39:3-6), and causes Eliphaz to wrap her in his purple robe (39:7), a subtle sign of recognising her royal dignity. That she had fled her servitude against her master's express command may cast her in a bad light, but, again, would also be heard with some sympathy, given Job's protestation about her plight. The author had recorded no response from her to Job's confrontation in 26:1-6, so that she re-enters the narrative as one who voiced Satan's will, but also as one still respected by Job, as we have seen. Her act of throwing herself at the feet of the kings asking that they remember her former station may be heard as another desperate act by someone who has lost much of their sympathy. Kugler and Rohrbaugh may be right that it exposes her as concerned about her own honor and shame again in a way that would not win approval.[383] Alternatively, or at least for others, concern for one's honour and shame would be very appropriate and serve primarily to underline how lowly and humiliated she had become.

---

[383] Kugler and Rohrbaugh, "On Women and Honor," 60.

Her attempt to solicit their assistance in recovering her children's remains for a memorial (39:8-10) reflects values highly cherished in the ancient world, and is unlikely to be dismissed as inappropriate preoccupation with mundane matters.[384] Her actions are ill-informed[385] and might be seen as blameworthy given Job's words to her about trusting God's mercy for a better future. Kugler and Rohrbaugh scold her concern with her own honour,[386] but this reflects *their* disapproval of such values, rather than attitudes of the world of the first hearers, who would surely see such concerns as appropriate. Indeed, Job does not rebuff her, but rather halts the diggers with the assertion that the children have been taken up into heaven (39:11-12). They, not Sitidos, respond by suggesting Job is mad (39:13).[387] He then asks to be lifted up, expresses a prayer of praise, and points them to the east where they can see his children "crowned with the splendour of the heavenly one" (40:1-3). When she saw them, Sitidos "fell to the ground worshipping and said, 'Now I know that I have a memorial with the Lord'" (40:4). This cannot be anything other than positive and would appear to rehabilitate Sitidos. It also depicts her children as receiving a heavenly reward. In this sense Sitidos finally sees heavenly things as will the daughters of Dinah, and Sitidos' children are as blessed in their future as those of Dinah.

The sequel is that she departs, returns to her servitude (perhaps also part of her rehabilitation), to working among the cows, lies down by a manger and dies in good spirits (καὶ τετελεύτηκεν εὐθυμήσασα) (40:6).[388] The great lamentation which greets her death both by the people of the city and the animals appears positive. Both Garrett and Kugler and Rohrbaugh, however, see the association with the animals as a negative reflection on her being.[389] It may, however, belong to the lowliness. Van der Horst comments: "kind she may be, she is dull, and it is

---

[384] Cf. Garrett, "Weaker Sex," who denies that the author sees any virtues in her actions: "Contra van der Horst, Sitidos's expressions of concern for her husband and for burying the dead would *not* have been seen as displays of virtue by the author and by ancient readers who shared the author's ideological construction of the female" (63); similarly 57, 65-66.

[385] So rightly van der Horst, "Images of Women," 99.

[386] Kugler and Rohrbaugh, "On Women and Honor," 60.

[387] Cf. Chesnutt, "Revelatory Experiences," who wrongly inculcates Sitidos (117).

[388] So MS P; MSS S and V read ἀθυμήσασα ("dispirited"). On internal grounds one would expect the positive, here. The negative may reflect interpretation of her image, followed also by some modern interpreters.

[389] Garrett, "Weaker Sex," writes: "She symbolizes for the author of the Testament of Job those who focus on the earthly and transient and so remain ignorant of the heavenly and eternal. At her own passing, she is mourned by animals – a symbol of the irrational" (66). This ignores the account of Sitidos' enlightenment, her worship, and also the blessed state of her children. Similarly Kugler and Rohrbaugh, "On Women and Honor," 60.

only fitting that it is the cows that are the first to bewail her death".[390] I do not read the note that the animals wept over her (40:11) along with "all who saw her", including her master (40:9), including "the poor of the city", far from a despised group in this document, as negative. The author has the city's poor mourn her death in procession: "Look! This is Sitidos, the woman of pride and splendour! She was not even considered worthy of a decent burial!" (40:13). She has died without seeing the end of misery (cf. already 1:6).[391] Unlike Job and in the book of Job she is not restored to blessing and abundance on earth. Given what happened to her children, the hearers might well have concluded that ultimately she would share their heavenly reward, but the author leaves that as a loose end. Given the revelation through Job (in some sense paralleling the sashes given to the daughters) and her response of worship, it would be seem very unlikely that the author means the hearers to see her humble end as divine rejection.

The characterisation of Sitidos is quite complex. She cares about the needy Job, an attitude towards the needy espoused by Job, himself. She cares about burial of the dead. She is prepared to sacrifice her own comfort to help meet his needs. By her own assessment her error was to allow herself to be shaved in public for the sake of bread. In itself it is hard for the modern reader to see why that was so bad, but in the world of the time it was associated with public shame, often sexual disgrace. It was almost as bad as had she performed an act of prostitution to pay for bread, though it is noteworthy that the author shows her doing no such thing and does not identify her sexuality as a point of vulnerability. This shameful act is only indirectly connected to her becoming the spokesperson for Satan, urging Job to curse God. In it, however, she crossed the boundary of despair into disbelief, instead of trusting in God's mercy and promise of heavenly wealth. The author does not appear to condemn her for wanting to help Job, but has her condemn herself for losing control, symbolised in loosing her hair to be cut. It is important to see that her final reappearance comes without any evidence of change, positively or negatively. She remains dutiful, this time towards her children, but in this instance by implication still failing to believe in hope beyond, until she is enlightened by Job. She does, then, see and believe and dies at peace, though without our hearing that a heavenly reward followed, as it had for her children.

Garrett detects a thoroughly negative assessment of womanhood in the image of Sitidos: "Sitodos' wifely and maternal passions bound her to the corruptible earthly realm and provided an easy avenue for access for Satan"[392] whereas she might have chosen the mastery of passions exhibited by the mother of the seven in

---

[390] Van der Horst, "Images of Women," 101.

[391] Kugler and Rohrbaugh, "On Women and Honor," argue that the final scene with Sitidos also shows her concerned with her own honour, as it had been (39:4), and as it will be if she does not bury her children (39:8b-10) (60).

[392] Garrett, "Weaker Sex," 63.

4 Maccabees.[393] It seems to me that while this is true, Garrett dismisses too quickly van der Horst's observation that there is nevertheless a certain sympathy present in the tragic portrait, indeed, it helps generate the sense of tragedy.[394] It is hard to deny a component of sympathy in Sitidos' story. Unlike in the story of the door maid there is no act of disobedience in her initial support for Job, but only compassion. It is hard to believe that the author would expect the hearer to be dismissive of Sitidos' endeavours to feed Job from the very beginning, as though this represented blameworthy behaviour or actions typical of women and to be despised on the assumption that the hearers knew that Job's future hope was already secured by divine promise in a heavenly world and her actions a waste of time and effort. While, like Garrett, van der Horst rightly notes that such an image of women is widely known in Jewish writings of the period "as creatures who can easily be misled and seduced (and themselves easily seduce)",[395] it is interesting that nowhere is Sitidos' story sexualised. There is nothing about her being seduced by Satan or of her sexuality being a cause even of her final desperate and wayward advice to Job.

Sitidos exercises the virtues of a good wife according to biblical standards. Her failure arises not from wilful disobedience in response to her compassion and perhaps her concern with her own shame, as with the door maid, but from her not knowing. For her ignorance about the identity of the seller, she can scarcely be blamed. The point where she crossed the boundary into despair was when she let loose her hair for sale, knowing this was wrong. It belongs to her tragic image, that in seeking to do what was virtuous she did what was culpable. The author connects the transgression into despair with its sequel: to counsel Job to despair and die, no longer to trust God. It is therefore unlikely that the author meant Sitidos to bear a gendered message about women as ignorant, since men, too, fail to see. Nor is the issue one of the appropriateness of compassion and wifely duties as the world of the time understood them, but unbelief and despair which causes people to lose their way and more generically allowing them to override all else. There is also no indication that women's sexuality is problematic.

---

[393] Garrett, "Weaker Sex," 64-65.

[394] Kugler and Rohrbaugh, "On Women and Honor," comment: "What Garrett misses is that this emphasis highlights the *true* essence of womanhood in the Greco-Roman imagination: she had to be *encouraged* to devotion, frugality, and self-restraint because it was in her *true nature* to be loyal above all to herself, overweening in her desire for possessions and profligate in her use of them, and sinister in her sexual, corporeal self-expression" (52).

[395] Van der Horst, "Images of Women," 100. See also Garrett, "Weaker Sex," who draws attention to the image of women in Philo (66-68).

Job's Final Instructions

After the account of Sitidos' burial the action continues with further exchanges
with the four kings, who are depicted as more hostile. The author depicts one of
their number, Elihu, as "inspired by Satan" in insulting Job. This puts him on a
level with Sitidos in her allegiance with Satan. God declares the sin of the other
three from on high and Job offers sacrifice for their forgiveness. One of them,
Eliphas, then condemns Elihu in a hymn, who then emerges as the worst sinner in
the book. The other three kings, like Sitidos, are rehabilitated.

The work portrays Job as finding hope in belief in the heavenly world, which
can also be described as the holy land. On this basis he addresses not only Sitidos'
concerns (39:11-13; 40:3), but also the questions of the kings. In response to the
lament over Job with its refrain, "Where then is the splendour of your throne?"
(32:1-12), Job asserts that his throne "is in the upper world ... in the holy land ...
in the world of the changeless one ... my kingdom is forever and ever, and its
splendour and majesty are in the chariots of the Father" (33:3-9). The focus on
"heavenly concerns" (36:3; 38:2) continues. Earlier he spoke of "the city" about
which an angel had spoken, presumably also in the heavenly world (18:8). The
location of hope not on earth but in heaven raises the question about how the
author might have understood human life in the heavenly world and what place
sexual relations might have had there, but this is not addressed.

The narrative moves quickly without detailed explanation to report that Job
and the kings re-entered the city and Job recommenced his good works for the
poor and instructed others to do similarly (44:1-5). Only later do we learn that
Job's restoration came when God had Job get up, gird his loins, and be ready to
respond (citing Job), but, instead of confronting him with overwhelming questions,
he gave him three sashes, which brought immediate relief, and revealed to him
"things present and things to come" (47:5-9).

Job's final words to his children in 45:1-3 express the same instructions as in
44:3-5, with the addition: "Do not take to yourselves wives from strangers" (μὴ
λάβετε ἐαυτοις γυναῖκας ἐκ τῶν ἀλλοτρίων) (45:3). This exhortation comes
somewhat as a surprise.[396] It is possible to view it as underlying the preceding
narrative just as much as does the exhortation to support the poor. Does it reflect
on Sitidos, implying that she was a Gentile? Kugler and Rohrbaugh, though not
citing the instruction about intermarriage, suggest that the Jew – non-Jew divide is
significant.[397] Only the daughters of Dinah, Jacob's daughters, truly see and can

---

[396] Collins, *Between Athens and Jerusalem*, notes that, despite the absence of reference
to circumcision or conversion or the Mosaic law as the basis of religion, "the prohibition of
intermarriage shows that the social reality of the Jewish community was important to the
author" (246).

[397] Kugler and Rohrbaugh, "On Women and Honor," 62.

resist Satan. We also noted the significance of that divide in the opening sections of the work. On the other hand, Sitidos does come to see in response to Job's revelation and her children are elevated to heaven. Similarly the daughters show themselves similarly fixed on earthly concerns and see only by Job's intervention, giving them magical sashes which change their hearts. Is the motif of their changed hearts sufficient to differentiate the quality of their change from the effect of the revelation which Sitidos received, as van der Horst insists,[398] and is this based on the demarcation between Jew and non-Jew, as Kugler and Rohrbaugh suggest? This may play a role, but the difference is not as stark as they suggest. If it does exist, then one would have to say that the author nevertheless appears to envisage that non-Jews can receive revelation, engage in worship, and find heavenly reward. In this sense Sitidos reminds us of the acceptance of the Gentile proselyte, Aseneth, in *Aseneth*. Nonetheless the warning against intermarriage to non-Jews may still reflect the view that such relationships are problematic, and certainly where no true conversion has taken place.

Job's Daughters

The final instruction includes matters of inheritance (45:4; 46:1-2), which become problematic and introduce the account of Job's daughters. In the closing verses of the Book of Job we read of the settlement and of the daughters: "In all the land there were no women so beautiful as Job's daughters; and their father gave them an inheritance along with their brothers" (καὶ οὐχ εὑρέθησαν κατὰ τὰς θυγατέρας Ιωβ βελτίους αὐτῶν ἐν τῇ ὑπ' οὐρανόν ἔδωκεν δὲ αὐταῖς ὁ πατὴρ κληρονομίαν ἐν τοῖς ἀδελφοῖς) (42:15). The author makes two major changes. He omits reference to their beauty. He also contradicts the second part by having Job exclude the daughters from inheritance: "He did not present any of the goods to the females" (46:2). This might bring the account into line with traditional expectations about inheritance with which the author was more comfortable, but it also provides the author as storyteller with the basis for depicting them as receiving a quite different inheritance, far superior to that of their brothers (46:1 – 50:3).

It is important to note that the author does not portray the daughters as particularly virtuous.[399] Rather they reflect the values of the kings: they want earthly goods (46:2), and even when they receive the greater inheritance, one of them, Kasia, complains that the sashes are of little use: "we cannot gain a living

---

[398] Van der Horst, "Images of Women," 104; similarly, Chesnutt, "Revelatory Experiences," 118-19.

[399] Cf. Chesnutt, "Revelatory Experiences," who claims of women in these chapters: "only in the latter are they depicted in a complimentary fashion" (115).

from them, can we?" (47:1). In that sense Collins is surely right that these women also lack insight, though he expresses it in a conflicted generalisation which implies the fault is gendered when he writes: "In the *Testament of Job*, womankind symbolizes, like the three kings, the human state of ignorance".[400] Job persuades the daughters that the sashes will function as protection against Satan, as an amulet (φυλακτήριον) (47:11). In addition we read that when each put on these sparkling shining sashes, their hearts were changed, they "no longer minded toward earthly things" (48:2; similarly 49:1; 50:2) and praised God in the dialect of angels (48:1 – 50:3).[401] These also make music as some come from above in gleaming chariots to take Job's soul (52:1-6).[402]

Van der Horst notes the striking image of these women as exercising spiritual leadership,[403] sees them as contrasted with the door maid and Sitidos, and as perhaps reflecting use by the author of a tradition originating in groups where women exercised prominent leadership. As Nickelsburg notes of their transformation, "This action ascribes a higher religious status to these women than to their male contemporaries".[404] The notion of women as prophets and as exercising spiritual leadership was not unknown in the ancient world, from the Sibyl to the daughters of Philip and also among the Therapeutae beside men.[405]

---

[400] Collins, *Between Athens and Jerusalem*, 244.

[401] Cf. Spittler, *OTP*, who sees *T. Job* 46 – 53 as later interpolations from Montanism (1.834). On the integrity of the work see the extensive analysis of Berndt Schaller, "Zur Komposition und Konzeption des Testaments Hiobs," in *Studies on the Testament of Job* (ed. Michael A. Knibb and Pieter W. van der Horst; SNTSMS 66; Cambridge: Cambridge University Press, 1989) 46-92, who explains inner inconsistencies as typical of such literature written for spiritual edification. See also van der Horst, "Images of Women," 108-109.

[402] This appears to be the author's understanding of resurrection from the dead to which he refers in 4:9 (cf. Job 42:17a LXX).

[403] Van der Horst, "Images of Women," appropriately draws attention to the role of Rebecca in *Jubilees* (115), to which one might add, women in general there.

[404] Nickelsburg, *Jewish Literature*, 320. He surmises that this may reflect the role of women in the author's religious community. Spittler, *OTP* 1.836, sees further indications of a positive attitude towards women in the fact that the *Testament of Job* apparently exonerates female slaves, compared to Job 31:31 LXX, by excluding them from being among the complainants. But cf. van der Horst, "Images of Women," who notes that this is neutralised in 14:4-5, which depicts female slaves murmuring in complaint (96).

[405] On the supposed connection with the Therapeutae of Philo, proposed by M. Philonenko, "Le Testament de Job et les Therapeutes," *Sema* 8 (1958) 41-53, see Spittler, *OTP*, 1.833-34, who notes that they allowed women a significant role, prayed towards the east (40:3; Philo, *Contempl.* 89), wrote hymns, favoured the number, 50 (cf. 10:7), and were also located in Egypt (cf. 28:7), but, unlike the Therapeutae, the *Testament of Job* assumes slavery (13:4; 14:4), and contains laments and glossalalic singing. See the critical

The image of women in leadership in this work is clearly positive and they reflect its consistent emphasis on the heavenly world as being the focus of spiritual people. The image of the daughters is not as rounded as Job's whose spirituality is shown as freeing him to be generous with earthly goods and to persevere through hardship and assault.[406]

Garrett reads the celebration of their heavenly focus as a negation of the earthly, in particular, things seen as preoccupations of the feminine. Thus she sees their turning from "earthly matters" as having less to do with issues such as wealth and property and more to do with "their corporeal nature and corresponding preoccupation with such matters as the conception and bearing of children, the nurturing of family, death, and burial".[407] This implies also their sexuality. She then makes this her hermeneutical construct for interpreting the door maid and Sitidos. So she sees the author implying that they were too concerned with female preoccupations, such as caring for Job. As we have noted above, however, the author does not call into question the validity of acts of practical caring. They are, after all, the hallmark of Job's spirituality. This must also include those activities which society of the time saw as particularly the roles of women or wives, including sexual relations.

There is no indication that the author calls into question women's sexuality or the normal processes of conception, birth, and marriage. We do not read that the daughters were virgins or remained celibate, for instance. The author's value system is probably reflected, however, in both changes made over against Job 42:15, namely excluding women from inheritance and deleting reference to their beauty. In replacing their inheritance with what he hails as a superior heavenly one and replacing the reference to their physical beauty (which would include sexual attractiveness) with a spiritual one, by implication he reinforces a stance which supports a patriarchal system on earth and downplays and probably devalues natural beauty and sexual attractiveness. To that extent I think Garrett is right that the work, including its final elevation of the three daughters, is not really good news for women – at least as many of us would see this today.[408]

---

discussion in van der Horst, "Images of Women," who concludes that the agreements and similarities are too slender (114-15).

[406] On the relation of heavenly wealth, care for the poor, and endurance, see the discussion in Patrick Gray, "Points and Lines: Thematic Parallelism in the Letter of James and the *Testament of Job*," *NTS* 50 (2004) 406-24, 419-20.

[407] Garrett, "Weaker Sex," 69.

[408] See also Rebecca Lesses, "The Daughters of Job," in *Searching the Scriptures: A Feminist Commentary* (ed. Elisabeth Schüssler Fiorenza; London: SCM, 1994) 139-49, who notes that the final section of the *Testament of Job* "describes only women as seeing visions and participating in the heavenly liturgy" and the testament itself depicts both women and

Conclusion

When we then return to consider the document as a whole in its treatment of women, some matters emerge more clearly in the light of detailed consideration of the text. It is not correct to depict the author as seeing all women as flawed by lack of knowledge, in particular, failure to recognise Satan or the heavenly realities, for this is equally true of the kings. Nor it is correct to characterise the author's view of women as one of faulting them for their passions and involvement in day to day caring or in sexual relations, conception, childbirth, marriage and family. What drives the door maid and Sitidos is not passion, but the kind of compassion which the author hails as an attribute of Job and has him espouse. Nor is it evident that the author faults either woman for her concern with honour and dishonour for herself or for Job. Nowhere is women's sexuality depicted as their flaw or a site of vulnerability, even though the author prefers to focus on their spiritual beauty than on their physical attractiveness. It is not even clear that the author attributes the failure of the first two to their being non-Jewish and the blessing of the daughters to their being Jewish, since Sitidos also receives revelation and her children find a place in heaven.

The door maid's sin was disobeying Job's instruction, which set necessary limits on his responses of compassion, which she should have followed. Failing to set limits to compassion in the light of one's ability to respond remains as much a problem today. A sense of shame in giving a beggar burnt bread was surely not inappropriate, but wrong came when in the light of it she chose to disobey. Her innocence of the beggar's identity is tragic but not her fault. Similarly Sitidos' sin is not shown to be her compassion, for which she would have deserved sympathy, but her doing what she knew was wrong in paying too high a price in her compassion by engaging in an act of shamelessness worthy of an adulteress. Her fault is not failure to recognise Satan, but falling into his power by doing what she admits she knew was wrong. At the same time her desperate action became despair based on disbelief, a disbelief she embodied not because she was female, since the kings exhibited the same disbelief, but because she forgot what were (divinely sanctioned) limits and like the Satan-inspired Elihu became Satan's mouthpiece. It is also not the case that she was abandoned, whether because of her gender, her race, or her failure. Rather she received grace through Job's initiative, giving her a heavenly vision of her children's bliss, enabling her to die in peace despite her wretched circumstances.

---

men as involved in heavenly life, sharing this with *Aseneth* and Philo's Therapeutae (147). See also Garrett, "Weaker Sex," 58.

The daughters were also not faultless or exempt from failure because of their race. Rather their father Job pre-empted their descent into the bitterness of receiving no inheritance by imparting magical sashes which compensated them with greater possessions, guaranteed them protection, and gave them a spiritual beauty which enabled the author to pass over their physical attractiveness. The difference between these and the other two women lies not in their virtue but in Job's ability to respond to their needs, and ultimately divine management of the resources of grace which we might see as problematic, but which the author embraces for purposes of his edificatory work.[409] This all belongs however within a document whose focus is not sexuality, nor women, but response to the plight of suffering.[410]

Sexuality as such plays a relatively minor role. Aside from the author's reworking of Job 42:15 which draws attention away from the daughters' attractiveness in favour of spiritual beauty, reflecting some devaluing of the natural, nothing else suggests the earthly engagement in sexual relations as part of marital partnership and producing children is unworthy or dishonourable. There may be reference to the danger of potential sexual abuse in 39:2. There are brief references to the processes of birth, expressed in a manner which sees them as normal. Thus Job speaks of the afflictions which await him using the familiar image of birth pains: "I was unable to utter a thing; for I was exhausted – as a woman numbed in her pelvic region by the magnitude of birth pangs" (17:4-5). Sitidos also refers to childbirth (24:2; 39:10). Finally Job's closing instructions to his sons include instruction about intermarriage (45:1-3). Marital partnership is a significant underlying theme, modelled by Job and Sitidos, and depicted as one of empathy despite the failures. Whether the heavenly hope which generates patient endurance also includes sexual engagement is not clear. Resurrection (4:9) appears to be understood as ascent of the soul (52:1-2, 7-12). Importantly, the focus on women and their tragic failures which they share with more blameworthy males at no point faults their sexuality or sees in it their vulnerability to Satan.

---

[409] Kugler and Rohrbaugh, "On Women and Honor," show them making a transition from concern with possessions and honour (46:2; 47:1) to affirming the honour given by God alone (61), but this occurs only through Job's initiative.

[410] This point is well made by Kugler and Rohrbaugh, "On Women and Honor," who speak of it "as a work about what stands at the forefront in its storytelling: the proper response to the sudden and wrenching loss of wealth and honor" (46). They focus in particular on "the decline of Jewish fortunes in Egypt" (49) in the second half of the first century C.E. as a likely setting. Their argument that the focus is loss of honour (53-56) seems to me, however, not sufficiently to take into account that, while this is true, more than honour was involved. There was actual suffering.

1.4.4   Testament of Abraham

The so-called *Testament of Abraham*, probably composed in Egypt in the first century C.E., [411] presents not Abraham's parting instruction as in a testament, but his reluctance to surrender his soul in death when summoned by the divine envoy Michael, a motif probably derived from Moses traditions.[412] It focuses especially on what Abraham saw of future judgement during his heavenly journey and reports this to promote greater tolerance and to depict the nature of judgement.[413] Material pertinent to issues of sexuality occurs only in the course of Michael's granting Abraham's request that he see the inhabited earth. In Recension A, which may better preserve the contents of the common ancestor it shares with Recension B,[414] Abraham sees the activities of humanity, grouped as contrasting pairs:[415] ploughing and leading wagons, pasturing flocks and dancing, sporting, playing music; wrestling and pleading at law, and, significantly for the narrative: weeping, bearing the dead, in contrast with newly weds. The last activity reads: "And he also saw newly weds being escorted in procession" (εἶδεν δὲ καὶ νεονύφους ὀψικευομένους) (10:3). These are all depicted as normal and appropriate activities.

The narrative then continues with depictions of three kinds of sin: murder, adultery, and theft, according to recension A, matching the sequence of the Decalogue in Exod 20:13, 14, 15 and Deut 5:17-19 (MT) and adultery, slander, and murder, according to recension B.[416] Of adultery it writes:

---

[411] See the overviews in Nickelsburg, *Jewish Literature*, 322-27; and Collins, *Apocalyptic Imagination*, 251-55; and the extensive treatment in Dale C. Allison, Jr *Testament of Abraham* (CEJL; Berlin: de Gruyter, 2003) 28-42; also Phillip B. Munoa III, *Four Powers in Heaven: The Interpretation of Daniel 7 in the Testament of Abraham* (JSPSup 28; Sheffield: Sheffield Academic Press, 1998) 16-17.

[412] So E. P. Sanders, "Testament of Abraham," *OTP*, 1.879; Nickelsburg, *Jewish Writings*, 326; see also Samuel E. Loewenstamm, "The Testament of Abraham and the Texts concerning the Death of Moses," in *Studies on the Testament of Abraham* (ed. George W. E. Nickelsburg; Missoula: Scholars, 1976) 219-25. See, however, the critical assessment of Davila, *Provenance*, who argues that a plausible case can be made for a Christian origin of the writing from a later period (199-207).

[413] So Sanders, *OTP*, 1.879.

[414] So Nickelsburg, *Jewish Writings*, 322. See the discussion in Allison, *Testament of Abraham*, 12-27

[415] See Allison, *Testament of Abraham*, 218-19.

[416] Cf. Exod 20:13-15 LXX: adultery, theft, murder; Deut 5:17-19 LXX: adultery, murder, theft.

8 καὶ εἶδεν εἰς ἕτερον τόπον ἄνδρα μετὰ γυναικος εἰς ἀλλήλους πορνεύοντας, 9 καὶ εἶπεν· Κύριε, κύριε, κέλευσον ὅπως χάνῃ ἡ γῆ καὶ καταπίῃ αὐτούς. καὶ εὐθὺς ἐδιχάσθη ἡ γῆ καὶ κατέπιεν αὐτους·

8 And he saw in another place a man with a woman, engaging in sexual immorality with each other, 9 and he said, "Lord, command that the earth open and swallow them up". And immediately the earth split in two and swallowed them up. (A 10:8-9)

2 καὶ κατανοήσασ 'Αβραὰμ ἐπὶ τὴν γῆν, εἶδεν ἄνθρωπον μοιχεύοντα γυναῖκα ὕπανδρον. 3 καὶ στραφεὶς λέγει 'Αβραὰμ πρὸς Μιχαήλ· Θεωρεῖς τὴν ἁμαρτίαν ταύτην; ἀλλα, κύριε, πέμψον πῦρ ἐξ οὐρανοῦ, ἵνα καταφάγῃ αὐτούς. 4 καὶ εὐθὺς κατῆλθεν πῦρ καὶ κατέγαγεν αὐτούς·

2 And when Abraham looked down upon the earth, he saw a man committing adultery with a married woman. 3 And Abraham turned and said to Michael, "Do you see this sin? But, lord, send fire from heaven that it may consume them". 4 And immediately fire came down from heaven and consumed them. (B 12:2-4)

The punishment of the earth swallowing them up recalls the judgement on the sons of Korah in Numbers 16, and that of being consumed by fire, Elijah's calling down fire in 2 Kgs 1:9-12.[417] Nothing more is made of the allusion beyond its inclusion as an instance of sin. The description, "a man with a woman, engaging in sexual immorality with each other" (A 10:8), need not be restricted to adultery, though the B recension makes it explicit as adultery.[418] While not in any way absolving such sinners, the author has God command Michael to stop Abraham's destructive zeal:

13 For if he were to see all those who pass their lives in sin, he would destroy everything that exists. 14 For behold, Abraham has not sinned and he has no mercy on sinners. But I made the world, and I do not want to destroy any one of them, but I delay the death of the sinner until he should convert and live. (A 10:13-14)

Indeed Abraham is to "repent over the souls of the sinners which he destroyed" (A 10:15).[419] Abraham's zeal recalls that other "friend of God", Phinehas (Num 25:6-8; cf. Ps 106:30-31; Gen 15:6; *Jub.* 19:9; 30:20). He will later change his ways and

---

[417] On the variations between the long and short recension both with regard to the order of what is seen and the applied punishments, see Allison, *Testament of Abraham*, 220.

[418] Allison, *Testament of Abraham*, draws attention to the parallel in *Apoc. Zeph.* 2:1-5 where the seer looks down to earth and sees a man and a woman on a bed (225).

[419] On the humour which the author employs in depicting Abraham's over-the-top zeal, see Jared W. Ludlow, *Abraham Meets Death: Narrative Humor in the Testament of Abraham* (JSPSup 41; Sheffield: Sheffield Academic Press, 2002) 132.

intercede for sinners (A 14:5) and acknowledge his destructive zeal as sin (A 14:10-12).[420]

Apart from the slight variation in what Abraham had asked as punishment, Recension B contains additional material in its account of judgement, which it depicts before rather than after Abraham's tour of the world. Here the narrative features the judgement of a woman who is accused of having murdered her daughter, against which she pleads innocence. The judge (identified later as Abel) then confronts her:

> O wretched soul, how can you say that you have not committed murder? Did you not, after your husband's death, go and commit adultery with your daughter's husband and kill her? (B10:13)

The focus here, too, is on adultery not as a particular theme, here including incest, but as an instance of sin. Allison argues that it is a secondary addition.[421]

It belongs within the overall universal emphasis of the writing (comparable to *2 Enoch* and *3 Baruch*)[422] that it makes no distinction between Jew and Gentile at the judgement (Israel features only in A13:6 where the twelve tribes exercise one of the three levels of judgement) and sees the basis of judgement as adherence to moral law and repentance or premature death, and not rites of atonement.[423] Accordingly such themes as intermarriage with Gentiles and disregard of purity laws pertaining to sexuality are absent. Hope beyond death appears to be a disembodied existence (with the exception of B 7:16) in an other-worldly paradise, but nothing enables us to discern the place of sexual relations in this realm.

---

[420] On the parallel engagement with Elijah's violent response in Luke 9:54-55, though independent and differently argued, see Jan Dochhorn, "Die Verschonung des samaritanischen Dorfes (Lk 9.54–55): Eine kritische Reflexion von Elia-Überlieferung im Lukasevangelium und eine frühjüdische Parallele im *Testament Abrahams*," *NTS* 53 (2007) 359-78.

[421] Allison, *Testament of Abraham*, 259-60.

[422] See Sanders *OTP*, 1.875-77.

[423] See Sanders *OTP*, 1.877-78; Allison, *Testament of Abraham*, 30.

1.4.5 Testament of Solomon

The *Testament of Solomon*[424] is widely considered to be a product of the third or fourth century C.E.,[425] so properly beyond our scope. It has, however, been recently argued that at least 18:1-42 belongs to the period before the middle of the first century C.E. and that chapters 1 – 15, with the exception of Christian additions, are probably also an originally independent work which stems from the period 75 – 125 C.E.[426] We will therefore limit our comments to these sections.

The work presents Solomon's report of encounters with demons in the context of the building of the temple and the way he bound them to his will and had them serve the construction. The first encounter is with the demon, Ornias, who had been robbing a boy of half his wages and provisions and sucking his right thumb (1:2, 4). The demon's explanation of his activity includes that he strangles those men of his star sign, Aquarius, who burn with passion for women belonging to the star sign of Virgo (the goddess of love) (τοὺς ἐν Ὑδροχόῳ κειμένους διὰ ἐπιθυμίαν τῶν γυναικῶν ἐπὶ τὴν Παρθένον ζῴδιον κεκληκότας ἀποπνίγω) (2:2), thus not a statement about sexual passion itself,[427] but about its direction,[428] and that he takes different shapes, including becoming as "a man who

---

[424] Unless otherwise indicated the translation is that of Dennis C. Duling, "Testament of Solomon," *OTP*, 1.935-87, and the Greek text that of David M. Miller and Ken M. Penner, ed. "'Testament of Solomon': Edition 1.0," in *The Online Critical Pseudepigrapha* (ed. Ken M. Penner, David M. Miller, and Ian W. Scott; Atlanta: SBL, 2006) no pages; online: http://www.purl.org/net/ocp/TSol.html.

[425] So, again, most recently Todd E. Klutz, *Rewriting the Testament of Solomon: Tradition, Conflict and Identity in a Late Antique Pseudepigraphon* (LSTS 53; London: T&T Clark, 2005) 34-35; Peter Busch, *Das Testament Salomos: Die älteste, christliche Dämonologie, kommentiert und in deutscher Erstübersetzung* (*Texte und Untersuchungen zur Geschichte der altchristlichen Literatur* 153; Berlin: Walter de Gruyter, 2006) 19-20. See also Sarah Schwarz, "Reconsidering the Testament of Solomon," *JSP* 16 (2007) 203-37, who argues that the work is most probably a rather late collection of traditions which circulated independently in late antiquity.

[426] So Klutz, *Rewriting the Testament of Solomon*, 95, 107-109. Of the latter he writes that unlike 18:1-42 it "identifies demons most closely not with physical illness but rather with sexual passion and unregulated desires of the flesh" (109; similarly 50). He sees Christian interpolations in 6:8; 12:3, and 15:10-11, including the addition of the Ephippas motif, and considers 19-26 and 16-17 Christian writing (108). See also Todd E. Klutz, "The Archer and the Cross: Chorographic Astrology and Literary Design in the *Testament of Solomon*," in *Magic in the Biblical World: From the Rod of Aaron to the Ring of Solomon* (ed. Todd E. Klutz; JSNTSup 245; London: T&T Clark, 2003) 219-44, 238.

[427] On the unparalleled lineage between Aquarius and Virgo here see Busch, *Testament Salomos*, 97-98.

[428] On this see Klutz, *Rewriting the Testament of Solomon*, 49.

craves the bodies of effeminate boys" (ὡς ἄνθρωπος ἔχων ἐπιθυμίαν εἴδους παιδίων θηλυκῶν ἀνήβων) (2:3), adding: "and when I touch them, they suffer great pain" (καὶ ἁπτομένου μου ἀλγῶσι πάνυ) (2:3). The word translated "touch" ἁπτομένου is also used to describe sexual relations (as 1 Cor 7:1; Prov 6:29) and should be understood in this way here, thus identifying pederastic rape. The allusion is probably to abuse of young effeminate boys. This is more likely than that θηλυκῶν means "feminine" here so that παιδίων θηλυκῶν would refer to young girls, though this is not impossible.[429] The claim of Ornias, that he "descended from an archangel of the power of God" (2:4) presupposes the myth of the Watchers, according to which angels produced offspring which gave rise to demons.

The second encounter is engineered through Ornias and is with Beelzeboul, who then responds to Solomon's question whether there were female demons (though in 1:7 Michael had already spoken to him of male and female demons), by introducing Onoskelis, a female demon of mixed form, a human woman with the legs of an ass (4:1-2). The allusion is to a myth involving anal intercourse with a donkey which gave rise to such a mixed form.[430] This emphasis reappears in the account of her actions: "Sometimes I strangle men; sometimes I pervert them from their true natures" (4:5), the latter probably including an allusion to bestiality and male same-sex relations.

The next demon summoned is Asmodeus, known to us from Tob 3:8. He, too, alludes to his "heavenly origin", reflecting the Watcher myth: "I was born of a human mother, I (am the son) on an angel" (5:3). Matching the role attributed to him in Tobit, he declares that his roles include "hatching plots against newly weds" (νεονύμφων ἐπίβουλός εἰμι) (5:7) and to "mar the beauty of virgins and cause their hearts to grow cold" (παρθένον κάλλος ἀφανίζω καὶ καρδίας ἀλλοιῶ) (5:7). Both relate to marriage. The former might include causing the death of husbands before they consummate their marriage as in Tobit (3:8, 16-17; 8:2-3),[431] though it might include much else not only relating to men. The second element has two aspects. Marring a virgin's beauty would also be a way of making marriage less attractive (cf. Tob 6:12). Causing their hearts "to grow cold" καρδίας ἀλλοιῶ may depict dampening of their sexual desire, but the Greek means literally "change their hearts" and is probably best read as indicating change of mind or disposition.[432] On the other hand, neither aspect (marring beauty or

---

[429] On the alternative possibilities see Duling, *OTP*, 1.963.

[430] On the legend of Onoskelis see Busch, *Testament Salomos*, 111. A certain Aristonymos of Ephesus uninclined towards women sodomised a donkey, which gave birth to Onoskelis, half human, half donkey.

[431] On this see Busch, *Testament Salomos*, 126-29.

[432] So Busch, *Testament Salomos*, 127, who points to its use in Dan 4:35 LXX.

changing disposition) should be read in contemporary western perspectives where romantic rather than arranged marriage prevails. The depiction reflects a valuing of virginity, which the demonic accordingly assaults.[433] Asked about further activity Asmodeus reports that he "spread madness about women through the stars" (Διὰ τῶν ἄστρων στρώνω θηλυμανίας) (cf. 4:5)[434] and that he has "often committed a rash of murders" (καὶ ἔπειτα εἰς τρικυμίας καὶ ἕως ἑπτὰ ἐφόνευσα) (5:8). These may be unrelated or might allude to crimes of passion committed by men because of their passion for women, a familiar motif. Alternatively "through the stars" may not indicate agency but location, in which case Asmodeus would be claiming responsibility for spreading among the stars the lust which originally led the Watchers to their deeds with women.[435]

The myth of the Watchers returns in Beelzeboul's explanation of his status: "I am the only one left of the heavenly angels" (6:1). This distinguishes him from the other demons, who are their descendants.[436] His roles include bringing destruction through tyrants, and promoting worship of demons (6:4), but also sexual wrongdoing: "I arouse desire in holy men and select priests" (καὶ τοὺς ἁγίους καὶ τους ἐκλεκτους ἱερεις εἰς ἐπιθυμίαν ἐγείρω) (6:4). Here "desire" most probably refers to sexual desire. The passage belongs in a tradition of such accusations against the priestly establishment, reflected already in Enoch literature, *Jubilees*, *Psalms of Solomon*, and early sectarian writings at Qumran. The words τοὺς ἁγίους "the holy ones" could refer to heavenly beings. The continuation, "I bring about jealousies and murders in a country, and instigate wars" might also reflect the effects of such activity, as in *1 Enoch*, though it could simply be a further role. MS P includes within the sins: "envy, murder, wars, sodomy, and other evil things", thus an allusion to particular male same-sex relations.

Solomon's next demon is Lix Tetrax, also claiming to be an offspring of a heavenly one (7:5), thus son of a Watcher. He declares as among his roles: "I make households non-functional" (οἴκους καταργῶ) (7:5). The focus here appears to be the bringing of fever not sexual wrongdoing. Then come seven demons. The seventh is "the Worst" and threatens to bind Solomon "with the

---

[433] Klutz, *Rewriting the Testament of Solomon*, 142-43.

[434] Busch, *Testament Salomos*, notes that Philo *Abr.* 135, uses the term in describing the men of Sodom (129).

[435] So Duling, *OTP*, 1.966.

[436] On this see Philip S. Alexander, "Contextualizing the Demonology of the Testament of Solomon," in *Die Dämonen: Die Dämonologie der israelitisch-jüdischen und frühchristlichen Literatur im Kontext ihrer Umwelt – Demons: The Demonology of Israelite–Jewish and Early Christian Literature in Context of their Environment* (ed. Armin Lange, Hermann Lichtenberger, and K.F. Diethard Römheld; Tübingen: Mohr Siebeck, 2003) 613-35, 630-31.

bonds of Artemis"[437] and speaks of his "desire" (8:11). This points to Solomon's own sexual wrongdoing which the final version of the work rehearses in 26:1-5. Sexual wrongdoing thus receives special prominence as the seventh of seven and as the cause of Solomon's fall from wisdom.[438]

Other demons presented include a headless murder demon, a demon in the form of a gigantic dog, a lion-shaped demon (this account interpolated with material reflecting the story of the Gerasene demoniac), a three headed dragon (similarly with Christian interpolations), and Obyzouth, a woman with dishevelled hair. She explains her task as strangling newborns at birth (13:3)[439] and divulges that a scrap of papyrus inscribed with her name is enough to send her away (13:6).

The Winged Dragon, a mixed human-dragon form, who explains: "I do not copulate with many women, but only a few who have beautiful bodies, who possess a name of Touxylou [or: of the wood][440] of this star. I rendezvous with them in the form of a winged dragon, copulating (with them) through their buttocks" (οὐ συγγίνομενος πολλαῖς γυναιξίν. ὀλίγαις δὲ καὶ εὐμόρφοις, αἵτινες τουξύλου τούτου τοῦ ἄστρου ὄνομα κατέχουσι, καὶ ἀπέρχομαι πρὸς αὐτας ὡσεὶ πνεῦμα πτεροειδες συγγινόμενον διὰ γλουτῶν) (14:3-4). Sexual intercourse through the buttocks might be thought to be vaginal rather than anal, on the ground that it produces offspring, and may then reflect disapproval of this manner of intercourse as demonic, but this need not be so.[441] The demon continues: "One woman I attacked is bearing (a child) and that which is born from her becomes Eros. Because it could not be tolerated by men, that woman perished" (καὶ ἡ μὲν βαστάζει ᾗ ἀφώρμησα καὶ τὸ γεννηθὲν ἐξ αὐτῆς Ἔρως γίνεται· ὑπ' ἀνδρῶν δὲ μὴ δυνηθὲν βασταχθῆναι ἀψόφησεν ἄρα καὶ ἡ γυνὴ ἐκείνη) (14:4). This not only confirms the aggression, so probably rape, but also makes Eros, representing sexual love, something problematic in itself and even has also the woman die. The account of the demon stands under the influence of the Eros myth, such as we find it expressed in the tale of Amor and Psyche in Apuleius *Metam.* 4:28 – 6:24.[442] There Amor is identified with a dragon (4.33.1-2; 5.17; 5.22.2) and as winged cupid (5.22.6). As here Amor seeks out particularly

---

[437] Busch, *Testament Salomos*, see the reference to bonds here as indicative that the seventh power in no way will let itself be bound (150).

[438] Busch, *Testament Salomos*, writes that because this failure is based in sexual desire, it likely reflects the hostility towards sexuality in the *Grundschrift* (150). See also Klutz, *Rewriting the Testament of Solomon*, 66-67.

[439] On the notion that demons attack babies at birth, especially Lilith, see Busch, *Testament Salomos*, 185-87.

[440] On the possibility that the text originally referred to Sagittarius, and so belonged closely with Aquarius in 2:1 see Klutz, *Rewriting the Testament of Solomon*, 44-45.

[441] Busch, *Testament Salomos*, interprets it as anal intercourse (196-97).

[442] On this see Busch, *Testament Salomos*, 193-200.

beautiful women (4:28:2), of whom Psyche is the prize example (6.22.1) and with whom he has forced sexual intercourse (5.4.2), the resultant child being Voluptas (=Eros). For the *Testament of Solomon*, therefore, Eros and therefore human sexual desire has demonic origins. Klutz sees reflected in 4:6 and 14:3-4 the notion that women are "a crack in the wall between the demonic realm and the ideal form of human being", but notes that the work contains nothing about women's impurity as danger.[443] He also notes that 14:1-4 and 2:1-7 both depict sexual predation, in both the demons possess wings, and both are associated with a god or goddess of love (Virgo and Eros).[444] Ornias and the Winged Dragon also form a triad of zodiacal allusions with Onoskelis, providing a framework for chapters 1 – 15, corresponding to Aquarius, Sagittarius, and Capricorn, each with an interest in sexual intercourse.[445] The next demon, Enepsigos, in the shape of a woman, probably reflects Hecate, the moon goddess, but here no sexual motif is apparent.

In 18:1-42 we appear to have an independent work consisting of a list of 36 demons classified according to the zodiac and mostly related to physical afflictions. The only one of possible relevance for issues of sexuality is the eighteenth, who declares: "I am called Modebel. I separate wife from husband" (Ἐγὼ Μοδεβήλ καλοῦμαι. γυναῖκα ἀπὸ ἀνδρὸς χωρίζω) (18:22). This probably refers to breakdown of marriage, namely divorce, but might simply refer to separation through distance or death.

In these two earlier sources of the *Testament of Solomon* the emphasis varies. In 18:1-42 there is at most an indirect reference to issues pertaining to sexuality in the allusion to wives being separated from their husbands. By contrast, in chapters 1 – 15 we find that sexual wrongdoing belongs firmly within the repertoire of the demonic, which also includes other forms of violence, and that sexual desire, itself, is called into question. As Klutz observes, "Erotic desire is repeatedly put in a negative light by association with the demons".[446] While Ornias' murderous behaviour towards men in Aquarius desiring women in Virgo has more to do with demarcation issues than sexual desire itself, he nevertheless engages in sexual violation with pain of the young, probably effeminate boys, thus pederastic rape. Onoskelis traces her origin to bestiality and delights in perversion, probably both bestiality and male same-sex relations. The Winged Dragon rapes attractive women by anal intercourse and thus brought Eros into the world.

These acts of sexual violence are demonic, but the author broadens the scope. Asmodeus undermines marriage by undermining both the beauty and the minds of virgins and either in the stars or through the stars spreads mad desire for women. Beelzeboul leads priests and holy men astray through such sexual desire

---

[443] Klutz, *Rewriting the Testament of Solomon*, 142.

[444] Klutz, *Rewriting the Testament of Solomon*, 46.

[445] Klutz, *Rewriting the Testament of Solomon*, 46-47.

[446] Klutz, *Rewriting the Testament of Solomon*, 56.

(according to one manuscript also into sodomy among other things) and the seventh demon, notably the Worst, threatens he will use sexual desire to bring Solomon's fall. Since the Winged Dragon's predation produced Eros, then sexual desire, itself, is called into question. The two references to marriage assume a place for sexual relations, perhaps even for having passion for women within the appropriate zodiacal zone, and the reference to marring virgins implies a valuing of virgins in relation to marriage, but the overwhelming emphasis is on sexual desire as dangerous and demonic. If as Klutz suggests the focus of the zodiac in chapters 1 – 15 is chorological, that is, related to geographical territories and their peoples,[447] then we might see here a reference also to prohibition of intermarriage across such boundaries. This might connect also to the depiction of Beelzeboul's activity of leading holy ones and elect priests astray.

The myth of the Watchers informs chapters 1 – 15 at a number of points.[448] A number of demons claim their descent from the Watchers (Ornias, 2:4; Asmodeus, 5:3; Lix Tetrax, 7:5) and Beelzeboul claims to be the only survivor of the angels who descended (6:1).[449] Asmodeus may claim to be still seeking to excite the stars with mad lust for women, though this is uncertain, and Beelzeboul may be engaged in leading not only priests but also heavenly ones, but this too is uncertain. On the other hand, it is interesting that we do not find the demons' actions depicted as specifically emulating the Watchers. For the testament, nevertheless, sexual wrongdoing is one of the major manifestations of the demonic, features in all key figures including the triad of the zodiac, and arises from sexual desire, itself a primary danger and in that sense at least half demonic.

---

[447] Klutz, *Rewriting the Testament of Solomon*, 47-50; Klutz, "Archer," 239-42.

[448] See also Alexander, "Contextualizing," 628-29. He notes that the demons are offspring of angels but not themselves angels and so can be male or female and can procreate (630).

[449] Noted also by Alexander, "Contextualizing," 630-31.

PART TWO

Attitudes towards Sexuality in Histories, Legends, and Related Writings

2.1 Septuagintal Literature

2.1.1 "The Tale of the Three Youths" (1 Esdras 3:1 – 5:6)

According to Zipora Talshir the work known as 1 Esdras represents a rearrangement and rewriting of parts of Chronicles, Ezra and Nehemiah, in which the "Tale of the Three Youths" (3:1 – 5:6) forms an essential element in the author's attempt to depict the restoration as the work of Ezra and Zerubbabel, rather than Ezra and Nehemiah.[1] Our concern is not the duplication thus generated and the impossible sequence of events[2] in what will have been a composition in

---

[1] Zipora Talshir (with David Talshir), *1 Esdras: From Origin to Translation* (SBLSCS 47; Atlanta: SBL, 1999) 1-109, 46-47, 54-57, 108-109. "1 Esd was created in order to interpolate the Story of the Youths into the story of the restoration" (58; similarly 106). "The section is the peak of this Hellenistic-Jewish account of how a Jewish youth, the king's bodyguard, successfully secured an advantage for his people, thus joining the ranks of various figures in the Books of Nehemiah, Esther, Daniel, Judith, 2 Macc, etc." (79). Similarly also Kristin De Troyer, "Zerubbabel and Ezra: A Revived and Revised Solomon and Josiah? A Survey of Current 1 Esdras Research," *CurBR* 1 (2002) 30-60, 52; Ulrike Mittmann-Richert, *Einführung zu den Jüdischen Schriften aus hellenistisch-römischer Zeit: Historische und legendarische Erzählungen* (JSHRZ 6.1.1; Gütersloh: Gütersloher Verlagshaus, 2000) 12.

[2] On this see Talshir, *1 Esdras* (1999), 42-43. See also her discussion of theories that the original speeches may have been in the sequence: king, wine, women (67-68, 80),

Aramaic sometime in the second century B.C.E.[3] and now preserved in Greek,[4] but what the work reveals of attitudes towards sexuality. For this the "Tale of the Three Youths" is of particular significance inasmuch as the contest among Darius' bodyguards about what is most powerful touches on sexual themes. In this playful story, which may well be recycling an originally non-Jewish tale,[5] the three mount arguments for wine, kings, and women, before the third, alone identified, as Zerubbabel, adds a final and superior option, truth, and so wins Darius' support to return as a Jewish hero with authority and resources to rebuild the temple. Other material in 1 Esdras related to sexuality is based on Ezra (8:68-90; 9:5-36; cf. Ezra 9:1-15; 10:9-44) and will not receive further comment here.

The case for wine's superior power (3:18-24) is made without the common link between wine and seduction (cf. "Wine and women lead intelligent men astray" Sir 19:12), though hearers might well have heard this as implied in its power to lead minds astray and to turn every thought to feasting and mirth. This is not, however, said. The case for the king as superior (4:1-12) is also devoid of sexual allusions, surprisingly, since the third speech alludes to his sexual behaviour.

The third speech, hailing women's power (4:13-32), is more extensive. The case for women's superior influence in contrast to kings and wine includes that they give birth to men, therefore also to kings (4:15), and bring up the men who make wine (4:16). The argument is reiterated in the words, "from women they came" (ἐξ αὐτῶν ἐγένοντο; cf. 1 Cor 11:12), and expanded with reference to their making men's clothes, bringing them glory, and being essential to their existence (probably in the sense of livelihood) (4:17). None of this relates directly to sexuality but rather to traditional expectations of the role of women in the patriarchal household.

---

concluding that there is insufficient proof. See also the review of research in De Troyer, "Zerubbabel and Ezra". She concludes that the insertion of the tale occurred at the time of the reorganisation of the material and before it was translated into Greek (52), but is to be seen not really as an insertion but as a rewriting of the whole story. "Zerubbabel revives King Solomon. Zerubbabel resembles King Solomon" (55). See also Kristin De Troyer, *Rewriting the Sacred Text: What the Old Greek Texts Tell Us About the Literary Growth of the Bible* (SBLTCS 4; Leiden: Brill, 2003) 120.

[3] On this see Talshir, *1 Esdras* (1999), 81-105.

[4] I have used the Greek of Robert Hanhart, ed., *Esdrae liber I* (SVTG 8.1; Göttingen: Vandenhoeck & Ruprecht, 1974). I have used the *NRSV* translation.

[5] So Harrington, *Apocrypha*, 153-54; Nickelsburg, *Jewish Literature*, 29; but cf. Mittmann-Richert, *Einführung*, who argues plausibly that the story may well be developed on the basis of similar stories in Daniel (12), while acknowledging the possible influence from popular folktales about speech competitions (13).

This changes however in 4:18-19, where the author turns to beautiful women in response to whom men give up gold and silver and things of beauty, gape at them and with open mouths[6] stare at them (18 ἐὰν δὲ συναγάγωσιν χρυσίον καὶ ἀργύριον καὶ πᾶν πρᾶγμα ὡραῖον καὶ ἴδωσιν γυναῖκα μίαν καλὴν τῷ εἴδει καὶ τῷ κάλλει 19 καὶ ταῦτα πάντα ἀφέντες εἰς αὐτὴν ἐγκέχηναν καὶ χάσκοντες τὸ στόμα θεωροῦσιν αὐτήν).[7] This is scornful and humorous,[8] but not an indication of disapproval of sexual attraction nor of response to it, provided it is not inappropriate and excessive. On the contrary, the argument continues in 4:20 with a loose allusion to Gen 2:24, expressed in terms of a man who leaves his own father who brought him up, and his own country, and clings to his wife (ἄνθρωπος τὸν ἑαυτοῦ πατέρα ἐγκαταλείπει ὃς ἐξέθρεψεν αὐτόν καὶ τὴν ἰδίαν χώραν καὶ πρὸς τὴν ἰδίαν γυναῖκα κολλᾶται). This also assumes a positive evaluation of response to sexual attraction and its consummation in marriage. The orientation is evident also in the statement that "with his wife he ends his days, with no thought of his father or his mother or his country" (NRSV) (καὶ μετὰ τῆς γυναικὸς ἀφίησι τὴν ψυχὴν καὶ οὔτε τὸν πατέρα μέμνηται οὔτε τὴν μητέρα οὔτε τὴν χώραν) (4:21), a further elucidation of Gen 2:24. Here is lifelong marital partnership (cf. Ps.-Phoc. 195-197).

On the other hand, the translation of leaving father and mother in Gen 2:24 into "with no thought of his father or his mother" (οὔτε τὸν πατέρα μέμνηται οὔτε τὴν μητέρα) twists the original into something negative, contrary to the Genesis text, and brings it into conflict with values about honouring parents. Similarly, there is a negative tone in the additional idea that a man abandons and gives no thought to his country. These playful assertions which focus on excess serve the conclusion, "Therefore you must realize that women rule over you!" (4:22). This is "boys' humour" which contains two demeaning aspects: women, in particular for their sexuality, are dangerous;[9] and men cannot help themselves, a

---

[6] On the likely Aramaic behind ἐγκέχηναν καὶ χάσκοντες τὸ στόμα see Zipora Talshir (with David Talshir), 1 Esdras: A Text Critical Commentary (SBLSCS 50; Atlanta: SBL, 2001) 194.

[7] For theories that the Jewish author who added Zerubbabel also added the Genesis allusions to what was originally about beautiful women, see Talshir, 1 Esdras (1999), 69-70.

[8] So James L. Crenshaw, "The Contest of Darius' Guards," in Images of Man and God: Old Testament Stories in Literary Focus (ed. Burke O. Long; Sheffield: Almond, 1980) 74–88, 119–20, who writes: "The image of a man carrying in his hand his most precious possessions and dropping them to gaze open-mouthed at a beautiful woman, both funny and profound (4:18-19), witness to man's ultimate priorities" (81).

[9] As Lewis John Eron, "'That Women Have Mastery Over Both King and Beggar,'(TJud. 15.5) – The Relationship of the Fear of Sexuality to the Status of Women in

tacit espousal of sexual irresponsibility. In this sense Talshir is right in claiming that the author "presents a very low opinion of women",[10] especially if it implies that women are to be blamed for men's responses. She also notes: "In actual fact, the entire argument is directed against men, who behave as they do when women are involved, and not against women themselves".[11] The speech really does assume that men bear responsibility. Its attack on men's irresponsibility and foolishness in response to sexual attraction also does not, of itself, call sexual attraction and response to it into question. Nevertheless, it probably assumes that women's sexuality is so out of control and dangerous that men must be especially careful to control their responses (and by implication to control women's sexuality).[12]

The power of women, according to the speech, lies not just in their sexual attraction. Zerubbabel had intimated that already in his opening statements. Their sexuality also belongs to who they are as persons in what is depicted as a loving lifelong relationship. Thus in 4:22 he depicts the husband working and bringing everything to give to his wife, reflecting her role as household manager, and continues with playful hyperbole in depicting the husband travelling abroad with his sword to rob, steal, sailing sea and rivers, facing lions, walking in darkness, to gather plunder to bring it back "to the woman he loves" (τῇ ἐρωμένῃ) (4:23-24). This may be any lover, but given the context of Gen 2:24, it more likely refers to the wife. While the rhetoric is designed to win the argument about women's superior power by describing men's excessive behaviour,[13] it nevertheless embodies the valuing not only of the marriage and household, but also of romantic love both before and during marriage. Thus the author then returns to Gen 2:24, which he summarises as affirming such love: "A man loves his wife more than his father or his mother" (καὶ πλεῖον ἀγαπᾷ ἄνθρωπος τὴν ἰδίαν γυναῖκα μᾶλλον ἢ τὸν πατέρα καὶ τὴν μητέρα) (4:25). Perhaps the author disapproves of these priorities, but that is not clear.

The author turns again to the argument from excess when he reports that "many men have lost their minds because of women, and have become slaves

---

Apocrypha and Pseudepigrapha: 1 Esdras (*3 Ezra*) 3-4, Ben Sira and *the Testament of Judah*," *JSP* 9 (1991) 43-66, observes, "The threat which women pose to men through their sexuality lies just below the surface" (48).

[10] Talshir, *1 Esdras* (2001), 188.

[11] Talshir, *1 Esdras* (2001), 189. I do not find the statement in 4:37 about all being unrighteous as a "vindictive summary" (189).

[12] As Eron, "Women Have Mastery," notes, "the normal order is that men have authority over women" (47).

[13] So Talshir, *1 Esdras* (2001), who speaks of the "man's deplorable behaviour when it comes to women" (201). She then sees the return to Gen 2:24 as "quite out of place" (201).

because of them. Many have perished, or stumbled, or sinned because of women" (καὶ πολλοὶ ἀπώλοντο καὶ ἐσφάλησαν καὶ ἡμάρτοσαν διὰ τὰς γυναῖκας) (4:26-27; cf. *T. Jud.* 15:5-6). The same issues arise as to who shoulders the blame. Probably some blame lies in the author's assumptions about the nature of women's sexuality, but, as noted above, the mockery is directed not towards women but towards men. Again the attack is not on sexual desire but on sexual desire misdirected, and is done with humour.

The speech concludes with a daring allusion to the king and the liberties he allows his concubine, Apame,[14] to sit at his right hand, put on his crown, and slap him with her left hand (4:29-30). In an echo of the speech's beginning, thus bringing the king down to the level of other men also with a touch of humour,[15] the author then reports the king as gazing at her with mouth agape, responding to her smile with laughter or her temper with flattery (καὶ πρὸς τούτοις ὁ βασιλεὺς χάσκων τὸ στόμα ἐθεώρει αὐτήν καὶ ἐὰν προσγελάσῃ αὐτῷ γελᾷ ἐὰν δὲ πικρανθῇ ἐπ' αὐτόν κολακεύει αὐτήν) (4:31). Here, too, there is no note of disapproval of the king's having a concubine nor of the sexual element in that relationship, but a rather confronting exposé of the extent to which such sexual attraction produces tolerance in the king of what would otherwise be seen as disrespectful and outrageous behaviour. The argument is, itself, cleverly seductive, since if the king takes offence, he would be acknowledging his behaviour as inappropriate and so ceding the argument. But, then, in seeing his own behaviour as appropriate, he would nevertheless have to allow that he has chosen to grant such liberties in the light of his valuing of that kind of sexual relationship.

The report of the narrator that "the king and the nobles looked at one another" (4:33) indicates shock at so direct an illustration,[16] but this soon gives way to Zerubbabel's second claim, namely that truth is superior to all three (4:34-40).[17] By contrast, "wine is unrighteous, the king is unrighteous, women are unrighteous,

---

[14] On attempts to identify her with an historical figure see Talshir, *1 Esdras* (2001), who notes that the names do not "match any historically known figures" (204).

[15] So Crenshaw, "Contest," 81.

[16] So George W. E. Nickelsburg, "The Bible Rewritten and Expanded," in *Jewish Writings of the Second Temple Period: Apocrypha, Pseudepigrapha, Qumran Sectarian Writings, Philo, Josephus* (ed. Michael E. Stone; CRINT 2; Philadelphia: Fortress, 1984) 89-156, 132.

[17] For the possibility that Jewish tradition of lay wisdom has influenced the account see Crenshaw, "Contest," 77. He also notes the possible influence of Jewish wisdom traditions concerning wine and the king (78-79). Thus on women as a man's most prized possession, more than gold, he cites Prov 31:10-31; Sir 7:19; 26:1-4, 16-18; 36:22-25, and on concern with mastery by a woman, Sir 9:1-9 (79). "The step from such material to that characterizing the dialogue under consideration is a tiny one" (79).

all human beings are unrighteous, all their works are unrighteous, and all such things" (4:37; cf. Eccl 7:20; Rom 3:10).

The distinctive addition which marks 1 Esdras out from its sources, the "Tale of the Three Youths", is now a Jewish story hailing Zerubbabel's wisdom, but incidentally affirming women in their traditional role of mothers and wives as household managers, and affirming sexuality and marriage. As Eron notes, "the purpose of the story is to entertain and not instruct".[18] In the speech about women, therefore, we can at most identify embedded values about sexuality. These appear to assume sexual response as something to be valued in itself, including even in a king's relation to a concubine. Part of that positive valuing is reflected in the use of Gen 2:24 both to depict consummation of sexual love in a lasting relationship and to describe ongoing love and support which supplants loyalty to parents and land. The negative aspects relate in part to seeing women's sexual attractiveness as potentially dangerous, but primarily to men's inappropriate and excessive responses to women's sexuality; in other words, failure to control themselves, and, probably by implication, also failure to control women and especially their sexuality. Sexual passion can drive men crazy over women, but the author clearly assumes that in their responses to women this need not be so.

2.1.2   Tobit

The Book of Tobit, composed in Aramaic[19] probably in the early second century B.C.E.,[20] either in the eastern diaspora[21] or in Palestine,[22] bears traits of a

---

[18] Eron, "Women Have Mastery," 48.

[19] So Matthew Morgenstern, "Language and Literature in the Second Temple Period," *JJS* 48 (1997) 139-40; Joseph A. Fitzmyer, *Tobit* (CEJL; Berlin: de Gruyter, 2003) 22-27, who argues against suggestions that the original may have been in Hebrew; similarly Beate Ego, "Das Buch Tobit," in *Einführung zu den Jüdischen Schriften aus hellenistisch-römischer Zeit: Unterweisung in erzählender Form* (ed. Gerbern S. Oegema, JSHRZ 6.1.2; Gütersloh, Gütersloher Verlagshaus, 2005) 115-50, 125-27; similarly Robert J. Littman, *Tobit: The Book of* Tobit *in Codex Sinaiticus* (SCS; Leiden: Brill, 2008) xxvi-xxvii.

[20] See the discussion in Fitzmyer, *Tobit*, 51-52; Ego, "Tobit," 130-31.

[21] This is the most commonly assumed location. See the review in Benedikt Otzen, *Tobit and Judith* (GAP; London: Continuum, 2002) 58-59; Ego, "Tobit," 134-35.

[22] Fitzmyer, *Tobit*, 52-54. John J. Collins, "The Judaism of the Book of Tobit," in *The Book of Tobit: Text, Tradition, Theology: Papers of the First International Conference on the Deuterocanonical Books, Pápa, Hungary, 20-21 May, 2004* (ed. Géza G. Xeravits and József Zsengellér; JSJSup 98; Leiden: Brill, 2005) 23-40, notes Tobit's interest in the tribe of Naphtali and the lack of interaction with Gentiles as counting against a diaspora setting (39).

folktale,[23] but is much more than that. Fragments survive at Qumran in Hebrew and one in Aramaic and these are closer to the Greek version preserved in Sinaiticus, designated GII (the text followed in this discussion), compared with the shorter version, GI, in addition to which a later GIII version exists.[24] The author wants us to believe Tobit's words that "everything that was spoken by the prophets of Israel, whom God sent, will occur" (14:4) and that "those who commit sin and injustice will vanish from all the earth" (14:7). The focus is particularly upon prophetic predictions that the exile will end, that all faithful Israelites "will be gathered together; they will go to Jerusalem and live in safety forever in the land of Abraham, and it will be given over to them" (14:7).

Collins rightly notes that it is not accurate to describe Tobit's and Sarah's plight as typical of suffering in the exile.[25] Sparrows' droppings (2:10) and demonic interference (3:8) can happen anywhere. Even the distress and danger depicted in Tobit's struggle to care for fellow Jews need not necessarily depict conditions of the exile, since Antiochus Epiphanes brought such oppression to Jerusalem, including banning burials of slain Jews (2 Macc 9:15).[26] The stories of Tobit and Sarah seem depicted less as instances of living in the diaspora and more

---

[23] See Carey A. Moore, *Tobit* (AB 40A; New York: Doubleday, 1996) 11-14, 197-98, for discussion of the folktale elements woven into the story and the loose threads such as Tobias' dog (6:1; 11:4). Expressing the alternative versions of the nature of the work as a necklace, collecting various elements, or a tapestry, weaving diverse elements together, he convincingly argues for the latter (17-21). Littman, *Tobit*, however, notes that dogs have high moral standing in Zoroastrianism (107). On folkloric background see also the more extensive review in Otzen, *Tobit and Judith*, who posits three stages: pagan fairytale, Jewish fairy tale, and finally Jewish Tobit Legend (8-20), based on biblical and nonbiblical Jewish sources and the Ahikar legend: pp. 21-26. Cf. Fitzmyer, *Tobit*, who concludes that "these ancient tales provide interesting parallels, but I find it difficult to conclude that the author of the Book of Tobit was deliberately imitating them or using them as a source, since there is practically no evidence that the tales predate the Tobit story" (41). See also Dennis Ronald MacDonald, "Tobit and the *Odyssey*," in *Mimesis and Intertextuality in Antiquity and Christianity* (ed. Dennis Ronald MacDonald; Studies in Antiquity and Christianity; Harrisburg: Trinity, 2001) 11-40 and in the same volume the discussion by George W. E. Nickelsburg, "Tobit, Genesis and the *Odyssey*: A Complex Web of Intertextuality," 41-55.

[24] In this discussion I have followed the GII text as recently set out in Christian J. Wagner, *Polyglotte Tobit-Synopse: Griechisch – Lateinisch – Syrisch – Hebräisch – Aramaisch* (Abhandlungen der Akademie der Wissenschaften in Göttingen; Philologisch-Historische Klasse Dritte Folge, Band 258; Göttingen: Vandenhoeck & Ruprecht, 2003), and the *NRSV* translation, unless otherwise indicated. On the textual tradition see also Littman, *Tobit*, xv-xvi, xix-xxv. See also Robert Hanhart, ed., *Tobit* (SVTG 8.5; Göttingen: Vandenhoeck & Ruprecht, 1983).

[25] Collins, "The Judaism of the Book of Tobit," 26-29.

[26] On this see Frank Zimmermann, *The Book of Tobit* (JAL; New York: Harper, 1958) 24.

as instances of facing adversity in general. The instructions about burying the dead, giving alms, and maintaining family solidarity would have been especially relevant in diaspora contexts, but not exclusively so. If the primary focus had been life in the midst of Gentiles one might have expected much more emphasis on not intermarrying with them, rejecting idolatry, remaining separate, upholding circumcision and sabbath, and not eating their food.[27] Some of this is present, to be sure, in the introductory chapter, but it is largely incidental and assumed.[28] The real focus is Jewish life and faith. That includes Tobit's concern with issues of purity, such as washing after touching corpses (cf. Num 19:11-12), burying them after sunset, then sleeping outside the house, all apparently reflecting concern with impurity,[29] as also the double washing in 7:9, καὶ ὅτε ἐλούσαντο καὶ ἐνίψαντο καὶ ἀνέπεσαν δειπνῆσαι ("When they had bathed and washed themselves and had reclined to dine").[30]

The story of Tobit and Sarah, as we have it, does appear to make a connection with the exile, not, however, by portraying all their problems as typical of the exile, but by portraying their responses as models for responding to Israel's needs as a whole. Just as divine providence met their need, so divine providence will bring restoration, and therefore despair and disbelief is to be set aside. Thus Ego writes: "The salvation of Tobit and Sara however is not only to be seen on an

---

[27] See Collins, "Judaism of the Book of Tobit," 30.

[28] As Gruen, *Diaspora*, observes, there is "more discord within the households than without" (158). Living in a Gentile world does not appear to be greatly problematic. Cf. Amy-Jill Levine, "Diaspora as Metaphor: Bodies and Boundaries in the Book of Tobit," in *Diaspora Jews and Judaism: Essays in Honor of, and in Dialogue with, A. Thomas Kraabel* (ed. J. Andrew Overman and Robert S. MacLennan; SFSHJ 41; Atlanta: Scholars, 1992) 107–17, who sees Tobit addressing the issue of diaspora as a chaotic place of unstable boundaries, represented symbolically in the text, and depicting the stability of endogamy with "women properly domiciled" in it as the solution (105). "Sarah represents what could be its fate in the diaspora: ignorant, childless, and in the undesired embrace of idolatry represented by the demon" (112), whereas Tobit represents the hope of the nation (113).

[29] So Ida Fröhlich, "Tobit against the Background of the Dead Sea Scrolls," in *The Book of Tobit: Text, Tradition, Theology: Papers of the First International Conference on the Deuterocanonical Books, Pápa, Hungary, 20-21 May, 2004* (ed. Géza G. Xeravits and József Zsengellér; JSJSup 98; Leiden: Brill, 2005) 55-70, 67.

[30] Moore, *Tobit*, argues against GII as preserving the original reading in 7:9 because having two verbs describing washing is superfluous, rejecting the notion that the second might indicate washing before eating, because the Old Testament knows no such requirements (219-20). See also the review of various explanations in Fitzmyer, *Tobit*. 229-30. More recent discoveries of stone jars and immersion pools indicate, however, that the practice of washing hands before meals may indeed have been more widespread than earlier thought. On this see Eyal Regev, "Pure Individualism: The Idea of Non-Priestly Purity in Ancient Judaism," *JSJ* 31 (2000) 176-202, 177-86.

individual level, but has also to be regarded as representing the fate of the people of Israel at large",[31] a hope which she sees reflected in 14:5-6. Thus, while exile also forms the backdrop of the story and an end to exile informs its hope, the story itself functions less as a model of how to live in the diaspora and more as encouragement in the faith that God will act also for his people bringing an end to exile just as he acted to heal Tobit, save Sarah from the demonic thwarting of her marriage, and bring each of the story's pious but fallible figures[32] to happiness and fulfilment.[33] The hope is bound up with the understanding of true piety as observing Torah in the midst of pressures not to do so. Within this context we find, then, references to sexual behaviour, both as part of general exhortations and in relation to key aspects of the story itself.

Defining the Proper Marriage Partner

The account begins by depicting Tobit as standing over against his fellow members of the tribe of Naphtali who worshipped Jeroboam's calf in Dan and

---

[31] Beate Ego, "The Book of Tobit and the Diaspora," in *The Book of Tobit: Text, Tradition, Theology: Papers of the First International Conference on the Deuterocanonical Books, Pápa, Hungary, 20-21 May, 2004* (ed. Géza G. Xeravits and József Zsengellér; JSJSup 98; Leiden: Brill, 2005) 41-54, 52; see also pp. 45-46.

[32] On the fallibility of both Tobit and Sarah see David McCracken, "Narration and Comedy in the Book of Tobit," *JBL* 114 (1995) 401-18; Lawrence M. Wills, *The Jewish Novel in the Ancient World* (Ithaca: Cornell Univ. Press, 1995) 68–92, 69; and Gruen, *Diaspora*, who writes: "The narrator takes pleasure in exposing the foibles of his creatures: Tobit's pompous piousness, Sarah's self-absorption, Tobias' naiveté and anxieties, Raguel's dread of neighbourly disapproval" (158). Against this see J. R. C. Cousland, "Tobit: A Comedy in Error?" *CBQ* 65 (2003) 535-53, arguing that such a reading would have been unlikely in the ancient world.

[33] On the underlying deuteronomistic theology, see Moore, *Tobit*, 20-21. See also George W. E. Nickelsburg, "Torah and the Deuteronomic Scheme in the Apocrypha and Pseudepigrapha: Variations on a Theme and Some Noteworthy Examples of its Absence," in *Das Gesetz im frühen Judentum und im Neuen Testament: Festschrift für Christoph Burchard zum 75. Geburtstag* (ed. Dieter Sänger, Matthias Konradt; NTOA 57; Göttingen: Vandenhoeck & Ruprecht; Fribourg: Academic Press, 2006) 222-35, 227. While Collins, "Judaism of the Book of Tobit," rightly observes however that neither Tobit's nor Sarah's plight is to be explained on the basis of Deuteronomic theology (28-29), this is not the case with the broader experience of distress which Tobit's prayer depicts as the result of Israel's sin (3:3-5). On this see Ego, "Diaspora", 44-45. At most one can speak of an underlying theology of that kind in the belief that ultimately God will reward the righteous. On the importance of the theme of providence and the reward of the faithful see also Fitzmyer, *Tobit*, 46.

remaining faithful to Jerusalem and its temple.[34] Its image of Tobit's piety may be assumed to reflect ideals which would have resonated with the work's hearers[35] and so reflect also their values.[36] He is a model in offering the required tithes, but also in his first comment which pertains to sexuality: "When I became a man I married a woman, a member of our own family (ἐκ τοῦ σπέρματος τῆς πατριᾶς ἡμῶν), and by her I became the father of a son whom I named Tobias" (1:9). Proper marriage is a major concern in the work.[37] Thus Tobit instructs his son, Tobias, similarly:

---

[34] Levine, "Diaspora as Metaphor," notes that "the choice of tribes is not accidental. Naphtali was geographically separated from the other Rachel tribes even in Palestine ... was closely connected with the local population, as Judges 1:33 makes clear: 'Naphtali dwelt among the Canaanites, the inhabitants of the land'" (107). Naphtali receives unusual attention in *Jubilees*, which is probably to be explained in relation to the Tobiad family, as seeking to support its claim to Jewish ancestry. The same may also lie behind its presence in Tobit. This is not to go as far as J. T. Milik, "La Patrie de Tobie," *RB* 73 (1966), 522-30, who suggested that the story originated in Samaria and was to enhance the Tobiad family. See also Wills, *Jewish Novel*, 72. It may however suggest a Palestinian context for the composition.

[35] McCracken, "Narration and Comedy," points to the discrepancy between Tobit's claims for himself in 1:6 that he alone went up to Jerusalem and his acknowledgment before Azariah that Azariah's kinsmen also went (409), but, as Cousland, "Tobit: A Comedy in Error?" notes, this is overstated and fails to give weight to the πολλάκις ("often") in Tobit's claim (542). While from our world *we* might see Tobit's self-description as arrogant and pompous, as Gruen, *Diaspora*, among others, asserts (151), the text does not suggest such implied disapproval of Tobit's narration any more than of the virtues espoused in 1:3-9.

[36] So Beverly Bow and George W. E. Nickelsburg, "Patriarchy with a Twist: Men and Women in Tobit," in *"Women Like This": New Perspectives on Jewish Women in the Greco-Roman World* (ed. Amy-Jill Levine; SBLEJL 1; Atlanta: Scholars, 1991) 127-43, who note that while the extent to which this is so remains uncertain, nevertheless Tobit "provides a glimpse of the everyday life and belief of families in the period of formative Judaism" (127).

[37] So also Helen Schüngel-Straumann, *Tobit* (HTKAT; Freiburg: Herder, 2000) 58; and Thomas Hieke, "Endogamy in the Book of Tobit, Genesis, and Ezra-Nehemiah," in *The Book of Tobit: Text, Tradition, Theology: Papers of the First International Conference on the Deuterocanonical Books, Pápa, Hungary, 20-21 May, 2004* (ed. Géza G. Xeravits and József Zsengellér; JSJSup 98; Leiden: Brill, 2005) 103-20. On the Vulgate's replacement of concern about endogamy by concern about sexual lust see Beate Ego, "'Denn er liebt sie' (Tob 6,15 Ms. 319): Zur Rolle des Dämons Asmodäus in der Tobit-Erzählung," in *Die Dämonen: Die Dämonologie der israelitisch-jüdischen und frühchristlichen Literatur im Kontext ihrer Umwelt - Demons: The Demonology of Israelite-Jewish and Early Christian Literature in Context of their Environment* (ed. Armin Lange, Hermann Lichtenberger, K. F. Diethard; Tübingen: Mohr Siebeck, 2003) 309-17, 315. See also Tobias Nicklas, "Marriage in the Book of Tobit: A Synoptic Approach," in *The Book of Tobit: Text,*

12 Beware, my son, of every kind of fornication (ἀπὸ πάσης πορνείας). First of all, marry a woman from among the descendants of your ancestors (ἀπὸ τοῦ σπέρματος τῶν πατέρων σου); do not marry a foreign woman (μὴ λάβῃς γυναῖκα ἀλλοτρίαν), who is not of your father's tribe (ἐκ τῆς φυλῆς τοῦ πατρός σου); for we are the descendants of the prophets. Remember, my son, that Noah, Abraham, Isaac, and Jacob, our ancestors of old, all took wives from among their kindred (ἐκ τῶν ἀδελφῶν αὐτῶν). They were blessed in their children, and their posterity will inherit the land. 13 So now, my son, love your kindred (τοὺς ἀδελφούς σου), and in your heart do not disdain your kindred, the sons and daughters of your people (ἀπὸ τῶν ἀδελφῶν σου καὶ τῶν υἱῶν καὶ θυγατέρων τοῦ λαοῦ σου), by refusing to take a wife for yourself from among them. (4:12-13)

Like the Hebrew זנות the word πορνεία which can be narrowed to prostitution encompasses a broad range of sexual wrongdoing and here denotes illicit marriage.[38] Not marrying a "foreign" woman, that is, a woman from elsewhere (γυναῖκα ἀλλοτρίαν) relates to three levels. He must marry neither a non-Jew, nor just any Israelite, but one belonging to his own tribe, and then not just any descendant of Naphtali, but a woman belonging to his father's extended family, from among his kindred,[39] just as Noah, Abraham, Isaac, and Jacob did ("from among their kindred, ἐκ τῶν ἀδελφῶν αὐτῶν),[40] and just as Tobit had done ("a

---

Tradition, Theology: Papers of the First International Conference on the Deuterocanonical Books, Pápa, Hungary, 20-21 May, 2004 (ed. Géza G. Xeravits and József Zsengellér; JSJSup 98; Leiden: Brill, 2005) 139-54, who compares the approaches to endogamy in GI and GII, arguing that the emphasis on endogamy with close kin comes through more strongly in GII (as in 6:16), but it is certainly strongly present in 4:12-13 which is missing from the Sinaiticus manuscript.

[38] Moore, *Tobit*, notes that it refers to "*all* sexual misconduct outside of marriage" (168). He observes that there is no specific mention of adultery or prostitution, sacral or otherwise. The focus here, however, is not just misconduct outside of marriage, but illicit marriage which it then goes on to define. See also Fitzmyer, *Tobit*, 172, who cites the broad use of πορνεία in Paul (Gal 5:19; 1 Cor 7:2); Littman, *Tobit*, 91; Ellis, *Sexual Desire*, 45.

[39] Ego, "Denn er liebt sie," appropriately defines this as meaning descendants of a common father three to six generations back (311 n. 5). See also the detailed discussion of kinship issues as a key to understanding Tobit in Littman, *Tobit*, xxxvii-xli.

[40] Hieke, "Endogamy," writes: "The shining example of the Patriarchs underscores this notion" (108). On the function of the Genesis narratives as a source of "Torah" see pp. 114-16 and the discussion in Irene Nowell, "The Book of Tobit: An Ancestral Story," in *Intertextual Studies in Ben Sira and Tobit: Essays in Honor of Alexander A. Di Lella* (ed. Jeremy Corley and Vincent T.M. Skemp; CBQMS 38; Washington: CBA, 2005) 3-13, 9-11. See also Pekka Pitkänen, "Family Life and Ethnicity in Early Israel and in Tobit," in *Studies in the Book of Tobit* (ed. Mark Bredin; London: T&T Clark, 2006) 104-17, who notes both

member of our own family" ἐκ τοῦ σπέρματος τῆς πατριᾶς ἡμῶν) (1:9). That Noah did so derives not from Genesis, but probably from *Jubilees* which reports it (4:33) or from a shared tradition.[41]

Moore notes that ἀλλοτρία is used of forbidden marriage partners also in Ezra 10:2 and Neh 13:27 to refer to non-Israelites (Ezra 9:1-2) and in Prov 5:20 and 6:24 to refer to "the unknown woman, or sexual adventuress"[42] (168-69). In her depiction of Tobit as addressing the challenge of the diaspora, Levine, writes: "In order to distinguish the Israelite from the Gentile, the Book of Tobit advances a program centred on endogamy".[43] This is so, only if we see the focus on endogamy as seeking to deal with stability of kin and its property, not if it implies countering intermarriage with Gentiles as an aim, since the latter is already assumed as out of the question in Tobit and so not addressed. Nor is its concern about intermarriage linked with idolatry.[44] The focus in Tobit is much more defined and much stricter. Marriage is to be only within one's extended family, the strict sense of endogamy.

This narrow band of licit partners finds confirmation in the account of Sarah's plight, who, having had seven men die on the wedding night before consummating their marriage to her, declares of her father: "he has no close relative or other kindred for whom I should keep myself as wife" (οὐδὲ ἀδελφὸς αὐτῷ ἐγγὺς οὔτε συγγενὴς αὐτῷ ὑπάρχει ἵνα συντηρήσω ἐμαυτὴν αὐτῷ γυναῖκα)[45]

---

the prevalence of endogamy in deeply divided societies, present also in early Israel, but also the distinctively Jewish issues of identity which inform both early Israel and Tobit.

[41] On the relation between *Jubilees* and Tobit see Moore, *Tobit*, who argues that *Jubilees* is dependent on Tobit (194); similarly John C. Endres, *Biblical Interpretation in the Book of Jubilees* (CBQMS 18; Washington: CBA, 1987), 95-96. See also Nickelsburg, "Tobit, Genesis and the *Odyssey*," 50-51; Gabriele Fassbeck, "Tobit's Religious Universe Between Kinship Loyalty and the Law of Moses," *JSJ* 36 (2005) 173-96, 194-95; and our discussion in the conclusion below.

[42] Moore, *Tobit*, 168-69). He also cites warnings against adultery and prostitution in ancient Egyptian and Akkadian wisdom (177-78).

[43] Levine, "Diaspora as Metaphor," 105. Cf. also Bow and Nickelsburg, "Patriarchy with a Twist," who relate the emphasis on endogamy to the problem of the diaspora where "it would have been more difficult to find an eligible, non-gentile spouse" (133); similarly William Michael Soll, "The Family as Scriptural and Social Construct in Tobit," in *The Function of Scripture in Early Jewish and Christian Tradition* (ed. Craig A. Evans, James A. Sanders; JSNTSup 154; Sheffield: Sheffield Academic Press, 1998) 166-75, writes: "Tobit's anxiety on the subject does seem to indicate that at least some Jews in the Hellenistic Diaspora married Gentiles" (170).

[44] Cf. Levine, "Diaspora as Metaphor," 112.

[45] So GII: συγγενής; OL *propinquus*. Cf. GI which reads υἱός; similarly 4QpapTob[a] ar/4Q196 6.12: לבר.

(3:15). This value is fundamental to the story's plot, since Tobias becomes part of the answer to Sarah's prayer, for "Tobias was entitled to have her before all others who had desired to marry her" (3:16), because she is the daughter of Raguel, of whom the angel, Raphael, later declares to Tobias: "He is your relative" (αὐτὸς συγγενής σού) (6:11). He then repeats Tobias' claim to her: "you, as next of kin to her, have before all other men a hereditary claim on her. Also it is right for you to inherit her father's possessions ... You have every right to take her in marriage" (6:12). The requirement is then reinforced by Raphael's declaration:

> I know that Raguel can by no means keep her from you or promise her to another man without incurring the penalty of death according to the decree of the book of Moses. Indeed he knows that you, rather than any other man, are entitled to marry his daughter. (6:13)

The value of kinship marriage is further reinforced in the narrator's comment:

> When Tobias heard the words of Raphael and learned that she was his kinswoman, related through his father's lineage (ἀδελφὴ ἐκ τοῦ σπέρματος τοῦ οἴκου τοῦ πατρὸς αὐτοῦ), he loved her very much, and his heart was drawn to her (ἐκολλήθη εἰς αὐτήν). (6:18)

The story then reinforces the fact of kinship, as Raguel remarks to his wife: "How much the young man resembles my kinsman Tobit" (7:2). The hearers are to be left in no doubt! Identification follows and long separated kin greet each other (7:3-9). We then find Raguel complying fully with this law as he declares to Tobias:

> οὐ γάρ ἐστιν ἄνθρωπος ᾧ καθήκει λαβεῖν Σαρραν τὴν θυγατέρα μου πλὴν σοῦ ἄδελφε ὡσαύτως δὲ καὶ ἐγὼ οὐκ ἔχω ἐξουσίαν δοῦναι αὐτὴν ἑτέρῳ ἀνδρὶ πλὴν σοῦ ὅτι σὺ ἔγγιστά μου.
> No one except you, brother, has the right to marry my daughter Sarah. Likewise I am not at liberty to give her to any other man than yourself, because you are my nearest relative. (7:10)

Raguel also tells us that previous men had also been "kinsmen" (τῶν ἀδελφῶν ἡμῶν) (7:11). The designation is then applied to Tobias and Sarah, for they, too, are kin (τὴν ἀδελφήν σου 7:11; τὴν ἀδελφήν μου 8:7).

Thus, central both to the plot and to the piety is the strict requirement of marrying only within one's extended family at the pain of death. When we look for the rationale for such restrictions we find on the one hand appeals to biblical law, but on the other, concern with inheritance. This is explicit in 4:12 which notes that the patriarchs who married their kin "were blessed in their children, and their posterity will inherit the land" and in 4:13 where the exhortation to marry kin is followed abruptly by the statement: "For in pride there is ruin and great confusion. And in idleness there is loss and dire poverty, because idleness is the mother of famine", possibly suggesting that doing otherwise by following one's own whims is pride[46] and creates confusion perhaps by mixing up claims to inheritance, possibly linked also to loss and poverty. Certainly Sarah's prayer links her father's lack of an heir with her lack of a husband (3:18), as do Raphael's instructions: "you, as next of kin to her, have before all other men a hereditary claim on her. Also it is right for you to inherit her father's possessions" (6:12). Already in 8:21 Tobias receives the first half of that inheritance (see also 10:10).[47] The concern with restricting marriage to kin, unlike the broader concern with intermarriage to non-Jews where idolatry and sexual wrongdoing are the fears, appears then to be about stable households and inheritance, protecting the wealth and welfare of the extended family, a value surely also espoused by the work's hearers.[48] The concluding words which report that Tobias "inherited both the property of Raguel and that of his father Tobit" (14:13) reflect not simply reward for piety, but also the rationale for keeping marriage within the extended family.[49]

---

[46] Collins, "Judaism of the Book of Tobit," writes that Tobit sees "the temptation to marry outside the tribe as a matter of pride rather than of idolatry or purity" (31).

[47] As Bow and Nickelsburg, "Patriarchy with a Twist," note concerning Raguel's reference not only to his own death, but also to that of his wife, "the implication of this is that if a husband dies first, the wife inherits" (132).

[48] Thus Collins, "Judaism of the Book of Tobit," writes: "Tobit's concern is not the danger of intermarriage with foreigners, but the desire to maintain the traditional social structure" (31). Nicklas, "Marriage,": "To marry one's relatives prevents poverty because the inheritance does not get lost to foreign families" (144). Similarly Sabine van den Eynde, "One Journey and One Journey Makes Three: The Impact of the Readers' Knowledge in the Book of Tobit," *ZAW* 117 (2005) 273-80, 278; Hieke, "Endogamy," 112, who goes on to speculate that concern with property may also have played a role in the attack on mixed marriages in Ezra and Nehemiah if they reflected principles evident in the Elephantine papyri according to which wives could inherit (116-18). Ego, "Diaspora," deals with endogamy as a response to being in exile, "to prevent assimilation" (50), but this applies only in the indirect sense that stronger cohesive Jewish households where marriage is kept within one's extended family better enable them to survive, not in the direct sense of not marrying Gentiles, since Tobit already assumes this and goes far beyond it with its focus on which Jews one may marry. See also her "Denn er liebte sie," in which she argues that Asmodeus represents the reverse of endogamy: the total outsider (315).

[49] Soll, "Family as Scriptural," notes that such endogamous marriage in the narrow sense of marrying within the extended family was common among the Herodians, which he sees reflecting the favourable light in which endogamy is depicted in Tobit, Judith, and *Jubilees*, concluding: "Tobit's view of the matter seems to me in many ways an aristocratic one, designed to preserve the wealth and traditions of prominent families" (174).

The appeal to "the decree of the book of Moses", including for "the penalty of death" (6:13) raises a number of questions. The right referred to might relate to the provisions for levirate marriage in Deut 25:5-10. Thus Fitzmyer argues that, "in effect, Tobias is related to Sarah as a distant levir would be, i.e., a husband's brother, who was to raise up progeny for a widow after the death of a husband, if she had no children by him".[50] But as Soll points out, the application here of levirate provisions is problematic since the relationship between Tobias and the dead husbands is unclear, Sarah is never assumed to be a widow, and the levirate rationale of perpetuating the name of the dead husband is never invoked in Tobit.[51] The rightness appears rather to relate to inheritance and the provisions to retain inheritance by a surviving daughter marrying within her clan as set out in Num 27:1-11; 36:8-9, according to which the inheritance of a man without a male heir may go to daughters provided they marry within their father's extended family.[52]

The penalty of death goes beyond what either Deut 25:5-10 or Num 36:6-8 requires. It recalls *Jubilees* which imposes the penalty of death for intermarriage with non-Jews on the basis of having extended what were originally restrictions applying to priests, to all the people (30:7-10; cf. Lev 18:21; 20:2; 21:9). Here the penalty appears to relate not just to the much narrower restriction of marrying only kin, but also to contravention of the provisions concerning inheritance. One must assume an understanding of the Mosaic law to include more than simply the written pentateuch, but also to include its exposition, such as we also find in the *Temple Scroll*.[53]

A further question arises in relation to Sarah's husbands which may indicate an even stricter narrowing of restrictions on marriage. The summary which the author provides in 3:16-17 indicates that "Tobias was entitled to have Sarah[54]

---

[50] Fitzmyer, *Tobit*, 212.

[51] Soll, "Family as Scriptural," 171.

[52] So Collins, "Judaism of the Book of Tobit," 31; Hieke, "Endogamy," 106-107; Similarly Otzen, *Judith and Tobit*, 38-39.

[53] So Mark A. Christian, "Reading Tobit Backwards and Forwards: In Search of 'Lost Halakhah'," *Henoch* 28 (2006) 63-95, 82-84. He also draws attention to *Jubilees* (66-70), suggesting that what we have in Tobit reflects oral halakhic innovation from a diaspora setting (90-92). Collins, "Judaism of the Book of Tobit," also notes that "'the book of Moses' in Tobit does not point to a specific biblical law, but rather to ancestral traditions, which derive authority from Moses even when they go beyond what is written in the Torah" (32). He sees this in 6:13 and 7:12 and points to similar claims made by Philo *Hypoth.* 7.1-9 and Josephus *Ap.* 2.190-219 which go beyond the written law (32-34).

[54] Nicklas, "Marriage," notes that while GII speaks of Tobias' right to take her as inheritance (σοὶ κληρονομία καθήκει λαβεῖν τὴν θυγατέρα αὐτοῦ), GI simply speaks of his right to receive the inheritance (τὴν κληρονομίαν σοὶ καθήκει λαβεῖν) (145), and suggests that GI's focus is the property, not Sarah (145), but in 3:17 both read: Τωβια ἐπιβάλλει κληρονομῆσαι αὐτήν.

before all others who had desired to marry her" (διότι Τωβια ἐπιβάλλει κληρονομῆσαι αὐτὴν παρὰ πάντας τοὺς θέλοντας λαβεῖν αὐτήν). This could be taken as referring not just to these currently eligible men, but to all, including the seven who died. Accordingly Levine reads those marriages as representing the chaos produced by exogamy on the basis that the seven "are not explicitly described as members of her family or tribe".[55] Such a reading is possible only if one prefers the GI reading of 7:11, and even then problematic, since nowhere do we find the suggestion that these would have been exogamous marriages.[56] In 7:11 (GII) Raguel plainly states that the previous would-be husbands were of his family ("I have given her to seven men of our kinsmen"; ἔδωκα αὐτὴν ἑπτὰ ἀνδράσιν τῶν ἀδελφῶν ἡμῶν). One might speculate about why they met this fate. Was it divine judgement because they approached Sarah with lust or greed? (cf. 8:7)[57] or were not as close kin as Tobias?[58] The text indicates neither. They appear to have been properly eligible. As Nicklas notes, "the text never refers to the death of seven bridegrooms as God's will. Sarah's seven husbands are not described in negative colours. Their death is a disaster which has to be overcome".[59]

They did, however, fall short in one respect. Only of Tobias is it said – indeed by the angel Raphael – that Sarah was set apart for him before the world was made (6:18; cf. Gen 24:44), perhaps already suggested in GII 6:13 ("It has been determined for you to take her in marriage";[60] καὶ εἶπεν δεδικαίωταί σοι λαβεῖν αὐτήν). The notion of divine will appears in the same statement of Raguel who declares that they are to be married because "it has been decreed from heaven" (καὶ ἐκ τοῦ οὐρανοῦ κέκριταί σοι) (7:11).[61] The motif belongs to many intertextual relations with the story of Abraham's servant seeking a wife for Isaac, where he declares: "let her be the one whom you have appointed for your servant Isaac" (Gen 24:14). The problem with the other husbands was simply that

---

[55] Levine, "Diaspora as Metaphor," 108.

[56] So Hieke, "Endogamy," 111. Nicklas, "Marriage," suggests GI is "not as much interested in the kinship of the first husbands as GII" (147).

[57] Cf. Moore, *Tobit*, 158.

[58] So Fassbeck, "Tobit's Religious Universe," who then goes on to suggest that the demon acts for God in punishment of the other kinsmen (179-80).

[59] Nicklas, "Marriage," 153.

[60] As translated by Fitzmyer, *Tobit*, 201, 212.

[61] Nicklas, "Marriage," notes that whereas GI contains the allusion to divine determination only in 6:18 ("because she was prepared for you before the world was made"; ὅτι σοὶ αὐτὴ ἡτοιμασμένη ἦν ἀπὸ τοῦ αἰῶνος; cf. GII: "for she was set apart for you before the world was made"; σοὶ γάρ ἐστιν μεμερισμένη πρὸ τοῦ αἰῶνος), only GII has the further reference to divine decree in 6:13 and 7:11 and in 8:21 draws the conclusion on that basis that the marriage is to be indissoluble (152).

they were not in accordance with divine will.[62] This, in turn, raises other problems because it was not divine will but a demon that prevented their consummation.

The tension remains unresolved. It arises from use of such language to affirm rightness and value, but which when pressed creates major difficulties. In this sense it recalls the language of predestination to salvation which functions doxologically as a way of affirming divine grace (or polemically to demarcate against others or explain their dissent), but has considerable consequences when treated as objective description. It remains questionable whether we should press for strict consistency in Tobit, which might entail attributing a divine function to Asmodeus or divine aim to sparrows' droppings.[63] The narrative does not appear to see Asmodeus or the sparrows in this way, but rather to assume the kind of limited dualism we find in the *Book of the Watchers*, where the world is also inhabited by destructive assailants, demonic and otherwise.[64]

Fitzmyer notes in relationship to Tobit's depiction of marriage, "The new element is the idea that the marriage of the two young people has been foreseen by God's providence and so their joining together is heaven-blest".[65] Used in the context of marriage – in days of romantic understandings of marriage even more – it underlies notions of the indissolubility of marriages (cf. 8:21) which can only be dissolved if the affirmation can be shown to have been false and so the marriage never licit. This puts enormous strain on all involved. Alternatively one might reason that divine providence will always ensure that one meets the right marriage partner, assuming Asmodeus is still active in destroying inappropriate ones! But this too presses the logic of the narrative too far. The assumption in Tobit is that by restricting oneself to eligible partners within the extended family and remaining open to divine guidance the right partner will be found – viewed of course from a male perspective.[66]

---

[62] Schüngel-Straumann, *Tobit*, notes that the effect in the story is to makes room for the fulfilment in the marriage of Sarah and Tobias (127). Similarly Fitzmyer, *Tobit*, who writes: "the seven earlier suitors were removed by Asmodeus in order that she might be preserved for Tobiah" (48).

[63] Cf. Gruen, *Diaspora*: "his pompous sanctimoniousness was punished with bird droppings" (152). Cf. also Fröhlich, "Tobit," who writes, "Nothing is accidental in Tobit" (62).

[64] Birds, however, are sometimes seen as demonic agents. See Mark 4:15; *Apoc. Abr.* 13:3-8; possibly also *Jub.* 14:12.

[65] Fitzmyer, *Tobit*, 48.

[66] As Bow and Nickelsburg, "Patriarchy with a Twist," note, this reflects typical androcentricity, expressed in the bride being decreed for the groom rather than both for each other (135).

The Marriage of Tobit and Anna

Marriage features in Tobit not only in instruction, but also in the narrative itself where we find two sets of parents who project an image of marriage and the beginning of a third. To both belong the giving birth to children, Tobias and Sarah, respectively. Beyond that, in the case of Tobit and Anna we find that "Anna earned money at women's work" (2:11). Citing Sir 25:22, Moore notes the shame which may be implied in the report that here Anna is supporting her husband.[67] She apparently wove cloth, selling what she had made to "the owners", presumably those who supplied the raw materials. This is a small window on what was probably a common practice and not simply a desperate measure upon which she had to embark because of Tobias' blindness which had reversed Tobias from being a helper of the poor to one whose family became poor, the plight of anyone with a disability in the ancient world.

This marriage is not however ideal. Tobit, himself, reports as a fact that Anna had received a goat as additional payment. He, however, had not believed her, thinking she had stolen it, and "became flushed with anger against her" (2:14). In response she confronts him: "Where are your acts of charity? Where are your righteous deeds? These things are known about you!" (2:14), as she does on two other occasions, about his priorities in risking Tobias' loss by seeking more money (5:17-19), and about his dismissal of her fears that he might indeed be lost (10:17).[68] The initial exchange has received diverse interpretations. Gunkel suggested that the goat was understood as payment for prostitution, as in the story of Judah and Tamar (Gen 38:17).[69] Against this Tobit, himself, is reporting that it was part of her wages (2:12).[70] This makes it also difficult to argue that Tobit's accusation is to believed.[71] For Tobit the narrator does not now believe it. Rather

---

[67] Moore, *Tobit*, 133; similarly Cousland, "Tobit: A Comedy in Error?" 544. Cf. also Levine, "Diaspora as Metaphor," who argues that the underlying assumption is that marriages become dysfunctional when wives go out to work (111).

[68] On this see Bow and Nickelsburg, "Patriarchy with a Twist," 137.

[69] Hermann Gunkel, *Genesis* (HAT 1/1; Göttingen: Vandenhoeck & Ruprecht, 1917) 416. As Schüngel-Straumann, *Tobit*, notes, as a Torah-faithful Jew Tobit would hardly have continued to live with her thereafter (74).

[70] So Irene Nowell, "The Book of Tobit," in *The New Interpreter's Bible: A Commentary in Twelve Volumes: Volume Three: The First and Second Books of Kings; The First and Second Books of Chronicles; The Book of Ezra; The Book of Nehemiah; The Book of Esther; The Book of Tobit; The Book of Judith* (Nashville, Abingdon, 1999) 975-1071, who argues that nothing indicates that in reporting his suspicions Tobit justifies them (1003). Cf. Cousland, "Tobit: A Comedy in Error?" 543.

[71] Cf. Schüngel-Straumann, *Tobit*, 71-72.

he was wrong in his suspicion,[72] but then so is Anna, for she is virtually saying: all your good deeds have been of no benefit to you – and everyone knows it! By implication: you should be ashamed![73]

The loss of honour is a final straw as is his wife's turning against him. It recalls the response of Job's wife to their common plight (2:9),[74] though Job's wife is angry primarily with God.[75] In the later *Testament of Job* Job's wife has done as Anna: worked to keep her husband alive, even sold her hair, and finally confronts Job only to be dismissed in anguish for acting as foolish women do.[76] Anna has added to the distress and insults which make Tobit want to die (3:6). In the narrative she represents response to suffering which chooses despair. It is not atypical of the time to turn women into models of negative behaviour. At the same time, as it stands, Tobit the narrator is nevertheless also acknowledging his own fallibility. His prayer as a character also espouses despair.[77] Its virtue is that he does, at least, pray about it, so that like Sarah, whose trust and sense of responsibility exceeds his,[78] he models an appropriate response to distress.

---

[72] So Moore, *Tobit*, 133. Similarly McCracken, "Narration and Comedy": "Tobit-the character- is in the wrong" (406). "He is a *flawed* paragon" (406), which, as he argues, must to some degree also apply to his pious prayer where he claims "undeserved insults, when in fact he has brought his wife's insults upon himself by his false and groundless accusation" (406); Gruen, *Diaspora*, 151-53.

[73] Fitzmyer, *Tobit*, suggests she sees his works of righteousness and good deeds as hypocritical (141). I find no indication of this. He does, however, capture her representative function when he writes: "Hannah's retort poses the real question in this book: Does God reward those who are righteous?" (141). Her accusative answer must be shown by the author to be wrong.

[74] Cf. Schüngel-Straumann, *Tobit*, who argues that Anna's rebuke primarily addresses Tobit's unjust treatment of herself. She argues that to see Anna as reflecting lack of trust is a male perspective (113). I agree, but think that is likely to be the author's stance, which we should be under no obligation to share.

[75] So Moore, *Tobit*, 135, though he overemphasises the difference, since in both cases God's providence is being called into question.

[76] See our discussion above and also Schüngel-Straumann, *Tobit*, who notes the parallel (74-76).

[77] See the comparison of the two prayers in Bow and Nickelsburg, "Patriarchy with a Twist," 129-30.

[78] See also Bow and Nickelsburg, "Patriarchy with a Twist," who describe Tobit's Prayer as "self centred and whining" (130). They contrast Tobit's will to die with Sarah's restraint at the thought, Tobit's fear that God has turned away with Sarah's confidence that he has not (130). See, however, Anathea Portier-Young, "Alleviation of Suffering in the Book of Tobit: Comedy, Community, and Happy Endings," *CBQ* 63 (2001) 35-54, who notes that Tobit's cry of despair and his aloneness (1:6) connect him to Moses (Num 11:15) and Elijah who also seek death (1 Kgs 18:22; 19:10) (43-44).

The book of Tobit has no equivalent of Job's rebuke of his wife. Instead we next find Tobit instructing Tobias to ask that he ensure he has a proper burial but then adds: "Honour your mother and do not abandon her all the days of her life. Do whatever pleases her, and do not grieve her in anything" (4:3). The spat produced by his failure to trust her word and the resultant bitter exchange has not undermined what appears to be respect and caring in the relationship.[79] Thus he continues: "Remember her, my son, because she faced many dangers for you while you were in her womb. And when she dies, bury her beside me in the same grave" (4:4). They are still together and to be together in death. Motivating respect for mothers on grounds of gratitude for what they have experienced during pregnancy and in giving birth is a common motif.[80]

Anna reappears in the text as the weeping mother like Rebecca when Jacob sets out to find his wife (5:18 – 6:1). She confronts Tobit's desire to put money before the security of Tobias: "Why is it that you have sent my child away? Is he not the staff of our hand as he goes in and out before us? Do not heap money upon money, but let it be a ransom for our child. For the life that is given to us by the Lord is enough for us" (5:18-20). As in the version of the story of Isaac and Rebecca retold in *Jub.* 27:13-18, like Isaac, Tobit comforts Anna.[81] The irony is not lost in Tobit's assurance spoken in unwitting trust: "a good angel will accompany him; his journey will be successful, and he will come back in good health" (5:22). In this way the narrator colludes with the hearer[82] to dismiss Anna's human fears in a manner probably not likely to have evoked in its day the distaste it deserves.[83] The message is clear: trust like Tobit and all will be well.

---

[79] Bow and Nickelsburg, "Patriarchy with a Twist," observe: "Despite the rebukes, the narrator gives the impression that the couple care for each other" (137).

[80] Schüngel-Straumann, *Tobit*, notes the close parallel in Sir 7:27, where the focus is on the pain of giving birth rather than of pregnancy, but both works stemming from around the same period. She also notes the theme in the early Hellenistic period and in much older Egyptian traditions which appeal for such respect towards mothers (99-100). See also Moore, *Tobit*, for this "characteristic feature of Near-Eastern Wisdom literature" (165). As Levine, "Diaspora as Metaphor," rightly observes, it still depicts women primarily in relation to their reproductive capacity (110).

[81] On this see Nickelsburg, "Tobit, Genesis and the *Odyssey*," 41-55, who also notes similarities with account of the servant's return in *Jub.* 31:3-9 (48-49).

[82] On the importance of 3:16-17 in informing the hearer and so creating dramatic tension in the narrative see van den Eynde, "One Journey," 274.

[83] As Schüngel-Straumann, *Tobit*, observes, we need not see Anna's weeping in a negative light, as have some commentators (112), although this is not to say that the author might not have seen it so, especially since she has symbolised the inappropriate response of anger and despair in 2:11-14. Cf. Gruen, *Diaspora*, who sees the author deliberately portraying Tobit as hypocritical, seeking money, while having enjoined trust (153-54).

Tobias is concerned for both his father and his mother when confronted with the possible dangers of marrying Sarah (6:15). The greater importance of the male as head of the household is reflected in the moment of recognition of kinship between Tobias and Sarah's parents (7:1-6): they ask only about Tobit. Nothing is said of Anna. The same is true of the meeting with Gabael (9:6). We find Anna and Tobit in 10:1-7 expressing anxiety that Tobias has not returned, but, again, there is a sharp interchange. Tobit seeks to console her by suggesting Tobias would soon come. Anna responds abruptly: "Be quiet yourself! Stop trying to deceive me! My child has perished" (10:7). Here as in the earlier conflicts Anna is giving voice to despair and hopelessness. While hearers would doubtless have felt empathy – that is its seductive effect for the author – the point in Tobit is that such despair is unwarranted, ultimately because on the basis of the work's theology it fails to believe that God is in control and will work things out.[84]

Tobias urges that he return and in the process expresses concern for both his father and his mother (10:7). When he finally arrives in Nineveh it is Anna who first sees him and the text somewhat enigmatically has her say to the blind Tobit: "Look, your son is coming!" (11:6). If the blindness is also symbolic of failure to hope, perhaps Anna's last earthy observation is an appeal to believe in what is promised.[85] The story then has Anna run to her son to embrace him. It could easily have concentrated only on Tobit and his healing, but Anna keeps her place. She has no place, however, in what follows. Finally we hear of her death and burial beside Tobit.

This marriage is notable for the assertiveness of Anna. Her concerns are practical and caring. The narrator even depicts her as unjustly accused by himself, her husband, Tobit. But from the narrator's perspective, for all her admirable qualities, perhaps the best he can imagine in a wife, she is tragically lacking the spiritual awareness which would give her hope. Even with his foibles Tobit has this awareness and so models the hope which the work espouses. The depiction of Anna as missing the dimension of trust in divine providence should not be generalised as typical for the author's view of women since Sarah is clearly not

---

[84] Nickelsburg, *Jewish Literature*, observes: "Tobit is paradigmatic in his movement from despair (or rather a vacillation between despair and faith) to doxology. The author is addressing the Tobits of his time" (33).

[85] Portier-Young, "Alleviation of Suffering," suggests that Tobit's blindness relates to "his inability correctly to perceive and appreciate the extent of his connectedness in this human community" (41). Both Tobit and Sarah fail to appreciate the support of those around them (48). Humour also helps (54). The overall framework of the work suggests that much more is at stake than these individual concerns. Israel's hope of restoration provides that wider perspective. Cf. Fassbeck, "Tobit's Religious Universe," who argues that Tobit functions as a metaphor for Israel: its hopes, his prayers, and his blindness (187-89).

like this, as we shall see. In a marriage which includes conflicts which we might view from a very different perspective as positive and healthy the author depicts ongoing caring between husband and wife. Nothing is said of the sexual aspect of their relationship, but that probably means it was also part of their shared intimacy.

The Marriage of Raguel and Edna

The other marriage is that of Sarah's parents. We meet her father in 3:7 which reports "Sarah, the daughter of Raguel, was reproached by one of her father's maids". She retreats to her father's upper room to hang herself, only to relent out of concern for him: "Never shall they reproach my father, saying to him, 'You had only one beloved daughter and she hanged herself because of her distress'. And I shall bring my father in his old age down in sorrow to Hades" (3:10). Concern about bringing shame to her father before others is crucial. There is no indication of concern for her mother, in part probably reflecting the fact that she would not be as exposed before others in her traditional role but also that she is not to be valued in the same way as the head of the household.

In her prayer Sarah extends her concern from disgracing her father to disgracing her own name, but still makes no mention of her mother. Similarly Raphael's instruction to Tobias reports only that Raguel has a daughter, indicating that he will speak to him about his daughter (6:11-13). Sarah is frequently described as Raguel's daughter (3:7, 17; 7:10, 12; 8:20; 10:7, 17; 11:15), reflecting not only the superior parental importance of Raguel, but also the notion that a father possesses his daughter and what happens to her is a matter of negotiation with him.

It is only when Tobias asks Raphael to be introduced to Raguel that we hear of Edna and then in what appears to be aside from the hearing of the others: "He said to his wife Edna, 'How much the young man resembles my kinsman Tobit!'" (7:2). This appears to reflect a pattern of communication in privacy between a husband and his wife since she does not properly belong in the public sphere as he does. On the other hand, Raguel's addressing her appears to allow her then to speak and she becomes active, questioning them about their origins (7:3-6), eliciting the crucial information that the Tobit of whom she and Raguel know is Tobias' father. Again, Tobias' mother is not mentioned, though Tobias himself had concern for both (6:15). In response to Tobit's blindness all three wept: Raguel, Edna, and Sarah (7:7-8).

Tobias reminds Raphael of his intention to ask for Sarah, is overheard by Raguel, and the men agree, Edna having no part, who therefore must be summoned to provide writing materials for the contract (7:13) and then to prepare the other room and take Sarah there (7:15). Her responsibilities include preparing her daughter for marriage. Her weeping as she does so (7:16) may reflect fear or solidarity with Sarah's sad history, but may also indicate grief at the impending separation as she is losing her daughter to a new household. Edna does all this while the men eat and drink (7:14; 8:1). After the wedding night Raguel's behaviour reflects the pattern of his exercising control of the household as he instructs Edna to send one of the maids to find out if Tobias, too, has died (8:12). Similarly Raguel instructs Edna to make bread (8:19). In his asseveration to Tobias Raguel grants him half his inheritance, the rest to follow after he and his wife die, and, addresses Tobias in a way that makes him part of his family: "Take courage, my child, I am your father and Edna is your mother, and we belong to you as well as to your wife now and forever. Take courage, my child" (8:21). Here Edna is not forgotten. He later reminds Sarah that the same applies to her in relation to Tobias' parents (10:12).

In the farewell Raguel acts first, befitting his superior position (10:10-12), but Edna also speaks. She addresses Tobias as "My child and dear brother", expressing the hope that she will see offspring in her lifetime and entrusting her daughter to him with the exhortation: "do nothing to grieve her all the days of your life", concluding: "Go in peace, my child. From now on I am your mother and Sarah is your beloved wife. May we all prosper together all the days of our life" (10:12). This indicates a certain status of authority for the mother, which, while subordinate to the male head of the household, is nevertheless sufficient for her to be able to speak in this authoritative way to her son-in-law. The narrative continues with the report that she kissed them both, probably to be understood as belonging to her farewell communication of word and action and more than simply saying goodbye. This may explain why Raguel is not reported as doing the same at this moment. He had already kissed her in farewell in 10:12. The next verse shifts to the more general comment of Tobias' taking leave, but concludes with a reciprocal blessing: "Finally, he blessed Raguel and his wife Edna, and said, 'I have been commanded by the Lord to honour you all the days of my life'" (10:13). In this we see that the Decalogue command to honour one's parents is being applied equally to parents-in-law. Apart from an allusion to Sarah as Raguel's daughter in 11:15, Raguel and Edna disappear from view in the concluding chapters until 14:12 where the author reports that, having buried both his father and his mother, Tobias "and his wife and children returned to Media and settled in Ecbatana with Raguel his father-in-law", again passing over Edna in silence. The next verse enables us to see that she was still alive and would have her wish to see grandchildren fulfilled: "He treated his parents-in-law with great respect in their old age, and buried them in Ecbatana of Media" (14:13), a model of true piety.

The second marriage, that of Raguel and Edna, lacks the turbulence developed by the author in the first to epitomise the responses of trust and despair to Israel's plight. Rather we are shown a marriage in which Raguel carries out the father's responsibilities, notably in relation to inheritance and the daughter, and Edna is more subservient.[86] She is supportive, as private confidant, an assistant with material and provisions, in the deployment of household staff, and in preparing both the room and her daughter for the wedding night. In these instances she exercises an authority delegated by her husband, but her status also gives her the right to question Tobias about his origins and to instruct him as her son-in-law, who in turn is to honour her along with Raguel as much as he is to honour his own parents. Her authority may be compared with that of Deborah who, Tobit tells, gave him instruction about proper fulfilment of the Law (1:9). She did this, however, in place of her son, Tobiel, who had died (nothing being said about his mother), and while it reflects the assumption that women, too, could be sufficiently knowledgeable of Torah to be able to so,[87] the authority exercised here is different from that of Edna's actions in relation to Tobias, where in part she exercises an authority in her own right.

It is important not to read more into the reference to Deborah's instruction than what is said. Tobit is referring to how they would eat the third tithe: "we would eat it according to the ordinance decreed concerning it in the law of Moses and according to the instructions of Deborah, the mother of my father Tobiel" (ἠσθίομεν αὐτὰ κατὰ τὸ πρόσταγμα τὸ προστεταγμένον περὶ αὐτῶν ἐν τῷ νόμῳ Μωσῆ καὶ κατὰ τὰς ἐντολάς ἃς ἐνετείλατο Δεββωρα ἡ μήτηρ Ανανιηλ τοῦ πατρὸς ἡμῶν) (1:8). Apparently Deborah's instructions related to how this was to happen in practice, probably passing on what had been previous practice from her own generation. She may presumably have had such knowledge also in relation to other laws on the basis of seeing how things had been done. It need mean no more than this.

Responses to the depiction of Edna vary according to various modern sensibilities. Whereas Levine sees her as another typically marginalised woman,[88] Moore, for instance, emphasises that she emerges "as a distinct and caring person as she quizzes the travellers … is moved to tears" and speaks of the development of her character as one of warmth,[89] describing her parting words to Tobias as "both touching and memorable".[90] In a sense both are right. Within the system of marriage which saw women's place as subordinate, the ideal woman would carry such positive traits. The author had also identified positive and practical traits in Anna, though they were tragically (and comically) deficient.

---

[86] See Bow and Nickelsburg, "Patriarchy with a Twist," 137-38.

[87] See Bow and Nickelsburg, "Patriarchy with a Twist," who note that 1:8 indicates that both that women could know the Law and that they could take on religious roles, but only in the absence of a male (133).

[88] Levine, "Diaspora as Metaphor," 111.

[89] Moore, *Tobit*, 225.

[90] Moore, *Tobit*, 218.

The account of the marriage is apparently untouched by the didactic concerns which contrast practical Anna and spiritual Tobit and probably reflects what the author and presumably his hearers would have considered proper and normal. The positive assessment of marriage reflected in both marriages reflects the assessment of the patriarchal marriages in Genesis which influence the narrative,[91] and whose marriages are especially valued in *Jubilees*.[92] Again, as with Tobit and Anna's marriage, we find no specific reference to sexual relations though they may be assumed to have formed natural part of this marriage. Perhaps, however, there is a subtle reference in Edna's name. Edna (עדנה), means "pleasure", including "sexual pleasure" as in Gen 18:12.[93] This may reflect the author's playfulness, but also what he sees as its proper place: in marriage.

The Marriage of Tobias and Sarah

The third marriage calls for more differentiated comment, and unlike the depiction of the parents' marriages also includes some elements pertaining more directly to sexuality. The tale embodies detail about what needed to happen to bring two people together in marriage, presumably reflecting what hearers of the work would consider as normal. It is therefore a valuable window into the marriage practices of its setting. As noted above, there are strict parameters. Marriage must be within the extended family at the pain of death and this is strongly rooted in concern with property, wealth, and welfare.

Our first indications of significance come with the report about Sarah in 3:7-9. The name, Sarah, will surely be a deliberate allusion to the matriarch of Israel just as Tobit and Tobias symbolises the "good", deriving from the long and short form,

---

[91] Nowell, "Ancestral Story," notes the common values which Tobit and Raguel share with one or more of the patriarchs: righteousness, prayer, testing, longevity, blindness, sending off a son, offering parting instruction, hospitality, welcoming angels unawares, calling on the "God of heaven" in relation to seeking a spouse for a son (4-6) and similarly shows connections between Anna, Edna, and Sarah, and the matriarchs: childlessness, reproaches, levirate marriage and accusations of murder (with Tamar), having a blind husband, acts of (alleged) deception relating to goats, grief at sons' departures, baking loaves and "pleasure" (Edna) (6-7).

[92] On this see Betsy Halpern-Amaru, *The Empowerment of Women in the Book of Jubilees* (JSJSup 60; Leiden: Brill, 1999), 33-73; Loader, *Enoch, Levi, and Jubilees*, 249-75.

[93] See Moore, *Tobit*, 192. He notes Levine's assessment that this name and the links between Sarah and (H)anna and barrenness, together with the use of theophoric names exclusively for men, reflect their marginalisation with regard to religious duties. He disagrees, however, that this is particularly so in Tobit, arguing that it reflects common practice in the ancient near east (192-93). Cf. Levine, "Diaspora as Metaphor," 111-12.

טוביה and טובי meaning "Yahu-is-good".[94] Both then represent Israel in its afflictions and serve the author's didactic purpose in assuring the hearers that God indeed hears their prayers. Both, like Israel, are far from perfect. Sarah apparently beats her maids (3:9)[95] and Tobit wrongly accused Anna over the goat. Sarah's plight is described as follows:

διότι ἦν ἐκδεδομένη ἀνδράσιν ἑπτὰ καὶ Ασμοδαῖος τὸ δαιμόνιον τὸ πονηρὸν ἀπέκτεννεν αὐτοὺς πρὶν ἢ γενέσθαι αὐτοὺς μετ' αὐτῆς, καθάπερ ἀποδεδειγμένον ἐστὶν ταῖς γυναιζίν.

For she had been married to seven husbands, and the wicked demon Asmodeus had killed each of them before they had been with her as is customary for wives. (3:8)

While not knowing the cause of the seven husbands' deaths, the maids reproach Sarah on the one hand for killing them and, significantly, on the other for not bearing children: "See, you have already been married to seven husbands and have not born the name of a single one of them" (3:9). Failure to bear children is accordingly something of which to be ashamed. Rachel had spoken of "her reproach" based on her not bearing children (Gen 30:23). More significantly, Sarah's namesake was barren and was similarly treated with contempt by her maid, Hagar (Gen 16:1-5). There are intertextual links also with Tamar, who, while shown by the narrator to be innocent of the death of her first two husbands, is believed by Judah to be the cause (Gen 38:11).[96] The obligation to bear children was grounded in concern for future stability of the household, its welfare and survival.

Ida Fröhlich, suggests that the maid's comment in 3:9, "May we never see a son or daughter of yours", might indicate that she believes that the demon may have had sexual relations with Sarah and so would fear the offspring.[97] In the

---

[94] On the names in Tobit see Moore, *Tobit*, 25-26. See also Littman, *Tobit*, 54; Richard Bauckham, "Tobit as a Parable of the Exiles of Northern Israel," in *Studies in the Book of Tobit* (ed. Mark Bredin; London: T&T Clark, 2006) 140-64, 150-51. He sees in both Tobit's and Sarah's plight and restoration a parable of hope, of Israel and Jerusalem respectively (147-50).

[95] This seems assumed to be true and so gives us a glimpse of the kind of treatment meted out to slaves. See Gruen, *Diaspora*, who notes this as underlining her flawed character (152). See also Jennifer A. Glancy, "The Mistress-Slave Dialectic: Paradoxes of Slavery in Three LXX Narratives," *JSOT* 72 (1996) 71-87, who notes that the narrator shows no sign of disapproval (81). She notes also the treatment of slaves as property (82).

[96] See the discussion in Schüngel-Straumann, *Tobit*, who notes beside this the equivalent numbers, three and seven, as sacred numbers, and that both women were faced with having no future prospects (84-85). The motif of the goat in 2:11-14 may also derive from Genesis 38, but it is not understood in the same way.

[97] Fröhlich, "Tobit," 64.

narrative, however, the maid knows nothing of a demon, but assumes that Sarah herself had killed her husbands. Nevertheless for the hearers of the story the spectre of such intercourse and its offspring might well have evoked the myth of the Watchers and their dreaded offspring and perhaps connect also to traditions about Eve's seduction by the serpent.[98] On the other hand, as Fröhlich notes, the hearers soon learn that Sarah has not had such relations, but has retained her virginity (so 3:15).[99]

Accordingly, in her prayer Sarah, herself, addresses a different kind of shame from that of not having children when she declares that she has not shamed her name or that of her father[100] because she is "innocent of any defilement with a man" (καθαρά ... ἀπὸ πάσης ἀκαθαρσίας ἀνδρός) (3:14).[101] This is not about ritual uncleanness after sexual intercourse, but about the kind of defilement of which *Jubilees* speaks which occurs through illicit sexual intercourse. Thus not only has she not had intercourse with any of her husbands, as 3:8 indicates, but she has also not had intercourse with anyone else (including Asmodeus), which would constitute defilement. She has therefore not engaged in any kind of sexual wrongdoing just as Tobias is exhorted to beware of every kind of sexual wrongdoing, where the focus is marriage outside the family. The other references to the seven husbands also imply that no intercourse took place, though some translations, including *NRSV*, do not make that sufficiently clear.[102] In both 6:14 (ἀπέθανον ἐν τοῖς νυμφῶσιν αὐτῶν τὴν νύκτα ὁπότε εἰσεπορεύοντο πρὸς αὐτή)[103] and 7:11 (πάντες ἀπέθανον τὴν νύκτα ὁπότε εἰσεπορεύοντο πρὸς αὐτήν) the use of the preposition πρός may indicate approach ("toward" *NETS*), but not actual sexual penetration in intercourse, or, alternatively, as Littman suggests, we should understand the imperfect εἰσεπορεύοντο as conative: "they were trying to have intercourse with her".[104]

---

[98] On this see Fassbeck, "Tobit's Religious Universe," 190-91.

[99] Fröhlich, "Tobit," 64.

[100] Gruen, *Diaspora*, deplores her concern about shameful insults from her maid (152), but hearers of the time in a culture where shame and honour mattered so much would probably not share his judgement.

[101] 4QpapTobᵃ ar/4Q196 מן] כ[ל טמאת (6.9); OL: *ab omni immunditia viri*; cf. GI: ἀπὸ πάσης ἁμαρτίας ἀνδρός; V: *ab omni concupiscentia*. On Jerome's expansion here which has a second denial of *concupiscentia*, see Moore, *Tobit*, 151.

[102] Moore, *Tobit*, notes that the translation "went in to her" (7:11) is thus misleading, since it refers to "their entrance into the bridal chamber, not consummation of the marriage" (223).

[103] 4QpapTobᵇ ar/4Q197 reads: כ]די עליין עליה הוו "when they (lit.) went onto her" (4 ii.8); (cf. OL: *ea hora, qua cum illa fuerunt*), which can also mean "have intercourse with her". So Littman, *Tobit*, 114.

[104] Littman, *Tobit*, 114-15.

It is typical of the superior status of the father especially in the public domain, assumed throughout Tobit, that Sarah makes no mention of shaming her mother. Within the framework of values espoused by the author and, we may assume, his hearers, Sarah offers a model of appropriate response to distress, showing even more hope than Tobit, in not remaining with the wish to die.[105] Like fallible Tobit, and, we may assume, like the work's hearers, the occasionally violent Sarah at least knows what the rules are and knows where to turn, thus displaying a dimension missing from Anna. Accordingly God responds.

The summary in 3:17 of God's answer to Tobit's and Sarah's prayer reports that Raphael "was sent to heal both of them". In Sarah's case that is expressed as: "by giving her in marriage to Tobias son of Tobit, and by setting her free from the wicked demon Asmodeus" (δοῦναι αὐτὴν Τωβια τῷ υἱῷ Τωβιθ γυναῖκα καὶ λῦσαι Ασμοδαιον τὸ δαιμόνιον τὸ πονηρὸν ἀπ' αὐτῆς). The word λῦσαι, translated "setting ... free", can sometimes indicate "divorce", but that is hardly the intention here.[106] GI formulates differently, speaking instead of Raphael coming "to bind the evil demon Asmodeus" (δῆσαι Ασμοδαυν τὸ πονηρὸν δαιμόνιον) (as 8:3 in both GI and GII).

While the appearance in the story of the angel Raphael as a young man[107] has to do initially with helping Tobias find his way to Media to retrieve money, he comes to play an essential role in the marriage of Tobias and Sarah because he claims in response to Tobit's insistence: "I am Azariah, the son of the great Hananiah, one of your relatives" (5:13).[108] The narrative does not depict this as

---

[105] On the similarity between Tobit's and Sarah's prayer of distress see Schüngel-Straumann, *Tobit*, 88-90, who notes that at the same time they reflect different emphases characteristic of their gender, Tobit the man confessing sin and concerned with the people and God's justice, and Sarah affirming her innocence and concerned with family, including her and her father's honour (90).

[106] Cf. Ego, "Denn er liebte sie," who writes that in the light of the demon's love and the context concerned with marriage, the driving away of the demon is effectively like a divorce (314). The use of the word and its Aramaic equivalent פטר both in relation to divorce and in relation to release from demons, and its use in Babylonian ritual texts in a manner that sees the demonic possession as analogous to marriage, to which she points (313-14), may indicate at least some play on this association in Tobit.

[107] Moore, *Tobit*, writes of a power struggle between Raphael, on the one hand, and, on the other, Tobias, who tries to order him around (5:8, 10) and Tobit who interrogates him (5:11-14) (190-91). He also notes that there is no indication given of Tobias' age, which he understands might be around 18 or 20, assuming this to be the marriageable age (200). See, however, the discussion in Michael L. Satlow, *Jewish Marriage in Antiquity* (Princeton: Princeton University Press, 2001), who suggests that the evidence of realities suggests around 30.

[108] On the parallels between this narrative and Genesis 24 where Abraham's servant is led by an angel to find Rebecca, see Schüngel-Straumann, *Tobit*, who notes both how the

deceit, but rather appears to assume that an angel can descend and somehow incarnate himself in this way,[109] and may be deliberately alluding to this role in his name, which means, "Yahweh has helped".[110] Special angelic knowledge then enables Raphael to inform Tobias about burning fish liver and heart to ward off demons and using gall to heal blindness (6:1-9). When the text reports that "a large fish leaped up from the water and tried to swallow the young man's foot" (6:3), it may be employing euphemism and indicate an assault on his genitals, reflecting another expression of the demonic in league with Asmodeus' attacks on Sarah's husbands,[111] but this is speculation.[112] Nowell sees the fish as a symbol of death, associated with the waters of chaos.[113] Littman notes, however, that the Tigris salmon can grow to two metres in length, even providing a photograph.[114]

The dual identity, Raphael/Azariah, becomes crucial for the next step towards marriage because as another male member of the extended family Raphael/Azariah can negotiate with Raguel about the marriage of his daughter in the absence of Tobit. This reflects the practice of arranged marriage as based on such negotiations.[115] An essential basis of such negotiations is clarity that the proposed marriage is legitimate and that any other would not be. Raphael knows this is so (6:11-13). In 6:12 4QpapTob[b] ar/4Q197 also includes the exhortation: "Take her to

---

story informs Tobit but also the contrast between the passive Sarah and the active and assertive Rebecca (129-31). See also Paul Deselaers, *Das Buch Tobit: Studien zu seiner Entstehung, Komposition und Theologie* (NTAO; Göttingen: Vandenhoeck & Ruprecht, 1982) 293-302.

[109] See Moore, *Tobit,* 192 saying such changes of roles were nothing extraordinary.

[110] Fitzmyer, *Tobit*, 192-93.

[111] So Moore, *Tobit*, 199.

[112] "Sheer eisegesis" – so Fitzmyer, *Tobit*, 206.

[113] Nowell, "Book of Tobit," 1029.

[114] Littman, *Tobit*, 108, 193.

[115] Cf. 4QpapTob[b] ar/4Q197, which speaks not of Raphael/Azariah making the approach but Tobias, himself: "You will speak about this [you]ng girl tonight; you will engage her (תקימנה) and take her for your wif[e]] (4 ii.3); similarly OL: *et loquere de illa hac nocte*; V: *Pete ergo eam a patre eius.* קום here in haf. means "set up" in the sense of arrange for her to be one's wife, hence appropriately translated "engage" or "betroth". On the probability that תקימנה should be read in the light of the third verb ותסבינה being clearly in the 2nd person, see Joseph A. Fitzmyer, "Tobit," in *Qumran Cave 4: Parabiblical Texts, Part 2* (ed. M. Broshi et al.; DJD 19; Oxford: Clarendon, 1995) 1–79, 49. Later in 6:13 Raphael similarly speaks of himself and her father: "and we shall engage her for you" (ונקימנה [לך]); similarly GII: καὶ μνηστευσόμεθά σοι αὐτήν; OL: *et desponsemus illam tibi*). Cf. Satlow, *Jewish Marriage*, who argues that in the light of Exod 22:15 תקימנה is better understood as referring to arranging the marriage itself, not betrothal (71).

yourself as a wife; to you belongs the right", attested also in OL and Vg.[116] As noted above in discussing the "proper marriage partner", the right relates in particular to provisions for an only daughter to marry within her father's clan.

Raphael also describes Sarah as "sensible, brave, and very beautiful" (6:12),[117] the latter reflecting an affirmation of what would include sexual attractiveness[118] and the former, like the description of Abraham's Sarah in the *Genesis Apocryphon*, emphasising her wisdom (1QapGen ar/1Q20 20.6-7). Raphael/Azariah also assures Tobias that Sarah was set apart for him before the world was made (6:18; cf. Gen 24:44; perhaps already suggested in 6:13), later echoed by Raguel (7:11). We discussed above the issue of predestined partners, both in relation to the previous husbands and in relation to Tobit's understanding of marriage.

Jerome's free translation has expanded Raphael's advice to include the comments:

> 17 For they who receive matrimony in such a manner as to shut out God from themselves and from their mind and to give themselves to their lust as the horse and mule which have no understanding, over them the devil has power. 18 But you, when you shall take her into the chamber, for three days keep yourself continent from her and give yourself to nothing else but prayer with her. ... 21 And the third night you shall obtain a blessing that healthy children may be born to you. 22 And when the third night is over, you shall take the virgin with the fear of the Lord, moved out of love of sons rather than out of lust, that in the seed of Abraham you may obtain a blessing in sons. (6:17-18, 21-22)

The distancing from sexual intimacy, through equating sexual desire with animal lust, reducing the role of sexual intercourse primarily to procreation, and interposing three days of prayer and continence as though sexual intimacy and holiness stand in tension, does not cohere with the positive attitude towards sexuality reflected in the earlier form of the narrative.[119]

---

[116] So Fitzmyer, *Tobit*, 211.

[117] In addition 4QpapTob[b] ar/4Q197 already describes her as "beautiful" in 6:11: לה ברה שפירה "he has a beautiful daughter" (4 i.17); similarly GIII: καὶ θυγάτηρ μία ὑπάρχει αὐτῷ καὶ αὐτὴ καλὴ τῷ εἴδει); OL: *et habet filiam speciosam.*

[118] So rightly Ellis, *Sexual Desire*, 46.

[119] See the discussion in Moore, *Tobit*, 206-207; Otzen, *Judith and Tobit*, 39-40. Fitzmyer, *Tobit*, concludes: "there is no way of ascertaining whether the three nights of abstinence were in Jerome's Aramaic *Vorlage* or whether they are a pious addition made by him" (244).

On the other hand, matching the spirit of the ancient world, the story certainly depicts marriage primarily within the context of households and inheritance, though not without love[120] and affection, including love before first sight:

καὶ ὅτε ἤκουσεν Τωβιας τῶν λόγων Ραφαηλ καὶ ὅτι ἔστιν αὐτῷ ἀδελφὴ ἐκ τοῦ σπέρματος τοῦ οἴκου τοῦ πατρὸς αὐτοῦ λίαν ἠγάπησεν αὐτήν καὶ ἡ καρδία αὐτοῦ ἐκολλήθη εἰς αὐτήν.

When Tobias heard the words of Raphael and learned that she was his kinswoman, related through his father's lineage, he loved her very much, and his heart was drawn to her. (6:18)

The word translated "drawn to", ἐκολλήθη, echoes Gen 2:24 which speaks of marriage: καὶ προσκολληθήσεται πρὸς τὴν γυναῖκα αὐτοῦ, and is used similarly in 1 Esdr 4:20. It includes sexual union in a way by no means restricted to the functionality of procreation. Nicklas observes: "So GII not only says that endogamous marriage does not exclude love, it even clarifies that the family relationship between both partners is *the reason of* Tobias' love".[121] Love, here, includes a positive sexual response, depicted as just as appropriate as the depiction of Sarah as beautiful affirms her sexual attractiveness. Tobias has fallen in love even before seeing her. This may also offer an explanation for the tension in the text between 6:13, which declares that the marriage will take place after they return from Rages, and what actually happens in 7:9 – 9:1 according to which the trip to Rages takes place after the wedding festivities. One might speculate that the author is deliberately playing with the notion that Tobias' passion was enough to subvert original plans. Certainly 7:11 shows him impatient to proceed and determined to change Raguel's plans: "'But now, my child, eat and drink, and the Lord will act on behalf of you both.' But Tobias said, 'I will neither eat nor drink anything until you settle the things that pertain to me'."[122]

It probably reflects a standard procedure that Raphael introduces Tobias to his prospective parents-in-law (7:1-8). That scene presumes that Sarah, the prospective bride, is present, though in the background (7:8).[123] As the norms of

---

[120] Moore, *Tobit*, notes that though the Greek expressions for love vary in Tobit, they all appear to reflect the one Aramaic word, רחמה (209).

[121] Nicklas, "Marriage," 153. He also claims that in 4:12 and 8:7 the concept of love depicted in 6:18 "is opposed to πορνεία" (153). See also Ellis, *Sexual Desire*, 46.

[122] On the tension in the text see Moore, *Tobit*, 205.

[123] On the text of GI which has Sarah greet the guests first, a reading not supported by 4QpapTobᵇ ar/4Q197, see Moore, *Tobit*, 217, who suggests the change was inspired by patriarchal narratives of seeking brides where the future bride is first to receive the guests (Gen 24:15; 29:9) (217). See also Nowell, "Book of Tobit," 1038; and the discussion of the links between Tobit 7 and Genesis 24 and 29 in Nowell, "Ancestral Story," 9-11 and of the allusions to Genesis 2 (12-13).

hospitality dictated, the meeting is expanded by a meal of welcome (7:9). In the narrative Raguel overhears Tobias' request that Raphael approach him about Sarah and shortcircuits what was probably the normal pattern, namely that the father or his representative first addresses the father of the daughter about prospective marriage, including the grounds of legitimacy, and that then the father addresses the prospective son-in-law (7:10). Nothing is said here of gifts, although these are probably to be assumed. In the story Raguel explains the past problems (cf. the requirement to disclose all blemishes as in any fair trade according to the *Damascus Document* (4QD^f/4Q271 3 8). Ragael seeks to put Tobias off for a time, perhaps reflecting what might often have occurred with reluctant fathers, but here the grounds are well-founded.[124] Similarly we might assume that Tobias' insistence reflected common practice. We may well be seeing here a pattern of "haggling" considered to belong to a wide range of transactions of this kind.

Raguel then makes a declaration: "She is given to you in accordance with the decree in the book of Moses, and it has been decreed from heaven that she is to be given to you" (7:11). We may well be hearing what either in substance and perhaps in formulation[125] was considered an essential step in the process. To this the following declaration may have also belonged: "Take your sister; from now on you are her brother and she is your sister. She is given to you from now on forever" (7:11). As Fitzmyer notes, the passive, "is given" is a "theological passive";[126] God is the giver. He then observes: "the girl thus became the possession of her husband, and any aberration or infidelity on her part was a violation of his rights".[127] With regard to addressing them both as brother and sister, Raguel has similarly addressed his wife as "sister" in 7:15, as had Tobit, Anna in 5:21 (cf. also 1QapGen ar/1Q20 2.9, 13; Cant 4:9-10, 12; 5:1-2).[128] It is a transaction legitimised by appeal to Mosaic law and heavenly decree in which

---

[124] As in 6:13 the reference to the husbands does not indicate that they did have sexual intercourse with her, but that they tried to. So Littman, *Tobit*, 121; and see the discussion of 6:13 above.

[125] On Jewish marriage contracts and their reference to the Law of Moses see Moore, *Tobit*, 205. See also Collins, "Judaism of the Book of Tobit," 32.

[126] Fitzmyer, *Tobit*, 233.

[127] Fitzmyer, *Tobit*, 234.

[128] McCracken, "Narration and Comedy," takes the frequent reference to brothers and sisters as indicating the author's attempt to pour scorn on the preoccupation with what he calls tribalism (413-15). According to Wills, *Jewish Novel*, it "becomes a *reductio ad absurdum*" (78). According to Gruen, *Diaspora*, "Focus on the family as the bonding link for diaspora Jews is carried to a point bordering on the burlesque ... This is endogamy with a vengeance – one big, happy family ... Maintenance of kinship ties might bring some stability to an otherwise fragmented diaspora existence. But churlishness, when carried to excess, prompts ridicule" (157). *We* might indeed see it this way, but I am not convinced that the author does. See also Cousland, "Tobit: A Comedy in Error?" 545-46.

Sarah passes from the authority of Raguel to the authority of Tobias in which they now become permanent companions, represented by their designation as siblings. The latter equates to the treatment of each other's parents as their own (8:21). Raguel's blessing may also reflect a step in the usual procedure: "May the Lord of heaven, my child, guide and prosper you both this night and grant you mercy and peace" (7:11).

Similarly the summoning of Sarah, who to this point will presumably have been absent or in the background, taking her by hand and giving her[129] to Tobias (7:12) will have reflected a known ritual act.[130] She has not been consulted in the process, nor has Edna, reflecting the patriarchal practices of the day.[131] The words accompanying the gesture are also likely to have represented in substance if not formulation what hearers would recognise as belonging to the ritual: "Take her to be your wife in accordance with the law and decree written in the book of Moses" (7:12).[132] The Mosaic decree is probably Gen 2:24, though it leaves no trace in the formulations. Alternatively it has the specific situation in mind related to inheritance and so invokes Num 36:8-9, but this is less likely. Perhaps the additional words, "Take her and bring her safely to your father", may be more than instructions adapted to the story. They might reflect the practice of taking the wife to the husband's household within the complex of his father's household.[133] This may also apply to the sending in peace.

The mention in 7:13 of the writing of a marriage contract by the father of the bride "to the effect that he gave her to him as wife according to the decree of the law of Moses" will reflect common practice.[134] It is one of our earliest references to a written marriage contract, though written bills of divorce are attested as early as Deut 24:1-4; Isa 30:1; Jer 3:8.[135] The Elephantine papyri preserve contracts with

---

[129] As Nicklas, "Marriage," notes, in λαβὼν τῆς χειρὸς αὐτῆς παρέδωκεν αὐτὴν τῷ Τωβια γυναῖκα (7:13 GII) the αὐτήν could be read as indicating either Sarah or her hand (148).

[130] On the customs and rituals of marriage, see Satlow, *Jewish Marriage*, 162-81, who notes that Tobit provides much useful detail, especially in relation to the consummation (173-74).

[131] See Schüngel-Straumann, *Tobit*, 127; Bow and Nickelsburg, "Patriarchy with a Twist," 135, 138-39.

[132] So Moore, *Tobit*, who speaks of the ritual of "giving the bride away" (222), noting the basis for Raguel deciding this by himself lies in Exod 21:7; 22:16.

[133] Similarly Moore, *Tobit*, 222, who cites Matt 25:1-12.

[134] Moore, *Tobit*, notes that this is "a *šetār*, a legal document drawn up by the bride's father, rather than a *ketubbah*, a marriage agreement drafted by the groom to protect the bride", as rabbinic halakha required (223). See also Satlow, *Jewish Marriage*, 87, 200-204, 213-16; David Instone-Brewer, *Divorce and Remarriage in the Bible: The Social and Literary Context* (Grand Rapids: Eerdmans, 2002) 1-19.

[135] So Moore, *Tobit*, 223.

the words: "She is my wife, and I am her husband from this day on and forever".[136] Fitzmyer cites P. *Murab.* 20:3 [ושה] מ כדין לאנתה לי תהוה י[את] "[yo]u are my wife according to the Law of M[oses]" and the traditional *ketubah* includes the words: הואי לי לאנתו כדת משה וישראל "Be to me a wife according to the law of Moses and Israel".[137] One might also expect that something would have been written about what happened on divorce and how possessions might be split, but nothing is said of that. GI adds in 7:13 that "they sealed it" (ἐσφραγίσαντο; similarly GIII; and OL: *signavit*), which Moore argues has slipped from the GII text through haplography, and reflects usual practice relating to such documents (cf. 9:5; 5:3).[138]

We may assume that the preparation of a room where the couple would spend their first night also reflected normal custom. Here it is in the wife's parents' house. In situations where both households are not so far apart the pattern may have been for the first night to be spent in the groom's household, though this is not necessarily clear,[139] since Deut 22:16-17 assumes that the bride's parents would have access to cloth showing that the woman was a virgin at her first intercourse, which presumably then will have taken place in their house. Where this was the case, one might imagine that the report that Edna prepares her daughter and wishes her well reflected common practice.[140]

It will also reflect common practice that a feast takes place with eating and drinking, that the bride is not present,[141] but waits for her husband in the bedroom, and that eventually he appears, as 7:14; 8:1 indicates. The abnormality in our story is the account of the exorcism, where the smell of burning fish expelled the demon (as it might expel anyone!) and Raphael chases it down to the remotest parts of Egypt and binds it, an echo of his role in *1 Enoch* 10:4.[142] There is no indication

---

[136] Pap 2 3-4; Pap 7 4 in Emil Kraeling, *The Brooklyn Museum Aramaic Papyri: New Documents of the Fifth Century B.C. from the Jewish Colony at Elephantine* (New Haven: Yale University Press, 1953) 143, 205. See also Moore, *Tobit*, 221, 230-32.

[137] Fitzmyer, *Tobit*, 234; Littman, *Tobit*, notes the husband writes the *ketubah* (123).

[138] Moore, *Tobit*, 224.

[139] Satlow, *Jewish Marriage*, notes that "precisely at the climax of the wedding our sources become annoyingly discrete" (173).

[140] So Satlow, *Jewish Marriage*, 174.

[141] Moore, *Tobit*, notes, that it was "in keeping with etiquette of much of the ancient Near East" that "neither Sarah nor her mother (so vv. 13, 15) ate with the men on formal occasions, but stayed in a nearby room, possibly the kitchen" (222). The situation is well illustrated by the party of Herod Antipas, which presumes that his wife was not present in the main feast (Mark 6:24).

[142] As Robert Doran, "Serious George, or the Wise Apocalypticist – Response to 'Tobit and Enoch: Distant Cousins with a Recognizable Resemblance,' and 'The Search for Tobit's Mixed Ancestry: A Historical and Hermeneutical Odyssey'," in *George W. E. Nickelsburg in Perspective: An Ongoing Dialogue of Learning* (ed. Jacob Neusner and Alan

that in addition the incense was used to fumigate Sarah's body by having the smoke go under her dress as some later Hebrew and Aramaic translations of Tobit intimate[143] nor that it functioned to help generate sperm, as Levine speculates.[144] What follows is probably a return to what the author sees as desirable practice even if not necessarily common practice. Here the bedroom door is shut leaving the couple in private. Then having got into bed, Tobias gets out of bed again, and has Sarah do the same, asking that they pray for safety. In this he is following Raphael's instructions (6:18). This probably reflects the peculiar situation which the couple faced rather than a particular custom. On the other hand, the prayer is not about safety and more likely reflects the kind of prayer which the author commended and perhaps knew, in substance if not in exact formulation. It may normally have come earlier, but be placed here because of the specific need to deal with Asmodeus.

The prayer begins by acclaiming God and calling on "the heavens and the whole creation" to do so. The link with the Genesis creation account continues in the reference to Adam and Eve:

σὺ ἐποίησας τὸν Αδαμ καὶ ἐποίησας αὐτῷ βοηθὸν στήριγμα Ευαν τὴν γυναῖκα αὐτοῦ καὶ ἐξ ἀμφοτέρων ἐγενήθη τὸ σπέρμα τῶν ἀνθρώπων
καὶ σὺ εἶπας ὅτι οὐ καλὸν εἶναι τὸν ἄνθρωπον μόνον ποιήσωμεν αὐτῷ βοηθὸν ὅμοιον αὐτῷ.

You made Adam, and for him you made his wife Eve as a helper and support.

From the two of them the human race has sprung.

You said, "It is not good that the man should be alone; let us make a helper for him like himself" (8:6)

18 ויאמר יהוה אלהים לא טוב היות האדם לבדו אעשה לו עזר כנגדו ...
20 ולאדם לא מצא עזר כנגדו

J. Avery-Peck; Leiden: Brill, 2003) 254-62, notes, binding was also common terminology in magical incantations (258), but that specifically Raphael does so makes influence from the Watcher myth likely.

[143] For the Hebrew and Aramaic texts see Stuart Weeks, Simon Gathercole, and Loren Stuckenbruck, *The Book of Tobit: Texts from the Principal Ancient and Medieval Traditions: With Synopsis, Concordances, and Annotated Texts in Aramaic, Hebrew, Greek, Latin, and Syriac* (Fontes et Subsidia ad Bibliam pertinentes 3; Berlin: de Gruyter, 2004) 220-21. See Moore, *Tobit*, 236, and Fitzmyer, *Tobit*, 242, both referring to the Aramaic on the basis of the edition of Adolf Neubauer, *The Book of Tobit: The Text in Aramaic, Hebrew and Old Latin with English Translations* (Ancient Texts and Translations; Eugene: Wipf & Stock, 2005; originally Oxford: Clarendon, 1878).

[144] Levine, "Diaspora as Metaphor," referring to the role of heat in generating sperm according to Aristotle, *Gen. an.* 717b24;717a5; Plato *Timaeus* 69c-72d, 86c (116 n. 41).

18 καὶ εἶπεν κύριος ὁ θεός οὐ καλὸν εἶναι τὸν ἄνθρωπον μόνον ποιήσωμεν αὐτῷ βοηθὸν κατ᾽ αὐτόν ...

20 τῷ δὲ Αδαμ οὐχ εὑρέθη βοηθὸς ὅμοιος αὐτῷ.

18 Then the LORD God said, "It is not good that the man should be alone; I will make him a helper as his partner." ...

20 but for Adam there was not found a helper like him. (Gen 2:18, 20)

The first part summarises the creation of Adam (Gen 1:27a; 2:7) and the creation of woman (Gen 2:20-24), picking up the word "helper" (βοηθόν) and supplementing it with the word "support" (στήριγμα), and noting that they are the origin of the human race. The significant emphasis lies on the word "helper" (βοηθόν), indicated both by its supplementation and by the following words which in the Greek conflate Gen 2:18 and 2:20, taking God's resolution from 2:18, but the formulation "a helper like him" (βοηθὸς ὅμοιος αὐτῷ) from 2:20. The Hebrew text is identical in Gen 2:18 and 20 (עזר כנגדו) and so the Aramaic of Tobit may well simply have cited 2:18. The Genesis text may well have been the point of reference in the appeals to the decree of the book of Moses in 7:11-12, although in 6:13 it will have been to Num 36:8-9. Nowell notes that among the prayer's allusions to the creation story no reference is made to sin or disobedience, to turning away from God, to mutual recrimination or "curse".[145] The focus is in fact threefold: having a wife as helper and support; procreation, and companionship. Neither βοηθός nor the Hebrew word it translates עזר need imply subordination, since both are used elsewhere of God, but the broader and immediate context indicates that subordination is implied here. The allusion to Adam and Eve having been the origin of the human race implies an emphasis on procreation. Tobias and Sarah are to continue the mandate of Gen 1:28. The author has merged the two perspectives of the creation stories. The citation of 2:18 retains the emphasis on companionship which is more than having a helper and having a reproductive mate. It will have included the kind of caring intimacy which the author depicts in the two senior marriages and will also include sexual intimacy.[146]

Tobias then makes his declaration, which I translate as follows: "I am now taking (λαμβάνω) this sister of mine, not because of sexual immorality (διὰ πορνείαν), but with sincerity/in truth/legitimately" (ἐπ᾽ ἀληθείας) (8:7). The διὰ πορνείαν recalls Tobit's warning: "Beware, my son, of every kind of sexual wrongdoing (ἀπὸ πάσης πορνείας)" (4:12). It refers in both cases to illicit

---

[145] Nowell, "Ancestral Story," 12.

[146] Fassbeck, "Tobit's Religious Universe," suggests a further reason for the allusion to Adam and Eve, namely the ancient tradition that the serpent seduced Eve (190-91). Nothing in the present context suggests this, though it may have occurred to hearers back in 3:8, as discussed above.

sexual relations.[147] The word λαμβάνω means here take by having sexual intercourse (cf. Gen 6:2). The target is not sexual desire, as if to say I am having sexual intercourse with my wife without sexual desire, but illicit expression of sexual desire through engaging in illicit sexual relations, which include sexual relations with prostitutes, for instance, but also with any who are forbidden marriage partners.

The frequent translation of πορνεία here as "lust" creates an ambiguity, leading many not to differentiate between sexual desire wrongly directed and sexual desire rightly directed. Moore, for instance, sees here a negative stance towards sexual passion comparable with what Philo and Josephus report of the Essenes and with what he therefore believes was the view of the Qumran community. On that basis he argues that there may even be some justification for claiming that Jerome was using sources when he depicted a stay of three days before marital consummation, though that is not his conclusion.[148] As our recent review has shown, the Qumran documents, including the sectarian documents, do not reflect the negative stance attributed to the Essenes by Josephus and Philo.[149] Tobit has much more in common with *Jubilees* which differentiates between appropriate sexual intimacy which it strongly affirms – especially in the creation story where it long precedes sexual intercourse for procreation – and illicit sexual relations, including illicit marriages, both of which it strongly condemns. The author of Tobit has shown no hesitation in depicting Sarah's attractiveness and Tobias' passion for her. To find here a denial of such love's validity is to import a jarring element into the text.

So the statement amounts to a declaration of legitimacy. Now part of the prayer, it may well have normally been an element in the formal declarations made in response to the declaration made by the father of the bride. Actual practice may be irrecoverable, so that the possibility should also be considered that the groom's declaration could be expressed in the form of a prayer. The prayer that they may find mercy and may grow old together and the responsive, "Amen, Amen" (8:7-8), may well also reflect part of a standard ritual of marriage.[150] One may interpret what immediately follows, "Then they went to sleep for the night" (καὶ ἐκοιμήθησαν τὴν νύκτα) (8:8), as indicating that they did not engage in sexual

---

[147] As Otzen, *Judith and Tobit*, puts it: "any relationship between man and woman that is not according to the divine will, and 'sincerity' (for 'truth') is the divine will as it is found in the Mosaic Law" (39). Similarly Ellis, *Sexual Desire*, 47.

[148] Moore, *Tobit*, 238, 242-44.

[149] See Loader, *Dead Sea Scrolls on Sexuality*, 369-76.

[150] Schüngel-Straumann, *Tobit*, observes that typically Sarah has nothing to say, but "Amen" (134).

intercourse, but this is not likely to have been what the author intended.[151] All other instances to the wedding nights of previous grooms suggest that sexual intercourse was intended but that the men died before it took place (3:8; 6:14; 7:11). Now Tobias and Sarah will have become one flesh in fulfilment of the Genesis archetype.[152]

While Raguel's thanksgiving prayer in 8:15-17 follows the information that Tobias survived the night,[153] nothing in its content (aside from "it has not turned out as I expected") requires this, so that it should probably be understood as another element of what will have been traditional marriage liturgy. Thus after the groom responds, the father of the bride blesses the couple. The marriage celebration continues with feasting for a further fourteen days, twice the normal practice (cf. Gen 29:27; Judg 14:12; cf. also Tob 11:19),[154] which is also a time for handing over some possessions, here, half of what Raguel owns (8:21), a substantial dowry,[155] and cementing of the new family bond (as in the declarations of parenthood in 8:21).[156]

The apparent resistance to having Tobias leave after completion of the fourteen days may well reflect a hospitality game which was commonly played rather than a problem. Raguel's enormous gift is assembled, "half of all his property: male and female slaves, oxen and sheep, donkeys and camels, clothing, money, and household goods" (8:19), farewells are said and Tobias and Sarah set off for Tobias' family. This would appear to reflect the usual transition from the

---

[151] Some later Hebrew and Aramaic translations say so explicitly. See Weeks, Gathercole, Stuckenbruck, *Book of Tobit*, 228-29. See also Fitzmyer, *Tobit*, 246-47; Littman, *Tobit*, 126; Ellis, *Sexual Desire*, 47-48. Moore, *Tobit*, adds that "otherwise the bride's parents would, presumably, have learned about it the next day when there would have been no 'proof of virginity'" (239).

[152] Wills, *Jewish Novel*, points to the "*Book of Tobit*'s reserve about the consummation of the wedding night" (79), arguing that "sexual love disappears almost completely" (78) and so "they are not indulging their lust but performing a sacred duty" (79). "The fantasies of the full realisation of erotic bliss, which the Greek romance conveys, are not explored in Tobit, but a hope is expressed that the conjugal pair can re-create the divine sanction to be fruitful and multiply" (83). This is surely correct about reserve, but not in posing the alternative as duty or lust. Sexual desire has not completely disappeared, as his own qualification still acknowledges.

[153] Gruen, *Diaspora*, depicts the humorous episode of Raguel digging a grave just in case as indicating the author's disapproval of "Raguel's dread of neighborly disapproval" (158). I doubt hearers in a world concerned with shame would see it that way.

[154] Moore, *Tobit*, suggests the doubling to emphasise Raguel's joy (246).

[155] So Littman, *Tobit*, 129.

[156] Soll, "Marriage as Scriptural," sees 8:21 as a dowry and based on a commitment to endogamy, understood in the strict sense, of marrying cousins or close kin, and assuming a daughter may inherit (172-73).

bride's to the groom's household. Another party awaits. This too was standard practice. There may be echoes of special rites of acclaiming the groom's arrival in the account of Anna seeing Tobias from afar. The healed Tobias and Anna welcome Sarah as a daughter to her new home (11:16-17).[157] Then the seven day feast begins, again probably reflecting common practice (11:18). It may have been, as some manuscripts indicate, an occasion for further giving gifts to the husband (gifts to either of them would count as gifts to him).

Tobit reflects many of the practices which accompanied and constituted weddings.[158] These include the possibility of a man negotiating with his prospective father-in-law (otherwise it could be parents), usually agreeing on a bride price (mohar), not mentioned here. Similarly Tobit apparently fails to mention a dowry (but cf. 8:21; 9:10) and witnesses to the agreement. Concern for offspring and inheritance features strongly, but again nothing is said of what would usually be part of the contract, namely provisions for dealing with financial arrangements in the eventuality of a divorce or death. The story assumes a monogamous marriage, which was the common pattern for all but the rich. The story does not limit marriage functionally to procreation and producing offspring, but in the depiction of all three marriages includes intimate companionship and especially in the case of Tobias and Sarah also has room for love,[159] which includes sexual love. Moore notes the unusual feature that the marriage is kept private for fear for further shame coming upon the family through an eighth casualty, but otherwise the pattern of men feasting, women preparing the bridal suite, the couple engaging in sexual intercourse the same night, festivities for a period (here 14 days), before then the bringing of the bride to the groom's house and further feasting, reflects common patterns.

Raphael's Wisdom

After the wedding festivities are over, and probably only then, because people would appreciate that they would have demanded so much attention, the account has Tobias undertake to pay Raphael (12:1-5). This gives occasion for Raphael finally to disclose his identity as "one of the seven angels who stand ready and

---

[157] Bow and Nickelsburg, "Patriarchy with a Twist," note that while Edna addressed Tobias as a brother, Tobit calls Sarah "daughter" and so "keeps her in a dependent position" (142).

[158] See the review of ancient Near Eastern and Jewish material in Moore, *Tobit*, 225-32, who cites a range of ancient documents.

[159] Moore, *Tobit*, notes of the marriages that "the narrator shows the reader, not only their love and kindness to one another …, but their warts and all (2:13-14; 5:18-20; 10:3-7)" (241).

enter before the glory of the Lord", known to us also from *1 Enoch*.[160] His authoritative exhortations offer nothing further related to marriage.[161] He had

---

[160] On the common elements with *1 Enoch* see George W. E. Nickelsburg, "Tobit and Enoch: Distant Cousins with a Recognizable Resemblance," in *George W. E. Nickelsburg in Perspective: An Ongoing Dialogue of Learning* (ed. Jacob Neusner and Alan J. Avery-Peck; Leiden: Brill, 2003) 1.217-39, who notes that in Tobit "holy angels" or "holy ones" attend the divine presence (8:15; 11:14), seven of them, including Raphael, serving as witnesses and intercessors (3:16-17; 12:12-15), and being sent to aid humans in need, Raphael as healer (3:17; 12:14). This matches the ideas of *1 Enoch* where Raphael is the heaven-sent healer (10:4-8). As there angels accompany Enoch's journeys, so Raphael accompanies Tobias, protects him from danger and teaches him medicine (6:3-8). Like the Watchers, Asmodeus has fallen in love with a woman, and like Asael is "bound" by Raphael (8:3; cf. *1 Enoch* 10:4). Nickelsburg sees a difference in the impartation of "magical information" by Raphael, something for which the Watchers were condemned in *1 Enoch* (223). He also notes that Tobit's main explanation for suffering, unlike in *1 Enoch*, is human sin (224). Hope in Tobit includes healing and divine help in the present against all appearances in contrast to *1 Enoch's* hope for the eschatological undoing of primordial disaster (224). Tobit does, however share much in common with the eschatology expressed in the *Apocalypse of Weeks* including the rebuilding of the temple after its burning and the people's dispersion, the conversion of the Gentiles and the removal of the wicked, though the latter, unlike Tobit, does not view the post-exilic cultus favourably (228). The *Epistle of Enoch* and Tobit share a concern for the poor and social justice, but with the rest of *1 Enoch* differ with regard to the Mosaic Law (232-33). They also share some liturgical vocabulary (234). Nickelsburg does not suggest dependence but possible use of common tradition, including notions of angelic revelation and instruction (236). He notes also that both have Mesopotamian and Upper Galilean associations (238). Nickelsburg revisits the issue in George W. E. Nickelsburg, "The Search for Tobit's Mixed Ancestry: A Historical and Hermeneutical Odyssey," in *George W. E. Nickelsburg in Perspective: An Ongoing Dialogue of Learning* (ed. Jacob Neusner and Alan J. Avery-Peck; Leiden: Brill, 2003) 241-53; and in his response to Doran, "Wise Apocalypticist," in the same volume: "Response to Robert Doran," 263-66. In "Search for Tobit's Mixed Ancestry," Nickelsburg broadens the search beyond *1 Enoch* but nevertheless underlines the commonality in the allusion to the seven angels and their roles, the primordial demons, and eschatology. Two further items not noted by Nickelsburg seem significant: a common concern with illicit marriage and Tobit's depicting demonic activity as sexual, not among their repertoire in *1 Enoch* (for instance in *1 Enoch* 15:9), surprisingly so, when one considers what gave rise to them in the first place.

[161] McCracken, "Narration and Comedy," takes Raphael's failure to address marriage as an indication that he disapproves of the narrow endogamy which Tobit espouses (414-15) and finds some support for this in Raphael's first encounter with Tobit, where Tobit's interrogation is depicted as excessive. But Raphael had earlier emphasised Sarah's close kinship links to Tobias, so that the silence in his parting words should not be read negatively. See also Soll, "Family as Scriptural," who cautions: "Raphael's initial reluctance to answer Tobit should not lead us to believe that Tobit is being fussy or

however made brief comments earlier. He had identified Sarah as "sensible, brave, and very beautiful" (6:12),[162] the latter reflecting an affirmation of what would include sexual attractiveness. After instructing Tobias how to banish the demon and how then to pray, he declares: "Do not be afraid, for she was set apart for you before the world was made" (6:18). It coheres with the belief in providence which pervades the work.

More significant is Raphael's equipping Tobias to deal with Asmodeus. In 3:7 we read of "the wicked demon Asmodeus" who had killed seven husbands thus far before they had consummated their marriages. Tobias reports what he had heard: "It was a demon that killed them. It does not harm her, but it kills anyone who desires to approach her" (6:15). By following Raphael's advice Tobias succeeds in expelling the demon to remotest parts of Egypt where Raphael bound him hand and foot (8:3). What may derive like much of Tobit's story from folktale in which sometimes serpents representing the demonic come out of virgins and attack men[163] is retold with sparse detail. The wider background of the story reflects male fears of women's sexuality, focused in particular on the act of sexual intercourse and especially on the wedding night.[164] The name Asmodeus was possibly familiar to the hearers and appears to have Persian origins.[165] No explanation is given of where the demon resides nor of its connection to Sarah. It does not depict her as possessed by the demon nor as seduced by it. No specific connection is made between the demon and sexual intercourse, although clearly the demon is understood to intervene to prevent it. The author show no interest in the ways the two relate, such as whether the demon may come from her mouth or her vagina or elsewhere.[166]

---

snobbish ... Raphael's challenge is not a rebuke, but a kind of test which Tobit passes" (169).

[162] In addition 4QpapTob[b] ar/4Q197 already describes her as "beautiful" in 6:11: לה ברה שפירה "he has a beautiful daughter" (4 i.17); similarly GIII: καὶ θυγάτηρ μία ὑπάρχει αὐτῷ καὶ αὐτὴ καλὴ τῷ εἴδει); OL: et habet filiam speciosam.

[163] See the examples cited by Otzen, Tobit and Judith, 10-11.

[164] On this see Schüngel-Straumann, Tobit, 82-85, who traces such fear to the sense that women are seen as having advantage over men in being more closely connected to life and death (84).

[165] On the name see Fitzmyer, Tobit, 150, who notes two possible explanations: "Old Persian or Avestian, equalling aēšma daēva, "demon of wrath," an associate of Ahriman, the god of evil, known from Avestan literature" or from Hebrew שמד, "destroy, exterminate", on the basis of popular etymology concocted to keep the tradition closer to home" (150-51). See also Moore, Tobit, 147 and on the motif of seven husbands, p. 145.

[166] Similarly Moore, Tobit, notes that there is "no description of the demon's entering the bridal chamber (assuming that Asmodeus was not already, quite literally, inside Sarah) ... nor is there any description of the demon's size or appearance" (241).

On the other hand, 4QpapTob[a] ar/4Q196 provides further information as a comment of Tobias in 6:15, reconstructed by Fitzmyer as: די ר[ח]ם לה "which is [in lo]ve with her" (14 i.4)[167] (also GIII ὅτι φιλεῖ αὐτήν; OL: *quoniam diligit illam*). This may suggest that the demon's aggression arises from sheer jealousy.[168]

The notion of a spiritual being in love with Sarah recalls the myth of the Watchers, who fell in love with women and whose offspring became the demons which plague humankind (Gen 6:1-4; *1 Enoch* 6 - 8).[169] This would be one of the rare instances where the activity of the angels' offspring is depicted in sexual terms.[170] It is noteworthy that, as Levine points out, by contrast Raphael, as a good angel, is depicted never speaking with a woman, avoiding their company, even sometimes ignoring their existence (11:2-3; 12:6).[171] Conversely, as Bow and Nickelsburg observe, "Only the male characters have 'good' contact with supernatural beings".[172]

The chief interest beside the story itself is the overcoming of the demonic, symboliszing the overcoming of the demonic in all contexts for those who do God's will, not least in overcoming the demonic which leaves Israel suffering. In that sense Sarah's plight, perhaps enhanced by her very name, and Tobit's plight, represent for the author the people, Israel. Both, despite their failings, know to cry out appropriately to God in prayer, whereas Anna's partly understandable responses represents despair. The work then employs a tale about finding a marriage partner, reminiscent of patriarchal narratives, combined with folkloric elements which provide many elements of the story, including the demonic Asmodeus, to encourage hope. It does so with a theology informed by what is embedded in the *Book of the Watchers* and in *Jubilees*, namely that the afflictions of this world are the directly or indirectly the work of demonic forces who will one day be overcome and Israel restored, but who may now be countered with remedies taught by angels, not least the healer archangel, Raphael, who meets us

---

[167] Fitzmyer, *DJD* 19, conjectures שדא די [רחמה "demon who loves her" also in 4QpapTob[b] ar/4Q197 4 ii.9-10 (48-49); but see also GI: ὅτι δαιμόνιον φιλεῖ αὐτήν; G III: ὅτι φιλεῖ αὐτήν; OL: *quoniam diligit illam*.

[168] So Moore, *Tobit*, 205.

[169] Moore, *Tobit*, 206.

[170] This is strikingly not the case in the *Book of the Watchers* and most traditions of which I am aware which stand under their influence. See my discussion in William Loader, "Attitudes towards Sexuality in Qumran and Related Literature – and the New Testament," *NTS* 54 (2008) 338-54, 339-42.

[171] Levine, "Diaspora as Metaphor," 110.

[172] Bow and Nickelsburg, "Patriarchy with a Twist," 134. They then exaggerate: "In fact, in Tobit's world the realm of the supernatural is off-limits to women" (134), which discounts Sarah's prayer.

in *1 Enoch*. These remedies belong not to forbidden magic but to ancient medical practice, which as in Sir 38:1-15 and *Jub.* 10:10-12, is affirmed.[173]

Conclusion

Within the framework of what serves to enhance hope in the midst of affliction the work provides us with much incidental information about what must have been common practices with regard to marriage and what were the author's strictures about legitimate marriages. The standard requires marriage within the extended family and not beyond with any women of the tribe, let alone a non-Jew and claims this is required by Mosaic law at the pain of death, thus taking a far stricter line than *Jubilees*, *Aramaic Levi Document*, and *4QMMT*, which also include illicit marriage within their notion of what was originally the word for prostitution. Here this concern appears related not to idolatry nor to immoral influence, but to inheritance and thus the stability and welfare of the household. Its devotion to Jerusalem also set it apart from texts critical of the temple and its practices such as we find in Enochic literature.

The incidental material on marriage invites comparison with other evidence of marriage practices of the time. It is clearly affirming of marriage, tracing its foundation to Genesis 2, even claiming divine predestination, and, for all the tensions developed for symbolic reasons in the marriage of Tobit and Anna, depicts a valuing of lifelong marital partnership, which it understands in a way that sees the man as the head of the household and his wife as supportive companion serving his interests. Sexual relations, blocked by the demonic, belong within the context of such marriage. Anything else is defilement and sexual wrongdoing.

Its positive attitude towards marriage, albeit patriarchal marriage, and its intertextual links with both the archetypal marriages of Genesis and its primal archetype, is close to what we find in *Jubilees*.[174] It appears even to know some of the expansions of those narratives now preserved in *Jubilees* (Noah's wife,

---

[173] On this see Bernd Kollmann, "Göttliche Offenbarung magisch-pharmakologischer Heilkunst im Buch Tobit," *ZAW* 106 (1994) 289-99, who puts the apotropaic use of odour to expel demons into the category of the genuinely magical (292-93) and the use of gall to cure blindness into the category of medical, citing parallels from the ancient Near East (293-97). See also Moore, *Tobit*, 201-202. Using odour, incense, or smoke to expel demons would not have been seen as forbidden magic and survives well in liturgical practices to our day.

[174] So also Fassbeck, "Tobit's Religious Universe," 194. She concludes: "While Tobit does not display the strong anti-gentile sentiments and many of the other features that characterize *Jubilees* and related literature, it may be placed in the same general social context if at a somewhat earlier time" (195). See also Nickelsburg, "Tobit, Genesis and the *Odyssey*," 50-51.

Rebecca's grief), perhaps drawing on common tradition, and assumes a similar cosmology in which the faithful are confronted by demons and in which an angel of the presence intervenes with countermeasures and gives instruction.[175] It shares with *Jubilees* the concern about illicit sexual relations and proper marriage, but also differs in many respects. For Tobit proper marriages are not just with other Israelites as in *Jubilees* where intermarriage with Gentiles and so exposure to their sexual and other wrongdoing is attacked in the interests of preserving the people, the temple and land from defilement. Rather proper marriages are those which preserve the tight knit extended families, including their inheritance, and so their welfare. Demarcation from Gentiles is assumed in both, but presupposed in Tobit, whose concerns lie elsewhere, and which does not display anti-Gentile sentiments.[176] Unlike *Jubilees*, for Tobit calendar is of no concern and nor are particular cultic practices,[177] though it reflects careful observance of tithes, corpse impurity, almsgiving, and food laws.

At most the story's diaspora context may indicate that the author's and hearers' context is the diaspora, but the focus is more on temple- and Jerusalem-based restoration than it is on being rescued from any hardship which the diaspora poses. Within this hope, family stability, understood as patriarchal marriage lived in mutually caring but unequal partnership and preserving inheritance through offspring, is foundational. In this context sexual relations find their place, as expression of properly directed love and desire, intimate companionship, and the producing of children.

2.1.3   Judith

The Book of Judith survives probably only in translation,[178] its presumably Hebrew original version[179] leaving no trace at Qumran and probably nowhere

---

[175] Fassbeck, "Tobit's Religious Universe," 194.

[176] So Fassbeck, "Tobit's Religious Universe," 195.

[177] Fassbeck, "Tobit's Religious Universe," 195.

[178] In what follows I use the text edition of Robert Hanhart, ed., *Iudith* (SVTG 8.4; Göttingen: Vandenhoeck & Ruprecht, 1979) and the *NRSV* translation, indicating by an asterisk translations which I have modified.

[179] On Hebrew as the likely original language of the work see Erich Zenger, *Historische und legendarische Erzählungen: Das Buch Judit* (JSHRZ 1.6; Gütersloh: Mohn, 1981), 430-31; Carey A. Moore, *Judith* (AB 40; Garden City: Doubleday, 1985) 66-67; Frank Zimmermann, "Aids for the Recovery of the Hebrew Original of Judith," *JBL* 57 (1938) 67-74. Cf. Ida Fröhlich, *"Time and Times and Half a Time": Historical Consciousness in the Jewish Literature of the Persian and Hellenistic Eras* (JSPSup19; Sheffield: Sheffield Academic Press, 1996) 112-32, who argues that the Hebraisms in vocabulary and syntax "only prove that the native language of the author may have been

else.[180] We know it primarily from the Greek translation, but it survives also in Old Latin, in Jerome's free translation, and in Syriac.[181] The attempts to date and place the work on the basis of treating it as history have long been abandoned in favour of recognising the confusion of times, personages, and places as part of the author's generalising concern to depict the conflict between God and evil on a universal scale,[182] lending it more easily relevant to his own context. That setting is usually identified as some time following the Maccabean period where Antiochus Epiphanes matches the protagonist, Nebuchadnezzar, well, probably not later than the early years of Alexander Janneus.[183] The work makes extensive use of biblical stories, not least, those of heroes and especially heroines who faced adversity on behalf of their people,[184] and appears also to depend on the account in 1 and 2 Maccabees of Judas' victory over Nicanor (1 Macc 7:26-49; 2 Macc 15:1-37).[185]

Aramaic or Hebrew. Other characteristics indicate that the author used Greek sources, and it is likely that the text of the book of Judith surviving in the LXX had also been written in Greek" (114). Similarly Claudia Rakel, "Das Buch Judit: Über eine Schönheit, die nicht ist, was sie zu sein vorgibt," in *Kompendium Feministische Bibelauslegung* (ed. Luise Schottroff, Marie-Theres Wacker; Gütersloh: Gütersloher Verlagshaus, 1999) 410-21, 410.

[180] On the later Hebrew paraphrased versions see Otzen, *Tobit and Judith*, 137-40; Moore, *Judith*, 101-108.

[181] Otzen, *Tobit and Judith*, 140-42; Moore, *Judith*, 91-101.

[182] See Otzen, *Tobit and Judith*, 81-93; Zenger, *Judit*, 438-39; Moore, *Judith*, 38-56; Fröhlich, *Time*, 112-32. Nickelsburg, *Jewish Literature*, contemplates that "a tale that originated in the Persian period has been rewritten in Hasmonean times" (101). On development of research see Toni Craven, "The Book of Judith in the Context of Twentieth Century Studies of the Apocryphal/Deuterocanonical Books," *CurBR* 12 (2003) 187-229.

[183] See Mittmann-Richert, *Einführung*, who notes that 2:28 must reflect a time before the annexation of the coastlands during the time of Alexander Janneus (103 – 76 B.C.E) and that 4:6-8 appears to reflect the political structures of the later Hasmoneans, thus suggesting composition of the work during the time of John Hyrcanus (142-104 B.C.E.) (85). See also *Tobit and Judith*, 132-34; Moore, *Judith*, 67-70. This counts against the otherwise attractive suggestion of Philip Francis Esler, "Ludic History in the Book of Judith: The Reinvention of Israelite Identity?" *BibInt* 10 (2002) 107-43, that it might allude to the defeat of Demetrius in 88 B.C.E. and celebrate the leadership of Salome (121).

[184] See for instance Zenger, *Judit*, 440-46; Otzen, *Tobit and Judith*, 74-79, 111-12.

[185] See Mittmann-Richert, *Einführung*, 86; Zenger, *Judit*, 442-43; Esler, "Ludic History," 118-20.

The first half of the Book of Judith sets the scene for Judith's appearance,[186] depicting Nebuchadnezzar's plan of vengeance against those nations who had refused to support him in his war against the Persians. The account is rich in anomalies and inaccuracies. Thus: "Nebuchadnezzar is introduced as king of the Assyrians (1:1), who makes war on Israel *after* their return from the exile (5:18-19; 4:3)".[187] This already raises a number of questions. Would the author have been unaware of making such blatant errors or is this deliberate? The author's obvious familiarity elsewhere in the book with biblical writings suggests that the running together of such diverse material is deliberate and that he would have expected well-informed hearers to recognise what he was doing.[188] That, then, raises the further question: was this then simply entertainment where such accuracy did not matter or has the author a serious intent?

Certainly the work exhibits great playfulness and is rich in irony, but its references to God go beyond the burlesque. Saying something about God is central to its concerns.[189] The creative and often confused setting notwithstanding, the work addresses issues which the author apparently wants his hearers to take seriously. As Gruen notes, "the solemn religiosity of Judith underpins the whole tale ... Judith's piety is its most conspicuous characteristic".[190] This means that in listening to the work with a view to detecting attitudes towards sexuality we need to be aware of both the playful and the serious and to seek to hear them as far as possible within the world in and beyond the text. We do so also aware that the work has produced its own rich history of interpretation, not least in art,[191] but more recently in the reactions positive and negative from within contemporary

---

[186] On the careful literary structure in which the apparently useless overload of information in chapters 1 – 7 functions as one half of a chiastic structure in the work, see Toni Craven, *Artistry and Faith in the Book of Judith* (Chico: Scholars, 1983) 47-112, but also Mittmann-Richert, *Einführung*, whose model gives greater weight to the three major speeches: Judith's before her people as the centrepiece (Judith 8) and matching each other: Achior's in Judith 5 and Judith's before Holofernes in Judith 11 (83).

[187] Nickelsburg, *Jewish Literature*, 100.

[188] John Craghan, *Esther, Judith, Tobit, Jonah, Ruth* (OT Message 16; Wilmington: Glazier, 1982) 70 "The historical and geographical blunders may very likely be the author's use of irony" (70); Fröhlich, *Time*, 120-21; Esler, "Ludic History," 117.

[189] So Rakel, "Judit," 411.

[190] Gruen, *Diaspora*, 162, who then goes on to demonstrate that wit and humour pervade it (163-69).

[191] On this see the studies of N. Stone, "Judith and Holofernes: Some Observations on the Development of the Scene in Art," in *"No One Spoke Ill of Her": Essays on Judith* (ed. James C. VanderKam; SBLEJL 2; Atlanta: Scholars, 1992) 73-93; Margarita M. Stocker, *Judith: Sexual Warrior: Women and Power in Western Culture* (New Haven: Yale University Press, 1998).

perspectives which seek to engage critically what ancient texts say about women.[192]

The long introduction depicts Israel as one of those who refused to support Nebuchadnezzar and so now faces the might of Holofernes, his general, with his 120000 men and 12000 cavalry.[193] The oddly concocted account of invasion and assault, riddled with inaccuracies and anachronism, nevertheless depicted a reality with which the author and his hearers were well familiar. They are not far from the days of Antiochus' oppression and subsequent generations had to live with the fluctuating threat of his successors. Concretely, they would have had no difficulty identifying again with the fear for Jerusalem and the temple which the story presents (4:1-4), nor with the fear of what it meant for people, expressed in their prayer in 4:12 "not to allow their infants to be carried off and their wives to be taken as booty, and the towns they had inherited to be destroyed, and the sanctuary to be profaned and desecrated to the malicious joy of the Gentiles". Violence and rape were the lot of conquered women in such war, as still so often today.[194] The detail may already serve to evoke what is to come, certainly for those already familiar with the story. Judith would be confronted by such violation. This is part of the larger threat.

The first element in Israel's response is to secure its borders to the north, reflecting, as it appears, the assumption that the areas of Samaria also belong to its territory.[195] In this context we first hear of Bethulia (4:6), pictured as near Dothan on the south side of the plain of Esdraelon, and the command to them "to seize the mountain passes, since by them Judea could be invaded; and it would be easy to stop any who tried to enter, for the approach was narrow, wide enough for only two at a time to pass" (4:7). We shall return to its potential symbolism, but the

---

[192] See for instance the discussion in Rakel, "Judit," 410-21; Pamela J. Milne, "What Shall We Do With Judith? A Feminist Reassessment of a Biblical 'Heroine'," *Semeia* 62 (1993) 37-58 and our discussion especially in the conclusion below.

[193] The numbers may be playful numerology to depict the enemy of the 12 tribes of Israel. Already 1:16 reports that Nebuchadnezzar celebrated for 120 days. Cf. also 1 Macc 15:13 which pictures Antiochus with 120000 infantry, but 8000 cavalry.

[194] See the discussion of Judith in the context of abuse of women in war in Claudia Rakel, *Judit über Schonheit, Macht und Widerstand im Krieg: Eine Feministisch-Intertextuelle Lektüre* (BZAW 334; Berlin: de Gruyter, 2003) and on rape in war: pp. 56-62. See also Rakel, "Judit," where she emphasises that the book links imperialistic oppression with rape (413-14); and Glancy, "Mistress-Slave Dialectic," 83.

[195] Fröhlich, *Time*, 124, 128-29. Cf. Mittmann-Richert, *Einführung*, who suggests that locating the exchange at Bethulia in Samaritan land is meant to imply that Nebuchadnezzar's army did not even make it to the holy land (94). See also the discussion in Moore, *Judith*, 150-51.

measures made good sense and may even have reflected techniques of resistance fighters of the period.[196]

Israel's response was also to turn to God in their desperation: "They and their wives and their children and their cattle and every resident alien and hired laborer and purchased slave – they all put sackcloth around their waists" (4:10). Clothing animals in sackcloth may seem to us to be deliberate humour,[197] but that would be jarring. As Moore notes,[198] it has a precedent in Jonah 3:8-9, and so for hearers more likely serves to enhance the extent of distress. Nothing suggests that the author means us to see the response of the Israelites, their prayers, fasting, sackcloth, prostrations and offerings (4:8-15), in anything but a positive light. This is confirmed in the only direct reference to God's action in the work: "The Lord heard their prayers and had regard for their distress" (4:13).[199] It is pivotal for the plot, since what follows will by implication demonstrate what God did in response.[200]

The tension builds as the author depicts Holofernes consulting the traditional neighbours and enemies of Israel, Moab and Ammon (5:1-4), whom he addresses in similarly evocative language as "Canaanites" (5:3). The author thus connects his hearers to Israel's ancient and continuing struggles with its neighbours. He then has Achior, an Ammonite, give Holofernes a potted summary of Israel's history, depicting them as having come to know the God of heaven, on his command settling in Canaan, in response to famine going to Egypt, and by God's help being rescued from its oppression to take possession of all the hill country driving out its inhabitants (5:9-16). In splendid anachronism Achior then reports the destruction of temple (in real history by Nebuchadnezzar!) and the exile as God's punishment for departing from the way prescribed for them, their return and resettling in the hill country and Jerusalem with their sanctuary (5:17-19). In accordance with his Deuteronomic review of its history, which also clearly informs the author's

---

[196] On this see Marie-Françoise Baslez, "Polémologie et histoire dans le livre de Judith," *RB* 111 (2004) 362-76, who suggests that the author was well informed.

[197] So Craven, *Artistry*, 115; Gruen, *Diaspora*, 164.

[198] Moore, *Judith*, 152.

[199] Rakel, "Judit," 412, uses this single occurrence as counter to the thesis of Milne, "What Shall We Do With Judith?" that God rather than Judith is the hero of the story and that Judith is just his helper (54). Within the world of the author and his text, unlike our world, one would expect that no hero would eclipse God. That still left room, however, for those who served God to be hailed as heroes, as in the case of Judith.

[200] So also Sabine van den Eynde, "Crying to God: Prayer and Plot in the Book of Judith," *Bib* 85 (2004) 217-31: "The actual effect of these prayers on the plot is clear: God hears their prayer (Jdt 4,13). Actually, this is the only direct action of God mentioned in the whole book" (220).

theology, Achior cautions Holofernes, that Israel will be defeated only if it has sinned (5:20-21).

The peoples of the sea coast and of Moab want to cut Achior to pieces, declaring Israel no match for Holofernes, but Holofernes, himself, then ups the stakes, by identifying the ultimate conflict: "What god is there except Nebuchadnezzar? He will send his forces and destroy them from the face of the earth. Their God will not save them" (6:2). There are echoes of the account of Sennacherib's siege of Jerusalem (Isaiah 36 – 38; 2 Kings 18 – 20).[201] The author then uses the depiction of God as universal Lord in Second Isaiah[202] to have Holofernes attribute his declaration of victory to Nebuchadnezzar: "So says King Nebuchadnezzar, lord of the whole earth. For he has spoken; none of his words shall be in vain" (6:4). The ultimate battle is between Nebuchadnezzar, who represents war and violence, and the God of Israel. This is something much more than a competition among deities and would-be deities. For it plays itself out in the threat of war and violence which confronts the people and the author thereby encourages his hearers to see their own situation in this light. Thus the author depicts Achior condemned, bound, and delivered to the people of Bethulia (6:5-13).

Hearing from Achior Holofernes' intent, the people of Bethulia cry out to the true "Lord God of heaven" (6:19), and the next day see for themselves his terrifying forces (7:1-4). They, in turn, follow the military advice of the coastland peoples, the Moabites, joined by that other traditional foe, the Edomites, to seize their water supply. The shift in the narrative from the profoundly theological dimension to details of military strategy connect the two. The merciless cruelty of war has a theological dimension. "They and their wives and children will waste away with famine, and before the sword reaches them they will be strewn about in the streets where they live" (7:14). The author is evoking what would have been real fears with which his hearers could identify, and connects them to their faith. The effects were as predicted: "Their children were listless, and the women and young men fainted from thirst and were collapsing in the streets of the town and in the gateways; they no longer had any strength" (7:22).

First the author depicts them crying out again to God (7:19), but then in despair urging surrender: better to be slaves and live than witnessing "our little ones dying before our eyes, and our wives and children drawing their last breath" (7:27). The author is not sparing in depicting human suffering. The people again

---

[201] Fröhlich, *Time*, contemplates that perhaps the story originated as a tale based on Jerusalem (as in later Hebrew paraphrases) and Sennacherib's siege in 701 B.C.E. (125-26). Cf. also Zenger, *Judit*, who argues that Bethulia is a cryptogram for Jerusalem (435).

[202] Mittmann-Richert, *Einführung*, notes that Judith depicts Nebuchadnezzar as having the traits of Zion's God, invisible to the world beneath him, declaring by his word, and coming from all directions (90).

cry out in prayer and Uzziah proposes holding out another five days with the theological assurance that God will not abandon them entirely (7:30). The author sustains the focus on their need: "The women and children he sent home. In the town they were in great misery" (7:32). To this point there is no letting up on the prediction of distress. There is, however, an intertextual echo of the people's cry to Moses at Massah and Meribah in Exodus 17, to turn back to Egypt. That will also shape what Judith will expound as a testing of God in Uzziah's proposal.[203] For all that, the author has depicted the situation in a way that evokes a considerable degree of empathy and solidarity.

To this point the focus has been on the "god" Nebuchadnezzar and his general's army inflicting suffering on an innocent people and threatening more. Sexual violation is an element of that threat, especially against women, but as part of a larger picture of the violence of war. This will change as the story proceeds, but the broader threat from such invading forces remains an important backdrop for the story and its significance.

Enter Judith. Her name, not unknown at the time,[204] meant "Jewess" or "woman of Judea".[205] It is especially suitable for one who acts on behalf of Judea. It may also be meant to echo the name of Israel's hero against Antiochus Epiphanes, Judas Maccabeus, who similarly against great odds defeated Nicanor, who was also decapitated and his head hung up for display (1 Macc 7:33-50).[206] Her name might suggests she functions also as a symbol of Israel.[207] We shall return to the issue once her story has been fully explored.

Her introduction in 8:1 is strange: "Now in those days Judith heard about these things". She could not but have heard about them had she been a member of Bethulia's besieged community, for "all the people" had gathered around Uzziah (7:23). So we are left with the impression that Judith lived somewhere else, though sufficiently nearby to hear of what was happening.[208] This stands in some tension with 8:10 where she is said to summon "the elders of her town" and 16:21 which depicts Bethulia as her home town. Storytellers and their listeners were probably

---

[203] On the intertextual allusion to Exodus 17 see Jan W. van Henten, "Judith as Alternative Leader: A Rereading of Judith 7-13," in *A Feminist Companion to Esther, Judith and Susanna* (ed. Athalya Brenner; Sheffield: Sheffield Academic Press, 1995) 224-52, 232-38.

[204] So Tal Ilan, *Jewish Women in Greco-Roman Palestine* (TSAJ 44; Tübingen: Mohr Siebeck, 1995) 54.

[205] So Mittmann-Richert, *Einführung*, 89, 94.

[206] So Nickelsburg, *Jewish Literature*, 101; Mittmann-Richert, *Einführung*, 94.

[207] So Nickelsburg, *Jewish Literature*, 101.

[208] L. Day, "Faith, Character and Perspective in Judith," *JSOT* 95 (2001) 71-93, asks why Judith only gets involved later, implying that it is to be seen negatively (76); but this is surely not so from the author's perspective.

well able to cope with a not too statistical use of "all" and would assume that not absolutely everyone made it to the reported gatherings.

Her genealogy (8:1) differs from that of all other biblical women by its length[209] and contains a mixture of names of various tribal groups.[210] It gives her special prominence by the fact that it pertains to her, not her husband, and by its length. In 8:2 we then learn that she is a widow and that she had been married to Manasseh. By contrast with the description of Judith the author has given him no genealogy, instead defining him in relation to her, as from her tribe and family.[211] The latter detail probably belongs to the author's conviction of what is right: namely endogamous marriage, such as we find emphasised in Tobit. We also learn that he died from heatstroke during the barley harvest (8:2-3): ὁ καύσων ἦλθεν ἐπὶ τὴν κεφαλὴν αὐτοῦ ("the burning heat came upon his head"). The detail may be extraneous, but might be in some way symbolic of what is to come, to which we will return in the conclusion.

We are next told she had remained a widow wearing sackcloth and dressed in widow's clothing for the three years and fourth months since his death (8:4). Nothing is said of her having children, so that one might have expected her to marry her husband's brother or someone of near kin for the sake of the inheritance, as Sarah married Tobit, but the author shows no sign of seeing her behaviour as problematic.[212] Instead, her remaining unmarried appears to be seen as more virtuous. Viewed from a male perspective of the time, it might be seen as especially honouring of his memory. Viewed from a woman's perspective this might have condemned some women to poverty and exploitation, but this is not the author's focus.

She also "set up a tent for herself on the roof of her house"[213] and, wearing sackcloth and widow's clothing, followed an extreme regime of fasting, with

---

[209] For discussion of its possible function beyond elevating Judith, including mocking contrived genealogies in the author's setting, see Moore, *Judith*, 187-88; Gruen, *Diaspora*, 165; Amy-Jill Levine, "Sacrifice and Salvation: Otherness and Domestication in the Book of Judith," in *A Feminist Companion to Esther, Judith and Susanna* (ed. Athalya Brenner; Sheffield: Sheffield Academic Press, 1995) 208-23, 214.

[210] On this see van Henten, "Judith as Alternative Leader," 247-48.

[211] A. A. Di Lella, "Women in the Wisdom of Ben Sira and the Book of Judith," in *Congress Volume: Paris 1962* (ed. J. A. Emerton; Leiden: Brill, 1991) 39-52, notes the irony that Manasseh is identified as belonging to *her* tribe (51).

[212] Cf. Sidnie White Crawford, "Esther and Judith: Contrasts in Character," in *The Book of Esther in Modern Research* (ed. Sidnie White Crawford, Leonard J. Greenspoon; JSOTSup 380; London: T&T Clark, 2003) 61-76, 73. Di Lella, "Women," notes that her apparently not having had a child is not treated as a disgrace (51).

[213] Linda Bennett Elder, "Judith," in *Searching the Scriptures: Volume Two: A Feminist Commentary* (ed. Elisabeth Schüssler Fiorenza; London, SCM, 1995) 455-69 suggests that the tent "introduces her as a solitary ascetic" like Aseneth (457). She also

exceptions determined by the religious calendar (8:5-6), in a normal week descending to her house (cf. 10:2) and eating only on two days. This would have to be understood as a partial fast. Otherwise, as Gruen notes, "that should have brought her to the brink of starvation".[214] It is unlikely that the author is deliberately subverting his image of Judith's devotion by inserting ludicrous claims.

We are then told that "she was beautiful in appearance, and was very lovely to behold" (καὶ ἦν καλὴ τῷ εἴδει καὶ ὡραία τῇ ὄψει σφόδρα) (8:7), echoing the description in the Septuagint of Rachel: καλὴ τῷ εἴδει καὶ ὡραία τῇ ὄψει (Gen 29:17; cf. also Sarah: Gen 12:11; and Esther: Esth 2:7). Such beauty includes sexual attractiveness. It remains a constant feature in her story, featuring centrally in her strategy of liberation, and present in subsequent years when many men responded to her attractiveness, finding her sexually desirable: καὶ πολλοὶ ἐπεθύμησαν αὐτήν (16:22). At all three stages we are dealing with male perceptions but, as we shall see, Judith also owns her own sexual attractiveness, but decides herself how she will express it. The author clearly sees it as something to be valued.[215]

In 8:7 we also learn that Judith was the female head of a substantial household: "Her husband Manasseh had left her gold and silver, men and women slaves, livestock, and fields; and she maintained this estate". The author does not, therefore, depict her as a poor widow.[216] She is a relatively prosperous one. As Linda Elder observes, "Judith's social location as a wealthy, landed widow, a solitary religious ascetic, and an educated woman was not anomalous in the social-historical ambient of the author".[217] It was nevertheless unusual and placed Judith

---

notes that τὰ ἱμάτια τῆς χηρεύσεως αὐτῆς "widow's garments" can also be translated "garments of her solitude" (458) though this is unlikely given the word, χηρεύουσα, in the previous verse. She also compares her to the female ascetics of Philo's Therapeutae (458).

[214] Gruen, *Diaspora*, 165.

[215] Monika Hellmann, *Judit - eine Frau im Spannungsfeld von Autonomie und göttlicher Führung: Studie über eine Frauengestalt des Alten Testaments* (Europäische Hochschulschriften; Reihe XXIII. Theologie 444; Frankfurt: Peter Lang, 1992), notes possible influence from Hellenistic romance literature in accounting for the presence of erotic traits in Jewish writings of the Hellenistic period like Esther, Tobit, and Judith, but sees influence rather from within Jewish tradition, particularly Canticles, as more probable (115), and then interprets it symbolically of Israel's chastity over against the Gentile world (120). Within its own Jewish tradition, however, Judith embraces also the literal.

[216] So, rightly, Esler, "Ludic History," 130; Cf. Craghan, *Judith*, 76.

[217] Elder, "Judith," 456; similarly 458-59. She notes that widows could inherit, citing Elephantine texts, Babatha archives, Sir 22:4; 25:21-22; *T. Job* 46-52; *Asen.* 24:5; 6:1-4; 12:15; and Josephus (459). This is also assumed in Tobit.

in a distinct position with society where as head of a household she will already have fulfilled roles traditionally performed by males. As Esler notes,

> As an Israelite woman, Judith was expected to conform to local conventions which required her to remain in the domestic sphere and leave it to Israelite males to wage war against Holofernes, the alarmingly powerful enemy of their *ethnos*. A failure to appreciate the underlying force of such conventions would seriously hamper our ability to comprehend the thoroughly radical nature of her actions.[218]

Levine observes that "close to the deity in spirit and in physical location, she is removed from the people both religiously and spatially".[219] She is exceptional, though in her time not unique. This means that it is difficult to see in the author's depiction an endeavour to address women's situations in general. While Judith's exploits will be larger than life, her image to this point must have been sufficiently credible to the author's hearers for us to conclude that such women were conceivable, that is, attractive and religiously devout widows heading up prosperous households, complete with male and female slaves, livestock and land and viewed positively.

Judith's unusual status gives her the right to have a say in public affairs. This is confirmed by Uzziah's remarks after her address, in which he declares, "Today is not the first time your wisdom has been shown, but from the beginning of your life all the people have recognized your understanding, for your heart's disposition is right" (8:29). The book shows her doing so again by summoning the town's leaders and, like Moses, rebuking them for agreeing on oath to surrender in five days on the grounds that it amounted to putting God under pressure,[220] testing God instead of recognising that God was testing them, as he had, Abraham, Isaac, and Jacob (8:11-27). It is significant that she does not depict the dangers as acts of God's punishment for Israel's sin (as she will do later in speaking to Holofernes, when she speaks of impending sin) or God's abandoning Israel.[221] Indeed she makes a point of asserting that they had not sinned: "For never in our generation, nor in these present days, has there been any tribe or family or people or town of ours that worships gods made with hands, as was done in days gone by" (8:18). This is one half of a Deuteronomic theology. She stops short of the other half which would guarantee deliverance for the faithful, or, she at least, qualifies it. For her cosmology assumes a world in which evil is at large, here in the form of Holofernes and his master, Nebuchadnezzar, setting itself up in direct opposition

---

[218] Esler, "Ludic History," 129.

[219] Levine, "Sacrifice and Salvation," 216.

[220] Van Henten, "Judith as Alternative Leader ," 232-38.

[221] Moore, *Judith*: "with some justification, one might describe Judith as the sole female theologian in the Old Testament" (186).

to God (cf. 6:2, "What God is there except Nebuchadnezzar?").[222] There is no other god but the Lord, who will ultimately overcome all resistance, but one must not be presumptuous about when God will intervene.[223] Judith enjoins trust in the interests not just of the town but of the nation and its temple (8:21, 24).

Uzziah then relents, in the process speaks of Judith's wisdom from the beginning of her life (8:28) and urges that she pray for rain (8:29). The narrative then indicates that Judith has more than that in mind, as she cautions the leaders not to try to find out what she is about to do: ὑμεῖς δὲ οὐκ ἐξερευνήσετε τὴν πρᾶξίν μου ("Only, do not try to find out what I am doing") (8:34). This may already belong to the author's playful use of double meaning which will especially characterise her interchange with Holofernes, since πρᾶξις is also the word used for a sexual "affair".

First we hear Judith's prayer, offered in true piety at the time of the evening offering of incense. In it Judith identifies herself with her tribal ancestor, Simeon, who with Levi executed vengeance on the people of Shechem (Gen 34:25-29).[224] The prayer gives a distinctive version of the events which differs in some respects from the account in Genesis 34. Only Simeon is mentioned, not Levi, probably because Simeon is her ancestor. Simeon plays the lead role also in the account in *Theodotus* (frag. 6). Other names are missing. Shechem's seizing Dinah and having forced intercourse with her (34:2) becomes: ἀλλογενῶν οἳ ἔλυσαν μήτραν παρθένου εἰς μίασμα καὶ ἐγύμνωσαν μηρὸν εἰς αἰσχύνην καὶ ἐβεβήλωσαν μήτραν εἰς ὄνειδος (lit "of strangers who violated a virgin's womb bringing defilement, and exposed her thighs bringing shame, and polluted her womb bringing disgrace" (9:2)[225] and expanded: τὴν στρωμνὴν αὐτῶν ἣ ἠδέσατο τὴν ἀπάτην αὐτῶν ἀπατηθεῖσαν εἰς αἷμα "their bed, which was ashamed of the deceit they had practiced" (9:3). While the allusion to defilement picks up Gen 34:13 and εἶπας γάρ οὐχ οὕτως ἔσται ("for you said, 'It shall not

---

[222] On the similarity to apocalyptic thought in this respect but also the differences from apocalyptic literature see Otzen, *Tobit and Judith*, 82-83.

[223] Day, "Faith," calls the integrity of Judith into question, noting that she chides the Bethulians though they had been praying (4:13), that we should we feel more sympathy with them (77), and that while she claims that they are testing God, her own actions would do the very same thing (78). But these are Day's critiques, not, it seems to me, the way the author sees it.

[224] Nickelsburg, *Jewish Literature*, notes the similar appeal to Phinehas by Mattathias in 1 Macc 2:24-26 (100).

[225] Mary Anna Bader, *Tracing the Evidence: Dinah in Post-Hebrew Bible Literature* (Studies in Biblical Literature 102; New York: Peter Lang, 2008), notes that the key words μίασμα and αἰσχύνη reappear in 13:16 where Judith indicates that her fate is the reverse of Dinah's (119-20). She notes "numerous thematic and vocabulary links between Genesis 34 and Judith" (121, and generally, in her discussion, 115-37.

be done'") (9:3) picks up 34:7, nothing is said of the detail in Genesis about the location, the negotiations which followed, the circumcision ploy, nor Jacob's rebuke, reflected later also in Gen 49:5-7 where Jacob curses the anger of Simeon and Levi. Here in Judith God gives Simeon a sword, thus commissioning the act (similarly *T. Levi* 5:3 speaks of a sword and shield given by an angel; cf. also *Asen.* 23:14).[226] *Aramaic Levi Document* and *Jubilees* similarly hail Levi's actions (*ALD* 1c 2; 78-81; *Jub.* 30:1-26), *Jubilees* also omitting reference to the circumcision ruse.[227] On the other hand, the author appears to assume that his hearers know of the deceit, since Judith will be shown similarly engaging in deceit. They may well also assume knowledge of the location which would be in the same area as Bethulia.[228]

Judith is depicted as hailing the slaughter of the men, the captivity of their wives and daughters and all their booty as divine action (9:4). The author apparently approves and expects his hearers to approve of what we today must recognise as unwarranted abuse and violence.[229] Hailing divine providence and design, she appeals for strength to bring similar vengeance against those who threaten her people and the temple (9:5-7). In doing so she addresses God as κύριος συντρίβων πολέμους κύριος ὄνομά σοι σύ ("the Lord who crushes wars; the Lord is your name") (9:7), an allusion to Exod 15:13 LXX (κύριος συντρίβων πολέμους κύριος ὄνομα αὐτῷ) (cf. יהוה איש מלחמה יהוה שמו "The LORD is a warrior; the LORD is his name"), which Judith repeats in 16:2.[230] Read in the light of what precedes this is not an espousal of pacifism; it appears, rather, to assume that peace will come once Israel's enemies have been destroyed.

---

[226] James L. Kugel, "The Rape of Dinah, and Simeon and Levi's Revenge," in James L. Kugel, *The Ladder of Jacob: Ancient Interpretations of the Biblical Story of Jacob and his Children* (Princeton: Princeton University Press, 2006) 36-80, 231-39, notes the notion of being given a heavenly sword may derive originally from the attempt to explain how two kill a whole town and possibly because of Gen 49:5 (40-41).

[227] See the discussion in Loader, *Enoch, Levi, and Jubilees*, 88-91, 105, 165-75.

[228] See Fröhlich, *Time*, 124, 128-29.

[229] Day, "Faith," observes: "Though noting Judith's emphasis upon vengeance and violence, a reader has no suggestion at this point that Judith is needlessly violent or deceitful outside what she may feel her mission requires." When she continues: "In her prayer, what is significant is that she clearly reveals that she is not the pious, quiet, grieving widow whom the narrator portrayed through the initial description. We may begin to wonder who this character really is and whose appraisal of her is the most accurate", we hear Day's and our own questions, not, I believe those of the author. The same is true of her valid observation that the God of Judith appears violent and capricious (78-79) – again, not likely to be the author's view.

[230] Moore, *Judith*, notes that this also appears in the Vulg of 16:2, suggesting either that Jerome's Aramaic sources were translations from the Greek or that they had a different Hebrew text, otherwise unattested (247-48).

More directly, Judith appeals to what these enemies might do to the temple: "for they intend to defile your sanctuary, and to pollute the tabernacle where your glorious name resides, and to break off the horns of your altar with the sword" (9:8; similarly 9:13), recalling for the hearers the intervention of Antiochus. She then portrays herself as God's instrument of wrath: "Look at their pride, and send your wrath upon their heads. Give to me, a widow, the strong hand to do what I plan" (9:9).[231] By juxtaposing the reference to herself as "a widow" and "strong hand" she associates herself with the weak. This contrast reappears in 9:11, "For your strength does not depend on numbers, nor your might on the powerful. But you are the God of the lowly, helper of the oppressed, upholder of the weak, protector of the forsaken, savior of those without hope". It is also fundamental to her appeal: θραῦσον αὐτῶν τὸ ἀνάστεμα ἐν χειρὶ θηλείας ("crush their arrogance by the hand of a female") (9:10), one of many intertextual echoes of the account of Jael's slaying Sisera in Judges 4 (cf. esp. 4:9). She will return to this formulation in reporting her triumph: ἐπάταξεν αὐτὸν ὁ κύριος ἐν χειρὶ θηλείας ("The Lord has struck him down by the hand of a female") (13:15) and in her hymn of praise: κύριος παντοκράτωρ ἠθέτησεν αὐτοὺς ἐν χειρὶ θηλείας ("But the Lord Almighty has foiled them by the hand of a female") (16:5). In the latter we again see the contrast of power: the almighty, all-powerful, employs the powerless. Judith refers to herself as a female, primarily in order to emphasise relative powerlessness, just as she had used "widow" to indicate the same, and at the other end of the spectrum had emphasised the greatly increased force of the Assyrians, their horses and riders and foot soldiers with their weapons (9:7). The image of "hand" also belongs to the discourse of power.[232]

In the author's understanding being "female" and being a "widow" means being weak. These are relative terms. For while Judith is a widow and that will have brought disadvantage she is still relatively prosperous and already has respect and social power in her community. As a "female" the author depicts her as weaker in physical strength than males, a reasonable generalisation to which she is not seen as an exception. God uses the weak to overcome the strong, a mythic defiance of the established order, of which the Judith story is just one of many examples, which need not be gendered. It was a matter of shame to be defeated by one weaker than oneself. Transferred into the sexual realm it was a matter of shame for a man not to be the penetrator but the penetrated. Within Judith's prayer there is hope for reversal, which will entail shame coming to Holofernes (and his

---

[231] I doubt if the author meant us to see hypocrisy in Judith's approach, as Day, "Faith," suggests, when she argues that Judith's interest is not God's plan but her own (83).

[232] On the extent of the image in Judith see P. W. Skehan, "The Hand of Judith," *CBQ* 25 (1963) 94-109.

mighty men) both because he, the stronger, is overcome by the weaker, a woman, but also because he who planned rape is himself at the receiving end of violence.

The intertextual allusion to Abimelech's death, having been hit on the head by a millstone dropped on him by a woman, and his instruction to his armour bearer: "Draw your sword and kill me, so people will not say about me, 'A woman killed him'" (Judg 9:54), illustrates the shame. It is not immediately apparent from Judith's prayer that to be killed by a woman would be the equivalent in shame to being killed by a boy (as Goliath was by David). In other words, the extent to which gender, itself, emphasised here through use of the word "female", and not just woman,[233] plays a role beyond the emphasis on relative weakness is not clear. Nothing suggests that women are shameful independent of the issue of their strength or because of their sexuality. The latter certainly seems not to be the case. On the contrary, the author sees it as one of Judith's positive strengths. Judith is also larger than her sexuality. As Elder observes, her prayer "provides insight into the inner landscape of a patriotic woman who refuses to be a victim either sexually or politically".[234] Judith is not just pictured outwardly by the author but also in her subjective reality, thus displaying "a full range of human emotion and capacity for experience that is not just bound by gender".[235]

Within the prayer Judith offers the first hearer further clues to her strategy. For she will achieve it, as she puts it, "by the deceit of my lips" (ἐκ χειλέων ἀπάτης μου) (9:10) and "my deceitful words" (λόγον μου καὶ ἀπάτην) (9:13). There is an intertextual link here to the deceit of Levi and Simeon which led to the slaughter she just hailed.[236] Here the Greek words, ἀπάτη ἀπατάω, can also carry the meaning "seduction, seduce", including in a sexual sense, somewhat lost in the English translation, "deceit". The sexual meaning is clearly present in 12:16 where Holofernes "was waiting for an opportunity to seduce her from the day he first saw her" (καὶ ἐτήρει καιρὸν τοῦ ἀπατῆσαι αὐτὴν ἀφ' ἧς ἡμέρας εἶδεν αὐτήν). In a typical reversal she seduces him, as she reports: "it was my face that seduced him to his destruction" (ἠπάτησεν αὐτὸν τὸ πρόσωπόν μου εἰς ἀπώλειαν αὐτοῦ) (13:16) and then acclaims in her hymn: "put on a linen gown to beguile

---

[233] Rightly emphasised by Moore, *Judith*, 193.

[234] Elder, "Judith," 462.

[235] Elder, "Judith," 460. This insight then informs her discussion which follows (460-65).

[236] So van den Eynde, "Crying to God," 222. She notes that "the reference to the answered prayer of Simeon has, as far as the plot is concerned, a double function. On the one hand, it raises the readers' expectation that Judith's prayer will be answered too, meanwhile guiding their interpretation by suggesting that in the ensuing events, God is at work through Judith. On the other hand, this part of the prayer offers the readers concrete keys as regards Judith's plans of action." (222).

him" (ἔλαβεν στολὴν λινῆν εἰς ἀπάτην αὐτοῦ) (16:8).[237] Her "deceit with the lips" is not only sexual[238] but refers to the series of lies and ambiguous statements with which she in effect seduces Holofernes into thinking that she is sexually available and can also be trusted (11:5-19; 12:14, 17). Such deceit would have been seen by the author and his hearers as not inappropriate where the honour of one's nation and one's own was at stake,[239] much as it offends those who read the text from our different worlds.[240]

She has evoked the Dinah story, not to focus on the sexual wrongdoing, though this is dramatically elaborated, but to affirm the vengeance and justify her own as divinely mandated. At the same time her own strategy will place her also in a position of sexual vulnerability like Dinah, only that she will avert violation. The lack of names perhaps gives the account wider applicability. The "strangers" (ἀλλογενεῖς) might mean any non-Jew. The assault is what one might expect from them. This is part of the generalising which enables the work to speak to new situations where oppression is faced, in the case of Judith, probably looking back at the Maccabean period and the continuing threats of the Hasmonean period.

Judith then abandons her isolation, descends to her house, removes her sackcloth and widow's attire and sets about making herself sexually attractive, beyond what had already been noted as her natural beauty (10:1-3). Thus she

> bathed her body with water, and anointed herself with precious ointment. She combed her hair, put on a tiara, and dressed herself in the festive attire that she used to wear while her husband Manasseh was living. (10:3)

Her bathing assumes she still had water, the author giving no indication that this reveals her as acting selfishly with regard to the dearth of water.[241] Making herself

---

[237] On ἀπάτη, ἀπατάω as a "Leitwort", a key concept, in the work, see Zenger, *Judit*, 434.

[238] Elder, "Judith," cautions against seeing it as primarily sexual here (463).

[239] So rightly David A. deSilva, "Judith the Heroine? Lies, Seduction, and Murder in Cultural Perspective," *BTB* 36 (2006) 55-61, 56-57, who writes of her as "a champion of honor" (58). See also Toni Craven, "Women Who Lied for the Faith," in *Justice and the Holy* (ed. D. A. Knight and P. J. Paris; Atlanta: Scholars, 1989) 35-49, who notes the deceit practised by Rebecca (38), Tamar (38-39), midwives in Egypt (39-41), Rahab (41), Jael (42-43), and women of Tekoa (44-45), beside Judith (45-46), who lied as people faithful to the tradition (48).

[240] Cf. Gruen, *Diaspora*, who writes: "Judith is an adherent of law and ritual, but has no hesitation in contriving artifice and trickery" (169); Moore, *Judith*, "Judith was a saint. She was also – for the sake of her God and her people – a shameless flatterer (11:7-8), a bold-faced liar (11:12-14, 18-19), and a ruthless assassin (13:7-8), with no respect for the dead (13:9-10, 15)" (61); Day, "Faith," 73.

[241] Cf. Levine, "Sacrifice and Salvation," 215; Day, "Faith," 83.

sexually attractive was something positive and appropriate. There is no hint here that enhancing one's sexual attractiveness is something negative, a pandering to passions.[242] These are not prostitute's regalia which she has secretly stored, but clothing which belonged to her self-expression within her marriage to Manasseh.[243] The description of her attire continues:

> She put sandals on her feet, and put on her anklets, bracelets, rings, earrings, and all her other jewelry. Thus she made herself very beautiful, to entice the eyes of all the men who might see her. (10:4)

In the right place and the right time such assertion of one's sexuality is natural and normal, presumably for both the author and his hearers. One might see her change of clothing in symbolic terms, as Bar 5:1 depicts Zion putting aside sackcloth and putting on splendid robes (cf. also Isa 52:1-2).[244] However here in Judith the focus is not celebration of hope but preparation for a particular undertaking. The supplies given to the maid (a skin of wine and a flask of oil, and a bag filled with roasted grain, dried fig cakes, and fine bread; 10:5) will be her alternative to the forbidden delicacies which Holofernes will offer (12:1-2).[245]

Judith has made herself attractive as a strategy and will use her sexual attractiveness to her ends.[246] She is neither out of control nor reduced to a sex object, though some male views will see her as the latter, if not the former.[247] Fear

---

[242] Cf. Jerome's apparently revisionist translation which replaces 10:4 with the words, "And the Lord also gave her more beauty because all this dressing up did not proceed from sensuality but from virtue and therefore the Lord increased her beauty so that she appeared to all men's eyes incomparably lovely" (cited from Otzen, *Tobit and Judith*, 109).

[243] Rightly noted by Gruen, *Diaspora*, 166.

[244] Craghan, *Judith*, 88; Moore, *Judith*, 200.

[245] White Crawford, "Esther and Judith," writes: "The Book of Judith remedies all the religious deficiencies of Hebrew Esther: God is central to the story, the Law is observed, the purpose of ritual observance (prayer, fasting, sacrifice) is understood and emphasized, and the heroine is not defiled by sexual relations with a Gentile" (69). She notes the same process going on in the additions to Esther, especially Addition C. See also the discussion below. The rape of Dinah to which Judith serves as a counterpoint also became a basis for dealing with concerns about sexual relations with Gentiles, as shown especially in *Jubilees* and *Aramaic Levi Document*, and ironically reversed in *Aseneth* (see our discussion below).

[246] Rakel, "Judit," 415-16.

[247] Rakel, "Judit," observes that Judith exploits male views of women, playing the expected role (416). It is not clear to me that her claim is justified that Judith thus exposes men who are made to look ridiculous, especially if this refers to their positive sexual response to her sexuality. It is true, however, of how they fantasise that they might express that response (10:19) and certainly of how Holofernes plans to. The issue is not having a sexual response, but how one expresses it. See also the note of ridicule in the *Tale of the Three Youths* above.

of the former informs the projection that she is dangerous and depictions of her as a *femme fatale*. She remains Judith, a woman, with all of the qualities which the author has already celebrated, beautiful and wise, competent manager and devout.[248]

Her endeavours are noted by the author as successful: the town's leaders are astounded at her beauty (10:7). The author is not degrading them as though to recognise sexual attractiveness is something unworthy. They are comfortable placing her sexuality fully within their spirituality, as is she, as they wish her well: "'May the God of our ancestors grant you favor and fulfill your plans, so that the people of Israel may glory and Jerusalem may be exalted'. She bowed down to God" (10:7). Far from seeing her out of control, they follow her instructions and allow her out through the gate (10:9-10).[249] The Assyrian patrol who interrogate her, who "heard her words, and observed her face – she was in their eyes marvelously beautiful" (10:14), are not thereby demeaned. Nor are those who gathered around Holofernes' tent who also "marveled at her beauty" (10:19). The author even claims for Israel some of the credit when he reports that they not only "marveled at her beauty", but also "admired the Israelites, judging them by her. They said to one another, "Who can despise these people, who have women like this among them?" (10:19). The author then drives his description of their response to the extreme in reporting their conclusion that it then makes sense to kill the men of Israel (10:19), οἳ ἀφεθέντες δυνήσονται κατασοφίσασθαι πᾶσαν τὴν γῆν ("for if we let them [the men] go they will be able to beguile the whole world!"). Oddly, the text speaks of men not women beguiling the whole world, but is probably to be understood as what men might do with such women's help. The exaggeration is part of the author's playfulness, but also reflects the common practice of war which killed men and exposed women to slavery and sexual exploitation, a feature already alluded to in 4:12 and 9:4.[250] The text keeps the hearer aware of the larger conflict.

Admiration for Judith's beauty continues with Holofernes and his entourage (10:23; 11:20-23). There is nothing untoward in either Judith's beauty or their

---

[248] Day, "Faith," sees her dressing up as evidence that her prayer about deceiving with lips was itself deceit (84), but the author shows no such concern and the remark seems hypercritical.

[249] Gruen, *Diaspora*, assumes that Judith's departure for Holofernes' camp must have taken place in the dead of night (166), so hardly able to be the spectacle which Craghan, *Judith*, describes: "The trek from Bethulia to the Assyrian camp is a beauty pageant" (91). Supporting Gruen's view is the note in 9:1 that the sequence of events began with evening prayer. The storyteller may simply have ignored the implications rather than intending to parody the responses.

[250] Moore, *Judith*, translates according to sense in both places referring to rape (152, 191).

admiration. The issue is how men choose to respond.[251] Judith's strategy of deception entails much more than her making herself sexually attractive. But first Holofernes begins with his lie: "Take courage, woman, and do not be afraid in your heart, for I have never hurt anyone who chose to serve Nebuchadnezzar, king of all the earth" (11:1; "no one will hurt you" 11:4). His response to her sexual attractiveness is to want to rape her (12:12), which first hearers might suspect and subsequent hearers know well.

In her response, Judith mouths a false acclamation of Neduchadnezzar's divine power and Holofernes' wisdom (11:7-8), but first ambiguously declares: "If you follow out the words of your servant, God will accomplish something through you, and my lord will not fail to achieve his purposes" – her Lord, of course! (11:6).[252] She then promises to reveal the way to overcome Israel in its hill country and the right moment (11:18), namely when they will have sinned, recalling positively the advice of Achior (11:9-11). They will sin by killing their livestock and eating what is unlawful for them even to touch: "the first fruits of the grain and the tithes of the wine and oil" (11:13).[253] Despite the deceit Judith continues to affirm her faith in God and even wins Holofernes to possible belief if her predictions come true. He and his entourage affirm her as both beautiful and wise, an ideal combination, which would also win the approval of the author and his hearers, though understood differently: "No other woman from one end of the earth to the other looks so beautiful or speaks so wisely!" (11:21); "You are not only beautiful in appearance, but wise in speech" (11:23). In this exchange Judith's sexual attractiveness remains in the background. Her deception is by flattery, promise, and argument. This is further reason for rejecting a reduction of her role to sexual seductress. Her sexual attractiveness made her worth preserving in the first place, but then her deceptive persuasion stands on its own and could have been voiced by any captive, male or female.

In contrast to the unlawful eating predicted of her compatriots (11:12-13) Judith refuses Holofernes delicacies and eats only what she brought with her (12:1-4), perhaps indirectly reinforcing Holofernes' belief in her genuineness.[254] Bathing to purify herself before eating (12:7-9) belonged to her piety and presumably will have been considered proper practice by the author and his hearers,[255] a practice which appears to be assumed as widespread by the time of

[251] As Rakel, "Judit," notes, one clear message in Judith is that that "women's attractiveness does not justify male sexual exploitation" (417).

[252] On the use of ambiguities see Moore, *Judith*, 208-209.

[253] Moore, *Judith*, suggests that the author implies they would have eaten the cattle, including their blood (210).

[254] Moore, *Judith*, 219.

[255] Cf. Moore, *Judith*, who suggests purification after menstruation or defilement from contact with Gentiles (219).

Jesus (cf. Mark 7:1-5; Luke 11:38; John 2:6).[256] Her permission to bathe at the spring becomes crucial for her later escape (13:10).

Only after the proverbial three days do matters come to a climax when Holofernes instructs his eunuch quite explicitly:

πεῖσον δὴ πορευθεὶς τὴν γυναῖκα τὴν Ἐβραίαν ἥ ἐστιν παρὰ σοί τοῦ ἐλθεῖν πρὸς ἡμᾶς καὶ φαγεῖν καὶ πιεῖν μεθ᾽ ἡμῶν. 12 ἰδοὺ γὰρ αἰσχρὸν τῷ προσώπῳ ἡμῶν εἰ γυναῖκα τοιαύτην παρήσομεν οὐχ ὁμιλήσαντες αὐτῇ ὅτι ἐὰν ταύτην μὴ ἐπισπασώμεθα καταγελάσεται ἡμῶν.

Go and persuade the Hebrew woman who is in your care to join us and to eat and drink with us. 12 For it would be a disgrace if we let such a woman go without having intercourse with her. If we do not seduce/rape her, she will laugh at us. (12:11-12)[257]

The instruction tells us about norms which would have applied to many such captive women. They would be raped. It also reflects fear of loss of face. There is no thought for Judith as a person. She is a sex object and unraped a potential threat to Holofernes' honour. The narrative brings us therefore to a situation both analogous to Dinah's, but also to all women threatened with violence through war, to whom the author has previously alluded (4:12; 9:4). Judith also stands representatively for the situation in which Israel found itself, though she is never just a symbol.

In conveying his master's wishes Bagoas, his eunuch, is similarly explicit:

μὴ ὀκνησάτω δὴ ἡ παιδίσκη ἡ καλὴ αὕτη ἐλθοῦσα πρὸς τὸν κύριόν μου δοξασθῆναι κατὰ πρόσωπον αὐτοῦ καὶ πίεσαι μεθ᾽ ἡμῶν εἰς εὐφροσύνην οἶνον καὶ γενηθῆναι ἐν τῇ ἡμέρᾳ ταύτῃ ὡς θυγάτηρ μία τῶν υἱῶν Ασσουρ αἳ παρεστήκασιν ἐν οἴκῳ Ναβουχοδονοσορ.

Let this pretty girl not hesitate to come to my lord to be honored in his presence, and to enjoy drinking wine with us, and to become today like one of the Assyrian women who serve in the palace of Nebuchadnezzar. (12:13)

The word, παιδίσκη, has a range of meanings including, "maiden, maid, prostitute",[258] hardly befitting the Judith whose wisdom and experience the author has extolled. She is reduced to being a "girl" (still a common practice), her

---

[256] See Regev, "Pure Individualism," 177-86.

[257] Moore, *Judith*, notes that ἐπισπασώμεθα can also indicate rape (223-24). Bader, *Tracing the Evidence*, contemplates that the author may intend the first person plural to include the eunuch and so engage in irony here (131). The more likely alternative is that the reference is only to Holofernes and employs the royal "we". On the other hand, eunuchs should not be assumed to be sexually inactive. On this see J. David Hester, "Eunuchs and the Postgender Jesus: Matthew 19.12 and Transgressive Sexualities," *JSNT* 28 (2005) 13-40, 17.

[258] Moore, *Judith*, 224.

attractiveness now making her in these males' eyes just "a pretty thing", who can be like the harem women who serve Nebuchadnezzar's sexual needs. The rape has begun. The author shows Judith resisting such humiliation and instead responding with a clever ambiguity that asserts her dignity: "Who am I to refuse my lord? Whatever pleases him I will do at once, and it will be a joy to me until the day of my death" (12:14) – her Lord![259] The author exploits the common delusive male fantasy that she would find joy in the act. She then makes out to ready herself for the encounter, having her maid spread the lambskin rugs.

The double meaning continues when Judith responds to Holofernes' invitation, "Have a drink and be merry with us!" (12:17): "I will gladly drink, my lord, because today is the greatest day in my whole life" (12:18). Before describing the scene the author depicts Holofernes' approach:

ἐξέστη ἡ καρδία Ολοφέρνου ἐπ᾿ αὐτήν καὶ ἐσαλεύθη ἡ ψυχὴ αὐτοῦ καὶ ἦν κατεπίθυμος σφόδρα τοῦ συγγενέσθαι μετ᾿ αὐτῆς καὶ ἐτήρει καιρὸν τοῦ ἀπατῆσαι αὐτὴν ἀφ᾿ ἧς ἡμέρας εἶδεν αὐτήν.
Holofernes' heart was ravished with her and his passion was aroused, for he had been waiting for an opportunity to seduce her from the day he first saw her. (12:16)

The words, ἐξέστη ἡ καρδία, indicate that he became obsessed with her, ἐσαλεύθη ἡ ψυχὴ αὐτοῦ, that he lost his balance, and κατεπίθυμος σφόδρα τοῦ συγγενέσθαι μετ᾿ αὐτῆς, that he had very strong sexual urges and wanted to have sexual intercourse with her.[260] He had been looking for the chance to seduce her ever since he saw her. The storyteller gives us no indication of what had stopped him doing so before now, probably leaving that to the hearers' imagination, rather than trying thereby to make fun of his own story.[261] Of course, Holofernes, the author allows us to imagine, would probably have been happiest if Judith had done what she apparently said and welcomed having sex with him. In reality she hardly had a choice and the hearers would see the consequences clearly. She faced being raped. Holofernes experienced sexual passion. It is doubtful that the author disapproves of sexual desire as such. Judith's beauty was such that men would have sexual feelings in response. Her husband, Manasseh, will have fully engaged his sexual responses in a relationship, presumably of respect, albeit patriarchal. Holofernes, however, chooses to respond to his sexual feelings by exploiting Judith's vulnerability as captive. His is an approach of violence, at one

---

[259] Moore, *Judith*, notes that 12:10 – 13:10 displays "a masterful blend of directness, brevity, and subtle irony" (228).

[260] Moore, *Judith*, notes the use of συγγενέσθαι ("to be with") to refer to sexual intercourse in Gen 39:10 LXX; Tob 3:8; and Sus 20-21 (225).

[261] Cf. Gruen, *Diaspora*, 167.

with the broader approach of war and violence which as Nebuchadnezzar's general he promotes.[262]

Holofernes proceeds to get drunk, too drunk, dead drunk, leaving him vulnerable. When evening came, the attendants had left, and the expected time for sex had come, Judith upheld before God what she was doing for the exaltation of Jerusalem, decapitated Holofernes, collapsed the canopy and then set off with her maid for Bethulia, his head in her food bag (13:6-10),[263] to display it in triumph to her compatriots and report her deed (13:15).

The story is rich in intertextual allusion, recalling Jael's assassination of Sisera (Judg 4:21), David's beheading of Goliath by his own sword (1 Sam 17:51) and the triumphant display of Nicanor's severed head (1 Maccabees 7; 2 Maccabees 15).[264] It is the myth of the weak defeating the strong reflected in its many intertextually related variants. These include also the tale of Esther, the exploits of Ehud (Judg 3:12-31), Abraham's defeat of the Mesopotamian kings (Genesis 14), the miraculous defeat of the besieging Assyrians (2 Chr 32:1-23), Jehoshaphat's victory over the people of Moab, Ammon, and Meun (2 Chr 20:1-30), and not least the Exodus, also celebrated, as in Judith, with a hymn.[265]

It is appropriate to attend first to what the author reports as Judith's explanation of the event. She displays the head and the canopy, reports his drunken stupor and declares: "The Lord has struck him down by the hand of a female" (13:15).[266] Alert hearers will have recalled her prayer where she asked God to help her "crush their arrogance by the hand of a female" (9:10). As there, the contrast is the weak and the strong, Judith identifying herself as a female and

---

[262] See also Rakel, "Judit," who notes that the author depicts Holofernes' act as one both of power and of sexual passion (415).

[263] Stocker, *Judith*, observes that this reflects "one of the story's classic mythic-primitive ingredients, ingestion of the enemy being a traditional method of acquiring the power of his spirit" (9).

[264] Moore, *Judith*, 227; Wills, *Jewish Novel*, 140-41; Esler, "Ludic History," 128-29, who emphasis David and Goliath in particular; and on the parallel with Jael and Deborah, see Hellmann, *Judit*, 96-103.

[265] See Zenger, *Judit*, 440-46; Otzen, *Tobit and Judith*, 74-79, 111-12; Fröhlich, *Time*, 125-27.

[266] There is no need, with Day, "Faith," 86-90, to see here a symptom of Judith's deceit, as though the author is playing off her claims that God acts, against her having executed her own strategy. She clearly connects the two throughout and nowhere does the author indicate this should be called into question. When she writes, "It appears as though Judith can do no wrong in anyone's eyes. Yet it is such unvarying adulation that it should sound alarm bells for a reader, for the inability to see ambiguity in another speaks as much about the viewer's judgment as the disposition of the one so evaluated" (90), this may well apply, as it should, to *our* critical engagement, but it is another matter to assume authorial intent.

therefore relatively weak in physical strength in comparison to men and so not able to claim the same level of honour in a culture where the strong are honoured. In that world Holofernes, close to the top of such a scale of honour, had wanted sex and to preserve his honour. Instead, she had brought him shame, as Bagoas later exclaims: "A Hebrew woman has brought disgrace on the house of King Nebuchadnezzar" (14:18) and escaped his violation. "As the Lord lives, who has protected me in the way I went, I swear that it was my face that seduced him to his destruction, and that he committed no sin with me, to defile and shame me" (13:16). This both protects her from what otherwise would have been great shame in her day, even it had not been her fault, and affirms that she had employed her sexual attractiveness to bring his end. Her own sexual being is not called into question, but implicitly affirmed. She remained in control. Holofernes lost control both of sexuality and of himself in combination with alcohol.[267] Hearing her report, the people blessed God for humiliating the people's enemies (13:17) and Uzziah declares:

> O daughter, you are blessed by the Most High God above all other women on earth; and blessed be the Lord God, who created the heavens and the earth, who has guided you to cut off the head of the leader of our enemies. (13:18)

This acclamation which sets Judith above all women (but notably not men) and goes on to speak of perpetual honour wins the people's praise (13:19-20). As at the beginning of the venture after her first exchange with the elders and as she set out (8:32-35; 10:9-10), so here, Judith assumes the authority to instruct the people about what should follow, including hanging up the head for display, as Judas had done with the head of Nicanor (1 Macc 7:33-50),[268] and the strategy to kill the fleeing Assyrians (14:1-4).[269] Judith continues to exercise the authority which she had as a respected householder already in 8:9-27 and before (8:29), now greatly enhanced by her achievements.

Her instruction also has Achior summoned, who converts, and is circumcised, an act which the author and his hearers must have known violated Deut 23:2, but perhaps was meant to support granting an exception to someone of note known to

---

[267] As deSilva, "Judith the Heroine?" notes, "The ancient audience will not chasten Judith when they hear the story; they will chasten Holofernes for his foolishness in letting his guard down" (59).

[268] So Nickelsburg, *Jewish Literature*, 101; Mittmann-Richert, *Einführung*, 94.

[269] Elder, "Judith," notes that "Hellenistic and Hasmonean queens frequently demonstrated personal expertise in military strategy" (461) and concludes that the author wants us to assume that she was well educated (462).

them but not to us,[270] though the author gives no indication of being aware of the conflict.[271] The Assyrians discover the assassination and flee, with the Israelites, including those from far beyond Bethulia, following Judith's instructions in pursuit. The Israelites return with success and much booty (15:7). The author continues to make connections with all Israel as he has the high priest Joakim and the Jerusalem elders bless Judith as "the glory of Jerusalem ... the great boast of Israel and ... the great pride of our nation" (15:10). The women then dance to celebrate in traditional fashion (cf. Exod 15:20-21; 1 Sam 18:6-7),[272] with Judith at their head, and then men following with arms and garlands (15:12-13).

As in the stories of the Exodus, and of Jael, Deborah and Sisera, Judith ends with a song of praise which picks up key emphases of the story. Judith begins by returning to the allusion to Exod 15:13 LXX, to which her prayer in 9:7 had alluded: θεὸς συντρίβων πολέμους κύριος ("the Lord is a God who crushes wars") (16:2a), expounded as setting up camp with his people and as having liberated her from her pursuers (16:2b). It is apparent that this song of praise has its own persona. Judith speaks as personified Israel. Thus in speaking of liberation she refers to the people of Israel and goes on to speak of the threat "to burn up my territory, and kill my young men with the sword, and dash my infants to the ground, and seize my children as booty, and take my virgins as spoil" (16:4). Here again the violence of war receives emphasis, especially its effects on the young and on young girls who would be raped.[273]

The hymn then returns to the familiar motif: κύριος παντοκράτωρ ἠθέτησεν αὐτοὺς ἐν χειρὶ θηλείας ("But the Lord Almighty has foiled them by the hand of a female") (16:5), the all-powerful using the relatively powerless to

---

[270] Cf. Gruen, *Diaspora*, who writes, "At the very moment of triumph for those faithful to the Law, they violate it by welcoming the alien into their midst. This is no inadvertent slip; the author knew exactly what he was doing" (168), but offers the unlikely explanation that this is comic subversion of the narrative on the part of the author, for whom "from the outset that amusement would be more important than didacticism" (169). Terence L. Donaldson, *Judaism and the Gentiles: Jewish Patterns of Universalism (to 135 CE)* (Waco: Baylor University Press, 2007), suggests that the author may have embraced the more idealised hope which one finds in Isa 56:3, which similarly saw the inclusion of eunuchs, also in tension with Deut 23:2 (62). See also his discussion of Achior's importance in the narrative and so his symbolic importance of a different kind of Gentile from those symbolised by Holofernes (57-62).

[271] The Vulgate of Tob 11:19 has Achior in place of Ahikar, giving rise to the speculation that Achior in Judith is the Greek form of Ahikar, but in Tobit Ahikar is Jewish, whereas here Achior is Ammonite. See the review of the discussion in Otzen, *Tobit and Judith*, 108.

[272] On this see Rakel, "Judit," 420.

[273] So Rakel, "Judit," who also notes that this is usually understood as robbing men of their women (414).

stop the powerful oppressor. This contrast of power continues in what follows, which reflects knowledge both of Greek[274] and Enochic tradition when it declares:

> For their mighty one did not fall by the hands of the young men, nor did the sons of the Titans strike him down, nor did tall giants set upon him; but Judith daughter of Merari with the beauty of her countenance undid him. (16:6)

The hymn then focuses on Judith's sexual attractiveness. Her report to the Bethulians had spoken similarly: ἠπάτησεν αὐτὸν τὸ πρόσωπόν μου εἰς ἀπώλειαν αὐτοῦ ("my face ... seduced him to his destruction") (13:16). So here: ἐν κάλλει προσώπου αὐτῆς παρέλυσεν αὐτόν ("with the beauty of her countenance undid him"). This is then elaborated to include a fuller picture:

> She anointed her face with perfume; 8 she fastened her hair with a tiara and put on a linen gown to beguile him. 9 Her sandal ravished his eyes, her beauty captivated his mind, and the sword severed his neck! (16:7-9)

The song's account of celebration speaks of "the oppressed people" and "the weak people" and, still composed with an eye to gender, declares: "sons of slave-girls pierced them through" (16:12). Judith hails God as creator, but again, as Levison notes, with a particular echo of Ps 104:30 and woman's creation in the words: ἀπέστειλας τὸ πνεῦμά σου καὶ ᾠκοδόμησεν ("You sent forth your spirit, and it formed them") (16:14), the only other use of the verb οἰκοδομέω in this way being at the creation of woman in Gen 2:22.[275] The song concludes by affirming that to fear the Lord is greater than offering sacrifices, and by pronouncing woes against enemy nations (16:16-17).

The concluding narrative reports that Judith brought the booty from Holofernes' tent as an offering to Jerusalem, including the canopy from his bedchamber (16:19), but more significantly depicts in summary the rest of her life. Everyone went home, including Judith, who returned to Bethulia, to her estate, as a person honoured through all the country (16:21). It is noteworthy that the author has not lost sight of her sexuality, for he reports:

> καὶ πολλοὶ ἐπεθύμησαν αὐτήν καὶ οὐκ ἔγνω ἀνὴρ αὐτὴν πάσας τὰς ἡμέρας τῆς ζωῆς αὐτῆς ἀφ' ἧς ἡμέρας ἀπέθανεν Μανασσης ὁ ἀνὴρ αὐτῆς.

---

[274] Moore, *Judith*, notes that 2 Kgs 5:18, 22 LXX translates רְפָאִים by τῶν τιτάνων (248).

[275] J. R. Levison, "Judith 16:14 and the Creation of Woman," *JBL* 114 (1995) 467-69, who notes that original Hebrew would have read ותבנה (467).

Many men desired her [i.e. to have sexual intercourse with her/to take her as wife] but no man had sexual intercourse with her all the days of life since the day her husband Manasseh died. (16:22)

Judith remains a sexually attractive woman, but remains by her decision not to engage in sexual intercourse with anyone else. Neither her sexuality nor that of the men who wanted her is called into question. Here as earlier the author appears to see in her remaining celibate, an indication of voluntary devotion to her husband, like Anna in Luke 2:36.[276] Thus she remained in her husband's house, dying at 105 years of age in Bethulia, where she was buried in her husband's cave.[277]

Apparently among her last acts was the dispersal of her property. This includes her maid, whom she frees. Her namelessness in the narrative and lack of praise, despite her also having engaged in dangerous and courageous feats, reflects the inequality and abuse of the times.[278] We not only know no name. We also cannot be certain of her origins, whether Gentile or Jew, though had she been the latter, according to the Law she should have had her released much earlier.[279] Had she been a Gentile, which is more probable, she would probably be understood to have been a victim of Jewish victories in battle.[280] The careful dispersal by Judith of the other property to her husband's next of kin and her own, all within the extended family, will, on the other hand, reflect the Law and breathes the same air as the Book of Tobit.[281]

Conclusion

There are a number of aspects pertinent to sexuality in the book. First, indirectly, the work affirms a woman and so women as valued agents of divine will.[282] The

---

[276] Levine, "Sacrifice and Salvation," notes that while she is domesticated back onto her estate, she is not the same as before. Nothing is said of her ascetic religiosity and she presumably had greater social contact, hence the suitors (222).

[277] Levine, "Sacrifice and Salvation," comments: "in death, she is made to conform to her traditional role as wife" (222).

[278] See Glancy, "Mistress-Slave Dialectic," 85-87, who notes that freeing her in her old age was not necessarily kind.

[279] Glancy, "Mistress-Slave Dialectic," who notes the requirement that she should then have been released much earlier, according to Deut 15:12, which stipulated the 7th year (cf. also Jer 34:12-22) (85-86).

[280] Glancy, "Mistress-Slave Dialectic," 84.

[281] Nickelsburg, *Jewish Literature*, notes that both depict their protagonists as genuine Israelites of exemplary piety, bring people from despair to doxology, employ extensive intertextual references, and conclude with a hymn (102).

[282] Di Lella, "Women," indeed suggests that one of the author's aims is "to challenge, among other things, many of Ben Sira's sexist biases" (52).

author certainly gives Judith prominence, identifying her in terms of her own genealogy, not her husband's, having her challenge the male elders, act with her own independent strategy, successfully carry it out against the enemy's most powerful man, and then issue instructions to fetch Achior and pursue the fleeing troops. Male leaders of prominence acclaim her, the elders, Uzziah, the high priest, and Achior.

The hymn of praise has her speak in the persona of Israel and some traits support a symbolic or representative reading of her character.[283] Her name also suggests a possible representative function. Its relation to the name of the Maccabean male hero, Judas, may be consciously contrived to this end, but perhaps also in reaction to Hasmonean ideology and rule of the time, celebrated in 1 and 2 Maccabees.[284] On the other hand, she is clearly also a woman in her own right.[285] The author portrays her not as a poor widow, but a relatively prosperous one, who runs a large household with her maid as manager. Before any of her exploits she is shown as having status in the community and being treated with respect.

Judith's world was one where men and women were not equal. Despite her uncommonly strong position she is depicted as being in a man's world. She is hailed only as the greatest among women, not men. She exercises a kind of charismatic leadership but afterwards returns to her estate.[286] We do not read of her becoming an elder.[287] Worse still, we observe that her maid remained almost to the end in subservience, receiving no praise or appreciation from the author. Recognising that world's inequality should prevent us from finding anything too contrary in the work of the author. He shows no signs of trying to subvert the unequal society of his day, though within it he clearly calls abuse, including sexual

---

[283] Mittmann-Richert, *Einführung*, argues that in her exploits Judith is in effect a collective figure, representing the daughter of Zion, and also for that reason female (89). See also Nickelsburg, *Jewish Literature*, 101.

[284] See van Henten, "Judith as Alternative Leader," who notes that Hasmoneans also appealed to Judges in their propaganda (243-45); Esler, "Ludic History," 121.

[285] Rakel, "Judit," 414.

[286] Wills, *Jewish Novel*, notes that traditionally heroes are never able to integrate into the societies they have rescued (144-45), but it is not clear that the author indicates this is so with Judith.

[287] Cf. White Crawford, "Esther and Judith," who claims that finally "she does not resubmit herself to patriarchal norms. She retains her anomalous status as a widow, her control over her wealth, and her female servant as her second-in-command" (75). This is true of her exceptional position, but in a broader sense this must be seen as still within an overarching patriarchal system.

abuse, into question, and takes sides against the oppression he recognises. Judith is a hero but within a man's world and in service to the God of Israel.[288]

On the other hand, from within his world we do not see him indicating fear about Judith as a threat to men either before her exploits or after them.[289] Here it is important to distinguish between what we see the author articulating and what our social analysis would cause us to suspect, namely that any woman seen as taking men's power would have been a threat. It is probably right to conclude that to allow her to continue in a leadership role would have been unacceptable for the author, but this is nowhere expressed.[290] To read the depiction of her return (like everyone else) to her former estate as a deliberate attempt on the part of the author to avert the threat of female leadership[291] is to read something into the text which might well have been true in the author's world, but the author does not bring it to expression in the text.[292] The common assertions that she changes gender roles and

---

[288] Thus Stocker, *Judith*, declares: "When Judith decapitates Holofernes – man, lover, ruler, commander – she beheads patriarchy", but then notes she remains only an instrument of the true patriarchal power – God (8-9). See also Milne, "What shall we do with Judith?" who argues that Judith remains a man's woman (54), identifies with male models, does not identify with women and is "the very antithesis of a woman-identified woman" and not the hero but "a helpmate to the male deity" (55). Similarly Deborah F. Sawyer, "Gender Strategies in Antiquity: Judith's Performance," *Feminist Theology* 28 (2001) 9-26, who speaks of Judith as "merely a literary device that serves the higher cause of God" (14). "The shadowy God ... is the key operator" (15). This confronts the more fundamental issue of the implications of understanding God in male-gendered terms for both women and men, issues clearly beyond the author's purview.

[289] Cf. Levine, "Sacrifice and Salvation," who writes: "Judith's being a woman who nonetheless speaks and acts in the world of Israelite patriarchy creates a crisis" (209).

[290] White Crawford, "Esther and Judith," may be right when she speculates that "the character of Judith herself made the patriarchal societies forming the canons uncomfortable, so uncomfortable that she was excluded from the Jewish canon without a fight, while in Christian circles a lot of interpretation took place to allay this discomfort" (70).

[291] Cf. Levine, "Sacrifice and Salvation," who says of Judith that she is "safely returned to her proper place" (213). Similarly Wills, *Jewish Novel*, 152. So, indeed, is everyone else: "After this they all returned home to their inheritances" (16:21). We may also assume that the author would have seen their not doing so as a breach of the order he considered appropriate, which included limiting the roles of women and retaining a male-dominated society. In this sense she rightly observes that for the story Manasseh needed to be removed because otherwise he would be disgraced by being outshone by his wife (213) and that "only by remaining unique and apart can Judith be tolerated, domesticated and even treasured by Israelite society" (218-19). See also White Crawford, "Esther and Judith," who writes: "Judith can be acceptable as a Jewish heroine only because her danger is turned away from Israel, toward the enemy" (75).

[292] See Nickelsburg, *Jewish Literature*, who questions whether the author "sidelined her at the end" (100).

acts like a male or becomes a phallic woman[293] are too simple. Gender roles in the author's day should not be too quickly stereotyped. While one might assume that the author's understanding of gender saw male as might and female as beauty, seduction, and treachery,[294] this needs heavy qualification and while typified by Judith is nowhere generalised by the author. Women were known to run estates, even though mostly it was men who did so. Men were certainly the warriors, but Judith's strategy did not entail her behaving as men did in the role of warrior. She remained fully a woman in turning defeat to victory, a role usually achieved by men's armies, but she did it her way. Judith crossed some of the boundaries which normally typified men's and women's roles, but she did so as a woman, not by artificially assuming a male persona.[295] She is allowed to be exceptional and celebrated as such and not in a way that seeks to imply that in her exploits she swapped roles to become male.[296] She remains a powerful woman, but in a man's world.

Reduction of her portrait to the dangerous woman of male fantasy does not do justice to her multifaceted character and makes her bad news for women[297] and is at worst misogynistic.[298] She is shown to be not only a respected and apparently competent leader of a household to whom the town's elders have listened, but also something of a theologian as she challenges their assessment of how God relates to

---

[293] Cf. Wills, *Jewish Novel*, 148,152; Levine, "Sacrifice and Salvation," 218.

[294] See Rakel, "Judit," who writes that in Judith women are defined by external categories and are given only specific roles, typically deceit and seduction, gender driven. Accordingly what makes a woman in Judith is framed by males, though the work opts for a female rather than a male mode of dealing with conflict (412-13).

[295] Sawyer, "Gender Strategies," speaks of "mercurial gender transitions" as Judith "strides across the gender spectrum" (20) and stands outside the usual male–female categories (19). For all that, as she notes, Judith remains active and assertive (23).

[296] Esler, "Ludic History," rightly notes her liminal position as a wealthy. widow "outside the usual male-controlled kinship patterns" (130). "It is difficult to think that Israelites who had taken the step of imaginatively entering the powerful liminality produced by the story of Judith could ever return unchanged to the rituals of diurnal normality. The explosion of alternative possibilities set off by the book could not be contained so easily" (138). He concludes that "the author of this ludic history was seeking to reinvent Israelite identity around the issue of gender" (139).

[297] On this see Betsy Meredith, "Desire and Danger: The Drama of Betrayal in Judges and Judith," in *Anti-Covenant: Counter-Reading Women's Lives in the Hebrew Bible* (ed. Mieke Bal; Bible and Literature Series 22; Sheffield: Almond , 1989) 63-78, who assuming such a reading notes its negative effects (76). See also Milne, "What Shall We Do With Judith?" 47.

[298] So Elder, "Judith," 464, who writes: "The complexity of the beautiful, prayerful young widow who fasts night and day and assassinates a general to save her nation is explained away by a traditional misogynism that focuses on 'feminine' beauty as a weapon" (463).

their situation. She is also devout, extremely so, and from the author's perspective to be admired because she remained an unmarried widow, probably something which would have been far from what was in women's real interest at the time.

Among her many traits she is beautiful. That includes that she is sexually attractive. Her sexual attractiveness is a constant in the narrative, before, during, and after her exploits. Thus long after her dramatic exploits men respond to her sexually. The author apparently has no problems with sexual attractiveness and appropriate sexual responses. Judith is a sexual being who is in control of her sexuality. Mostly men as sexual beings are also not problematic. They become so however when they respond to women and their sexuality inappropriately, especially with violence. This was a constant feature of war, where rape and abduction were common. Holofernes is depicted as determined to get his way with Judith, prepared to rape. The author is also depicting men's responses to women as sometimes also stupid when like Holofernes they lose control of themselves through alcohol.

The juxtaposition of sexuality and death plays itself out in the assassination.[299] Tobit also juxtaposes them in the account of Sarah's seven husbands (3:8-9). While one might generalise that we see here an underlying fear of women's sexuality, it is clear in the case of both Sisera and Holofernes that both men meet their end primarily because of their own stupidity,[300] not because of any danger posed to them by women's sexuality. This is also the case with Samson and Delilah. On the other hand, the narrative assumes that women's sexuality is powerful, but does not blame women for that. It is up to men to take responsibility for their engagement with both women's sexuality and their own. A similar perspective was noted in the speech of the youths in 1 Esdras 3 – 4 (cf. also *LAB*).

Wills suggests that the narrative may be telling us much more about the encounter with Holofernes than its characters report. Taking his clue from Freudian perspectives he not only suggests that decapitation may symbolise castration, prefigured by having Bagoas as a eunuch, and by Manasseh's head suffering heatstroke,[301] but also by Judith entering Holofernes' tent as a vagina and

---

[299] On this juxtaposition see Otzen, *Tobit and Judith*, 111-12. White Crawford, "Esther and Judith," asserts that "the mixture of sex and death in this scene is both irresistible and appalling to a male audience, while many women find it empowering" (73), a claim about male audiences which surely also needs the qualification "many".

[300] Levine, "Sacrifice and Salvation," exaggerates, however, when she writes: "The men are weak, stupid, or impaired" (214). Holofernes is. Men who respond sexually to women are only "weak, stupid, or impaired" when they act inappropriately. I do not see the author calling either women's or men's sexuality as such into question.

[301] Wills, *Jewish Novel*, 148, citing Alan Dundes, "Response [to Alonso-Schöckel]" in *Protocol of the Colloquy of the Center for Hermeneutical Studies in Hellenistic and Modern Culture* 11 (Berkeley: Graduate Theological Union, 1975) 27-29; cf. Luis Alonso-Schöckel,

tearing down his canopy like a hymen and her offering it in Jerusalem as presentation of the signs of virginity (10:21; 13:9; 15:11; 16:19).[302] Is the depiction of Bethulia meant to evoke the Hebrew word for virgin, *bethulah* בתלה,[303] and the threat to its narrow entry pass an image of the threat of rape? It is difficult to know how one might verify such claims. One might ask, for instance, whether the outburst of joy at Judith's entry into Bethulia might represent orgasmic intercourse and why not. Such speculation may far exceed the author's scope and go far beyond what the evidence allows us to determine. There is certainly a sense in which the oppressive assault of Nebuchadnezzar's army is analogous to a sexual assault. Factors such as rape in war connect the elements of the analogy to reality.

2.1.4   Susanna

The work known as Susanna comes to us in two different Greek versions, the Septuagint Old Greek (OG), and so-called Theodotion (TH).[304] Both may be independent translations of semitic originals, with some indication that TH's was already an expanded original which it translated partly in dependence on the OG.[305] In the OG the work is appended to Daniel; in TH it precedes it. While the

---

"Narrative Structures in the Book of Judith," 1-20; similarly, Stocker, *Judith*, 7. See also Levine, "Sacrifice and Salvation," 212; Otzen, *Tobit and Judith*, 111-12.

[302] Wills, *Jewish Novel*, 149. "Judith has not only castrated Holofernes; she has penetrated him. Robbing him of his virginity, and has taken the 'tokens of virginity' as a trophy fit for a triumphant man. The net-as-hymen renders the 'manning' of Judith and the 'unmanning' of Holofernes balanced symbols" (150). Otzen, *Tobit and Judith*, notes a number of reversals in relation to sexuality which characterise the book of Judith: Judith is a widow, but celibate; a female, but acts like a male; personifies virtue but ventures into the spheres of indecency and laxity; Holofernes wants to seduce, but is seduced himself; seeks potent intercourse, but is rendered impotent in his drunken state; wants to penetrate both Judith and Bethulia, but Judith penetrates both his camp and tent; by decapitation he is castrated like Bagoas the eunuch; Achior is circumcised, Manasseh hit by head stroke, and Holofernes loses his head; Judith in her dress moves from death to life, whereas Holofernes moves from life to death; and Judith's bag first carries nourishment for life and then the dead head of Holofernes (111-12).

[303] Wills, *Jewish Novel*, 148; Levine, "Sacrifice and Salvation," 211.

[304] In what follows I use the text edition of Olivier Munnich, *Susanna – Daniel – Bel et Draco* (Septuaginta XVI.2; 2d ed.; Göttingen: Vandenhoeck & Ruprecht, 1999) and the *NETS* translation. I indicate with an asterisk translations which I have modified.

[305] So Moore, *Additions*, 79-83, 114-16; L. Timothy McLay, *The OG and Th Versions of Daniel* (SBLSCS 43; Atlanta: Scholars Press, 1996) 15. John J. Collins, *Daniel: A*

story of Susanna may rest on an older folktale,[306] the work was probably composed in the Hasmonean period and in a Hasmonean setting, but it is difficult to be more specific without engaging in speculation.[307]

I shall briefly review the two versions of the story before examining pertinent detail in each and discussing key themes. It is striking that some key statements in the story are preserved in either identical or close to identical wording, suggesting that these were deliberately kept unchanged whereas storytellers felt free to change other elements of lesser significance. Thus the citation about "lawlessness" coming from Babylon (5), reflecting an authoritative source, and its initial link to people coming to seek judgement (6a) is identical. The initial depiction of Susanna is also very close, though in a different sequence:

ὄνομα Σουσάνναν θυγατέρα Χελκίου γυναῖκα Ιωακιμ, περιπατοῦσαν ἐν τῷ παραδείσῳ τοῦ ἀνδρὸς αὐτῆς named Susanna daughter of Chelkias, wife of Joakim – walking about in her husband's garden.* (OG 7)	ἀνὴρ οἰκῶν ἐν Βαβυλῶνι καὶ ὄνομα αὐτῷ Ιωακιμ 2 καὶ ἔλαβε γυναῖκα, ᾗ ὄνομα Σουσαννα θυγάτηρ Χελκίου a man living in Babylon, and his name was Joakim. 2 He took a wife named Susanna daughter of Chelkias.* (TH 1-2) περιεπάτει ἐν τῷ παραδείσῳ τοῦ ἀνδρὸς αὐτῆς. (she) would walk about in her husband's garden. (TH 7)

Commentary on the Book of Daniel (Hermeneia; Minneapolis: Fortress, 1993), proposes that TH has an already expanded version of OG to hand (426). See also Mittmann-Richert, *Einführung*, 116; and R. Timothy McLay, "Sousanna: To the Reader," in *NETS*, 986-87.

[306] So Moore, *Additions*, 84-89; Gruen, *Diaspora*, 171; Wills, *Jewish Novel*, 55. Collins, *Daniel*, 438, notes that the story could have its origins at any time in the Hellenistic or late Persian period. See also the discussion in Lorenzo DiTommaso, *The Book of Daniel and the Apocryphal Daniel Literature* (SVTP 20; Leiden: Brill, 2005) 59-64, who sees Susanna as originally an independent work, but "redacted in some close relationship with" the court tales of Daniel 2 – 6 (62).

[307] Mittmann-Richert, *Einführung*, sees the work belonging together the other additions to Daniel, reflecting a process of reworking Daniel's heritage in Palestine during the reign of Simon (143-134 B.C.E.) looking back on the disaster of Antiochus (118-37). Dan W. Clanton, Jr. "(Re)Dating the Story of Susanna: A Proposal," *JSJ* 34 (2003) 121-40 combines the proposal of Nehemiah Brüll, "Das apokryphische Susanna Buch," *Jahrbuch für jüdische Geschichte und Literatur* 3 (1877) 1-69, that the story reflects conflicts between Pharisees and Sadducees at the time of Simeon ben Shetah, with the proposal of Tal Ilan, "'And Who Knows Whether You have not Come for a Time Like this?' (Esther 4:14): Esther, Judith and Susanna as Propaganda for Shelamzion's Queenship" in Tal Ilan, *Integrating Women into Second Temple History* (TSAJ 76; Tübingen: Mohr Siebeck, 1999) 127-53, that Esther, Judith and Susanna were composed as propaganda to support having a woman, Salome, as queen (76-67 B.C.E.). Cf. Gruen, *Diaspora*, 149-50, 324.

Identical words describe the distraction of the two elders from their responsibility (9) and almost identical words, their being besotted with her:

ἀλλὰ ἀμφότεροι ἦσαν κατανενυγμένοι περὶ αὐτῆς	καὶ ἦσαν ἀμφότεροι κατανενυγμένοι περὶ αὐτῆς
but both were transfixed by her (OG 10)	and both were transfixed by her (TH 10)

Susanna's response when confronted by them is similarly almost identical:

22 οἶδα ὅτι ἐὰν πράξω αὐτό, θάνατός μοί ἐστι, καὶ ἐὰν μὴ πράξω, οὐκ ἐκφεύξομαι τὰς χεῖρας ὑμῶν· 23 κάλλιον δέ με μὴ πράξασαν ἐμπεσεῖν εἰς τὰς χεῖρας ὑμῶν ἢ ἁμαρτεῖν ἐνώπιον κυρίου. 22 I know that if I do it, it is death for me, and if I do not, I will not escape your hands. 23 But it would be better for me to fall into your hands by not doing it than to sin before the Lord. (OG 22-23)	22 στενά μοι πάντοθεν· ἐάν τε γὰρ τοῦτο πράξω, θάνατός μοί ἐστιν, ἐάν τε μὴ πράξω, οὐκ ἐκφεύξομαι τὰς χεῖρας ὑμῶν· 23 αἱρετόν μοί ἐστιν μὴ πράξασαν ἐμπεσεῖν εἰς τὰς χεῖρας ὑμῶν ἢ ἁμαρτεῖν ἐνώπιον κυρίου. 22 Things are narrow for me on all sides. For if I do this, it is death for me; if I do not, I will not escape your hands. 23 It is preferable for me to fall into your hands by not doing it than to sin before the Lord. (TH 22-23)

The summoning of Susanna before the court is similarly almost identical:

ἀποστείλατε ἐπὶ Σουσάνναν θυγατέρα Χελκίου, ἥτις ἐστὶ γυνὴ Ιωακιμ· Send for Susanna daughter of Chelkias, who is the wife of Joakim.* (OG 29)	ἀποστείλατε ἐπὶ Σουσάνναν θυγατέρα Χελκίου, ἥ ἐστιν γυνὴ Ιωακιμ· Send for Susanna daughter of Chelkias, who is the wife of Joakim.* (TH 29)

The concocted false testimony and its acceptance by the assembly is very close, with minor variations (36-41), in part reflecting TH's elaboration of the garden scene. The inspired cross examination by Daniel in 52-59 with its Greek puns[308] is also very close with only minor plusses or variants. The outcome is also identically expressed: καὶ ἐσώθη αἷμα ἀναίτιον ἐν τῇ ἡμέρᾳ ἐκείνῃ ("and guiltless blood was saved that day") (62b).

It is noteworthy that such exact correspondence does not occur in incidental detail, but in elements which are at the core of the story and its meaning. The extent to which further details coincide varies, although further key elements in

---

[308] On the Greek puns as not necessarily indicating a Greek original, as first argued by Julius Africanus, see Moore, *Additions*, 84, 111.

common include the elders' plot, their attempt to implement it, and then to cover it up.

The Story in OG

The first lines of OG are missing, though on the basis of P967 probably included the mixed citation of 5.[309] They probably made mention of the two elders, as those to whom the word οὗτοι (7) refers. The surviving text begins as TH with the citation about lawlessness and immediately reports the elders seeing the attractive Susanna (whom it identifies through her husband and family) walking in her husband's garden and sexually lusting after her, which, it then declares, as TH, diverted their minds from heaven (God) and corrupted their judgments. They are each secretly befuddled with her without the other's knowing and Susanna's knowing, and try each morning to be first to come and speak with her, until one confronts the other about their early arrival and both confess what OG calls their distress. They resolve to force her to have sex with them. We then hear her refusal as a woman of Judah (ἡ Ἰουδαία) to sin and they plan to kill her. Then "the two elders and judges" have her summoned in the assembly (τὴν συναγωγὴν) of the city where they sojourn, where she arrives with over 500 supporters including her parents and servants. They then have her stripped (or perhaps only unveiled), and "the elders and judges" place their hands on her head, but she utters a prayer to God who knows all to help her against the false accusations. The elders then allege that they were walking in the garden and happened to see a couple having sex, looked to see who they were, noticed it was Susanna and a young man, who then fled, and that Susanna refused to divulge his identity. They are believed, given that they are "elders and judges". They were also two witnesses. OG then tells us that as she was being taken off to be executed an angel gave insight to a young man called, Daniel. He accosts the crowd as fools for proceeding to execution before examining the truth, demands the elders be separated, summons each, condemns them and then through interrogation exposes inconsistencies of their stories by asking under what tree the deed took place. The crowd acclaims the young man. They then do to the elders what they had wanted to do through their false testimony to Susanna in accordance with Deut 19:19. The elders are thrown into a ravine and burned up and so no innocent blood is shed. The version concludes with an affirmation that this is why "youths are beloved by Jacob because of their simplicity" (62) and should be watched over as those who are pious and wise.

---

[309] On this see Moore, *Additions*, 95.

The Story in TH

TH differs in a number of details. It begins with Joakim and his wife, Susanna, her beauty, her religious devotion, and her parents who taught her the Law. TH makes Joakim's house the location for court hearings, thus accounting for the two elders' regular appearance there. This also has the effect of relocating the trial of Susanna from the city synagogue to Joakim's house, his own wife being tried on site. TH has greatly altered and expanded the account of the elders' encounter with Susanna.[310] Their mutual secrecy is broken not as they arrive early in the morning but after they have agreed to go off for lunch but both returned separately to the garden. TH then adds the motifs that she was bathing on a hot day, sent her maids to get oil and soaps, and had them close the gates. It has the elders voice to her their threat to concoct false testimony if she didn't consent. TH then depicts a shouting match between her and the elders and has one of them open the gates, with the result that the servants return and are ashamed as the elders allege what has happened. TH has the elders the next day have Susanna summoned, but now in her husband's house. They have her unveiled, apparently just her head, and as in OG place their hands on her head. Where OG then brings her prayer, TH mentions that she prays, relocating a version of the prayer till after the sentence has been passed when she prays again. Their concocted testimony now contains detail about the maids and about shutting the gates, but in a further falsification reports that the young man opened the gates to flee. TH makes explicit that the assembly condemns her to death and her prayer follows. TH then has divine response to Susanna's prayer follow immediately, but makes no mention of an angel equipping Daniel; Daniel already has a holy spirit which God then awakens[311] and he declares his innocence of "this woman's blood" (46). TH then stays very close to OG, but has Daniel ask the people to return to the court and the leaders acknowledge that he has the right to act as an elder, enhancing Daniel's status in the account. The interrogation of each elder runs very much as in OG as does the judgement. TH concludes by noting the family's relief that Susanna had not been found guilty of a shameful deed and by highlighting Daniel's status: "Daniel became great in the presence of the people from that day onward", an ideal introduction for the Book of Daniel which in TH follows.

---

[310] Helmut Engel, *Die Susanna-Erzählung: Einleitung, Übersetzung und Kommentar zum Septuaginta-Text und zur Theodotion-Bearbeitung* (OBO 61; Fribourg: Universitätsverlag; Göttingen: Vandenhoeck & Ruprecht, 1985), notes that TH has enhanced the psychologised and erotic aspects of the story (181-82).

[311] Ilse von Loewenclau,"Das Buch Daniel: Frauen und Kinder nicht gerechnet" in *Kompendium Feministische Bibelauslegung* (ed. Luise Schottroff, Marie-Theres Wacker, Claudia Janssen, and Beate Wehn; Gütersloh: Gütersloher Verlagshaus, 1999) 291-98, notes that in depicting Daniel as having the spirit the author reflects Dan 5:12; 6:4 (297).

Leadership and Corruption

For all the common elements the versions function differently. The different endings make this clear.[312] In OG the account emphasises the wisdom of the young, of whom Daniel is an example, thus setting the young over against both the corrupt elders and the establishment which is willing to follow them.[313] This emphasis may well reflect real tensions in the historical context of its composition where the author champions young leadership over against the establishment. While TH also depicts corrupt elders and an establishment willing to follow them, its interest appears to be on establishing the status of Daniel,[314] most likely in the interests of enhancing the status of his works or, at least Danielic literature. These enhancements may even belong to the stage when it was being used as an introduction to the Book of Daniel. While in both Daniel appears late in the narrative (45), to some degree this is dictated by the sequence and need not have been a problem for TH. Daniel's role as judge may have been inspired by his name which means: "God has judged". None of this pertains to issues of sexuality, nor to Susanna, who is left behind in both narratives in the interests of these other concerns. Apparently in OG, unlike TH, Susanna does not appear in the opening lines, which are also concerned with leadership.

In both, however, there is an overriding concern about corruption, which first comes to expression in an authoritative manner through what is presented as the words of ὁ δεσπότης "the Lord" (5). In OG this stands over the entire narrative before any mention of Susanna. In TH it comes after she has been presented, but as both beautiful and as φοβουμένη τὸν κύριον ("fearing the Lord") and well-instructed in Torah by her parents (2-3), so that the citation now stands in contrast to Susanna's piety and also carries major weight as a kind of title for what is to come.

> ἐξῆλθεν ἀνομία ἐκ Βαβυλῶνος ἐκ πρεσβυτέρων κριτῶν οἳ ἐδόκουν κυβερνᾶν τὸν λαόν.
> Lawlessness came forth from Babylon, from elders who were judges, who were supposed to govern the people. (5)

---

[312] On the different function and form of the two versions see the discussion in Engel, *Susanna*, 175-83.

[313] So Moore, *Additions*, 113-14; Wills, *Jewish Novel*, 56; von Loewenclau, "Daniel," 295; Engel, *Susanna*, 180.

[314] So Moore, *Additions*, 108-109; von Loewenclau, "Daniel," 295.

The alleged citation appears nowhere known to us, but probably alludes to Jer 29:22-23 (36:22-23).[315]

> 22 And on account of them this curse shall be used by all the exiles from Judah in Babylon: "The LORD make you like Zedekiah and Ahab, whom the king of Babylon roasted in the fire," 23 because they have perpetrated outrage in Israel and have committed adultery with their neighbors' wives
> (יען אשר עשו נבלה בישראל וינאפו את נשי רעיהם δι' ἣν ἐποίησαν ἀνομίαν ἐν Ισραηλ καὶ ἐμοιχῶντο τὰς γυναῖκας τῶν πολιτῶν αὐτῶν), and have spoken in my name lying words that I did not command them; I am the one who knows and bears witness, says the LORD. (Jer 29:22-23 [36:22-23])

It may also allude to Jer 23:14-15:

> 14 But in the prophets of Jerusalem I have seen a more shocking thing: they commit adultery and walk in lies; they strengthen the hands of evildoers, so that no one turns from wickedness (נאוף והלך בשקר וחזקו ידי מרעים לבלתי שבו איש מרעתו μοιχωμένους καὶ πορευομένους ἐν ψεύδεσι καὶ ἀντιλαμβανομένους χειρῶν πονηρῶν τοῦ μὴ ἀποστραφῆναι ἕκαστον ἀπὸ τῆς ὁδοῦ αὐτοῦ τῆς πονηρᾶς); all of them have become like Sodom to me, and its inhabitants like Gomorrah. 15 Therefore thus says the LORD of hosts concerning the prophets: "I am going to make them eat wormwood, and give them poisoned water to drink; for from the prophets of Jerusalem ungodliness has spread throughout the land"
> (כי מאת נביאי ירושלם יצאה חנפה לכל הארץ ὅτι ἀπὸ τῶν προφητῶν Ιερουσαλημ ἐξῆλθεν μολυσμὸς πάσῃ τῇ γῇ). (Jer 23:14-15)

The likelihood of an allusion to Jer 29:21-23 is strengthened by the fact that there we have reference to two prophets who committed adultery, as the two judges/elders were intent to do, and that in OG they too meet a fiery end (60-62). It also preserves the word ἀνομία. The connection with Jer 23:14-15 is not as strong, though there, too, we have reference to prophets committing adultery, but in addition: lying and the verb ἐξῆλθεν. What these texts allege of prophets, Susanna alleges of elders who are judges.[316] Thus already the authoritative citation would, for those catching the allusions, make the link between corruption and sexual wrongdoing.

---

[315] So Moore, *Additions*, 96. Marti J. Steussy, *Gardens in Babylon: Narrative and Faith in the Greek Legends of Daniel* (SBLDS 141; Atlanta: Scholars, 1993) points to Zech 5:5-10 LXX which also speaks of ἀνομία in connection with going out and Babylon (146-51).

[316] Mittmann-Richert, *Einführung*, 127-28. She also sees Hab 1:1-4, which rails against violence, though not against sexual wrongdoing, as having influenced if not inspired the work (129).

In its opening TH has already set Susanna in contrast to such corruption (2-3). OG also emphasises Susanna's devotion to the Law (23). Both emphasise that she knows that to do what the elders want would be to commit a sin for which the punishment is death (Deut 22:21-24; Lev 20:10; cf. John 8:4-5) and is prepared to face the consequences of not sinning (22-23), recalling Joseph's response in Gen 39:9. Both have her cry out to God in prayer and find her prayer answered (OG 35; TH 35, 42-44). The idealisation of Susanna's piety may account for OG's additional information that she did not know of the elders' attitude towards her (11), that her family support numbered 500 people (30b) and, for TH's note, that her family and all who knew her wept (33), presumably because they held her in high regard. TH 24 tells us that she also knows that she must cry out with a loud voice (cf. Deut 22:24 in the case of a virgin) and further reinforces her status by reporting that the slaves were ashamed because they had never heard of such a report about her (27).[317] Perhaps by making explicit that Susanna was veiled TH helps support this observant modest image (32).

Both bring Daniel's challenge to "the sons of Israel" that they are fools in proceeding to execute "a daughter of Israel" without examining the evidence (48), but also the charge to the second man which contrasts daughters of Israel and a daughter of Judah 57):

οὕτως ἐποιεῖτε θυγατράσιν Ισραηλ, καὶ ἐκεῖναι φοβούμεναι ὡμιλοῦσαν ὑμῖν, ἀλλ' οὐ θυγάτηρ Ιουδα ὑπέμεινε τὸ νόσημα ὑμῶν ἐν ἀνομίᾳ ὑπενεγκεῖν· And thus you used to treat the daughters of Israel, and they, being afraid, would have intercourse with you, but a daughter of Judah did not tolerate bearing your sickness in lawlessness.* (OG 57)	οὕτως ἐποιεῖτε θυγατράσιν Ισραηλ, καὶ ἐκεῖναι φοβούμεναι ὡμίλουν ὑμῖν, ἀλλ' οὐ θυγάτηρ Ιουδα ὑπέμεινε τὴν ἀνομίαν ὑμῶν· Thus you used to treat the daughters of Israel, and they, being afraid, would have intercourse with you, but a daughter of Judah did not tolerate your lawlessness.* (TH 57)

The contrast may allude to the northern and southern kingdoms (cf. Hos 4:15)[318] or perhaps even to Jews and Samaritans,[319] but is more likely making a distinction

---

[317] Glancy, "Mistress-Slave Dialectic," notes that the author does not make clear whether the female body slaves were ashamed because they believed the report or because it was given, though notes that for the author slaves are treated as an extension of their owners as invisible as plumbing is to us in the functions they performed (78-80).

[318] Mittmann-Richert, *Einführung*, 129. The MT has Israel contrasted with Judah, using sexual imagery: אם זנה אתה ישראל אל יאשם יהודה "Though you play the whore, O Israel, do not let Judah become guilty"; whereas LXX reads: σὺ δέ Ισραηλ μὴ ἀγνόει καὶ Ιουδα μὴ εἰσπορεύεσθε εἰς Γαλγαλα "But you, O Israel, stop being ignorant, and you, O Ioudas, stop going to Galgala".

[319] Cf. Moore, *Additions*, 112; Collins, *Daniel*, 434.

within Israel, especially since she has shortly before been referred to as a daughter of Israel (48).[320] It does, however, reflect a differentiation which is probably less ethnic than religious and so the equivalent of "a true daughter of Judah" (cf. also the contrast between Canaan and Judah in 56).[321] This again reinforces Susanna's status. The reference to Susanna in 22 as ἡ Ἰουδαία ("The Judean woman") implies the same, especially because it coheres with her claim to know God's will. In this sense Susanna is at least a model, however else her image may function, to which we return below.

Within the framework of "lawlessness" and faithful observance, we find then an account of transgression of the Law. At one level the focus is corrupt judgement. Accordingly Daniel confronts the two elders with the charge that as those entrusted to hear and adjudicate on capital cases they have acquitted the guilty and condemned the innocent, contrary to the biblical command, "You shall not kill an innocent and righteous person" (53). With the confronting words, "You that have grown aged in wicked days, your sins have now come, which you have committed formerly" (52), the storyteller indicates that Daniel is about to expose longstanding corruption. The conclusion which affirms that "guiltless blood was saved that day" (62), also reflects the focus on avoiding such corruption. The allusion to age fits the emphasis in OG on the contrasting wisdom of the young (62b). To this point the sin against Susanna, herself, except in the sense that she was threatened with unjust execution, remains unmentioned. The elder is not condemned for trying to force her to have sexual intercourse.[322]

The sexual dimension, however, is strongly present in the interrogation of the second elder.

διὰ τί διεστραμμένον τὸ σπέρμα σου, ὡς Σιδῶνος καὶ οὐχ ὡς Ιουδα; τὸ κάλλος σε ἠπάτησεν [ἢ μικρὰ ἐπιθυμία]· οὕτως ἐποιεῖτε θυγατράσιν Ισραηλ, καὶ ἐκεῖναι φοβούμεναι ὡμιλοῦσαν ὑμῖν,	σπέρμα Χανααν καὶ οὐκ Ιουδα, τὸ κάλλος ἐξηπάτησέ σε, καὶ ἡ ἐπιθυμία διέστρεψεν τὴν καρδίαν σου· 57 οὕτως ἐποιεῖτε θυγατράσιν Ισραηλ, καὶ ἐκεῖναι φοβούμεναι ὡμίλουν ὑμῖν,

---

[320] Engel, *Susanna*, draws attention to Jer 29:22-23 (125-26).

[321] See Shaye J. D. Cohen, "Ioudaios: 'Judaean' and 'Jew' in Susanna, First Maccabees, and Second Maccabees," in *Geschichte-Tradition-Reflexion: Festschrift für Martin Hengel zum 70. Geburtstag: Bd 1: Judentum* (ed. Hubert Cancik, Hermann Lichtenberger, and Peter Schafer; Tübingen: Mohr Siebeck, 1996) 211-20, who notes that it means more than simply "Jewess" in OG 22, since her assailants are also Jews, but rather is depicting her as one who as a true "daughter of Judah" or "Judean" resists evil (212-13).

[322] Alice Bach, *Women, Seduction, and Betrayal in Biblical Narrative* (Cambridge: Cambridge University Press, 1997), is only half right when she writes that the elders "are condemned for bearing false witness against her; nothing is said of their lascivious designs on her" (71). The issue does return with the second elder.

ἀλλ' οὐ θυγάτηρ Ιουδα ὑπέμεινε τὸ νόσημα ὑμῶν ἐν ἀνομίᾳ ὑπενεγκεῖν· Why is your seed twisted, like that of Sidon, and not like that of Judah? Beauty has deceived/seduced you, [paltry lust]. 57 And thus you used to treat the daughters of Israel, and they, being afraid, would have intercourse with you, but a daughter of Judah did not tolerate bearing your sickness in lawlessness.* (OG 56-57)	ἀλλ' οὐ θυγάτηρ Ιουδα ὑπέμεινε τὴν ἀνομίαν ὑμῶν· O seed of Canaan and not Judah, beauty has beguiled/seduced you, and lust has twisted your heart. 57 Thus you used to treat the daughters of Israel, and they, being afraid, would have intercourse with you, but a daughter of Judah did not tolerate your lawlessness.* (TH 56-57)

Here we learn that the instance with Susanna is only one of many in a pattern of longstanding sexual exploitation. The statement that a daughter of Judah would never put up with their lawlessness, which OG, interestingly, depicts as "sickness in lawlessness", implies that in the past some had submitted to their pressure and invites the hearers' disapproval.

While only OG describes them as "sick" (though not in a way that absolves them of responsibility), both depict them as corrupted. OG depicts them as corrupted like (presumably) the men of Sidon. The hearers apparently need no further explanation. It assumes that men of Sidon were generally corrupt, unlike those of Judah, and probably in a sexual sense. It may include a reference to women if hearers recall that Jezebel and Athaliah come from there (1 Kgs 16:31; 2 Chr 21:6; 22:10-12).[323] TH instead simply accuses them of being Canaanites, also traditionally accused of sexual corruption, and more traditionally Israel's enemy. Ham, Sidon's grandfather and Canaan's father, brought the curse on his seed for looking at his father's nakedness (Gen 9:22-27).[324]

TH links corruption not with the seed, here of Canaan, but as something which ἡ ἐπιθυμία has done to their minds. OG (though not P967) also apparently has reference to μικρά ἐπιθυμία ("paltry desire/lust") and has it stand in apposition to the statement both versions share: τὸ κάλλος σε ἠπάτησεν ("beauty has deceived/seduced you") (OG); τὸ κάλλος ἐξηπάτησέ σε ("beauty has beguiled/seduced you") (TH). Both reflect a certain psychology of men's sexual responses.

---

[323] Amy-Jill Levine, "'Hemmed in on Every Side': Jews and Women in the Book of Susanna," in *A Feminist Companion to Esther, Judith and Susanna* (ed. Athalya Brenner; Sheffield: Sheffield Academic Press, 1995) 303-23, 321. See also Engel, *Susanna*, 125.

[324] See also Moore, *Additions*, 111-12.

Men's Sexuality and Corruption

This "psychology" of sexual corruption comes to expression earlier in the narrative. TH describes Susanna as καλὴ σφόδρα ("very beautiful") (2) and OG as γυναῖκα ἀστείαν τῷ εἴδει ("a woman elegant in appearance"*) (7). Both again report her beauty when summoned to trial: she is τρυφερὰ σφόδρα ("very refined") to which TH adds: καὶ καλὴ τῷ εἴδει ("beautiful in appearance") (31). Her beauty, which includes her sexual attractiveness, is something positive which in TH sits comfortably beside καὶ φοβουμένη τὸν κύριον ("fearing the Lord") (2).[325] There is no indication that the author blames Susanna for her sexuality, as though she is to be made partly accountable for the men's responses.[326] When Daniel charges them with having been beguiled by a woman's beauty (56), he is not implicating Susanna in guilt, as we shall show below.[327] When Glancy asks with allusion to 9, "Does looking at a beautiful woman render a man unfit to look at heaven?",[328] the author's answer is almost certainly: no. Ilan captures more accurately the focus of the work when she writes: "Instead of concentrating on the negative aspects of women's sexuality and temptation for men, it chose to highlight the danger of men's sexuality for women".[329]

---

[325] Similarly Ellis, *Sexual Desire*, 54.

[326] Cf. Levine, "Hemmed in," who writes: "Once we see her as desirable, we are trapped; either we are guilty of lust, or she is guilty of seduction" (313). This antithesis does not, I believe, accurately reflect the author's perspective who apparently has no discomfort in affirming Susanna's beauty. None of the details to which Levine points (313-18) within the text (the garden, bathing) or beyond it (e.g., the story of Bilhah, who is in any case not blamed in *Jub.* 33:2-9, which she cites) supports the view that the author is blaming women. Similarly negative are Susan Starr Sered and Samuel Cooper, "Sexuality and Social Control: Anthropological Reflections on the Book of Susanna," in *The Judgment of Susanna: Authority and Witness.* (ed. E. Spolsky, EJL 11; Atlanta: Scholars, 1996) 43-55, who write: "The significance of Susanna's beauty is quite simply to 'seduce' the reader into thinking that rape is a consequence of male sexual arousal precipitated by female beauty, rather than a product of culturally condoned patriarchal control of female autonomy" (50); "women 'ask for it'" (50).

[327] Jennifer A. Glancy, "The Accused: Susanna and her Readers," in *A Feminist Companion to Esther, Judith and Susanna* (ed. Athalya Brenner; Sheffield: Sheffield Academic Press, 1995) 288-302, 293-94. She rightly notes that such a belief "is often used to excuse men from responsibility for their actions since women's beauty is considered the cause of men's lust" (298).

[328] Glancy, "Accused," 294. Her assertion that Daniel "resists the temptation of looking at the lovely Susanna himself" at the trial is argument from silence with no foundation in the text (296).

[329] Ilan, "And Who Knows," 149. Similarly Gail Corrington Streete, *The Strange Woman: Power and Sex in the Bible* (Louisville: Westminster John Knox, 1997) "Clearly,

OG simply speaks of the elders seeing her (ἰδόντες), but TH of seeing her on a daily basis because of their place of work (ἐθεώρουν αὐτὴν), as she went for her walk in the garden. Both then speak of a further development:

καὶ ἐπιθυμήσαντες αὐτὴν 9 διέστρεψαν τὸν νοῦν αὐτῶν καὶ ἐξέκλιναν τοὺς ὀφθαλμοὺς αὐτῶν τοῦ μὴ βλέπειν εἰς τὸν οὐρανὸν μηδὲ μνημονεύειν κριμάτων δικαίων· 10 ἀλλὰ ἀμφότεροι ἦσαν κατανενυγμένοι περὶ αὐτῆς. Being sexually attracted to her, 9 they diverted their minds and turned away their eyes in order not to look to heaven nor to remember to make right decisions, 10 but both were transfixed by her.* (OG 8-10)	καὶ ἐγένοντο ἐν ἐπιθυμίᾳ αὐτῆς 9 καὶ διέστρεψαν τὸν ἑαυτῶν νοῦν καὶ ἐξέκλιναν τοὺς ὀφθαλμοὺς αὐτῶν τοῦ μὴ βλέπειν εἰς τὸν οὐρανὸν μηδὲ μνημονεύειν κριμάτων δικαίων. 10 καὶ ἦσαν ἀμφότεροι κατανενυγμένοι περὶ αὐτῆς. And they became sexually attracted to her. 9 And they diverted their own minds and turned away their eyes in order not to look to heaven nor to remember to make right decisions. 10 And both were transfixed by her.* (TH 8-10)

Here we find four stages of development. At the first they respond to her sexual attractiveness with sexual desire ἡ ἐπιθυμία. Presumably her husband did, similarly, so that the issue is what happens next, what they do with their sexual feelings?[330] ἡ ἐπιθυμία, potentially neutral, then becomes negative, and given what follows this may be assumed here. As Collins notes, it then contravenes Exod 20:17.[331] One could therefore already imply the negative in translating 8b, by using the language of lust.

The second stage indicates that they turn or divert (διέστρεψαν) their minds. The verb will be used in OG in Daniel's charge that their seed is corrupted (56). It is important to note that they are the subject of the verb, not ἡ ἐπιθυμία, though in 56 we read: ἡ ἐπιθυμία διέστρεψεν τὴν καρδίαν σου ("desire/ lust has twisted your heart"). The assumption is not that they cannot help themselves. They pervert their minds with their sexual desire instead of responding to it in ways that would not have this effect. In describing the effect as including that they turn their eyes from heaven, the author is probably playing with the connection between looking, and looking with sexual desire with a view to wanting to fulfil that sexual desire. Looking to heaven means looking to God, including, looking to God's commandments and the prohibition of adultery and sexual assault. The additional

---

however, the onus is not on Susanna but on the foolish, lustful elders, who pervert the good, both of Wisdom and the law" (118).

[330] As Ellis, *Sexual Desire*, observes, "the story makes it clear ... that the elders are responsible for their desire's leading them into sin" (54).

[331] Collins, *Daniel*, 430.

detail that they are not mindful of just judgements is probably more than that they are distracted and don't do their work well. In the light of the charges laid by Daniel, it will include behaviour that is directly corrupt including sexual exploitation through their position of power.

We reach the third stage of development where both texts describe them as having become κατανενυγμένοι περὶ αὐτῆς. Κατανυσσω means "to pierce to the heart", usually in sorrow. Here the author apparently means to convey the idea that they had become so obsessed with their sexual desire that they had made themselves sick.[332] OG preserves this sense in using the word, νόσημα, in 57, noted above. The same sense is conveyed, when the text has them speak of τὴν ὀδύνην αὐτῶν (TH 10; similarly OG 14), best translated "their distress".

The account of their behaviour coheres with this depiction, in which we recognise patterns familiar from every age where sexual desire and guilt meet. Thus they are secretive over against each other about their desire to have sex with her (ἠσχύνοντο ἀναγγεῖλαι τὴν ἐπιθυμίαν αὐτῶν ὅτι ἤθελον συγγενέσθαι αὐτῇ ("because they were ashamed to tell of their lust, that they wanted to have sex with her"*) (TH 11), and deceived each other, in TH pretending once that they were going off to lunch (13), but then finding their way back to the same place (14), where they finally had to acknowledge what they were really after: ὡμολόγησαν τὴν ἐπιθυμίαν αὐτῶν ("they acknowledged their lust") (14). Here their sexual desire had moved a long way from a feeling of being sexually attracted; it had become deliberate intention to fulfil that desire by having sex with Susanna. OG also depicts their secrecy (10/11) and their competitiveness by trying to be first to arrive at their workplace where they could speak to her (12), and depicting such earliness as the cause for finally acknowledging what was going on, here described as their distress (ὀδύνην; 14). The depiction of their antics also belongs to the entertainment of the story: men laughing at themselves or at their colleagues for being stupid. Such humour works because it assumes men could behave differently and so are responsible for their foolishness. Women are not to blame.

OG then takes us straight to stage four: καὶ εἶπεν εἷς τῷ ἑτέρῳ πορευθῶμεν πρὸς αὐτήν· καὶ συνθέμενοι προσήλθοσαν αὐτῇ καὶ ἐξεβιάζοντο αὐτήν ("And one said to the other, 'Let us go to her!' So having

---

[332] See Frank Zimmermann, "The Story of Susanna and Its Original Language," *JQR* 48 (1957-58) 236-41, on the possible confusion reflected in the translation between חלה ("to wound") and חלל ("to be sick"), who suggests that the original Hebrew of 10 probably read ויחלו באהבתה, but that the translator read it as deriving from חלה rather than חלל (239-40).

agreed, they approached her and tried to force her") (19).[333] Two sets of uncontrolled passions make such situations all the more dangerous. Compacting for rape they try to force her to have sex. TH fills out the scene: the elders hide, then, when the doors are shut, converge on Susanna, declaring: ἰδοὺ αἱ θύραι τοῦ παραδείσου κέκλεινται, καὶ οὐδεὶς θεωρεῖ ἡμᾶς, καὶ ἐν ἐπιθυμίᾳ σού ἐσμεν. διὸ συγκατάθου ἡμῖν καὶ γενοῦ μεθ' ἡμῶν. ("Behold the garden doors are shut, and no one can see us, and we want [to have sex with] you. So go along with us and have sex with us"*) (20). Far from consensual sex διὸ συγκατάθου ἡμῖν ("So go along with us") is pressure to submit. Having sexual desire for you (ἐν ἐπιθυμίᾳ σού) is no justification (διὸ) for forcing submission. The violence and abuse of power then manifests itself in TH by their threat to concoct a false story and in both OG and TH by their desire to kill her.

Sexual love as affirming life stands in stark contrast to sexual exploitation, deceit and murder. This is not a scene of attempted seduction but of attempted rape.[334] These are not lovers; they are violent predatory males with no thought for Susanna as anything other than a means of their sexual gratification. The author has the elders continue to indulge their sexually predatory behaviour in depicting their desire that she be unveiled before them as motivated by their sexual exploitation (ἵνα ἐμπλησθῶσι κάλλους ἐπιθυμίας αὐτῆς ("so that they could be sated with lust for her beauty") (OG 32); ὅπως ἐμπλησθῶσιν τοῦ κάλλους αὐτῆς ("so that they could be sated with her beauty") (TH 32) even at the point where if they succeed she will die, like rapists who go on to kill (cf. also Ammon whose resisted lust provokes hate 2 Sam 13:10-15).[335]

While TH suggests removing a veil, adding that she was veiled, thus uncovering her head (οἱ δὲ παράνομοι ἐκέλευσαν ἀποκαλυφθῆναι αὐτήν ἦν γὰρ κατακεκαλυμμένη) (32), OG, which mentions no such veiling (καὶ προσέταξαν οἱ παράνομοι ἀποκαλύψαι αὐτήν) (32), may mean stripping her

---

[333] Sarah Pearce, "Echoes of Eden in the Old Greek of Susanna," *Feminist Theology* 11 (1996) 10-31, notes that P967 has not the imperfect ἐξεβιάζοντο but the aorist ἐξεβιάσαντο, which could be read as indicating that they actually raped Susanna (as Esth 7:8 LXX), though this need not be the case, especially since in Deut 22:25-28 LXX, to which Susanna 24 also alludes, the middle form of the simple verb is used to refer to seizing prior to sexual assault: βιασάμενος κοιμηθῇ μετ' αὐτῆς ("seizes her and lies with her") (22:25, 28) (14). In addition Susanna's response in 22-23 does not indicate rape has taken place.

[334] On this see Glancy, "Accused," 289, 298. She also calls into question the author's assumption that death is to be preferred to submitting to rape and so, by implication, that doing so is sin (290). As she points out, such a stance feeds the widespread prejudice that rape victims are thus by definition guilty (298). The major focus, however, is not blaming the sexually exploited, though that is there, but blaming the exploiters.

[335] So Moore, *Additions*, 102.

naked, such as we read of in Ezek 16:37-39; Hos 2:3, 10.[336] Some uncovering to expose at least some of the body is reflected in later rabbinic tradition about adulterous women (*m. Sot.* 1.5),[337] though not allowed in the case of attractive women.[338] On the other hand, OG may simply reflect the formulation in Num 5:18 LXX according to which the priest hearing a charge of adultery against a woman among others things ἀποκαλύψει τὴν κεφαλὴν τῆς γυναικός ("shall uncover the head of the woman"). Pearce challenges the applicability of the later rabbinic material and also points to the highly metaphorical use in Ezekiel and Hosea, where the stripping of prostitutes and adulteresses occurs after their condemnation.[339]

This may cohere, however, with a second irregularity, namely the laying of hands on her head, which in Deut 24:14 also belongs to a declaration of condemnation, not an act of testimony. The author apparently intends us to see the elders as judges simultaneously doing both (emphasised more in OG by its persistence in identifying them as both elders and judges: 29, 34) and thereby leaving no room for further testimony, certainly none from Susanna[340] and also none for her husband, who could have asked for the test of bitter waters.[341] Daniel's challenge to the people does indeed address improper procedure: οὕτως μωροί υἱοὶ Ισραηλ; οὐκ ἀνακρίναντες οὐδὲ τὸ σαφὲς ἐπιγνόντες ἀπεκτείνατε (OG)/ἀπεκρίνατε (TH) θυγατέρα Ισραηλ; ("Are you such fools, O sons of Israel? Without examining or learning the plain truth, do you kill (OG)/condemn (TH) a daughter of Israel?"(48). The elders acted as judges effectively pronouncing the verdict and then articulating its grounds. OG thus sees no need for a declaration of Susanna's guilt; the assembly simply believed them (41). Only TH adds that they then condemned her to death.

The Role of Susanna

While the author is clearly concerned with the injustice which kills the innocent and sets the guilty free, and to follow the principle of reciprocity in applying to

---

[336] So Moore, *Additions*, 103; Wills, *Jewish Novel*, 55-56, who writes that in this way she becomes "a permissible object of male erotic attention who is then to be stoned by the community" (57).

[337] So Zimmermann, "Story of Susanna," 236-37 n. 2.

[338] Collins, *Daniel*, 432.

[339] Pearce, "Echoes of Eden," 15-16.

[340] So Bach, *Women, Seduction, and Betrayal*, 68; von Loewenclau, "Daniel," 295.

[341] As Streete, *Strange Woman*, notes, the text assumes that because the woman had allegedly been witnessed in the act (cf. Num 5:13) the test with bitter waters (Num 5:16-28) would not apply (117).

them what they saw sought to apply to her (61),[342] this has not submerged an equally clear concern with abuse of power for sexual advantage, including the gullibility with which allegations are assumed to be so.[343] Nevertheless the story is more concerned to describe the outcome of judgement on the elders than to report what happened for Susanna. Once her prayer has elicited God's engagement of Daniel she disappears from the story.[344] It presumes that, her innocence confirmed, she returns to her husband,[345] though, as Wills notes, only the ending of TH mentions him.[346] No interest is shown in the trauma such an experience would have brought, nor the shame of having to face trial and be humiliated.[347] As Glancy observes, "What is at stake in the story is not Susanna's physical well-being as she is threatened with rape and death but the honor of Joachim's household".[348] Nor is it interested in changing the patriarchal structures,[349] provided all abide by Torah.

The suggestion that Susanna (and Judith and Esther) was designed as propaganda to support the validity of Salome's rule as a woman as proposed by Ilan and Clanton[350] would be more convincing if Susanna showed some leadership. It is certainly, as Ilan observes, "a blatant critique of traditional male

---

[342] On the dispute between Sadducees and Pharisees on whether Deut 19:18-21 applied not only to performance of murder but intent, as here, and espoused by the Pharisees, see *m. Mak.* 1.6. The Jerusalem Talmud reports the story of Simeon ben Shetach and his son who was willing to die an unjust death because of false witnesses in order to have them executed on the basis of Saducean law (*y. Sanh.* 6.3.23c). On this see Moore, *Additions*, 87.

[343] As Ilan, "And Who Knows," notes, "in the society in which they live (which generates the view that women are sexually loose) such allegations are believable" (149).

[344] Glancy, "Accused," 302. As Levine, "Hemmed in," observes, "Ethnic pride, not women's liberation, is at the heart of Daniel's speech" (320). Sered and Cooper, "Sexuality and Social Control," note that Daniel, who combines both traditionally male and female strengths, also leaves Susanna behind as passive and inadequate (55).

[345] Sered and Cooper, "Sexuality and Social Control," 51.

[346] Wills, *Jewish Novel*, 55.

[347] So Levine, "Hemmed in," 318-19.

[348] Glancy, "Accused," 292.

[349] So also Gruen, *Diaspora*, who notes that the work is also not a social challenge about the elite, because Susanna belongs to the elite (173); similarly Wills, *Jewish Novel*, 58. Sered and Cooper, "Sexuality and Social Control," write: "The Book of Susanna contrasts two types of strength: structural and moral. Structural strength is associated with maleness, and is presented as both inconsistent with moral strength, and inferior to it. Moral strength is associated with femaleness, and is presented as the antithesis of structural strength, and superior to it" (45), but then recognise that Daniel breaks the pattern (46) and functions as the trickster, a role usually performed by the female (46-47). They see this as part of ensuring patriarchal control – women are still dependent on men (49). "For better or for worse, men control women's sexuality" (49).

[350] Ilan, "And Who Knows," 127-53; Clanton, "(Re)Dating" 135-40.

leadership".[351] However Susanna's disappearance from the narrative, itself, which celebrates the leadership of young men (OG) and Daniel (TH), and within the story back to her husband's charge might serve just as well as propaganda on behalf of those who opposed having a woman in a role beyond the domestic scene.

The story of Susanna matches stories of persecution and deliverance.[352] Her piety makes her a model. She may at the same time function as a representative, and perhaps a metaphor, for Israel, though, as in Judith, both levels of meaning, literal and metaphorical may be at play. In OG she is designated ἡ Ιουδαία ("The Judean woman").[353] Her name, Susanna, means a lily and may evoke Hos 14:6 which describes Israel as a lily: אהיה כטל לישראל יפרח כשושנה; ἔσομαι ὡς δρόσος τῷ Ισραηλ ἀνθήσει ὡς κρίνον "I will be like the dew to Israel; he shall blossom like the lily".[354] Mittmann-Richert suggests that the author is employing the imagery of Israel being unfaithful to Yahweh, familiar from the prophets.[355] Levine writes:

> Susanna is the projection of the threatened covenant community. Part of the diaspora whose (b)orders have been shattered, she faces the temptation to lose self-integrity, self-respect and self; to submit to being raped; to refuse will likely lead to a death sentence.[356]

Reinhartz takes this even further, arguing that the garden represents Susanna and is to the household of Joakim as the diaspora Jewish community is to Babylon.[357] If she is a symbol of Israel under duress from Gentiles, as a diaspora setting might suppose, we should expect to find signs of this tension in the narrative itself. Instead we find nothing about tension with Gentiles.[358]

---

[351] Ilan, "And Who Knows," 149.

[352] Wills, "Jewish Novel," notes that "the overall structure of threat and vindication is very similar to the court conflicts of Daniel 3 and 6, Esther, and Bel and the Dragon" (55).

[353] Von Loewenclau, "Daniel," 296.

[354] Mittmann-Richert, Einführung, 137

[355] Mittmann-Richert, Einführung, 129.

[356] Levine, "Hemmed in," 311. On p. 319 she writes: "As a metaphor for the community, she is ultimately an example of the protection fidelity to the Law of Moses provides: she is unpenetrated and unpenetrable".

[357] Adele Reinhartz, "Better Homes and Gardens: Women and Domestic Space in the Books of Judith and Susanna," in Text and Artifact in the religions of Mediterranean Antiquity: Essays in Honour of Peter Richardson (ed. Stephen G. Wilson and Michael Desjardins; SCJ 9; Waterloo: Wilfred Laurier University Press, 2000) 325-39, 335-37, noting some similarity in the way in which the Song of Songs came to read symbolically as a corporate metaphor.

[358] So Moore, Additions, 91; Wills, "Jewish Novel," 55.

The story has many intertextual links. In many ways Susanna is a female Joseph, who was also confronted with sexual manipulation.[359] Both respond similarly with reference to sinning against God: ἁμαρτεῖν ἐνώπιον κυρίου ("to sin before the Lord") (23); cf. πῶς ποιήσω τὸ ῥῆμα τὸ πονηρὸν τοῦτο καὶ ἁμαρτήσομαι ἐναντίον τοῦ θεοῦ ("How then could I do this great wickedness, and sin against God?") (Gen 39:9). Potiphar's wife spoke to Joseph daily (ἡμέραν ἐξ ἡμέρας) as did the elders with Susanna (OG 12), but still he refused καθεύδειν μετ᾽ αὐτῆς τοῦ συγγενέσθαι αὐτῇ ("to sleep with her in order to have sex with her"*) (39:10), as in TH Susanna rejected their demand: συγκατάθου ἡμῖν καὶ γενοῦ μεθ᾽ ἡμῶν ("So go along with us and have sex with us") (20). Failing in her attempt she concocts a false allegation (39:14-15), as do the elders. At her cry, she claims, Joseph fled (39:18), just as did, allegedly, the young man in the elders' testimony (39). The parallels serve to enhance Susanna's status by association with the famed Joseph. In adding the details of Susanna's bathing TH evokes the story of Bathsheba with whom then Susanna stands in contrast.[360]

More significant are the links to Genesis 2 – 3, which Brooke highlights,[361] as does Pearce,[362] independently a few years later. Common elements include the garden (a term loaded with symbolic meaning), mention of trees (two), prohibition, death, a woman under pressure, temptation, deceit, shame, hiding, nakedness, walking about and a judgement. Brooke concludes: "When the story in Susanna is understood with Genesis 2-3 in mind, then it is possible to see that part of the purpose of the story is to portray the possibility of Paradise regained and in Susanna herself a Second Eve".[363] The term, "second Eve", might recall Paul's depiction of Jesus as a second Adam, but here the term could carry no such weight. At most the storyteller is deliberately portraying Susanna as not having succumbed as Eve did, in that sense, offering a model for women's faithfulness to Torah. This corresponds to Pearce's assessment who writes: "Susanna's action is not to be seen essentially as a defence of chastity, but as obedience to the divine

---

[359] Moore, *Additions*, 98. See also Nickelsburg, *Jewish Literature*, who notes that elements of Genesis appear with the male/female roles reversed in Susanna: 12, cf. 39:10; 23, cf. 39:9; 26, cf. 39:14-15; 39, cf. 39:18 (23). See also Bach, *Women, Seduction, and Betrayal*, 67-72.

[360] Von Loewenclau, "Daniel," 296; Collins, *Daniel*, 431.

[361] George J. Brooke, "Susanna and Paradise Regained," in *Women in the Biblical Tradition* (ed. George J. Brooke; Lewiston: Edwin Mellen, 1992) 92-111.

[362] Pearce, "Echoes of Eden," 10-31.

[363] Brooke, "Susanna," 109.

command. If this is the case, then we have in Susanna the first (and thoroughly Jewish) 'Second Eve'".[364]

Taking her inspiration from Levine's observation that "the immediate comparison of Susanna to Eve uncovers much",[365] Pearce, who is dealing with the OG version, notes that Susanna is depicted as περιπατοῦσαν ἐν τῷ παραδείσῳ τοῦ ἀνδρὸς αὐτῆς τὸ δειλινόν ("walking about daily in her husband's garden"*) (7), echoing the description of God in the garden of Eden: περιπατοῦντος ἐν τῷ παραδείσῳ τὸ δειλινόν ("walking about in the garden daily"*) (3:8).[366] While also noting that the elders, too, are depicted as doing the same, she suggests that by introducing Susanna as first doing so, with the intertextual echo of Genesis, the author is indicating in advance that "she belongs to the side of godliness; even, perhaps, that she represents the way in which God walks",[367] walking being a common term to describe living according to Torah, ironically the opposite of what the elders claimed to do. The reference in 10 to Susanna simply as ἡ γυνὴ may enhance the links.

Like Brooke, she takes particular note of the verb ἠπάτησεν in Daniel's charge: τὸ κάλλος σε ἠπάτησεν ("Beauty has deceived/seduced you") (56), suggesting plausibly that it echoes what Eve alleges the serpent did to her: ὁ ὄφις ἠπάτησέν με (Gen 3:13). Here the reverse is the case: Susanna is the subject and the elders the object.[368] Here she notes the tradition in 4 Maccabees according to which the snake sexually seduced Eve, where the mother of the seven sons declares: οὐδὲ ἔφθειρέν με λυμεὼν ἐρημίας φθορεὺς ἐν πεδίῳ οὐδὲ ἐλυμήνατό μου τὰ ἁγνὰ τῆς παρθενίας λυμεὼν ἀπάτης ὄφις ("No seducer or corrupter on a desert plain corrupted me, nor did the seducer, the snake of deceit, defile the purity of my virginity") (18:8).[369] Paul also makes this assumption, possible only on the basis of the Greek translation (2 Cor 11:3; cf. also *Prot. Jas.* 13:1).[370] She concludes that this tradition probably lies behind the Susanna story.[371] In addition she points to OG's reference to the angel with sword and fire in 59-62, echoing the cherubim with flaming sword in Gen 3:24 and

---

[364] Pearce, "Echoes of Eden," 21. She rejects defence of chastity with reference to Steussy, *Gardens in Babylon*, 118, and Collins, *Daniel*, 438.

[365] Levine, "Hemmed in," 315; Pearce, "Echoes of Eden," 21.

[366] She notes that τὸ δειλινόν is in MSS 88 and Syh, but missing in P967, but argues that its presence cannot be explained by the very different μέσον ἡμέρας in TH, but derives from Gen 3:8 LXX. Pearce, "Echoes of Eden," 23.

[367] Pearce, "Echoes of Eden," 23.

[368] Pearce, "Echoes of Eden," 24-25; Brooke, "Susanna," 105-106.

[369] Pearce, "Echoes of Eden," 29.

[370] On this see Loader, *Septuagint*, 105.

[371] Pearce, "Echoes of Eden," 29. She also notes the strong possibility that Philo *Cher.* 14-17 stands under the influence of the Susanna story (30-31).

possibly the Eden tradition in Ezek 28:13.[372] The intertextual link has been employed by the author to depict Susanna as a counter-model to Eve, one who upheld the commandments.

Susanna may be an ideal figure and example for the author, but this has also been questioned. Gruen notes that she appears to lack the faith that God will deliver her and suggests that daily walks in the garden enflaming the desires of onlookers, her seeking oils to beautify herself, and her showing no surprise at the elders' response may suggest she is not a paragon of virtue.[373] I find no indication of the author's disapproval and arguing from no mention being made of surprise is speculation about silence. His critical observations about Daniel's procedure, in pronouncing judgement before cross-examination, are valid,[374] but nothing suggests they are meant to detract from Daniel's status; he acts, the author would have us believe, by divine inspiration. Comedy certainly plays a role in the storytelling, as Gruen notes,[375] and recalls similar entertainment in the speech of the three young men, making fun of men's foolishness in response to women's beauty (1 Esdr 4:13-22). The author does employ humour, but in a serious cause. Part of what would have constituted its entertainment value for male hearers of the day would have been its erotic themes (more especially in TH).[376] These were always in danger of turning Susanna into an object of male gaze and so repeating the elders' behaviour, as a history of Susanna in art has shown.[377] To some degree the narrator has also reduced Susanna to an object,[378] who scarcely acts for herself,[379] though within the framework of patriarchal values of his day he still portrays her with respect and does ultimately make her prayer a turning point and her faithfulness the cause of exposing corruption and its impact, no small feat.[380]

---

[372] Pearce, "Echoes of Eden," 25-27.

[373] Gruen, *Diaspora*, 171-72, 324.

[374] Gruen, *Diaspora*, 172.

[375] Gruen, *Diaspora*, 172-73.

[376] So Wills, *Jewish Novel*, 56.

[377] See the studies of M. Miles, *Carnal Knowing: Female Nakedness and Religious Meaning in the Christian West* (Boston: Beacon, 1989) 117-44; Mieke Bal, "The Elders and Susanna," *BibInt* 1 (1993) 1-19; and B. Bohn, "Rape and the Gendered Gaze: Susanna and the Elders in Early Modern Bologna," *BibInt* 9 (2001) 259-86.

[378] So Levine, "Hemmed in," 308; Richard I. Pervo, "Aseneth and Her Sisters: Women in Jewish Narrative and in the Greek Novels," in *"Women Like This": New Perspectives on Jewish Women in the Greco-Roman World* (ed. A. J. Levine; Atlanta: Scholars, 1991) 145-60, 148.

[379] So Glancy, "Accused," who writes: "the mechanisms of gender representation render the character of Susanna almost entirely as object" (301). See also pp. 290-91.

[380] Von Loewenclau, "Daniel," notes that in this sense Susanna is still central: it all happens because of her. God intervenes for a woman and will intervene for God's faithful people (297).

Wills notes that in OG she is more an examplar and in TH more an individual.[381] In Pearce's assessment of OG while Susanna "is described very much as defined by her relation to men" (7, 29), the perspective of the corrupt, she steps out of that role in her resistance when she is designated as ἡ Ιουδαία ("The Judean woman") (22) and described by Daniel as "daughter of Israel" and "daughter of Judah" (50-51), contrasted with the elder whose seed is not of Judah (56), and within biblical literature is uniquely depicted as calling on "the Lord her God" (35).[382] Similarly in 60-62 the author has adapted the law of Deut 19:19 LXX on requiting a false witness with what he planned κατὰ τοῦ ἀδελφοῦ αὐτοῦ to now refer to the "sister": κατὰ τῆς ἀδελφῆς.[383]

There are further elements which make this story of interest. One is the surprising absence of the husband in the deliberations over the allegations. He is not listed among the many (OG 500!) who accompany her to the hearing. In TH where it is taking place in his own house he is invisible.[384] Normally the elders' endeavour would have been seen as assault on his property and, as adultery, therefore theft from him. He appears again only in TH at the conclusion of the work where we read: Χελκίας δὲ καὶ ἡ γυνὴ αὐτοῦ ᾔνεσαν τὸν θεὸν περὶ τῆς θυγατρὸς αὐτῶν Σουσαννας μετὰ Ιωακιμ τοῦ ἀνδρὸς αὐτῆς καὶ τῶν συγγενῶν πάντων ὅτι οὐχ εὑρέθη ἐν αὐτῇ ἄσχημον πρᾶγμα ("Then Chelkias and his wife expressed praise concerning their daughter together with her husband Joakim and all the relatives, because no shameful deed was found against her") (63). It is tendentious to cite only the second part as though the chief concern was relief that nothing shameful has been found in her.[385] They do in fact praise her. We are left having to make up our own stories about the husband: would he have seen it as inappropriate to speak up in his own house? Was he feeling bound to run with the outcome, perhaps out of respect for the reliability of the witnesses?[386] Did the absence of the male partner mean he had no one to prosecute? We are probably right to assume that the welfare and esteem of his household would have had greater priority for him than Susanna's.[387] This coheres with the values of the time.

---

[381] Wills, *Jewish Novel*, 59-60.

[382] Pearce, "Echoes of Eden," 19-20.

[383] Pearce, "Echoes of Eden," 20.

[384] Levine, "Hemmed in," 312-13; Bach, *Women, Seduction, and Betrayal*, 71.

[385] Cf. Gruen, *Diaspora*, 173; Glancy, "Accused," 292, on this, cited above; Levine, "Hemmed in," 313.

[386] Von Loewenclau, "Daniel," contemplates that the family may have doubted her (298).

[387] Glancy, "Accused," reflects those values when she writes: "preservation of women as intact property is more important than the preservation of women's lives" (295).

Another is the assumption, perhaps just for the story and not reflecting practice, that someone engaged in adultery would face the penalty of death (both in her words and in the sentence passed on her) (Deut 22:21-24; Lev 20:10; cf. John 8:4-5). The tale is interesting also for its sexual vocabulary. Sexual intercourse is variously described. συγγενέσθαι αὐτῇ TH 11; ὄντας σὺν ἑαυτοῖς OG 54; ὁμιλοῦντας ἀλλήλοις OG 37; similarly 57, 58; TH 54, 57, 58;[388] ἀναπαυομένην μετὰ ἀνδρὸς OG 37; ἀνέπεσε μετ᾽ αὐτῆς Th 37; by force: ἐξεβιάζοντο αὐτήν OG 19. In addition, TH describes the instance as an ἄσχημον πρᾶγμα 63, echoing the language of Deut 24:1 (cf. also Gen 34:7). The verb πράσσω is used in 22-23 to describe the act of adultery which Susanna refuses (ἐὰν πράξω τοῦτο θάνατός μοί ἐστι καὶ ἐὰν μὴ πράξω οὐκ ἐκφεύξομαι τὰς χεῖρας ὑμῶν 23 κάλλιον δέ με μὴ πράξασαν ἐμπεσεῖν εἰς τὰς χεῖρας ὑμῶν ἢ ἁμαρτεῖν ἐνώπιον κυρίου; cf. also οὐδὲ ἡ γυνὴ ἔγνω τὸ πρᾶγμα τοῦτο) (OG 11). OG also describes it as τὸ κακὸν τὸ ἔχον αὐτοὺς περὶ αὐτῆς (10). The elders describe it as ἀνομίαν which they allegedly saw (TH 38; cf. also 57).

Conclusion

The relevance of Susanna in relation to attitudes towards sexuality lies in its depiction of both male and female sexuality. The latter is clearly affirmed and not held to blame for men's behaviour. Susanna is sexually attractive and fears the Lord, affirmed by TH, and this also coheres with the image in OG. Much more is said or implied about men's sexuality. Nothing suggests that finding women sexually attractive is problematic. The author assume this of the largely invisible Joakim. With humour the author depicts how men can respond to women's sexuality in ways that make them look stupid, a theme present elsewhere, not least in the speeches of the three young men (1 Esdr 4:13-22; see above), but also in Judith. More seriously, the author depicts men who do not take responsibility for their sexual responses, follow them to meet their own needs in disregard of heaven's commands and at the expense of women, and exhibit the violence of their attempted violation by deceit, hate, and corruption. Probably inspired by Jeremiah's attack on corruption manifesting itself in sexual wrongdoing among prophets and priests, loosely cited in the opening lines, the author mounts an attack on corrupt sexual behaviour of two elders and judges, indicating that the instance of Susanna was one of many. *Psalms of Solomon* 4 addresses similar corruption (see below).

---

[388] Pearce, "Echoes of Eden," notes that the verb is used in this way also in Judg 12:12, but usually means simply, "converse with", "to associate with" (17). On the language of intercourse see also Moore, *Additions*, 97-98.

Equally serious, the author not only exposes the corruption of the two, but the corruption of the assembly and its leaders, who wittingly or unwittingly collude in corrupt practices, denying due legal procedures and being too willing to believe charges about the sexual depravity of women. This is a substantial challenge to prevailing authority and would sit uncomfortably with those in power in its context, certainly if the author has a real social context in mind and is not just telling stories. The likelihood that the work, Susanna, is designed for such subversion is enhanced when we take seriously the conclusion of OG, which, as in Daniel's confrontation of the elders as aged in wickedness, appeals to the hearer to recognise the wisdom and leadership of the younger generation.

This is a case, however, for new male leadership,[389] not a case for female leadership. Under their leadership Susanna can assume her proper place in what the author assumes is a society rightly ordered, where Susanna can walk freely in her husband's garden, beautiful and devout as ever, but unmolested by men who cannot control their sexuality. The orientation changes only to some degree in TH which is no longer concerned to promote leadership from the younger generation, develops the entertaining aspects of men poking fun at other men's stupidity, and has Susanna's story serve not to elevate her beyond her proper place in domestic security, but to elevate Daniel (and presumably the Danielic corpus which it now in TH introduces) as a source of ongoing wisdom for the future.

2.1.5   Additions to Esther

Both Greek versions of Esther, Old Greek (B-Text)[390] and the shorter so-called Alpha-Text (A-Text) (shorter even than the Hebrew text), contains six substantial Additions, designated A-F.[391] Addition C, in particular, contains matters pertaining

---

[389] On this see Engel, *Susanna*, 180-81 and Steussy, *Gardens*, 134-35. By contrast Engel describes TH as using the story of Susanna for purposes of edification (181).

[390] Its colophon dates the translation to 114/113 B.C.E. or 78/77 B.C.E. or 48 B.C.E. Ilan, "And Who Knows," argues that not only was the translation made in 78/77 B.C.E., but that also the original belongs to this period and that both, along with Judith and Susanna, are Hasmonean and will have sought to support Salome Alexandra's ascent to the throne (127-53).

[391] On this see Moore, *Additions*, who sees the A-Text as an independent translation of the Hebrew and as being dependent on the B-text of the LXX for the Additions (164-65); similarly Karen H. Jobes, "Esther: To the Reader," in *NETS* 2007, 424-25. See, however, De Troyer, *Rewriting the Sacred Text*, who argues that the A-Text reflects not a translation of the Hebrew, but a reworking of the B-Text, the LXX (76-88). See also Kristin De Troyer, "Der lukianische Text: Mit einer Diskussion des A-Textes des Estherbuches," in *Im Brennpunkt: Die Septuaginta: Studien zur Entstehung und Bedeutung der Griechischen*

to sexuality. Apart from Additions B and E, which purport to be copies of decrees and are composed in florid Greek, the others have been variously explained as deriving from semitic additions made to the Hebrew text of Esther in the second century B.C.E, but now preserved only in translation,[392] or as also composed in Greek, and added to one of the Greek versions and copied to the other.[393] In what follows I first review briefly the story of Esther as preserved in the shorter Hebrew version before addressing relevant material in the modifications in the two Greek versions and in the Additions.

Esther's Story in the Hebrew Text

The Book of Esther recounts a tale in which sexual issues play a significant role. This is already the case in Queen Vashti's refusal to answer the summons of her drunk husband, King Ahasuerus, who wanted "to show the peoples and the officials her beauty; for she was fair to behold" (1:11).[394] No explanation is given for her refusal, but the author most likely would expect his hearers to see in it her resistance to being treated as a sex object on display. His need, then, to dismiss her is depicted as a matter of his being shamed by such a refusal, then expanded to a fear that other women might similarly act so shamefully and shamingly. "Every man should be master of his own house" (1:21).[395] For women not to remain in subservience is an issue of shame.

The king's sexual whims are then met by the proposal of his advisors to assemble "beautiful virgins" (2:2) from across his realm, with a view to seeking replacement for Vashti. This strategy catches up Esther, who, without any indication of resistance or disapproval from herself or her cousin, Mordecai, who

---

Bibel: Band 2 (ed. Siegfried, Kreuzer and Jürgen Peter Lesch; BWANT 161; Stuttgart: Kohlhammer, 2004) 229-46, 237-44.

[392] So Moore, *Additions*, 166-67.

[393] So Jobes, "Esther: To the Reader," 424-25. See also Mittmann-Richert, *Einführung*, 99-100; Kristin De Troyer, "Esther in Text- and Literary-Critical Paradise," in *The Book of Esther in Modern Research* (ed. Sidnie White Crawford, Leonard J. Greenspoon; JSOTSup 380; London: T&T Clark, 2003) 31-49, where, on the basis of her studies there and earlier, suggests that "first there was a short Hebrew text. Then, it was translated into Greek" (48), the translator adding "A,12-17, (Add. B,) Add. E, and Add. D" (48-49), but she leaves open her assessment of Addition C, F, and the first part of A.

[394] The Greek text is that of Robert Hanhart, ed., *Esther* (SVTG 8.3; Göttingen: Vandenhoeck & Ruprecht, 1983). The English translation of Esther is that of the *NRSV*, of the LXX versions, that of *NETS*, unless otherwise indicated by an asterisk where I have modified the translation.

[395] Cf. B-Text: ὥστε εἶναι φόβον αὐτοῖς ἐν ταῖς οἰκίαις αὐτῶν ("so that they had fear in their homes").

had adopted her on her parents' death, joins a harem of women, who are prepared
with cosmetics and oil of myrrh for a year "under the regulations for the women"
(2:12). The account had the potential to incite male fantasy and probably did.[396]
Each woman would then be tried out, as it were, for a night, then placed in the
harem of concubines (2:14), and only those who satisfied the king would be asked
to return. Within this framework of what we recognise as sexual exploitation, but
is told without any such perspective expressed by the author, Esther wins favour
and succeeds in becoming Queen Vashti's successor, all the time an incognito Jew
(2:17). The author apparently has no qualms about her having sexual intercourse
with a Gentile and dining on Gentile food at the feasts which follow (2:18).

The story then takes us to Mordecai's exposing a plot, Haman's plan for an
anti-Jewish pogrom throughout the realm when he notes Mordecai's refusal to
bow to him and discovers his race, the intervention of Esther, the rescinding of
Haman's pogrom decree, some mass executions and killings instead by Jews, and
the laboured insistence that this should be celebrated as the feast of Purim.

The work is notable for not mentioning the name of God.[397] It probably
implies a theology in depicting Mordecai's refusal to bow (presumably to any
other than God) (3:2),[398] but much else is missing, including issues of Law relating
to non-Jews, such as food laws and sexual intercourse and marriage. Its celebration
of escape and vengeance will have been written against a background where
people saw pogroms as a possibility.

The Additions and the Translation

It is not surprising that later generations sought to improve the work's
perspectives. This is apparent in the six additions contained in the Greek versions
and in modifications in the process of translation. The revision is also apparent in
changes (or possible variants) in the text outside the additions, such as the
introduction of reference to God in 2:20; 4:8; 6:1, 13; and only in the A Text: 4:14,

---

[396] Kristin De Troyer, "An Oriental Beauty Parlour: An Analysis of Esther 2.8-18 in
the Hebrew, the Septuagint and the Second Greek Text," in *A Feminist Companion to
Esther, Judith and Susanna* (ed. Athalya Brenner; Sheffield: Sheffield Academic Press,
1995) 47-70, notes: "It seems that this text is written by a man who states what women must
be if they want to please men" (55).

[397] On whether אחר ממקום "from another place" in 4:14 implies a reference to God,
see De Troyer, *Rewriting the Sacred Text*, 1-21, where she argues this is unlikely, but that
in the Septuagint text it certainly carries this meaning (22-27), the translation by its
modifications and the additions creating a religious text.

[398] As Moore, *Additions*, notes, refusing to bow "does not reflect the actual practice in
either the Persian or Hellenistic periods" (204), though Addition C 13:12-14 assumes it
would be an affront to faith in God.

16; 7:2.[399] The first and last Addition (A and F), inserted at either end of the text, depict Mordecai's dream and its meaning, revealing that the story in between is indeed in God's control. Its employment of the dream motif and its imagery recalls Daniel. Two further expansions, B, inserted after 3:13 and E, inserted after 8:12, supply texts of the two decrees sent to the provinces, also with theological references, especially the latter which espouses "a kingdom quiet and peaceable for all", and respect for the Jews, who "are governed by most righteous laws and are children of the living God" (E 15-16), but which dubs Haman a Macedonian and therefore "quite devoid of our kindliness" (E 10). More significant are additions C and D, inserted sequentially together after 4:17, and preserved in both B- and A- text with little variation of significance. Addition C presents the prayers of Mordecai and Esther, transposing their strategies into divinely blessed initiatives.

Esther's prayer is especially important, since its author makes every effort to reshape her image. It shows her removing her splendid apparel and putting on garments of distress and sackcloth (C 12-13/14:1-2). It also has her acknowledging that ever since she was born she had heard that God had taken Israel out of all the nations as an everlasting inheritance: "that you, O Lord, took Israel out of all the nations and our fathers from among all their forebears, to be an everlasting inheritance" (ὅτι σύ, κύριε, ἔλαβες τὸν Ισραηλ ἐκ πάντων τῶν ἐθνῶν καὶ τοὺς πατέρας ἡμῶν ἐκ πάντων τῶν προγόνων αὐτῶν εἰς κληρονομίαν αἰώνιον) (C 16/14:5). She mentions also that she learned this within the tribe of her family (ἐγὼ ἤκουον ἐκ γενετῆς μου ἐν φυλῇ πατριᾶς μου) (C 16/14:5 B-Text). These references reinforce the kind of family solidarity espoused in Tobit and Judith (Tob 1:9; 4:12; Jdt 8:2). They also focus more sharply than the original Esther text on the qualitative aspect which separates Israel from the nations, which is here much more than the status of a persecuted minority, and fits more the spirit of *Jub.* 2:19-20 about Israel's election above all other nations at creation.[400] This is enhanced by C 17-21/14:6-10, which confesses sin and attributes to Israel's sin their being delivered into the hands of their enemies, especially the sin of idolatry: "And now we have sinned before you, and you have delivered us into the hand of our enemies, because we honoured their gods" (καὶ νῦν ἡμάρτομεν ἐνώπιόν σου, καὶ παρέδωκας ἡμᾶς εἰς χεῖρας τῶν ἐχθρῶν ἡμῶν, ἀνθ' ὧν ἐδοξάσαμεν τοὺς θεοὺς αὐτῶν) (C 17-18a/14:6-7a) (cf. *Jub.* 1:8-14; 23:13-14, 22-23). The consequences are then spelled out:

---

[399] On this see Moore, *Additions*, 158.

[400] See also Donaldson, *Judaism and the Gentiles*, who notes the particularistic tendencies also in Additions B and E, which contrast Israel and the nations (36).

19 καὶ νῦν οὐχ ἱκανώθησαν ἐν πικρασμῷ δουλείας ἡμῶν,
ἀλλὰ ἔθηκαν τὰς χεῖρας αὐτῶν ἐπὶ τὰς χεῖρας τῶν εἰδώλων αὐτῶν
20 ἐξᾶραι ὁρισμὸν στόματός σου
καὶ ἀφανίσαι κληρονομίαν σου
καὶ ἐμφράξαι στόμα αἰνούντων σοι
καὶ σβέσαι δόξαν οἴκου σου καὶ θυσιαστήριόν σου
21 καὶ ἀνοῖξαι στόμα ἐθνῶν εἰς ἀρετὰς ματαίων
καὶ θαυμασθῆναι βασιλέα σάρκινον εἰς αἰῶνα.

19 And now they were not satisfied that we are in bitter slavery,
but they have put their hands into the hands of their idols,
20 to annul the stipulation of your mouth
and to destroy your inheritance
and to stop the mouths of those who praise you
and to extinguish the glory of your house and your altar,
21 to open the mouth of the nations for the mighty deeds of vain things,
and that a mortal king be admired forever. (C 19-21/14:9-10 B-Text)

The threat to the temple appears to allude to the Maccabean crisis, but could also fit the invasion of Pompey. Moore notes that C 17-21/14:6-12 is absent from the Old Latin and seems not to have been present in the version paraphrased by Josephus and so may have been a later expansion.[401] The focus is, in any case, not sexual sins, but idolatry.

When mentioning her husband, Ahasuerus, Esther now speaks of him as "the lion" (C 24/14:13; cf. 4QpNah/4Q169 3-4 i.4-6). This is part of the distancing also evident from the beginning of Addition C where she flees to the Lord in fear for her life (κατέφυγεν ἐπὶ τὸν κύριον ἐν ἀγῶνι θανάτου) and in Addition D, which has the king respond to her intervention first with anger (A-Text "like a bull"), unlike in original Esther, and Esther faints with fear (D 7/15:7).[402] The reshaping of Esther's image in her prayer has her distancing even further as she lists what she hates and abhors about her situation, quite in contrast to the Hebrew account which depicts no such discomfort:

26 καὶ οἶδας ὅτι ἐμίσησα δόξαν ἀνόμων καὶ βδελύσσομαι κοίτην
ἀπεριτμήτων καὶ παντὸς ἀλλοτρίου. 27 σὺ οἶδας τὴν ἀνάγκην μου, ὅτι
βδελύσσομαι τὸ σημεῖον τῆς ὑπερηφανίας μου, ὅ ἐστιν ἐπὶ τῆς κεφαλῆς μου
ἐν ἡμέραις ὀπτασίας μου· βδελύσσομαι αὐτὸ ὡς ῥάκος καταμηνίων καὶ οὐ

---

[401] Moore, *Additions*, 166.

[402] See Michael V. Fox, "Three Esthers," in *The Book of Esther in Modern Research* (ed. Sidnie White Crawford, Leonard J. Greenspoon; JSOTSup 380; London: T&T Clark, 2003) 50-60, who sees Esther's "frailty, overwhelming emotions and fainting", used to evoke the king's "gracious condescension", but also her piety, as reflecting influences from Hellenistic novels (59), and the reduction of her self-assuredness as reflecting a "progressive deterioration in the status of women in Hellenistic culture" (59).

φορῶ αὐτὸ ἐν ἡμέραις ἡσυχίας μου. 28 καὶ οὐκ ἔφαγεν ἡ δούλη σου
τράπεζαν Αμαν, καὶ οὐκ ἐδόξασα συμπόσιον βασιλέως οὐδὲ ἔπιον οἶνον
σπονδῶν.

26 And you know that I hate the glory of the lawless and abhor the bed of the
uncircumcised and of any foreigner. 27 You know my predicament – that I abhor the
sign of my proud position that is upon my head on days when I appear in public. I
abhor it like a menstrual cloth, and I do not wear it on the days when I am in private.
28 And your slave has not eaten at Haman's table, and I have not honoured the king's
banquet nor drunk the wine of libations. (C 26-28/14:15-17)

She hates her adornment (her royal turban unclean as menstrual rags; cf. Lev
15:19-24), and has restricted her eating and drinking, thus, for the author of the
addition, going some way toward keeping food laws and avoiding idolatry. The
original story does not allow him to claim she refused to eat with king or touch
Gentile foods at all (so 2:9) and so she falls short of Daniel's abstinence,
abstaining primarily from the toasts at drinking parties and the libations to the
gods.[403]

More significantly for our analysis, she hates "the bed of the uncircumcised
and of any foreigner", which has to mean that she abhors the indisputable fact that
she has been having sexual intercourse with an uncircumcised man. The presence
of the additional words "and of any foreigner" (καὶ παντὸς ἀλλοτρίου) beyond
"the uncircumcised" (ἀπεριτμήτων) probably indicate that, like *Jubilees*, she goes
further[404] to despise sexual relations also with a circumcised foreigner, that is,
proselyte,[405] unless we read the two designations as equivalent. The author of the
expansion is making his point as best he can in the face of what is undeniable in
the story.

His reading directs us by implication to seeing Esther as forced into sexual
service against her will, a valid reading of the tale, but one its original authors did
not intimate,[406] but which is now reflected in the translations. Accordingly De

---

[403] Moore, *Additions*, 212.

[404] Cf. Moore, *Additions*, who notes only the general prohibition on intermarriage
found in Deut 7:3-4; Ezra 10:2; Neh 13:23-27 (212).

[405] This appears to be implied in its retelling of the abduction of Dinah, where the
circumcision ruse is ignored. See Christine E. Hayes, *Gentile Impurities and Jewish
Identities: Intermarriage and Conversion from the Bible to the Talmud* (Oxford: Oxford
University Press, 2002) 77.

[406] Moore, *Additions*, notes that with the Additions Esther becomes more the hero than
Mordecai and the enemy less Haman than all Gentiles (212). See also his notes on the
parallel created with Judith, who similarly prayed out of concern for the temple, and Israel's
inheritance, then dressed herself up for the dangerous crucial encounter, was welcomed by
Holofernes and ate (though her own kosher food), through her courage saved the nation,
and made possible the slaughter of their enemies (221-22).

Troyer notes that the B-Text employs a number of passive verbs in the translation of the passage depicting Esther's incorporation into the harem, indicating a more passive role on her part.[407] Some of these changes in the LXX (B-Text) include: Esther is brought directly to Gai and that girls become women in his hands (2:8); no reference is made to "the law for women" (2:12); nor does Esther return to a different harem (2:14); her crown becomes a "diadem of women" (2:17); and her becoming queen in place of Vashti is omitted (2:17).[408] The A-Text abbreviates and reorders, including omitting the beautification treatment and the twelve month wait.[409] This would be consistent with the perspective in Addition C which sees her as a victim. Similarly B-Text portrays Mordecai as training her to become his wife (2:7), implying that her being taken to Susa was a virtual abduction. This would also cohere with the depiction in Addition C according to which Esther goes on to declare: καὶ οὐκ ηὐφράνθη ἡ δούλη σου ἀφ᾽ ἡμέρας μεταβολῆς μου μέχρι νῦν ("Your servant has not rejoiced since the day of my change until now") (C 29/14:18). This will include denial that sexual intercourse was ever anything other than a negative experience.

Taken as whole, therefore, the expanded Esther still brings us into the world of sexual exploitation, though the B-text has virtually removed this element from the detail about the presentation of Vashti, shifting the focus to her proclamation as queen and making the feast in 1:5 "wedding feast" (τοῦ γάμου).[410] Young women are assembled in the sexually exploitative context of a harem, and Esther becomes the chosen one decked out with all the trappings. Unlike the Hebrew tale, however, which offers no hint of Esther's resistance or distress in being so enlisted, the expanded tale of the B-text (and to some extent also the A-Text) portrays her as thereby forced against her will into sexual service, given a diadem but not a crown, and having much greater fear, which is focussed in particular upon dangers not only to the people, but also to the temple.

---

[407] De Troyer, "Oriental Beauty Parlour," 56.

[408] De Troyer, "Oriental Beauty Parlour," 55-64.

[409] De Troyer, "Oriental Beauty Parlour," 66-68.

[410] This differs significantly from the Hebrew which reads להביא את ושתי המלכה לפני המלך בכתר מלכות להראות העמים והשרים את יפיה כי טובת מראה היא ("to bring Queen Vashti before the king, wearing the royal crown, in order to show the peoples and the officials her beauty; for she was fair to behold") (1:11; similarly the A-Text). The B-Text reads instead: εἰσαγαγεῖν τὴν βασίλισσαν πρὸς αὐτὸν βασιλεύειν αὐτὴν καὶ περιθεῖναι αὐτῇ τὸ διάδημα καὶ δεῖξαι αὐτὴν πᾶσιν τοῖς ἄρχουσιν καὶ τοῖς ἔθνεσιν τὸ κάλλος αὐτῆς ὅτι καλὴ ἦν ("to bring the queen to him in order to proclaim her queen and to place a diadem on her and show her to the rulers and her beauty to the people, because she was beautiful").

A number of factors make it probable that the expanded Esther belongs in the setting of the Hasmonean dynasty, probably in the second century B.C.E. These include the proximity to Daniel in Additions A and F, [411] to the Book of Judith whose hero also observed the law meticulously,[412] and to *Jubilees*, which shares the extreme view of rejecting sexual intercourse and marriage not only with the uncircumcised but also with any foreigner, if that is the likely reading. This view appears to inform a number of writings from, the period, including *Aramaic Levi Document*, *4QMMT*, earlier Ezra and Nehemiah, and later *Pseudo-Philo (LAB)* (cf. also *T. Job* 45:3; *2 Bar.* 41:3-4; 42:4; 48:22-24; possibly *T. Mos.* 8:3), and the hardliners whom *Aseneth* seeks to counter by subverting their symbolic spokesperson, Levi, into an advocate of the opposite, as the discussion below will show. The reflection on the disaster of Antiochus IV Epiphanes' assault on the temple and Judaism, and, more broadly, the designation of Hamann as a Macedonian, also suggest a setting in the second century B.C.E.[413] Like Judith, the expanded Esther now depicts Esther in a context of sexual exploitation, which in her case is realised, but which she cannot resist. The revision thus not only adds a strong theological dimension to the story which was absent, but also attempts to bring it into harmony with an emphasis on upholding Torah[414] which now depicts Esther as not transgressing Torah or doing so only under duress. In relation to sexuality, it both exposes the sexual exploitation and may well espouse a hardline stance on intermarriage, opposing marriage even to proselytes.

2.1.6   1 and 2 Maccabees

I deal with both works within the framework of a single section because they overlap in dealing with the revolt and what preceded and followed it, though with differences, 2 Maccabees treating the history only up to the death of Judaism but offering greater detail of the period between 175 and 167 B.C.E., and 1 Maccabees taking history down to the succession of John Hyrcanus in 134 B.C.E. Each is

---

[411] Moore, *Additions*, 166-67, who notes the similarity of the dream (A and F), to Daniel (166). See also Mittmann-Richert, *Einführung*, 110.

[412] Moore, *Additions*, 166-67, who notes that "the spirit and details of Additions C and D are similar to those in the Book of Judith, a Hebrew work composed in the same century" (166).

[413] Moore, *Additions*, notes that "the theology of the Additions and their anti-Gentile spirit (especially A 6, C 26,28, F 5,8) are quite compatible with a second-century B.C. date" (166). See also Mittmann-Richert, *Einführung*, 100, 104, who also notes the link made in 2 Macc 15:36 between Purim and the celebration of Nicanor's defeat (100-101).

[414] Mittmann-Richert, *Einführung*, 105-106.

discussed separately, but with an eye to the other where overlaps and differences occur.[415]

2.1.6.1   1 Maccabees

Issues pertaining to sexuality play only a minor role in the pro-Hasmonean 1 Maccabees, composed originally in Hebrew some time late in the second or early in the first century B.C.E., but surviving only in translation.[416] They may surface indirectly already in the report in 1:11-15 about the παράνομοι "renegades", "those who disregarded the Law":

11 ἐν ταῖς ἡμέραις ἐκείναις ἐξῆλθον ἐξ Ισραηλ υἱοὶ παράνομοι καὶ ἀνέπεισαν πολλοὺς λέγοντες πορευθῶμεν καὶ διαθώμεθα διαθήκην μετὰ τῶν ἐθνῶν τῶν κύκλῳ ἡμῶν, ὅτι ἀφ᾽ ἧς ἐχωρίσθημεν ἀπ᾽ αὐτῶν, εὗρεν ἡμᾶς κακὰ πολλά. 12 καὶ ἠγαθύνθη ὁ λόγος ἐν ὀφθαλμοῖς αὐτῶν, 13 καὶ προεθυμήθησάν τινες ἀπὸ τοῦ λαοῦ καὶ ἐπορεύθησαν πρὸς τὸν βασιλέα, καὶ ἔδωκεν αὐτοῖς ἐξουσίαν ποιῆσαι τὰ δικαιώματα τῶν ἐθνῶν. 14 καὶ ᾠκοδόμησαν γυμνάσιον ἐν Ιεροσολύμοις κατὰ τὰ νόμιμα τῶν ἐθνῶν. 15 καὶ ἐποίησαν ἑαυτοῖς ἀκροβυστίας καὶ ἀπέστησαν ἀπὸ διαθήκης ἁγίας καὶ ἐζευγίσθησαν τοῖς ἔθνεσι καὶ ἐπράθησαν τοῦ ποιῆσαι τὸ πονηρόν.

11 In those days certain renegades came out from Israel and misled many, saying, "Let us go and make a covenant with the Gentiles around us, for since we separated from them many disasters have come upon us." 12 This proposal pleased them, 13 and some of the people eagerly went to the king, who authorized them to observe the ordinances of the Gentiles. 14 So they built a gymnasium in Jerusalem, according to Gentile custom, 15 and removed the marks of circumcision, and abandoned the holy covenant. They joined with the Gentiles and sold themselves to do evil. (1:11-15)

These are Jews (ἐξ Ισραηλ) whom many followed. "In those days" relates to Antiochus Epiphanes' ascending the Seleucid throne in 175 B.C.E., as 1:10 reports. The assertion that separation from the Gentiles had been the cause that many disasters had come upon them probably alludes to Deut 31:16-17.[417]

---

[415] The Greek texts are those of Werner Kappler and Robert Hanhart, ed., *Maccabaeorum liber I* (SVTG 9.1; Göttingen: Vandenhoeck & Ruprecht, 1990) and Werner Kappler and Robert Hanhart, ed., *Maccabaeorum liber II* (SVTG 9.1; Göttingen: Vandenhoeck & Ruprecht, 1976). The translation is from *NRSV*. I indicate by an asterisk translations which I have modified.

[416] See the overview in John Raymond Bartlett, *1 Maccabees* (GAP; Sheffield: Sheffield Academic Press, 1998) 13-34; Mittmann-Richert, *Einführung*, 22-23.

[417] So Jonathan A. Goldstein, *1 Maccabees* (AB 41; Garden City: Doubleday, 1976) 200, who also points to Deut 13:7-8, which contains the phrase: "Let us go worship other gods"; similarly 13:13. Katell Berthelot, "The Biblical Conquest of the Promised Land and the Hasmonean Wars according to 1 and 2 Maccabees," in *The Books of the Maccabees:*

16 Then this people will begin to prostitute themselves to the foreign gods in their midst, the gods of the land into which they are going; they will forsake me, breaking my covenant that I have made with them. 17 My anger will be kindled against them in that day. I will forsake them and hide my face from them; they will become easy prey, and many terrible troubles will come upon them. In that day they will say, "Have not these troubles come upon us because our God is not in our midst?" (Deut 31:16-17)

The reference to the practice of separation from surrounding peoples (μετὰ τῶν ἐθνῶν τῶν κύκλῳ ἡμῶν) (1:11), which the renegades are reported as rejecting, must include among other things intermarriage, which had been a key element in keeping separate (Exod 34:15-16; Deut 7:2-4; Ezra 9:1-2; 10:11; Neh 9:2; 10:31; 13:1-3).[418] Making a covenant, here, refers to an agreement or alliance, not to marriage. These Jews are not just talking about an alliance with one particular nation, such as the Seleucid or Ptolemaic kingdoms, but are rejecting separateness. The words, καὶ ἡγαθύνθη ὁ λόγος ἐν ὀφθαλμοῖς αὐτῶν ("and the proposal pleased them") reinforces what has already been indicated, namely that they persuaded many. The κακὰ πολλά "many disasters" probably refer not to particular crises, but rather to economic and other hardship.[419] Here we read that τινες ἀπὸ τοῦ λαοῦ "some of the people" were very keen and approached Antiochus.

The point in approaching him was that any relaxing of the commandments which require separation (for instance, over food and marriage) would only be possible if Antiochus revoked or modified the decree of Antiochus III which stipulated that Jewish Law was to be in force (Josephus *A.J.* 12.138-146).[420] We are almost certainly hearing 1 Maccabees' version of what is described in greater detail in 2 Maccabees as a corrupt initiative for personal gain on the part of Jason, brother of the high priest Onias III, who did not support the move for greater openness and whom he usurped as high priest, having offered Antiochus money.

History, Theology, Ideology: Papers of the Second International Conference on the Deuterocanonical Books, Pápa, Hungary, 9-11 June, 2005 (ed. Géza G. Xeravits and József Zsengellér; JSJSup 118; Leiden: Brill, 2007) 45-60, emphasises the impact of Deuteronomy on 1 Maccabees, in contrast to 2 Maccabees, which sees "the wrath of God turned away from Israel because of the blood shed by the martyrs", not as in 1 Maccabees under the influence of Deut 13:18, "because of the killing of impious or idolatrous ones" (51).

[418] So Goldstein, *1 Maccabees*, who draws attention also to Hecataeus of Abdera's observation of rigid Jewish separation from Gentiles as deriving from their Mosaic law (199-200).

[419] David S. Williams, "A Literary Encircling Pattern in 1 Maccabees 11," *JBL* 120 (2001) 140-42, notes that the reference to many ills coming upon the people correlates with 1:9 and 1:52.

[420] Goldstein, *1 Maccabees*, 200.

Apart from gaining the high priesthood, 2 Maccabees tells us that Jason obtained permission to register Jerusalem citizens as Antiochenes or "to found an Antiochene citizenship community in Jerusalem with gymnasium and ephebic institutions, exempt from Jewish law" (4:7-20).[421] It then reports that τῆς ἀρχῆς κρατήσας εὐθέως πρὸς τὸν Ἑλληνικὸν χαρακτῆρα τοὺς ὁμοφύλους μετέστησε ("he at once shifted his compatriots over to the Greek way of life") (4:10) and goes on to mention setting laws aside and introducing what were institutions typical of a Hellenistic city, including a gymnasium.

When 1 Maccabees reports that Antiochus ἔδωκεν αὐτοῖς ἐξουσίαν ποιῆσαι τὰ δικαιώματα τῶν ἐθνῶν ("authorized them to observe the ordinances of the Gentiles"), it is referring to the same processes rather than to individual moral commands. Accordingly the passage goes on to record: καὶ ᾠκοδόμησαν γυμνάσιον ἐν Ἱεροσολύμοις κατὰ τὰ νόμιμα τῶν ἐθνῶν ("So they built a gymnasium in Jerusalem, according to Gentile custom") (1:14). These were centres of education closely associated with an ἐφηβεῖον, a structure for sports (mentioned specifically in 2 Macc 4:9).[422] For those familiar with the implications of this development, including the introduction of sporting activities carried out naked, the next detail draws attention to a predictable consequence: καὶ ἐποίησαν ἑαυτοῖς ἀκροβυστίας ("and removed the marks of circumcision") (1:15). Had all been circumcised, one would imagine that no problem would have arisen, but this is clearly not assumed to be the case. Accordingly, some engaged in epispasm, a way of stretching the skin to create the appearance of having a foreskin on the penis.[423] This must have been because uncircumcised people,

---

[421] Goldstein, *1 Maccabees*, 162. "Jason and Menelaus are certainly included among the wicked of I 1:11-15. Their names do not occur because our author observes the principle of *damnatio memoriae* for wicked Jews" (73). On the tension between the two accounts, Goldstein suggests that the naming of the two by Jason was to distinguish them "from his hero Onias III" (87).

[422] On the gymnasium and its significance see János Bolyki, "'As soon as the signal was given' (2 Macc 4:14): Gymnasia in the Service of Hellenism," in *The Books of the Maccabees: History, Theology, Ideology: Papers of the Second International Conference on the Deuterocanonical Books, Pápa, Hungary, 9-11 June, 2005* (ed. Géza G. Xeravits and József Zsengellér; JSJSup 118; Leiden: Brill, 2007) 131-39, 135-37, who notes also the unifying function of games cultivated in the *ephebium*, bringing together peoples of different language and ethnic backgrounds (136). See also Robert Doran, "Jason's Gymnasium," in *Of Scribes and Scrolls: Studies on the Hebrew Bible, Intertestamental Judaism and Christian Origins* (ed. H. W. Attridge, J. J. Collins and T. H. Tobin; Lanham: University Press of America, 1990) 99-109, 99-106.

[423] Doran, "Jason's Gymnasium," disputes that "they removed the marks of circumcision", and argues that both it and the reference to the brimmed hat are meant metaphorically (107-108); but cf. Robert Doran, "The High Cost of a Good Education," in *Hellenism in the Land of Israel* (ed. John J. Collins and Gregory E. Sterling; Christianity

presumably uncircumcised Gentiles, also used the gymnasium. We hear a likely echo of this in the warnings preserved in *Jubilees*, which attack nudity (3:31) and also incomplete circumcision (15:33-34; cf. also *T. Mos.* 8:3). The practice of epispasm was not novel nor confined to this period. As Hall shows, it "prevailed throughout the Hellenistic and Roman ages and attained a plateau in popularity in the first century".[424] In addition 2 Maccabees mentions the wearing of the broad-rimmed hat during exercises, an element of the attire of devotees of Hermes, which would be seen by some, therefore, as idolatry, but not by others.[425] The establishment of a gymnasium did not necessarily entail idolatry.[426] The assertion that ἀπέστησαν ἀπὸ διαθήκης ἁγίας ("they abandoned the holy covenant") reflects the understanding of circumcision as the sign of the covenant.

The final two statements in 1:11-15 are less explicit: ἐζευγίσθησαν τοῖς ἔθνεσιν καὶ ἐπράθησαν τοῦ ποιῆσαι τὸ πονηρόν ("They joined with the Gentiles and sold themselves to do evil"). These may simply summarise the substance of what precedes, adding nothing of substance, themselves. They probably, however, indicate more. If, as is likely, the separation to which the dissenters from Law referred included intermarriage, then one would expect that their stance now would allow it, so that ἐζευγίσθησαν ("they joined with") would assume also marriage. The word, ζευγίζω, occurs only here in the LXX. It is related to ζευγός "yoke", "carriage" or "pair, couple" (e.g. of doves; Lev 5:11); ζυγός or ζυγόν, meaning "yoke" (of animals: Num 19:2; Deut 21:3; figuratively to indicate hardship: Gen 27:40; Lev 26:13; Isa 9:3; 10:27; 2 Chron 10:4. 9, 10, 11, 14; 1 Macc 8:18, 31; 13:41; Sir 28:19-20; of positive teaching: Sir 51:26; Jer 2:20; 5:5; Zeph 3:9; Lam 3:27) or "scale" (Lev 19:35-36; Ps 61:10; Prov 11:1; 16:11; 20:23) and is related to ζεύγνυμι or ζευγνύω, "to harness, to yoke" (Gen

---

and Judaism in Antiquity 13; Notre Dame: University of Notre Dame Press, 2001) 94-115, 107, where he appears to take the reference to circumcision literally. See also Gruen, *Heritage and Hellenism*, who notes that Josephus interprets it this way (*A.J.* 12.241), and suggests that 2 Maccabees' making no mention of nudity or removing circumcision may indicate that it referred originally to the period of Antiochus' persecution (30).

[424] Robert G. Hall, "Epispasm and the Dating of Ancient Jewish Writings," *JSP* 2 (1988) 71-86, 71.

[425] See Bolyki, "Gymnasia," 137.

[426] Cf. Elias Bickerman, *The God of the Maccabees: Studies in the Origin and Meaning of the Maccabean Revolt* (Leiden: Brill, 1979) 41. Martha Himmelfarb "Levi, Phinehas, and the Problem of Intermarriage at the Time of the Maccabean Revolt," *JSQ* 6 (1999) 1-24, notes that there is no mention of idolatry in relation to the gymnasium in 1 and 2 Maccabees or Daniel and points instead to evidence in 2 Macc 4:18-20, that efforts were undertaken to avoid idolatry by using money sent by Jason for a sacrifice to Hercules to equip triremes for Tyre (21).

46:29; Exod 14:6; 1 Sam 6:7, 10; 2 Sam 20:8) and ζυγόω "to yoke, to join together" (of structures: 1 Kgs 7:43; Ezek 41:26). Doran notes also that the Aquila and Theodotion translations have used ἐζευγίσθη to translate צמד in Num 25:3.[427]

> 1 While Israel was staying at Shittim, the people began to have sexual relations with the women of Moab. 2 These invited the people to the sacrifices of their gods, and the people ate and bowed down to their gods. 3 Thus Israel yoked itself (צמד ἐζευγίσθη; cf. LXX ἐτελέσθη) to the Baal of Peor, and the LORD's anger was kindled against Israel. (Num 25:1-3; cf. Ps 106:28 referring to the same event)

Bearing in mind that the Hebrew of 1 Maccabees is not extant, it is very possible that this passage lies behind the allusion, particularly since the following statement, καὶ ἐπράθησαν τοῦ ποιῆσαι τὸ πονηρόν ("and sold themselves to do evil") appears also to be an allusion to scripture:

> 17 They made their sons and their daughters pass through fire; they used divination and augury; and they sold themselves to do evil (ἐπράθησαν τοῦ ποιῆσαι τὸ πονηρόν) in the sight of the LORD, provoking him to anger. (2 Kgs 17:17)

The allusion to Num 25:3 recalls a situation of illicit relations with gentiles, expressed, in particular, through sexual relations with Moabite women. It was the occasion for Phinehas' zealous execution of judgement (Num 25:6-8). It is therefore highly probably that this is also implied here. The image of yoke, while denoting oppression, can also denote partnership and marriage as in Sir 26:7 (βοοζύγιον σαλευόμενον γυνὴ πονηρά, "an evil wife is (like) a shaking ox yoke"; cf. also 2 Cor 6:14). The verb ἐπράθησαν "sold themselves" might refer to selling oneself to oppression, but in 2 Kgs 17:17 it alludes to idolatry and refers in the context to making one's sons and daughters pass through fire and using divination and augury. This might connect to the concern with intermarriage expressed in the *Book of the Watchers*, where marriage to foreign women is seen as the conduit for such forbidden practices (cf. also *Jub.* 11:7-8, 14-17; 22:16-17).[428] This is more likely than that selling oneself might refer to prostitution,

---

[427] Doran, "Jason's Gymnasium," 107. Similarly Kugel, "Rape of Dinah," who in relation to ἐζευγίσθησαν in 1:15 writes: "The original Hebrew text (not preserved) appears to have used the same verb as Num. 25:3 (ויצמד), and perhaps in the same sexual sense; even if not, it would be hard to exclude exogamy from the sorts of 'being joined' condemned by this verse" (79). Cf. Satlow, *Jewish Marriage*, who sees no reference to intermarriage here on grounds of the ambiguity of the verb and the nature of its indirect object (326).

[428] See the discussion in Loader, *Enoch, Levi, and Jubilees*, 47-48.

heterosexual or homosexual, such as one might have expected where Hellenistic lifestyle is being affirmed and which Jason of Cyrene reports occurred among Gentiles in the temple after Antiochus' act of suppression (6:3-6).

If 1 Macc 1:15 does indeed allude to intermarriage,[429] then 1 Macc 1:11-15 is not reducing the complaints against the reform movement to the mere setting up of the gymnasium and its associated activities.[430] Concern with such links as intermarriage is, as we argued, already to be assumed in the earlier allusion to separateness, so that relaxing these restrictions would have led to intermarriage with Gentiles, even though, as Himmelfarb notes, this is not said explicitly here, nor reported elsewhere in either 1 or 2 Maccabees, not even in association with the figure of Phinehas referred to in Numbers 25, who is elsewhere famous for his zeal on such issues.[431] I am not convinced that the silence implies any more than that it was not deemed significant enough to report by either author.[432]

It is notoriously difficult to discern the extent to which what the author depicts corresponded to reality and how it related to Hellenism and to the figures involved. Bickerman argued that Jason was intent on reforming Judaism.[433] Tcherikover, on the other hand, argued that his concern was largely economic and structural.[434] Hengel noted that the evidence for extensive Hellenism in Jerusalem before Jason is not strong compared with other cities.[435] On the other hand, Jason's initiative must reflect that it was already widely espoused among some.[436] This need not,

---

[429] So also Léonie J. Archer, *Her Price is Beyond Rubies: The Jewish Woman in Greco-Roman Palestine* (JSOTSup 60; Sheffield: JSOT, 1990) 129, 131.

[430] Cf. Doran, "Jason's Gymnasium," 99.

[431] Himmelfarb, "Levi, Phinehas," 20-21.

[432] Cf. Himmelfarb, "Levi, Phinehas": "In the absence if evidence for the hellenizers' embrace of marriage to foreign women, should we not assume that even supporters of the gymnasium would not lightly have ignored the traditional prohibition of such marriages?" (22). Having denied any allusion to it in 1 Maccabees, she writes: "*2 Maccabees* is also silent on the subject of intermarriage, which surely would have caused its author considerable agitation had he known of such behaviour" (21).

[433] Bickerman, *God of the Maccabees*, 85-88.

[434] Victor Tcherikover, *Hellenistic Civilization and the Jews* (Peabody: Hendrickson, 1999) 167-70. See also in agreement John J. Collins, "Cult and Culture: The Limits of Hellenization in Judea," in *Hellenism in the Land of Israel* (ed. John J. Collins and Gregory E. Sterling; Christianity and Judaism in Antiquity 13; Notre Dame: University of Notre Dame Press, 2001) 38-61, 46, who writes "there is little evidence that their deeper motives were cultural or religious" (46).

[435] Martin Hengel, *Judaism and Hellenism: Studies in their Encounter in Palestine during the Early Hellenistic Period* (2 vols; London: SCM, 1974) 1.88-99, 199.

[436] Collins, "Cult and Culture," rightly points to the evidence of engagement with Hellenistic culture in the Book of the Watchers, citing *1 Enoch* 8:1-2 (54), and one could add much more.

however, have been seen as a threat to Judaism in a religious sense, at least by those who might have supported Jason. It is not to be confused with Antiochus' act of repression, which probably had more to do with frustration than with ideology, and was the cause of the Maccabean revolt, rather than Hellenism.[437]

It would inevitably, however, have created boundary issues, especially concerning the extent to which one engaged the non-Jewish world and in particular where mores clashed. This is likely to have occurred around circumcision and the naked sports associated with the gymnasium, not over the gymnasium itself,[438] and only, as noted above, because of the presence of uncircumcised males whose significance was enough to have some Jewish men want to emulate them. It would have arisen in relation to foods and also in relation to sexual practices, both with regard to marriage to non-Jews and with regard to forbidden practices likely to have been present where traditions of Hellenism were strong, namely prostitution and male same-sex relations, both of which were traditionally associated with the Hellenistic lifestyle of symposia and the equivalent.

After reporting the initiative of the Hellenists 1 Maccabees gives a brief account of acts by Antiochus (1:20-40), leading finally to his decree of 167 B.C.E. to suppress Jewish religion (1:41-64). In none of this do themes of sexual wrongdoing appear. Its poetic pieces employ the imagery of lament including the mourning of bridegroom and bride (1:27), a standard topos (cf. Joel 2:16) in depicting the opposite of the joy which people valued in marriage. The author does not ignore women and children in the descriptions of war and plunder. Thus 1:32 reports that Antiochus and his men ἠχμαλώτισαν τὰς γυναῖκας καὶ τὰ τέκνα καὶ τὰ κτήνη ἐκληρονόμησαν ("They took captive the women and children, and seized the livestock"), reflecting the common patriarchal understanding of a man's possessions. In 2:30 the men took their sons, their wives, and their livestock into the wilderness, who then died as they refrained from fighting on the sabbath (2:38). In 3:20 we similarly read of the threat to women and children. In these instances women are portrayed as the weak and dependent. As Oegema notes, "Jewish women are considered to be first of all Jewish and only secondarily female".[439]

The poetic imagery depicting Jerusalem's plight uses the common topos (cf. Lam 5:2) of depicting her as a woman estranged from her offspring and abandoned by her children: ἐγένετο κατοικία ἀλλοτρίων, καὶ ἐγένετο ἀλλοτρία τοῖς γενήμασιν αὐτῆς, καὶ τὰ τέκνα αὐτῆς ἐγκατέλιπον αὐτήν ("she became a

---

[437] See the discussion in Collins, "Cult and Culture," 49-52.

[438] So Collins, "Cult and Culture," 46-47.

[439] Gerbern S. Oegema, "Portrayals of Women in 1 and 2 Maccabees," in *Transformative Encounters: Jesus and Women Re-viewed* (ed. Ingrid Rosa Kitzberger; BIS 43; Leiden: Brill, 2000) 244–64, 254.

dwelling of strangers; she became strange to her offspring, and her children forsook her") (1:38). The image of Jerusalem as mother returns in the poetic material of Mattathias' lament, which speaks of her infants and youths, of her adornments, and her becoming a slave (2:7-13). Being sold into slavery was a common fate for women in war.[440]

The account of what the king required, which included setting the Law aside, includes the words:

καὶ ἀφιέναι τοὺς υἱοὺς αὐτῶν ἀπεριτμήτους, βδελύξαι τὰς ψυχὰς αὐτῶν ἐν παντὶ ἀκαθάρτῳ καὶ βεβηλώσει 49 ὥστε ἐπιλαθέσθαι τοῦ νόμου καὶ ἀλλάξαι πάντα τὰ δικαιώματα.

and to leave their sons uncircumcised. They were to make themselves abominable by everything unclean and profane, 49 so that they would forget the law and change all the ordinances. (1:48-49)

If 1:15 has sexual references, then they would be likely to be in mind here. Thus to "forget the law and change all the ordinances" might include allusion to non-observance of sexually related purity laws. The notion of changing ordinances plays a significant role in addressing sexual wrongdoing in documents found at or associated with Qumran, including *4QThe Wiles of the Wicked Woman*/4Q184 and the *Damascus Document*. The reference to circumcision would recall 1:15a. It finds it sequel in 1:60-61, which reports that "they put to death the women who had their children circumcised, and their families and those who circumcised them; and they hung the infants from their mothers' necks".[441] According to 2:46 Mattathias and friends "forcibly circumcised all the uncircumcised boys they found within the borders of Israel".

Mattathias' farewell speech (2:49-68) lists zealous forebears. Abraham's faithfulness when tested may have been the sacrifice of Isaac, but perhaps more likely refers to his rejection of his father's idolatry.[442] Joseph is hailed for his zeal

---

[440] On the role of women in 1 Maccabees see Claudia Rakel, "Das erste Makkabäerbuch: Frauenexistenz an den Rändern des Textes," in *Kompendium Feministische Bibelauslegung* (ed. Luise Schottroff, Marie-Theres Wacker, Claudia Janssen, Beate Wehn; Gütersloh: Gütersloher Verlagshaus, 2007) 384-91, 385-87.

[441] Goldstein, *1 Maccabees*, reads these verses not as indicating that women performed circumcisions, but that they were responsible for ensuring circumcision happened (139). Cf. however Ilan, *Jewish Women*, who assumes the verb is not causative, but indicates that these women circumcised their own sons (182).

[442] Friedrich V. Reiterer, "Die Vergangenheit als Basis für die Zukunft Mattathias' Lehre für seine Söhne aus der Geschichte in 1 Makk 2:52-60," in *The Books of the Maccabees: History, Theology, Ideology: Papers of the Second International Conference on the Deuterocanonical Books, Pápa, Hungary, 9-11 June, 2005* (ed. Géza G. Xeravits and József Zsengellér; JSJSup 118; Leiden: Brill, 2007) 75-100, notes that 1 Macc 2:52 is

in rejecting sexual wrongdoing: "Joseph in the time of his distress kept the commandment" (2:53).[443] Phinehas (2:54), already cited in 2:26 for his zeal, executed those who engaged in sexual relations with foreigners, perhaps directly relevant to one of the key issues.[444]

The accounts which follow depict Judas' exploits, who is presented as being like a giant (3:3), apparently not on the basis of his size, but of his warrior qualities, reflecting a neutral interpretation of the giants in Gen 6:4a, c (cf. *1 Enoch* 7:3-5). In recruiting for battle, we are told, he observed the biblical requirement that "those who were building houses, or were about to be married (μνηστευομένοις γυναῖκας), or were planting a vineyard, or were fainthearted, he told to go home again" (3:56; cf. Deut 20:7).

Wives and children feature again in the plundering. The Gentiles in Gilead captures the Jewish wives, their children and goods (5:13), but Simon rescues "the Jews of Galilee and Arbatta, with their wives and children, and all they possessed" (5:23). Judas kills all the males in Bozrah (5:28) and Maapha (5:35). Nothing is said of the women. Judas then rescues the Israelites of Gilead "the small and the great, with their wives and children and goods" (5:45), and kills all the non-Jewish males there (5:51). He may have taken the women captive to serve as slaves and captive brides. In 8:10 we read in positive tones of the victorious Romans who took captive the wives and children of the Greeks. A wedding becomes an occasion of vengeful slaughter for members of the family killing John (9:37-42). Simon will avenge his nation, including "wives and children" (13:6), but spares the men, women and children of Gazara (13:45).

Alliance through marriage appears in Ptolemy's marriage of his daughter Cleopatra to Alexander Epiphanes (10:51-58) and then her transfer to his rival, Demetrius (11:8-12), reflecting a widespread practice among rulers.[445] Simon liberates the citadel, putting Gentiles out of the country so that they could no longer "sally forth and defile the environs of the sanctuary doing great damage to its purity" (ἐξ ἧς ἐξεπορεύοντο καὶ ἐμίαινον κύκλῳ τῶν ἁγίων καὶ ἐποίουν

---

similar to the image of Abraham in Sir 44:20d and that both see testing in association with "religiöser Bedrängnis" (87).

[443] So Reiterer, "Vergangenheit," 88-89.

[444] On the relevance here of the allusion to Phinehas as justifying the stance of Mattathias as his faithful descendant and the legitimacy of the Hasmoneans, see Reiterer, "Vergangenheit," 89-91.

[445] Goldstein, *1 Maccabees*, suggests that mention of the two marriages may reflect coming to terms with the unfulfilled prophecy of Dan 2:43-44, which speaks of marriages between two dynasties (415).

πληγὴν μεγάλη) (14:36). Nothing in the context suggests particular acts of sexual wrongdoing.[446]

2.1.6.2 2 Maccabees

There are few relevant references in 2 Maccabees.[447] Much detail is incidental. Thus in 1:14 we read in a supposed letter to Aristobulus in Egypt of the death of Antiochus, who had sought a large dowry on the pretext of marriage. In the account of the arrival of Heliodorus in Jerusalem to confiscate temple funds for the royal treasury, we read that some monies belonged to "widows and orphans" (3:10), indicating that widows could own property[448] as in Judith, and then that in response to his incursion: "women, girded with sackcloth under their breasts, thronged the streets. Some of the young women who were kept indoors ran together to the gates, and some to the walls, while others peered out of the windows. And holding up their hands to heaven, they all made supplication" (3:19-20). This incidentally reflects the pattern of restraining girls to remain indoors (cf. 3 Macc 1:18; Sir 42:11; *Ps.-Phoc.* 215-217).[449] In 4:30 we read of cities given as a present to Antiochis the king's concubine. In 5:13 we read of a "massacre of young and old, destruction of boys, women, and children, and slaughter of young girls and infants". Antiochus sent Apollonius "to kill all the grown men and to sell the women and boys as slaves" (5:24). The drowning of Jews with their wives and children at Joppa evokes Judas' vengeance (12:2-4). In 12:21 we find a further reference to women, children, and baggage in the context of war. Finally confronted by Nicanor, Judas is moved by "concern for wives and children, and also for brothers and sisters and relatives" (15:18).

We find more specific detail in the account of the evil perpetuated in the temple in the aftermath of Antiochus' decree to suppress Judaism.

---

[446] Goldstein, *1 Maccabees*, suggests contamination through corpses of pious Jews (506).

[447] On the authorship and date of 2 Maccabees, see Mittmann-Richert, *Einführung*, 44-48, who contemplates that the work of the author in excerpting Jason of Cyrene probably occurred in the late 2d century B.C.E., perhaps around the date of 124 B.C.E. identified in 1:10a. See also the review of the issues in David S. Williams, "Recent Research in 2 Maccabees," *CurBR* 2 (2003) 69-83.

[448] Noted by Christine Gerber, "Das zweite Makkabäerbuch: Was die Geschichte lehrt," in *Kompendium Feministische Bibelauslegung*, (ed. Luise Schottroff, Marie-Theres Wacker, Claudia Janssen, Beate Wehn; Gütersloh: Gütersloher Verlagshaus, 1999) 392-400, 395.

[449] Archer, *Her Price*, 120-21. On the possibility of women's quarters, at least in more wealthy houses, see Ilan, *Jewish Women*, 132-34; Satlow, *Jewish Marriage*, noting it as a sign of claim to respectability and class (313).

3 χαλεπὴ δὲ καὶ τοῖς ὅλοις ἦν δυσχερὴς ἡ ἐπίτασις τῆς κακίας. 4 τὸ μὲν γὰρ ἱερὸν ἀσωτίας καὶ κώμων ὑπὸ τῶν ἐθνῶν ἐπεπληροῦτο ῥᾳθυμούντων μεθ' ἑταιρῶν καὶ ἐν τοῖς ἱεροῖς περιβόλοις γυναιξὶ πλησιαζόντων, ἔτι δὲ τὰ μὴ καθήκοντα ἔνδον εἰσφερόντων. 5 τὸ δὲ θυσιαστήριον τοῖς ἀποδιεσταλμένοις ἀπὸ τῶν νόμων ἀθεμίτοις ἐπεπλήρωτο. 6 ἦν δ' οὔτε σαββατίζειν οὔτε πατρῴους ἑορτὰς διαφυλάττειν οὔτε ἁπλῶς ᾽Ιουδαῖον ὁμολογεῖν εἶναι.

3 Harsh and utterly grievous was the onslaught of evil. 4 For the temple was filled with debauchery and reveling by the Gentiles, who dallied with prostitutes and had intercourse with women within the sacred precincts, and besides brought in things for sacrifice that were unfit. 5 The altar was covered with abominable offerings that were forbidden by the laws. 6 People could neither keep the sabbath, nor observe the festivals of their ancestors, nor so much as confess themselves to be Jews. (6:3-6)

Here in 2 Macc 6:3-6 we are dealing with the effects of Antiochus' resolution to suppress Judaism and transform the temple to a place where the Olympian Zeus would be worshipped. First mentioned among the objectionable happenings at the temple which the Gentiles initiated are acts of sexual wrongdoing. While the text speaks only of Gentiles, it probably assumes participation also of supportive Jews.[450] Such activity is not previously reported either in the author's own account of the activities of the Hellenists in 4:7-20 or in the account found in 1 Macc 1:11-15. The accounts of Antiochus' oppression and the earlier activities of the Hellenists should not be equated, as though Jason and his supporters were seeking to implement what Antiochus imposed. Antiochus required a cessation of the temple rituals, rather than just the superficial syncretism which made Jews acknowledge that their God could be described with other names, something which some Jews in other contexts happily conceded,[451] and required a setting aside of those things which made Judaism distinctive: circumcision, foods, and the sabbath. As 1 Maccabees puts it,

the king wrote to his whole kingdom that all should be one people, 42 and that all should give up their particular customs. 43 All the Gentiles accepted the command of the king. Many even from Israel gladly adopted his religion; they sacrificed to idols and profaned the sabbath. (1 Macc 1:41-43)

---

[450] Cf. Himmelfarb, "Levi, Phinehas," who speaks of it as "all-gentile sex" (21). John Kampen, "The Books of the Maccabees and Sectarianism in Second Temple Judaism," in *The Books of the Maccabees: History, Theology, Ideology: Papers of the Second International Conference on the Deuterocanonical Books, Pápa, Hungary, 9-11 June, 2005* (ed. Géza G. Xeravits and József Zsengellér; JSJSup 118; Leiden: Brill, 2007) 11-30, speaks of 1 Maccabees depicting two covenants in its opening chapter so that "Antiochus was not merely an invader, he was supported by a substantial Jewish population" (13), pointing to the level of support indicated in 1:43 and 52. Similarly Reiterer, "Vergangenheit," 77.

[451] So Collins, "Cult and Culture," who points to *Pseudo-Aristeas* and *Aristobulus* (48).

The "enlightened" would have seen this as a removal of divisive and separatist practices. What that meant concretely for Jews is then explained:

> he directed them to follow customs strange to the land, 45 to forbid burnt offerings and sacrifices and drink offerings in the sanctuary, to profane sabbaths and festivals, 46 to defile the sanctuary and the priests, 47 to build altars and sacred precincts and shrines for idols, to sacrifice swine and other unclean animals, 48 and to leave their sons uncircumcised. They were to make themselves abominable by everything unclean and profane, 49 so that they would forget the law and change all the ordinances. (1 Macc 1:44-49)

The debauchery and revelry referred to in 2 Macc 6:3-6 includes prostitution and sexual intercourse in the temple (not to be confused with temple prostitution). This would have been an abhorrence and to be contrasted with the opposite stance of the author of the *Temple Scroll* and the *Damascus Document* who demand that sexual intercourse not even occur in the holy city (11QTᵃ/11Q19 45.11; CD 12.1-2). It is not to be assumed that Jason and Menelaus would have condoned such activity. It goes far beyond their openness to Gentiles which would have included intermarriage. In its equivalent report of the impact of Antiochus' decree 1 Maccabees makes no reference to debauchery and sexual wrongdoing in the temple (1 Macc 1:41-64). Accordingly Goldstein reads the report as a false allegation on the part of the historian Jason, possibly under the influence of a misreading of זרעים Dan 11:31 to refer not to arms but to seed and of prophetic denunciation of such practices (Lev 19:29; 21:9; Amos 2:7-8).[452] The context may suggest otherwise.

The account then reports that to celebrate the king's birthday "a festival of Dionysus was celebrated, they were compelled to wear wreaths of ivy and to walk in the procession in honor of Dionysus" (6:7). This continues the image of debauchery, for which the Dionysiac cult was notorious. As Goldstein notes, Dionysus would probably have been seen in the syncretistic cult as "the son of Lord God of Israel and the Queen of Heaven".[453] As in 1 Maccabees we hear of suppression of circumcision, instanced in 2 Maccabees by two women whom the oppressors publicly paraded around the city "with their babies hanging at their breasts, and then hurled them down headlong from the wall" (6:10; cf. 1 Macc 1:60-61). The violence continues in the report of the killing of seven brothers. The author then pictures their mother: as πεπληρωμένη φρονήματι καὶ τὸν θῆλυν λογισμὸν ἄρσενι θυμῷ διεγείρασα "Filled with a noble spirit, she reinforced her woman's reasoning with a man's courage" (7:21). She recalls to her son her

---

[452] Jonathan A. Goldstein, *2 Maccabees* (AB 41a; Garden City: Doubleday, 1983) 274-75.

[453] Goldstein, *2 Maccabees*, 276.

maternal care: "My son, have pity on me. I carried you nine months in my womb, and nursed you for three years, and have reared you and brought you up to this point in your life, and have taken care of you" (7:29).[454] Thus while 2 Maccabees like 1 Maccabees considers women as victims, it also portrays some as taking initiatives and acting with great courage for their faith and their nation in the face of great adversity.[455]

It is interesting that in 14:23 Nicanor is shown urging Judas "to marry and have children": παρεκάλεσεν αὐτὸν γῆμαι καὶ παιδοποιήσασθαι and that Judas is shown as complying: ἐγάμησεν εὐστάθησεν ἐκοινώνησεν βίου "he married, settled down, and shared the common life".

In 14:37-38 we find reference to a certain Razis, who had in earlier days been accused of "Judaism". The author adds that this was "in former times, when there was no mingling" (ἦν γὰρ ἐν τοῖς ἔμπροσθεν χρόνοις τῆς ἀμειξίας). A similar temporal reference occurs in 14:3 about Alcimus who "had wilfully defiled himself in the times of separation" (ἑκουσίως δὲ μεμολυσμένος ἐν τοῖς τῆς ἀμειξίας χρόνοις). The times of separation most likely refer to the immediate aftermath of the Revolt when Jews re-asserted the separateness which Antiochus was partly wanting to quash. That separateness would have included prohibiting intermarriage, probably included in the allusion to "mingling" (ἀμειξίας), but here the focus is general. Accordingly, Razis "had been accused of Judaism, and he had most zealously risked body and life for Judaism", presumably resisting the attempts to force compliance with Antiochus' imposition. The story adds no further detail about this, but rather describes in gory detail his suicide when Nicanor acts after a tip-off to try to execute him.

Goldstein considers what Jason might have meant by Alcimus' defilement, reported in 14:3, ruling out defilement by blood guilt or idolatry, since otherwise the pious would not have accepted him.[456] The same would apply to any sin of mixing, that is, sexual intercourse, which μειξία can connote. On the other hand, Jason's account of Alcimus differs from that of 1 Maccabees and portrays him as conspiring against both the pious and Judas, so that it would be credible, that, true or not,[457] Jason is alleging that he had defiled himself through inappropriate mixing, which could include sexual wrongdoing and would then make him a candidate, for instance, to be considered as the target of *Jub.* 23:21, which refers to contamination of the holy of holies, presumably by a high priest.

---

[454] For similar emphasis on maternal care, especially through pregnancy, birth and breast feeding, see the expansion in the retelling of the story in 4 Macc 13:19-22; 15:4-7; 16:7-8.

[455] On this see also Oegema, "Portrayals of Women," who notes that the mother becomes a model for Christian martyrs (258-59).

[456] Goldstein, *2 Maccabees*, 481.

[457] Goldstein, *2 Maccabees*, deems it another falsehood (482).

Goldstein notes the textual variants A V q, reading ἀμειξίας and L' 58 311 La-^BM Sy, reading ἐπιμειξίας.[458] ἀμειξία can mean "unwillingness to mix with foreigners" as Josephus *A.J.* 13.245, 247, but ἐπιμειξία can mean the opposite and so would fit well as description of what those in 1 Macc 1:11-15 sought. He then argues that 14:38 requires the former meaning, noting that in Greek literature ἐπιμειξία can mean a time of peace after war and suggests that we should see 14:3 and 14:38 differently, the former referring to times of peace, the latter to times of war.[459] The alternative reading, however, is equally possible and would then give us two references to the time of separation. If Alcimus was guilty of an alleged crime of sexual wrongdoing, then the reference to this happening at a time when Israel was committed to separation would be particularly appropriate.

Conclusion

1 and 2 Maccabees are important sources for our reconstruction of the momentous events of the first half of the second century B.C.E. Both agree in depicting the impact of Hellenisation. Historical reconstruction needs to take into account a much longer period of Hellenistic influence and the impact of other factors on the crisis, including economic need and greed. In the lead up to Antiochus' act of suppression we find some groups wanting closer relations with the Gentile peoples of their world and rejecting the long tradition of separateness, marked among other things by prohibition of intermarriage. The new freedom probably included intermarriage, though this is never articulated as such despite intertextual allusions. The reported attempts to hide one's circumcision are plausible given the establishment of the gymnasium and associated naked sports with participation also by uncircumcised people. These earlier events are to be distinguished from the forced changes imposed by Antiochus. His decrees apart from forbidding circumcision, sabbath, and cult, and erecting the offensive altar, may also have led to desecration of the temple also through Gentiles and presumably their Jewish friends engaging in sexual wrongdoing in the temple precincts, probably not in the form of temple prostitution, but rather as an adjunct of feasting and revelry. On the whole, however, sexual issues play a minor role in these works. Both allow us to see women and children as victims of war, probably taken as slaves, some to be captive brides, significantly, on both sides (see their assumed place in 11QT^a/11Q19 63.10-15;[460] Deut 21:10-14; but probably attacking the practice: *4QMMT* C 6-7).[461]

---

[458] Goldstein, *2 Maccabees*, 483.

[459] Goldstein, *2 Maccabees*, 484.

[460] See Loader, *Dead Sea Scrolls on Sexuality*, 30.

[461] See the discussion in Loader, *Dead Sea Scrolls on Sexuality*, 79-80.

The author of 1 Maccabees, apart from offering his brief version of the events prior to and during Antiochus' repression, uses poetic images with biblical roots, which depict lament as turning what is valued like the joy of the wedding to mourning and portray Jerusalem as a bereft woman. Beyond that it recalls Joseph's defiant chastity, has Judas apply biblical law to those about to be married, reports a massacre at a wedding, and dynastic political marriages. The accusation of altering the ordinances has echoes in later generations, where disputes arise over laws relating to sexuality, but are not so specifically defined in the work.

2 Maccabees has more detail about the years leading up to the revolt, but says nothing about sexual wrongdoing then. Its account of desecration of the temple through sexual profligacy is fittingly followed by mention of the Dionysian parade. Its other pertinent references are largely minor: royals seeking large dowries or benefiting their concubines, Nicanor advising Judas to settle down and start a family, Alcimus' pollution of the high priesthood possibly through sexual wrongdoing, and reference to both his and Razis' behaviour during the times when separation from the Gentiles was observed, probably including rejection of intermarriage. Its expression of lament portrays women in sackcloth and girls kept indoors making public outcry and depicts the mother of the seven martyrs recalling their birth and nurture.

Neither depicts sexual wrongdoing as a major issue in the conflicts of the period. At most we must assume that the new engagement with Gentiles must have raised such issues, including intermarriage, prostitution, male same-sex relations, but the most we hear of is an instance of profligacy and the shame of some about their circumcision and their initiatives to deal with it.

2.2   *Beyond the Septuagint*

2.2.1   The Book of Biblical Antiquities *Liber Antiquitatum Biblicarum (LAB)*/Pseudo-Philo

This extensive work, referred to as *LAB* in what follows, which rewrites the biblical story from Adam to the death of Saul, survives in Latin, being a translation from Greek of a work written in Palestine in Hebrew[462] in the first century C.E.,

---

[462] See the arguments for a Hebrew original in Daniel J. Harrington, "The Original language of Pseudo-Philo's 'Liber Antiquitatum Biblicarum'," *HTR* 63 (1970) 503-14. The text of the Latin used in this discussion is that found in volume one of Daniel J. Harrington, Jacques Cazeaux, Charles Perrot, Pierre-Maurice Bogaert, *Pseudo-Philon: Les Antiquités Bibliques* (2 vols; SC 229-30; Paris: Cerf, 1976), also reproduced in Howard A. Jacobson, *A Commentary on Pseudo-Philo's Liber Antiquitatum Biblicarum with Latin Text and English Translation* (AGAJU 31; 2 vols.; Leiden: Brill, 1996) 1-87. The translation is that

probably in the period just before[463] or in the decades after[464] the Jewish War, 66-70 C.E. It rewrites the material, sometimes summarising, sometimes omitting large sections (e.g. most of Genesis, Leviticus, Numbers, Deuteronomy and Joshua), while giving special emphasis to Judges and to leaders generally, and occasionally adding completely new material.[465] It has a strong sense of Israel's uniqueness, speaking of an eternal covenant, while at the same time grappling with Israel's failure and the fear that Israel may one day go too far. Israel's dangers are, above all, idolatry, but also intermarriage with non-Jews. Its hope includes resurrection, judgement, and punishment of the wicked. Within these concerns the work also addresses issues pertaining to sexuality.

Creation and Genealogies

It begins with a genealogy from Adam to the sons of Noah (1:1-22), followed by a more detailed, annotated, genealogy from Cain (2:1-10). Halpern-Amaru notes that *LAB* "provides the names of non-firstborn male and female children who are omitted in the biblical narratives", supplementing "not only Genesis, but also *Jubilees*".[466] She notes that *LAB* also provides alternative data to *Jubilees*, a

---

of Daniel J. Harrington, "Pseudo-Philo," *OTP*, 2.304-77 (unless otherwise indicated by "lit."), who uses italics to indicate biblical quotations.

[463] For a general introduction see Gerbern S. Oegema, "Pseudo-Philo: Antiquitates Biblicae (JSHRZ II/2)," in *Einführung zu den Jüdischen Schriften aus hellenistisch-römischer Zeit: Unterweisung in erzählender Form* (ed. Gerbern S. Oegema; JSHRZ 6.1.2; Gütersloh: Gütersloher Verlagshaus, 2005) 66-77, who argues that the absence of clear references to the momentous event of the Jewish War makes a date after that time unlikely (69-70); similarly Harrington, *OTP*, 2.299-300.

[464] Louis H. Feldman, "Josephus' Jewish Antiquities and Pseudo-Philo's Biblical Antiquities," in *Josephus, the Bible, and History* (ed. Louis H. Feldman and Gohei Hata; Leiden: Brill, 1989) 59-80, suggests that among other things the emphasis in the work on the importance of leadership and of God's continuing faithfulness despite Israel's failure "may well suggest that *LAB* dates from the chaotic period just before or just after the destruction of the Temple" (76). Jacobson, *Commentary*, even suggests a date as late as after the Second Revolt, 132-35 C.E. (199-210). See also Bruce N. Fisk, *Do You Not Remember? Scripture, Story and Exegesis in the Rewritten Bible of Pseudo-Philo* (JSPSup 37; Sheffield: Sheffield Academic Press, 2001) 34-41; Nickelsburg, *Jewish Literature*, 265-70.

[465] Feldman, "Josephus' Jewish Antiquities and Pseudo-Philo's Biblical Antiquities," notes "the number of unique elements in *LAB* that differentiate it from both Josephus and rabbinic tradition and, indeed, from any other extant work" (76).

[466] Betsy Halpern-Amaru, "Portraits of Women in Pseudo-Philo's *Biblical Antiquities*," in *"Women like This": New Perspectives on Jewish Women in the Greco-Roman World* (ed. Amy-Jill Levine; SBLEJL 1; Atlanta: Scholars, 1991) 83–106, 84.

different wife for Cain, no sibling marriages, and a different wife for Reu, Melcha.[467] Cain's wife, significantly, bears the same name, Themech, as Sisera's mother (31:8).

LAB passes over the first three chapters of Genesis, though later the author alludes to paradise (9:10-13; 11:15; 13:8-9, 25:10; 26:4, 8), the formation of humankind (16:5; cf. also the seed's beginning, 15:7), the creation of Adam (26:6); the creation of woman (32:15), the deception of Eve by the serpent and her persuasion of Adam to sin (13:8); and sin in the garden (19:10).[468] So it omits the foundational passages about male and female and marriage.

Lamech and Sexual Wrongdoing

The first reference to evil among humankind after Cain, whose deed is reported only incidentally: "after he had killed Abel his brother" (2:1; alluded to also in 16:2), is particularly related to Lamech and concerns sexual wrongdoing, thus giving it particular prominence. Accordingly the author goes beyond Genesis in writing: "In that time, when those inhabiting the earth began to do evil (each one with his neighbor's wife) and they defiled them (*contaminantes eas*), God was angry" (2:8a). The Genesis account of Lamech (4:19-24) says nothing of sexual wrongdoing. Here *LAB* specifies adultery not as offence against another man, but as defilement, reflecting the notion in Deut 24:1-4 that a woman who has had sexual relations with another man becomes unclean in relation to her husband. Jacobson notes that the opening words of 2:8 (*cum iniciassent habitantes terram operari iniqua*; "In that time, when those inhabiting the earth began to do evil deeds") may well deliberately echo Gen 6:1 ("When people began to multiply on the face of the ground").[469] He writes: "LAB's sentence recounts the beginnings of immorality, in particular sexual immorality".[470] This may also relate to what immediately precedes: "*Jobal, who was the first to teach all kinds of musical instruments*" (2:7; similarly Gen 4:21), because what immediately follows reads: "And he began to play the lyre and the lute and every instrument of sweet song and to corrupt the earth" (2:8b).[471] The following verse mentions another son of

---

[467] Halpern-Amaru, "Portraits of Women," 85.

[468] On the use of flashbacks in *LAB* see Jacobson, *Commentary*, 240-41.

[469] Jacobson, *Commentary*, 299.

[470] Jacobson, *Commentary*, 299.

[471] On attempts to overcome the awkwardness of the syntax (the singular *cepit*) and to bring both references together, separating them from the references to sexual wrongdoing, see the discussion in Jacobson, *Commentary*, who argues that it is better to stay with the transmitted text (perhaps changing *cepit* to *ceperunt* or understanding *cepit* collectively as אדם in Gen 6:1) and to recognise here a link between music and sexual immorality (300-303). Sirach assumes a link when he warns against singing girls in the context of warning

Lamech, Tubal, who taught metallurgy. "Then those inhabiting the earth began to make statues and to adore them" (2:9). Lamech then declares to his wives:

> *I have destroyed men* on my own account (*corrupi pro me*) and snatched sucklings from the breasts, in order to show my sons and those inhabiting the earth how to do evil deeds. And now *Cain will be avenged* (lit. punished)[472] *seven times, but Lamech seventy-seven times*. (2:10)

> I have killed a man for wounding me, a young man for striking me. 24 If Cain is avenged sevenfold, truly Lamech seventy-sevenfold. (Gen 4:23-24)

While the second sentence reproduces Gen 4:24, what precedes is without parallel, and replaces Gen 4:23. The words, *corrupi pro me*, could have a sexual reference and allude to male same-sex relations or/and rape, as James' literal translation suggests: "I have corrupted men for myself".[473] Snatching sucklings from the breast may allude to child sacrifice or to warfare. Thus the author highlights adultery, behaviour associated with certain kinds of music (possibly debauchery, possibly foreign cults), and idolatry (made possible through metallurgy). One might contrast the myth of the Watchers where metallurgy enhances warfare and female seduction and where sexual wrongdoing consists of the Watchers' relations with women. In *LAB* not the Watchers, but Lamech takes the major blame. It is consistent with this that when it comes to the account of the myth of the Watchers the work limits itself to the version as reported in Genesis 6 (with minimal change such as making the women not just beautiful but very beautiful) (3:1-3), though it appears to know the Enochic tradition about the angels teaching magic before their condemnation (34:3) and shares the use of the flood as a model for future eschatological judgement (3:10).[474] It may be deliberately shifting attention away from the descent of the Watchers to the earlier period, perhaps already indicated in the apparent use of Gen 6:1 in 2:8.

---

against loose women (9:3-4), connected in the wider context with banquets (9:9) and probably to be assumed as part of what was present at banquets (cf. also 31:12 –32:13; 18:30 – 19:3). I acknowledge Ibolya Balla for these references (email 24 April, 2008).

[472] So Jacobson, *Commentary*, 304.

[473] M. R. James, *The Biblical Antiquities of Philo* (London: SPCK, 1917; Eugene: Wipf and Stock, 2006) 79; similarly Harrington, Cazeaus, Perrot, Bogaert, *Pseudo-Philon*. Jacobson, *Commentary*, notes that *Gen. Rab.* 23:2 condemns Lamech for sexual corruption (1.306). He argues that it would be hard to see how *LAB* might have seen homosexuality in איש הרגתי לפצעי ("I have killed a man for wounding me"; Gen 4:23) (306). We appear to be dealing here, however, with deliberate rewriting.

[474] So Fröhlich, *Time*, 176.

The Flood, New Beginnings, and the Eschaton

The truncated account of the flood goes beyond the detail in Genesis in having God destroy not only human beings but also "all the things that grow on the earth (*omnia que germinate sunt in terra*)" (3:3). As Hayward notes, this effectively sets up Noah as the beginning not only of a new humanity, but also of a new a creation, a new Adam.[475] In 3:10 we find the eschatological discourse linked to the story of the flood. It speaks of judgement, resurrection and then declares: "And the earth will not be without progeny or sterile for those inhabiting it (*et non erit sine fetu terra, nec sterilis habitantibus in ea*); and no one who has been pardoned by me will be tainted. And there will be another earth and another heaven, an everlasting dwelling place". Jacobson argues that the text as it stands (*non erit sine fetu terra*) speaks of "absolutely perfect agricultural fertility", but also notes that it may have originally indicated more than that, if the word *in* is missing before *terra* or if behind it lies בארץ, thus ולא תהיה הארץ, rather than הארץ.[476] Then, he points out, the second part of the text would refer to sterile women and thus the statement reflect Exod 23:26: לא תהיה משכלה ועקרה בארצך ("No one shall miscarry or be barren in your land"; *non erit infoecunda nec sterilis in terra*). This would assume a future which includes progeny, thus, by implication, marriage and sexual relations, but nothing more specific is said. As it stands *terra* is not used here to refer to earth's people, but to something which will benefit them by being fruitful. It says nothing of human fruitfulness. The eschatology envisaged here includes resurrection, thus embodiedness, in "another earth and another heaven, an everlasting dwelling place" (3:10), but says nothing to indicate sexual relations, procreation or progeny, a surprising omission if it is envisaged and perhaps indicative of their absence in the age to come, a possibility which we shall address below in relation to the promise that the resurrected will dwell in the place of sanctification (19:13).

As in Gen 9:1, Noah echoes the instruction to be fruitful and multiply in Gen 1:28 (which *LAB* had omitted) (3:11), adding: "like a school of fish multiplying in the waves". No mention is made of Ham's seeing Noah naked (cf. Gen 9:22-27).[477] The work elaborates the genealogies of Japheth, Ham and Shem, has the sons of Peleg takes wives from the daughters of Joktan (4:10), reflecting the

---

[475] Robert Hayward, "The Figure of Adam in Pseudo-Philo's Biblical Antiquities," *JSJ* 23 (1992) 1-20, 9.

[476] Jacobson, *Commentary*, 326.

[477] Louis H. Feldman, "Questions about the Great Flood, as Viewed by Philo, Pseudo-Philo, Josephus, and the Rabbis," *ZAW* 115 (2003) 401-22, writes of the author: "Apparently, he is disturbed by the idea that Noah, the perfect man, could have descended to such a low level as to become drunk and to have cursed not the person who saw him naked but the latter's son, who was apparently innocent" (418).

requirement of endogamous marriage, and adding the prediction of Melcha that from one of Reu's descendants would come one "born in the fourth generation who will set his dwelling on high and will be called perfect and blameless; and he will be the father of nations, and his covenant will not be broken, and his seed be multiplied forever" (4:11). As Halpern-Amaru notes, "the prediction makes a prophetess of Melcha, and at the same time, creates the annunciation scene lacking in Genesis for the first patriarch".[478] In the time of Lot it reports that "those who inhabited the earth began to observe the stars and started to reckon by them and to make predictions and to have their sons and daughters pass through the fire" (4:16), an allusion to astrology and pagan practices. There are no sexual references here. The census of Noah's descendants reported in what follows counts males, but regularly with the note: "apart from women and children" (5:4, 5, 7; cf. Matt 14:21; 15:38).

From Abram to Moses

Apart from the legend about Abram's refusal to participate in building the tower of Babel (6 – 7), the entire sweep of history from Abram up to Moses is compressed within a single chapter (8). There *LAB* shows a regular interest in marriage, childbirth and sterility (8:1, 4, 6; cf. already 4:10).[479] There is, however, no discussion of Sodom and Gomorrah (Gen 19:1-29), though it is known, as 8:2 (reproducing Gen 13:13 about their wickedness) and 45:2 (about stopping the men of Sodom) show, no mention of the incest of Lot's daughters (Gen 19:30-38), nor of Abraham and Sarah's encounters with Pharaoh (Gen 12:10-20) and with Abimelech (Gen 20:1-18) or Isaac and Rebecca's with the latter (Gen 26:1-16), probably to avoid all contact between the matriarchs and foreign men,[480] nor of Isaac's and Jacob's finding a wife from within the extended family (Gen 24:1-67; 27:46 – 29:30), nor of Rebecca, in contrast to her prominence in *Jubilees*.[481]

---

[478] Halpern-Amaru, "Women in Pseudo-Philo," 87.

[479] Halpern-Amaru, "Women in Pseudo-Philo," notes that the author consistently emphasises the role of women as vehicles of the divine either through annunciation and miraculous birth: Sarah (88-89), Rebecca (89), Eluma (96-97), Hannah (97), or by divine plan: Tamar (93); and Moses' mother, whose pregnancy is announced by Miriam (93-94). "Sarah is significant to Pseudo-Philo solely in terms of her role as a vehicle for the miraculous birth of a son to Abraham" (89).

[480] So Mary Therese Descamp, "Why Are These Women Here? An Examination of the Sociological Setting of Pseudo-Philo through Comparative Reading," *JSP* 16 (1997) 53-80, 61.

[481] On this see Halpern-Amaru, "Women in Pseudo-Philo," 89-90. Descamp, "Why Are These Women Here?" notes that *LAB* has chosen not to emulate *Jubilees* which links Rebecca with Abraham as key tradents of the covenant, but instead reduces her role, and thus "removes all direct reference to this woman who tricked her husband" (62). She also

Perhaps the author wanted to avoid suggestions that intermarriage with people of Aram was acceptable. Halpern-Amaru notes that *LAB* calls Bilhah and Zilpah not handmaids, but concubines and depicts only Judah, Levi and the tribes descended from Rachel as trusting in God for help (10:3).[482] The document mentions the rape of Dinah and the revenge of Levi and Simeon (without hint of reproof), but very briefly and without mention of the circumcision trick (8:7).[483] She becomes Job's wife (8:8, 11), as in *T. Job* 1:5, but, unlike there, his only wife. Nothing is said of her having been rendered unclean for Job.[484] There is no account of Reuben's incest with Bilhah (Gen 35:22) nor of Joseph's virtuous resistance to temptation (though it is alluded to in 43:5) (Gen 39:1-20) or his saga in Egypt, nor of Judah's using Tamar as a prostitute and so unwittingly committing incest (Gen 38:1-30), though we find a flashback to Tamar in 9:5-6 as part of the next chapter.

The Elders, Amram, and Tamar

The author depicts the Egyptians' response to the growth of the people of Israel: "Let us kill (*interficamus*)[485] their males, and we will keep their females so that we may give them to our wives as slaves" and declares: *et hoc est quod pessimum visum est coram domino* ("and this is what seemed wicked before the Lord") (9:1). Jacobson discusses what *hoc* means here, considering that it could refer to sexual immorality, sexual intercourse with Gentiles, the breeding of slaves, or the treatment of the girls, noting that to the author "the killing of the boys was less criminal in God's eyes than their treatment of the girls".[486] This coheres with the

---

notes that whereas *LAB* tends to add women's names to genealogies, it deletes references to Rebecca from its genealogies (62).

[482] Halpern-Amaru, "Women in Pseudo-Philo," 90.

[483] Jacobson, *Commentary*, notes that behind the Latin *rapuit ... et humiliavit eam* lies the Hebrew ויקח ויענה "and he seized and raped her" (391). On the brevity of the account and the omissions see Louis H. Feldman, *"Remember Amalek!": Vengeance, Zealotry, and Group Destruction in the Bible according to Philo, Pseudo-Philo, and Josephus* (Cincinnati: Hebrew Union College Press, 2004), who notes that the author removes anything that "might create sympathy for Shechem and the Hivites" and is more concerned to report that Dinah became Job's wife (155-56). Similarly Halpern-Amaru, "Women in Pseudo-Philo," 91.

[484] See the discussion of the passage in Bader, *Tracing the Evidence*, 97-99.

[485] Jacobson, *Commentary*, notes that this, the reading of the MS Δ is less likely than the simple future of MS π *interficiemus* ("we shall kill"), indicating compliance with the pharaoh's command (401).

[486] Jacobson, *Commentary*, 402.

interest elsewhere in what concerns women. By contrast the narrative plays down the physical persecution and enslavement.[487]

The people of Israel then complain:

> The wombs of our wives have suffered miscarriage; our fruit is delivered to our enemies. And now we are lost, and let us set up rules for ourselves that a man should not approach his wife lest the fruit of their wombs be defiled and our offspring serve idols. For it is better to die without sons until we know what God may do. (9:2)

Descamps summarises the logic of the elders' argument thus: "the birth of children is causal for the death of male children and marriage of female children to Egyptian slaves, and the marriage of females to Egyptian slaves is causal for idolatry".[488] Here we see the double concern: the defilement of the fruit of their wombs through sexual intercourse with foreign men, and idolatry. This dual concern far outweighs all else, including the death of male children and the enslavement itself. This matches also the declaration which the author gives to Tamar whose chief concern is also to avoid sexual intercourse with foreigners (9:5). *LAB* had thus introduced concern about female offspring (not present in the biblical text) as a basis for developing one of his key themes.[489] As Descamps notes, the expression "fruit of their wombs" belongs to the author's "preoccupation with children and birth" which shows itself in the occurrence in this context of "seven terms in six verses related to childbirth: wombs, miscarriage, fruit, fruit of their wombs, offspring, fruits of her womb, fruit of our wombs".[490]

The response to the crisis is in some sense similar to the situation faced at the Sea of Reeds in 10:2-3, as Olyan notes, where the choices may have matched options faced in the author's time (perhaps the Jewish War): mass suicide, return/assimilation, or resistance, with the author's strong preference for resistance.[491] It is also interesting that we find in 9:1 an espousal of celibacy, which may also be addressing an option of the author's time where some may have been espousing celibacy in the face of danger before divine intervention.[492] One

---

[487] Jacobson, *Commentary*, 402.

[488] Mary Therese Descamp, *Metaphor and Ideology: Liber Antiquitatum Biblicarum and Literary Methods through a Cognitive Lens* (BIS 87; Leiden: Brill, 2007) 204. See her discussion of the passage, pp. 203-20.

[489] So Descamp, "Why Are These Women Here?" 64.

[490] Descamp, "Why Are These Women Here?" 64 (see also 77), who sees this as suggestive among other indicators of authorship by a woman.

[491] Saul M. Olyan, "The Israelites debate their options at the Sea of Reeds: *LAB* 10:3, its Parallels, and Pseudo-Philo's Ideology and Background," *JBL* 110 (1991) 75-91, 86, 89-90.

[492] On similar arguments for celibacy to avoid having children not able to keep Torah, linked to Rabbi Ishmael, see *b. B. Bat.* 60b and *t. Sot.* 15.10, and Jacobson, *Commentary*

might recall one of Paul's arguments for that preference in 1 Corinthians 7, namely duress and adversity (7:26-31), though in the immediate context of *LAB* the concern is more specifically sexual intercourse with foreigners and resultant idolatry as the inevitable consequence of their plight. It is in that sense very different from celibacy because of a special place or time or proleptically in view of a universal celibacy or because of ascetic attitudes towards sexuality or to avoid the demands of family responsibility to be free to undertake special tasks.

Amram counters with dramatic rhetorical flourish to decry the elders' proposal and its prospect "that the race of the sons of Israel will be ended": better rather for the age to end, the world sink, or the abyss rise up to touch the sky! (9:3). He also appeals to the covenant and the near completion of the predicted 400 year stay in Egypt (9:3)[493] and so rejects this advice, instead asserting that he will take his wife and produce sons, to ensure Israel multiplies on earth, and trust God who will not "cast forth the race of Israel in vain upon the earth" (9:4; cf. also 9:6), a daring allusion to Onan's sin.[494] There is an implied allusion here also to the command to be fruitful and multiply, passed over from Gen 1:28, but reproduced in 3:11, citing Gen 9:1.

Amram then supports his argument with a reminder about pregnancy and an appeal to Tamar: "For when our wives conceive, they will not be recognized as pregnant until three months have passed, as also our mother Tamar did" (9:5).[495] The reference to pregnancy not showing for three months is straightforward, as is the allusion to Tamar's pregnancy which first became apparent after three months according to Genesis. Beyond that, however, the allusion is far from straightforward. This is already the case in relation to why not being seen as pregnant should help the women who faced the prospect that their offspring would

---

(403). Apparently only here is Amram depicted as resisting the plan. So Louis Feldman, "Prolegomenon," in M. R. James, *The Biblical Antiquities of Philo* (New York: KTAV, 1971) i-clxix, xcii; Jacobson, *Commentary*, 403-404.

[493] Jacobson, *Commentary*, observes that by elevating Amram's piety the author provides missing background for Moses' calling to his special role (404).

[494] As Descamp, *Metaphor and Ideology*, notes, the focus is not on *coitus interruptus* in itself, but on the effects of avoiding normal intercourse (187; see also 207); cf. Donald C. Polaski, "On Taming Tamar: Amram's Rhetoric and Women's Roles in Pseudo-Philo's *Liber Antiquitatum Biblicarum* 9," *JSP* 13 (1995) 79-99, 89-91.

[495] Jacobson, *Commentary*, observes that the point of this comment about pregnancy not being noticed till after three months is not clear within Amram's argument (408). Is it perhaps an aetiology? But, as the author states, Tamar was recognised as pregnant only after three months. The author notes that "her intent saved her". Perhaps similar intent is being hailed as likely to save the women and their offspring in Egypt.

be killed or abducted.[496] Bauckham has suggested that behind it may lie an interpretation of Exod 2:2 to remove the difficulty of how Jochabed could have concealed Moses for three months, thus accounting for the depiction of the concealment as having happened in her womb.[497] Jacobson notes that rabbinic tradition explains it on the basis that the Egyptians could not see that she was pregnant until after three months and so could not therefore calculate the birth.[498]

The flashback to Tamar does more than illustrate when pregnancy becomes visible. Tamar is not just another woman, but described by Amram as "our mother" (9:5), probably alluding to her role as David's forebear (cf. Ruth 4:18-22).[499] Van der Horst notes that *LAB* has thus significantly elevated Tamar, recalling "our father, Abraham", and by saying nothing of Judah, effectively raised her to the level of the patriarchs.[500] More seriously, an appeal to Tamar must deal with what was seen as her sinful deed, albeit not as sinful as Judah's (cf. the accusation in Gen 38:24 and also the prohibition in Lev 18:15; 20:12). Thus the author immediately explains:

> *Quia non fuit consilium eius in fornicatione, sed nolens recedere de filiis Israel recognitans dixit: Melius est mihi socero meo commixta mori, quam gentibus commisceri.*
>
> For her intent was not fornication, but being unwilling to separate from the sons of Israel she reflected and said, "It is better for me to die for having intercourse with my father-in-law than to have intercourse with gentiles". (9:5)

This both exonerates her as "our mother" (*mater nostra*) and makes a point about intermarriage to Gentiles which will return in 18:13-14; 21:1; 30:1; 44:7; 45:3, and which also concerned the elders.[501] Its point also appears to be that to perpetuate the promised people is better than abstinence, which would fit the analogy with

---

[496] So Jacobson, *Commentary*, who notes that it would at most protect the wives from any interference in the first months (408).

[497] Richard Bauckham, "The Liber Antiquitatum Biblicarum of Pseudo-Philo and the Gospels as 'Midrash'," in *Gospel Perspectives Vol 3: Studies in Midrash and Historiography* (Sheffield: JSOT, 1983) 33-76, 55.

[498] Jacobson, *Commentary*, 409.

[499] So Jacobson, *Commentary*, 409.

[500] Pieter W. van der Horst, "Tamar in Pseudo-Philo's Biblical History" in *A Feminist Companion to Genesis* (ed. Athalya Brenner; Sheffield: Sheffield Academic Press, 1993) 300-304, 301-302; cf. Polaski, "Taming Tamar," who argues that depicting her as "our mother" has more to do with the pious adaptation of her potentially troublesome image than to do with her elevation to matriarchal status (92-93).

[501] On the complications of the story, given what the hearers would have assumed of marital law, including levirate marriage, see Descamp, *Metaphor and Ideology*, 210-18.

Amram.[502] Polaski sees the allusion to Tamar as thus effecting the equivalent of a role play, where the elders are like Judah, less righteous than Tamar, "abandoning their obligations out of fear of losing sons" and like Onan spilling his semen, and God is the opposite to Onan and like Judah in the sense of being reminded of what is appropriate.[503] More significantly Amram is like Tamar, whom *LAB* must have Amram represent for an appropriate match, thus denying sexual pleasure, his, licit, hers, illicit, as motivation.[504] This is not a denial of sexual pleasure as such but of its role in this instance where Israel's progeny and survival is uppermost and sexual intercourse with foreigners (and idolatry) is to be avoided at all costs. As Feldman puts it, *LAB* is here indicating, "in effect, that it is preferable, under extraordinary circumstances, even to have incestuous relations than to marry outside of the Jewish faith".[505] Thus *LAB* has Tamar be the first to give expression to its major theme of prohibiting intermarriage with Gentiles, and clearly does so on the basis that it assumes that she herself was an Israelite.[506] The connection between the story of Tamar and intermarriage is not entirely novel, as commonly supposed,[507] since in *Jubilees'* depiction, this chaotic situation arose in the first place because Judah chose to marry a Canaanite wife (41:2-3).[508] While the story begins with fear both of sexual relations with non-Jews and idolatry, the focus falls more on the former than the latter.

In this context the rest of the story of Amram is told (9:6). His strategy wins divine approval, which *LAB* uses to explain the basis for the promise of Moses' birth and of God's works through him. This includes, not least, the revealing of the covenant, the giving of the Law, bringing light, and thus making him a mediator

---

[502] Descamp, *Metaphor and Ideology*, rightly argues that "covenant fruitfulness" is the cognitive frame "throughout Amram's review of the Tamar narrative" (189). "Tamar's story is linked to this situation because Tamar, in the biblical story, chose an Israelite child over no child or a child fathered by gentiles; and she chose that Israelite child in the face of possible death" (189).

[503] Polaski, "On Taming Tamar," 90-93. He also speculates that the author may have suppressed reference to the female children in the analogy lest it evoke the idea that an alternative for the Israelites would have been the kind of incest which in which Tamar was involved, "a time bomb ready to go off, destroying the framework of patriarchal Israelite family" (97), but nothing in the text indicates this as a concern. So rightly Descamp, *Metaphor and Ideology*, 188.

[504] Polaski, "On Taming Tamar," 92-93.

[505] Feldman, "Josephus' Jewish Antiquities and Pseudo-Philo's Biblical Antiquities," 75. A similar logic enabled *Jubilees* to contemplate sibling marriages as an alternative to marrying into evil lines. See Loader, *Enoch, Levi, and Jubilees*, 156.

[506] So van der Horst, "Tamar," 302-303.

[507] Cf. Feldman, "Introduction," lxxii; Frederick J. Murphy, *Pseudo-Philo: Rewriting the Bible* (New York: Oxford University Press, 1993) 57.

[508] See Loader, *Enoch, Levi, and Jubilees*, 180-86.

among human beings, envisaged as far back as the time of sin after the transgression of the angels (9:7-8; cf. Gen 6:3). Amram is not only a key link in the divine plan but also a model of appropriate behaviour: "Amram *of the tribe of Levi went out and took (accepit) a wife* from his own tribe *(de tribu sua)*" (9:9) (cf. Exod 2:1 וילך איש מבית לוי ויקח את בת לוי "Now a man from the house of Levi went and married a Levite woman"), reflecting what the author saw as the ideal (cf. also Tob 4:12-13; Jdt 8:2). It could imply a belief that priests only marry within priestly families, but this may not be intended or be intended to apply to all as in Tobit, not just to priests. The statement also reads as though at this point Amram marries, whereas in 9:4-5 he already refers to his wife. Therefore "*took*" (*accepit*) here, as often, refers rather to having sexual intercourse (e.g., Gen 6:1). Thus the others also "take" their wives in this sense, following his example rather than the proposal of abstinence.

Miriam, Amram's daughter, also becomes a key link in the divine plan,[509] instructed in a dream to tell her parents of Moses' birth. Thus "the spirit of God came upon Miriam one night" who had a dream that a man stood by her and told her that a man to be born from her parents would "be cast forth into the water" and will save his people (9:10), though her parents do not believe her. Then 9:12 mentions Jochabed conceiving from Amram, giving birth and naming the child Moses (9:16). Nothing is said of the technically incestuous marriage between Amram and his aunt, Jochabed (Lev 18:12; cf. Exod 6:20). Divine plan, not happenstance, surrounds the story of the discovery of Moses by Pharaoh's daughter, also instructed in a dream (reminiscent of the Matthean birth narratives), and she recognises the baby Moses as a Hebrew, since, as *LAB* attests, he was apparently circumcised from birth, born in the covenant of God and "the covenant of the flesh" (9:15; cf. *b. Sot.* 12a; *Exod. Rab.* 1:24).

Sinai and the Law

After its account of the crossing of the Reed Sea after typical divisions over response to adversity (mass suicide, compliance, or resistance) and a brief account of the wilderness wanderings, *LAB* takes us to the giving of the Law at Sinai, depicted, as predicted, as bringing light (11:1; cf. 9:8). It includes the prohibition of Exod 19:15 about men approaching their wives for three days beforehand: *tribus diebus non ascendat vir ad mulierem* (lit. "for three days let no man approach a woman") (11:2).[510] It cites the Decalogue, including: "*You shall not*

---

[509] On *LAB*'s additional material about Miriam, the prediction of Moses' birth (9:10, 15) and Miriam's well (10:7; 11:15; 20:8), see Cheryl A. Brown, *No Longer Be Silent: First Century Jewish Portraits of Biblical Women* (Louisville: Westminster/John Knox, 1992) 17.

[510] Harrington, *OTP*, translates on the basis of emending the reading attested in all MSS, *ascendat*, to *accedat* (2.318). Similarly Jacobson, *Commentary*, who argues that while in

commit adultery" (11:10), reflecting the order of the Decalogue in the LXX in Exodus and the Nash Papyrus of having it precede the prohibition of murder (but in reverse order in 44:6-7),[511] adding as grounds: "because your enemies did not commit adultery against you, but *you came forth with a high hand*" (11:10). This is a strange addition. It may be indicating that the Egyptians did not get the chance to commit adultery with the Israelites because they escaped.[512]

Jacobson suggests the *non* has mistakenly come into the text because of its frequent use in the context, so that originally the text spoke of the opposite, namely that the Egyptians had sexually abused the Hebrews. In support he cites (i) the use of ויענונו in Deut 26:6 to describe the Egyptians' oppression, which can also mean sexual assault; (ii) the grounds given for forbidding murder which also appeal to the Egyptians' killing; and (iii) the reciprocal command of Exod 23:9 not to oppress the stranger the way the Egyptians oppressed them. The commandments would thus have been reformulated along the lines of the golden rule.[513]

The prohibition of false testimony receives the argument: "lest your guardians (*custodes*) speak false testimony against you" (11:12), an allusion to angels in prosecution in the heavenly court. Angels are referred to as "guardians" (*custodes*) also in 59:4 (cf. also 15:5). *Custodes* might suggest "Watchers", though the role is different.[514] The prohibition against coveting mentions only the "*neighbor's house and what he has*" (11:13), not specifying "his wife" (cf. Exod 20:17; Deut 5:20-21; but present in 44:10).

The author supplements the Exodus account about Sinai with the report that Moses was shown the tree of life (11:15), relating it to the event in Exod 15:25 according to which Moses made the waters at Marah sweet. This alludes to the tree of life of paradise, indicating that Moses looked into paradise. This is probably an elaboration of his seeing the pattern after which he was to construct

---

Latin, Greek, and Hebrew, *ascendere*, ἀναβαίνω, and לעלות are used in a sexual sense, this occurs in relation to animals, not humans (449). There are, however, examples of application to humans (e.g. Gen 49:4), so there is no need for the emendation. "Going up onto" depicts what was the common "male-superior" position. Jacobson, *Commentary*, notes that the three days are linked directly to the abstinence here, rather than to the preparation, which would also imply it, but could allow some to argue for more permanent celibacy or abstinence only on the third day (448-49).

[511] See Loader, *Septuagint*, 5-9. Jacobson, *Commentary*, notes the reverse order in 44:6-7 and also the absence in 11:7-13 of the prohibition of theft, suggesting possible corruption of the text (473).

[512] So Harrington, *OTP*, 2.319.

[513] Jacobson, *Commentary*, 473-74.

[514] Jacobson, *Commentary*, rejects the link (475); cf. Christian Dietzfelbinger, *Pseudo-Philo: Antiquitates Biblicae (Liber Antiquitatum Biblicarum)* (JSHRZ 2.2; Gütersloh, Gütersloher Verlagshaus, 1979) 131.

the sanctuary and its cult, important elements for the author (Exod 25:9) to which 19:10 later refers.

Moses' distress at the incident with the golden calf is described thus: "And his hands were opened, and he became like a woman bearing her firstborn who, when she is in labor, her hands are upon her chest and she has no strength to help herself bring forth" (12:5).[515] The use of female imagery is noteworthy and coheres with the author's interest in portraying women elsewhere. *LAB* makes no reference to the activity which accompanied the making of the golden calf in Exod 32:6, "the people sat down to eat and drink, and rose up to revel" (also 32:19a "dancing"), but on the other hand like Exod 32:20 connects the resultant confrontation with the testing of the accused adulteress in Num 5:11-31, having the people drink the dust mixed with water (12:7).[516] The focus is not sexual sin, but idolatry and the effect of the measure is to have "Moses distinguish between two levels of guilt: wilful defiance and fearful compliance".[517] The faces of the latter will shine as did Moses when he descended (transferred from his second descent to his first). The result is a depiction of Israel's sin of idolatry as adultery.[518]

Moses now intercedes for the people, depicted as a vine here (12:8-9) as commonly in *LAB* (18:10-11; 28:4; 30:4), urging God not to root it out, reasoning in a manner reminiscent of Exod 33:12-16, but also 4 Ezra 3:20-36; 4:22-25; 5:21-30 and *2 Bar.* 3:1-9; 14:1-19. God relents and Moses descends to set up the sanctuary and establish the laws about the cult and its festivals. In another flashback *LAB* then has God address Moses telling him of the time of Noah when, he says,

I showed them the place of creation and the serpent ... This is the place concerning which I taught saying, "If you do not transgress what I have commanded you, all things will be subject to you", but that man transgressed my ways and was persuaded by his wife, and she was deceived by the serpent. And then death was ordained for the generation of men. 9 And the Lord continued to show him the ways of paradise and said to him: "These are the ways that men have lost by not walking in them, because they have sinned against me". (13:8-9)

---

[515] Christopher T. Begg, "The Golden Calf Episode according to Pseudo-Philo," in *Studies in the Book of Exodus: Redaction, Reception, Interpretation* (ed. M. Vervenne; BETL 126; Leuven: Peeters, 1996) 577-94, notes similar imagery in 2 Kgs 19:3; Isa 37:3 (585).

[516] On this see the discussion in Fisk, *Do You Not Remember?* 176-90.

[517] Fisk, *Do You Not Remember?* 179, noting a similar differentiation in 22:5-6 (180).

[518] Fisk, *Do You Not Remember?* suggests a similar allusion to Num 5:11-31 in the context of charging Israel with adultery may be present in Ezek 16:17, 38 and 23:31-34 (184-85).

In a double flashback the author takes the hearers back to the garden of Eden. The assumption here is that Noah's generation was shown paradise (13:8), as Moses was shown the ways of paradise (13:9; similarly *2 Bar.* 4:5)[519] and earlier, the tree of life (11:15). As Hayward notes, *LAB* implies that observance of the cult can undo the effects of Adam's sin, for, had Adam not sinned, the ways to paradise would still be open.[520] This, he argues, assumes also the widespread link between paradise and the temple, citing *Jub.* 8:19; 1QS/1Q28 8.1-11; Sir 24:8-27; 1QH[a] xvi.4-20, and is written over against views which saw Adam as having been a priest.[521] Accordingly, the author portrays Adam in a largely negative light as the one who lost things and depicts in Noah a totally new beginning of creation and in Moses the basis for sustaining the new order.[522] Thus the cult and promise of fertility belong to Noah and Moses not Adam, who is at best simply the ancestor of Israel. It assumes that at the giving of the Torah Moses was taken to the place of light, paradise.[523] In the words, "that man transgressed my ways and was persuaded by his wife, and she was deceived by the serpent" (13:8), the author summarises the event of sin, but without further specific reflection, for instance, on the nature of the deception, including whether it was to be understood as sexual seduction, which nothing in the text indicates.

LAB then has God declare that if the people walk in his ways (which entails also observance of the cult), then he "will bless their seed (*semen*) and the earth will quickly yield its fruit" (13:10). This is more than an agricultural reference, but, as in Exod 23:26 and Deut 7:13, also a reference to abundant human progeny.[524] Its focus is life in the present, not life in the eschaton, when it seems the author assumes no need of human progeny. The issue of seed remains in focus in the prediction that they will be abandoned because of sin (13:10) and the recalling of the promise of seed like the stars of heaven (14:2; cf. Gen 22:17). When in response to the spies, Israel falls into despair and God threatens to abandon them, Moses responds to God with extraordinary frankness: "Before you took the seed from which you would make man upon the earth, was it I who did

---

[519] On the likelihood that the reference in 13:9 is to Moses, see Jacobson, *Commentary*, 521-22.

[520] Hayward, "Figure of Adam," 6.

[521] Hayward, "Figure of Adam," 6-8, 16.

[522] Hayward, "Figure of Adam," 9-10. He also draws attention to the tradition about the precious light-bearing stones which derive from paradise in 26:6, which according to *LAB* are replaced by the gems on the high priest's ephod and will be given to the righteous at the eschaton (12-13).

[523] Hayward, "Figure of Adam," 13-14. He notes also that 37:3 contrasts Adam and Moses and light, by playing on the thornbush, a result of Adam's sin, but then the place of light in the disclosure of the divine name (18).

[524] Cf. Jacobson, *Commentary*, 523.

establish their ways?" (15:7), appealing for mercy.[525] This incidental reference to creation goes beyond the Genesis accounts in depicting God as beginning human creation with a seed. The assumption is that the seed continues to be passed down.

Korah

In a creative reworking of the Korah episode (16:1-7; cf. Num 16:1-35) the author uses the second creation story to speak on the one hand of man being formed from the earth (16:2, 5), which he then connects with the earth swallowing up the dissenters, as the man's curse was to return to the ground (Gen 3:19). It also has God recall Cain's shedding of blood (16:2), but nothing is picked up here from the creation story of relations between the sexes or sexual issues. The revolt is now not Levites against Moses' leadership, but Korah and only some of his sons against the Law (cf. 16:5) and is directly linked to the requirement which precedes the episode in Num 15:37-40, namely, the wearing of tassels to symbolise adherence to Torah.

Balaam and Balak

The author has greatly elaborated the account of the incident with Balaam and Balak, enhancing Israel's special status as God's chosen people (18:5-6), in particular, again using the image of the vine (18:10). Balaam, who initially resists Balak (18:7-10), loses the Spirit (18:10, 11) and then connives against Israel, proposing the following mode of temptation:

> Pick out the beautiful women who are among us and in Midian, and station them naked and adorned with gold and precious stones before them. And when they see them and lie with them, they will sin against their Lord and fall into your hands. (18:13)

> And afterward the people were seduced after the daughters of Moab. (18:14)

Thus the theme of intermarriage returns. *LAB* has thereby forged a close connection between the story of Balaam and Balak and the accounts of intermarriage with the women of Moab in Num 25:1-5 (linked to the idolatry of serving Baal of Peor) and with a woman of Midian by an Israelite recounted in Num 25:6-9, where Phinehas displays his zeal by spearing both. The latter two stories, not connected with the Balaam–Balak accounts in Numbers, now serve the author's theme of warning against intermarriage as the enemies' strategy to

---

[525] Murphy, *Pseudo-Philo*, notes the parallel with "4 Ezra 3:20-36 where Ezra tells God that God did not remove humanity's 'evil heart'" (79). He suggests that *LAB* nevertheless alludes to the evil heart in 3:9 and 33:3 (79).

undermine Israel.[526] In the original story in Numbers there is a strong link between the intermarriage and idolatry (Baal Peor), but at this point in *LAB* no reference is made to idolatry,[527] unlike in the further allusion to Num 25:1 in 30:1. This should caution us against seeing intermarriage only or primarily as a problem in relation to idolatry. Traditions of Phinehas were widely used in relation to the dangers of intermarriage and not always in relation to idolatry. Phinehas will assume significant status as high priest in *LAB* (46:1 – 48:5).

Moses and Paradise, the Place of Sanctification

In 19:10 we find further reference to Moses' seeing paradise: "and he showed him the place from which the manna rained upon the people, even unto the paths of paradise" (cf. 13:8-9). There, apparently, he is also shown the pattern for the temple and the astrological signs which are forbidden for humans to know because of their sin (19:10). Moses then receives the promise of resurrection:

> I will raise up you and your fathers from the land of Egypt in which you sleep and you will come together and dwell in the immortal dwelling place that is not subject to time. (19:12)

Using apocalyptic imagery, shortened times and sun and moon failing, the author repeats the promise of resurrection so that "all who can live may dwell in the place of sanctification (*locum sanctificationis*) I showed you" (19:13).[528] The *locum sanctificationis* refers to the temple as in:

> מי יעלה בהר יהוה ומי יקום במקום קדשו
> Who shall ascend the hill of the LORD? And who shall stand in his holy place? (Ps 24:3)

The promise assumes an embodied future state of the righteous who will sleep until the time of God's visitation, when they will be raised from the dead. They will then dwell "in the place of sanctification I showed you". This must be a

---

[526] On the linking together of these stories with the Balaam–Balak stories also in Josephus *A.J.* 4.126-130, Philo *Mos.* 1.294-299 and rabbinic sources, see Jacobson, *Commentary*, 608. He sees the connection suggested by Num 31:16 which connects Balaam and the scandal of the Midianite women. On Balaam and Balak see also Fisk, *Do You Not Remember?* 227-49.

[527] So Jacobson, *Commentary*, who notes that the connection with idolatry is maintained in the retellings in Philo, Josephus, and rabbinic literature (610); similarly Fisk, *Do You Not Remember?* 51; Halpern-Amaru, "Women in Pseudo-Philo," who notes also that *LAB* shows no interest in developing the characters of Gentile women (94).

[528] Jacobson, *Commentary*, cites as parallels Isa 52:1; 60:13; Ps 24:3; Eccl 8:10 (645).

reference to paradise (so 11:15; 13:8-9), where Moses was shown the pattern for the cult and the tree of paradise, and so is understood as a temple, hence "place of sanctification", as in *Jubilees*. This would have implications, in turn, for sexual relations, since they would have no place there. We noted above that the promise of progeny in the eschaton in 3:10 refers only to the earth and the animals, not earth's inhabitants who are depicted as beneficiaries, and that the promise of abundant seed in 13:10 refers to life prior to the eschaton. In describing that "immortal place" as "not subject to time" (19:10), the author probably envisages a timeless existence without day and night, sun and moon, much as in Rev 21:22-27; 22:5, where we find a similar timelessness and the combining of temple and paradise imagery, the whole, being conceived as a temple with similar implications. The same may be implied in *2 Enoch* and *Sibylline Oracles* 2 and thus provides an important parallel to Mark 12:25, which speaks of there being no marrying or being given in marriage in the age to come.

Joshua and the Women

When the author has God tell Joshua that after he dies the people "will be intermingled (*commisceatur*) with those inhabiting the land and *they will be seduced (seducentur) after strange gods*" (21:1), the reference, which in its latter part alludes to Deut 31:16,[529] doubtless includes intermarriage, and is here closely connected to idolatry. In 22:1-2 *LAB* has Joshua confront the tribes of Reuben, Gad and half of Manasseh for constructing an altar beyond the Jordan, citing Moses' warning about corrupting their way (22:2).[530] Joshua's final major speech begins with an image of a rock from which were hewn two men, Abraham and Nahor, but also two women, Sarah and Melcha, again reflecting the emphasis on women (23:4).[531] The author then recounts Sarah's sterility which God reverses when Abraham offers a calf, a she-goat, a ram, a turtledove and a dove (as in Gen 15:9-10). The author uses these as images for Abraham, himself; the prophets; the wise men; the multitude of peoples; and the she-goat for "the women whose

---

[529] On this see Hofmann, *Assumptio Mosis*, 116-17, 290. Jacobson, *Commentary*, draws attention also to Exod 34:15-17, which refers to those inhabiting the land (676).

[530] The term occurs in *Jubilees* of wickedness at the time of the Watchers, based on Gen 6:12 (5:2, 3, 10, 17; 25:7, 10). On this see Loader, *Enoch, Levi, and Jubilees*, 130-32.

[531] Fisk, *Do You Not Remember?* notes that the author appears to assume identification of Sarah with Iscah in Gen 11:19, thus both Sarah and Milcah having the same grandfather, Terah (297). This identification is apparently deliberately avoided in *Jubilees* because it would make her Abraham's niece (cf. *Jub.* 12:9) and see Loader, *Enoch, Levi, and Jubilees*, 249-50. Halpern-Amaru, "Women in Pseudo-Philo," notes that while the identification with Iscah appears in *LAB* 23:4, it is not supported by *LAB*'s genealogies (87).

wombs I will open and they will give birth" (23:7).[532] This underlines the importance of abundant progeny in the author's understanding of covenant promise (cf. also 8:1-3), but may also have in mind the three matriarchs who struggled with sterility.[533] He then returns to Isaac and Sarah, reporting God's words:

> And I gave him Isaac formed him in the womb of her who gave birth to him and commanded her to restore him quickly and to give him back to me (restituens eum redderet mihi) in the seventh month. And therefore every woman who gives birth in the seventh month, her son will live, because upon him I have brought my glory and revealed the new age. (23:8)

Again we see the special emphasis given to women and women's issues. The tradition that Isaac was born in the seventh month is known from later rabbinic tradition (b. Rosh ha-Sh. 11a).[534] Restituens eum redderet mihi ("to give him back to me") is best taken as reference to birth,[535] but is unusual.

Kenaz and the Confessions

After the death of Joshua we read of the Philistine threat and divine guidance under the newly chosen leader Kenaz to use lots to identify those who are defiled and who must be excluded from battle, and are to be burned (25:1, 3, 6). Nothing initially indicates the nature of the defilement, "the deeds that they have done with cunning" (25:6). They are given hope that in the resurrection they will receive mercy (their death atones for them is the assumption) (25:7). Only then do we have an account of what constitutes the defilement. Each tribe confesses before Kenaz its sins. These may be taken, in turn, as an indication of LAB chief concerns.[536] Most confessions are about idolatry, but also include testing the holiness of the tent of meeting (Levi), neglect of the sabbath (Manasseh), cannibalism (Zebulun), making sons and daughters pass through fire (Ephraim), questioning the Law of Moses (Benjamin), but Gad declares: "We have committed

---

[532] Jacobson, Commentary, notes that the link between goats and women giving birth may derive from Cant 4:1-2, which speaks of goats bearing twins and not losing offspring (719).

[533] So Jacobson, Commentary, 719.

[534] On children born in the seventh month, see Feldman, "Prolegomenon," cx; Pieter van der Horst, "Seven Months' Children in Jewish and Christian Literature from Antiquity," ETL 54 (1978) 346-60, 357-58; Jacobson, Commentary, 721.

[535] On whether it might also allude to the binding of Isaac in the seventh month of the year, see Jacobson, Commentary, 720.

[536] On the confessions see Michael Tilly, "Die Sünden Israels und der Heiden: Beobachtungen zu L.A.B. 25:9-13," JSJ 37 (2006) 192-211, 197-200.

adultery with each other's wives" (25:10) (recalling its prominent position as the first designated sin in 2:8).[537]

The Sacred Stones and Paradise

The men of Asher confess to worshipping Amorite idols called the sacred nymphs, probably virgin goddesses of the Canaanite cult,[538] and decorated with seven sacred stones which emit light, to hiding them with their stones, defiled by the idols, under Shechem (an anti-Samaritan reference) (25:10).[539] The seven sacred stones are then found and God has angels cast them into the depths of the sea and twelve new stones from the same source (26:4) implanted in the high priest's breastplate (25:10-12; 26:5-15; referred to already in 11:15; 13:1). The fact that these stones will be light rather than sun and moon (26:13; cf. also 25:12) matches the image of paradise as a place of timelessness and eternal light without stars, sun and moon in 19:12-13. The sacred stones, both the original seven and the twelve, described as brought from the land of Havilah, appear to derive from the garden of Eden, paradise, as a source of holy things and so probably a holy place, recalling its designation as a "place of sanctification" (19:13). Jacobson notes that Ezek 28:13 implies that there were sacred stones in paradise.[540] All the sinners then face death by fire (26:1-5). The accounts of their sins are also burned with fire after they have been blotted out by "dew from the ice of paradise" (26:8), another reference indicating belief in a paradise located above in the heavenly world. The references to paradise, like those in 19:10-13, assume a heavenly paradise understood as a temple, and so an age to come within that temple and so without sexual relations.

In his dying vision (28:6-9) Kenaz addresses the theme of resurrection, speaking of the generation of two foundations, one solid and one of foam, depicting human beings as coming from a place of invisible light, apparently some through sin failing and others apparently finding a place in the upper foundation. Nothing in the vision allows us to see the nature of that resurrection, but it assumes a transformed embodiedness and probably another reference to paradise as the place of those raised from the dead.

---

[537] Tilly, "Sünden Israels," suggests that the meaning is not only literal, but also metaphorical (199), but this does not seem necessary given the literal meaning in 2:8.

[538] So Jacobson, *Commentary*, 751.

[539] So Tilly, "Sünden Israels," 208.

[540] Jacobson, *Commentary*, 754.

Deborah and Jael

In 29:2 we read that Kenaz had only three daughters, no sons, but in view of his achievements his successor Zebul gave each an inheritance and arranged husbands for them.[541] After Zebul leadership failed and, according to *LAB*, as a consequence the people "*were led astray after the daughters* of the Amorites and served their gods" (30:1). This reflects again (cf. 18:13) the situation of Num 25:1-2 ("the people began to have sexual relations with the women of Moab. These invited the people to the sacrifices of their gods, and the people ate and bowed down to their god"), which goes on to report Phinehas' execution of a man who brought a Midianite woman into his family (Num 25:6-8). There is also an intertextual allusion to Judg 3:6 which reports: "they took their daughters as wives for themselves, and their own daughters they gave to their sons; and they worshiped their god". Here, too, in 30:1, intermarriage leads to idolatry, a connection which, as we noted, was not expressed in 18:13-14, which also draws on Numbers 25.

God's angry response expresses itself in rousing Israel's enemies against them and having "a woman rule over them and enlighten them for forty years" (30:2), apparently seen negatively as punishment,[542] though without calling into question either the rule or the enlightenment. The assumption is that it was humiliating for men. As a consequence, as Brown notes, *LAB* significantly enhances Deborah's status. This includes the innovation of having an angel announce her, attributing ruling and teaching roles to her and associating her with Moses who also led Israel for forty years.[543]

In the face of defeat and humiliation by Hazor and his general, Sisera, the people finally turn to God with fasting and God sends them Deborah, who, like Judith (8:9-27) confronts them with what God has done, who gave them the Law, sent them prophets, did wonders, gave them leaders, and comforts them with God's covenant faithfulness and the promise of more wonders (30:5-7). In 30:4-5 *LAB* adds that she was sent on the seventh day, portrays her as like a shepherdess, and in 30:7 has her echo Moses' words of warning about corruption when she is gone (cf. Deut 31:29), suggesting she is like a female Moses.[544] She enlists Barak to attack Sisera assuring him that the stars and lightning support his cause (31:1a). The author then cites Sisera's arrogant intentions, to attack Israel with a mighty

---

[541] Brown, *No Longer Be Silent*, notes that the author appears to have built this episode on the basis of Moses' ruling about Zelopehad's daughters in Numbers 36 (41).

[542] Jacobson, *Commentary*, 250.

[543] Brown, *No Longer Be Silent*, 43-45. See also Pieter W. van der Horst, "Deborah and Seila in Ps-Philo's Liber Antiquitatum Biblicarum," in *Messiah and Christos: Studies in the Jewish Origins of Christianity Presented to David Flusser* (ed. I. Gruenwald, S. Shaked, and G. Stroumsa; Tübingen: Mohr Siebeck, 1992) 111-17, 111.

[544] Brown, *No Longer Be Silent*, 48-49.

arm, to divide the spoils among his men, and to take the beautiful women as concubines (31:1b), an allusion, as Jacobson notes, to Judg 5:30 ("Are they not finding and dividing the spoil? – A girl or two for every man").[545] *LAB* then has Deborah cite divine reversal: "And on account of this the Lord said about him that the arm of a weak woman would attack him and maidens would take his spoils and even he would fall *into the hands of a woman*" (31:1c; whose fulfilment is noted in 31:9).[546]

Thus the author highlights the issue of abuse of women far beyond what is implied in the biblical text. Sisera sees Jael who, in the author's elaboration, probably under the influence of Judith (see Jdt 12:15; cf. also 10:3 Vg), had deliberately adorned herself, making herself "beautiful in appearance" (31:3), responds to her invitation and decides that once rescued he wants to go to his mother and have her as his wife (31:3).[547] On Sisera's need to go to his mother, Jacobson doubts it means seeking her approval, suggesting it refers to her need to prepare a wedding or perhaps just to his returning home.[548] Sisera's mother, Themech (significantly the same name as Cain's wife), does indeed have some prominence, since she speaks of his wanting to make Hebrew daughters into concubines (31:8), typical of the fate of women captives of war.[549] His shame is that he is overcome by "the arm of a weak woman" and falls "*into the hands of a woman*" (31:1, 7). Jael taunts him to tell that to his father (31:7). Consistent with his emphases elsewhere, the author has concentrated in particular on the role of women, both as potential victims of war, but also in leadership and heroic acts, much more than in the biblical account and partly inspired by the story of Judith. Unlike in Judges, Jael is not instructed by Sisera, but instructs him.[550] Now in *LAB*, like Judith (13:4-5), Jael prays, indeed twice, before performing her execution (31:5, 7).[551] The story of her killing Sisera is retold but without the sexual symbolism.[552]

---

[545] Jacobson, *Commentary*, 844.

[546] On the role of reciprocal punishment see Brown, *No Longer Be Silent*, 51; Rhonda Burnette-Bletsch, "At the Hands of a Woman: Rewriting Jael in Pseudo-Philo," *JSP* 17 (1998) 53-64, 56, 60.

[547] On the allusions to Judith see Brown, *No Longer Be Silent*, 50, 53; Burnette-Bletsch, "At the Hands of a Woman," 59.

[548] Jacobson, *Commentary*, 849.

[549] Burnette-Bletsch, "At the Hands of a Woman," notes *LAB*'s typical depiction of a woman faced with spoils and sexual vulnerabilities of war, though not to evoke sympathy (63).

[550] So Burnette-Bletsch, "At the Hands of a Woman," 60.

[551] So Burnette-Bletsch, "At the Hands of a Woman," 61.

[552] Brown, *No Longer Be Silent*, notes that *LAB* does not allow us to imagine that he fell between her legs, as Judg 5:27 (55).

Deborah, Barak and the people then sing a hymn, again reminiscent of the song of Moses.[553] It amounts to an extensive speech. It includes reference to *LAB*'s account of Babel and Abraham's deliverance from the fire and also to the sterility of Rebecca, though, as elsewhere in *LAB*, unnamed:

> And he gave Isaac two sons, both also from a womb that was closed up. And their mother was then in the third year of her marriage; and it will not happen in this way to any woman, nor will any female so boast. But when her husband approached (*appropinquans*) her in the third year, to him there were born two sons, Jacob and Esau. (32:5)

Again we note the interest in women's issues,[554] including an aetiological concern. Approached (*appropinquans*) clearly refers to sexual intercourse. The author's perspective reflects the values of his time is depicting the birth as for Isaac, not for Isaac and Rebecca.

It also reports the activity of stars acting on Israel's behalf (32:11, 14, 15 cf. also 31:2; 32:13). It then addresses the earth: "Not unjustly did God take from you the rib of the first-formed, knowing that from his rib Israel would be born" (32:15). This allusion to the creation story focuses in particular on women's role in giving birth to future generations.[555] The author then depicts Deborah in a final address drawing attention to her being a woman: "Behold I am warning you as a woman of God (cf. "man of God" in Deut 33:1) and am enlightening you as one of the female race; and obey me like your mother and heed my words as people who will also die" (33:1). While having roots in the biblical story, this assertion of Deborah's womanhood goes far beyond the biblical text. Deborah's speech mentions the desire to sin as ceasing in hell (33:3), not in order to raise hope, but rather as a warning that no repentance is possible after death, nor indeed its opposite. Her final words hold out the promise to the obedient that in future will be like the stars in heaven (33:5), an astral image of future life attested already in Dan 12:2-3 (cf. also *1 Enoch* 104:2-6; 1QS/1Q28 5.8; 4Q184 1.7-8). Finally a dirge praises her as "a *mother from Israel*" (33:6; cf. Judg 5:7, "you arose, Deborah, arose as a mother in Israel"), but goes beyond it in designating her as "the holy

---

[553] Brown, *No Longer Be Silent*, 56.

[554] On the problem posed by having Rebecca conceive in her third year, mentioned twice here, whereas Gen 25:20, 26, implies that it must have been after twenty years, including for suggested emendations, see Jacobson, *Commentary*, 871-73.

[555] Noting the awkwardness of having the rib taken from the earth, Jacobson, *Commentary*, proposes that behind the Latin is Greek which had the first formed man taken from the earth (892). Descamp, *Metaphor and Ideology*, notes that the passage may be in reaction to belief that women are a cause of sin. Their reproductive capacity warrants their existence (334-35).

one", and as having "firmed up the fence about her generation" and she is mourned not the usual thirty but a full seventy days, like Jacob (Gen 50:3).[556]

Aod and Gideon

In 34:1-5 *LAB* adds to the story of Judges an account of a magician called Aod from Midian who challenged Israel's adherence to the Law, offering them an alternative and promising to show them the sun by night. The account reports that angels had taught magic before they were condemned, but that since their judgement they have no power. This recalls the Watcher myth. The author depicts a cult sacrificing to these angels and a magician gaining the power of magic by doing so. Nothing links these to issues of intermarriage nor to sexual wrongdoing as in the myth of the Watchers. Nor is the link with the Midianites here depicted as happening through intermarriage. Its effects for Israel are that they are shown falling again into slavery. Gideon is then summoned to rescue Israel as in Judges, but he sins by taking gold from the booty of the defeated Midianites and making idols (as in Judg 8:24-27). As in Judg 8:31 *LAB* reports the birth to Gideon of a son, Abimelech, by a concubine (37:1), whose reign is cut short when a woman throws a millstone on him (37:5; as Judg 9:53).

Jephthah and Seila

LAB then offers an account of Jephthah and his virgin daughter, Seila.[557] In introducing Jephthah it mentions his being sent away by his brothers, but not because he was the son of a prostitute (cf. Judg 11:1). Jephthah, summoned to help the people of Israel, becomes the preacher urging obedience to the Law (39:6). This has the desired effect: the people then turn to God. God, in turn, strengthens Jephthah for his task (39:7-8). In *LAB* God is reported as immediately disapproving of Jephthah's fateful vow on the grounds that it could easily have led

---

[556] Brown, *No Longer Be Silent*, 69-70. See also van der Horst, "Deborah and Seila," 113-14, who notes that declaring her "a holy one in the house of Israel" (33:6) "has no parallel in any other ancient Jewish writing" (114).

[557] On the transformation of the story in its retelling by *LAB* see Cynthia Baker, "Pseudo-Philo and the Transformation of Jephthah's Daughter," in *Anti-Covenant: Counter-Reading Women's Lives in the Hebrew Bible* (ed. Mieke Bal; Bible and Literature Series 22; Sheffield: Almond, 1989) 175–209. She notes that *LAB* "dissipates the horror and perplexity" of the story by obscuring character interaction and "creating an aura of 'individual destiny' and 'honor' around the victim" (196). Thus *LAB* omits reference to the Spirit of the Lord coming upon Jephthah (cf. Judg 11:29) (196). "Questions of culpability and victimization are dulled by the author's use of impersonal constructions which blur the interaction between characters" (198). Seila is not a victim but makes a noble choice (199).

to him sacrificing a dog. In his anger God resolves to make Jephthah sacrifice his daughter (39:11).[558] Thus *LAB* removes the element of chance that Jephthah's daughter happens to be the first whom he sees and puts God in control, who deliberately targets Jephthah's daughter as a means of punishing Jephthah. Instead of just his daughter meeting him after his defeat of the Ammonites (Judg 11:34), others also dance to greet the victor, but his daughter comes out as the first of them (40:1).

LAB then has him reflect on her name, Seila, probably meaning "she who was demanded" (40:1).[559] It then greatly elaborates Seila's response, whose compliance is now expressed as analogous to the sacrifice of Isaac[560] and in terms of wanting to ensure that the father's vow will be seen by God as properly fulfilled by her being willing. As in Judges, she seeks only to go away into the mountains with her virgin companions to lament with them not for herself, but for her father (40:3; cf. Judg 11:37 "to bewail her virginity"). *LAB* adds that the wise were not able to respond to her report, but that God thought about her in the night and declared that he had stopped the wise from saying anything. God adds that she was wiser than her father and wiser than the wise, that her death would be precious to him and that she was about to "fall into the bosom of her mothers" (40:4).[561]

The author then provides an account of Seila's alleged lament. In it she affirms her willingness to die, acknowledging that "a father did not refuse (*expugnet*) the daughter whom he has sworn to sacrifice, that a ruler granted (*audiat*) that his only daughter be promised for sacrifice" (40:5)[562] and then declares:

> But I have not made good on [lit. I have not been satisfied, given the satisfaction of] my marriage chamber, and I have not retrieved [lit. I have not been filled with] my wedding garlands. For I have not been clothed in splendour while sitting in my woman's chamber, and I have not used the sweet-smelling ointment. And my soul has not rejoiced in the oil of anointing that has been prepared for me. O Mother, in vain have you borne your only daughter, and Sheol has become my bridal chamber. And may all the blend of oil that you have prepared for me be poured out, and the white

---

[558] Brown, *No Longer Be Silent*, 97. Descamp, "Why Are These Women Here?" notes that in *LAB* "Jephthah is transformed from a tragic hero into a fool" (70).

[559] Brown, *No Longer Be Silent*, suggests "she who was dedicated, or offered" (101).

[560] Van der Horst, "Deborah and Seila," describes it as "a second *aqedah*, completely on a par with the first" (115). Similarly Brown, *No Longer Be Silent*, 97-99, 102. See also the extensive discussion in Fisk, *Do You Not Remember?* 249-63.

[561] Van der Horst, "Deborah and Seila," notes this unique expression, "bosom of the mothers" (115).

[562] Baker, "Pseudo-Philo," disputes this translation arguing that *expugnet* is better translated "overrule" or "fight against" and *audiat*, "hear", giving stronger indication of Seila's volition (204-205).

robe that my mother has woven, the moth will eat it. And the crown of flowers that my nurse plaited for me for the festival, may it wither up; and the coverlet that she wove of hyacinth and purple in my woman's chamber, may the worm devour it. (40:6)

This passage, unique in *LAB*, for its passionate depiction, has long been recognised as standing under the influence of Greek lamentation traditions, recalling Sophocles' *Antigone* and Euripides' *Iphegeneia*, as well as language of epitaphs depicting the netherworld as a bridal chamber.[563] The detail reflects elements which hearers would have recognised as belonging to wedding rituals.[564] These include the bridal chamber where the bride awaits the new husband on the wedding night, in which her mother has prepared her with perfumed oils and with a white dress (see also Tob 7:15). The garland and crown of flowers will have been worn in the celebrations. The coverlet appears to relate to decoration within the bridal chamber. Deborah's lament assumes that getting married is the main hope of young women to which they can look forward, reflecting at least the view of the author but also most likely that of his contemporary hearers, male and female.

The account in *LAB* concludes as in Judges with the report that the mourning of Jephthah's daughter became the basis for four days of mourning every year, which *LAB* sets on the fourteenth of the month.[565] Brown speculates that *LAB* is using the story metaphorically to convey the message that God also willed the destruction of Jerusalem: "It appears that Pseudo-Philo, by introducing specific

---

[563] See van der Horst, "Deborah and Seila," 116, who refers to the detailed studies of M. Alexiou and P. Dronke, "The Lament of Jephtha's Daughter: Themes, Traditions, Originality," *Studi medievali* ser. 3, 12 (1971) 825-51; Ida Fröhlich, "Historiographie et Aggada dans le Liber Antiquitatum Biblicarum du Pseudo-Philon," *Acta Antiqua Academiae Scientarum Hungaricae* 28 (1980) 353-409, 394-401.

[564] On the chiastic structure of the lament, centred on her address to her mother, see Baker, "Pseudo-Philo," 200. In relation to the wedding imagery within this she notes that "each item, introduced negatively and abstractly in the first half, becomes, in the second, the work of a woman with whom Seila shares an intimate bond" (201). The portrait of the daughter's intimate connection to her mother (absent in Judges) contrasts with the realm of the father which is impersonal and traditionally threatening (202). "Thus Seila's lament embodies both a sense of the ideological and social constraints that the Judges fabula presumes, namely the immutability of vows, the immanence of God, and the power of a father – divine or otherwise – over the life of his child. At the same time, Seila's volition, her autonomy and the appeal to her mother in the lament are a response to that ideology within those constraints" (202).

[565] Howard Jacobson, "The *Liber Antiquitatum Biblicarum* and Tammuz," *JSP* 8 (1991) 63-65, noting that 40:8 indicates a four day lament commencing on the fourteenth of the month, suggests that the author may have depicted the mourning to have it coincide with the day of mourning for Tammuz, which occurred on the seventeenth of Tammuz, perhaps to indicate that that festival is only commemoration of a human death.

motifs and imagery applied elsewhere to the destruction of Jerusalem and the Temple, presents Seila's death as in part a symbol for what the Jewish people had suffered in their recent past",[566] a sacrifice "decreed by God, yet ultimately for the good of the Jewish people".[567] The problem with this speculation is that unlike the parallel texts she cites we find here no specific connection linking Seila and Jerusalem.

Eluma and Manoah

In 42:1-10 we read of Manoah and Eluma, his wife (cf. Judg 13:1-23). The author elaborates the story by reporting that in response to her infertility Manoah kept saying to her every day, that she should let him go (*nunc dimitte me*; "let me go") and take another wife lest, he says, "I die without fruit" (42:1). The word *dimitte* can indicate divorce, so that Manoah could be asking that she divorce him. The text would then provide evidence for women being able to divorce men. It would then seem strange that he would not, himself, initiate divorce. It is more likely that *dimitte* means "allow" and that Manoah is asking for Eluma's agreement that he take another wife, thus reflecting polygyny (also in 50:1) and for which Gen 16:1-3 provides some precedent (though there the maid Hagar becomes a surrogate not a wife).[568] The dispute also reflects the importance of bearing children. The latter was important both for passing on inheritance and for having a younger generation to care for the older one.

The account depicts conflict between the two, with Eluma blaming Manoah for being impotent ("Not me has the Lord shut up that I may not bear children, but you that I may not bear fruit" (42:1). Finally Eluma takes the initiative of going to the upper chamber (*solarium*) to pray (cf. Jdt 9:5), seeking an answer from God. Her question identifies the issue: are people infertile because they have sinned or because God has simply ordained it? (42:2). This is more than a tale. It probably tells a story that was existential for couples facing similar situations and coheres with the focus elsewhere in *LAB* on issues concerning women, especially those faced with the prospect of having another wife join them. In reply God owns up to being responsible ("you are the womb that is forbidden so as not to bear fruit")[569] and here the author returns to the account in Judg 13:3, having the angel announce that she will conceive and bear Samson (42:3). This is a further intertextual echo with the story of Hagar, where an angel announces the birth of Ishmael (Gen 16:11). *LAB* then has the angel require that she impose a regime on her child in

---

[566] Brown, *No Longer Be Silent*, 115.

[567] Brown, *No Longer Be Silent*, 117.

[568] So Jacobson, *Commentary*, 980.

[569] Describing women as a womb finds parallels in *4QInstruction* which speaks of a man's womb, meaning his wife (4QInstr^a/4Q415 9; cf. also 4QInstr^g/4Q423 3a).

view of his future role (42:3; cf. Judg 13:4, 7, 14, where this requirement is imposed on her).

The author then continues his elaboration, having Eluma return to Manoah and apologise for blaming him, and then, as in Judg 13:6, announce the promise of conception and birth of a son (42:4). Having a son would have been deemed more important than having a daughter. In Judges the focus is much more on the impressiveness of the angel and his not giving his name (13:17-23). Unlike in Judges, the author depicts Manoah's disbelief and sadness and only then has him resort to prayer (42:5). As in Judges, the answer from God through an angel comes not to him but to his wife, giving her particular prominence (42:6). She calls him and he goes out to her to be met by the angel who in the author's elaboration instructs him to have sexual intercourse: "Go into your wife (*ingredere ad mulierem tuam*) and do all these things" (42:7). Manoah says, "I am going", but first seeks reassurance. The rest of the story deals with Manoah's sacrifice and the angel's return, with slight modifications from Judges, including a first reference to the angel's name, which is given as Fadahel, which may mean "my name is a mystery",[570] fitting for the way it features in the story. The author's elaborations still serve to prepare for Samson, but give far more attention to issues of fertility and infertility, depicting them as a source of marital conflict including where polygyny is one solution.

Samson

In 43:1-2 *LAB* reports briefly that Samson marries a Philistine wife whom the Philistines then burn. It omits the report in Judges of the exchange with his parents who preferred that he marry someone of his own family and not someone from among the uncircumcised and the narrator's assurance there that they were unaware that this was God's plan (Judg 14:1-4). This is surprising given *LAB*'s clear disapproval of such marriages, but it will make the point about intermarriage in relation to Delilah (43:5). *LAB*'s abridgement also passes over Samson's finding a new wife (Judg 14:5-10), and his visiting a prostitute in Gaza (Judg 16:1), but picks up his relation with Delilah (Judg 16:4), whom by conflation with the woman of Gaza it describes as a prostitute (43:5; similarly Josephus *A.J.* 5.306),[571] adding

> he was led astray after her and took her to himself for a wife. And God said, "Behold now Samson has been led astray through his eyes and he has not remembered the

---

[570] On this see Jacobson, *Commentary*, 992-93.

[571] So Jacobson, *Commentary*, 997. Murphy, *Pseudo-Philo*, notes that by conflating the prostitute of Judg 16:1 with Delilah (Judg 16:4-22) *LAB* produces the contrast between Samson's beginning as good and his downfall, attributing it to this relationship (172).

mighty works that I did with him; and he has mingled with the daughters of the Philistines and has not paid attention to Joseph my servant who was in a foreign land and became a crown for his brothers because he was not willing to afflict (*contristare*) his own seed … And now Samson's lust (*concupiscentia*) will be a stumbling block for him, and his mingling (*commixtio*)[572] a ruin". (43:5)

We note the motif of sexual wrongdoing arising through the eyes (how men respond to women's sexual attractiveness)[573] and the reference to Samson's lust as becoming his stumbling block. The comment about intermarriage makes up for its omission earlier. The example of Joseph is somewhat problematic because Joseph married the Egyptian Aseneth, but *LAB* never reports that and the focus here is on his resisting the sexual advances of Potiphar's wife. In then writing that thereby he did not afflict his own seed, the author provides a genealogical ground for rejecting intermarriage.[574]

Micah

In its account of Micah (*Michas filius Dedila*; probably: Micah son of Delilah)[575] and his idols (44:1-10; cf. Judg 17:1 – 18:31) *LAB* adds that people wanting a wife would ask about it through the idol shaped in the image of a dove (44:5),[576] but, more significantly, has God despairing of Israel's disobedience. God's statement alludes to the Decalogue as something which Israel accepted but then refused to obey, including the words:

> I commanded them not to commit adultery (*ne mecharent*), and they did not oppose this. And I ordered them not to speak false testimony and not to covet (*ne concupiscerent*) each one his neighbor's wife or his house or all his possessions. (44:6)

> And though I commanded them not to commit adultery, they committed adultery with their zeal. And whereas they chose not to speak false testimony, they accepted false

---

[572] Jacobson, *Commentary*, notes: "by the second or third century this noun is used of sexual relations" (999).

[573] Halpern-Amaru, "Women in Pseudo-Philo," "a matter of lust not love" (100).

[574] Cf. Jacobson, *Commentary*, who sees it referring to depression among Samson's descendants (999). He notes that Lev 21:15 speaks of a priest profaning his seed, but that the verb here does not suggest defilement.

[575] So Jacobson, *Commentary*, 1003.

[576] On the association of the dove and marriage see Jacobson, *Commentary*, who notes rabbinic praise for doves as forming faithful pairs, and the role of doves in the cult of Aphrodite (1008).

testimony from those whom they destroyed. And they lusted for foreign women (*concupierunt mulierea alienas*). (44:7)[577]

Here the prohibition of adultery is listed in the order in which it appears in Deut 5:17-21, in contrast to 11:10-13, where it matches the order found in Exod 20:14-17 LXX.[578] Also in contrast to 11:10-13 we see not only the prohibition, but also the issue of intermarriage, which *LAB* connects with the prohibition of coveting. In Deuteronomy 5 coveting one's neighbour's wife is listed separately from coveting his house and other chattels (5:21; but also in Exod 20:17 LXX). This eases the possibility of interpreting the prohibition as referring not only to wanting to possess but as desiring, thus in a sexual sense, reflected then in the Greek translation of חמד ("want to possess") by ἐπιθυμέω. Perhaps *LAB* was influenced by the second verb used in relation to coveting house and chattels, namely אוה, which has a stronger sense of having a craving for.[579] *LAB* then applies the prohibition of coveting one's neighbour's wife in a directly sexual sense (found also in Matt 5:28), but gives it an application not present in the Decalogue, namely, as prohibition against lusting after foreign women. *LAB* returns a third time to adultery and coveting in 44:10.

And if anyone wishes to covet the wife of his neighbor (*concupiscere rem proximi sui*),[580] I will command death and it will deny them the fruit of their womb. (44:10)

The text may have read *uxorem* ("wife"), as Harrington conjectures and so translates, but even the attested *rem* ("thing, possession") may be assumed to include an allusion one's neighbour's wife. Here the focus is adultery, a key theme already in 2:8 and 25:10. At the same time, the exposition has also focussed on the theme of intermarriage, here in the wider context seen not as something leading to idolatry, but as something apparently resulting from it .[581]

The Rape at Nob

In retelling the gruesome story of the rape of the concubine in Gibeah (45:1-6; cf. Judg 19:1-30) *LAB* relocates it to the city of Nob (45:1). In its much truncated

---

[577] Halpern-Amaru, "Women in Pseudo-Philo," notes that this sin "has nothing to do with the story of Dedila, but one which is quite pertinent to the story of Delilah" (99) and they were probably "joined in the author's imagination" (99-100 n. 52).

[578] On this see Loader, *Septuagint*, 5-8.

[579] On the use of the different verbs and their translation, see Loader, *Septuagint*, 8-11.

[580] Harrington, *OTP*, 2.359. See also Jacobson, *Commentary*, 1025.

[581] On this development of the Micah story see Feldman, "Josephus' Jewish Antiquities and Pseudo-Philo's Biblical Antiquities," 75.

account, it has not an old man like Judges, but another Levite called Bethac offer hospitality to his fellow tribesman, whom it names, Beel, and to his concubine. In material unparalleled in Judges, *LAB* has Bethac forewarn him of the wickedness of those who lived in the city, expressing the hope that: "the Lord will shut up their heart before us as he shut up the Sodomites before Lot" (45:2). *LAB* thus made the connection between what it was about to relate and the threat to Lot's angelic visitors in Sodom, the common aspect being forced sexual violation (Gen 19:10-11). There is no explicit reference here, as in Judg 19:22, to intended male rape, though it was probably implied (45:3).[582] The author appears also to have made a connection between this event and the massacre of the priests of Nob reported in 1 Samuel 22, soon to be related (47:10; 63:2).[583]

Regev disputes a link between the two episodes and so the explanation of the massacre as punishment for what would have been a much earlier sin.[584] Rather he sees the massacre as intended to show punishment of non-Zadokite priests for cultic misdeeds, perhaps under the influence of disputes over priesthood in the author's time. He sees the relocation of the rape of the concubine, on the other hand, as resulting from the confusion of two geographically similar adjacent sites, perhaps aided by a reading of גבעה not as a name "Gibeah", but as a description, "hill". In discussing the massacre he draws attention to the polemic in CD 3.18 – 4.12, in which the author sees his own as true successors of Zadokite priesthood in conflict with opponents depicted as belonging to the house of Eli.[585] For the *Damascus Document*, however, sexual wrongdoing plays a major role in that conflict,[586] so that it is thinkable that the sexual abuse now attributed apparently to the priestly population of Nob also reflects *LAB*'s espousal of similar allegations.

The author's account of what happens omits reference to the host's daughter (cf. Judg 19:24), has the assailants respond to Bethac's pleading by declaring, "It has never happened that the strangers gave orders to the natives" (45:3) and then continues:

---

[582] Cf. Innocent Himbaza, "Israël et les nations dans les relectures de Juges 19,22-25: débats sur l'homosexualité," *BibNot* 131 (2006) 5-16, who argues that the author has eliminated the homosexual focus (7).

[583] So Jacobson, *Commentary*, 1027-28. See also Feldman, *Remember Amalek!* 186. Murphy, *Pseudo-Philo*, notes that rejection of hospitality in two Benjaminite cities doubles the negative light shed on the tribe (177).

[584] Eyal Regev, "The Two Sins of Nob: Biblical Interpretation, an Anti-priestly Polemic and a Geographical Error in *Liber Antiquitatum Biblicarum*," *JSP* 12 (2001) 85-104, 100.

[585] Regev, "Two Sins of Nob," 97.

[586] See Loader, *Dead Sea Scrolls on Sexuality,* 97-107.

They entered by force and *dragged* him and *his concubine out, and they cast him off.* And when the man had been let go, *they abused* his concubine until she died, because she had transgressed against her man (*trangressa fuerat virum suum*)[587] once when she committed sin with the Amalekites, and on account of this the Lord God delivered her into the hands of sinners. (45:3-4)

Beel goes out, finds her dead, cuts her up and sends the pieces to the twelve tribes urging war against Nob (45:4; Judg 19:29-30). The retelling changes the original, however, so that the concubine is declared to have deserved the atrocity "because she had transgressed against her man once when she committed sin with the Amalekites" (45:3).[588] The author is thereby interpreting Judg 19:2 as indicating infidelity, which it need not mean.[589] It certainly says nothing of Amalekites, so that this is to be seen as another instance of *LAB* introducing the theme of sexual relations with foreigners. It also coheres with its apparent concern to explain events as meaningful and deserving, rather than random, to preserve its notion of God being in control (but at great moral cost!).

Whereas Judges reports Israel's success against the Benjaminites after two initial failures (Judg 20:1-20), the author has God refuse to support Israel because it had not suppressed Micah and his idols (45:6) and has God deliberately mislead them through Umim and Thummim to expect success (46:1). Phinehas, appealing to his former zeal in punishing evildoers, an allusion to Num 25:6-18, where he slew the one engaging in sexual relations with a Midianite woman, challenges God to reveal the truth (47:1). In reply God speaks in a parable about senseless slaughter and reprimands Israel both for neglecting to deal with Micah and his idols and for their overreaction about the concubine:

And now on seeing how this man's concubine, who had done wicked deeds, died, you were all disturbed and came to me saying, "Will you deliver the sons of Benjamin into our hands?" Therefore I have deceived you. (47:8)

The author appears to be wanting to make a point about unnecessary conflict within Israel and about idolatry and does so at the expense of dismissing the significance of the concubine's violation as something deserved and so less offensive. Only then does God relent and Israel is victorious. This implies that the wickedness being punished is not what happened to the woman, but the failure of the city to provide hospitality to strangers.

---

[587] Jacobson, *Commentary*, notes as parallel Sir 23:18, which speaks of a man transgressing against his bed: παραβαίνων ἀπὸ τῆς κλίνης αὐτοῦ (1034).

[588] On this see Feldman, *Remember Amalek!* 23.

[589] See the discussion in Jacobson, *Commentary*, 1033-34.

The sons of Benjamin who had been devastated in the final battle are told by the sons of Israel: "Go up and get wives for yourselves, *because we cannot give you our daughters. For we made a vow* in the time of our anger" (48:3; cf. Judg 21:17-18), but omits the proposed strategy of abducting dancing girls from the Shiloh vineyards (Judg 21:23). It may be that the author disapproved, but including the exhortation underlines the importance of marriage for survival of the tribe.

Hannah and Elkanah

In 49:1-8 the author moves towards the material of 1 Samuel, with the legend of casting lots to find a leader and the reluctance of Elkanah upon whom the lot fell to assume control. The people appeal to God's promise to multiply their seed (49:6; cf. Gen 16:10) and God promises that Elkanah's son by his sterile wife will be leader (49:8). The author has God allude to Isaac: "I will love him as I loved Isaac" (49:8), probably also with allusion to Sarah and Rachel's sterility and the taunts they faced. For the other wife, Penninah, who has borne Elkanah ten sons, ridicules the sterile Hannah daily:

> What does it profit you that Elkanah your husband loves you, for you are a *dry tree*? I know that my husband will love me, because he delights in the sight of my sons standing around him like a plantation of live trees. (50:1; echoing Isa 56:3; Ps 128:3 LXX; 144:12)

> A wife is not really loved even if her husband loves her or her beauty. *Let* Hannah *not boast in her* appearance; *but she who boasts, let her boast* when she sees her offspring before her. And when the fruit of her womb is not so, love will be in vain. For what did it profit Rachel that Jacob loved her? And unless the fruit of the womb had been given to him, his love would have been in vain. (50:2)

This takes us into the world of polygynous marriage, perhaps the experience of some of the author's hearers. It also serves in the story to enhance the dramatic effect of the reversal of Hannah's fortune. The focus is not non-procreative sex as something wrong in itself, but the stigma of sterility on the basis of the claim that husbands want offspring. The author also reinforces for the hearer the fact that Hannah's sterility is not on account of sin, portraying her as "fearing God from her youth" (50:2). We then have an account of Hannah's prayer which includes further reflection on wives and reproduction: "I know that neither she who has many sons is rich nor she who has few is poor, but whoever abounds in the will of God is rich" (50:5; similarly Sir 16:1-4).[590] Eli reassures Hannah that he knows what she was praying about in silence and that her prayer is heard, though not adding the rest of his information, namely about the prophet whom she would bear (50:7-8). Only when Samuel has been born and reached two years of age does Eli declare that not only her prayers but those of the people have been answered in this child: "And through this boy your womb has been justified so that you might provide advantage for the peoples and set up the milk of your breasts as a fountain for the twelve tribes" (51:2).[591]

The imagery of breasts continues in Hannah's acclamation:[592]

> Drip, my breasts, and tell your testimonies, because you have been commanded to give milk. For he who is milked from you will be raised up, and the people will be enlightened by his words, and he will show to the nations the statutes, and his *horn will be exalted* very high. (51:3)

She is both the one to announce Samuel who will be a prophet, bear wisdom and be a light for the nation (51:6), but is herself, like Moses (20:2), bearer of that wisdom, represented in the image of milk.[593]

Philistines, Saul and David

The account of the sins of Eli's sons, as in 1 Samuel, makes no mention of sexual sins (52:1-4), nor do sexual issues feature in the account of the Philistines' capture of the ark (54:1-5). The Philistines complain that the ark causes death to the pregnant and nursing mothers and babies (55:4, 6, 10).[594] The author follows 1 Samuel in reporting Saul's failure to carry out instructions to destroy the

---

[590] Brown, *No Longer Be Silent*, notes as a parallel Wis 4:1 and its context, 3:13-14, which links the image of the barren woman with the eunuch, with echoes of Isa 56:3, 5, suggesting that it "may provide a link between the passages in Isaiah and *Biblical Antiquities*" (147).

[591] Brown, *No Longer Be Silent*, suggests that Hannah functions here as an image of Wisdom (155-56), but as much as the imagery is used this way elsewhere, it is not clearly used like that here. I am not convinced that women's prominence in *LAB* has to do with the figure of Wisdom as Brown suggests (e.g. of Deborah, p. 54). See also the critique in Descamp, *Metaphor and Ideology*, 313, which she relates to seeing Seila as a cipher for Jerusalem.

[592] According to Halpern-Amaru, "Women in Pseudo-Philo," rewritten "to celebrate her maternity and role as God's wondrous instrument" (98).

[593] On this see Joan E. Cook, "Pseudo-Philo's Song of Hannah: Treatment of a Mother in Israel," *JSP* 9 (1991) 103-14, 106-107, 113.

[594] As Jacobson, *Commentary*, notes: "LAB's emphasis on pregnant women and nursing mothers is totally absent in the Bible" (1141).

Amalekites by letting Agag still live, adding also mention of his wife (58:2-3).[595]
This then makes possible the elaboration that God allows them to have sexual
intercourse together for one night before having him killed the next day and that
the offspring would then be the one to kill Saul (58:3-4).

The author provides words of a song alleged to have been sung by David
before Saul to drive off his demons (60:2-3). It addresses the demon "as one
created on the second day" (60:3; cf. *2 Enoch* 29:1), and connected with Tartarus
and chaos, but contains no sexual references. The document makes David and
Goliath cousins, the former addressing the latter in the words:

> Hear this word before you die. Were not the two women, from whom you and I were
> born, sisters? And your mother was Orpah, and my mother Ruth. And Orpah chose for
> herself the gods of the Philistines and went after them, but Ruth chose for herself ways
> of the Most Powerful and walked in them. (61:6)

This might reflect some attempt to come to terms with Philistine neighbours and
their successors, reflecting both distance and yet also some affinity.[596] Might the
author have also been aware that the sisters were Gentile and that in the case of
Ruth we have therefore an example of intermarriage with a Gentile?

In depicting David and Jonathan, the author has Jonathan declare that their
separation will be "like an infant who is taken away from the milk of its mother"
(62:10). He portrays the love between the two similarly. In depicting the witch of
Endor the author gives her the name, Sedecla, and makes her the daughter of the
Midianite diviner who led Israel astray with sorceries (64:3).

Conclusions

Sexual relations regularly feature in *LAB* within the context of relations among
human beings. This is so despite the omission of so much from its sources in
Genesis to 1 Samuel pertaining to sexuality. Such omissions are numerous: Ham's
seeing Noah naked; Lot and his daughters; Abram and Sarai with Pharaoh and
Abimelech; Isaac with the latter; Isaac's and then Jacob's finding a wife;
Rebecca's manoeuvres; Reuben's incest; including minor details such as Amram's
incestuous marriage; revelry around the golden calf; and Jephthah's expulsion as
son of a prostitute. Sometimes significant episodes are missing in their narrative
place, but are referred to in flashbacks, such as Sodom's sin; Judah and Tamar;
Joseph's chastity; and Phinehas' zealous deed. A striking omission is the account

---

[595] On this see Feldman, *Remember Amalek!* 24-26.

[596] The same connection is made in later rabbinic tradition. On this see Jacobson,
Commentary, 1184.

of creation and sin in Eden from the beginning of the work, though among flashbacks are allusions to: the formation of the man from the ground (16:5); the creation of Adam (26:6); the descent of human beings from the rib (32:15); the deception of Eve by the serpent and her persuasion of Adam to sin (13:8); sin in the garden (19:10); the seed's beginning (15:7); and, not least, the equation of Eden with paradise containing the tree of life (11:15) and seen by Noah and Moses (9:10-13) and source of special stones (25:10; 26:4).

Despite the omissions much remains which indicates that sexual relations are a normal part of human life. Specifically, Amram resolves to engage in sexual intercourse with his wife, Jochabed (9:9); Deborah's song mentions Isaac's sexual intercourse with (unnamed) Rebecca (32:5); an angel tells Manoah to have sexual intercourse with his wife (42:7); and God instructs Saul to spare Agag one night to have sexual relations with his wife before execution (58:3-4), from which Saul's killer was born. Sexual intercourse, while depicted as a normal part of life, is capable of both positive and negative consequences, and of being licit or illicit. Licit sexual intercourse is assumed to take place in licit marriages. Licit marriage is depicted as the chief aspiration of young women, illustrated by Seila's plaintive cry that she will not have the joy of a wedding and the pleasure of sex (40:6). Seeking a wife is a normal aspiration for young men. Sisera wants to tell his mother about Jael, possibly for wedding arrangements (31:3). The Benjaminites are told to find themselves wives (though abducting dancing virgins from the vineyards of Gibeah falls to the author's censorial cut) (48:3; cf. Judg 21:23) and we hear also of some seeking the wrong kind of advice in the process by consulting Micah's idol (44:5). *LAB* also reflects attention to issues of inheritance, such as when Kenaz's daughters are given lands and husbands (29:2).

Marriage can by polygynous as both the story of Elkanah and Hannah (50:1-5) and, indirectly, that of Manoah and Eluma (42:1-10) indicate, and may apparently include concubines, the designation of Bilhah and Zilpah as concubines (61:6) apparently removing what the author must have seen as unacceptable: sexual relations with handmaids (Abram's with Hagar is significantly missing, though indirectly alluded to in the account of Eluma and Manoah, 42:1-3). At the same time concubines and those born of concubines, like Abimelech from Gideon's concubine (39:1), have lesser status. Concubines are known to be often the result of the spoils of war, as the hopes of Sisera and his mother Themech illustrate (31:1, 8). Perhaps the lower status of the Levite's concubine helped the author to his dreadful portrayal of her violation as something not so abhorrent (47:8), though he does primarily on the grounds that she had sexual relations with an Amalekite. Prostitution makes an occasional appearance directly or indirectly, but is not approved. *LAB* omits reference to Jephthah having been driven from home because he was son of a prostitute, makes no specific reference to Judah's visiting what he thought was a prostitute, and conflates the stories of Samson to make Delilah a prostitute (43:5).

In the relations among wives and their husbands *LAB* paints an image of tensions, which probably reflected the realities of experience with which the author was familiar. These include conflict among wives, particularly the disparagement of those who had not been able to bear children (50:1-5), extending also to recriminations between wife and husband about which of the two was to blame (42:1-10). Typically, in the case of Manoah and Eluma, the woman is to blame, though, for *LAB*, not outside of divine control and purpose. Hannah's defence is to assert that there is more to sex than procreation: doing the will of God is the true measure of richness, not numerous offspring (50:5).

On the other hand, there is more to sex than pleasure, as *LAB* has Amram explain of Tamar (9:5). Her deliberate sin of incest is the lesser evil compared with being a woman of Israel and not bearing its seed. This drove her act, not the desire for illicit sex. So it drove Amram similarly to persist in sexual engagement and procreation with his wife (9:5, 9) despite external threat of death to male offspring and of abduction of female children which would end up having Israelite women having sex with non-Israelites and being exposed to their idolatrous influence. Celibacy on pragmatic grounds and to avoid sexual relations with foreigners and idolatry, as here, let alone ascetic or eschatological grounds, is not an option (9:2-3), perhaps reflecting the author's critique of espousal of celibacy in his own time. The mandate to multiply, missing along with the author's omission of the creation stories, holds its place in the retelling of new beginnings after Noah, and remains prominent (3:11). In an allusion to Onan's sin, no seed is to be spilt (9:4). This plays into the dramatic tension created by the numerous accounts of sterile women, including the matriarchs (8:1; 23:7), beside Eluma and Hannah, and the reversals by divine intervention (8:2-3; 23:8) and promise of special progeny (cf. also 4:11; 9:10).

As an aspect of sexual relations, sexual desire and sexual attractiveness are also part of normal life. They can be rightly or wrongly directed. Most references to women's beauty occur in relation to inappropriate responses: those of the angels to beautiful women, over against Genesis heightened to very beautiful (3:1-2); the Israelites' response to the beautiful naked and bejewelled women of Moab and Midian staged by Balaam (18:13); Jael's self-adornment to attract Sisera to his demise (31:3); and Samson's misdirecting of his sexual passion aroused through his eyes (43:5), a common and natural motif. We must presume that there were also beautiful women whose visual attractiveness evoked appropriate responses and fulfilled themselves in licit marriage, though such depictions as Rachel's beauty in Gen 29:17 do not appear in the narrative.

Misdirected sexual passion relates to some of the author's major concerns about sexual wrongdoing. In contrast to Genesis where the sin in the garden is foundational and the *Book of the Watchers* where the angels descend to have illicit sexual relations with women, the first major treatment of sin in *LAB* after the brief incidental mention of Cain's murder of Abel, is the report about Lamech, which highlights adultery (2:8-10). While the angels' sin is reported much as in Genesis and flashbacks indicate knowledge of the wider tradition that they taught magic before their condemnation (34:1-5), teaching metallurgy was part of Lamech's legacy and, more significantly, his generation's engagement in adultery. The latter thus wins considerable prominence and appears related to the invention of music which helped corrupt the earth. If the author's model is the wild parties which characterised the Hellenistic Roman world, the suggestion that Lamech's words, "I have corrupted men for myself", might refer to buggery has some credibility. The author later connects his account of the gang rape of the Levite's concubine (which he nevertheless plays down) to the attempted male rape by the men of Sodom (45:2). Women's vulnerability, especially in time of war, features in the work (e.g., 31:8) and may be the context also for what Lamech confesses here. *LAB* has in any case elaborated the note in Genesis which makes Lamech's sin be tenfold worse than Cain's (cf. Gen 4:24). The specific sin of adultery is depicted here not as wronging a woman's husband, but defiling a woman, on the assumption that she is rendered unclean for her husband, the assumption behind Deut 24:1-4 (though not reflected in the account of Dinah's marrying Job in 8:8).

In Kenaz's review of the tribes, Gad acknowledges the sin of adultery (25:10). Adultery is one of the key aspects in the relating of the Decalogue, in the first instance, 11:10, given prior place before murder and theft and supplemented with a rationale about the Egyptians (perhaps not having been able to do so against Israel before Israel escaped) and in the second, 44:6-7, 10, in the usual order, but with the prohibition of coveting now, unlike in the first instance, including reference to a neighbour's wife and relating adultery also to the major theme of intermarriage: they lusted after foreign women. The application of testing procedures derived from the trial of women for alleged adultery to the calf worshippers (12:7), as in Exodus (32:20), reflects the widespread use of adultery also as a metaphor for apostasy.

Though *LAB* already depicts Peleg's sons as forming appropriate marriages by taking wives from the daughters of his brother, Joktan (4:10), the issue of intermarriage first arises in the elders' fear that by abducting their newborn daughters the Egyptians would defile them (by having sexual intercourse with them) and lead them to idolatry (9:1-2). Sex with foreigners was probably depicted as defiling because it defiled the holy seed of Israel, as in *Jubilees* (25:3, 12, 18; 16:15-19; 30:15-16; 33:20)[597] and *4QMMT* B 75-82.[598] *LAB* has Amram reject

---

[597] On this see Loader, *Enoch, Levi, and Jubilees*, 155-96.

[598] On this see Loader, *Dead Sea Scrolls on Sexuality*, 65-74.

their solution of celibacy, but not their underlying concern with the purity of Israel's seed, and then cite Tamar as the champion of rejecting intermarriage, implicitly on grounds that it does not produce seed to Israel, as well as that it would be defiling (9:3-5). Amram, himself, then models appropriate behaviour in having a wife from his own tribe, going one step further than marrying any Israelite but not as far as Tobit in limiting choice to the immediate family within the tribe (9:5, 9; Tob 1:9; 4:12-13).

The juxtaposition of intermarriage with idolatry, firmly rooted in Exod 34:16 and Deut 7:3-4, reappears in Joshua's prediction (21:1), the report about taking Amorite wives (30:1), reflecting Numbers 25, and thus by association also in the depiction of Balaam's strategy of exposing Israelite men to Moab and Midian's naked women (18:13-14), though there the focus is much more on intermarriage in itself. In the case of the idolatrous Micah we find the reverse sequence: idolatry leads to intermarriage (44:1-7). God's frustration in response rehearses the Decalogue, enhancing its emphasis both on adultery, in act and desire, and adding reference to lusting after foreign women (44:6-7, 10). Idolatry is a major theme of the work and dominates the sins in Kenaz's review of the tribes (25:7-13), where intermarriage does not appear. On the other hand, in the retelling of the Samson saga the focus is primarily on intermarriage (43:1-8), with Joseph's resistance cited in support (43:5) but his marriage to Aseneth, which leaves a loophole in such arguments, ignored. Similarly, *LAB*'s affirmation of Ruth (61:6) does not address her non-Jewish background. The converted Ruth generates good David; the unconverted Orpah, bad Goliath (as Delilah produced Micah, 44:2). *LAB* has God confront the tribes' aggressive punishment of Benjamin by refocussing the emphasis from what was done to the Levite's concubine to idolatry, thereby suggesting that she in some sense deserved her fate. She deserved it because she had engaged in sexual relations with the Amalekites (45:3; 47:8). Thus *LAB* sustains its theme of outlawing intermarriage, but does so at the expense of justifying an appalling rape, reflecting its underlying values which are to explain that God is in control, which also accounts for *LAB*'s making the sacrifice of Jephthah's daughter not an accidental fruit of his rash oath, but a strategy of divine vengeance.

LAB has long been recognised as giving particular attention to women. This is true from its supplements to genealogies, to the prominence it gives to Deborah as like Moses, sent on the seventh day from God, a shepherdess, mother and mourned 70 days (30:5; 33:1, 6); its idealisation of Seila, Jephthah's daughter, wiser than the wise, going to the bosom of her mothers, a female Isaac (40:3-5); the key role given to Tamar ("our mother") in articulating one of its key themes, intermarriage (9:5); the concern about daughters in relation to Egyptians (9:1); and the special role of mothers in predicting or receiving predictions about significant offspring

(4:11; 9:10; 23:7). Women, too, are hewn from the rock, Sarah and Melcha, not just Abraham and Nahor (23:4).

At a number of points we noted indirect engagement with what would have been themes of existential relevance especially for women. These included issues which might arise in polygynous marriages, which it assumes, such as whether one's husband should add another wife if one could not have children (42:1-3) and the rivalry among wives which might express itself in despising another for her infertility (50:1-2). Thus the author has Hannah declare that there is something more to marital companionship than simply bearing children (50:5). Other issues include women giving birth in the seventh month (23:8); not giving birth till the third year of one's marriage (32:5); the snatching of suckling infants from the breast (2:10); the emphasis on the rib as the origin of humankind (32:15); regular depiction of children as "fruit of the womb", and ensuring they are not missed in counting numbers (characteristically by the addition: "apart from women and children"); the noted concern of Philistines with deaths of pregnant and nursing mothers and their babies (55:4, 6, 10); the intimacy of breastfeeding and milk as an image both of teaching (51:2-3), and of the closeness of David and Jonathan, 62:10), and the image of Moses like a pregnant woman in difficult labour with her first child (12:5). As Halpern-Amaru notes, women are mostly described in relation to the processes of motherhood and giving birth, which is true even of its major heroic figures, Deborah, Jael, and Seila.[599]

Such awareness of women's existential issues has suggested female authorship as a possibility to some,[600] although it might also just reflect a male author sensitive to such issues, such as we find from the same period in 4 Ezra, where the author exhorts the hearers on some issues to ask a woman to appreciate the strength of the analogies he constructs (4:40-42; 5:46-52; 8:9-11). One might speculate that in the post-war period, if this is *LAB*'s setting, women would inevitably have come more to the fore because of the devastation of the likely reduction of the male population. The period of the Judges in particular offered

---

[599] So Halpern-Amaru, "Portraits of Women," who writes: "The maternal role – giving birth, nurturing, or chastening – is a major theme in his depiction of women" (105). "Pseudo-Philo reserves the role of female protagonist for Israelite women who serve as God's agents/partners. These women confidently act out their parts, fully aware of their significance in the divine plan for Israel. Heroic mothers acquire their awareness in the contexts of the wonder births of their sons" (103). By contrast, "when the biblical story offers no context for a maternal characterization, Pseudo-Philo either underdevelops the portrait or portrays the woman as ineffective and dependent" (106).

[600] See especially Descamp, "Why Are These Women Here?" 79, who writes: "the view of this text is a view from the inner room, the women's court, where marriage, babies, nursing, pregnancy, and motherhood are the main concerns"; see also Descamp, *Metaphor as Ideology*, 17.

rich potential for developing legend and for enhancing women heroes, and also offered perhaps the best analogy to the new situation in which the community found itself with a desperate need for leadership, another of the author's key themes.

LAB's women heroes retain their domestic concerns and reflect a range of values which would have been equally espoused by men. These include the notion of being compliant and subservient in doing what is seen as God's will, even if it means, as in the case of Jephthah's daughter, allowing oneself to be offered as a sacrifice, in *LAB* a vengeful response of the author's God, apparently unable to release an oath and more worried about the cultic reach of offering a dog as a sacrifice than about poor Seila's welfare (39:10-11). This is somewhat striking given pentateuchal laws which make sure that rash oaths, at least by women, could be overturned (Lev 5:4-6; cf. Num 30:13-15). Seila's lament also highlights the major role which marriage is seen to play in the hopes of women, especially the celebration of entering marriage with the celebration of the wedding so colourfully portrayed in contrast to Judges' terse summary that she was to die without having had sexual intercourse (11:39), a tragic deprivation also assumed in *LAB*. The hero Judith stands behind some depictions, especially of Seila, but also of Deborah. But even so, Deborah's forty year rule is still deigned to be punishment (30:2), by implication, as a humiliation for men, though not nearly so dramatic as Sisera's humiliation at being slain by a woman (31:1, 7, 9). The dramatic impact of such humiliations requires that the hearers share the author's view of women as weak and also that any placement of them in a position superior to men is shameful.

Thus *LAB*, on the one hand, shows awareness of a number of issues which would have been of existential significance especially for women of its day, while at the same time operating within a frame of reference which saw elevation of women beyond the household tasks as exceptional and potentially shameful and insulting to men's dignity. There is a very wide gulf between the author's values both in relation to God and in relation to women and women, on the one hand, and contemporary values which acknowledge human rights, recognise violation, and affirm the dignity of all.

Finally, *LAB* presents an enigma in its depiction of the future. It strongly espouses cult (e.g. 13:1-10; and the confessions in 25:9 on the holiness of the tent of meeting and in 25:13 on keeping the sabbath) and depicts Eden/paradise as the place of sanctification in a manner which suggests it sees paradise as a sanctuary (19:10-13; 11:15), the source of the revelation of Sinai giving forth its scent (19:10; 13:8-9; 32:8), and the source of sacred stones, both the seven and the twelve which replaced them, which will be its everlasting source of light making the sun, moon, and stars redundant (25:10-13; 26:1-15; cf. also 13:1). It seems that the details about the making of the tabernacle and its accompaniments essential for the cult and festivals are something for which Moses saw the pattern in paradise along with the precious stones and the tree of life from which he received also the rod to make the bitter waters sweet and which was placed in the ark of the covenant (11:15). Paradise is above and real and also a source for blotting out the account of sins by "dew from the ice of paradise" (26:8). Adam, affirmed as progenitor, is depicted as a failure, not as the first priest, as in *Jubilees*. He forfeited paradise for humanity, but this is reversed only through the new beginning with Noah and its regulation revealed to Moses. The promise, then, to all who live by Torah is ultimately entry into this holy paradise and, by implication, access to the tree of life (11:15) and so to everlasting life.

Hope in *LAB* also speaks of embodied existence, presuming a future resurrection, captured in Kenaz's final vision as a transformed heavenly existence (28:6-9), though elsewhere *LAB* espouses the notion of a new heaven and new earth (3:10). While a synthesis is difficult and may not do justice to the diversity of ideas found in the work which the author may not have integrated into a systematic whole, it appears probable that the emphasis on paradise as the destiny of the righteous and as a sanctuary, implies that sexual relations would cease to exist, being out of place in holy space. Neither 3:10, which refers to future fertility of the earth and its creatures for human beings in the age to come, nor 13:10 which speaks of the promise of abundant seed in the present, contradicts this conclusion. This makes it likely that in *LAB* we have evidence of a notion of eschatological fulfilment as living in paradise, understood as a place of sanctification, in eternal light, and where sexual relations do not take place.

Overall, *LAB* assumes sexual relations, including sexual attractiveness and desire, as something positive, which is open however to abuse through illicit relations, doing what is good with the wrong people. Its focus is not so much wrong place in relation to sexuality in the present (e.g. holy space, with the exception of the requirement of temporary celibacy before Sinai, 11:2), nor wrong time (such as the sabbath), but wrong people and thus wrong associations, not least with idolators. The emphasis on wrong people is not incest (of which it is aware) or prohibited degrees in marriage (such as nieces, let alone nephews – it ignores the issues with Amram and Jochabed, his aunt) or monogyny, which it does not presume, but adultery, and especially intermarriage with non-Jews. Where the reason for the latter is articulated, it is predominantly fear of idolatry, but not exclusively so. It is also concerned about maintaining Israel's seed, but not, apparently, with potential immoral influence from foreign cultures, especially sexual immorality, as in *Jubilees*. Israel's survival, based on God's covenant faithfulness, matters most, including as a community which observes cultic law. This overrides all else, justifying an image of God as taking the initiative to have Seila sacrificed as punishment for Jephthah's lack of care about cult and playing down the violation of the Levite's concubine. Future promise focuses on paradise, understood as a place of sanctification and where accordingly sexual relations have no place.

2.2.2   Joseph and Aseneth

Joseph and Aseneth (hereafter just *Aseneth*),[601] preserved in manuscripts that date from the sixth century C.E. onwards, and surviving in a long text and what appears to be a secondarily abridged form,[602] is most probably a Jewish work composed in Greek somewhere in the first century B.C.E. or first century C.E. in Egypt,[603] and written primarily for performance to a Jewish audience.[604] An account of

---

[601] I use the edition of the Greek text found in Christoph Burchard with Carsten Burfeind and Uta Barbara Fink, *Joseph und Aseneth* (PVTG 5; Leiden: Brill, 2003) and the English translation of Christoph Burchard based on this text in "Joseph and Aseneth," *OTP*, 2.177-247. I use his versification. When referring to the shorter text I use the slightly different versification of Marc Philonenko, *"Joseph et Aséneth": Introduction, texte critique, traduction et notes* (SPB 13; Leiden: Brill, 1968), indicated by the abbreviation, Ph. See now also the revised edition of the Greek text in Uta Barbara Fink, *Joseph and Aseneth: Revision des griechischen Textes und Edition der zweiten lateinischen Übersetzung* (FSBP 5; Berlin: de Gruyter, 2008), which arrived too late to be taken into account in what follows.

[602] See the detailed discussion of the two forms in Burchard, *Joseph und Aseneth*, who provides convincing evidence for the priority of the long text (39-46). See also Christoph Burchard, "The Text of *Joseph and Aseneth* Reconsidered," *JSP* 14 (2005) 83-96; Christoph Burchard, "Joseph und Aseneth: Eine jüdisch-hellenistische Erzählung von Liebe, Bekehrung und vereitelter Entführung," *TZ* 61 (2005) 65-77; Edith M. Humphrey, *Joseph and Aseneth* (GAP; Sheffield: Sheffield Academic Press, 2000) 18-23. See also the caution of Davila, *Provenance*, about attributing Jewish or Christian authorship (194-95).

[603] So Gerbern S. Oegema, "Joseph und Aseneth (JSHRZ II/4)," in *Einführung zu den Jüdischen Schriften aus hellenistisch-römischer Zeit: Unterweisung in erzählender Form* (ed. Gerbern S. Oegema; JSHRZ 6.1.2; Gütersloh: Gütersloher Verlagshaus, 2005) 97-114, 100-101.

[604] On earlier attempts to link Aseneth with the Essenes or the Therapeutae, see the recent review in Randall D. Chesnutt, "The Dead Sea Scrolls and the Meal Formula in *Joseph and Aseneth*: From Qumran Fever to Qumran Light," in *The Bible and the Dead Sea Scrolls: The Princeton Symposium on the Dead Sea Scrolls: Volume 2: The Dead Sea Scrolls and the Qumran Community* (ed. James H. Charlesworth; Waco: Baylor University Press, 2006) 397-425, who concludes that "the persistent claims of kinship between *Joseph and Aseneth* and the Essenes or Therapeutae emanate more from Qumran fever than from compelling evidence" (409). He notes the absence in *Aseneth* of characteristics of one or both of these groups: orders of initiation and seniority (404-405, 408), separation of men and women (408), a spirituality of withdrawal (409), and special communal order (409), and notes the very different approaches to proselytes (406) and the depiction of Levi as

conversion, it makes better sense to see it composed before the revolt under Trajan in 117 C.E. and Hadrian's suppression of circumcision in 135 C.E.[605] and arguably the relatively positive depiction of relations with Egyptians and Egyptian authorities and absence of allusion to Rome would make better sense early in the first century C.E.[606] or perhaps even late in the first century B.C.E., but evidence remains circumstantial.[607]

The work is an elaboration of a single verse in Genesis: "Pharaoh gave Joseph the name Zaphenath-paneah; and he gave him Aseneth daughter of Potiphera, priest of On (LXX: Petephres, priest of Heliopolis) as his wife. Thus Joseph gained authority over the land of Egypt" (41:45).[608] This fanciful story in the form of a romance, rich in motifs characteristic of Hellenistic romances,[609] including the *Metamorphosis* of Apuleius with its links to mystery religion,[610] begins with a

---

prophet (406), observing also that the link with angels is found in a range of documents beside those attributed to these groups (407).

[605] So Oegema, "Joseph und Aseneth," 101; John J. Collins, "*Joseph and Aseneth*: Jewish or Christian?" *JSP* 14 (2005) 97-112, 109.

[606] So Collins, *Between Athens and Jerusalem*, 109; Randall D. Chesnutt, *From Death to Life: Conversion in Joseph and Aseneth* (JSPSupp 16; Sheffield: Sheffield Academic Press, 1995) 85. For the case for identifying its context as the period before 38 C.E. see Dieter Sänger, "Erwägungen zur historischen Einordnung und zur Datierung von 'Joseph und Aseneth'," *ZNW* 76 (1985) 86-106, and the playful but critical response in Edith M. Humphrey, "On Bees and Best Guesses: The Problem of *Sitz im Leben* from Internal Evidence as Illustrated by *Joseph and Aseneth*," *CurBS* 7 (1999) 223-36, 228-29.

[607] For discussion of the radical proposal of Gideon Bohak, *Joseph and Aseneth and the Jewish Temple in Heliopolis* (SBLEJL 10; Atlanta: Scholars, 1996) to situate the writing in relation to the foundation of the temple at Leontopolis by Onias IV in the first half of the second century B.C.E., see Humphrey, *Joseph and Aseneth*, 33-36, 51; Collins, "Joseph and Aseneth," 107-108. Apart from details of matching the events such an early date is problematic in the light of the extensive use of the LXX.

[608] More specifically its chaps. 1 – 21 fit between Gen 41:46-49 and 50, and 21 – 29 between Gen 41:53-54 and 46:5-7. On this see Burchard, "Joseph und Aseneth," 70.

[609] See Oegema, "Joseph und Aseneth," who sees it as most comparable to "Amor and Psyche" (Apuleius *Metam.* 4:28 – 6:24), but also similar to Ruth, Esther, Tobit, and Judith (97-98); Burchard, *OTP*, 2.183-85; Humphrey, *Joseph and Aseneth*, 39-40; Wills, *Jewish Novel*, 176; Bach, *Women, Seduction, and Betrayal*, who notes the comparative lack of the overtly erotic in *Aseneth* (102); similarly Chesnutt, *From Death to Life*, 88-90; Gruen, *Heritage and Hellenism*, 93; Barclay, *Jews in the Mediterranean Diaspora*: "rather prudish" by comparison (205).

[610] The major review of the relevance of parallels with the mysteries and especially with the oft cited Apuleius, *Metamorphosis*, remains that of Dieter Sänger, *Antikes Judentum und die Mysterien: Religionsgeschichtliche Untersuchungen zu Joseph und Aseneth* (WUNT 2.5; Tübingen: Mohr Siebeck, 1980) 88-117, on Apuleius: pp. 117-47, and

depiction of the eighteen year old daughter of "the exceedingly rich and prudent and gentle" Pentephres, priest of Heliopolis, Aseneth (1:3; Ph 1:4). Her positive qualities include that she was a virgin, "very tall and handsome and beautiful to look at beyond all virgins of the earth" (1:4; Ph 1:6). In addition she "had nothing similar to the virgins of the Egyptians, but she was in every respect similar to the daughters of the Hebrews,[611] and was as tall as Sarah and handsome as Rebecca and beautiful as Rachel" (1:5; Ph 1:7-8).[612] Already here we see the agenda of addressing why, despite her being Egyptian, she was a suitable wife for Joseph. The issue of intermarriage between Jews and Gentiles informs the account.[613] In portraying both Pentephres and Aseneth the author works with soft boundaries.[614]

The fairy tale quality continues as the author reports that "the fame of her beauty spread all over the land and to the ends of the inhabited (world)" and that she was much in demand from suitors who also fought among themselves over her (1:6; Ph 1:9-10). At this point the author also notes that among them is the son of Pharaoh, who preferred her to the daughter of the king of Moab to whom he was

---

comparison with *Aseneth*: pp. 148-90. Among other things he notes that *Aseneth* lacks the structural pattern of a mystery (188); has change effected by God not by a rite (189); and lacks the motifs of secrecy (189), shipwrecks and others forms of separation (190), and subsequent searching (190).

[611] Angela Standhartinger, *Das Frauenbild im Judentum der Hellenistischen Zeit: Ein Beitrag anhand von 'Joseph und Aseneth'* (Leiden: Brill, 1995), prefers a reading from the shorter text which makes her similar to neither Egyptians nor Hebrews (44 n. 210).

[612] P. Battifol, *Le livre de la prière d'Aseneth* (Studi Patristica: Études d'ancienne littérature chrétienne, 1-2; Paris: Lerous, 1889-90), proposed that Aseneth reflected the tradition later preserved in rabbinic sources that Aseneth was the illegitimate daughter of Dinah (10-14); similarly Victor Aptowitzer, "Asenath, the Wife of Joseph: A Haggadic Literary-Historical Study," *HUCA* 1 (1924) 239-306, 266-68. It could explain her appearance, but also the reference to her being Joseph's sister in 7:7-8, but there the focus is their common virginity not consanguinity and here the author is softening the boundaries. In any case the author makes very clear that she is Egyptian and the daughter of Pentephres. For further discussion see Standhartinger, *Frauenbild*, 151-55; Ross Shepard Kraemer, *When Joseph Met Aseneth: A Late Antique Tale of the Biblical Patriarch and His Egyptian Wife, Reconsidered* (New York: Oxford University Press, 1998) 309-12; Ross Shepard Kraemer, "When Aseneth Met Joseph: A Postscript," in *For a Later Generation: The Transformation of Tradition in Israel, Early Judaism, and Early Christianity* (ed. Randal A. Argall, Beverly A. Bow, and Rodney Alan Werline; Harrisburg: Trinity, 2000) 128-35, 130-31.

[613] On this and the treatment which follows see also William Loader, "The Strange Woman in Proverbs, LXX Proverbs and *Aseneth*" in *Septuagint and Reception: Essays Prepared for the Association for the Study of the Septuagint in South Africa* (ed. Johann Cook; VTSup 127; Leiden: Brill, 2009) 97-115, 110-15.

[614] Humphrey, *Joseph and Aseneth*, 82.

betrothed (1:7-9; Ph 1:11-14). This introduces into the narrative the basis for what must wait for the final chapters of the work, his aggressive but foiled attempt to seize her for himself (23 – 29).

The author then draws attention to Aseneth's failings: "Aseneth was despising and scorning every man (ἐξουθενοῦσα καὶ καταπτύουσα πάντα ἄνδρα), and she was boastful and arrogant (ἀλαζὼν καὶ ὑπερήφανος) with everyone" (especially her suitors) (2:1).[615] The narrative goes on to note that no man had ever seen her, since she was protected in a tower of ten chambers, continuing its storytelling hyperbole. The first of these was filled with Egyptian idols to which she was devoted (2:3; Ph 2:4-5). Seven virgins born on the same day as her, with whom no man ever conversed, served her, and were very beautiful like the stars of heaven (2:8; Ph 2:10-11). Thus the fairy tale superlatives continue, but already here the detail is suggestive of allegory, though it stands without interpretation. The note that no one, not even her virgin attendants, ever sat on her bed, indicates her pristine virginity (2:9; Ph 2:16).[616]

The description of the courtyard surrounding the house, with its four gates each attended by 18 men, but especially the handsome trees with fruit ripe for plucking, and the spring, cistern and river, is highly suggestive, evoking images of Eden.[617] The images appear suggestive rather than systematic. Hearers might see the tower, courtyard and gates as representing her body, the fruit but also the spring as promising sexual fulfilment, and the gates and tower, the protections of her virginity. Here they might recall for hearers the imagery of Cant 4:12 – 5:1 about gardens, fountains, and fruit, including, "A garden locked is my sister, my bride, a garden locked, a fountain sealed" (4:12); "I come to my garden, my sister, my bride" (5:1). The tower, with its three inner chambers, is also suggestive of a temple,[618] but its holiest chamber is contaminated by idols. Aseneth is a person of mixed virtues: her virginity is valued, but her hating men and arrogance are not, and her idolatry is an abomination.

Joseph, whose projected arrival the author had announced in his opening words (1:1-2; Ph 1:1-3), now becomes the focus of attention (3:1; Ph 3:1). The author has Pentephres depict him as "the powerful one of God" (3:4; Ph 3:6). The motif of harvest is further enhanced (cf. 2:11; Ph 2:18-20) in the report of

---

[615] This negative note about her as boastful and arrogant is absent in the shorter version, although it reports these traits in Ph 12:7 (σοβαρὰ καὶ ὑπερήφανος); cf. also Ph 4:16 (ἀλαζονεία).

[616] On the comic dimension of the author's depiction of Aseneth's super-virginity see Humphrey, *Joseph and Aseneth*, 86, 90-91.

[617] So Anathea E. Portier-Young, "Sweet Mercy Metropolis: Interpreting Aseneth's Honeycomb," *JSP* 14 (2005) 133-57, 140.

[618] So Andrea Lieber, "I Set a Table before You: The Jewish Eschatological Character of Aseneth's Conversion Meal," *JSP* 14 (2004) 63-77, 67.

Aseneth's parents having returned from harvest fields (3:5; Ph 3:7-8, but no reference to harvest), whom Aseneth descends to greet, dressed splendidly, but replete with idolatrous images (3:6; Ph 3:9-11). She is "adorned like a bride of God" (4:1; Ph 4:2). Again, the narrative combines the storyteller's excess with symbolic allusion, since at stake in the narrative is not only marriage to Joseph, but also conversion to God. Her enjoying the fruits of the harvest brought by her parents (4:2; Ph 4:3 "good things") further enhances the narrative's erotic suggestiveness.

The marital motif continues as Pentephres exercises what was seen as a father's responsibility in finding a mate for his daughter. He proposes Joseph, whom he again describes as "the powerful one of God" (4:7; Ph 4:8; cf. 3:4; Ph 3:6), but also as "a man who worships God (θεοσεβής), and self-controlled (σώφρων), and a virgin (πάρθενος) like you today" and "powerful in wisdom and experience, and the spirit of God is upon him, and the grace of the Lord (is) with him" (4:7; Ph 4:9). For the alert Jewish hearer Pentephres' proposal raises the problem of intermarriage between a Jew and a Gentile, but also recalls the known fact from the Genesis account that Joseph did in fact marry Aseneth, the Egyptian. So the narrative takes the knowing hearer to the heart of an issue of considerable debate in Jewish communities, as reflected in a wide range of Jewish literature, from Exodus 32 and Deuteronomy 7 to Ezra and Nehemiah, *Jubilees*, *Aramaic Levi Document*, and *4QMMT* to *LAB*.[619]

The author exploits the tension through the irony of Aseneth the idolator's response, which effectively voices the hardline position of prohibiting such marriages. She is outraged at her father's proposal, to hand her over "like a captive", to a man who is "an alien (ἀνδρὶ ἀλλοφύλῳ),[620] and a fugitive (φυγάδι), and (was) sold (as a slave) (πεπραμένῳ) ... a shepherd's son from the land of Canaan, and he himself was caught in the act (when he was) sleeping with his mistress" (κοιμώμενος μετὰ τῆς κυρίας αὐτοῦ) and released from the darkness of prison when, like old women, he interpreted dreams (4:9-10; Ph 4:11-14), her preference being to marry "a king's firstborn son" (4:11; Ph 4:15). There is some evidence that earlier attacks on intermarriage sometimes focussed on captive wives.[621] This is in part the reverse: Joseph is a foreign slave. The author highlights her response to her father as boastful and angry (4:12; Ph 4:16), thus illustrating the description in 2:1. Allusion to the king's firstborn, whose own intention the author has reported in 1:7-9 (Ph 1:11-14), keeps the dramatic tension alive, which will later issue in violence, but also matches the designation of

---

[619] On this see Loader, *Enoch, Levi, and Jubilees*, 91-94, 100-104 (*ALD*); 155-96 (*Jubilees*); Loader, *Dead Sea Scrolls on Sexuality*, 53-90 (*4QMMT*); and on *LAB* above.

[620] Possibly ἀλλογενεῖ. See Burchard, *Joseph und Aseneth*, 373.

[621] See Loader, *Dead Sea Scrolls on Sexuality*, 79-80.

Joseph, so that her dream of marrying a king's firstborn son will in fact come to fulfilment. Having a Gentile articulate the hardline position is an attempt on the part of the author to expose to hearers its unacceptability, indeed, to portray it as arrogant. They, like her, must be persuaded.

Hearing of Joseph's arrival, Aseneth flees to her windowed chamber (5:2; Ph 5:2). The account of Joseph's arrival is again rich with storyteller's excess, but also with suggestive symbolism which presumably would not have been lost on the hearers. For he comes from the east, in resplendent royal attire, dressed like the sun god, having come to Heliopolis, sun city. There are also echoes of the depiction of the sun in Psalm 19 as like a bridegroom: "In the heavens he has set a tent for the sun, which comes out like a bridegroom from his wedding canopy" (19:4-5). His bearing a fruiting olive branch (5:5; Ph 5:7) continues the erotic suggestiveness. His entering the gates prefigures his entry of Aseneth in sexual intercourse. The divine attire is not idolatrous, but reflects the author's eclectic use of diverse motifs. Indeed it strengthens the image of Joseph as one aligned to the true God.

The romantic motif of a protagonist falling madly in love plays itself out as Aseneth espies Joseph out her east facing window (6:1; Ph 6:1), but is transcended with spiritual motifs as she gives poetic utterance to her regret at having spoken wickedly and foolishly (6:2-8; Ph 6:2-8 similar but shorter and reordered). In case the hearer has missed the message, the author has her declare: "Behold, the sun from heaven has come to us on its chariot" (6:2; Ph 6:5), and that he is "son of God" (6:3, 5; Ph 6:6, 2), so the real "king's son" (cf. (4:11; Ph 4:15). Her words include imagery of birth: "For who among men will generate such beauty, and what womb of woman will give birth to such light?" (6:4; Ph 6:7). Significantly she calls on the Lord, God of Joseph, to be gracious towards her because she has "spoken wicked words against him in ignorance" (6:7; Ph 6:4) and declares herself willing to become Joseph's "maidservant and slave" and to "serve him for ever (and) ever" (6:8; Ph 6:8), reversing the denigration with which she disdained Joseph. The narrator will have us see this response as genuine and so the beginning of a process which will change her life. It is, however, only a confession of sin based on ignorance in denigrating Joseph, not a turning from idolatry. In the author's narrative world idol-worshipping Egyptians like Pharaoh and Pentephres seem quite happy to acknowledge the existence of a God of Israel beside their gods (3:3-4; Ph 3:4, 6; 4:7; Ph 4:9; 6:7; Ph 6:4; 21:4, 6; Ph 21:3-4).

Meanwhile "Joseph entered the house of Pentephres and sat upon the throne (ἐπὶ τοῦ θρόνου)" (7:1; Ph 7:1), had his feet washed and a separate table set up for himself "because Joseph never ate with the Egyptians, for this was an abomination (βδέλυγμα) to him" (7:1; Ph 7:1). Two elements may suggest some arrogance on Joseph's part, a character trait perhaps already intimated in his depiction in the Genesis narrative. It may have struck some hearers as arrogant that

Joseph enters and sits on Pentephres' throne and similarly that he eats in isolation, considering meals with Egyptians an abomination, which seems a deliberate reversal on the part of the author of Gen 49:32, which has the Egyptians objecting to eating with the Hebrews as abominable.[622]

This kind of behaviour, probably to be seen as arrogant, continues in the report that Joseph catches sight of Aseneth and demands her removal, fearful of harassment, because, as the author tells us, all the noble wives and daughters of Egypt pester him wanting to sleep with him (7:2-3; Ph 7:3-4). His superlative sexual attractiveness belongs to the stuff of the entertaining romance. The detail coheres with Aseneth's own response, falling in love at first sight. The story, however, is entertainment with intent.[623] There is probably a touch of arrogance in Joseph's treating such suitors with contempt (nicely matching the description of Aseneth's arrogance). More seriously, Joseph is depicted as embodying the hardline position of those who oppose all intermarriage with Gentiles, based on the words of his father, Jacob:

Φυλάξασθε τέκνα μου ἰσχυρως[624] ἀπὸ γυναικὸς ἀλλοτρίας τοῦ κοινωνῆσαι αὐτῇ. ἡ γὰρ κοινωνία αὐτῆς ἀπωλειά ἐστι καὶ διαφθορά.
My children, guard strongly against associating with a strange woman, for association (with) her is destruction and corruption. (7:5; Ph 7:6 minor variation)

This echoes the warnings about the strange woman and the consequences in Proverbs (5:1-23; 6:26 – 7:27).[625] In the broader narrative context its focus is on women who are not Israelite, though it also alludes to sexual wrongdoing, since these women include wives and daughters who just want to have sexual intercourse with him, as 7:3 (Th 7:4) indicates. They are multiples of Potiphar's wife. The account of his response recalls Joseph's appeal to the teaching of Abraham in resisting Potiphar's wife in *Jub.* 39:7.

It is hard to imagine that the author expects Joseph's stance to receive an unsympathetic hearing. That is its subtlety. Joseph acts appropriately, though with a touch of arrogance, that might suggest to the hearer that there are other options. After all, the hearers know the outcome, so know that what sounds absolute and

---

[622] So Gruen, *Heritage and Hellenism*, who writes: "Joseph's fussiness bespeaks a cramped disposition, and his public display of abstinence borders on the offensive" (96) and "The hero of this saga evidently did not prize graciousness or even civility" (97).

[623] As Humphrey, *Joseph and Aseneth*, observes: "It is important to remember that the ancient world did not divide 'entertainment' from 'religious meaning'" (45) and later, "The reader must not abandon Aseneth to the world of sheer aesthetics – here is a tantalizing story that pronounces its riddles and asks to be understood, not merely enjoyed" (82).

[624] Possibly ἀσφαλῶς. On this see Burchard, *Joseph und Aseneth*, 374.

[625] On the dependence of *Aseneth* on Proverbs LXX see Kraemer, *When Joseph Met Aseneth*, 21-25; see also Humphrey, *Joseph and Aseneth*, 87.

the conclusion of the matter and was seen by the hardliners as such is not the end of the story. The author is being playfully subversive of the prohibition of intermarriage by having Joseph articulate it so strongly, when the hearers know the outcome is otherwise. Joseph must relent. He does so only when Pentephres assures him that Aseneth "is a virgin hating every man (παρθένος μισοῦσα πάντα ἄνδρα)" and that no other man has ever seen her: "our daughter is like a sister to you" (ἡ θυγάτηρ ἡμῶν ὡς ἀδελφή σού ἐστιν) (7:7; Ph 7:8-9).

Joseph's response indicates acceptance of Pentephres' argument. "He rejoiced exceedingly and with great joy" (7:8; Ph 7:10), to which one might have expected a ripple of laughter, since its very intensity suggests something more is at stake than relief from molestation. The author does, however, give the latter as Joseph's reason and has him declare to Pentephres and his family: "If she is your daughter and a virgin, let her come, because she is a sister to me, and I love her from today as my sister" (7:8; Ph 7:11), doubtless evoking more laughter among the knowing hearers.[626] While sustaining the demarcation from women with improper sexual intent, the author loosens the demarcation about foreignness and has Joseph embrace a notion of family that transcends the bounds of Israel. How could one be of one family with a Gentile just because she is apparently a non-molesting virgin? The author will have lost the hardliners at this point. Their cause is not, however, lost. It receives what must be mocking articulation in what immediately follows.

Thus the issue of intermarriage moves further into focus in what would probably be heard by listeners as Pentephres' matchmaking manipulation, who suggests that at least since they are brother and sister it is appropriate for Aseneth to greet and kiss Joseph. After all, not so far back the listeners had heard of her being love-struck. The author enhances the irony in the words he gives to Pentephres: "Greet (ἄσπασαι) your brother, because he, too, is a virgin like you today and hates every strange woman (πάσαν γυναῖκα ἀλλότριαν), as you, too, every strange man (πάντα ἄνδρα ἀλλότριον)" (8:1; Ph 8:1). For a moment the narrative holds us in suspense as Joseph and Aseneth bless each other. Then Pentephres urges what would belong to a normal greeting, but, as listeners would sense, is anything but a normal greeting: "Go up and kiss (καταφίλησον) your brother" (8:4; Ph 8:3). This becomes another occasion for the author to articulate the hardline position his narrative will steadily undermine. Thus the author has Joseph push her away, but depicts him as doing so by placing his hand "on her chest between her two breasts" (πρὸς τὸ στῆθος αὐτῆς ἀνάμεσον τῶν δύο μασθῶν αὐτῆς). The shorter text simply reads: προς τὸ στῆθος αὐτῆς ("on her chest/breast") (Ph 8:4), but is already sufficiently suggestive. Burchard's text continues: "and her breasts were already standing upright like handsome apples"

---

[626] On earlier suggestions that the passage may allude to the legend that Aseneth was Dinah's illegitimate child, see the discussion of 1:5 above.

(καὶ ἦσαν οἱ μαθοὶ αὐτῆς ἤδη ἑστῶρες ὥσπερ μῆλα ὡπαῖα) (8:5), thus entertaining the hearers with erotic allusion,[627] consistent with Aseneth's portrait this far.

By contrast the author has Joseph assert his refusal:

> It is not fitting for a man who worships God, who will bless with his mouth the living God and eat blessed bread of life (ἐσθίει ἄρτον εὐλογημένον ζωῆς) and drink a blessed cup of immortality (πίνει ποτήριον εὐλογημένον ἀθανασίας) and anoint himself with blessed ointment of incorruptibility (καὶ χρίεται χρίσματα εὐλογημένῳ ἀφθαρσίας) to kiss a strange woman (φιλῆσαι γυναῖκι ἀλλοτρίαν) who will bless with her mouth dead and dumb idols and eat from their table bread of strangulation (ἐσθίει ἐκ τῆς τραπέζης αὐτων ἄρτον ἀγχόνης) and drink from their libation a cup of insidiousness (πίνει ἐκ τῆς σπονδῆς αὐτῶν ποτήριον ἐνέδρας) and anoint herself with ointment of destruction (χρίεται χρίσματι ἀπωλείας). (8:5; Ph 8:5; cf. 10:13; Ph 10:14)

Joseph's declaration continues with the assertion that kisses belong only within the family: mother, born sister, clan sister, and wife (8:6; Ph 8:6), focusing only on women because of the context, and the reverse: "Likewise for a woman who worships God it is not fitting to kiss a strange man, because this is an abomination (βδέλυγμα) before the Lord" (8:7; Ph 8:7).

The references to bread, wine, and oil, have occasioned much discussion which is beyond the present investigation to review. It is now widely recognised that they refer to Jewish meals, not the Christian eucharist and chrismation.[628] They serve here to describe what is entailed in being a worshipper of God and thus will serve later to depict what Aseneth also has access to as a convert. Bread, wine, and oil, common elements of life in the ancient world, clearly attain a blessed status within Israel and as such convey "life" (ζωῆς), "immortality" (ἀθανασίας) and "incorruptibility" (ἀφθαρσίας). These are set in contrast to blessing idols, eating strangled food, drinking libations (an insidious influence?) and anointings linked with destruction. Touching the lips of one who does such things defiles the lips and so the person of the true worshipper, a general application of purity concerns and is "an abomination" (βδέλυγμα) .

Once again, it is unlikely that the author would expect hearers to dissent. They know that Joseph is serious, but also that a way will be found for the situation to

---

[627] Burchard, *Joseph und Asenath*, implausibly argues that the reference is not sexual but alludes to the fact that she is a grown woman, not a child (43). Cf. Ellis, *Sexual Desire*, who speaks of its "playful eroticism" 74. Humphrey, *Joseph and Aseneth*, notes MS B lacks these words and suggests it may be a secondary addition (73), but then assumes it as text in her own exposition (89). Yet it is well-attested (MSS APQ). On this see Burchard, p. 116.

[628] So Collins, "Joseph and Aseneth," 111, but see also the conclusion below.

be reversed. For hardliners Joseph's words have said all that needs to be said; entertaining conversion is to be ruled out. Such is the stance we see championed in *Jubilees* not least in association with Levi (30:18 in 30:5-23) and also in *Aramaic Levi Document* (3a; cf. also *T. Levi* 9:10).[629] The story of Joseph and Aseneth is a chink in their armour. They would not have sympathised with the author's report that Aseneth "was cut (to the heart) strongly and distressed exceedingly . . . eyes filled with tears" nor with his depiction of Joseph's response: "And Joseph saw her, and had mercy on her exceedingly, and was himself cut (to the heart), because Joseph was meek and merciful and fearing God" (8:8; Ph 8:9-10). But, subversive of their stance, the author evokes sympathy for both and has Joseph bless Aseneth in what in effect is a prayer for her incorporation into God's people – before she has given any indication of wanting to convert.

Joseph's prayer for Aseneth employs the contrasts, darkness–light, error–truth, death–life, to pray for Aseneth's renewal, new formation, revivification, and that she, too, may eat the "bread of life" and drink the "cup of blessing" and be numbered among God's people chosen before all things were made, enter God's "rest" (κατάπαυσιν) and have God's "eternal life" forever (8:9; Ph 8:11). The shorter text has Aseneth, herself, chosen before she was begotten (Ph 8:11). The prayer recalls Joseph's earlier demarcation, including the image of the blessed food and cup, refuses to see it as the end of the story, but rather seeks its solution in Aseneth's conversion. For the author, Joseph gets its right. The hardliners have got it wrong.

We then read of Aseneth's great joy over Joseph's prayer, but also her exhaustion and mixed emotions of joy and distress, especially her profound grief at worshipping other gods (9; Ph 9:1-2). The author notes that she "waited for the evening to come" (8; Ph 9:3), possibly understood by his listeners as looking forward to her first intercourse with Joseph, though this was mistaken and would have been inappropriate before marriage as we later hear (21:1; Ph 20:8). What follows proceeds, indeed, much more slowly. The author has Joseph turn down Pentephres' offer that he stay that night (thus quashing hopes Aseneth may have had), and instead set off on what he signals as the first day of creation, with the promise that he would return a full week later on the eighth day (9; 10:1; Ph 9:4-5; 10:1), a playful allusion to the new creation about to embrace Aseneth.

Aseneth has now gone beyond confession of her sin of ignorance in denigrating Joseph. She has also repented of her idolatry. One might imagine that this would suffice. She has converted. But given that intermarriage with a non-Israelite was a significant issue which the author appears to be addressing, it was important to underline the extent of that repentance and to elaborate the

---

[629] On this see Loader, *Enoch, Levi, and Jubilees*, 87-111.

significance of the change, not least given the imagery of Joseph's prayer.[630] This is, in turn, what we find in the following chapters, which go beyond this in making Aseneth not only the model proselyte, but also the symbolic refuge of all proselytes to come. The author not only wins the argument by citing the famed exception to the practice of forbidding intermarriage, but also exploits it as an aetiology and theological foundation.

The utter seriousness of Aseneth's seven day repentance may also be tinged with humour, as she more than fulfils expectations (9 – 10), thus adding more mockery of the hardliners' stance. As night falls the narrative tells us not of the lovers' first night, but of Aseneth's wakefulness and distress (10:1; Ph 10:2). Her first act is to slip downstairs to the gate and remove the skin from the window which hung there as a curtain (τὴν δέρριν τοῦ καταπετάσματος) (10:2; Ph 10:4). If the house and courtyard also function as a sexual symbol, then this act may symbolise removal of her hymen and so first intercourse. It becomes a container for ashes which she put on the floor of her chamber, before closing herself off and sending her inquiring virgins back to sleep.

We then read that she entered the second chamber, removed her "gold woven royal robe", her golden girdle, and tiara, dressed herself in mourning attire, and then threw her glorious garment with bracelets and diadem out the north window to the poor (10:11; Ph 10:12). Similarly she ground down her idols (like the Israelites after the episode of the golden calf; Exod 32:20), and threw them through the north window to the beggars and needy (10:12; Ph 10:13). She then did the same with her food, vessels, and cups, to the strange dogs (τοῖς κύσι τοῖς ἀλλοτρίοις) (10:13; Ph 10:14). The change of clothes represents rejection of an old way of being. The elements thrown out the window match that way of life with its idolatry and, significantly, its association with food and drink, already identified in Joseph's declaration of demarcation. The "strange dogs" probably also symbolise the Gentiles (cf. Mark 7:24-30). She then girded herself in sackcloth, sprinkled ashes on her head and on the floor, and spent the night weeping, sighing, and screaming (10:15; Ph 10:15-17), her tears mixing with the ashes to produce a muddy mess. The effect, doubtless the author's intention, is to establish Aseneth's worthiness as a penitent. Surely not all hearers would have kept a straight face, let alone a dour one, during this depiction. It is still storytelling and entertainment despite its earnest intent.

---

[630] Humphrey, *Joseph and Aseneth*, criticises the claim in Chesnutt, *From Death to Life*, 112, 124-25, that the epiphanic passage is merely confirming conversion, depicted as Aseneth's act (53), and claims that major change occurs at 15:5-6 (54). Cf. also Pervo, "Aseneth and Her Sisters, who writes: "her repentance and conversion derive from her own choice, insight, capacity to accept revelation, and courage" (151). These are probably false alternatives, such as reproduce themselves in later Christian controversy. Arguably the beginning is divine initiative but there is soon a synergy of interactions.

The hearers would also sense the change as the author takes us to the eighth day and fittingly depicts a new beginning: "And on the eighth day, behold, it was dawn and the birds were already singing and the dogs barking" (11:1). For we know that this is the day of Joseph's return (9; 10:1; Ph 9:4-5; 10:1). As Humphrey notes, the author has Joseph appearing in the city of the sun on the summer solstice.[631] But first we must wait for three further expressions of Aseneth's repentance, which take us across three chapters (11:3-14; 11:16-18; 12:1 – 13:15), only the last of which survives in the shorter version (Ph 12:1 – 13:12). To some extent they are like a musical interlude. They reflect the story, yet go beyond it in ways that suggest that they may have functioned also as independent pieces loosely based on the story. For while Aseneth's claim to be an orphan (11:3) might partly cohere with incidental detail thus far, at least the death of her younger brother (10:8), it can only make sense metaphorically in the sense that, as she goes on to claim, in contradiction to the story, that her parents hated her for giving up her idols (11:3-5).[632] This was probably a common experience for converts[633] which slips into the song by artistic licence. That all people hated her because she hated all men and suitors (11:6) is also new, but thinkable. While she depicts God as also hating her for her idolatry, she entertains that God is merciful, "does not count the sin of a humble person" and is "the father of orphans" (where the song began; cf. 11:3), "protector of the persecuted and of the afflicted a helper (βοηθός)" (11:13). The first prayer prayer while sitting is an utterance of the heart, not of her lips ("without opening her mouth" (11:3). The second prayer is on her knees but also only from her heart (11:15). In it she also speaks of her being an orphan and desolate, and as having a defiled mouth (τὸ στόμα μου μεμίαται) and speaks of forgiveness.

The third prayer, also prayed on her knees, now comes in spoken words (11:19; Ph 12:1). Longer and more elaborate, it confesses sins of "lawlessness and irreverence" (ἠνόμησα καὶ ἠσέβησα), speaking "wicked and unspeakable (things)" (πονηρὰ καὶ ἄρρητα) (similarly 13:13; Ph 13:9 against Joseph) and having a mouth defiled by food derived from sacrifice to idols (12:5; Ph 12:5). It, too, speaks of being an orphan and desolate, hated and abandoned (12:5), including by her parents (12:12-14; Ph 12:11), but speaks also of God as a compassionate father, but in more graphic and moving detail (12:8; also 12:14-15; Ph 12:11) . The shorter version compares God also to a mother (Ph 12:8), probably under influence from use of the Psalms in the immediate context and here: Ps

---

[631] Humphrey, *Joseph and Aseneth*, 82.

[632] Noting this in chap. 12, Collins, "Joseph and Aseneth," writes: "We may suspect that the prayer is a secondary addition" (107).

[633] So Chesnutt, *From Death to Life*, 115-17; Pervo, "Aseneth and Her Sisters," 151.

130:2 LXX.[634] There are no explicitly sexual themes. The concluding word repeats Aseneth's declaration of 6:8 Ph 6:8 that she is willing to be maid and slave for Joseph, but also to make his bed, wash his feet, and wait on him (13:15; Ph 13:12). The spoken and unspoken prayers reinforce Aseneth's repentance while also signalling key themes concerning conversion and the author's understanding of God. In relation to conversion they include the notion of moving from idolatry where food defiles the mouth. In relation to theology they put major emphasis on the nature of God as a compassionate parent. This element justified Joseph's willingness not to close the door on Aseneth. It clearly informs the author's argument against the hardline position which resists marriage under any circumstances to Gentiles.

After spending four chapters hearing the author describe Aseneth's repentance we might expect a matching elaboration of its effects. This comes in chapters 14 – 17. These, too, serve to enhance Aseneth's status as one worthy of intermarriage, but also much more than that; for she becomes the patroness of all future proselytes like her. These chapters are, indeed, central to the structure of the narrative, as Humphrey shows.[635] The account begins with Aseneth seeing the morning star and taking it as reassurance that God had heard her prayer, "because this star rose as a messenger and herald (ἄγγελος καὶ κῆρυξ) of the light of the great day" (14:1; Ph 14:2). So now the heavenly world is confirming her status. "The great day" is both the day of her conversion and the day of her marriage. Heavenly portents continue as "heaven was torn apart" (a motif reminiscent of Jesus' baptism in Mark 1:10) and a great light appeared and a man came to her from heaven (ἄνθρωπος ἐκ τοῦ οὐρανοῦ) breaching the closed doors of her chamber (14:3-7; Ph 14:4-6), then identifying himself as chief of God's house and commander of his host (14:8; Ph 14:7). He appears as "a man in every respect similar to Joseph" (ἀνὴρ κατὰ πάντα ὅμοιος τῷ 'Ιωσήφ), but with more shining features (14:9; Ph 14:8). It is hard to know if the author sees the man from heaven's entry into her chamber and later sitting on her bed as sexually allusive,[636] especially since he is like Joseph.

The man's first instruction is that she go into her second chamber, put off her black tunic and the sackcloth and ashes, wash her face and hands with living water, and put on "a new linen robe (as yet) untouched (ἄθικτον)" and gird herself with the twin girdle of her virginity (14:12; Ph 14:12-13), described in 14:14 Ph 14:16 as being "one girdle around her waist, and another girdle upon her breast".

---

[634] On this see Standhartinger, *Frauenbild*, 184.

[635] Humphrey, *Joseph and Aseneth*, 41.

[636] So Wills, *Jewish Novel*, who asks: "Is he a symbolic substitute for the sexual union one expects between Aseneth and Joseph?" 174, which becomes an assertion: "Thus the Man from Heaven is an example of an erotic substitute, just as Joseph is almost an erotic substitute himself" (175).

Change of clothes and washing were widespread indicators of transformation, here indicating confirmation of her acceptance. She followed the instructions, but in addition "took an (as yet) untouched (ἄθικτον) and distinguished linen veil and covered her head" (14:15; Ph 14:17). This earned the man's rebuke, who declared: "You are a chaste virgin today, and your head is like that of a young man (ὡς ἀνδρὸς νεανίσκου)" (15:1; Ph 15:1).

This description of her unveiled head as looking like that of a young male does not apparently require further elucidation for the hearers of the work, unlike for us as later interpreters. Removing the veil of the bride belonged then as now to rituals of marriage, but that does not appear to be the context here. It is not until 18:5-6; Ph 18:3-6 that she dresses in wedding attire. Kraemer tentatively observes: "For the moment, at least, Aseneth stands in a human-divine hierarchy as though she were male and as the direct image of the divine, as the primordial *anthrōpos* in Genesis 1.26-27 was the direct image or glory of God and perhaps also androgynous".[637] Nothing else, however, suggests she is from this point onwards androgynous, as though restored to a primeval state understood on the basis of one particular interpretation of Gen 1:27 in accord with Platonic thought as being both male and female.[638] Another possibility, widely attested in early Christian literature, but attested also in Philo and perhaps reflected in the presuppositions of Paul in 1 Corinthians 11, is that she has been "made male", an interpretation also based on Genesis in which the first human being is understood to have been male and as the primary reflection of God's image (cf. also *Gos. Thom.* 114).[639] This need mean neither denial of her femaleness (as if making her male implied unmaking her as female) nor androgyny. Aseneth remains a woman, a "chaste virgin", which, though theoretically also able to be seen as male, is clearly female when a few verses later she is depicted as a "chaste virgin" to be given to Joseph as a bride (15:6). Nor does it appear to imply the merging of masculine and feminine virtues, as reflected in the Hellenistic romances,[640] nor the ascetic denial

---

[637] Kraemer, *When Joseph Met Aseneth*, 197.

[638] See the discussion in Kraemer, *When Joseph Met Aseneth*, 197; and also Loader, *Septuagint*, 27-30, 52-55; William Loader, "Sexuality and Ptolemy's Greek Bible: Genesis 1-3 in Translation: '... Things Which They Altered For King Ptolemy' (Genesis Rabbah 8.11)," in *Ptolemy II Philadelphus and his World* (ed. Paul McKechnie and Philippe Guillaume; MnemSup 300; Leiden: Brill, 2008) 207-32, 215-18.

[639] Kraemer, *When Joseph Met Aseneth*, 197-98.

[640] On this see Kraemer, *When Joseph Met Aseneth*, who writes: "This transference of gendered valuation allows a different interpretation of the meaning of 'becoming male' in ancient texts, including, perhaps, *Aseneth* itself" (204; see also 201-202). She notes also that chasteness in the romances is focussed primarily on lovers' fidelity in suffering absence from one another, not a trait shared by *Aseneth*, though it probably shares to some extent the

of sexuality found in the Christian apocryphal Acts.[641] While here addressed as "chaste Virgin", after she marries Joseph and ceases to be a virgin, she will continue to hold her special status, including her role, to be announced, of being a City of Refuge. Therefore her special status here is something independent of her virginity. The focus here is not her virtues, nor her sexuality, but her special status in relation to God and the heavenly world, which, in turn, is a promise to all proselyte women. Her male head appears to be related to her being given equal status before God in the heavenly world. It does, of course, imply a world view which presupposes a hierarchy of being in which female is subordinate to male and that to be raised to male status is a privilege.

The next element includes the identification of her name as "written in the book of the living in heaven" and as having been written there from the beginning (15:4; Ph 15:3). This coheres with the shorter reading in Joseph's prayer, which depicts her as one whom God chose before she was begotten (Ph 8:11). We then hear the familiar language of her being "renewed and formed anew and made alive again", just as Joseph prayed (8:9; Ph 8:11), and that from that day (ἀπὸ τῆς σήμερον) she will "eat the blessed bread of life, and drink a blessed cup of immortality", and anoint herself "with blessed ointment of incorruptibility" (15:5; Ph 15:4; cf. 8:5; Ph 8:11). This refers to her ongoing status, not an initiation meal, and this status makes possible what the man goes on to declare: "Courage, Aseneth, chaste virgin. Behold, I have given you today to Joseph for a bride, and he himself will be your bridegroom for ever (and) ever" (15:6; Ph 15:5 without "for ever and ever"). Perhaps this also implies that marriage continues in the future place of heavenly rest.

Thus divine intervention through the man from heaven establishes two things: on the one hand, Aseneth's incorporation into the people of God, symbolised by her change of clothes, her name being identified as among the elect, and her assured future participation in the bread, wine, and oil that brings eternal life; and, on the other hand, her qualification, therefore, as an appropriate spouse for Joseph and therefore the divine blessing of their wedding. This makes clear on what basis intermarriage with Gentiles is possible and shows it as blessed by God, Aseneth being the prime exhibit.

The author then goes beyond making her a proof of valid intermarriage to make her also a shelter for all such people "who attach themselves to the Most High God in the name of Repentance" (15:7; Ph 15:6), having her renamed, "City of Refuge". As Portier-Young notes, Num 35:15 envisages that not only Israelites

---

male investment in perpetuating control of women through marriage by its conservative depictions (201, 205).

[641] So Kraemer, *When Joseph Met Aseneth*, 202-206.

but also aliens may find refuge in the cities of refuge and "the LXX translator has rendered the Hebrew גֵּר ('sojourner, resident alien') with προσήλυτος, which has the added connotation of 'proselyte' or 'convert'".[642] Jerusalem was also seen as a city of refuge both for Israelites and for aliens, particularly in the prophets (Isa 55:5-7) and especially Isa 54:15 LXX, which uses the word προσήλυτοι: ἰδοὺ προσήλυτοι προσελεύσονταί σοι δι' ἐμοῦ καὶ ἐπὶ σὲ καταφεύξονται, (lit. "See, proselytes shall approach you through me and flee to you for refuge").[643] Thus Aseneth is also being linked symbolically with Jerusalem.[644] Collins draws attention also to Zech 2:15 LXX, which says of the daughter of Zion: καὶ καταφεύξονται ἔθνη πολλὰ ἐπὶ τὸν κύριον ἐν τῇ ἡμέρᾳ ἐκείνῃ καὶ ἔσονται αὐτῷ εἰς λαὸν καὶ κατασκηνώσουσιν ἐν μέσῳ σου ("And many peoples will flee for refuge to the Lord on that day and they will be his [lit. for him a] people and dwell in your midst") (cf. also Isa 62:4).[645]

Extending the use of symbolic names, the author speaks of "Repentance" as an exceedingly beautiful virgin in the heavens who intercedes for all such repentant virgins, like Aseneth, preparing for them a place of rest (τόπον ἀναπαύσεως) in the heavens (15:7; cf. Ph 15:7).[646] This "Repentance" bears the traits of heavenly Wisdom,[647] and is described as loved by God and the angels and as the man from heaven's sister (15:8), an allusion to Prov 7:4 ("Say to wisdom, 'You are my sister,'"). Issues of marriage are central even to this depiction of the heavenly "Repentance", because she looks after virgin proselytes.

Fitting this concern, the man from heaven returns to the promise to Aseneth that she is to be Joseph's bride, tells her that he will inform Joseph of all that has happened, and instructs her: "Dress in your wedding robe, the ancient and first robe which is laid up in your chamber since eternity" (15:10; Ph 15:10), and so she is to present herself as a good bride for Joseph. This assumes miraculous provision of the wedding dress (as later the honeycomb), but, more significantly, declares by implication that even her marriage as a proselyte was in the divine plan from the beginning. The man thwarts Aseneth's attempt to find out his name (cf. Manoah in Judg 13:17-18), but this provides the author with the opportunity to underline the

---

[642] Portier-Young, "Sweet Mercy Metropolis," 135.

[643] So Gerhard Delling, "Einwirkungen der Sprache der Septuaginta in 'Joseph und Aseneth'," *JSJ* (1978) 29-56, 42.

[644] So Portier-Young, "Sweet Mercy Metropolis," 137.

[645] Collins, *Between Athens and Jerusalem*, 236.

[646] The shorter text at this point reads: "She has prepared a heavenly bridal chamber for those who love her" (τοῖς ἀγαπῶσιν αὐτὴν ἡτοίμασε νυμφῶνα οὐράνιον) (Ph 15:7). At Ph 8:11, however, it, too, speaks of a future place of "rest": (κατάπαυσίν σου).

[647] So Humphrey, *Joseph and Aseneth*, 70, 99; Angela Standhartinger, "Weisheit in *Joseph und Aseneth* und den paulinischen Briefen," *NTS* 47 (2001) 482-501, 488-89.

man's superior heavenly credentials as chief of God's house, and so further enhance the credibility of the author's claims (15:11-12; not in Ph).

Aseneth is then depicted following appropriate custom of the day (and as standing in succession to Abraham) in offering the heavenly man hospitality. She places her hand on his knee and invites him to sit on her bed, which she informs him "is pure and undefiled, and a man or woman never sat on it" (15:14; Ph 15:14 only a brief invitation). As noted above in relation to 14:9; Ph 14:8, some see a sexual reference here, as though the man, who looks like Joseph, is being invited to share her bed, but what immediately follows points in other directions as she promises him bread and wine with a wonderful bouquet. At this point we begin the curious episode where the man asks for a honeycomb and has it miraculously supplied in Aseneth's storeroom (16:1-8; Ph 16:1-4). It was "white as snow and full of honey. And that honey was like dew from heaven and its exhalation like a breath of life" (16:8; Ph 16:4). The author then has Aseneth twice wonder whether as breath it might have come from the man's mouth (16:10, 11; Ph 16:6 once) and for this insight win the man's approval (16:12; not in Ph). This is an important clue to its coded significance later. He then declares:

> Happy are you, Aseneth, because the ineffable mysteries of the Most High have been revealed to you, and happy (are) all who attach themselves to the Lord God in repentance, because they will eat from this comb. For this comb is full of the spirit of life (16:14; Ph 16:7)

If we assume that the man has revealed the "mysteries", then they will refer to her status as "City of Refuge" and to "Repentance" as intercessor of proselytes. This makes sense, then, of the reference to "all who attach themselves to the Lord God in repentance". Their eating of the comb is the same as her eating of it, and indicates what is elsewhere described as receiving the food which brings eternal life. This makes sense, in turn, of the statement which follows:

> And the bees of the paradise of delight have made this from the dew of the roses of life that are in the paradise of God. And all the angels eat of it and all the chosen of God and all the sons of the Most High, because this is the comb of life, and everyone who eats it will not die for ever (and) ever. (16:14; Ph 16:8 shorter)

Accordingly he has her eat from it: he "said to her, 'Eat'" (16:15; not in Ph). Kraemer suggests that this may be read as an inversion of the exchange in Eden, which she then interprets as undoing what Adam and Eve did and restoring patriarchal order.[648] The immediate context does not suggest this is the focus.

---

[648] Kraemer, *When Joseph Met Aseneth*, 208-209, who writes: "its subliminal message is that Paradise is restored when women are properly obedient to their husbands" (209).

Rather the man declares: "Behold you have eaten bread of life, and drunk a cup of immortality, and been anointed with ointment of incorruptibility" (16:16; not in Ph). Eating the honeycomb symbolically represents these three actions, which, in turn, represent the ongoing receiving of eternal life. This is therefore another way of indicating Aseneth's full integration into the people of God. As Chesnutt notes, "Aseneth's eating of the honey and her full participation in the blessings of life and immortality symbolized thereby, all under the direction of God's chief angel, prove this convert worthy to be received fully into the community of Israel and to be married to the revered patriarch".[649] To this point the image of the honeycomb appears best understood as related to the manna which is also depicted as white and tasting like honey (Exod 16:31), as the "food of angels" (Ps 77:25 LXX), as coming down with the dew (Num 11:9 LXX) and is used in later Jewish and Christian tradition to symbolise Wisdom and Torah.[650] The connection with the mouth, suggesting spoken word, supports this. Portier-Young proposes that the sweetness may also reflect the wider background of honey as an image of God's mercy, related to healing, the promise of the land and honey from the rock in Deut 32:10-13 where the word νοσσία referring to an eagle's nest can also mean beehive.[651] Aseneth embodies this sweet compassion in her advocating mercy towards the sons of Bilhah and Zilpah in 27.7–28.17.[652]

The words which follow speak in images of her flesh flourishing like flowers and her bones becoming strong like cedars, and reassure her that "untiring powers" would embrace her, her youth not see old age, and her beauty not fail (16:16; not in Ph). These references are apparently not to her earthly existence, but to her heavenly life. This makes sense of the following comment which declares: "You will be like a walled mother-city of all who take refuge in the name of the Lord God, the king of the ages" (16:16; not in Ph). She is then like a heavenly Jerusalem.[653] As Humphrey notes, "Aseneth, a locked garden, is here *verbally* transformed into a walled city; the virgin is pronounced a mother".[654]

---

[649] Chesnutt, "Dead Sea Scrolls," 413; Humphrey, *Joseph and Aseneth*, 97. So earlier Christoph Burchard, *Untersuchungen zu Joseph und Aseneth* (WUNT 8; Tübingen: Mohr, 1965) 129-30; Chesnutt, *From Death to Life*, 146.

[650] Collins, *Between Athens and Jerusalem*, 235.

[651] Portier-Young, "Sweet Mercy Metropolis," 147-52. She also draws attention to imagery of honey in Cant 4:11, 5:1, noting that "the association of honey with the sweet pleasures of love and marriage finds attestation across cultures and eras" (133). Cf. also M. Hubbard, "Honey for Aseneth: Interpreting a Religious Symbol," *JSP* 16 (1997) 97-110, who draws attention to the associations of honey and birth, so linking it to transformation imagery, as in *Let. Barn.* 6:8 – 7:2 (104-106).

[652] Portier-Young, "Sweet Mercy Metropolis," 155.

[653] Kraemer, *When Joseph Met Aseneth*, 29-30.

[654] Humphrey, *Joseph and Aseneth*, 95.

The image of the honeycomb continues as the author depicts the man making a cross of blood on the honeycomb (16:17; Ph 10-11), which might appear at first to be a Christian allusion, but seems better related to what follows. The man summons the bees from out of the honeycomb, tens of thousands of them "white as snow, and their wings like purple and like violet and like scarlet (stuff) and like gold-woven linen cloaks and golden diadems (were) on their heads, and they had sharp stings" (16:18; Ph 16:13).[655] Queen bees then made a honeycomb on Aseneth's lips (Ph: land on them; 16:14) and other bees ate from it before being sent off to their places in heaven (16:19-21). The shorter text has all the bees die then come alive and fly to the courtyard as 16:22 below (Ph 16:15-17). To this point nothing indicates that this impinged negatively on Aseneth.[656] Indeed, given the earlier reference to lips and mouth and the honeycomb coming from the man's mouth, it would appear that the somewhat bizarre image intends to depict Aseneth as now also a source of honey for others, perhaps another way of speaking of her special role for other proselytes who convert and marry Israelites.

Only in 16:22 (cf. Ph 16:14 perhaps not to harm) do we hear of some bees who want to harm her, but they fall to the ground dead and the man sends them into the fruit bearing trees of the courtyard. They clearly have no place in heaven. They thus belong in the earthly reflection of the true paradise, not in paradise itself. The fact that these are bees belonging in the honeycomb probably suggests that a demarcation is being made among those who are honey feeders, namely Israel. Some see this as prefiguring the divisions depicted in chaps. 23-27.[657] It is not too subtle to suggest that these may represent the opponents of intermarriage, even with a proselyte. Given the level of multivalent allusion in the work it is probable that both allusions are present, not least because both relate to opposition to Aseneth, which in the final chapters is ironically reversed so that the traditional champions of opposing intermarriage become its defenders.

---

[655] See the critique of Collins, "Joseph and Aseneth," of attempts to identify the bees as priests or souls of Neoplatonism (110-11). Cf. Bohak, *Joseph and Aseneth*, who points to the colours worn by priests in Exodus 28 (11); Kraemer, *When Joseph Met Aseneth*, 168-72.

[656] Cf. Angela Standhartinger, "Joseph und Aseneth: Vollkommene Braut oder himmlische Prophetin," in *Kompendium Feministische Bibelauslegung* (ed. Luise Schottroff, Marie-Theres Wacker, Claudia Janssen, and Beate Wehn; Gütersloh: Gütersloher Verlagshaus, 1999) 459-64, who contrasts the shorter text which has the honeycomb touch her lips, an image evoking prophetic calling (Ezek 3:1-3; Jer 1:9; Isa 6:6-7) and so an active Aseneth with the longer text, which she sees as restricting her to silence by effectively blocking her speech with honeycomb actually formed on her mouth (460). Similarly Kraemer, *When Joseph Met Aseneth*, 207. Standhartinger sees a stronger association between Aseneth and the image of Elisha in the short text's depiction of the man's departure as like Elijah's (460).

[657] Humphrey, *Joseph and Aseneth*, 23-26, 44, 98; Portier-Young, "Sweet Mercy Metropolis," 155; Chesnutt, *From Death to Life*, 114.

The man's final act is to respond to Aseneth's request that he bless her virgins (17:4). The author has him declare them seven pillars of Aseneth, the "City of Refuge" (17:6; Ph 17:5), an association of Aseneth with the image of Wisdom in Proverbs 9,[658] whose counterpart is Wisdom/"Repentance" in the heavenly world. The man then returns to heaven in a chariot like Elijah (17:8; Ph 17:7), while Aseneth rebukes herself for not realising that not a man but (a?) God had visited her chamber, apologising to God for speaking boldly and in ignorance (17:10). This regret, present also in the shorter text (Ph 17:7), probably serves not to tarnish but rather to enhance Aseneth's image as one who matched the best male models of the day of what is appropriate women's behaviour. Her ignorance excuses her and has in any case served the hearers well, since they are now very clear that God not only approves of intermarriage with Gentile proselyte women, but made Aseneth their representative for all time, supported by heavenly Wisdom herself who as "Repentance" intercedes for all Aseneth's successors.

We return to the literal narrative in 18:1; Ph 18:1 with the report that Joseph is about to return. It reads almost as though the events of chaps. 14 – 17 had not happened, indeed, could read as a sequel to chap. 10, since it depicts Aseneth as with a fallen face and her "foster-father", the steward managing her house, whom she asked to prepare a welcome dinner for Joseph, as distressed at the sight (18:1-4; Ph 18:1-2, but nothing about a fallen face).[659] But then we hear that "Aseneth remembered the man (from heaven) and his commandment" (given in 15:10; Ph 15:10-11) and so went off and dressed in her wedding attire, including the veil, with which "she covered her head like a bride", and a sceptre (18:5-6; Ph 18:3-6). Dressing like royalty for one's wedding appears to have been a common practice, which still survives.

Aseneth has been through a number of changes of clothes.[660] First she dresses to greet her parents (3:5-6; Ph 3:9-11); then she discards those clothes, throwing them out the window, and dons a black mourning gown with sackcloth and ashes (10:10-11, 14-15; Ph 10:11-12, 15-17), which she next replaces by an untouched linen robe and twin girdle with a veil which she is told to remove (15:1; Ph 15:1); and finally the present scene where she dresses in wedding attire with veil (18:5-6; Ph 18:3-6). Each marks a significant stage, from initial idolatry to repentance to acceptance to marriage.

Washing usually belonged to rituals of preparation for marriage. The author may be playing with this in having her summon water for washing her face (18:8;

---

[658] On the association of Aseneth with Wisdom see Sänger, *Antikes Judentum*, 204.

[659] Cf. Wills, *Jewish Novel*, who speculates that a form of the story once existed without the intervening allegorical treatment (177-80).

[660] On the changes of clothes as reflecting the processes of transformation see Rees Conrad Douglas, "Liminality and Conversion in Joseph and Aseneth," *JSP* 3 (1988) 31-48; Humphrey, *Joseph and Aseneth*, 101.

Ph 18:7). Its immediate context is her fear that Joseph will be put off by her fallen face. The storyteller is at work in depicting her worry, but also in cleverly conjuring up a mirror effect through the water in the basin, a rather incredible effect which those being entertained would have tolerated. The image she sees of herself (18:9; Ph 18:7 much shorter) is anything but a drawn, fallen face.

The description begins: "It was like the sun and her eyes (were) like a rising morning star" (18:9; Ph 18:7 much shorter). While the imagery speaks for itself, it is also rich in intratextual allusion. She now takes on some of the appearance of Joseph, presented as like the sun-god coming to sun-city. The "morning star" recalls the beginning of her visitation from the heavenly man and signals a new beginning. Indeed, as already 11:1 (not in Ph) intimated, this eighth day began with its dawn of promise, birds singing and dogs barking. The intratextual allusions continue: "and her cheeks like fields of the Most High, and on her cheeks (there was) red (color) like a son of man's blood". This recalls the markings of blood on the honeycomb which may symbolise people from all directions coming to it. The accounts continues: "and her lips (were) like a rose of life coming out of its foliage, and her teeth like fighting men lined up for a fight, and the hair of her head (was) like a vine in the paradise of God prospering in its fruits, and her neck like an all-variegated cypress, and her breasts (were) like the mountains of the Most High God" (18:9). This recalls the roses of paradise from whose dew the honeycomb was made which was placed on her lips (15:14; not in Ph) and the image of fruitfulness with which the story begins. The image of her breasts may simply indicate that they were fulsome or perhaps peaked, as once they stood up as apples at Joseph's first touch. Some parts of the anatomy are missing, like hands, arms, and feet, but this probably means no more than that they would not have been seen in the basin's image.[661]

Her glorious appearance belongs to the storyteller's entertainment as does the humour in having her not wash her face for fear lest she wash it all away (18:10; not in Ph) and her "foster-father" being stunned by her appearance (18:11; not in Ph). He is still looking at the same face which he saw as fallen in 18:3 (not in Ph), so that its transformation in the interim must be attributed to her remembering her visitation which, we may assume, not only reminded her to dress for the wedding, but also that she had been incorporated into the people of God. Her beauty but also her transformation as a proselyte warrant the foster-father's musing: "At last the Lord God of heaven has chosen you as a bride for his firstborn son, Joseph?" (μήτιγε κύριος ὁ θεὸς τοῦ οὐρανοῦ ἐξελέξατο σε εἰς νύμφην τῷ υἱῷ αὐτοῦ τῷ πρωτοτόκῳ Ἰωσήφ;) (18:11; not in Ph). The hearers, informed by the account of transformation and convinced by the author that such a marriage to a

---

[661] So Humphrey, *Joseph and Aseneth*, 72; Cf. Standhartinger, *Frauenbild*, 212-13; Standhartinger, "Joseph und Aseneth," 460-61.

Gentile proselyte is both legitimate and blessed by God, and perhaps recalling the irony of her earlier protestations about marrying a king's firstborn (4:11; Ph 4:15), might chant in response: "He has indeed!"

In 19:1; Ph 19:1 the author takes us back to the announcement in 18:1; Ph 18:1 that Joseph was arriving, but by now he is standing at the doors of the courtyard. Aseneth, who all this time has been busy in her chamber – clearly too busy to see Joseph's arrival! – hurries down to meet him and stands at the door (19:2; cf. Ph 19:1 only to meet him), while Joseph enters the courtyard closing the door on "all strangers" (πάντες ἀλλότριοι) outside (19:3; not in Ph), possibly a reference to the demarcation of Jews and Gentiles, although Aseneth's family clearly also belong inside.[662] Rather oddly, Joseph asks Aseneth: "Who are you?" (19:4; not in Ph). At the level of the entertaining story it means: she is so beautiful that he does not recognise her. More probably the intent is to focus on who she has become, almost like a liturgical invitation to a convert to give voice to their identity. The hearers can answer the question well, whom the author thus indirectly invites to do so. Aseneth gives her own brief answer:

> I am your maidservant Aseneth, and all the idols I have thrown away from me and they were destroyed. And a man came to me from heaven today, and gave me bread of life and I ate, and a cup of blessing and I drank. And he said to me, "I have given you for a bride to Joseph today, and he himself will be your bridegroom for ever (and) ever". And he said to me, "Your name will no longer be called Aseneth, but your name will be called City of Refuge and the Lord God will reign as king over many nations for ever, because in you many nations will take refuge with the Lord God, the Most High". (19:5; not in Ph)

This neatly summarises the import of chapters 10 – 17 in four steps: turning from idolatry, receiving eternal life (represented in the image of eating and drinking), being assured she is to be Joseph's bride, and being made a representative symbol of all Gentile women after her who become proselytes (and marry Jewish men). She reports also that the man reassured her that he would provide a full account to Joseph (19:6; not in Ph).

The well informed Joseph responds by acclaiming Aseneth as like a city: "The Lord God founded your walls in the highest, and your walls are adamantine walls of life, because the sons of the living God will dwell in your City of Refuge, and the Lord God will reign as king over them for ever and ever" (19:8; Ph 19:2 only briefly). He leaves what some might see as the most important aspect unsaid: yes, she will be his bride, and focuses instead on her symbolic role as a "City of Refuge". Thus far the "City of Refuge" has been described as serving those

---

[662] Kraemer, *When Joseph Met Aseneth*, notes that in the long text the meeting takes places within enclosure, symbolising a traditional understanding of enclosed women (210).

Gentile women who like Aseneth convert to Judaism as virgins and for whom also the virgin "Repentance" on high intercedes. Here we might see a much broader application if the symbol of "sons of the living God" refers to all. Perhaps more probable is that Joseph means angels by "sons of the living God" and so underlines the level of support for Aseneth's city.

The element of romance returns with some humour as Joseph follows his profundities by saying: "And now, come to me, chaste virgin, and why do you stand far away from me?" (19:9; not in Ph). "Joseph stretched out his hands and called Aseneth by a wink of his eyes" (19:10; not in Ph). Doing the same she "ran up to Joseph and fell on his breast. And Joseph put his arms around her, and Aseneth (put hers) around Joseph, and they kissed each other for a long time and both came to life in their spirit" (19:10; Ph 19:3 similar). This is as erotic as it gets, but even then entertainment with intent intervenes as we read of three gifts given by Joseph through the three kisses: life, wisdom, and truth (19:11; not in Ph). In the light of all that Aseneth has already received, these must be seen not as new gifts but as part of what being in the people of God now brings.[663] The mildly romantic returns in the note: "And they embraced each other for a long time and interlocked their hands like bonds" (20:1; cf. Ph 19:3). While not interested in developing the erotic as in Hellenistic romances, the author is clearly affirming of sexual love and show no signs of ascetic disapproval. His work is after all serving to justify marriage to Gentile proselytes.

Aseneth has Joseph enter her house and sit on her father's throne (20:1-2; Ph 20:1-2). In insisting against Joseph that she, not her maids, wash his feet, Aseneth echoes earlier sentiments (13:15; Ph 13:12), but also asserts: "Your feet are my feet and your hands are my hands, and your soul my soul, and your feet another (woman) will never wash" (20:4; Ph 20:3). This reflects the sentiment of Gen 2:24 of the two becoming one flesh. The exclusion of other women suggests that the washing here symbolises something more, namely sexual intercourse and so marital chastity. Perhaps the detail of having him enter her house and sit on her father's throne also symbolises sexual union and marriage as the beginning of a new household. Then the imagery continues in the depiction of Aseneth taking the typical position in households of the time, as at the right hand of the husband who is sitting on a throne, but also as a source of life. That would make sense of Joseph's seeing her hands as "like hands of life, and her fingers fine like (the) fingers of a fast-writing scribe" (20:5; not in Ph). The latter image probably

---

[663] So Sänger, *Antikes Judentum*, 205-208; Chesnutt, *From Death to Life*, 138; cf. Michael Penn, "Identity Transformation and Authorial Identification in *Joseph and Aseneth*," *JSP* 13 (2002) 171-83, who sees this as a ritual act and argues that as such it lacks parallels in Judaism and so counts in favour of seeing the work as Christian (182), but that a ritual act rather than a traditional threefold kiss is intimated here is improbable.

implies her ability to do the women's work which required nimble fingers, such as needlework.

Pentephres and his wife, returning from the fields of their inheritance, are also struck with Aseneth's beauty, which the author describes in ways which allude to her transformation: "like (the) appearance of light, and her beauty was like heavenly beauty" (20:6; not in Ph), noting similarly that they "gave glory to God who gives life to the dead" (20:7; not in Ph). Pentephres then accedes to Joseph's suggestion that Pharaoh marry them (20:8-10; Ph 20:6-7). There is no trace of their disowning her as in Aseneth's laments (11:3-5; 12:12-14; Ph 12:11). The author then makes a point of emphasising that while staying with Pentephres, Joseph did not sleep with Aseneth before the wedding, but has him declare: "It does not befit a man who worships God to sleep with his wife before the wedding" (21:1; Ph 20:8), which we may presume was a common value which the author would expect the hearers to share (cf. also *Jub.* 25:4).

The account of the wedding contains traditional elements. Thus Pharaoh asserts that Aseneth had been betrothed for Joseph from eternity (21:3; not in Ph; also 23:3; Ph 23:4; similarly Tob 6:18) and declares: "she shall be your wife from now on and for ever (and) ever" (21:3; Ph 21:3; similarly 15:6; 19:5; 21:21; none in Ph) and addresses Aseneth as "daughter of the Most High" just as Joseph is "the firstborn son of God" (21:4; Ph 21:3). The author is having Pharaoh declare one of his central themes: Aseneth and all such proselytes who follow her are as much God's children as ethnic Jews who follow the path of wisdom.[664] Pharaoh then sets Aseneth at Joseph's right side (21:6; prefigured in 20:5; neither in Ph), places his hands on both their heads and blesses them, including the hope of fruitfulness (21:6; Ph 21:5 similar). "And Pharaoh turned them around toward each other face to face and brought them mouth to mouth and joined them by their lips, and they kissed each other" (21:7; Ph 21:6 similar). A marriage feast and seven days' celebration follow, declared throughout the realm as a holiday (21:8; Ph 21:6-7; cf. Judg 14:12, 17).

Finally the author reports: "And it happened after this, Joseph went in to Aseneth, and Aseneth conceived from Joseph, and gave birth to Manasseh and Ephraim, his brother, in Joseph's house" (21:9; Ph 21:8). Both the consummation and the birth of offspring receive scant attention. That the marriage was consummated in Joseph's house after the celebrations were in hers appears to follow usual practice which would have seen a procession to his house after the celebrations, but such details are not the author's major concern.

---

[664] See Collins, *Between Athens and Jerusalem*, who points to the understanding of being God's children, reflected in Wis 2:13, 16, 18; 5:5 (236). See also Sänger, *Antikes Judentum*, 199-200, 202.

The long text then brings a poetic confession on the lips of Aseneth. Like the earlier pieces it seems like an interlude and one might imagine it sung. It does not really move the story on, but rather recapitulates it in verse, repeating in each stanza, "I have sinned, Lord, I have sinned". It is the most elaborate account of her sins and includes that she was "boastful and arrogant" (21:12, 16), related particularly to her despising suitors and all men (21:17-19) and had been an idolater, eating "bread from their sacrifices", "bread of strangulation", drinking "a cup of insidiousness", and not knowing or trusting God (21:13-15). The song ends with acclamation of Joseph, "the king's firstborn son" (cf. 4:11; Ph 4:15!), who, she declares, "pulled me down from my dominating position and made me humble ... by his beauty caught me ... by his power confirmed me and brought me to the God of the ages and to the chief of the house of the Most High, and gave me to eat bread of life, and to drink a cup of wisdom, and I became his bride forever" (21:21). Poetic licence allows the author to attribute all this to Joseph her husband, whereas in the narrative at most his prayer set these matters in train and they were performed by others. But this suits the author's purpose which has in mind Jewish men who help convert their Gentile would-be spouses.

Further confirmation of Aseneth's acceptance (and so further support for the author's argument) comes when Aseneth goes with Joseph to meet Jacob,[665] whose image is given God-like treatment,[666] enhancing the authority of the event (22:1-8; Ph 22:1-6 without an enhanced image). Jacob first addressed Joseph: "Is this my daughter-in-law, your wife? Blessed she will be by the Most High God" (22:8; not in Ph), then turning to Aseneth blessed and kissed her (22:9; Ph 22:5).

At this point in the narrative the author introduces Simeon and Levi in the beginning of an account heavy with irony. For Simeon and Levi, and Levi in particular, have been established in *Jubilees* and *Aramaic Levi Document* as the champions of opposition to marriage with Gentiles, including Gentile proselytes. The author "converts" them, particularly Levi, to be the supporters and sponsors of the Gentile proselyte, Aseneth. While some have noted that their support for Aseneth is like their support for Dinah,[667] this scarcely does justice to what the author is doing here, because Dinah is an Israelite and Aseneth a Gentile,[668] and it

---

[665] Collins, *Between Athens and Jerusalem*, rightly speaks of this as completing her transition (237); similarly Chesnutt, *From Death to Life*, 111.

[666] On this see Humphrey, *Joseph and Aseneth*, who notes that the author also describes Jacob as like the sun, and with feet of a giant (22:7), an allusion to the sun ὡς γίγας "as a giant" in Ps 18:6 LXX (108).

[667] So Bader, *Tracing the Evidence*, who also a notes a parallel between Shechem and Pharaoh's son in wanting their fathers to act for them (99-102, esp. 101).

[668] If the author knows the legend that she is the illegitimate daughter of Dinah, the author certainly does not share it. See the note in association with 1:5 above where the issue first arises.

is precisely the Dinah incident which formed the basis for extrapolating the hardline position which rejected intermarriage, deleted Jacob's disapproval of their extreme measures, and then saw its heroes in the zeal of Phinehas (*Jub.* 30:1-23; *ALD* 1c-3a; *4QMMT* C 31-32; cf. Ps 106:31; Num 25:7-13). For the same reason the author's depiction goes beyond just the kind of support given to Dinah; it depicts Levi as developing very special love of Aseneth consonant with the elevated status given her by the author as the champion, model, and refuge of Gentile proselyte brides.

Levi's transformed role appears already in 22:12 (Ph 22:8), where in contrast to the enmity and envy of the sons of Zilpah and Bilhah (22:11; not in Ph), Levi joins Joseph on Aseneth's right side with Joseph on the left. We then read that "Aseneth grasped Levi's hand. And Aseneth loved Levi exceedingly above all Joseph's brothers" (22:13; Ph 22:8). He was

> a prudent man and a prophet of the Most High and sharp-sighted with his eyes, and he used to see letters written in heaven by the finger of God and he knew the unspeakable (mysteries) of the Most High God and revealed them to Aseneth in secret, because he, himself, Levi, would love Aseneth very much, and see her place of rest in the highest, and her walls like adamantine eternal walls, and her foundations upon a rock of the seventh heaven. (22:13; Ph 22:8 shorter)

This apparently alludes to Levi literature in which Levi sees visions (such as we find in *Aramaic Levi Document*) with which we must assume the hearers were familiar (1b, 3a-7; cf. also *T. Levi* 5:1-2; 8:1-19; *Jub.* 32:21; *1 Enoch* 103:2; 106:19).[669] The author is underlining that Levi's affection derives from his knowledge about her special status as the model and refuge of Gentile proselyte brides. So the author has enlisted Levi to warrant his construction and argument, for Levi not only loves Aseneth; he also knows what she is about.

In what follows we have a relatively fast-moving narrative of intrigue in which both Aseneth and Levi play key roles, cementing the former's status. First we have the return of Pharaoh's son (cf. 1:7-9; Th 1:11-14) who tries to enlist Levi and Simeon to kill Joseph (23:1-6; Ph 23:1-6), citing their exploits against the Shechemites, further enhancing the irony in the author's transformation of Levi's character. Pharaoh's son wants Aseneth as his wife, who, he claims, "was betrothed to me from the beginning" (23:3; Ph 23:4), echoing what was apparently a common motif in marriages. Levi refuses, but also mollifies Simeon's violence, who wanted to strike Pharaoh's son dead, by standing on his foot, another touch of humour (23:7-17; Ph 23:7-16). Levi models gentleness rather than anger and reminds Pharaoh's son that Joseph "is like the firstborn son of God" (23:10; cf.

---

[669] Humphrey, *Joseph and Aseneth*, rightly notes that mysterious features occur here in the depiction of Levi and are not confined to chapters 14 – 17 (41-42).

4:11! Ph 23:10 only "loved of God"), thus outweighing his status, but warns of their achievements in slaughtering the Shechemites because of Dinah, which again alerts the hearers to their traditional role (23:14; Ph 23:13) and by implication sees it as approved by God, not as deserving rebuke (cf. Gen 34:30; 49:5-7).

Pharaoh's son persists, enlisting Dan and Gad through lies about Joseph (24:1-20; Ph 24:1-21), who are happy to let Pharaoh's son have Aseneth, as they put it, to "do to her as your soul desires" (24:19; Ph 24:18).[670] Pharaoh's son fails in his plot to kill his father (25:1-4; Ph 25:1-4). His claim to be going out "to harvest (the vintage of) my newly planted vineyard" (25:2; Ph 25:2) may be a not so subtle allusion to his true intentions in relation to Aseneth.[671] Naphtali and Asher warn that God's angels will fight for Joseph, "the apple of the eye" to God (25:5; Ph 25:5), but fail to dissuade Dan and Gad (25:5-6; Ph 25:5-7), who scorn the implication that they might "die like women" (25:7; Ph 25:7). Joseph goes off on his commission and is happy for the anxious Aseneth to go off to her inheritance, for she, too, will be guarded as "the apple of the eye" (26:2; Ph 26;2). Dan and Gad and their men ambush Aseneth and her 600 men (26:5; Ph 26:5). Levi sees her plight in a vision and alerts the sons of Leah (26:6; Ph 26:6-7). Aseneth escapes in her carriage only to be confronted by Pharaoh's son and his 50 horsemen (26:7; Ph 26:8), so she prays for help (26:8; not in Ph). Benjamin then hurls a stone at Pharaoh's son, wounding him, and kills the fifty with more stones (27:1-5; Ph 27:1-5), recalling the feat of David before Goliath. Leah's sons kill 2000 more (27:6; 27:6). The sons of Bilhah and Zilpah then confront Aseneth and Benjamin, swords drawn. Aseneth again cries out to the God who made her alive and rescued her "from the idols and the corruption of death" (27:7-10; Ph 27:7-8), "and at once the swords fell from their hands on the ground and were reduced to ashes" (27:11; Ph 27:8). They then confess their sin and beg mercy from Aseneth (28:1-6; Ph 28:1-3), reminding her that their "brothers are men who worship God and do not repay anyone evil for evil" (28:5; Ph 28:3).

Aseneth, now incorporated into Israel and clearly under divine protection, becomes the vehicle for expressing a core of the author's theology: eschewing vengeance and showing compassion.[672] Thus she agrees to their request and has

---

[670] On the role of Dan and Gad and its background in Gen 49:17 and 19, see Humphrey, *Joseph and Aseneth*, 109.

[671] See Humphrey, *Joseph and Aseneth*, 109.

[672] Humphrey, *Joseph and Aseneth*, writes: "The second story has served to put a now-integrated Aseneth into the vanguard: in the first tale, her role was less initiating, more receptive" (107-108). On the background to eschewing vengeance see János Bolyki, "'Never Repay Evil with Evil': Ethical Interaction between the Joseph Story, the Novel Joseph and Aseneth, the New Testament and the Apocryphal Acts," in *Jerusalem, Alexandria, Rome: Studies in Ancient Cultural Interaction in Honour of A. Hilhorst* (ed.

them hide in the thicket while she appeases their brothers' anger (28:7-8; Ph 28:4-7), then persuading Leah's sons not to do "evil for evil", despite Simeon's initial protestations (28:9-14; Ph 28:8-14). Levi, who goes up to her and kisses her hand (28:15-16; Ph 28:15), knows the brothers are hiding, but goes along with her (28:17; not in Ph). Levi then intervenes to stop Benjamin killing the injured son of Pharaoh (29:1-4; Ph 29:1-4), because "it does not befit a man who worships God to repay evil for evil nor to trample underfoot a fallen (man) nor to oppress his enemy till death" (29:3; Ph 29:3), bringing him to Pharaoh, who in response blesses Levi (29:5-6; Ph 29:5-7). The story ends with Joseph succeeding Pharaoh for 48 years before passing the reign to his younger offspring, but with no mention of Aseneth, who presumably took up her appropriate place in Joseph's household.

There is nothing particularly related to sexuality in this final section except the suggestion of sexual violation in Pharaoh's son having his desire with Aseneth (24:19; Ph 24:18) and the probable allusion to his wanting to "harvest her" (25:2; Ph 25:2). The whole, however, must be seen as a splendid irony in which the greatest opposer of intermarriage with Gentiles in *Jubilees* and Levi literature becomes the greatest protector of Aseneth and her intimate friend.

Conclusion

Aseneth is a playfully contrived piece of entertainment with intent. Taking its cue from the "loophole" in arguments against marriage to Gentile women, namely Joseph's marriage to Aseneth,[673] the work makes the case that Gentile women may be converted by their husbands-to-be and that as Gentile proselytes they are acceptable spouses for Jewish men.[674] The work not only employs Aseneth as an example, but also elevates her to representative and symbolic status, as the

---

Florentino García Martínez and Gerard P. Luttikhuizen; JSJSup 82; Leiden: Brill, 2003) 41-53, who points to its roots in Gen 50:20 and Prov 20:22 (50-52).

[673] Sänger, "Erwägungen," rightly observes that *Aseneth* is not the idle product of the artistic imagination nor simply Haggadah explaining a curiosity, namely that the pious Joseph married a Gentile (104-105). Cf. Susan Docherty, "*Joseph and Aseneth*: Rewritten Bible or Narrative Expansion?" *JSJ* 35 (2004) 27-48, who argues that it is written to address that very issue and so belongs to "the genre of rewritten Bible" (33). It does do that, but it does also much more.

[674] Sänger, *Antikes Judentum*, 214; Nickelsburg, *Jewish Literature*, who writes: "That the author chose to write a story in which a Jewish–Gentile marriage is at the center of the plot and in which erotic elements play a significant role suggests further that intermarriage and not just conversion to Judaism is of importance to that author" (336). Chesnutt, "Dead Sea Scrolls," writes: "a major purpose of *Joseph and Aseneth* was to enhance the status of converts within a community deeply divided over the perception of converts and especially over the propriety of marriage between a convert and a born Jew" (412).

protector and refuge of all such women in the future with Wisdom, herself, titled "Repentance", as intercessor on their behalf. Her elaborate repentance and confessions, unspoken and spoken, and her heavenly visitation by a man who confirms her acceptance, feeds her honeycomb, and reveals her special status, serve to ensure that the willing hearer knows that hers was a genuine conversion blessed by God and that her way as a path for future proselytes to follow into marriage has God's blessing.[675]

The work is rich in imagery as it depicts conversion and its effects, including changes of clothes, images of darkness and light, death and life, and employment of eating, drinking, and being anointed as means by which eternal life is imparted. Attempts to find here a Jewish initiation rite[676] or ongoing ritual meal entailing bread, wine, and oil,[677] or honeycomb, founder on the document's obvious symbolic employment of these terms, which equates eating honeycomb with eating bread and drinking wine, which it claims Aseneth has done, but nowhere reports her actually doing.[678] It remains however an issue whether just ordinary meals represent this nourishment which conveys eternal life or whether special communal meals of some kind do so, such as those which prefigure the eschatological banquet.[679] Imagery of garments, transfigurations, and the like, are widely attested in diverse forms of Judaism of the time and so also in New Testament writings.[680]

---

[675] So Chesnutt, *From Death to Life*, who writes: "the detailed narrative of Aseneth's self-abasement, asceticism and repudiation of idolatry serve to confirm the sincerity and genuineness of her conversion" (112); and: "in particular the visit of the man from heaven in chs. 14-17 serves to authenticate Aseneth's conversion by showing that her professed change corresponds to transcendent objective reality" (112); similarly earlier Sänger, *Antikes Judentum*, 156-57, 182.

[676] Against this *Aseneth* depicts Joseph as also eating this meal. So Chesnutt, "Dead Sea Scrolls," 411.

[677] On the special role of oil see Chesnutt, "Dead Sea Scrolls," who notes that it frequently occurs as a major medium of contamination, including at Qumran, and so like bread and wine belongs to categories where demarcation matters (410-25).

[678] So Chesnutt, "Dead Sea Scrolls," 411.

[679] Humphrey, *Joseph and Aseneth*, noting the particular association of the food with immortality and incorruptibility, argues that it cannot just be ordinary food, concluding: "For now we may suspect with reason that *Aseneth* has been informed by some of the mystical traditions that fed into traditions which we have documented only at a later time" (60); cf. also Peter Dschlunigg, "Überlegungen zum Hintergrund der Mahlformel in JosAs: Ein Versuch," *ZNW* 80 (1989) 272-75, who suggests a particular understanding of the passover meal such as we see reflected in 1 Corinthians 10 and John 6.

[680] See for instance, the recent discussion in George J. Brooke, "Men and Women as Angels in *Joseph and Aseneth*," *JSP* 14 (2005) 159-77, who draws attention to relevant Qumran material, both sectarian and non sectarian, in providing evidence for belief that

The author achieves the challenge to hardline positions on intermarriage with subtle irony, not only in having both Joseph and, paradoxically, Aseneth voice such opposition, but also in depicting Levi, the champion hardliner, according to the literature to which the author alludes, as affirming the author's own position and surrounding Aseneth with great affection and support. These are well attested Jewish issues, doubtless highly relevant for the first hearers.[681] If the work is written in the context of dispute over intermarriage, it is probably right to assume that this was a significant issue rather than simply one element in a wider debate. It would be the latter if, with Collins, we assume that the author espoused a Judaism reduced to little more than "monotheism, rejection of idolatry, chastity before marriage, and avoidance of social or sexual intimacy with 'aliens' – that is, people who worship other gods", in which it "is not clear that observance of the full Jewish law is required".[682] For then the conflict with the hardliners would be on a very broad front and the issue of intermarriage just one amid a myriad of conflicts. This does not appear to be the case. In addition, the author clearly reflects familiarity with purity language and concerns (e.g. oil), presumably not limited to metaphorical application. So in reading the silence, we are probably better to understand the image of wisdom and Torah on Aseneth's lips, not as a watered down Judaism for which we would struggle to find parallels, but as Jewish Torah interpreted with distinctively universal emphases. Such emphases would lead to particular controversies, one of them predictably being intermarriage. Indeed, as

---

humans and angels can commune and that the former through transformation can take on appearance of angels. These include the appearance of the bees as angelic priests, but also the angelic qualities attributed to Joseph (166-67), Aseneth (167-70), and Jacob (171). He cites Esth D 6 LXX which depicts Esther as having a face like an angel's; 4Q541 9.i.2-5, which depicts Levi as an angelic-like priest; the *Songs of the Sabbath Sacrifice*; the enigmatic 4Q491 11, and the blessing of the high priest in 1QSb/1Q28b 4.24-26 (163-64). A major argument which Kraemer, *When Joseph Met Aseneth*, uses in support of a late date and possible Christian authorship of *Aseneth* is its parallels with merkavah mysticism and magic and its depiction of Aseneth's adjuring a divine being. For a critical discussion of the latter claim see Collins, "Joseph and Aseneth," 110-11; Humphrey, *Joseph and Aseneth*, 35-37, 53-55. She concludes: "I see in *Aseneth* a major distinctive feature of merkavah mysticism – the centrality of a revelatory experience as constitutive of transformation … Far from reinforcing a third- to fourth-century date for *Aseneth*, the imperfectness of comparisons with merkavah texts suggests a time much earlier" (58).

[681] According to Collins, "Joseph and Aseneth," "the concern with intermarriage as a problem in the first story provides the basic argument for the view that the story is Jewish" (102). "The subject of intermarriage was a central Jewish concern and much less important in Christianity" (107).

[682] Collins, *Between Athens and Jerusalem*, 234. Similarly Donaldson, *Judaism and the Gentiles*, 149.

Collins rightly points out, these emphases would have allowed greater flexibility in weighing the importance of ethnic descent.[683]

Implied in the author's affirmation of intermarriage with Gentile proselyte women is an affirmation of marriage and, within it, sexual relations. Sexual attraction and erotic responses which ever so lightly spice up the narrative compared with its secular Hellenistic counterparts have their place in the world of the author and hearers.[684] Nothing suggests asceticism.[685] Sex out of place includes before marriage and with "strange women", which appears to mean especially women who are seeking illicit sex, whether as the wives of others or as unmarried women. The author's depiction of Joseph and Aseneth's marriage as lasting forever probably indicates that the author does not envisage a heavenly world or age to come where marriage and sexual relations cease to be.

There are some indications that the author also employs some detail in a way that is erotically suggestive, though sometimes we are left uncertain. It is very possible that the author understands Joseph's entry into Aseneth's courtyard and house as an image of sexual intercourse, her removal of the skin which covers the gate window as the rupturing of her hymen, and his being washed by her and no other woman as an allusion to sexual relations, perhaps echoing Gen 2:24. The richly suggestive imagery of Genesis 2 – 3 and Canticles is never far away. Possibly the man from heaven's entry into Aseneth's chamber and sitting on her bed is meant to be suggestive, especially since he is depicted as like Joseph. Similarly the honeycomb may include erotic allusion, though that is not its primary function in the narrative, unless the whole encounter with the man from heaven has an underlying erotic tenor. This would not be entirely novel since marital imagery had been employed in depictions of Israel's relation to God for

---

[683] Collins *Between Athens and Jerusalem*, 234, is responding to Barclay, *Jews in the Mediterranean Diaspora*, who, over against the first edition of Collins' book, argues that the work is "fiercely antagonistic to all non-Jewish religion" (207), anti-Egyptian (208) and so far from being non-ethnic Judaism (214-18). I can accept Collins' statement that Aseneth is not culturally antagonistic (238) towards Egyptians only to the degree that one not include its religion. Aseneth rings with a sense of superiority, while clearly remaining open and appreciative of Egyptians who acknowledge their God, but even more so those who deny their own. See also Chesnutt, *From Death to Life*, who notes that Aseneth is superior but not vengeful (107).

[684] On this see also Ellis, *Sexual Desire*, 71-73.

[685] Cf. Lawrence M. Wills, "Ascetic Theology Before Asceticism? Jewish Narratives and the Decentering of the Self," *JAAR* 74 (2006) 902-25, who identifies Aseneth's repentance as reflecting "a growing Jewish concern about sexuality and the sin inherent in the body" like that of later Christian asceticism (909).

centuries and the Canticles then served such elaboration.[686] Both the shorter and the longer texts affirm sexual relations, though the latter has more erotic allusions. The erotic also belongs to the entertainment of the story designed primarily for a male audience and so has raised issues for some, of its appropriateness in pandering to the "male gaze".[687]

Aseneth is given striking prominence, which shows itself differently in the longer and shorter versions, as Standhartinger has shown, though both depict her as ultimately subordinate to her husband.[688] She notes that in contrast to the long text the shorter text at 2:1 says nothing of her boastfulness and arrogance.[689] Aseneth's arrogance is not, however, absent from the short text (Ph 12:7; 4:16), although it lacks the special emphasis of the long text on Aseneth's failings, especially in the final prayer.[690] The long text she sees as typical of the values of the time which preferred women to be silent and submissive (as Sir 26:14),[691] and making their husband's bed (13:15).[692] Thus it has Aseneth give only silent utterance to her first two prayers in chap. 11, depicts hating men as a failing (11:6; 21:19-19), has her confess to arrogance (12:5; 21:12), depicts her as shy before the man from heaven and lacking understanding (16:2, 9, 13), only reaching understanding after his departure (17:8), which it depicts not as like Elijah's but like Joseph's (cf. 5:4-5), has bees make a honeycomb on her mouth blocking her speech (16:19), depicts her image in the basin without arms (18:9-10), so that Aseneth ends up being a passive woman, fitting for the values of the day.[693] Some of these contrasts are overdrawn.[694] Physical realities determine what the image in the basic could show. Nothing indicates that building a honeycomb on Aseneth's mouth is anything but positive. Aseneth is lacking knowledge also according to Ph 17:7. There is nevertheless a degree to which the longer text does tame Aseneth somewhat more.

---

[686] Humphrey, *Joseph and Aseneth*, observes: "Aseneth seemingly follows the traditional hermeneutic applied to the Song of Solomon – God's love for his people – while retaining a literal and human level of love" (91).

[687] On this see Kraemer, *When Joseph Met Aseneth*, 202.

[688] Standhartinger, *Frauenbild*, 76-219, presented in brief overview in Standhartinger, "Joseph und Aseneth," 459-64.

[689] Standhartinger, *Frauenbild*, 79-80, 214; Standhartinger, "Joseph und Aseneth," 461.

[690] Standhartinger, *Frauenbild*, 2121 similarly Kraemer, *When Joseph Met Aseneth*, 209.

[691] Standhartinger, "Joseph und Aseneth," 461; similarly Kraemer, *When Joseph Met Aseneth*, 207.

[692] Kraemer, *When Joseph Met Aseneth*, 208.

[693] Standhartinger, *Frauenbild*, 212-13; Standhartinger, "Joseph und Aseneth," 460-61. See also Kraemer, *When Joseph Met Aseneth*, 207.

[694] See the critical discussion in Humphrey, *Joseph and Aseneth*, 71-72.

In the short text Standhartinger sees the actions of Pharaoh's son as the reverse of those of Potiphar's wife, here problematizing the male not the female, an emphasis not nearly as clear in the long text.[695] It depicts her as chosen before she was born (Ph 8:10-11). The short text has Aseneth speak of God as like father and mother (Ph 12:7); the long text, only of God as father.[696] Both texts depict Aseneth as taking the initiative in acts of mercy in 28:1-17, though the longer text enhances Levi's role (cf. 28:17), but only slightly. "Repentance" is identified with Wisdom in both texts but the long text places her in a more subordinate position and at the same level as the man from heaven and lacks the notion of a heavenly marriage between the wise and wisdom.[697] She concludes that the long text depicts Aseneth as finally reduced to the role of the submissive, devoted wife, under the protection of her family, reflecting the conservative moral values of the time.[698] Kraemer, who also weighs the difference between the long and short text's portrait of women, reaches a slightly different conclusion:

> On the whole, both texts utilize constructions of gender that were fairly conventional in Greco-Roman antiquity. A complex hierarchy, both on earth and in heaven, is the norm. Women, at least proper women, are subordinate (and subservient) to men, as are slaves to their owners and subjects to their rulers.[699]

Accordingly both "utilize stereotyped associations of gender", with the male, "wise and self-controlled" as the self, and the female, "foolish, ignorant, and lacking in self-discipline", as the other. [700] Thus, she writes, "In *Aseneth* female chastity is precisely the feminine form of *sōphrosynē*, 'the virtue proper to a devoted, and fertile wife,' and Aseneth herself becomes precisely such a spouse".[701] On the other hand, she emphasises a certain egalitarian quality:

---

[695] Standhartinger, *Frauenbild*, 147-48; Standhartinger, "Joseph und Aseneth," 462; see also Lothar Ruppert, "Liebe und Bekehrung: Zur Typologie des hellenistisch-judischen Romans Joseph und Asenet," in *Paradeigmata: Literarische Typologie des Alten Testaments: I. Teil: Von den Anfängen bis zum 19. Jahrhundert* (ed. F. Link; Berlin: Duncker & Humblot, 1989) 33-42, 38-41.

[696] Standhartinger, *Frauenbild*, 183-85; Standhartinger, "Joseph und Aseneth," 461.

[697] Standhartinger, *Frauenbild*, 189-204.

[698] Standhartinger, *Frauenbild*, 214-16; Standhartinger, "Joseph und Aseneth," 463.

[699] Kraemer, *When Joseph Met Aseneth*, 212.

[700] Kraemer, *When Joseph Met Aseneth*, 212, similarly 215.

[701] Kraemer, *When Joseph Met Aseneth*, 205, citing Kate Cooper, *The Virgin and the Bride: Idealized Womanhood in Late Antiquity* (Cambridge: Harvard University Press, 1996) 65. On Kraemer's suggestion that 16:15 develops an intertextual link with instruction to eat in the garden of Eden in order to depict women's obedience to husbands as paradise restored (208-209), see our discussion of 16:15 above.

The concept of marriage in Aseneth seems to me very like the relatively egalitarian union of the harmonious couple, in which fidelity and concord (manifested here particularly in their devotion to the same God and in their attainment of similar mystical status) are of far more interest than the production and raising of legitimate heirs.[702]

Pervo also notes that in contrast to Hellenistic romances, in *Aseneth* the wedding is not a happy ending with return to seclusion, but rather it depicts Aseneth as strongly active in the final chapters, entrusted by her husband to act independently.[703]

Humphrey rightly cautions against reading the romance as reflecting or idealising social values, so that, "It is unlikely that the author intends his reader to envision or even to idealize married women gallivanting around the countryside"[704] and similarly that "virgins were totally secluded and married".[705] Neither extreme, she argues, "represents the social dynamics of the author's time".[706] The existence of many variant readings in the reporting of Aseneth's response to father, from polite to rude, reflects sensitivities of the day.[707] She also notes the precariousness of arguments for female authorship, given lack of specific evidence,[708] which must also apply, however, to exclusive claims of male authorship.

The primary significance of this work is its attempt to address the question of intermarriage and to subvert hardline positions, traditionally associated with Levi. It is in that sense daringly subversive, while providing humour and entertainment along the way as befitting its genre. Central to its structure and its thought is Aseneth's elevation. Her unveiled head, depicted as looking like that of a young man, serves not to deny her femaleness, nor revert her to androgyny, but to be a way of claiming that as a Gentile woman proselyte she and all who follow her will be able to stand before God sharing equal honour to men, that is, raised to the higher level which the author presumes is male. This affirmation of Gentile women proselytes in the context of intermarriage is at the same time a strong affirmation of marriage and sexual relations in marriage and something willed by God in the present and apparently also for the future. This positive stance provides also the basis for unabashed and playful affirmation of sexual attraction in the

---

[702] Kraemer, *When Joseph Met Aseneth*, 204.

[703] Pervo, "Aseneth and her Sisters," 153.

[704] Humphrey, *Joseph and Aseneth*, 75.

[705] Humphrey, *Joseph and Aseneth*, 76. See also Kraemer, *When Joseph Met Aseneth*, 213-15.

[706] Humphrey, *Joseph and Aseneth*, 76.

[707] Humphrey, *Joseph and Aseneth*, 76.

[708] Humphrey, *Joseph and Aseneth*, 77-78. See also Chesnutt, *From Death to Life*, 92; cf. Standhartinger, "Joseph und Aseneth," 463.

story itself, as the author subverts hardline opposition to intermarriage with ironic skill and a theology of divine generosity and compassion.

2.3 Later Works of Disputed Provenance

This chapter deals with a number of writings whose origins with varying degrees of probability are to be found in the second century or later, but have sometimes been placed earlier.

2.3.1 The Lives of the Prophets and the Martyrdom of Isaiah

This is now widely accepted as the case with the *Lives of the Prophets*, which most likely emanates from the fourth or fifth century.[709] It has, in any case little of relevance to our theme. In telling of Nathan it embroiders the story by having Nathan foresee David's sin with Bathsheba, but Beliar hinders him by having him find a dead man lying naked on the road (17:2). In telling of Abijah it reports that he warned Solomon that "his wives would change him" (18:4). The *Martyrdom of Isaiah*, embedded within the Christian *Ascension of Isaiah* 1 – 5, composed in the second century C.E.,[710] also has little that is relevant. "Sexual wrongdoing and adultery" are listed among the sins which increased through Manasseh, beside "sorcery and magic, augury and divination" and "persecution of the righteous", inspired by Beliar (2:5). In 2:7 the author also speaks of "wantonness" in Jerusalem.

2.3.2 The History of the Rechabites or the Story of Zosimus

This is a composite work, Christian in its present form, but possibly incorporating material of Jewish origin.[711] While chaps. 19 – 23 are recognised as Christian, attempts have been made to find Jewish sources behind the remaining material, such as 1 – 17 (with Christian interpolations)[712] or 8 – 10 (or 7 – 9) with further

---

[709] So David Satran, *Biblical Prophets in Byzantine Palestine: Reassessing the Lives of the Prophets* (Leiden: Brill, 1995) 118.

[710] Jonathan Knight, *The Ascension of Isaiah* (Sheffield: Sheffield Academic Press, 1995) 9.

[711] See the discussion in Davila, *Provenance*, 207-16 and the review of research in Chris H. Knights, "A Century of Research into the Story/Apocalypse of Zosimus and/or the History of the Rechabites," *JSJ* 15 (1997) 53-66.

[712] Brian McNeil, "Narration of Zosimus," *JSJ* 9 (1978) 68-82.

Jewish supplements consisting of 11 – 12 and 14 – 15 (minus Christian interpolations),[713] or 8 – 10 as a possibly Jewish work about Rechabites composed in Greek, the *History of the Rechabites*, and later interpolated with minor changes into a Christian document at whose core is another possibly Jewish document composed in Greek, the *Abode of the Blessed*, 11 – 12; 14 – 16:7.[714] Assuming the latter explanation, we find in the *History of the Rechabites* reference to the instruction of Aminadab to his family about abstinence in relation to food and drink, but also that they are to divest themselves of their clothes until God hears their prayer: καὶ ἀποδύσασθε τὰ ἱμάτια ὑμῶν ἐκ τοῦ σώματος ὑμῶν καὶ κεράμιον οἴνου ου πίεσθε· καὶ ἄρτον ἐκ τοῦ πυρὸς οὐ φάγεσθε· καὶ σίκερα καὶ μέλι οὐ πίεσθε· ἕως τοῦ εἰσακοῦσαι κύριον τῆς δεήσεως ὑμῶν· (8:3; similarly 8:5; 9:2).[715]

These apparent references to nakedness may well be secondary Christian insertions since such espousal of nakedness is unlikely in a Jewish work and are likely based on a misunderstanding of 12:3 which speaks of the blessed wearing only the garment of immortality.[716] The *History of the Rechabites* appears to speak of a community consisting of both men and women: "Our virtuous wives, who with us had surrendered themselves to God, now abide among us in this land, while remaining as we (do) in a fast and prayer and praise to God" (10:7a). This prompted McNeil to posit a link with the Therapeutae,[717] but, as Davila notes, there are also major differences, not least the absence in the document of any reference to the Law and observance of festivals and Sabbath.[718]

The *Abode of the Blessed* contains instruction about intercourse and celibacy:

6 οὔτε εἰσιν ἐξ ἡμῶν λαμβάνοντες ἑαυτοῖς γυναῖκας ἕως οὗ ποιήσωσιν δύο τέκνα· 7 καὶ μετὰ τὸ δύο τέκνα ποιῆσαι· ἀφίστανται ἀπ'ἀλλήλων καί εἰσιν ἐν ἁγνείᾳ μὴ γινώσκοντες <ὅτι ἦσάν ποτε ἐν> συνηθείᾳ τοῦ γάμου· ἀλλ' ὡς ὅτι ἀπ' ἀρχῆς ἐν τῇ παρθενίᾳ ὑπάρχοντες· 8 μένει τὸ ἕν τέκνον εἰς τὸν γάμον· καὶ τὸ ἕν εἰς τὴν παρθενίαν·

---

[713] James H. Charlesworth, "History of the Rechabites," *OTP*, 2.444-45.

[714] Knights, "Century of Research," 53-66; Chris H. Knights, "The *Abode of the Blessed*: A Source of the *Story of Zosimus*?" *JSP* 17 (1998) 79-93. Ronit Nikolsky, "The History of the Rechabites and the Jeremiah Literature," *JSP* 13 (2002) 185-207, considers the embedded text, the History of the Rechabites, as a fourth century C.E. Christian work (206).

[715] The text is that of David M. Miller, ed. "'The History of the Rechabites': Edition 1.0," in *The Online Critical Pseudepigrapha* (ed. Ken M. Penner, David M. Miller, and Ian W. Scott; Atlanta: SBL, 2006) no pages; online: http://www.purl.org/net/ocp/ HistRech.html.

[716] So Knights, "*Abode of the Blessed*," 85-86; Knights, "Century of Research," 62.

[717] McNeil, "Narration of Zosimus," 81.

[718] Davila, *Provenance*, 215.

And there are some among us who take for themselves wives until they have produced two children. 7 After they have produced two children they separate from each other and are in purity not knowing that they were once in the state of marriage, but as though they have been in a celibate state from the beginning. One child enters marriage and one enters celibacy. (11:6-8)

The passage is strikingly similar to a tradition preserved in the Jerusalem Talmud (y. Yeb. 6.6) about a man's producing two children before entering celibacy, though it says nothing of the fate of the offspring, which in the ruling of the *Abode of the Blessed* would, as Davila notes, lead to a fifty percent reduction in each generation and ultimately the extinction of the group, unlikely as a Jewish idea.[719] One proposed reading of the *Congregational Rule* preserved in 4Q249e interprets it as requiring that a man cease intercourse with his wife when he turns twenty, but is probably based on misunderstanding.[720] Such a provision might easily have arisen in monastic times.[721] It may preserve an earlier practice but this is hard to verify.

According to 12:3 the blessed ones address the issue of nakedness:

οὐκ ἐσμὲν δε γυμνοὶ τῷ σώματι ὡς δὴ ἀλογίζεσθε ὑμεις ἔχομεν γὰρ τὸ
ἔνδυμα τῆς ἀθανασίας καὶ οὐκ αἰσχυνόμεθα ἀλλήλους.

We are not physically naked as you wrongly conclude, for we have the garment of immortality and we do not cause each other shame. (12:3)

This assumes that the blessed return to the state of innocence of Adam and Eve before they sinned, including that they no longer engage in sexual relations, though 11:6-8 suggests that these continue, but only for the purpose of procreating children. In 14:1a we find the claim that among the blessed there is no "evil desire/lust" (αἰκισμὸς), listed beside "rage, jealousy" and "hateful thoughts".

2.3.3   The Life of Adam and Eve and the Apocalypse of Moses

The *Life of Adam and Eve*, comes to us in a number of versions, a Latin text known as *Vita Adae et Eva*, Armenian, Georgian and Slavonic texts, and an earlier Greek document, sometimes called the *Apocalypse of Moses*, reflecting the original language of composition and closest to the earliest form of the work, parts

---

[719] Davila, *Provenance*, 212 n. 81. He contemplates that this lack of realism may have prompted a scribe to delete 11:8 in Codex Mus. Brit. Add. 10073.

[720] See my discussion in Loader, *Dead Sea Scrolls on Sexuality*, 207-209.

[721] So Davila, *Provenance*, 212.

of which may at times still be better preserved in other ancient versions.[722] In his assessment of the evidence, Nickelsburg concludes that "the provenance of the versions of the Life of Adam and Eve is uncertain, but seems to tip in favor of Christian authorship of the Life of Adam and Eve in the versions in which it is now extant",[723] though recent exegetical study favours Jewish provenance.[724] In what follows I discuss the Greek text.[725]

There is some material of potential relevance for our theme. In Adam's initial retelling of his plight and the plight of humanity, the loss of Eden and the inevitability of sickness (7:1 – 9:1), issues of sexuality do not feature. Eve bears the blame for what happened there (7:2) and in 10:2; 32:2; and 29:9, but at no point is her sin portrayed as sexual seduction.[726] In her own much more extensive

---

[722] See Marinus de Jonge and Johannes Tromp, *The Life of Adam and Eve and Related Literature* (GAP; Sheffield: Sheffield Academic Press, 1997) 75-77. Michael D. Eldridge, *Dying Adam with his Multiethnic Family: Understanding the Greek Life of Adam and Eve* (SVTP 16; Leiden: Brill, 2002), argues that the Armenian and Georgian may reflect a form of the text at points more original than the Greek (127-33) and proposes a Jewish setting, having close affinity to *Joseph and Aseneth* and the *Testament of Job* (256, 263-64, 268).

[723] Nickelsburg, *Jewish Literature*, 332; a view espoused also by de Jonge and Tromp, *Life of Adam and Eve*, 67-75; see also Marinus de Jonge, "The Christian Origin of the Greek Life of Adam and Eve," in *Pseudepigrapha of the Old Testament as Part of Christian Literature: The Case of the Testaments of the Twelve Patriarchs and the Greek Life of Adam and Eve* (ed. Marinus de Jonge; Leiden: Brill, 2003) 181-200.

[724] So Eldridge, *Dying Adam,* who sets the parameters as 200 C.E. on the basis of usage in the *Cave of Treasures* dated to 250 C.E. and 100 B.C.E. because it uses *Jubilees* (30), hypothesising that the Greek *Life of Adam and Eve* may itself be dependent on "a work quite close to the *Greek Life*" (30); Thomas Knittel, *Das griechische 'Leben Adams und Evas': Studien zu einer narrativen Anthropologie im frühen Judentum* (TSAJ 88; Tübingen: Mohr Siebeck, 2002), who emphasises the closeness to *2 Enoch* and *4 Ezra* (62-63); and Jan Dochhorn, *Die Apokalypse des Mose: Text, Übersetzung, Kommentar* (Tübingen: Mohr Siebeck, 2005) 149-72, who sees the work as having been composed in Palestine in the late first or early second century C.E. (172). This also makes sense of clear dependence on the Hebrew text of Genesis, as indicated below. See also Otto Merk and Martin Meiser, "Das Leben Adams und Evas (JSHRZ II/5)," in *Einführung zu den Jüdischen Schriften aus hellenistisch-römischer Zeit: Unterweisung in erzählender Form* (ed. Gerbern S.Oegema; JSHRZ 6.1.2; Gütersloh: Gütersloher Verlagshaus, 2005) 151-94, 171-77.

[725] For the Greek text I use Johannes Tromp, *The Life of Adam and Eve in Greek: A Critical Edition* (PVTG 6; Leiden: Brill, 2005). The English translation is my own.

[726] We do find such an interpretation in the additional material found in MS C at 26:1 which clearly understands the encounter of the demon with Eve in sexual terms. On this see Jan Dochhorn, "Warum der Dämon Eva verführte: Über eine Variante in Apc Mos 26,2 – mit einem Seitenblick auf Narr Zos (gr) 18-23," in *Jüdische Schriften in ihrem antik-jüdischen und urchristlichen Kontext* (SJSHRZ 1; ed. Hermann Lichtenberger and Gerbern

report of what happened (15 – 30) (πῶς ἠπάτησεν ἡμᾶς ὁ ἐχθρός "how the enemy deceived us" 15:1), Eve reports more extensively on the encounter with the serpent. The devil first persuades the serpent to collaborate with having Adam expelled from paradise in revenge for his own expulsion through Adam (16:1-3), reassuring the anxious serpent that he would speak through him "to deceive them" (πρὸς τὸ ἐξαπατῆσαι αὐτούς) (16:5). Satan then appears over the wall of paradise looking like an angel (17:2; 2 Cor 11:14) and addresses Eve, which then becomes a conversation between the serpent and Eve in which the serpent draws attention to "the glory of the tree" (τὴν τιμὴν τοῦ ξύλου) (18:1), "its great glory" (δόξαν μεγάλην) (18:5). She lets him in, but initially going ahead, he threatens to change his mind unless she agrees on oath to give the fruit also to her husband (ἐὰν μὴ ὀμόσῃς μοι ὅτι δίδεις καὶ τῷ ἀνδρί σου) (19:1).[727] Dochhorn observes that the author appears to have derived the notion of an oath from reading not הִשִּׁיאַנִי but הִשְׁיאַנִי in Gen 3:13, thus also helping the author make sense of why, despite seeing the consequences in herself of nakedness, Eve nevertheless went on to give the fruit to Adam.[728] He also notes that the serpent gives the fruit to Eve, rather than her taking it as in Genesis, which he plausibly argues reflects an interpretation of גַם ("also") in Gen 3:7 as referring not to the indirect object but to the verb.[729]

In this context we find the appearance of sexual issues as Eve reports that before giving her the fruit the serpent sprinkled poison on it:

καὶ ἔθετο ἐπὶ τὸν καρπόν ὅν ἔδωκέν μοι φαγεῖν τὸν ἰὸν τῆς κακίας αὐτοῦ, [τοῦτ' ἔστιν τῆς ἐπιθυμίας· ἐπιθυμία γάρ ἐστιν κεφαλὴ πάσης ἁμαρτίας].
On the fruit, which he gave me to eat, he put the poison of his wickedness, [that is of his desire, for desire is the source of all sin]. (19:3)

S. Oegema; Gütersloh: Gütersloher Verlagshaus, 2002) 347-64, 352-55. There Eve is twelve years of age. It speaks of the demon seducing Eve, using ἀπατάω, as Gen 3:13 LXX, and having lust towards her, reporting that he had for a long time given attention to her body σκεῦος, but the main driver was envy because he had been in paradise first and resented the veneration given by the angels. This is clearly a later secondary addition, which takes the interpretation in a different direction. He notes here the influence of *Prot. Jas.* 13:1, which expounds Matt 1:18 (355-57), in 8:2, which says Mary was 12 (356), and in 16:3, which shows the devil was in paradise before Adam and Eve (355-57). He argues that the gloss is based on the *Protoevangelium of James* and the *Life of Adam and Eve* (359-60).

[727] Some manuscripts include at this point the words, ταῦτα δὲ εἶπεν θέλων εἰς τέλος δελεάσαι καὶ ἀπολέσαι με ("he said these things, wishing in the end to entice and ruin me"), but without any notion of sexual seduction which one could see in the translation of הִשְׁיאַנִי in the LXX by ἠπάτησεν.

[728] Dochhorn, *Apokalypse des Mose*, 345.

[729] Dochhorn, *Apokalypse des Mose*, 344.

The words which Tromp encloses in brackets are missing in some MSS, but well attested in others.[730] The word, ἐπιθυμία, may well be meant in a sexual sense, especially in the light of God's declaration to Eve (25:3), discussed below, which represents an elaboration of Gen 3:16. Again Dochhorn notes possible influence of the Hebrew, where the words describing the attractiveness of the tree, אֶרֶה חֶמֶד, unlike those in LXX, ὡραῖος ἄρεστος, relate to the words to desire or covet in Ex 20:17; Deut 5:21. These may have evoked the notion of desire here.[731]

Eve speaks of nakedness as the consequences of her sin because she lost the garment of glory with which she had been clothed up to that point (καὶ ἐν αὐτῇ τῇ ὥρᾳ ἠνεῴχθησαν οἱ ὀφθαλμοί μου, καὶ ἔγνων ὅτι γυμνὴ ἤμην τῆς δικαιοσύνης ἧς ἤμην ἐνδεδυμενένη. καὶ ἔκλαυσα λέγουσα· τί τοῦτο ἐποίησας, ὅτι ἀπηλλοτριώθην ἐκ τῆς δόξης μου (20:1-2), a notion alluded to in the *Abode of the Blessed* just considered above. Having Adam and Eve both clothed and in separate parts of the garden, accompanied by the male and female animals respectively (15:2-3), probably reflects, as Dochhorn suggests, the author's negative attitude towards sexuality.[732]

God's judgement on Eve places major emphasis on distress in childbirth as in Gen 3:16, but then interpolates into the Genesis account a prediction of Eve's future response, which then becomes grounds for her further condemnation:

ἐξομολογήσει δὲ καὶ εἴπεις· κύριε, κύριε, σῶσόν με, καὶ οὐ μὴ ἐπιστρέψω εἰς τὴν ἁμαρτίαν τῆς σαρκός. 4 δία τοῦτο ἐκ τῶν λόγων σου κρινῶ σε διὰ τὴν ἔχθραν ἥν ἔθετο ὁ ἐχθρὸς ἐν σοί· στραφεὶς δὲ πάλιν πρὸς τὸν ἄνδρα σου, καὶ αὐτός σου κυριεύσει.

And you will confess and say, "Lord, Lord, save me, and I shall never return to the sin of the flesh". 4 And because of this I will judge you against your word. Because of the enmity which the enemy placed in you, you will return to your husband, and he will rule over you. (25:3-4)

Here her returning to her husband is directly linked to the enmity ἔχθρα which the enemy (cf. ὁ ἐχθρός 2:4; 7:2; 28:4) has placed in her.[733] This in turn appears to be equated with the poison sprinkled on the fruit, which 19:3 explains as ἐπιθυμία.[734] What drives her back to her husband is this ἐπιθυμία.[735] But this, in turn, appears to be related to the grounds for condemning Eve out of her own

---

[730] See Tromp, *Life of Adam and Eve in Greek*, 144; Dochhorn, *Apokalypse des Mose*, 330-32.

[731] Dochhorn, *Apokalypse des Mose*, 346.

[732] Dochhorn, *Apokalypse des Mose*, 347.

[733] In 28:4, however, ὁ ἐχθρός places warfare (πόλεμον) in Adam.

[734] So also Dochhorn, *Apokalypse des Mose*, 394-95.

[735] Cf. *Apoc. Abr.* 23:10-11 where Eve herself is made to represent desire.

mouth, by her own words, namely that she will "never return to the sin of the flesh". The "sin of the flesh" appears then to be equated with returning to her husband, namely, in sexual intercourse and so becoming pregnant and bearing children in pain. In his important discussion,[736] Dochhorn sees here, too, the influence of the Hebrew text, which uses תשוקה, translated by LXX, ἀποστροφή ("return" or "refuge"), suggesting the similar Hebrew word, תשובה, will have played a role, inspiring the notion of Eve's future repentance. [737] תשוקה appears, however, already in documents at Qumran to have taken on the meaning "return".[738] Therefore the author may well have played with its range of meaning. His innovation is to equate תשוקה as sexual passion which has Eve constantly returning to her husband in sexual intercourse with the "sin of the flesh" and "enmity" understood as "desire".[739] The result is an assessment of sexual desire as something evil. That may indicate an espousal of celibacy, but could alternatively reflect a belief that sexual intercourse has only a procreative function and that any passion associated with it is sinful.[740]

Adam's attempt to return to the garden or to retrieve its healing oils is refused, but he receives the promise that at the resurrection he and those who remain faithful in humanity will return to the garden (28:4, also in some MSS in 13:1-6).[741] The document locates paradise in the third heaven (37:5). The document's depiction of future hope as resurrection to return to the garden, probably assumes return to the state of being clothed with the kind of garment of glory which Eve reports she lost, and which preceded the implanting of sexual

---

[736] Dochhorn, *Apokalypse des Mose*, 394-407.

[737] Dochhorn, *Apokalypse des Mose*, 403-406. He also draws attention to *Gen. Rab.* 20:7 which expounds Gen 3:16 with the two words in mind (407), but I would argue, with the two established meanings of the one word.

[738] See Loader, *Dead Sea Scrolls on Sexuality*, 198; William Loader, "The Beginnings of Sexuality in Genesis LXX and Jubilees," in *Die Septuaginta – Texte, Kontexte, Lebenswelten* (ed. Martin Karrer and Wolfgang Kraus; Tübingen: Mohr Siebeck, 2008) 300-12, 304.

[739] So also Dochhorn, *Apokalypse des Mose*, 395-97. He sees a similar meaning implicit in *2 Bar.* 56:6 (397). See also Levison, *Portraits of Adam*, who writes of the serpent as "an unadorned phallic symbol" and appropriately deemed "an ungrateful vessel" (169).

[740] Eldridge, *Dying Adam*, notes possible sexual connotations in what he sees as likely redactional addition by the author of the Greek *Life of Adam and Eve* over against what is preserved in Armenian/Georgian, where in 2:1 the author "adds slightly to the likely sexual connotation of the 'while they were sleeping' already found in the same verse" (141). "This neutral reference to sex needs to be borne in mind by those who would see an ascetic tendency in the *Greek Life*" (141). See also p. 122 on its secondary character.

[741] On 13:3b-5 preserved in MSS ATLC as on balance as secondary addition, see Eldridge, *Dying Adam*, 138-40.

desire and awareness of nakedness, thus to a state where sexual relations have no place, as apparently in *LAB*.

In summary, the Greek *Life of Adam and Eve* appears either to see sexual relations as inspired by the poison of Satan and so as evil, the sin of the flesh, or to see sexual relations as appropriate only for procreation and without passion. Concern with sexual issues appear also to have shaped its depiction of paradise in the beginning as having kept male and female humans and animals strictly separated and the former clothed, and in the end of a return to innocence, including absence of sexual desire and sexual relations. The latter appears to be motivated not by notions of paradise as a holy place, as in *LAB* and *Jubilees*, but by an understanding of sexual desire as Satanic poison.

PART THREE

Attitudes towards Sexuality in Psalms, Wisdom Writings, and Fragmentary Works

3.1 Psalms

3.1.1 The Psalms of Solomon

This collection of psalms, preserved in both Greek and Syriac translation,[1] was composed in Hebrew across the period of great upheaval in Jerusalem, ca 70 – 40 B.C.E.,[2] by members of an unidentifiable Jewish group caught up in its turmoils.[3]

---

[1] The Syriac may be a translation of the Greek, however this is far from certain. See especially the case for seeing it as a translation from the Hebrew, in Joseph L. Trafton, *The Syriac Version of the Psalms of Solomon* (SOCS 11; Atlanta: Scholars, 1985) 187-207; Joseph L. Trafton, "The Psalms of Solomon: New Light from the Syriac Version?" *JBL* 105 (1986) 227-37, 231-34.

[2] See the discussion in Robert B. Wright, *The Psalms of Solomon: A Critical Edition of the Greek Text* (JCTCRS 1; London: T&T Clark, 2007) 1-13. This text forms the basis for the discussion below, but I have preferred his more literal English translation in Robert B. Wright, "Psalms of Solomon," *OTP*, 2.639-70, except where his textual reconstruction differs. Where I have modified the translation to render it even more literal or clearer I have indicated this with an asterisk. Kenneth Atkinson has also produced a fresh translation in *NETS*, 763-76. On the date and setting see also Nickelsburg, *Jewish Literature*, 238-47; Oegema, *Einführung*, 22-33; H. Daniel Zacharias, ed. "'Psalms of Solomon': Edition 2.0," in *The Online Critical Pseudepigrapha* (ed. Ken M. Penner, David M. Miller, and Ian W. Scott; Atlanta: SBL, 2007) no pages; online: http://www.purl.org/net/ocp/PssSol.html. One should note also the caution of Svend Holm-Nielsen, *Die Psalmen Salomos* (JSHRZ 4.2;

Psalms 2, 8, and 17 allude to Pompey's entry into Jerusalem in 63 B.C.E., including such detail as his negotiations with leaders of competing groups and the disastrous aftermath, and in the case of Psalm 2 reporting his death in Egypt in 48 B.C.E.[4] The works are a rich source not only of allusions to political events, but also of religious ideas, including attempts to address theodicy and depictions of the future, seen as God's reign with his messianic deputy, the royal son of David, and as good news for the poor.

The material pertinent to issues of sexuality is to be found primarily in depictions of the reasons for the disaster which Pompey brought, but also to a limited degree in visions of the future. The investigation will focus therefore on the relevant passages, but also take into account a number of more general statements elsewhere which are probably to be fleshed out in the light of these passages.

Psalms of Crisis

The opening psalm, *Psalm 1*, may have been composed with Psalm 18 to enclose the collection.[5] It speaks in the persona of Jerusalem as a mother[6] suddenly

---

Gütersloh: Mohn, 1977), that some of the psalms may be even older and we should not assume that they were written either as a single collection or by a single author, given their diversity in use of language and biblical tradition (58-59).

[3] For discussion of earlier identification of the group as Pharisees, a view now largely abandoned, see Joseph L. Trafton, "The Bible, the *Psalms of Solomon*, and Qumran," in *The Bible and the Dead Sea Scrolls: The Princeton Symposium on the Dead Sea Scrolls: Volume 2: The Dead Sea Scrolls and the Qumran Community* (ed. James H. Charlesworth; Waco: Baylor University Press, 2006) 427-46, which includes a critique (431-34) of the most recent attribution of the work to Pharisees by Mikael Winninge, *Sinners and the Righteous: A Comparative Study of the Psalms of Solomon and Paul's letters* (Stockholm: Almqvist & Wiksell, 1995) 171-78. See also the earlier review in Joseph L. Trafton, "The Psalms of Solomon in Recent Research," *JSP* 12 (1994) 3-19, 7-8.

[4] So Kenneth Atkinson, *I Cried to the Lord: A Study of the Psalms of Solomon's Historical Background and Social Setting* (JSJSup 84; Leiden: Brill, 2004) who sees Psalm 2 as composed after Pompey's death in 48 B.C.E., but before Herod's appointment in 40 B.C.E. (52-53). Psalm 7 appears to stem from the time before Pompey's siege when it was merely a possibility that might have been averted; probably Psalm 9 similarly.

[5] So Atkinson, *I Cried to the Lord*, who points out that the first psalm is patterned on the first of the canonical collection in being the only one without a heading (205). See also Otto Kaiser, "Beobachtungen zur Komposition und Redaktion der Psalmen Salomos," in *Das Manna fällt auch heute noch: Beiträge zur Geschichte und Theologie des Alten, Ersten Testaments: Festschrift für Erich Zenger* (ed. Frank-Lothar Hossfeld and Ludger Schwienhorst-Schönberger; HBS 44; Freiburg: Herder, 2004) 362-78, who finds evidence

confronted with the cries of battle, reflecting on her inhabitants as having become numerous,[7] influential, and arrogant, exalting themselves to the stars and believing they would never fall. It assumes a connection between abundance, including of offspring, and righteousness, but this was in ignorance of the sins of the inhabitants. Having cited their arrogance, partly in allusion to the taunt against the King of Babylon as elevating himself to the stars of heaven in Isa 14:13, mother Jerusalem then declares:

7 αἱ ἁμαρτίαι αὐτῶν ἐν ἀποκρύφοις καὶ ἐγὼ οὐκ ἤδειν
8 αἱ ἀνομίαι αὐτῶν ὑπὲρ τὰ πρὸ αὐτῶν ἔθνη
ἐβεβήλωσαν τὰ ἅγια κυρίου ἐν βεβηλώσε.
7 Their sins were in secret; I knew nothing about them.
8 Their acts of lawlessness were worse than the Gentiles before them;
they profaned the Lord's sanctuary (or: the holy things of the Lord).* (1:7-8)

These three motifs, secret sins, transgression worse than Gentiles, and profaning the temple, reappear in other psalms, which may have been the reason for their presence here. Thus in Psalm 2 we again find reference to the people of Jerusalem profaning the temple,[8] juxtaposed to reference to their crimes (2:3) and in 2:9 the accusation that "no one had ever acted as they". Similarly, in Psalm 8, after depicting the profaning of the sanctuary the psalmist declares: "There was no sin they left undone in which they did not surpass the gentiles" (8:13). Psalms 2 and 8 also provide us with detail indicating that a significant aspect of such profaning sin had to do with sexual wrongdoing. The theme of hidden and secret sins, applicable to most sexual wrongdoing, features regularly in the psalms (2:17; 4:7; 8:8; 9:3; 14:8).

Psalm 2 begins quite abruptly with an account of Pompey's siege: "Arrogantly the sinner broke down the strong walls with a battering ram and you did not interfere" (2:1), recording that the Gentiles then trampled on the holy place

---

of careful composition of the collection as a whole, in which Psalms 2, 8, and 18, which focus on righteousness, form a structure for the rest of the material (365-67).

[6] On the image of Jerusalem as "mother" see also 11:2, 7, where the psalmist has Jerusalem encouraged to look at the return of her children and dress in glorious and holy attire.

[7] ἐλογισάμην ἐν καρδίᾳ μου ὅτι ἐπλήσθην δικαιοσύνης· ἐν τῷ εὐθηνῆσαί με καὶ πολλὴν γενέσθαι ἐν τέκνοις ("I considered in my heart that I was full of righteousness, because I had prospered and there was abundance in children") (1:3).

[8] τὰ ἅγια κυρίου which appears also in 2:3, may refer to "the holy things of the Lord", the temple itself, or the sacrifices (cf. Ezek 5:11; 23:38; 25:3; Mal 2:11; Lev 19:8). On this see Devorah Dimant, "A Cultic Term in the Psalms of Solomon in the Light of the Septuagint," *Textus* 9 (1981) 28-51.

of sacrifice (2:2). God's failure to intervene is then accounted for by the Jerusalemites' sin:

3 ἀνθ' ὧν οἱ υἱοὶ Ιερουσαλημ ἐμίαναν τὰ ἅγια κυρίου
ἐβεβηλοῦσαν τὰ δῶρα τοῦ θεοῦ ἐν ἀνομίαις
4 ἕνεκεν τούτων εἶπεν ἀπορρίψατε αὐτὰ μακρὰν ἀπ' ἐμοῦ
οὐκ εὐδοκῶ ἐν αὐτοῖς
3 because the sons of Jerusalem defiled the sanctuary of the Lord,
they profaned the gifts of God with acts of lawlessness.
4 Because of these things he said, "Take them far away from me."
He had no pleasure in them.* (2:3-4)

"The sons of Jerusalem" here will refer to priests who have defiled holy things, that is, sacrifices,[9] by becoming themselves defiled and not dealing with that defilement before commencing their duties.[10] The same is implied in 8:12. The result is that God rejects the offerings (αὐτά refers back to τὰ ἅγια κυρίου and τὰ δῶρα τοῦ θεοῦ),[11] and by implication rejects the validity of their temple worship. The notion of rejecting the validity of temple worship because the holy things have been defiled has precedent in *1 Enoch* 89:56 and *Jub.* 23:21; 30:15-16. "The acts of lawlessness" (ἐν ἀνομίαις) would include what the author goes on to describe in 2:11-13, namely prostitution, but could also include the transgressions listed in 8:9-13: incest, adultery, theft of temple belongings and menstrual intercourse, the latter specifically linked to defilement of priests which in turn defiled sacrifices.

The psalm continues with a description of the effects: God's glorious sanctuary was held in disrepute and Jerusalem's sons and daughters bore the mark of slaves among the Gentiles. Because they all sinned, old and young, God abandoned them, heaven was appalled and earth loathed them for their unprecedented disobedience – according to the author's theology, rightly so (2:5-10).[12] At this point we meet detail, but first in the context of Gentile ridicule:

---

[9] So Winninge, *Sinners and the Righteous*, 32.

[10] Cf. Winninge, *Sinners and the Righteous*, who on grounds of 2:6 and 11 argues that not only priests are in view (28).

[11] Atkinson, *I Cried to the Lord*, 20; Holm-Nielsen, *Psalmen Salomos*, 63.

[12] Atkinson, *I Cried to the Lord*, notes that the "classical accounts mention that Pompey only took Aristobulus's partisans, along with 'his two daughters and as many sons,' in chains to Rome as captives" (37). He also draws attention to 4QpNah/4Q169 3-4 iv.1-8 which describes the Sadducees as Manasseh, recording the slaughter and captivity (43-45). He notes that 1QpHab addresses the same situation, describing the last priest of Jerusalem as accumulating wealth by plunder (9 4-6) (45-46). He refers also to 4QPolemical Text/4Q471a which may reflect the imposing threat of Pompey's siege and defeat of the Sadducees as God's punishment for their sins (47-48). On the common

11 ἔστησαν τοὺς υἱοὺς Ιερουσαλὴμ εἰς ἐμπαιγμὸν ἀντὶ πορνῶν ἐν αὐτῇ
πᾶς ὁ παραπορευόμενος εἰσεπορεύετο κατέναντι τοῦ ἡλίου
12 ἐνέπαιζον ταῖς ἀνομίαις αὐτῶν καθὰ ἐποίουν αὐτοί,
ἀπέναντι τοῦ ἡλίου παρεδειγμάτισαν ἀδικίας αὐτῶν·
13 καὶ θυγατέρες Ιερουσαλὴμ βέβηλοι κατὰ τὸ κρίμα σου·
ἀνθ' ὧν αὐταὶ ἐμιαίωσαν αὐτὰς ἐν φυρμῷ ἀναμείξεως.

11 They (Gentiles) set up the sons of Jerusalem for ridicule because of prostitutes in it.
Everyone passing by went into (them) in the light of day.
12 They ridiculed their lawlessness more than what they themselves were doing;
in the light of day they exposed their wickedness
13 and the daughters of Jerusalem became profaned in your judgement,
because they defiled themselves with illicit intercourse.* (2:11-13)

The focus here is not secret sins, but the opposite: open daytime visits to
prostitutes, comparable to what is assumed in 2:12 as a common charge against
Gentiles. If this is the charge now laid against "the sons of Jerusalem", 2:13 is
probably laying a similar charge against "the daughters of Jerusalem", namely that
they are engaging in prostitution. This is more likely than that here a different
form of illicit intercourse is envisaged, such as incest, as in 8:9, where it takes
place in secret.[13] As Atkinson notes, while the captive sons and daughters of 2:6
include the population in general, the reference to sons and daughters in 2:11 and
13 may well refer to priestly families, given the close link with the denunciation of
priests,[14] and these we may assume were Sadducean.[15] The rest of the psalm
asserts that in allowing Pompey's devastation God was right, returns to the
distressed image of Jerusalem as a woman now in sackcloth,[16] and then focuses on
God's final avenging of Pompey, killed on the beach in Egypt.

The other major account of the sins that prompted God to give rein to
Pompey's siege is to be found in *Psalm 8*. Here the psalmist speaks in the first
person of the distress of Pompey's siege, but again emphasising that God was right

---

historical background of Psalm 2 and 4QpNah4/Q169 see also Shani Berrin, *"Pesher
Nahum, Psalms of Solomon and Pompey,"* in *Reworking the Bible: Apocryphal and Related
Texts at Qumran: Proceedings of a Joint Symposium by the Orion Center for the Study of
the Dead Sea Scrolls and Associated Literature and the Hebrew University Institute for
Advanced Studies Research Group on Qumran, 15-17 January, 2002* (ed. Esther G. Chazon,
Devorah Dimant, and Ruth A. Clements; STDJ 58; Leiden: Brill, 2005) 65-84.

[13] Cf. Holm-Nielsen, *Psalmen Salomos*, 64.

[14] Atkinson, *I Cried to the Lord*, 21.

[15] Atkinson, *I Cried to the Lord*, 37.

[16] Joachim Schüpphaus, *Die Psalmen Salomos: Ein Zeugnis Jerusalemer Theologie
und Frömmigkeit in der Mitte des vorchristlichen Jahrhunderts* (ALGHJ 7; Leiden: Brill,
1977), argues that the psalmist and his community see the plight of the sons and daughters,
with sympathy, despite condemning their sexual wrongdoing (28).

to allow it to happen and then detailing the cause. This time the concern is secret sins:

8 ἀνεκάλυψεν ὁ θεὸς τὰς ἁμαρτίας αὐτῶν ἐναντίον τοῦ ἡλίου·
ἔγνω πᾶσα ἡ γῆ τὰ κρίματα τοῦ θεοῦ τὰ δίκαια·
9 ἐν καταγαίοις κρυφίοις αἱ παρανομίαι αὐτῶν ἐν παροργισμῷ·
υἱὸς μετὰ μητρὸς καὶ πατὴρ μετὰ θυγατρὸς συνεφύροντο·
10 ἐμοιχῶντο ἕκαστος τὴν γυναῖκα τοῦ πλησίον αὐτοῦ·
συνέθεντο αὐτοῖς συνθήκας μετὰ ὅρκου περὶ τούτων.

8 God exposed their sins in the light of day
the whole earth came to know the just judgements of God.
9 In secret places underground was their lawbreaking, provoking (him),
son involved with mother and father with daughter.
10 Everyone committed adultery with his neighbour's wife;
they made agreements among themselves about these things with an oath.* (8:8-10)

The four lines of 8:9-10 appear to address four abuses, of which at least the second and third have to do with sexual wrongdoing. Atkinson suggests that "in secret places underground" (ἐν καταγαίοις κρυφίοις) is "not merely a poetic metaphor", but appears to allude to a practice of purification in an underground immersion pool, reported in *m. Tam.* 1.1 which has found confirmation through archaeology.[17] The author may be attacking use of the underground pool or may be attacking its use by priests in a manner that contravened Lev 22:4-7 by not then waiting till evening for complete purification. This provision relates indirectly to sexuality in the sense that its use as reported in *m. Tamid* relates to purification from seminal emission. It amounts to neglect of purity laws in the area of sexuality and relates particularly to priests.

The second instance is incest within the immediate family, between parents and children, which need not be limited to priests. The same is true of the third, which speaks of adultery on a broad scale: "Everyone committed adultery with his neighbour's wife". This finds a parallel in *LAB* which declares as a characteristic of the time of Lamech that "in that time, when those inhabiting the earth began to do evil (each one with his neighbor's wife) and they defiled them (*contaminantes eas*), God was angry" (2:8a). The fourth is directly related to the preceding sins (περὶ τούτων "about these things"), at least the third and second. Its most natural reading is that people swear on oath not to tell what has happened. It is difficult to find in it an allusion to the oath associated with the test for unfaithfulness administered on a woman suspected of adultery in Numbers 5, as Atkinson

---

[17] Atkinson, *I Cried to the Lord*, 65-66. It is not clear whether Atkinson sees the author attacking the practice itself or some abuse relating to it, when he writes "it is likely that the psalmist denounces the Temple priests for their improper purification rituals" (66).

suggests, unless it is ironic.[18] They are, as he notes "improper oaths",[19] but their purpose is far from obscure. They are designed to cover up the wrongs previously mentioned: συνέθεντο αὐτοῖς συνθήκας μετὰ ὅρκου περὶ τούτων ("they made agreements among themselves about these things with an oath").

The charges continue:

11 τὰ ἅγια τοῦ θεοῦ διηρπάζοσαν ὡς μὴ ὄντος κληρονόμου λυτρουμένου·
12 ἐπατοῦσαν τὸ θυσιαστήριον κυρίου ἀπὸ πάσης ἀκαθαρσίας καὶ ἐν ἀφέδρῳ αἵματος ἐμίαναν τὰς θυσίας ὡς κρέα βέβηλα·
13 οὐ παρέλιπον ἁμαρτίαν ἣν οὐκ ἐποίησαν ὑπὲρ τὰ ἔθνη.
11 They stole from the sanctuary of God as if there were no redeeming heir.
12 They walked on the place of sacrifice of the Lord, (coming) from all kinds of uncleanness; and (coming) with menstrual blood (on them), they defiled the sacrifices as if they were common meat.
13 There was no sin they left undone in which they did not surpass the gentiles.
(8:11-13)

Theft of things belonging to the temple (τὰ ἅγια τοῦ θεοῦ; similarly τὰ ἅγια κυρίου, 2:3) is likely to have been carried out by priests.[20] The reference to no redeeming heir appears to use the language of household inheritance to liken such theft to a man's squandering his property as though he has no heir to whom he might leave an inheritance. Priests will have been the target also in the allegations of disregard of various kinds of impurity (ἀκαθαρσία), since they were implied in the charge in 8:9 about secret underground transgressions. Again the charge is that they have been officiating in a state of uncleanness. The instance cited here is defilement with menstrual blood. This might conceivably be intercourse without the priest or his wife initially being aware that she was menstruating. More likely it is knowing. In either instance Lev 15:24 requires a seven day period of purification. Lev 18:19 and 20:18 treat this as more than incidental impurity. It is forbidden intercourse. Lev 15:31 relates neglect of such impurity directly to defiling the temple. The *Damascus Document* makes the connection clear by

---

[18] Atkinson, *I Cried to the Lord*, 77. He sees the reference to pouring out blood like dirty water by Pompey's forces in 8:20 as a play on temple rituals (76-77), including, he speculates, an allusion to debates over transmission of liquid impurity between vessels (79).

[19] Atkinson, *I Cried to the Lord*, 79.

[20] Atkinson, *I Cried to the Lord*, canvasses a number of possibilities about how this might have occurred, including improper commerce (75). He suggests also reading *4QMMT* C 4-9 as referring to misappropriation of temple property (75), but see my discussion in Loader, *Dead Sea Scrolls on Sexuality*, where I argue that in its context it could be referring to illicit sexual activity (77-78).

reading Lev 15:24 in the light of 18:19 and 20:18 and so adding the reference to sin (ע[ון]).[21]

האש[ה] [ ] [אשר י]קרב [ ] 2 [אל]יה ע[ון] נדה עלו

[   ] the wom[an   one who] approaches [her has the s]in of menstrual impurity upon him. (4QDᵃ/4Q266 6 ii.1-2)

The focus here in 8:12, however, is not the intercourse, but the neglect of proper purification on the part of the priest, who thereby brings defilement to the temple service.

The remainder of the psalm deals with the consequences of such sins: the advent of Pompey, described in some detail and apparently not yet with knowledge of his death. It includes the report that he took prisoners: ἀπήγαγεν τοὺς υἱοὺς καὶ τὰς θυγατέρας αὐτῶν ἃ ἐγέννησαν ἐν βεβηλώσει ("he led away their sons and daughters whom they have given birth to in defilement") (8:21). This may refer to children of prostitutes, if we read it in the light of 2:11, but more likely refers to a generation which the author sees as contaminated by the defiling activities of their parents. It is possible that the author could have in mind illicit marriages, for instance, as some saw it, between priests and ordinary people,[22] or between Jews and non-Jews (on this see the discussion of Psalm 17 below), or between uncles and nieces, for each of which the collection of writings at Qumran offers instructive parallels.[23]

The accusations of incest and menstrual intercourse bear some similarity to the charges in the *Damascus Document* against those wanting to modify the Law (5.6b-11), but there incest is specifically targeted at niece marriages. The concern with menstrual intercourse is however very close, namely that it leads to defilement of the temple, though this connection is given already in Lev 15:24-31. Wright points in addition to the three nets of Belial which CD lists as sexual wrongdoing, riches, and defiling the sanctuary (4.15-18), claiming that they recur in 8:11-12 in the same order.[24] The parallels are not close, however, since the latter

---

[21] On this Loader, *Dead Sea Scrolls on Sexuality*, 149, and on intercourse with menstruants in documents of the Qumran collection, p. 354.

[22] Atkinson, *I Cried to the Lord*, 69-70; and Kenneth Atkinson, "4QMMT and Psalm of Solomon 8: Two Anti-Sadducean Documents," *Qumran Chronicle* 11 (2003) 57-77, who sees *4QMMT* addressing marriage between priests and ordinary people (69-71), but see my detailed discussion in Loader, *Dead Sea Scrolls on Sexuality*, 53-90, where I argue that the primary concern is intermarriage with Gentiles.

[23] See my summary discussion in Loader, *Dead Sea Scrolls on Sexuality*, on intermarriage (356-59) and incest (354-56).

[24] Wright, *OTP*, 2.648-49. See also Atkinson, *I Cried to the Lord*, who suggests that "both Psalms of Solomon and CD 4.15-18 likely reflect some anti-Hasmonean propaganda

speaks of adultery, the former, not.[25] On the other hand, stealing from the sanctuary correlates broadly with greed for riches (emphasised in 1:4-6) and defiling the temple through menstrual intercourse is a match. Nothing indicates a relationship between the two or a common source. These are, however, concerns which are likely to have repeated themselves at various times of corrupt temple leadership during the Second Temple period (cf. *Jub.* 23:21).[26]

Psalm 17 also properly belongs to the psalms of crisis. In his earlier work Atkinson raised the possibility that 17:7-8 referred to Herod's execution of remaining Hasmoneans between 37-30 B.C.E. and that the siege referred to Herod's capture of Jerusalem with the Roman general Sosius in 37 B.C.E.[27] His most recent analysis, where he argues that the psalm has been composed in stages, relates it to Pompey's siege. Accordingly, it begins in 17:1-10 by affirming God's kingship, and by depicting the Hasmonean monarchy as illegitimate but allowed to be by God as punishment for Israel's sin. If, as Atkinson plausibly argues, the future tenses should be taken at face value, it predicts the siege of Pompey, but with the inaccuracy to be expected in such predictions, for it indicates that Pompey would exterminate the Hasmoneans, whereas in fact he reinstalled Hyrcanus II as high priest.[28] Unlike in Psalms 2 and 8 no account is given of the "sins" because of which it says "sinners rose up against us" (17:5).

According to Atkinson, 17:11-20 must have been "added to update the work to recount Pompey's removal of Aristobulus and his partisans 'to the west' (Ps. Sol. 17:12)".[29] He then sees a reference to Pompey's entering the Holy of Holies in the comment, "he did in Jerusalem what all the gentiles do for their gods in their

---

that circulated in Jerusalem which was appropriated independently by the writers of both texts to denounce Jerusalem's priests for their immoral conduct" (67).

[25] See the discussion in Loader, *Dead Sea Scrolls on Sexuality*, 122-23.

[26] Similarly Atkinson, *I Cried to the Lord*, 70, 73.

[27] Kenneth Atkinson, "Herod the Great, Sosius, and the Siege of Jerusalem (37 B.C.E.) in Psalm of Solomon 17," *NovT* 38 (1996) 313-22; Kenneth Atkinson, "Towards a Redating of the Psalms of Solomon: Implications for Understanding the *Sitz im Leben* of an Unknown Jewish Sect," *JSP* 17 (1998) 95-112, 106-107; Kenneth Atkinson, "On the Use of Scripture in the Development of Militant Davidic Messianism at Qumran: New Light from *Psalms of Solomon* 17," in *Interpretation of Scripture in Early Judaism and Christianity: Studies in Language and Tradition* (ed. Craig A. Evans; JSPSup 33; Sheffield : Sheffield Academic Press, 2000) 106-23, 109-10; Kenneth Atkinson, *An Intertextual Study of the Psalms of Solomon: Pseudepigrapha* (Studies in the Bible and Early Christianity; Lewiston: Mellen, 2001) 358-68; and still on p. 185 of Atkinson, *I Cried to the Lord*, where he writes: "*Psalms of Solomon* 2 and 17 recount different sieges of Jerusalem" (185).

[28] Atkinson, *I Cried to the Lord*, 136-37.

[29] Atkinson, *I Cried to the Lord*, 138.

cities" (17:14), indicating that he treated it just as a shrine,[30] and according to 17:15 locals followed suit. The "lawless one" (17:11) thus gave rise to "lawless ones" (17:18a) from whom the author's community had to flee, as birds from a nest (17:16-17; similarly 1QH[a] xii.8-9).[31] In 17:18b-20 we then read that creation itself withheld its waters and all, from the king to judge to people, engaged "in every kind of sin", but again without indicating further sins beyond the misuse of the temple and the violence implied in the preceding statements. Thus in his most recent discussion Atkinson sees these lines written before the brief renewal of kingship by Antigonus in 40-37 B.C.E.[32] Nowhere in the first half of the psalm do we find references to sexual wrongdoing.

In the second half of the psalm the author then sets his hope on the royal messianic Son of David, among whose achievements will be the restoration of the tribes and their being settled on their tribal lands, but also the driving out of Gentiles with the result that πάροικος καὶ ἀλλογενὴς οὐ παροικήσει αὐτοῖς ἔτι ("an alien and the foreigner will no longer live near them"*) (17:28). This goes beyond being delivered from profane enemies, enunciated in 17:45, ῥύσαιτο ἡμᾶς ἀπὸ ἀκαθαρσίας ἐχθρῶν βεβήλων ("may he deliver us from the pollution of profane enemies"). From it we may conclude with a high level of probability that the author would have opposed intermarriage with Gentiles, including proselytes.

The image of the future reflects a creative employment of Isaiah 11 and Psalm 2,[33] so that purging Jerusalem of Gentiles, subjugation of the nations, and resettlement of the tribes, come about as the Son of David acts on God's behalf. The city is restored to be "holy as it was from the beginning" (17:30). Gentiles are welcomed, but only as admiring visitors bearing gifts and to receive compassion.[34] This picture of the future apparently envisages normal life, centred on Jerusalem, presumably with a restored temple, though that is not specifically addressed in Psalm 17. It is however assumed in *Psalm 11* which alludes to the messenger

---

[30] Atkinson, *I Cried to the Lord*, 138.

[31] On the parallel with the *Thanksgiving Hymns* of Qumran see Trafton, "The Bible, the *Psalms of Solomon*, and Qumran,", who lists also "trees of life" (14:3; cf. 1QH[a] xvi.5-6); "fruit of the lips" (15:3; cf. 1QH[a] ix.28); wild beasts/lions that "break bones" (13:3; 1QH[a] xiii.7) (432). See earlier Svend Holm-Nielsen, "Erwägungen zu dem Verhältnis zwischen den Hodajot und den Psalmen Salomos," in *Bibel und Qumran: Beiträge zur Erforschung der Beziehungen zwischen Bibel- und Qumranwissenschaft* (ed. Hans Bardtke; Berlin: Evangelische Haupt-Bibelgesellschaft, 1968) 112-31.

[32] Atkinson, *I Cried to the Lord*, 139.

[33] On this see Atkinson, "On the Use of Scripture," who points to parallel use especially of Isaiah in scrolls at Qumran (112-23). See also Trafton, "Bible, Psalms of Solomon, and Qumran," 435-42.

[34] On this see also Donaldson, *Judaism and the Gentiles*, 139.

addressing Zion and declaring good news to the poor (11:1; cf. Isa 52:7).[35] It, too, envisages, the return of the dispersed from all directions and so the reclothing of mother Jerusalem in glorious and holy attire (11:2-7), probably drawing on Baruch (cf. also 8:28).[36] This vision of hope is similar to what we find in many documents of the Qumran collection, including sectarian documents, in envisaging the future as reflecting the present restored to its proper order. In this the boundaries of sacred space remain, so that with reference to sexual relations, these may be assumed to continue in their proper place.

Psalms of Community

The matter of adultery, already cited in 8:10, comes to expression above all in *Psalm 4*, but here not in the context of depicting the immediate causes for God allowing Pompey's siege. One might still see the perpetrator as belonging to such transgressors, but the focus is something going on in the community. For the psalm begins by confronting someone as "a profaner" (βέβηλε), who sits "in the council of the devout" (ἐν συνεδρίῳ ὁσίων) (4:1; cf. 17:16). The term, οἱ ὅσιοι ("the devout/holy ones"), is a favourite designation of the authors of these psalms, used to refer to themselves and their group (e.g., 4:6, 8; 8:23; 10:6), so we may be dealing within an internal confrontation or at least one in which a council is still held in high regard, since otherwise objection to the man's presence there (4:1, 6) would have no point. Absence of allusion to the crisis of Pompey may indicate that it stems from the earlier period. The word συνέδριον could refer to the governing council of Jerusalem,[37] but might also refer to a local council. Nothing suggests the man is the council's convener,[38] nor that objections to his presence are on

---

[35] As Atkinson, *I Cried to the Lord*, notes, the reference is probably to the jubilee trumpet (Lev 25:9-10) (199).

[36] On the relation of Psalm 11 to Baruch, see Atkinson, *I Cried to the Lord*, who wavers between seeing the latter using the former (4) and the former using the latter: "This composition draws heavily on both First Baruch 4:36 – 5:9 and Isaiah 40 – 66" (199), though in a footnote identifying the relationship as "uncertain" (199 n. 35). See also his discussion in Atkinson, *Intertextual Study*, 223-35. See also Pesch, "Abhängigkeit," who makes a strong case for the priority of Baruch (251-63), and our discussion above.

[37] Atkinson, *I Cried to the Lord*, 3. Winninge, *Sinners and the Righteous*, speculates that the term was used for the Sanhedrin dominated by Pharisees during the reign of Salome Alexandra and then continued to be used in the period 67 – 63 B.C.E., so that those accused are Sadducees and Hasmonean leaders (54-55). Holm-Nielsen, *Psalmen Salomos*, doubts the verse refers to historical relationships, suggesting that its formulations are rather to be seen as derived from biblical precedents like Pss 1:1; 50:16-17; and Isa 29:13 (69).

[38] Atkinson, *I Cried to the Lord*, 95. Similarly Atkinson, "Towards a Redating," 102. The words, περισσὸς ἐν λόγοις περισσὸς ἐν σημειώσει ὑπὲρ πάντας ("excessive in

grounds other than his hypocrisy (such as his party[39] or pedigree). That he exercises the role of a judge (4:2), probably along with others as a member of the council, enhances the hypocrisy to be described. Thus his hypocrisy recalls that of the two judges in the tale of Susanna, who are also exposed as engaging in a pattern of sexual predation through adultery and whose description also features their lustful eyes (12, 52-53, 57).

Beginning with a general charge that the man is ἔνοχος ἐν ποικιλίᾳ ἁμαρτιῶν καὶ ἐν ἀκρασίαις ("guilty of all kinds of sins and of lack of self control"*) (4:3), the latter often related to lack of control in the area of sexual behaviour, the psalmist then moves to specifics: οἱ ὀφθαλμοὶ αὐτοῦ ἐπὶ πᾶσαν γυναῖκα ἄνευ διαστολῆς ("his eyes looking at every woman indiscriminately"*) (4:4). We then enter the category of "secret sins" of which adultery is typical (cf. 1:7; 8:8-9):

ἐν νυκτὶ καὶ ἐν ἀποκρύφοις ἁμαρτάνει ὡς οὐχ ὁρώμενος·
ἐν ὀφθαλμοῖς αὐτοῦ λαλεῖ πάσῃ γυναικὶ ἐν συνταγῇ κακίας·
ταχὺς εἰσόδῳ εἰς πᾶσαν οἰκίαν ἐν ἱλαρότητι ὡς ἄκακος·
At night and in secret he sins as though not seen.
With his eyes he speaks to every woman in an affair of wickedness,
swiftly entering every house in grace as innocent.* (4:5)

Before continuing to explain where this leads, the author launches into a declaration of hope that God would expel such hypocrites, "those who please men, who deceitfully quote the Law" from among the devout and expose them (4:6-8). Nothing connects this to the crises facing Jerusalem addressed elsewhere. The hypocrisy, "the deeds of those who try to impress people", the desire to "please men" (ἀνθρωπαρέσκων) and the deceitful use of the Law, are general attributes, but the author then returns to an instance where potentially all these play a role. The author has more than one person in his sights, so moves from singular to plural and back again,[40] the singular making the account more graphic:

9 καὶ οἱ ὀφθαλμοὶ αὐτῶν ἐπ᾽ οἶκον ἀνδρὸς ἐν εὐσταθείᾳ·
ὡς ὄφις διαλῦσαι σοφίαν ἀλλήλων ἐν λόγοις παρανόμων·
10 οἱ λόγοι αὐτοῦ παραλογισμοὶ εἰς πρᾶξιν ἐπιθυμίας ἀδίκου·
οὐκ ἀπέστη ἕως ἐνίκησεν σκορπίσαι ὡς ἐν ὀρφανίᾳ·
11 καὶ ἠρήμωσεν οἶκον ἕνεκεν ἐπιθυμίας παρανόμου·

words, excessive in appearance above everyone") (4:2) indicates only that his pretentiousness exceeds that of others.

[39] So Atkinson, *I Cried to the Lord*, 96.

[40] Kaiser, "Beobachtungen," suggests that the plural reflects secondary redaction (370-73). This is possible, but need not be so.

παρελογίσατο ἐν λόγοις ὅτι οὐκ ἔστιν ὁρῶν καὶ κρίνων·
12 ἐπλήσθη ἐν παρανομίᾳ ἐν ταύτῃ·
καὶ οἱ ὀφθαλμοὶ αὐτοῦ ἐπ᾽ οἶκον ἕτερον ὀλεθρεῦσαι ἐν λόγοις
ἀναπτερώσεως·
13 οὐκ ἐμπίπλαται ἡ ψυχὴ αὐτοῦ ὡς ᾅδης ἐν πᾶσι τούτοις·

9 And their eyes are on a husband's peaceful house,
like a snake to destroy the wisdom of others with lawless words.
10 His words are arguments to lead to the activity of sinful lust.
He did not stop until he conquered to scatter them as orphans
11 and makes a house desolate because of immoral sexual desire.
He deceived with words because there was no one looking or judging
12 and was filled with lawlessness in this;
and his eyes turned to another house to destroy it with clamorous words.
13 His soul will not be satisfied in all these things until he reaches Hades.* (4:9-13)

The image of the snake suggests that the author sees such men as assuming the role of the snake in the garden of Eden as they speak with other men's wives. We see here the concrete instance of their attempts to impress and please people, noted in 4:7-8. The "lawless words" (ἐν λόγοις παρανόμων) are probably more specifically a reference to enticement to transgress Torah (picking up the general reference to deceitful use of the Law in 4:8), namely the prohibition of adultery. The expression εἰς πρᾶξιν ἐπιθυμίας ἀδίκου ("to lead to the activity of sinful lust") should not be read as implying all sexual desire is sinful, but that wrongly directed desire leads to sinful action.[41] As 4:11 indicates, it is ἐπιθυμίας παρανόμου ("desire that transgresses the Law"). The author depicts the effect of such adultery as scattering people as orphans and making a house desolate. This is not a different topic, but an implication of the adulterous liaisons. It has in view children bereft of parents whose marriage and household have collapsed. The author repeats the motif of supposed secrecy (4:11; cf. 9:3; 14:8) and the transgression of the Law a third time (4:12; cf. 4: 9, 11), returning to where the description began: the lustful eyes, which now look to ruin another house (4:12b). This attack on predatory adulterous behaviour emphasises its transgression of Law but equally argues against it on the basis of its destructiveness to households. The account stands on its own without any relation to the broader political crises addressed in other psalms and appears to address a danger within the author's own community in a council the author values.[42]

The author then returns to his appeal to God to act against the man, wishing upon him disgrace, cursing, groaning, pain, poverty, anxiety, sleeplessness, failure, an emptied household, even to the extent of wishing that his bones be scattered

---

[41] Similarly Ellis, *Sexual Desire*, 65.

[42] Cf 12:1-4 where the psalmist speaks of deceitful words of a man entering the houses of others, but here the focus is slander and inciting conflict between houses.

and crows pick out his eyes (ὀφθαλμοὺς ἐκκόψαισαν κόρακες ὑποκρινομένων) (4:14-20a). It bespeaks the venom of one who could well have been a victim of such a man's abuses. The author wishes all this on him because such men "disgracefully emptied many people's houses and scattered (them) in their sexual lust"* (ὅτι ἠρήμωσαν οἴκους πολλοὺς ἀνθρώπων ἐν ἀτιμίᾳ καὶ ἐσκόρπισαν ἐν ἐπιθυμίᾳ) (4:20b). Again the emphasis is on the devastating effects on households of uncontrolled sexual desire, but at the same time on disregarding God (4:21) and defrauding by pretence. The psalm ends with hope for those who fear the Lord, because he will rescue them ἀπὸ παντὸς σκανδάλου παρανόμου ("from every cause of stumbling by transgressing the Law"*) (4:23). The word σκάνδαλον will carry sexual connotations here, as it does in 16:7. When in 15:11 the psalmist writes: ἡ κληρονομία αὐτῶν οὐχ εὑρεθήσεται τοῖς τέκνοις αὐτῶν αἱ γὰρ ἁμαρτίαι ἐξερημώσουσιν οἴκους ἁμαρτωλῶν ("The inheritance shall not be found for their children, for sins have devastated the houses of sinners"*), we may have another reference to the effects of adultery.

I am aware that this interpretation flies in the face of numerous recent attempts to read the psalm as alluding to political turmoil. Atkinson reviews the main options among those who read the psalm in this way.[43] He favours a reading which sees an allusion to the Jerusalem Sanhedrin, rather than to a local assembly of the devout, as proposed by Schüpphaus,[44] preferring to take the reference to "the devout" as indicative that the author gives recognition to the body and "only denounces the current occupants for their crimes".[45] I am not convinced that the author would employ the word οἱ ὅσιοι ("the devout/holy ones") so differently here than elsewhere nor that the author is attacking the council's current occupants. Atkinson reads the devastation of houses not as the result of adultery and the break-up of marriages but more generally as attacks on the author's group.[46] He appears to overlook the references to the sexual predations of the adulterer (4:4, 5, 9, 12). Reading the text within a framework of assumptions about parties, Atkinson see "the sinners" on 4:2-3 as a party, rather than as victims of harsh rulings by a judge,[47] though he cautions later that "the author does not explicitly identify any individual or political party".[48] He also presumes that "the profane man" convened the council,[49] though the text nowhere indicates this.[50]

---

[43] Atkinson, *I Cried to the Lord*, 96-104.

[44] Schüpphaus, *Psalmen Salomos*, 33 n. 92.

[45] Atkinson, *I Cried to the Lord*, 95.

[46] Atkinson, *I Cried to the Lord*, 91.

[47] Atkinson, *I Cried to the Lord*, 95.

[48] Atkinson, *I Cried to the Lord*, 96.

[49] Atkinson, *I Cried to the Lord*, 95. Similarly Atkinson, "Towards a Redating," 102.

[50] Schüpphaus, *Psalmen Salomos*, argues explicitly that he a member of the council and not its leader, but as typical of the group (34). He speculates further that the situation

In his review he first considers Wellhausen's suggestion that Janneus is "the profane man",[51] noting also *Nahum Pesher*'s identification of him as the "lion of wrath" and the grounds for seeing him as ineligible to hold his position.[52] He considers that the absence of reference to his foreign campaigns and alliances makes this unlikely.[53] Next he considers Salome Alexandra, but she should be ruled out on grounds that the figure here is clearly male, not least in the light of the depiction of his adulterous exploits.[54] He sees an identification with figures who appear after Pompey's invasion improbable because of the psalm's silence about the crisis. This makes identification with Antipater[55] and similarly with Herod,[56] improbable, despite matching the lofty appearance. Atkinson sees an allusion to the period between Salome' death and Pompey's advent as more likely, when her two sons fought for the throne.[57]

It seems very likely that the psalm emanates from the period before Pompey, indeed before he is sufficiently on the horizon to be worth mentioning. The "profane man" may be a known figure, but the psalm gives us a profile of a judge in a council, not necessarily the only one or the convener, whose hypocrisy it exposes by contrasting the severity of his judgements on others with his own misbehaviour, in particular, in a pattern of adultery like Susanna's elders, which brings households to ruin, in which others also engaged.[58] This is not primarily if at all about political parties, but about sexual wrongdoing, adultery in particular.[59]

---

may have arisen in the light of the adversity brought by the Romans and reflects behaviour of some from within the author's own group looking for sinners to blame for why God allowed the disaster to come upon them (35).

[51] Atkinson, *I Cried to the Lord*, 97. Cf. Julius Wellhausen, *Die Pharisäer und die Sadducäer: Eine Untersuchung zur inneren Geschichte* (Greifswald: Bamberg, 1874) 146-47.

[52] Atkinson, *I Cried to the Lord*, 98.

[53] Atkinson, *I Cried to the Lord*, 98.

[54] Atkinson, *I Cried to the Lord*, 99-100.

[55] Atkinson, *I Cried to the Lord*, 102. Cf. M. Auerbach, "The Historical Allusions of Chapters IV, XI, and XIII of the Psalms of Solomon," *JQR* 41 (1951) 379-96, 381-91. His suggestion that the sexual references allude to Antipater's attempts to ingratiate himself with "successive rulers of the Eastern part of the Roman Empire" (385) does not do justice to the depiction of households as victims of his exploitation and ruined by his philandering.

[56] Atkinson, *I Cried to the Lord*, 103. Cf. Schüpphaus, *Psalmen Salomos*, 34 n. 94.

[57] Atkinson, *I Cried to the Lord*, 100, 103-104.

[58] Hence the shift from singular to plural and back again in 4:5 to 6; 4:9 to 10; 4:18-19. Schöpphaus, *Psalmen Salomos*, see the shift as indicating that the author sees the majority as so inclined (33), but this goes beyond the evidence.

[59] On the devastating effects of adultery, including the fate of their offspring see Wis 3:16; 4:3-6.

It belongs therefore with Psalms 3, 5, 6, 9, 10, 11, 14, 16, which Atkinson shows are best seen as not dealing with the political crises.[60]

The only other passage directly related to sexual wrongdoing is to be found in *Psalm 16*, which like Psalm 4, seems independent of concerns with Jerusalem's crises. In it the psalmist prays:

7 ἐπικράτησόν μου ὁ θεός ἀπὸ ἁμαρτίας πονηρᾶς
καὶ ἀπὸ πάσης γυναικὸς πονηρᾶς σκανδαλιζούσης ἄφρονα
8 καὶ μὴ ἀπατησάτω με κάλλος γυναικὸς παρανομούσης
καὶ παντὸς ὑποκειμένου ἀπὸ ἁμαρτίας ἀνωφελοῦς.
7 Keep me back from wicked sin
and from every wicked woman who makes the foolish stumble (sexually)
8 and let not the beauty of a woman who transgresses the Law deceive me
nor anyone subject to useless sin.* (16:7-8)

It is typical of the psalms that in speaking of serious sin (ἁμαρτίας πονηρᾶς) the author focuses on sexual sin. The concern about the wicked woman (γυναικὸς πονηρᾶς) is associated with the fool (ἄφρονα), suggesting a wisdom background, probably reflecting the admonition of Proverbs, which in Hebrew speaks of the "strange woman" also as the "evil woman" and then goes on immediately to speak of a woman's beauty (6:24). The adulterers' destructiveness is also described as undermining "the wisdom of others" (σοφίαν ἀλλήλων) (4:9), and is closely associated there as in Proverbs with deceptive speech (4:9-11; cf. Prov 2:16; 5:3; 6:24). The motif of being deceived (ἀπατησάτω) by a beautiful woman who wants you to transgress the Law (παρανομούσης), almost certainly here in a sexual sense, probably alludes to the garden of Eden, perhaps including use of the LXX, which has Eve use the same verb of what the snake did: ἠπάτησέν με ("deceived/seduced me" Gen 3:13). The same imagery appears in 4:9, also in the context of wisdom language. The prayer cites two instances of power: the woman and God, with little indication of individual responsibility. It is as though such women are so dangerous that only God can help, and the writer is otherwise a victim, a stance which inevitably leads to blaming women for men's irresponsibility. The fact that the man prays shows at least some need to address one's actions.

Elsewhere in the collection we do find direct assertion of human responsibility for wrongdoing: "Our works are in the choosing and power of our souls, to do right and wrong in the works of our hands" (9:4). It is not clear whether in 16:8 the author has any particular sin in mind, sexual or otherwise, in referring to the danger of παντὸς ὑποκειμένου ἀπὸ ἁμαρτίας ἀνωφελοῦς ("anyone subject to useless sin"). In 14:6-7 we read καὶ οὐχ οὕτως οἱ ἁμαρτωλοὶ καὶ παράνομοι

---

[60] Atkinson, *I Cried to the Lord*, 181-203.

οἳ ἠγάπησαν ἡμέραν ἐν μετοχῇ ἁμαρτίας αὐτῶν 7 ἐν μικρότητι σαπρίας ἡ ἐπιθυμία αὐτῶν καὶ οὐκ ἐμνήσθησαν τοῦ θεοῦ ("And not so the sinners and the transgressors who love to spend the day sharing their sin. Their desire is short and decaying and they are not mindful of God"*) (14:7). This reference to fleeting pleasures could well have included sexual pleasures.

Much discussion of sin is generic, including concern with unintentional sins (3:7-8). Other sins include arrogance (1:5-6; 17:6, 13), theft from the sanctuary (8:11), slander and deceit (12:1-4).[61] In 16:10 we have brief mention of anger and thoughtless rage and grumbling and discouragement in persecution. These are minor sins of the kind for which the righteous finds atonement through fasting and humility (3:5-8; similarly 13:7-10) unlike the sinner, who ends up cursing his life, the day of his birth, the author adding also: "his mother's pain" (3:9). Sexual wrongdoing is, however, foremost among the sins identified by the authors of these psalms (2:11, 13; 4:3-5, 9-12, 20; 8:9-12), sometimes directly related to others, such as profaning the sanctuary (8:12; cf. also 2:3; 8:9).[62]

Sexuality and the Future

The future perspectives of the authors may give some indication of positive attitudes towards sexuality. We noted in discussing Psalm 17 that it envisages a future which appears to be a restoration of the present structures of reality to proper order. That includes restoration of the tribes and their resettlement, banishing of foreigners (17:28) and by implication no mixed marriages with Gentiles and proselytes, and the city restored to holiness (17:30) and, presumably at its centre a restored temple. It is an image of the present order restored to peace, with the nations honouring Zion with gifts and living in submission to the Son of David. It apparently assumes, therefore, normal human life, which would include families, marriage, and sexual relations, or, at least gives no indication to the contrary.

Psalm 3 also envisages an embodied future existence, which then also assumes a resurrection for the righteous: οἱ δὲ φοβούμενοι τὸν κύριον ἀναστήσονται εἰς ζωὴν αἰώνιον καὶ ἡ ζωὴ αὐτῶν ἐν φωτὶ κυρίου καὶ οὐκ ἐκλείψει ἔτι ("but those who fear the Lord will rise up to eternal life, and

---

[61] Atkinson, *I Cried to the Lord*, along with others reads this closely with Psalm 4 by overlooking the latter's major theme of a corrupt adulterous council judge and seeing it as addressing conflict between parties. Psalm 12 fits the the conflict context better, at least in the sense that it depicts a slanderous transgressor who incites conflict through slander.

[62] See also Winninge, *Sinners and the Righteous*, who also notes that the primary sins in the *Psalms of Solomon* are sexual and cultic (126).

their lives will be in the Lord's light and it shall not go out"*) (3:12).[63] If one saw sexual relations as solely for procreation, then at least the need to reproduce to replace the dead would be redundant if all continue to live eternally (following the logic of the rebuke of the eternal angels in *1 Enoch* 15:5-7 and of Luke 20:34-36), but nothing indicates that this is assumed. The notion that there will be eternal day, thus presumably without sun and moon and stars, finds parallels elsewhere (cf. *1 Enoch* 58:3, 5-6; *2 Enoch* 65:7-11; 4 Ezra 7:39-42; *LAB* 19:10; 26:13; Rev 21:22-25; 22:5). It stands in some tension with the stronger sense of realism reflected in Psalm 17, though such visions commonly transcend the normal. We can only speculate about what this might mean for sexual relations.

Psalm 13 also says that "the life of the righteous (goes on) forever" (13:11), whereas sinners face only destruction (similarly 14:9, "Hades, and darkness and destruction"; 15:10).[64] According to 15:9 they bear the mark of destruction. Psalm 14 depicts "the Lord's holy ones" both as living forever and as being "trees of life", and apparently as "the Lord's paradise". Those to whom "The Lord is faithful" (14:1) are described as:

τοῖς πορευομένοις ἐν δικαιοσύνῃ προσταγμάτων αὐτοῦ
ἐν νόμῳ ᾧ ἐνετείλατο ἡμῖν εἰς ζωὴν ἡμῶν
3 ὅσιοι κυρίου ζήσονται ἐν αὐτῷ εἰς τὸν αἰῶνα
ὁ παράδεισος τοῦ κυρίου τὰ ξύλα τῆς ζωῆς ὅσιοι αὐτοῦ
4 ἡ φυτεία αὐτῶν ἐρριζωμένη εἰς τὸν αἰῶνα
οὐκ ἐκτιλήσονται πάσας τὰς ἡμέρας τοῦ οὐρανοῦ.
those who live in the righteousness of his commandments,
in the Law, which he has commanded us for our life.
The Lord's holy ones shall live by it (the Law) forever.
The Lord's paradise, trees of life, are his holy ones;
their planting is firmly rooted forever;
they shall not be uprooted all the days of heaven.* (14:3-4)

The imagery of "the Lord's holy ones" as a "planting" is relatively widespread (*Jub.* 7:34-35; 21:23-24; CD 1.7). One of the *Thanksgiving Hymns* at Qumran also speaks of "trees of life" (1QH^a xvi.5-6). The rather odd statement that they are "the Lord's paradise", not just in it, if not an error of syntax, may reflect an

---

[63] There may be an allusion to future resurrection in 2:31, ὁ ἀνιστῶν ἐμὲ εἰς δόξαν καὶ κοιμίζων ὑπερηφάνους εἰς ἀπώλειαν αἰῶνος ἐν ἀτιμίᾳ ὅτι οὐκ ἔγνωσαν αὐτόν ("he lifts me up to glory and puts to sleep the arrogant for eternal destruction in dishonour, because they did not know him"*). So Winninge, *Sinners and the Righteous*, 34; cf. Atkinson, *I Cried to the Lord*, 49-52.

[64] Atkinson, *I Cried to the Lord*, suggests that the promise that "the devout of the Lord will inherit life in happiness" (14:10) also alludes to resurrection, given the contrast with Hades in the context (203).

expansion of the imagery of planting to include paradise itself as an orchard, so that paradise is seen no longer (or not only) as a place but (also) a community. Harmonised with Psalm 17 it would be a way of describing the restored community focused on Jerusalem. It might, indeed, assume a collocation of paradise and Jerusalem, as in *1 Enoch* 25:2-6 and 4QpPs/4Q171 1-10 iii.1-2, 10-11. The centrality of the Law by which the righteous will live forever[65] coheres with the emphasis throughout the collection on sin as transgression and finds its echo in the closing lines of the final psalm, which highlights cosmic order, reflecting unwavering obedience to divine will.[66] As in *1 Enoch* 1 – 5, such unchanging cosmic order underlines the call to obey God's unchanging Law as the way to life. This, too, then assumes a future ordered as the Law prescribes, and so probably entailing all that it assumes about human community, including sexual relations. The evidence is, however, circumstantial. Unlike their concern with sexual wrongdoing, the authors show no indication that sexual "right-doing" is to be any different from what the Law prescribes. It nowhere treats sexual desire as problematic in itself.

Conclusion

If we take into account that this is a fairly coherent collection of psalms composed probably over three decades of turbulent history,[67] we can distinguish comments relating to sexuality made in relation to crises, and others made in the broad context of community instruction. In the collection, most likely a resource for worship,[68] they would serve as a warning beside the encouragement to obedience to the Law and to hope in God's goodness. Thus in relation to the crises sexual wrongdoing is seen as a major cause for God's allowing Pompey's intervention. The specific sins are open engagement in prostitution by men and women (Psalm 2), and the secret sins (1:7) of incest between parents and children, and adultery

---

[65] The importance of the Law is emphasised by Niebuhr, *Gesetz und Paränese*, who while noting that νόμος occurs only once (14:2) points to the abundance of related terms as indicating the Law's centrality (226-27). Cf. Schüpphaus, *Psalmen Salomos*, 122.

[66] Psalm 18:7b-12 are missing from the Syriac and are listed as a 19th psalm in MS 3004, but this runs contrary to reports that there were 18 psalms and probably reflects a later scribal innovation. On this see Atkinson, *I Cried to the Lord*, 208, and on the manuscript, Wright, *Psalms of Solomon*, 21-22.

[67] On the coherence see Bradley Embry, "The Psalms of Solomon and the New Testament: Intertextuality and the Need for a Re-evaluation," *JSP* 13 (2002) 99-136, who takes Atkinson, *Intertextual Study*, to task for treating the psalms too much in isolation from one another and so developing notions of alienation from the temple on the basis of absence of reference to it in some psalms (129, 132-34). Embry speaks of a "thematic concatenation" among the psalms (129).

[68] So Holm-Nielsen, *Psalmen Salomos*, 59.

(both in Psalm 8). These are characterised as sins in which Gentiles engage, thus adding to the shame that the sons and daughters of Jerusalem had outdone the Gentiles in their sinning (1:8; 8:9; cf. 2:13) and thus exposed themselves to Gentile ridicule (2:12). Sins relating to neglect of proper purification after seminal emission or after sexual intercourse with a menstruant may not have been current dangers, if this community did not include serving priests, but they would serve to reinforce the need to observe all such purity laws which still had application to their lives.

Adultery also features in community instruction, where in Psalm 4 we find an elaborate description of the predatory adulterous official or judge, whose deeds are condemned as transgressions of the Law, destructive acts which devastate households, and not least as hypocrisy. Beyond that we find a prayer, apparently inspired by Prov 6:24-25 and the story of Eden, in which the writer asks to be protected from the wicked woman who leads the foolish to transgression and from being seduced by a woman's beauty, the emphasis being on need for divine help to ward off such women, as though without it a man could be a helpless victim. The stereotype tends to diminish men's responsibility and ultimately lay the blame on the woman. The eyes feature in the account of the adulterer as medium of sexual transgression (4:4, 5, 9, 12) and by implication also in 16:8.

The link with Solomon (1 Kgs 4:32) may well have been imposed on the collection on the basis of the similarity between Psalm 17 and the biblical Psalm 72. A reference to Solomon now introduces each psalm except the first. Apart from that, nothing relevant to Solomon occurs.[69] One might expect to find some allusion to Solomon's own sexual wrongdoing had authors of the psalms sought to embody his persona, but of this there is no trace. On the other hand, in relation to what elsewhere is seen as one of Solomon's sins, we may assume on grounds of the image of the future ideal in Psalm 17 that intermarriage with Gentiles including proselytes was not tolerated in the community which composed and used these psalms. The image of the future variously reflected in these psalms appears to envisage a form of life matching how life should be when ordered by God's Law and centred on Jerusalem and its cult. This probably therefore envisages also normal sexual relations as provided for in the Law. We find nothing which suggests otherwise or which calls human sexual desire into question in the present when not misdirected and transgressing the commandments.

---

[69] So Holm-Nielsen, *Psalmen Salomos*, who sees the references to Solomon as probably having been introduced already to the Hebrew version, given their sharing the same linguistic awkwardness as the rest of the Greek (58).

3.2   Wisdom Writings

3.2.1   Ben Sira / Sirach   by Ibolya Balla

Based on information provided in the prologue supplied by Ben Sira's grandson to the Greek translation of his forebear's work, we are able to identify the date of his arrival in Egypt as 132 B.C.E., the thirty-eighth year of the reign of Ptolemy VII Physcon Euergetes II, and to calculate that the original work in Hebrew will have been composed in Jerusalem about two generations earlier, that is, between 190–175, probably around 180 B.C.E. The translation will have taken place some time after 132 B.C.E., possibly close to the time when the prologue was added in 117 B.C.E.[70]

Both the Hebrew text and the Greek translation have shorter and longer recensions. The textual witnesses are usually designated as HTI (the original Hebrew of Ben Sira),[71] HTII (the expanded Hebrew text of one or more recensions, also primarily the basis for GII), GI (the grandson's Greek translation of HTI, found primarily in the major uncial MSS ABCS and their cursives) and GII (the expanded Greek translation based on HTII, represented by a number of minuscule MSS, especially in the O and L recensions). HTII differs from HTI primarily by additions. Within HTI the overlapping Hebrew manuscripts sometimes present considerable textual differences. GII, probably originating from 50–150 C.E., also has additions compared with GI.[72] At times these additions reflect Christian interpolations.[73] The Greek translation at points also differs

---

[70] Richard J. Coggins, *Sirach* (GAP; Sheffield: Sheffield Academic Press, 1998) 18-20; Harrington, *Apocrypha*, 79-80; John J. Collins, *Jewish Wisdom in The Hellenistic Age* (Louisville: Westminster John Knox, 1997) 23; Patrick W. Skehan, *The Wisdom of Ben Sira: A New Translation with Notes, Introduction and Commentary by Alexander A. Di Lella* (AB 39; New York: Doubleday, 1987) 8-10.

[71] They consist of the medieval Cairo Geniza materials (MSS ABCDEF), the earlier Masada manuscript (MS M, 1st century B.C.E.), and the Qumran fragments (2Q18/2QSir, 1st century B.C.E., 11QPs^a/11Q5 xxi, 1st century C.E.); see Skehan, *Ben Sira*, 51-53; Warren C. Trenchard, *Ben Sira's View of Women: A Literary Analysis* (BJS 38; Chicago: Scholars, 1982) 4, 186-87, nn. 29-33.

[72] Skehan, *Ben Sira*, 55-58; Friedrich Vinzenz Reiterer, "Review of Recent Research on the Book of Ben Sira," in *The Book of Ben Sira in Modern Research* (ed. Pancratius C. Beentjes; BZAW 255; Berlin: de Gruyter, 1997) 23-60, 26; Pancratius C. Beentjes, "Prophets and Prophecy in the Book of Ben Sira," in *"Happy the One who Meditates on Wisdom" (Sir. 14,20): Collected Essays on the Book of Ben Sira* (ed. Pancratius C. Beentjes; CBET 43; Leuven: Peeters, 2006) 207-29, 209.

[73] Maurice Gilbert, "Wisdom Literature," in *Jewish Writings of the Second Temple Period: Apocrypha, Pseudepigrapha, Qumran Sectarian Writings, Philo, Josephus* (ed. Michael E. Stone; CRINT II/2; Assen: Van Gorcum, 1984) 283-324, 299-300.

substantially from the Hebrew text. As we shall see below, in certain passages relating to sexuality it seems to tone down the erotic content of the Hebrew original. For convenience I use the term "Ben Sira" to designate the book in general and also the author of the Hebrew text and "Sirach" to refer specifically to the Greek translation.[74]

In the way it addresses everyday issues, and deals with customs and manners, and with how one should behave toward God, one's fellows and the world at large, the Book of Ben Sira may be described as "recipe wisdom".[75] In its subject matter, language and imagery Ben Sira has much in common with the wisdom writings of the Hebrew Bible, Job, Proverbs, and Ecclesiastes, but also differences. It is more concerned with matters of sexuality, honour and shame, than are Job or Ecclesiastes, and even Proverbs. The same is true with regard to the Wisdom of Solomon and Baruch. The writer's anxiety regarding the chastity of daughters, for instance, is unparalleled in other wisdom writings. The author addresses various sexual issues across a wide range of locations. Therefore, while taking sequence and structure into account, this analysis will proceed on a thematic basis.

Fathers, Mothers and Widows

The most extensive teaching regarding one's parents is found in Sir 3:1-16. This passage demonstrates that honour and respect is required toward both father and mother on the basis of the fifth commandment in the Decalogue (Ex 20:12; Deut 5:16). However, while honouring both father and mother is atoning (3:3-4), 3:14-15 depict good deeds toward only the father as atoning. The passages give more attention to fathers than mothers. 3:11b, where the Greek is significantly different from the Hebrew, warrants particular attention:

ומרבה חטא מקלל[76] אמו (MS A)

and multiplies sin who curses his mother (3:11b)
καὶ ὄνειδος τέκνοις μήτηρ ἐν ἀδοξίᾳ
and for the children a mother in dishonour is a disgrace (3:11b GI)

---

[74] The Hebrew text is that of Pancratius C. Beentjes, *The Book of Ben Sira in Hebrew: A Text Edition of All Extant Hebrew Manuscripts and A Synopsis of All Parallel Hebrew Ben Sira Texts* (VTSup 68; Leiden: Brill, 1997), but I also take into account that of Israel Lévi, *The Hebrew Text of the Book of Ecclesiasticus* (SSS 3; Leiden: Brill, 1904). For the Greek text I use Alfred Rahlfs and Robert Hanhart ed. *Septuaginta: Id est Vetus Testamentum graece iuxta LXX interpretes* (2d ed.; Stuttgart: Deutsche Bibelgesellschaft, 2006), but also take into account Joseph Ziegler, ed. *Sapientia Iesu Filii Sirach* (SVTG 12.2; Göttingen: Vandenhoeck & Ruprecht, 1965). Translations are my own, but see also Benjamin G. Wright, "Sirach: Introduction and Translation," in *NETS* 2007, 715-62.

[75] Skehan, *Ben Sira*, 32.

[76] Trenchard, *Ben Sira's View*, 40, 216, n. 21, suggests מקלה ("he who treats with contempt", from קלה). Cf. Skehan, *Ben Sira*, 153-54.

While MS A does not describe the qualities of the mother, GI depicts her as a mother in dishonour. It does not say what dishonour means in this context. It may refer to an act of a sexual nature, such as adultery, which would bring shame on the children, but that is uncertain. It would certainly be a surprising comment in the context of honouring father and mother. While fathers are not connected explicitly with sexual wrongdoing in Sir 3:1-16, where in 3:10 the nature of the disgrace (בקלון, MS A; ἀτιμία, GI) is not specified, elsewhere Ben Sira condemns the immorality of old men in particular (25:2d; 42:8b).

Sir 23:14 also refers to disgraceful conduct, but without further specification, except that it can reflect negatively on both father and mother. By contrast, in 41:17a ("Before father and mother be ashamed of sexual immorality", אל זנות בוש מאב ואם, MS B) the term זנות (or פחז in MSS B^mg and M) clearly indicates shame of sexual wrongdoing. The sage may have intended a sexual focus in his concern for the vulnerability of widows and orphans (4:10; 35:17[14]-18[15]), but this is not explicit.

Sons and Daughters

Ben Sira has detailed instruction concerning the chastity of sons and daughters. Their sexuality, especially daughters', is a great cause for anxiety for fathers, as the passages to be treated here betray. We begin our investigation with Sir 7:23-25 and 22:3-5, which include teachings regarding both sons and daughters.

23 בנים לך יסיר[78] אותם   ושא להם נשים[77] בנעוריהם:
24 בנות לך נצור שארם   ואל האיר אלהם פנים:
25 הוצא בת ויצא עסק   ואל נבון גבר חברה: (MS A)

23 Do you have sons? Chastise them and take for them wives in their youth.
24 Do you have daughters? Guard their chastity (lit. body) and do not let your face shine upon them.
25 Give your daughter (in marriage) and you finish a task (lit. business, affair), and unite/join her with a sensible man. (7:23-25)

23 τέκνα σοί ἐστιν; παίδευσον αὐτὰ καὶ κάμψον ἐκ νεότητος τὸν τράχηλον αὐτῶν.
24 θυγατέρες σοί εἰσιν; πρόσεχε τῷ σώματι αὐτῶν καὶ μὴ ἱλαρώσῃς πρὸς αὐτὰς τὸ πρόσωπόν σου.
25 ἔκδου θυγατέρα, καὶ ἔσῃ τετελεκὼς ἔργον μέγα, καὶ ἀνδρὶ συνετῷ δώρησαι αὐτήν. (GI)
23 Do you have children? Admonish them and bow their neck from youth.

---

[77] Missing from MS C.
[78] MS C has יסר.

24 Do you have daughters? Be concerned for their chastity (lit. body) and do not let
your face be cheerful upon them.
25 Give (your) daughter (in marriage) and you will have finished a great task, and give
her to a sensible man. (7:23-25)

It is immediately clear in 7:23-25, that the translator has left the verses dealing
with daughters (7:24-25) almost completely unchanged, while he has made
significant modifications to the verse treating sons (7:23). The context in 7:23-25
in the Hebrew text suggests that the sage is concerned with the marriage of sons
and daughters, therefore with the sexuality of both male and female children.
Behind the expression "take for them wives in their youth" probably lies the
anxiety of the father that finding a suitable and chaste wife for his son at an early
age will reduce the risk of the son engaging in sex, especially with immoral
women (similarly 26:19-21 GII).

The translation in 7:23 lacks the idea of the marriage of sons and has a more
general comment on disciplining children (τέκνα). The marriage and sexuality of
daughters in 7:24-25 however remains a central theme in the Greek. On the one
hand the instruction to guard the chastity of daughters reflects the society in which
the author lived. A sexually promiscuous unmarried daughter if she became
pregnant in her father's house could bring shame on him. On the other hand, the
anxiety that the author exhibits concerning the sexuality of daughters in 7:23-25,
and also 22:3-5, 42:9-14 and 26:10-12, seems extreme. A picture of a loveless
relationship between father and daughter emerges from these comments. A father
is even urged in 7:24b not to shine his face upon his daughter (תאיר אלהם פנים
ואל, MS A).[79] This may suggest that if the father is too indulgent with the daughter
she may exploit it by using the lack of her father's supervision to misbehave
sexually. It is unlikely that this comment is a warning against a father's incestuous
intentions since none of the uses of the expression in 7:24b has such implications.

Sir 7:25a may refer to the reality that raising a female child has placed a
financial burden on the father, since the daughter was not a permanent member of
his family and upon marriage was transferred to the family of her husband. The
"bride price", given to the bride's father or guardian by the bridegroom or his
father (Gen 34:12; Exod 22:15(16)-16(17); Deut 20:7; 22:29; Hos 2:19-20; 3:2; 1
Sam 18:25, 27),[80] if returned with the dowry as part of the security for the wife in
case of divorce or the death of the husband,[81] was only a temporary financial

---

[79] The Greek is not significantly different here.

[80] E. Lipiński, "מֹהַר," *TDOT* 8.142-49, 143.

[81] John J. Collins, "Marriage, Divorce, and Family in Second Temple Judaism," in
Families in Ancient Israel (ed. Leo G. Perdue, Joseph Blenkinsopp, John J. Collins, and
Carol Meyers; Louisville: Westminster John Knox, 1997) 104-62, 113-14; cf. Lipiński,
"מֹהַר," 145.

advantage for the bride's father. The term "you finish a task" (MS A) may refer to ending one's financial responsibilities or to becoming free of the burden of supervising and controlling the daughter's chastity. To find a husband who is "a sensible man" may reflect genuine concern for the daughter's welfare. In the light of 22:3-5 and 42:9-14, however, the husband may be deemed sensible in the father's eyes according to his ability to take over control of her sexuality.

> 3 αἰσχύνη πατρὸς ἐν γεννήσει ἀπαιδεύτου, θυγάτηρ δὲ ἐπ' ἐλαττώσει γίνεται.
> 4 θυγάτηρ φρονίμη κληρονομήσει ἄνδρα αὐτῆς, καὶ ἡ καταισχύνουσα εἰς λύπην γεννήσαντος·
> 5 πατέρα καὶ ἄνδρα καταισχύνει ἡ θρασεῖα καὶ ὑπὸ ἀμφοτέρων ἀτιμασθήσεται.
> 3 (It is) a disgrace of a father to produce a (son)[82] who is uneducated/without discipline/without instruction, but a daughter is born to his loss.
> 4 A sensible daughter will inherit her husband, (and) a shameless one is a grief to him who begat (her);
> 5 An impudent daughter disgraces father and husband, and will be despised by both. (22:3-5)

Nothing explains why the son is considered undisciplined. Since his conduct brings disgrace to his father, it may include sexual promiscuity, or for instance rejection of an arranged marriage with a suitable future wife. 22:3b is an example of the extremely negative view of female children on the writer's part. Similarly to 7:25 it may refer to the financial difficulties of raising daughters, or the father's anxiety and loss of sleep over keeping the daughter chaste until marriage. 22:4a may imply that the daughter will accept any man as a husband selected by the father.[83] Nothing indicates why the daughter is called shameless (22:4b), but 22:5 confirms that her potential misconduct still causes concern to her father even after marriage. The fact that she is despised by both suggests that her misconduct may be of a sexual nature.

9ab בת לאב מטמנת[87] שקר[86] דאגה[85] תפ[...][84]:

---

[82] While the term the term ἀπαίδευτος ("unlearned", "undisciplined") could refer to both male and female, from the context it is fairly certain that the focus of 22:3a is on an undisciplined son.

[83] Cf. also Trenchard, *Ben Sira's View*, 138. 36:21a, ("[Any] man will a woman accept", MS B) may also describe a situation where the bride does not have a choice regarding the person of the groom.

[84] Lévi, *Hebrew Text*, 53, restores תפ[ריע שנתו]. MS M is restored from GI and MS B: [תפר]יד נומה ("drowsiness will part").

[85] MS B^mg: ודאגתה ("and anxiety for her").

9cd בנעוריה פן תגור⁹⁰   ובבתוליה⁸⁹ פן [...]⁸⁸:

10a, 10b(10c) בבתוליה פן תפותה⁹³   ובבית [...] לה⁹² [...]⁹¹:

10c(10b), 10d בבית אביה פן [...]⁹⁵   ובבית א[...]⁹⁴:

11ab [...] ל [...] ל [...]⁹⁷   [...] שם סרה⁹⁶:

11cd דבת עיר וק[...]ח¹⁰⁰ עם   והושבתך⁹⁹ [...] דח⁹⁸ שער:

11ef [...] קום¹⁰³ תגור אל יהי אשנב¹⁰²   ובית מביט מבוא סביב¹⁰¹:

12ab לכל זכר אל תתן¹⁰⁶ תאר   ובית¹⁰⁵ נשים אל תסתויד¹⁰⁴:

---

⁸⁶ The word seems corrupt. Skehan, *Ben Sira*, 477, 479, restores שקד ("keep watch", "be wakeful") on the basis of GI.

⁸⁷ MSS M and Bᵐᵍ: מטמון ("treasure").

⁸⁸ Lévi, *Hebrew Text*, 54, reconstructs תשנא ("lest she be hated"). Skehan, *Ben Sira*, 479, offers: תעצר, "(lest she be) childless".

⁸⁹ Probable dittography from 42:10; read: בעולה ("married woman"). See also Lévi, *Hebrew Text,* 54.

⁹⁰ גור II in Aramaic means "commit adultery". Cf. also Lévi, *Hebrew Text*, 54. MS M has ת[ה]מאס from מאס ("reject"): "(lest) she be rejected". Skehan, *Ben Sira*, 479, agrees.

⁹¹ MS M: [...]השט [פן] אישה ועל, where [ה]השט can be surmised (שטה = "to be/prove unfaithful").

⁹² Lévi, *Hebrew Text*, 54, reconstructs בע]לה].

⁹³ MS Bᵐᵍ: תתפתה from פתה ("deceive", "entice"). MS M: תחל from חלל ("defile").

⁹⁴ MS M restored from GI: ובעלה פן תעצר ("and when married, lest she be barren"). See Skehan, *Ben Sira*, 477, 480, who notes that בית from 42:10c (10b) does double duty for בעלה.

⁹⁵ Lévi, *Hebrew Text*, 54, reconstructs תזנה in the text and gives פחזה אל in the notes. The latter is supported by MS Bᵐᵍ. They suggest the following reading: "In her father's house lest she commit sexual wrongdoing". MS M: בית אביה פן תזריע: "(In) her father's house lest she become pregnant".

⁹⁶ All versions are too fragmentary to use. Read with GI: "Lest she make you a laughingstock to enemies".

⁹⁷ MS M: בני על] בת חז]ק[משמר] ("My son, keep a close watch on your daughter"). See also Skehan, *Ben Sira*, 477, 480.

⁹⁸ Lévi, *Hebrew Text,* 54, reconstructs בע]דת].

⁹⁹ MS Bᵐᵍ has והובישתך from בוש ("to be ashamed"). MS M has a lacuna.

¹⁰⁰ MS M has וקהלת here.

¹⁰¹ MS M has a lacuna.

¹⁰² MS M omits אשנב. If the Aramaic גור II ("commit adultery") is used here, then one could conjecture: "let there not be a place for adultery". Cf. similarly John Strugnell, "Notes and Queries on 'The Ben Sira Scroll from Masada'," *ErIsr* 9 (1969) 109-19, 116. However, מקום תגור is used in Sir 41:19a (MS B) in the sense "the place where you dwell".

¹⁰³ MS M has מקום.

¹⁰⁴ MS Bᵐᵍ: תסתיד.

13ab כי מבגד יצא עש[107]   ומאשה רעת אשה:

14ab מטוב רוע[111] איש [110] מטיב[109] אשה   ובית מחרפת תביע אשה:[108] (MS B)

9ab A daughter is a treasure for a father [],[112] anxiety[113] [][114]:

9cd in her youth lest she [][115] and while unmarried,[116] [];[117]

10a, 10b(10c) while unmarried, lest she be seduced,[118] and in the house of [][119]

10c(10b), 10d and in the house of her father lest [][120] and in the house of [][121]

11ab [][122] [][123]

11cd a byword in the city and the [][124] of the people, I made you dwell[125] in the city (lit. in the [congregation] of the gate).

---

[105] בין: "among", "in the midst"; see Trenchard, *Ben Sira's View*, 146, 303, n. 156.

[106] MS M: תבן from בין ("to understand"), as "to expose, show, reveal" in the context. Skehan, *Ben Sira*, 480, reads חפן ("to reveal").

[107] MS M has סס, "moth".

[108] Both MS B ("and a house which disgraces pours forth a woman") and MS B[mg] (ובית מחרפת תביע חרפה: "and a house which disgraces, pours forth disgrace") seem corrupt. MS M: ובת מפחדת מכול חרפה (where חרפה means "disgrace", פחד means fear [also of God]). For suggestions to read מבן instead of מכול in MS M, see Trenchard, *Ben Sira's View*, 304, n. 167. MS M would then read: "But better is a God-fearing daughter than a shameless son". Trenchard, *Ben Sira's View*, 304-305, nn. 165-66, offers the following translation for 42:14b: "And a daughter causes fear regarding disgrace more than a son". This way 42:14b would be the "culmination" of not only 42:14a, but the theme of 42:9-14.

[109] Both מטיב and מטוב are supported; see Trenchard, *Ben Sira's View*, 304, n. 164. The former would be closer to GI in meaning (מטיב אשה = "than a woman who does good"), while the latter would read: מטוב אשה ("than a woman's goodness").

[110] MS B[mg]'s insertion (מחפרת from חפר = to act shamefully) seems unnecessary.

[111] Read with MS M and MS B[mg]: טוב רע.

[112] Read "who keeps watch"/"who is wakeful"; see the note on the text.

[113] Read "anxiety for her"; see the note on the text.

[114] Read "takes away sleep"; see the note on the text.

[115] Instead of "commit adultery" the more probable reading is: "(lest) she be rejected"; see the note on the text.

[116] Read "when married"; see the note on the text.

[117] Read "lest she be hated"; for the other variant see the note on text.

[118] MS M reads: "lest she be defiled".

[119] Read "her husband"; see the note on the text. MS M reads: "[lest] she prove unfaithful to her husband".

[120] MS M reads: "(In) her father's house lest she become pregnant". For other variants see the note on the text.

[121] Read with MS M restored from GI: "and when married, lest she be barren"; see the note on the text.

[122] MS M reads: "My son, keep a close watch on your daughter".

[123] Read with GI: "Lest she make you a laughingstock to enemies".

[124] Read "assembly"; see the note on the text.

11ef In the []¹²⁶ of her dwelling let there be no window/lattice, and place that overlooks the surrounding entrance/entrance round about.

12ab Let her not give her beauty (lit. figure) to any male, or consort/associate []¹²⁸ women.

13ab For from a garment comes a moth, and from a woman, woman's wickedness.

14ab []¹²⁹ of a man than a woman who does good,¹³⁰ and a house which disgraces pours forth a woman.¹³¹ (42:9-14) (The numbers in brackets in the Hebrew text and its translation correspond to Skehan's verse numeration.)

9ab θυγάτηρ πατρὶ ἀπόκρυφος ἀγρυπνία, καὶ ἡ μέριμνα αὐτῆς ἀφιστᾷ ὕπνον·
9cd ἐν νεότητι αὐτῆς, μήποτε παρακμάσῃ, καὶ συνῳκηκυῖα, μήποτε μισηθῇ·
10ab ἐν παρθενίᾳ, μήποτε βεβηλωθῇ καὶ ἐν τοῖς πατρικοῖς αὐτῆς ἔγκυος γένηται·
10cd μετὰ ἀνδρὸς οὖσα, μήποτε παραβῇ, καὶ συνῳκηκυῖα, μήποτε στειρωθῇ.
11ab ἐπὶ θυγατρὶ ἀδιατρέπτῳ στερέωσον φυλακήν, μήποτε ποιήσῃ σε ἐπίχαρμα ἐχθροῖς,
11cd λαλιὰν ἐν πόλει καὶ ἔκκλητον λαοῦ, καὶ καταισχύνῃ σε ἐν πλήθει πολλῶν.
12ab παντὶ ἀνθρώπῳ μὴ ἔμβλεπε ἐν κάλλει καὶ ἐν μέσῳ γυναικῶν μὴ συνέδρευε.
13ab ἀπὸ γὰρ ἱματίων ἐκπορεύεται σὴς καὶ ἀπὸ γυναικὸς πονηρία γυναικός.
14ab κρείσσων πονηρία ἀνδρὸς ἢ ἀγαθοποιὸς γυνή, καὶ γυνὴ καταισχύνουσα εἰς ὀνειδισμόν. (GI)

9ab A daughter is a hidden sleeplessness to a father, and worry (over her) drives away sleep:

9cd in her youth, lest she overpass the prime of her life, and when married, lest she be hated;

10ab in virginity, lest she be defiled and in her father's house become pregnant;

10cd having a husband (lit. being with a man) lest she prove unfaithful, and when married, lest she be barren.

11ab Keep strict watch over a headstrong daughter, lest she make you a laughingstock to enemies,

11cd a common talk in the city and the assembly¹³² of the people, and bring shame to you in a multitude of many.

---

¹²⁵ It does not fit here. Read "and bring shame to you" on the basis of MS Bᵐᵍ.

¹²⁶ Read "place"; see the note on the text.

¹²⁷ Reading with MS M: "reveal", "expose"; see the note on the text.

¹²⁸ Read "among" on the basis of the corrected text. See the note on the text.

¹²⁹ Read "Better is the wickedness"; see the note on the text.

¹³⁰ For other variants see the note on the text.

¹³¹ On the basis of the corrected MS M text the most probable reading is "But better is a God-fearing daughter than a shameless son". See the note on the text.

¹³² The word "assembly" in the accusative seems out of place here. It may be that the accusative case of the noun is a mistake and the line should read: "a common talk in the city

12ab Do not look upon anyone in terms of beauty, and do not sit in the midst of women:

13ab for from garments comes a moth and from a woman, woman's wickedness.

14ab Better is the wickedness of a man than a woman who does good, and a woman brings shame leading to disgrace. (42:9-14)

Sir 42:9-14 is the closing section of Sir 41:14 – 42:14. Sir 41:14 – 42:8 has extensive teaching on behaviour of which one *should* or *should not* be ashamed. The longest passage concerns daughters (42:9-14), as if the author intended to demonstrate that shameful activity of daughter, whether unmarried or married, can cause the most damage to a man's, in this case, a father's, honour. If she is still in her father's house and seduced (42:10a, תפותה MS B; "defiled", תחל in MS M), or even pregnant (42:10c[10b], חזריע, MS M = 42:10b in GI),[133] the difficulties are obvious. If she is an unfaithful married woman (42:10b[10c], תשט[ה], MS M = 42:10c in GI), she brings shame not only on her husband and children if she had any, but also on her father. According to MS M in 42:10ab, defilement (תחל from תלל) is closely connected to unfaithfulness (תשט[ה] from שטה). Thus sexual wrongdoing is presented in strong and broad terms as profanation.[134] As the passage progresses, it suggests that not only the daughter's unfaithfulness to her husband, but even her barrenness is her father's problem (42:10d, תעצר, MS M = 42:10d in GI).[135] If she is divorced (probably the meaning of "hated" in 42:9d) and returns to her father's house, perhaps because of adultery or childlessness, she again becomes a financial burden on him.[136] Her behaviour, if shameless, reflects not only on herself, but gives her father a bad reputation for failing to fulfil his duty to keep his daughter chaste, as instructed in 7:24, and in 42:11a: "keep a close watch on your daughter". The consequences include the father being an object of scorn and shame before others, including his enemies (42:11bcd).

---

and in the assembly of the people". If however the accusative is to be expected we would have to assume that the text is not complete. The idea behind it would be something like this: the behaviour of the daughter, if she, for instance, committed a sexually illicit deed, would result in a public judgement, calling together those who are selected to judge in such matters. The following reading could then be surmised: "lest she make you a laughingstock to enemies ... and cause the assembly of the people". Wright, "Sirach," 754, translates "common talk in the city and summoned by the people", which reflects a related idea.

[133] The terms תזנה (reconstruction) and פחזה (MS B^mg) also suggest sexual wrongdoing.

[134] Cf. Joseph Jensen, "Does Porneia mean Fornication?" *NovT* 20 (1978) 161-84, 171. GI (42:10a, c) follows the terminology on defilement (βεβηλωθῇ from βεβηλόω) and unfaithfulness (παραβῇ from παραβαίνω, lit. "transgress").

[135] Also 42:9d if Skehan's suggestion is accepted; see the note on the text.

[136] Archer, *Beyond Rubies*, 27.

The solution then for some of these problems is to keep the daughter's sexuality within the household and under the control of her father (42:11-13) until her marriage, physically locking her in the house. Thus she can be prevented not only from seeing someone through the window, but also from being seen by a man (42:11ef). If her beauty is exposed to a man (42:12a), it might lead to seduction or even rape.[137] Bathsheba and David (2 Sam 11:1-5) and Susanna and the two lecherous elders are prime examples (Sus 5-25, esp. 5-8). Apparently Ben Sira sees contact with a man as inevitably leading to loss of chastity. According to Sir 42:11-12 a daughter without the supervision of her father means danger, namely illicit sexual behaviour. Thus her father must take necessary precautions to prevent her bringing disgrace on herself, but more importantly on her husband and himself.

The idea in 42:12b may be that if a virgin daughter spends time among married women she may become aware of her own sexuality.[138] It may also reflect the writer's concern that women living in a segregated world could use various means including their sexuality to gain power over men, sometimes to bring shame to them, an aspect of women's wickedness (42:13). A daughter may learn this from married women and use it to harm her father's reputation.

For Ben Sira, as Berquist observes, a daughter "is not the subject of her own sexuality; she possesses no possibility for self-control … she works by physiological instinct".[139] Her sexuality may create tensions within the household, therefore raising the possibility of incest with other males in this context, perhaps with her father.[140] This is a problematic issue in the book of Ben Sira. Even if the father depicted in 42:9-14 is tempted by the sexuality of his daughter, there is no explicit evidence that the sage is concerned with fathers committing incest with their daughters. It is more likely that the admonition in 42:9-14 to guard the chastity of the daughter is motivated purely by the fear that she will bring shame to the father. We may note regarding the text of 42:14, that if the second half of the verse (42:14b) is read with the corrected version of MS M ("But better is a God-fearing daughter than a shameless son"), then the fairly misogynist comment of 42:14a would be followed by a surprising ending: it would have a positive comment on daughters. In the book this would be the only example of a daughter being pious/religious, and it would have the only comment on sons within 42:9-14. Nevertheless, taking into account all the teachings on daughters, it appears that Ben Sira views daughters as women mainly in a sexual context, as if their main

---

[137] Cf. Trenchard, *Ben Sira's View*, 156.

[138] Collins, "Marriage," 143.

[139] Jon L. Berquist, *Controlling Corporeality: The Body and the Household in Ancient Israel* (New Brunswick: Rutgers University Press, 2002) 188.

[140] Jon L. Berquist, "Controlling Daughters' Bodies in Sirach," in *Parchments of Gender: Deciphering the Bodies of Antiquity* (ed. M. Wyke; Oxford: Clarendon, 1998) 95-120, 116. Incest is a major concern in CD 6.14 – 7.4; 8.3-8 and in *Jub.* 33.9-20; 41.23-26.

characteristic were their sexuality, and in this context his view is excessively negative. This, however, is not representative of his view on women, femininity, or sexuality, in general.

Sir 26:10-12 is found in the context of 26:7-12. Sir 26:7-9 treats wives: an evil wife (γυνὴ πονηρά, 26:7) later becomes a drunken wife (γυνὴ μέθυσος, 26:8a) whose drunkenness leads her into indecency/shamelessness (ἀσχημοσύνην, 26:8b). 26:9 explicitly describes her as a sexual wrongdoer ("a wife's sexual wrongdoing", πορνεία γυναικός). Suddenly in 26:10-12 the subject becomes a daughter who indiscriminately engages in sexual encounter. Unfortunately the text is not extant in Hebrew. In the discussion we will attempt to answer the question whether the real concern here is indeed the behaviour of daughters, or the Hebrew original may have had different ideas.

> 10 ἐπὶ θυγατρὶ ἀδιατρέπτῳ στερέωσον φυλακήν, ἵνα μὴ εὑροῦσα ἄνεσιν ἑαυτῇ χρήσηται·
> 11 ὀπίσω ἀναιδοῦς ὀφθαλμοῦ φύλαξαι καὶ μὴ θαυμάσῃς ἐὰν εἰς σὲ πλημμελήσῃ·
> 12 ὡς διψῶν ὁδοιπόρος τὸ στόμα ἀνοίξει καὶ ἀπὸ παντὸς ὕδατος τοῦ σύνεγγυς πίεται,
> κατέναντι παντὸς πασσάλου καθήσεται καὶ ἔναντι βέλους ἀνοίξει φαρέτραν.
> (GI)
> 10 Keep strict watch over a headstrong daughter, lest, finding an opportunity (i.e. relaxation of restraint), she make use of it.
> 11 Follow closely (her) bold eyes, and do not be surprised if she commits an offence against you/sins against you.
> 12 As a thirsty traveller opens his mouth and drinks from any nearby water,
> (so) she sits down in front of every peg and opens (her) quiver for (lit. before) an arrow.[141] (26:10-12)

As noted above, in the Greek text the subject of sexual wrongdoing becomes a daughter in 26:10. Skehan considers 26:10a a continuation of sayings concerning wives, and gives the following translation: "Keep strict watch over an unruly wife".[142] He argues that, although the GI version of 26:10a is identical to the GI version of Sir 42:11a, which deals with daughters in the context (42:9-14), the idea of daughter comes to 26:10a from 42:11a, where in turn the term ἀδιατρέπτῳ was added to the text. (Its Hebrew form is not present in the MS M version of 42:11a: "My son, keep a close watch on your daughter"). 26:10a is not extant in Hebrew,

---

[141] Syr. has "before every arrow", and also adds: "So is an adulterous wife, who opens her womb to every man"; see Trenchard, *Ben Sira's View*, 296-97, n. 101. Skehan, *Ben Sira*, 344, takes "sits" as a euphemism for "lies" in 26:12c and also translates "every arrow" in 26:12d.

[142] Skehan, *Ben Sira*, 344, 346.

but Skehan conjectures the term עזות פנים behind "unruly" (or "impudent", "insolent"), which, he argues, can be understood with regard to a wife rather than an unmarried person.[143] This expression occurs in Prov 7:13 regarding the adulteress and a similar term describes the wicked man in Prov 21:19.[144] While it is true that GI reads "daughter" in 26:10, the idea of "adulterous wife" is present in the Syriac text of 26:12d. Further, if "wife" is assumed in 26:10 instead of "daughter", 26:10-12 would fit into their context not only by content, but this way the number of the distichs on bad wives (26:5-12) and on good ones (26:1-4, 13-18) would be equal (10+10 distichs) in Sir 26:1-18. If the Hebrew original indeed had "wife" in this verse, this would raise the question as to why the Greek translator has changed the text.

Sir 26:10a warns that a close watch has to be kept on a "headstrong" (or "insolent") daughter, otherwise as soon as she finds an opportunity, she will commit an offence against her father (26:10b). The sexual nature of the offence is indicated by the use of the term "follow closely (her) bold eyes" (26:11a). Eyes or sight, and desire are commonly linked (e.g. Gen 39:7; Num 15:39; Job 31:1; Prov 6:25; Isa 3:16; Sus 8, 32; *Jub.* 20:4; *1 Enoch* 6:1; CD 2.16-17). A negative bias is reflected in the allusion itself that an "insolent" or "headstrong" daughter will automatically be promiscuous when she finds an opportunity. We noted above Berquist's comment that for Ben Sira a daughter cannot control her own sexuality.[145] Sir 26:12 also suggests this. The daughter is compared to "a thirsty traveller" who does not care from which water he drinks (26:12ab; cf. also Prov 9:17 linking water and adultery), as if the daughter does not care where she lies down for the purpose of sex. The symbolic use of the terms "peg" (πασσάλου) and "arrow" (βέλους) as penis, and "quiver" (φαρέτραν) as vagina (26:12cd) indicates this. It recalls Ezek 16:25 where unfaithful Jerusalem is described as promiscuous with anyone who passes by. Likening one's daughter to idolatrous Jerusalem betrays the author's great anxiety regarding the chastity of daughters.

On the other hand, as noted above, if we assume that the concern of the writer was an adulterous wife in 26:10-12, the language of 26:10-12 would be surprising. The anxiety reflected in it is more characteristic of comments on daughters, as shown in the discussion of 42:9-14. Even though wives may commit adultery (23:22-26), this concern is not expressed in Ben Sira in language as obscene as the description in 26:10-12 in Greek. The problem may be resolved if we surmise that the translator not only changed "wife" to "daughter", but made other changes as

---

[143] Skehan, *Ben Sira*, 344, 346.

[144] Trenchard, *Ben Sira's View*, on the other hand, translates "daughters", assuming identical Hebrew versions behind 26:10a and 42:11a except for בני that is present in the latter, and also argues that other examples of using related material can be found in both chaps. 26 and 42, pointing to 26:5c as similar in theme to 42:11c (140, 295, n. 84).

[145] Berquist, *Controlling Corporeality*, 188.

well, including the introduction of the obscene images. Accordingly Ben Sira may well have originally been condemning adulterous wives, but in much milder terms.

Marital Relations

Ben Sira has an interesting mixture of comments on marital relationships. Perhaps the most obvious feature of these passages is the paucity of advice to husbands on how they should behave, compared with the attention given to wives and the harm they may bring their husbands. While concrete instructions to men concerning issues of sexuality, passions/desires, do occur, most are not in the context of discussions of marriage and so we will not address them in this segment.

In the selection of a wife, beauty is important (36:21b, "yet [one woman is more] [pleasant] [than another]" from the reconstructed text אשה מאשה] [חנ[עם], [יש] אך, MS B[146]). 36:21a suggests that in the majority of cases unmarried women had little choice in the arrangement of their marriage, including their choice of husband ("[Any] man will a woman accept", כ]ל זכר תקבל אשה], MS B[147]). This may reflect reality but could depicts the author's and translator's ideals. Thus it could be another expression of the sage's negative view that women are not discriminating and will put up with anything. Sir 22:4a may also imply, as noted earlier, that a sensible daughter will receive a husband, i.e. without discrimination. This would be in contrast to the *Damascus Document* according to which a father could deem someone unfit for his daughter (4QD[f]/4Q271 3 9).[148]

Attractiveness as part of a woman's sexuality an be the cause of delight to her husband in a good marriage: "[charm] of a wife [delights/pleases] her husband", בעלה [149]יב[מט] אשה [150][חן], MS C; "A wife's charm will delight her husband", Χάρις γυναικὸς τέρψει τὸν ἄνδρα αὐτῆς, GI (26:13a). This is part of the comments on good wives/marital relationships in 26:1-4, 13-18. In this colon the words חן and χάρις can denote charm as attractiveness or as goodwill, favour. It is possible that in 26:13a it is the beauty of the wife that pleases her husband rather than her kindness, or perhaps both. This would suggest a sexual aspect. The verbs used here (מטיב and τέρφει) can mean "delights", "pleases". The latter can also be understood as "satisfies". This way 26:13a could read "the attractiveness of the wife satisfies her husband" (GI). Here the Greek translation seems to enhance the meaning of the original text.

---

[146] Reconstructed by Trenchard, *Ben Sira's View*, 19, 198, nn. 100-101.

[147] This text is based on Lévi, *Hebrew Text*, 38.

[148] Cf. Loader, *Dead Sea Scrolls on Sexuality*, 157-58.

[149] Restored text; see GI and Trenchard, *Ben Sira's View*, 9, 189, n. 10.

[150] Restored text; cf. GI and Trenchard, *Ben Sira's View*, 9, 189, n. 9.

The text of 36:22 is remarkable:

תואר אשה והליל¹⁵² פנים ועל כל מחמד עין יגבר:¹⁵¹ (MS B)

The beauty of a woman []¹⁵³ the face¹⁵⁴ and surpasses every desire of the eye.

κάλλος γυναικὸς ἱλαρύνει πρόσωπον καὶ ὑπὲρ πᾶσαν ἐπιθυμίαν ἀνθρώπου ὑπεράγει· (GI)

A woman's beauty gladdens the face, and surpasses every human desire. (36:22)

According to this verse beauty surpasses everything the eye can desire (MS B). This assertion not only places the desirable attribute "beauty" at the beginning of the description of a good wife within 36:22-24, but also states that in itself it can satisfy and even surpass what the human eye desires. The Greek text perhaps goes even a step further. It lacks the term "eye" and implies that beauty can satisfy not only the eye's desire, but every human desire. This is an example where the translation does not tone down the sexual content, but enhances it. However isolated, it is an important statement pertaining to sexuality: beauty in itself, as part of the woman's sexuality, brings pleasure to the husband and is affirmed.

Similarly significant in a positive sense are the statements in 26:16-18 where within the context of comments on good wives/marital relationships in 26:1-4, 13-18 the author compares that beauty to sacred space:

16 שמש [...] במרומי מעל¹⁵⁶ יפה א [...]¹⁵⁵ בדביר בחור

17 נר שרף על מנורת קדש הוד פנים על קומת תוכן:¹⁵⁷ (MS C)

16 The sun [...]¹⁵⁸ in the heights above, a beautiful [...]¹⁵⁹ in the chosen shrine.¹⁶⁰

---

¹⁵¹ The mutilated text of MS C agrees.

¹⁵² MS B^{mg} reads יהלל from הלל ("to shine", "to be bright"). Trenchard, *Ben Sira's View*, 198, n. 104, suggests the Hiphil form of the verb. Used together with פנים the most probable meaning of 36:22a is: "the beauty of a woman brightens the face". In the place of the verb MS C has מכל ("above all").

¹⁵³ See the footnote on the text. The correct reading is: "brightens".

¹⁵⁴ Cf. the footnote on text. Skehan, *Ben Sira*, 424, reads: "A woman's beauty makes her husband's face light up".

¹⁵⁵ Reconstructed text, read אשה ("woman"/"wife"); see Trenchard, *Ben Sira's View*, 9, 189, n. 20.

¹⁵⁶ Trenchard, *Ben Sira's View*, 189, n. 19, considers the text for this line equivalent with GI except for MS C having מעל ("above") instead of κυρίου ("of the Lord"). In this light verse 16a would read "the sun rising in the heights above" (MS C).

¹⁵⁷ Verse 18 is not extant in the Hebrew text.

¹⁵⁸ The probable reading is: "the sun [rising] in the heights above"; see the note on the text.

¹⁵⁹ Read "woman"/"wife"; see the footnote on the text.

17 (Like) a lamp burning on the holy lampstand, (so is) the splendour[161] of a face on the height of measurement. (26:16-17)

16 ἥλιος ἀνατέλλων ἐν ὑψίστοις κυρίου καὶ κάλλος ἀγαθῆς γυναικὸς ἐν κόσμῳ οἰκίας αὐτῆς·

17 λύχνος ἐκλάμπων ἐπὶ λυχνίας ἁγίας καὶ κάλλος προσώπου ἐπὶ ἡλικίᾳ στασίμῃ·

18 στῦλοι χρύσεοι ἐπὶ βάσεως ἀργυρᾶς καὶ πόδες ὡραῖοι ἐπὶ στέρνοις[162] εὐσταθοῦς. (GI)

16 (Like) the sun rising in the heights of the Lord, (so is) a good wife's beauty in the order of her house/home.

17 (Like) a shining lamp on the holy lampstand, (so is) a beautiful face on a firm figure.

18 (Like) pillars of gold on a silver base, so are shapely feet on the chest[163] of the firm/stable (woman). (26:16-18)

By comparing her beauty, which includes her sexual attractiveness to beautiful sacred objects in the temple (26:17-18; cf. also 1 Macc 1:22, 23; 4:49-50), whose sacred rites he highly regards (50:1-21), the author is making another very positive statement about sexuality.

Within this passage the remains of the corrupt Hebrew text of 26:16b simply praise the beauty of the wife (יפה א[שה]), while GI fills the comment with a moral evaluation: "(so is) a *good* wife's beauty in the order of her house/home" (καὶ κάλλος *ἀγαθῆς* γυναικὸς ἐν κόσμῳ οἰκίας αὐτῆς). All that is known from the Hebrew text is that the wife's beauty, which may include sexual beauty, in itself is praised and compared to the rising sun. In what context she is viewed is not certain.[164] It appears that the Greek text emphasises not only beauty but also goodness in her and places her in the domestic environment, where mainly her husband can delight in her beauty. This also suggests that only he can enjoy her

---

[160] Trenchard, *Ben Sira's View*, 189-90, n. 21, sees it as corrupt, together with the other variant: "in the shrine of a young man".

[161] Trenchard, *Ben Sira's View*, 190, n. 23, suggests יפי ("beauty") instead of הוד ("splendour"). Skehan, *Ben Sira*, 345, translates 26:17b as: "are her beauty of face and graceful figure".

[162] Literally means "breast", "chest", as "the seat of the affections", also "mood", "spirit". Both Skehan, *Ben Sira*, 345, 351, and Trenchard, *Ben Sira's View*, 10, 190-91, n. 27, suggest πτέρναις ("heels" or "feet" from πτέρνη, "heel").

[163] "Breast" or "chest" is not a likely word here. Πτέρναις from πτέρνη ("heel") would be more in context; see the footnote on the text.

[164] The remaining parts of this verse in MS C seem to be corrupt. The word דביר, "shrine" or "sanctuary" seems to be out of context whether it reads "chosen shrine" or "shrine of a young man" (בדביר בחור).

sexuality. Perhaps this is why she is called good: her sexuality is only available for her husband. Unlike in the Hebrew, in GI physical beauty or sexuality appears to be connected with chastity, moral behaviour. This way in 26:16b the ethical aspect may call into question natural beauty.

A woman's/wife's beauty, however, can also be negative. According to 25:21a ("Do not fall []^{165} a woman", אשה ^{166}יופי אל ^{167}אל תפול, MS C; "Do not fall down upon a woman's beauty", μὴ προσπέσῃς ἐπὶ κάλλος γυναικὸς, GI) a man should not be seduced by it. Since this verse is found in the context of bad marital relationships (25:13-26), it probably warns against selecting a beautiful but wicked woman, who can then make a man's life unbearable. The "woman of beauty/charm" (9:8a, חן אשת, MS A) in the context of 9:8-9 is probably another man's wife and thus desiring her represents danger. In 26:9 the (probably painted) eyelids of a wife are responsible for arousing men's desire, which may lead to adultery (cf. also Prov 6:25; 2 Kgs 9:30; Jer 4:30; Ezek 23:40).

Several conclusions may be drawn from these comments. The beauty of one's own chaste wife in a good marriage is positive. In this context a husband is to enjoy his wife's attractiveness as part of her sexuality. However, a man should not be caught in a bad marriage by falling for the beauty of a wicked woman (25:21a). This seems confirmed in 25:21b ("and [do not desire]^{168} her possessions (lit. what she has/owns)", ^{169}ד[תחמן אל] לה יש ועל, MS C; "and do not yearn after a woman", καὶ γυναῖκα μὴ ἐπιποθήσῃς, GI). The Hebrew may convey the message that just like beauty, wealth should also not be the decisive reason in selecting a wife. One should not marry someone for greed. Even if a wicked wife is rich, it will not compensate for the heartache she may cause to her husband. Another interpretation may be that the wife's wealth might prevent the husband from seeking divorce, if the woman could takes her possessions back with her. This way the husband might become trapped in an unbearable marriage (cf. also *Ps.-Phoc.* 199-200).^{170} If the situation in Ben Sira's time was similar to that of Rabbinic times, where the husband's property was a lien and guarantee for the payment of the marriage settlement for the woman in case of divorce, it made divorce more difficult for the husband.^{171} The Greek text of 25:21b lacks any reference to the financial aspect and advises against desiring a woman in general.

---

^{165} Read "through the beauty of"; see the note on the text.

^{166} Read with Lévi, *Hebrew Text*, 27: [ביפי].

^{167} Trenchard, *Ben Sira's View*, 58, 242, n. 66, supports לכד as a parallel to נפל which terms are used in Sir 9:3 I, II. He reads: "And do not be caught because of her possessions."

^{168} See the note on the text.

^{169} Restored by Lévi, *Hebrew Text*, 27. Beentjes, *Ben Sira in Hebrew*, 98, has תמהר.

^{170} Collins, *Jewish Wisdom*, 67; Collins, "Marriage, Divorce, and Family," 115.

^{171} On this see Satlow, *Jewish Marriage*, 87, 200-204, 213-16.

While similar advice is found regarding women belonging to someone else in Sir 9:8; 41:21c(23b), the context in 25:21 is most probably the selection of a wife. This line may mean that a man's desire for a woman should not take control of him, so as to ensnare him in a bad marriage. Another possibility is that the financial aspect is missing somehow, perhaps by mistake, or maybe the translator did not consider it necessary to include, since it follows in both versions of 25:22.

In the example where the Greek text adds the attribute "good" to the description "beautiful wife" (26:16b), it may not only reflect on the wife but also on the husband. It may imply that a husband is not to desire his wife for her beauty or sexuality alone, but also for her goodness, to be seen in the context of her home, where she is solely reserved for her husband and where she is also a homemaker and a mother. Perhaps for the translator, beauty in itself, viewed in parallel with sacred space, was unacceptable and he tried to direct the attention to "goodness". "Good" in the context of the sacred could read "virtuous" or "devout".

Certain passages emphasise that the sexuality of both wife and husband should be reserved exclusively for each other. On the sexuality of wives, apart from 26:16b, which has been discussed above, we see this in 26:15 and 40:23 (in the context of 40:19, 23).

15 חן ע [...]¹⁷² אשה ביישת ואין משקל לצרורת פה: (MS C)

15 Charm [...]¹⁷³ is a modest wife and there is no price (lit. weight) of a sealed mouth/a sealed mouth is priceless.

15 χάρις ἐπὶ χάριτι γυνὴ αἰσχυντηρά, καὶ οὐκ ἔστιν σταθμὸς πᾶς ἄξιος ἐγκρατοῦς ψυχῆς. (GI)

15 Charm upon charm is a modest wife, and priceless is (lit. there is no weight worthy/equal of) her self-controlled person/character. (26:15)

The traits of a good wife in the Hebrew version of 26:15 are modesty (26:15a) and a "sealed mouth" (26:15b). The latter is translated by the GI version as "self-controlled person/character", which can refer to various aspects of self-control. In MS C the term "sealed"/"restricted mouth" or "shut up mouth" (לצרורת פה, from צרר I = "to shut up", Qal I), need not refer exclusively to a closed mouth. The word, "to shut up", "to wrap up", apart from meaning among other things, is said of women withheld from marital intercourse as in 2 Sam 20:3, where the concubines of David are condemned to live in confinement without having sexual relations with David until the day of their death like widows. Skehan therefore argues that "restricted/shut up mouth" here is a euphemism for the closed

---

¹⁷² The text is restored, read על חן ("upon charm"); cf. GI and Trenchard, *Ben Sira's View*, 9, 189, n. 16.

¹⁷³ Read "upon charm"; see the footnote on the text.

vagina.[174] Then 26:15 is more than just a general reference to being disciplined, as the toned down version of GI suggests. Exactly what Ben Sira meant, however, is difficult to determine. It hardly implies her being unavailable even to her husband. More likely it means unavailable to other men. "Modest" in the first half of the verse would reflect this concern and mean her being reserved only for her husband and not attracting other men's attention or not exposing her sexuality to them.

19ab ילד ועיר יעמידו שם ומשניהם מוצא חכמה:[175]

19cd שגר ונטע יפריחו שם ומשניהם אשה נחשקת:[176]

23 [אוהב וחבר לעֶ]ת[177] ינהגו ומשניהם אשה משכלת: (MS B)

19ab A child and a city will establish a name, but better than both is he who finds wisdom.

19cd Cattle and plantation make a name[178] flourish, but better than both is a devoted wife.

23 [A friend and a companion at the right time][179] will lead, but better than both is a sensible wife. (40:19, 23)

19ad τέκνα καὶ οἰκοδομὴ πόλεως στηρίζουσιν ὄνομα,[180] καὶ ὑπὲρ ἀμφότερα γυνὴ ἄμωμος λογίζεται.

23 φίλος καὶ ἑταῖρος εἰς καιρὸν ἀπαντῶντες, καὶ ὑπὲρ ἀμφότερα γυνὴ μετὰ ἀνδρός. (GI)

19ad Children and the building of a city establish a name, but better than both is a woman/wife regarded blameless/without blemish or defect.

23 A friend and a companion meet at the right time, but better than both is a wife with (her) husband. (40:19, 23)

The difference between the Hebrew and Greek texts in 40:23 is noteworthy. According to MS B having a sensible wife (אשה משכלת) surpasses the guidance of friend and companion. GI employs a different word (ἀπαντάω), "meet" or "come near" instead of "guide", omits the expression "sensible wife", and has only "a wife with (her) husband". One might speculate that the translator found it inconceivable that a husband might value a sensible wife more than the guidance of friends. The comment in Greek "but better than both is a wife with (her)

---

[174] Skehan, *Ben Sira*, 350.

[175] MS M, while mutilated, agrees.

[176] The only extant word in MS M in 40:19cd is שאר ("flesh", "body", "self", also "flesh" as "food").

[177] Reconstructed by Lévi, *Hebrew Text*, 49.

[178] As noted above, MS M reads שאר ("flesh", "body", "self", "flesh" as "food"), which is translated by Skehan, *Ben Sira*, 463, 467, as "person": "Cattle and orchards make a person flourish" (40:19c).

[179] See the note on the text.

[180] 40:19bc is not extant in GI.

husband" is also puzzling. It may simply value marital union, or be focusing on the wife as *solely* her husband's, and not straying and looking for a (possible sexual) encounter with another. This may also shed some light on the Greek text of 40:19d ("a woman/wife regarded blameless/without blemish or defect"), which departs from the Hebrew text ("a devoted wife"): a wife is blameless so long as she remains *solely* her husband's.

Further comments that may pertain to the sexuality of wives include 7:19a ("Do not reject/despise a sensible wife",[181] אל תמאס אשה משכלת, MS A; "Do not depart from a wise and good wife", μὴ ἀστόχει γυναικὸς σοφῆς καὶ ἀγαθῆς, GI), where the unspecified term "sensible wife" (אשה משכלת) can include chastity.[182] As in 26:16b, GI has added "good" (ἀγαθῆς). While 7:19 advises against rejecting a sensible wife, 7:26 may refer to divorce when it declares: "Do you have a wife? Do not abhor her. But do not trust a wife who is hated",   בה אשה לך אל תתעבה ושנואה אל האמן, MS A; "Do you have a wife who pleases you (lit. who is according to your soul)? Do not cast her out; but do not trust yourself to one who is hated", γυνή σοί ἐστιν κατὰ ψυχήν· μὴ ἐκβάλῃς αὐτήν· καὶ μισουμένῃ μὴ ἐμπιστεύσῃς σεαυτόν, GI. The translation with its modified text may also imply that the exhortation "do not cast her out" applies only to a wife *who pleases* her husband, but in other cases casting her out may be justified. One can only surmise what constitutes a reason for casting out a wife. The reference to a hated woman may well also allude to divorce and so be cautioning against marrying a divorcee (cf. 4QMinor Prophets[a]/4Q76 where Mal 2:16 reads, כי אם שנתה שלח "for if you hate her, send her away"). The sage may be referring to divorce in 42:9c where he fears for a daughter: "lest she overpass the prime of her life, and when married, lest she be hated". Divorce comes into focus in 25:25-26 in the context of an extensive teaching on bad wives/marital relationships in 25:13-26: "Do not allow an outlet to water, nor outspokenness in an evil wife. If she does not go as you direct [or: according to your hands], cut her off from your flesh".[183] Here the grounds could apparently include both adultery and outspokenness.

---

[181] This reading is more probable than "Do not reject/despise the barren woman" (from שכל = "to prove barren").

[182] 25:8a ("Happy is the husband of a sensible wife", אשרי בעל אשה משכלת, MS C) is an isolated positive comment on marriage. While "sensible" may include "chaste", it is not explicit.

[183] G 248 adds: "give and send (her) away"; also see the extended Syriac version of it: "give to her and send her from your house": Trenchard, *Ben Sira's View*, 245, n. 87. Skehan, *Ben Sira*, 344, 346, also includes the following idea: "cut her away from your flesh with a bill of divorce".

The immediately preceding lines of the passage may also have relevance to this theme. There we read: "From a woman is the beginning of sin, and on her account we all die (lit. we die together)" (MS C) (25:24). This may allude to Eve (cf. Gen 3:1-15, esp. 3:6) and imply that women in general are the cause of sin and death in the world. Levison, however, argues that the context's concern with wicked wives suggests something much more directly related to the theme and so he translates: "From the [evil] wife is the beginning of sin, / and because of her we [husbands] all die". [184] The evil wife is the beginning of sin because she causes her righteous husband to sin. The issue throughout 25:21-26 is a husband's control of his wife. An uncontrollable wife should be divorced. Supporting this argument is the observation that attributing death to Eve would conflict with Ben Sira's view of the origin of death elsewhere, where mortality is seen as God's will for creation since the beginning (17:1-2a; 41:3b, 4a; 40:11) and that Ben Sira does not associate either sin or death with Adam's and Eve's disobedience (14:17; 17:2a). Accordingly in writing "we" in 25:24 Ben Sira speaks as one husband to others, convinced that women who gain control of men are deadly, at least in a metaphorical sense. An uncontrollable wife cuts short her husband's days by grief. Much in the context supports this reading.

On the sexuality of wives, we may finally refer to 42:6a, which encourages husbands to place a seal (חותם, MS B; σφραγίς, GI) on a wicked/evil wife to prevent her from foolishness, perhaps from sexual transgression.

Concerning the sexuality of husbands, we find this addressed in 36:24-26 (MS B, or 36:24-27 in GI) in the context of 36:21-26 (36:21-27 in GI):

24 קנה[188] אשה ראשית[187] קנין עזר ומבצר[186] ועמוד משען:[185]
25 באין גדיר יבוער כרם ובאין אשה נע ונד:[189]

---

[184] John R. Levison, "Is Eve to Blame? A Contextual Analysis of Sirach 25:24," *CBQ* 47 (1985) 617-23, 619, 620, 621.

[185] MS C, though mutilated, suggests משען. It is followed by העמיד.

[186] The term suggested by MS B (עזר ומבצר) lit. means "helper and fortification". MSS B[mg], C and D have עיר מבצר ("fortified city", MS D, where extant, agrees for the rest of the verse). Trenchard, *Ben Sira's View,* 19, 199, n. 114, uses the term עזר כנגדו ("a helper suiting him") employed also in Gen 2:18, 20. It is closer to GI. Skehan, *Ben Sira,* 424, 427, also supports the Greek version, and conjectures the term עזר כעצמו as original. עצם originally means bone/s, but it also expresses identity (Exod 24:10); see Ludwig Koehler and Walter Baumgartner, ed. *Lexicon in Veteris Testamenti Libros* (Leiden: Brill, 1958) 728. Thus Skehan translates: "a help like himself".

[187] It can mean "best", "first", "beginning".

[188] This form may be understood as imperative or a defective form of participle. Therefore the translation would be: "acquire" in the first case or "whoever acquires" in the second. MS B[mg] has the participial form: קונה ("whoever acquires").

26 מי יאמין גדוד צבא המדלג מעיר אל עיר:[190]

כן איש אשר לא קן[192] המרגיע באשר יערב:[191] (MS B)

24 Acquire[193] a wife: the best/first/beginning of his possession, a helper and fortification and a pillar of support.

25 Without a fence/hedge the vineyard will be destroyed, and without a woman a homeless wanderer.[194]

26 Who will trust a troop of soldiers that skips from city to city?

So is the man who has no nest, who settles where night sets in. (36:24-26)

24 ὁ κτώμενος γυναῖκα ἐνάρχεται κτήσεως, βοηθὸν κατ' αὐτὸν καὶ στῦλον ἀναπαύσεως.

25 οὗ οὐκ ἔστιν φραγμός διαρπαγήσεται κτῆμα· καὶ οὗ οὐκ ἔστιν γυνή στενάξει πλανώμενος.

26 τίς γὰρ πιστεύσει εὐζώνῳ λῃστῇ ἀφαλλομένῳ ἐκ πόλεως εἰς πόλιν;

27 οὕτως ἀνθρώπῳ μὴ ἔχοντι νοσσιὰν καὶ καταλύοντι οὗ ἐὰν ὀψίσῃ.

24 Whoever acquires a wife begins[195] a possession, a helper suiting him and a pillar of support (lit. "rest").

25 Where there is no fence, the property will be plundered, and where there is no woman/wife, he will sigh as he wanders.

26 For who will trust a swift robber that skips from city to city?

27 So is the man who has no nest and who lodges wherever night falls. (36:24-26)

For the husband the wife is "a helper and fortification and a pillar of support" (עזר ומבצר ועמוד משען, MS B) according to 36:24b. The word "helper" is supported by GI. "Fortification" seems perhaps out of place here, as it is usually and frequently used regarding cities (fortified city). It is not completely irrelevant, however, considering that the verses that follow use images of destroyed properties without fences. For the term "helper and fortification" the Greek provides the following reading: "a helper suiting him/according to him" (βοηθὸν κατ' αὐτόν). This reproduces the Greek of Gen 2:18, probably indicating that the translator made the connection with the Genesis account.

In what sense a wife is a helper and pillar of support is not specified. It may be understood generally in a broad sense, or specifically such as support in

---

[189] MSS C and D, though mutilated, agree, except they have גדר instead of גדיר.

[190] The text of MSS C and D, where extant, do not differ significantly.

[191]MS D is the same. MS C (המרגיע כאשר יסביב) does not fit here.

[192] The text of MS C and MS D do not have significant differences, except MS C has קין which does not fit here.

[193] The other option is "whoever acquires a wife"; see the footnote on the text.

[194] The subject from the context can be understood: "a man".

[195] Trenchard, *Ben Sira's View*, 199, n. 112, suggests that the word "begins" may be a misunderstanding in GI on the basis of the Hebrew term ראשית which means "first, best" and also "beginning". See the footnote on the text.

economic matters, or, since marriage includes the spheres of sexuality, it may imply that the wife is a suitable sexual counterpart to the husband. This seems to be certain from the last verses of the passage and would cohere with possible intertextual allusions to Genesis 2. In 36:25 the man as a wanderer and the destroyed vineyard (MS B) or property (GI) are images of ruination, including the ruination of the life of the man, if his household collapses. Wives are seen as persons who help build up a family with their sexuality, thus creating a household for the husband. When she fails, the household can collapse; the family line is not continued. In the last verse of the passage (36:26 in MS B = 36:26-27 in GI) the images of the "troop of soldiers"/"swift robber" and the man without a nest (home)[196] are only similar in that they go from one place to the other and are unreliable. Although there is no reference to women in 36:26 it is probable that, as the wife is the "best possession" (36:24a) and "suiting helper" (36:24b) to her husband, thus affecting her husband's life in a positive way, it would affect the man's life in a negative way when her support is missing (36:26).

By contrast 36:25-26 (MS B, or 36:25-27 in GI) can also suggest that if the wife is a matching helper, pillar of support, or partner in a sexual sense, her husband will have sex with her rather than wandering around, having sex wherever he settles. As such the wife stands at the border of the property as the "strongest defence" against the husband's "shameful tendencies".[197] In this sense she may be a "fortification" (36:24). The man himself who has no such "defence" may, himself, be the cause of a ruined property, if he engages in sexual wrongdoing wherever and whenever he can. He may wander from one household to the other, and by extramarital intercourse cross familial boundaries, destroying other households as well. He then becomes the potential thief of another man's wife, an idea especially relevant to the image of "swift robber" in the Greek text of 36:26a. We may conclude, therefore, that 36:24-26 (or 36:24-27 in GI) describes a good marriage as a guard against prostitution or adultery for the husband, whose sexuality should be reserved solely for his wife, foreshadowing a similar argument used by Paul in 1 Cor 7:2-4.

Other potentially relevant passages include 25:1d, where among the things in which the author takes pleasure are: a woman and a man ἑαυτοῖς συμπεριφερόμενοι, which may well mean: "engaging in sexual intercourse", thus be another positive affirmation of sex in marriage; and a set of references to rivalry among wives in a polygynous marriage, causing the husband heartache (26:5-6; 28:15; 37:11a), which may well have been about sexual issues.

---

[196] Cf. Sir 14:26a; Prov 27:8. Archer, *Beyond Rubies*, 124, suggests the word "nest" be understood as "wife".

[197] Cf. also Claudia V. Camp, "Wife," in *Women in Scripture: A Dictionary of Named and Unnamed Women in the Hebrew Bible, the Apocryphal/Deuterocanonical Books, and the New Testament* (ed. Carol Meyers; Grand Rapids: Eerdmans, 2001) 372-73, 372.

Illicit Sexual Relations, Prostitution, Adultery; Unruly/Unruled Passions

Ben Sira addresses unchastity in both men and women. Thus in 9:3 he uses the image of the "strange woman" which appears frequently in Proverbs 1 – 9.

אל תקרב אל־אשה זרה פן־תפול במצודתיה: (MS A)

Do not approach a strange woman, lest you fall into her snares. (9:3 I)

μὴ ὑπάντα γυναικὶ ἑταιριζομένῃ, μήποτε ἐμπέσῃς εἰς τὰς παγίδας αὐτῆς.

Do not meet a woman who is a prostitute, lest you fall into her traps/snares. (9:3 GI)

This verse is found among sayings on diverse types of women in the context of 9:1-9. This helps determine what "strangeness" means here. Sir 9:3 I (9:3 in GI) is closely related to the following bicolon:

II 3 [ע]ם [199] זונה אל־חסתייד פן־תלכד בלקותיה[198],[] (MS A)

4 עם מנגינת אל תדמוך פן ישרפך בפיפיחם

3 II Do not associate/consort [with][200] a prostitute, lest you get ensnared/caught
4 Do not sleep with female musicians, lest they burn you with their mouths[201] (9:3-4 II)

μετὰ ψαλλούσης μὴ ἐνδελέχιζε, μήποτε ἁλῷς ἐν τοῖς ἐπιχειρήμασιν αὐτῆς

With a female musician (lit. one who plays the harp or stringed instrument) do not (do something) constantly/regularly, lest you become caught in her endeavours. (9:3 GI)

---

[198] בלקותיה is problematic. Isa 30:10 uses חלקות of "flattering, smooth speech" and various forms of חלק are used in the warnings against adultery in Prov 2:16; 5:3; 6:24 and 7:5, 21. Lévi, *Hebrew Text*, 12, corrects בלקותיה to בחלקותיה in the Ben Sira passage. Therefore the reading "in her flattering/smooth speech" would make sense in Sir 9:3 II, where one aspect of the snares of the woman in 9:3 I could be her speech.

[199] Lévi, *Hebrew Text*, 12, restores עם.

[200] See the note on the text.

[201] This translation is based on the use of the Aramaic verb behind תדמוך ("to sleep"). Note that the term מנגינת is in the plural ("female musicians"), over which the singular in GI would be the preferred version. ישרפך בפיפיחם is a plural masculine. Neither the reading "lest they burn you with their mouths" nor the idea of burning with a double-edged sword (if פיפיה, "double-edge", "double-edged" is read) seems likely here. Skehan, *Ben Sira*, suggests יפי ("beauty", "charm") (218). It would fit well with the images used in the immediate context, especially if read with תלכד ("get ensnared", "caught") from 9:3 IIb (218). A probable reading of Sir 9:4 is: "Do not associate with a female musician, lest you be caught/captivated by her beauty/charm". This way after introducing another kind of "dangerous" woman as "female musician" after the ones in 9:3 I, II, another aspect of her snares, her beauty, would be listed here. Also the theme of a "woman's beauty" returns in 9:8abc as something that represents danger.

9:3 II and the Greek version (9:3) of 9:3 I clearly identify the woman in question as a "prostitute", or a sexually immoral woman (זונה and γυναικὶ ἑταιριζομένη, respectively), with whom one should not "consort/dally" (תסתייד).[202] In 9:4 the "female musician"[203] can also be understood as a prostitute. In Isa 23:15-16 Tyre is compared to a forgotten prostitute (זונה) playing a harp.[204] These comments lack any reference to the "strange woman". Prostitutes are the focus also of 9:6-7, "Do not give yourself to a prostitute [לזונה], lest you surrender [lit. "turn over"] your inheritance", MS A;[205] 9:7: "Do not look around in the streets of a city, nor wander about in its deserted places",[206] GI. There follows a warning regarding married women:

> Avert (lit. "hide") your eyes from a lovely woman (lit. "woman of beauty/charm", חן מאשת), and do not look intently at beauty that is not for you. Through a woman[207] many [have been ruined][208] and thus her lovers kindles in fire.[209] With a mistress[210] do

---

[202] The verb has the meaning "be confiding", "to confide a secret to someone", "to gossip". The noun סוד also means "secret", "confidential speech"; cf. also Koehler-Baumgartner, *Lexicon,* 651. The verb used here appears with medieval double ' and Aramaizing ֗ at the end; cf. Skehan, *Ben Sira,* 217.

[203] See the note above regarding this verse for translation issues.

[204] Cf. also O. J. Baab, "Prostitution," *IDB* (New York: Abingdon, 1962) 3.931-34, 934; Elaine Adler Goodfriend, "Prostitution," *ABD* (New York: Doubleday, 1992) 5.505-10, 509.

[205] GI is not significantly different. It has the plural πόρναις.

[206] The Hebrew text is corrupt. However, Lévi, *Hebrew Text*, 12, with its similar ideas במבואי עיר ("in the entryways of the city") and לשוטט ברחבותיה ("wandering in its wide places") supports this translation.

[207] The probable reading is "through a woman's beauty" based on the text in Lévi, *Hebrew Text*, 12: בתואר אשה.

[208] Based on Lévi, *Hebrew Text*, 12: [ה]שחתו.

[209] Trenchard, *Ben Sira's View*, 108, 273, n. 118, suggests the correction to אהבה ("love") instead of אהביה ("her lovers") in MS A. GI supports it. If באש is also corrected to כאש ("like fire"), as in GI and in Lévi, *Hebrew Text*, 12, then 9:8d should read: "thus love kindles like fire".

[210] Read בעולה ("married woman") with Lévi, *Hebrew Text*, 13; Skehan, *Ben Sira,* 215, 218, agrees.

not taste/eat/enjoy,[211] [and do not sit down][212] with him[213] at the table drunken, lest (your) heart incline/turn [toward her][214] and in blood you decline to the [pit].[215] (9:8-9).

In 9:9 the combination of wine and (married) women presents danger, indicating that just as a woman does not know shame when drunk (26:8) and may incline toward initiating an illicit relations, a drunk may do the same.

In short, Sir 9:3 I (9:3 in GI) is surrounded by references to prostitution and in the wider context by comments on adultery. Although there are suggestions that the prostitution of the "strange woman" of Proverbs 7 has something to do with the cult on the basis of 7:14, no similar allusion is found either in Sir 9:3 I (9:3) or in Sir 9:3 II, 4, 6-7, 8-9. The theme of intermarriage, an important issue in the work of Ezra and Nehemiah, seem not to worry Ben Sira, so the concern here seems also to have nothing to do with foreignness. In fact, in 47:19-21, which gives an account of Solomon's sin, the author refer neither to intermarriage, nor to his wives as foreign. His main accusation is that Solomon gave women dominion over his body. Thus Ben Sira's warning in 9:3 I (9:3) is most likely about either an ordinary prostitute, or a married woman, whose nationality or ethnicity is not clear, and seems irrelevant for him. The only passage where the term "strangers"/ "others" (ἀλλοτρίοις) may refer to non-Israelites is 26:19-21, but it focuses rather on the selection of a chaste wife who will provide legitimate children for the husband, and may also guard him against having sex outside of marriage.

It appears that, unlike in Proverbs 1 – 9, where the personifications of the strange or foolish woman serve both as symbols of folly and as concrete warnings against extramarital sexual liaisons, in Ben Sira they serve only the latter purpose. This seems to be the case in Sir 41:20b(22a) where one is to avoid the זרה (41:20b, MS M), translated as γυναικὸς ἑταίρας in GI (= 41:22a). In these warnings if the "strange woman" is a prostitute but not a married woman, she may be regarded strange as her way of life places her outside the prescribed social boundaries. If she is also a married woman, then her extramarital sexual activity makes her an outsider in relation to the prescribed familial boundaries, both in terms of her family and of the family of the man she consorts with, since compared with one's lawful wife she is an outsider, strange, different, the "other".[216]

---

[211] אל חט אצל ("do not stretch elbow") is also acceptable as suggested by Lévi, *Hebrew Text*, 13; Skehan, *Ben Sira*, 218; and Trenchard, *Ben Sira's View*, 109, 273-74, n. 121. A similar expression is found in Sir 41:19c.

[212] Based on the restored text in Lévi, *Hebrew Text*, 13: ואל [ת]סב.

[213] Read עמה ("with her"); cf. Lévi, *Hebrew Text*, 13.

[214] Based on the text in Lévi, *Hebrew Text*, 13: אליה.

[215] Based on the text in Lévi, *Hebrew Text*, 13: שחת.

[216] Cf. Mieke Heijerman, "Who Would Blame Her? The 'Strange' Woman of Proverbs 7," in *A Feminist Companion to Wisdom Literature* (ed. Athalya Brenner; Sheffield:

In Sir 9:3 I (9:3) the meaning of the expression "her snares" is not specified. The image comes from hunting. The noun without the suffix can be both מָצוֹד and מָצוּד ("hunting net", "trap" or "snare") and with this meaning is popular in wisdom literature in various forms (Job 19:6; Ps 116:3; Prov 12:12; Eccl 7:26; 9:12; but also found in Ezek 12:13; 19:8).[217] In the *Damascus Document* it includes the snare of sexual wrongdoing (4.15-21). In Sir 9:3 I the feminine מצודה is used. Images of snares, traps, bonds or restraints are used in a positive sense in Sir 6:24-25, 29-30 regarding the snares of personified wisdom.

Ben Sira does not specify the consequences of being caught by the snare of the strange woman in Sir 9:3 I (9:3). If the woman is only a prostitute, then the consequence might range from loss of money, to loss of one's inheritance through "the practice of purchasing sexual favours",[218] spiritual ruin,[219] or even death resulting from destructive life style. This may apply to 9:6-7 as well. If the woman is married (Sir 9:8-9, 41:21c[= 41:23b in GI]), the consequences will be more serious. The comment about the pit (9:9d) in MS A and destruction in GI is not elaborated. If as Skehan suggests, the death penalty might not have been in force anymore in Ben Sira's time,[220] the punishment could include compensation for the offended husband as suggested in Prov 6:33-35, which implies for the offender not only a beating, and loss of honour and disgrace in the community,[221] but also vengeance from the wronged husband, who will not be satisfied with compensation or bribe. 26:22b (GII) also emphasises the gravity of adultery compared to consorting with prostitutes (26:22a).[222]

Finally, although in Sir 9:3 I (9:3), 3 II, 4, 6-7, 8-9 the emphasis is on the husband's behaviour and on his approach to women with questionable virtues, the sage may also be concerned that, by being seduced and ensnared by a woman, a

---

Sheffield Academic Press, 1995) 100-109, 105. See also Loader, "Strange Woman in Proverbs," 97-101.

[217] Cf. Koehler-Baumgartner, *Lexicon*, 555-56.

[218] See Trenchard, *Ben Sira's View*, 121. He also assumes an unwanted long term relationship (120).

[219] Elaine Adler Goodfriend, "Adultery," *ABD* (New York: Doubleday, 1992) 1.82-86, 85.

[220] Skehan, *Ben Sira*, 325.

[221] Hilary B. Lipka, *Sexual Transgression in the Hebrew Bible* (HBM 7; Sheffield: Phoenix, 2006) 162-63.

[222] Although Sir 26:22b does not use παγίς, rendered "snare" in Sir 9:3, but the term πύργος θανάτου ("tower of death"), Skehan translates it as "deadly snare" instead of "tower of death", since, he argues, Eccl 7:26 also links "woman" and "snares". See Patrick W. Skehan, "Tower of Death or Deadly Snare? (Sir 26:22)," *CBQ* 16 (1954) 154.

man would come under the woman's control, a cause of great shame.[223] The fear of being controlled by a woman seems to be reflected not only in the verses discussed but also in Sir 9:2 and indirectly in 9:1. 9:2 can also suggest that a husband should not let even his wife have power over him, possibly through sexuality (9:2b, "to cause her to tread upon your heights", להדריכה על במותיך, MS A; or "your strength/power", τὴν ἰσχύν σου in GI).

The most extensive teaching on the sexual immorality, including adultery of men, is found in 23:16-21. It views the ἄνθρωπος πόρνος (23:16e, GI) in the context of sexual immorality (23:16-17), where the author sums up all the persons or activities that are despicable and cause anger. The comment on the burning passion that consumes everything (23:16cd) is not further specified. Nothing indicates whether the man is married nor what is the object of his passion (cf. Prov 6:27-29). According to 23:16-17 the consequences involve fire. 23:16 employs the image of fire a number of times.[224] While in 23:16c it describes passion, in 23:16d the very same fire can destroy a person, but it is not clear how. The expression "fire breaks forth" (23:16-17) may simply mean burning passion that kindles in the person committing sexual wrongdoing in 23:16e. In 23:17 for the sexual wrongdoer (ἀνθρώπῳ πόρνῳ) "all bread is sweet", implying that he frequently commits sin and is not selective in his liaisons, always looking for opportunities. In Prov 9:17, "stolen water" and "bread eaten in secret" serve both to symbolise folly and to warn about illicit sex. Sir 23:17 is concerned only with the latter.[225]

Unlike in 23:16-17, in 23:18-21 there is no doubt that the sexually immoral man is married. In 23:18 sinning against one's own female spouse is an issue: "The man who leaves his (marriage) bed/strays from his bed", ἄνθρωπος παραβαίνων ἀπὸ τῆς κλίνης αὐτοῦ (23:18a GI). This is remarkable since usually an adulterous man is seen as committing an offence against the woman's husband, not against the woman or his own wife, if he is married.[226] Although it is not stated that he transgresses with a married woman, this seems to be the case. Nothing is said here about wronging the other man by violating his exclusive right to the woman's sexuality which was reserved for him before and during marriage.[227] With the statement in 23:18e ("The Most High will not be mindful of

---

[223] Gale A. Yee, *Poor Banished Children of Eve: Woman as Evil in the Hebrew Bible* (Minneapolis: Fortress, 2003) 51-58.

[224] Fire appears frequently in Ben Sira's vocabulary, but it is used in the context of destruction only in 7:17; 16:6; 21:9; 36:8; 45:19 and in 9:8 to depict burning passion.

[225] On this see Loader, "Strange Woman in Proverbs," 100-101, 105-10.

[226] D. N. Freedman and B. E. Willoughby, "נאף," *TDOT* 9.113-18, 114.

[227] Cf. Phyllis A. Bird, "Prostitution in the Social World and Religious Rhetoric of Ancient Israel," in *Prostitutes and Courtesans in the Ancient World* (ed. Christopher A. Faraone and Laura K. McClure; Wisconsin: University of Wisconsin Press, 2006) 40-58, 42; Goodfriend, "Adultery," 82; Baab, "Adultery," 51.

my sins") the man acknowledges that what he is about to do is wrong in the eyes of the Lord, and at the same time he is aware that with his deeds he is about to cross communal boundaries (23:19a: "and he fears the eyes of humans").[228] 23:21 does not disclose anything about the penalty. As noted earlier, the death penalty was probably not in force anymore. Even though there is no reference to the revenge of an offended husband or compensation for the offence against him, they cannot be excluded, and would be accompanied maybe by public shaming, permanent disgrace, or loss of status.

While the adulteress (23:22-26), similarly to the adulterer, commits an offence against God (23:23a, "[she] has disobeyed the law of the Most High", ἐν νόμῳ ὑψίστου ἠπείθησεν, GI) and her own spouse (23:22a, "who leaves [her] husband", καταλιποῦσα τὸν ἄνδρα; 23:23b, [she] "has offended her husband", εἰς ἄνδρα αὐτῆς ἐπλημμέλησεν, GI), she also brings, or may bring children into the marriage who are not rightful heirs of the husband (23:22b, "provides [lit. brings into existence] an heir by someone else", παριστῶσα κληρονόμον ἐξ ἀλλοτρίου and 23:23d, "brought forth [lit. brought into existence] children by another man", ἐξ ἀλλοτρίου ἀνδρὸς τέκνα παρέστησεν, GI). Bringing forth illegitimate children was socially and economically an important aspect of adultery.[229] With an heir from someone else the family line would be defiled, the boundaries of the household as body would be crossed,[230] and as a consequence the inheritance, name and status of the offended party would go to the children from an illegitimate union (similarly *Ps.-Phoc.* 177-178). Keeping the inheritance within the husband's family appears to be Ben Sira's concern not only here but also in 26:19-21. 23:25 declares that the punishment also affects the adulteress's children. The latter and the motif of an accursed memory (23:26) are lacking in the description of the adulterer.

Other short comments that concern the sexual immorality of both men and women include 25:2d (γέροντα μοιχόν), 42:8b and 26:8-9. The first two condemn the adultery of old men. In 42:8b the term זנות ("sexual immorality", MS M) is used in a broad sense. Sir 26:8-9 describes a woman who is drunk, and whose drunkenness can lead to sexual wrongdoing. The term πορνεία γυναικός ("wife's sexual wrongdoing") seems to be a new term introduced by the author in 26:9 and has a meaning broader than prostitution.

Not only Sir 9:3, 4, 6-7, 23:16-17, but also the teachings on virgins/ maidservants suggest that the sage perhaps applied stricter ethical standards than

---

[228] Lipka, *Transgression*, 165, 169-99, 169.

[229] Cf. Goodfriend, "Adultery," 82; Anthony Phillips, "Another Look at Adultery," in Anthony Phillips, *Essays on Biblical Law* (JSOTSup 344; London: Sheffield Academic Press, 2002) 74-95, 79.

[230] See Berquist, *Controlling Corporeality*, 99-106.

those in the Hebrew Bible that tolerate prostitution or sexual intercourse with maidservants. Thus he declares: "Do not turn your attention to a virgin lest you be ensnared/trapped in fines because of her" (9:5, MS A) and "[Be ashamed of] [231] meddling [with a maidservant][232] of *yours*, and of violating her bed" (41:22ab MS M); cf. "of meddling with *his* maidservant, and do not approach her bed" (41:24ab, GI). Thus the Hebrew text in 41:22a forbids sex even with one's own maidservant.

All kinds of sexual wrongdoing are discouraged. Most of the passages that deal with extramarital sexual relations reflect anxiety about consequences: financial penalties, unwanted marriage in the case of a seduced virgin, losing one's inheritance to prostitutes or perhaps through compensation of the wronged husband in the case of adultery, ruination of one's health, mistaken paternity, and also shame before others. On the other hand, coming under the control of a woman through sexuality can also be an issue for a man, in the context of both licit and illicit relations.

Maintaining self-control is an important concern for the writer. It is perhaps best expressed in 6:1-3 (= 6:2-4 in GI); 18:30 – 19:3 and in 23:4-6. These passages suggest that Ben Sira may have been influenced by the Stoic and Cynic ideal of αὐτάρκεια (self-sufficiency, self-contentment), freedom from passions, but only in the sense that a person should not be controlled by desires.[233] At least for the grandfather, passions are not negative in themselves. This is also reflected in the comments on good marital relationships. Passions are only dangerous when they are excessive and take control of one's life (23:6a, "let neither gluttony [lit. longing of the belly] nor sexual intercourse take hold of me", κοιλίας ὄρεξις καὶ συνουσιασμὸς μὴ καταλαβέτωσάν με, GI). In 18:30 – 19:3 the combination of passions, drinking, and women, presents temptation and danger. The motivation behind these passages is, on the one hand, fear of negative consequences. Accordingly, 6:2(3) refers to a person who by following his sexual desires without restraint becomes like a dry tree (6:2b, יבש יעל‎ כען, MS A; 6:3b, ξύλον ξηρόν GI). The term is used in Isa 56:3; Ps 128:3 LXX; 144:12; *LAB* 50:1 of sexual impotence and implies that here. On the other hand, the fear is of being controlled by women through sexuality. The dual focus of these teachings is thus on managing one's own inner sexual desires, and on managing external dangers, women, in particular.

Finally, the sage makes two incidental references to eunuchs.

4 ἐπιθυμία εὐνούχου ἀποπαρθενῶσαι νεάνιδα,
οὕτως ὁ ποιῶν ἐν βίᾳ κρίματα.

---

[231] Supplied from 41:19b.

[232] Based on the restored text in Skehan, *Ben Sira,* 479: ע[ם ש]ח[זה‎.

[233] Cf. also Eron, "Women Have Mastery," 53.

4 a eunuch's desire to violate a virgin;
so is the one who executes judgments by force (20:4 GI).

20a בעינו [...] [234]
20b כאשר סירים[235] יחבק נערה ומתאנח
20c כן עושה באונס[236] משפט:

20a With his eyes []‍[237]
20b like a []‍[238] who embraces a young woman and sighs/groans.
20c So is the one who does judgment under compulsion. (30:20 MS B)

19a τί συμφέρει κάρπωσις εἰδώλῳ;
19b οὔτε γὰρ ἔδεται οὔτε μὴ ὀσφρανθῇ·
19c οὕτως ὁ ἐκδιωκόμενος ὑπὸ κυρίου.
20a βλέπων ἐν ὀφθαλμοῖς καὶ στενάζων
20b ὥσπερ εὐνοῦχος περιλαμβάνων παρθένον καὶ στενάζων,

19a Of what use is an offering to an idol?
19b For it will neither eat nor smell:
19c So is the one being punished by the Lord.
20a seeing with his eyes and groaning
20b like a eunuch embracing a virgin and groaning. (30:19-20 GI)

20c οὕτως ὁ ποιῶν ἐν βίᾳ κρίματα.
20c so is the one who executes judgments by force. (30:20 GII)

The comment in 20:4 addresses abuse by a judge, which it suggests will come to nothing, but implies that eunuchs also had sexual desire and could engage in sexually abusive behaviour. In 30:(19-)20 the analogy with idols also suggests impotence perhaps compared to failure of appetite through sickness,[239] though, again, it assumes sexual desire on the part of the eunuch. This is generally to be assumed. Both texts appear to relate to being able to resist and exercise justice properly. While the sexual desire of eunuchs may have diminished, it did not necessarily disappear entirely.[240]

---

[234] Lévi, *Hebrew Text*, 29, restores [רואה ומתאנח] בעינו.

[235] Read סרים; Lévi, *Hebrew Text*, 29.

[236] B[mg] has בגזל (by "robbery", "violent taking away"); Lévi, *Hebrew Text*, 29, agrees. אנס also means "rob".

[237] "he sees and groans"; see the note on the text.

[238] Read "eunuch"; see the note on the text.

[239] Skehan, *Ben Sira*, 382.

[240] B. Kedar-Kopfstein, "סָרִיס," *TDOT* 10.345-50, 346-47; also Hester, "Eunuchs," 17.

Wisdom Poems

The wisdom poems occupy ajn important place in the book (1:1-10; 4:11-19; 6:18-31; 14:20 – 15:10; chaps. 24; 51:13-30). While building on the tradition of other wisdom books in the personification of wisdom, Ben Sira exhibits unique features in these poems. In detailed descriptions of a love affair between wisdom and her suitor these poems express perhaps most clearly that Ben Sira is not shy about sexuality. 1:1-10 can be taken as an introduction to the rest of the poems to establish one of the main themes in the book: all wisdom is from the Lord, and only he knows her origin and can make her accessible for humans.

Sir 4:11-19 is more explicit: "Whoever obeys me [lit. hears/listens to me] will judge truly/safely, and whoever listens to me will dwell in my inmost chambers" (4:15, MS A). Living in wisdom's inmost chambers as a reward is part of the love affair between the seeker and wisdom. The Greek version, however, lacks this idea and suggests that those who listen to wisdom will live in confidence (κατασκηνώσει πεποιθώς, GI). It tones down the erotic. Crenshaw points out that, since the idea of judging nations is foreign to Ben Sira, some scholars read ישכן for ישפט in 4:15a which would result in the following translation: "whoever obeys me will dwell truly/safely". Then 4:15 would have a chiastic pattern: whoever obeys me will dwell truly/safely :: will dwell in my inmost chambers whoever listens to me. This would indicate that living in wisdom's chamber as a lover means safe dwelling, or we could even assume that only living with wisdom is true living.[241]

In 6:18-31 the author uses agricultural images to describe the student's and wisdom's erotic affair. Wisdom as a fertile field is pursued by her lover: "Like ploughing and reaping[242] draw near her and wait for her plentiful yield/crops" (6:19ab, MS A). The images of ploughing (חורש, MS A) and probably sowing (זורע, as suggested as the replacement for קוצר, "reaping" in MS A)[243] symbolise the act of sexual penetration and ejaculation (6:19).[244] The fertility of the soil ensures that with little labour (6:19c) the fruit/crop, the offspring, will be plentiful (6:19b) and will soon be available (6:19d).[245] The idea of a good field and sowing associated with the feminine is also used in 26:19-21. Sir 6:20-22 suggests that the

---

[241] James L. Crenshaw, *Defending God: Biblical Responses to the Problem of Evil* (Oxford: Oxford University Press, 2005) 105.

[242] Skehan, *Ben Sira*, 190-91, suggests וכזורע ("and like sowing").

[243] See the note on the translation.

[244] These images resemble courtship language; see Jessie Rogers, "'As ploughing and reaping draw near to her': A Reading of Sirach 6:18-37," *Old Testament Essays* 13 (2000) 364-79, 372-373, esp. 373, and Jane S. Webster, "Sophia: Engendering Wisdom in Proverbs, Ben Sira and the Wisdom of Solomon," *JSOT* 78 (1998) 63-79.

[245] Both text versions contain this idea.

foolish person who does not value her and casts her away will also cast away the possible intimate relationship with her.

In 6:24-25 the images of "fetters" (πέδας, 6:24a, only in GI) and "yoke" (κλοιὸν, 6:24b, only in GI) may symbolise the lovers' bonds. Wisdom dominates her lover. On the other hand in 6:29a ("And her fetters will become your strong shelter", GI) the "fetters" (πέδαι) as "strong shelter" (σκέπην ἰσχύος) may be the protection against immoral women, keeping the man from straying. In 6:28 ("For afterwards you will find rest in her and she will be transformed/changed for you into delight/comfort", MS A) rest (מנוחתה)[246] and delight (תענוג)[247] are also characteristics of love fulfilled. In this passage the translator has not made significant changes.

Sir 14:20 – 15:10 is also dedicated to the love relationship between wisdom and her suitor. It encourages the student to seek her out and camp near her house (14:20-27) as one "who looks behind her window and listens at her doors, who encamps near her house and drives [][248] into her wall, who puts up his tent by her side and dwells where it is good to dwell, who builds his nest in her foliage and in her branches spends the night, who seeks refuge in her shadow from the heat and dwells in her home" (14:23-27, MS A). Wisdom is virtually besieged.[249] The expression "drive his tent peg (the corrected יתדו, MS A; πάσσαλον, GI) into her walls" suggests sexual penetration (14:24b). This idea appears in both text versions. Wisdom is a tree in 14:26-27.[250] Living among her branches also implies, especially in the Hebrew, that her space is penetrated for the purpose of sex. Sir 14:27b further confirms that the person no longer lives just close to wisdom but in her home as her lover or spouse.[251] Among the rewards of the person who finds wisdom are motherly love (15:2a, אם, MS A) and the love of a young bride (15:2b, אשת נעורים, MS A). Wisdom offers food and drink in 15:3 (15:3a, "bread of knowledge/"insight"/"comprehension", לחם שכל, MS A; 15:3b, "water of [understanding]", מי [תבונה], MS A). Wisdom's house is full of choicest fruits in Sir 1:17, where a sexual connotation cannot be excluded. In Cant 2:3-5 food images symbolise the pleasure the man's body holds for the woman.[252] In

---

[246] ἀνάπαυσιν in GI.

[247] εὐφροσύνην in GI.

[248] Read "his tent peg" on the basis of the corrected text in Lévi, *Hebrew Text*, 23: יתדו ("his tent peg") from יתד ("peg", "tent pin").

[249] Judith E. McKinlay, *Gendering Wisdom the Host: Biblical Invitations to Eat and Drink* (JSOTSup 216; Sheffield: Sheffield Academic Press, 1996) 145.

[250] As in Sir 24:13-17.

[251] See also Webster, "Sophia," 71.

[252] Ken Stone, *Practicing Safer Texts: Food, Sex and Bible in Queer Perspective* (London: T&T Clark, 2005) 100.

Canticles the fruit and vineyard symbolism is connected with non-procreative sexual activity: "Seed and procreation give way to ripening, engorgement and taste".[253] Sexuality is not just something useful for goals beyond itself; it celebrates itself.[254] This may be the case also in Sir 15:3, in contrast to Sir 6:18-31, where the field/seed image focuses on fruit. Here there is no reference to producing offspring.[255] According to 15:4 whoever trusts in wisdom will not commit mistakes, shameful acts, which may include sexual wrongdoing. In Sir 15:6a "joy and gladness" (ושמחה שָׂשׂוֹן, MS A) may also include sexual joy. As in 6:18-31 the translator has not made significant changes to the erotic comments in 14:20 – 15:10.

Sir 24:1-22 follows immediately after the comments on the adulteress whose punishment includes public shaming (23:22-6, esp. 23:24). It begins with wisdom's self-praise in the assembly of the Most High.[256] The juxtaposition of the adulteress and wisdom may suggest an erotic background for the latter, which appears to be confirmed in the second half of the poem (24:13-15, 16-22). Wisdom, like plants or trees, offers food and symbolises fertility and abundance as she offers herself (24:13-15, 16-17, 19-21). The fragrance of these plants may also serve to awake one's desires (24:15). Myrrh, aloes and cinnamon are used as part of the adulteress' arsenal to seduce the unsuspecting man into her house in Prov 7:17. Throughout the Canticles images of fragrance are also symbols of sensuality (1:12-14; 4:6, 10, 13-14; 5:1, 5, 13). They attract the lover to enjoy the fruits in the garden of the beloved (Cant 4:16). In 24:17 wisdom, like a vine, produces fruits: "honour and wealth". Riches and honour are said to be wisdom's gifts in Prov 3:16, where it is connected with long life, and in Prov 8:18-19, 21 (cf. also also Prov 8:10-11). These passages imply, and Prov 3:18; 8:35a; Sir 4:12a confirm, that what wisdom offers is life with her, life that follows her instructions. This may include prosperity but also honour (Sir 4:21b) in the sense of good reputation before others. Prov 7:4-5 suggests that wisdom can also prevent a person from engaging in sexual wrongdoing. Indirectly this may be implied in Sir 6:29a (especially in Greek), 15:4 and 24:22.

Wisdom arouses unquenchable desire (24:21, "Whoever eats me will hunger still, and whoever drinks me will be thirsty still", οἱ ἐσθίοντές με ἔτι πεινάσουσιν, καὶ οἱ πίνοντές με ἔτι διψήσουσιν, GI). Intimacy with her has a lasting memory: "For the memory of me is sweeter than honey, and the

---

[253] Carey Ellen Walsh, *Exquisite Desire: Religion, the Erotic, and the Song of Songs* (Philadelphia: Fortress, 2000) 85.

[254] Berquist, *Controlling Corporeality*, 84.

[255] Cf. also David Carr, "Gender and the Shaping of Desire in the Song of Songs and Its Interpretation," *JBL* 119 (2000) 233-48, 241-42.

[256] Cf. J. C. H. Lebram, "Jerusalem, Wohnsitz der Weisheit," in *Studies in Hellenistic Religions* (ed. M. J. Vermaseren; Leiden: Brill, 1979) 103-28, 105-106.

inheritance of me is better than a honeycomb of honey" (24:20 GI). While the adulteress in Sir 23:26 leaves an accursed memory, the memory of wisdom's love is so desirable that once a person has tasted intimacy with her, he will desire more and will never be satisfied (24:21). The love of the adulteress is condemned; the love of wisdom is exalted. This seems to be confirmed in 24:22 ("Whoever obeys me will not be ashamed, and those who work with me will not sin", ὁ ὑπακούων μου οὐκ αἰσχυνθήσεται, καὶ οἱ ἐργαζόμενοι ἐν ἐμοὶ οὐχ ἁμαρτήσουσιν, GI). The latter may also imply that wisdom can prevent a person from committing a shameful, possibly sexual, act. This is followed by the identification of wisdom and Torah in 24:23. It is remarkable that language with a potential sexual connotation and the comment on the covenant of the Most High are in such close proximity.

Ben Sira's most erotically-charged wisdom poem is 51:13-30. It is a description in the first person of seeking and finding wisdom, and of the love affair with her. In 51:13a ("[When] I was young and before I went astray", 11QPs^a/11Q5 xxi) the expression "before I went astray" (בטרם תעיתי) may refer to innocence. It is suggested in 51:14 that wisdom is beautiful (בתאּרה, as reconstructed, 11QPs^a/11Q5 xxi).[257] GI lacks the reference to beauty. 51:15 in both versions uses the ripening of the grapes to depict a young man reaching maturity, who in 51:15d admits that he has known wisdom, probably sexually, from a young age (ידעתיה, 11QPs^a/11Q5 xxi). GI reads only "I sought her" (ἴχνευον αὐτήν).

In 51:16 ("I paid heed [lit. I turned/inclined my ear] [for] a little [time], and I found much instruction", 11QPs^a/11Q5 xxi) the word used for instruction is לקח, which may also mean "persuasive words" as in Prov 7:21.[258] Sir 51:17 is problematic. The reconstructed text of 11QPs^a/11Q5 xxi may read "And she became a nurse (from עול) for me and to my teacher I will give my manhood/vigour (הודי)".[259] The version in MS B without the erotic content may also be accepted for 51:17a ("her yoke became glory for me", היה לי לכבוד עלה) combined with the text from 11QPs^a/11Q5 xxi for 51:17b ("to my Teacher I will give my praise", למלמדי אתן הודי). With the reading "praise" a certain pattern can be maintained, i.e. all the three stanzas end with a reference to the praise of the Lord (51:17, 22, 29). GI reads: "I made progress in her; to him who gives me wisdom I will give glory/praise".

Wearing down wisdom, jealousy and burning with passion, expressed in 51:18ab, 19a, 11QPs^a/11Q5 xxi, are also characteristics of a love affair. GI is less explicit ("For I intended to practise her, and I have been jealous for the good, and I

---

[257] See also Skehan, *Ben Sira*, 572, 574.

[258] Cf. J. A. Sanders, "Sirach 51:13ff," in *The Psalms Scroll of Qumran Cave 11 (11QPS^a)* (DJD 4; Oxford: Clarendon, 1965) 79-85, 82.

[259] Cf. Sanders, "Sirach 51:13ff," 81-82.

will not be ashamed. My soul has wrestled with her", 51:18ab, 19a), although it retains the idea of jealousy. 51:20bcd seems to be the climax of wisdom's and the sage's relationship: their love is fulfilled. For the reconstructed text "[and on her heights (from מרום)] I am not at ease" (51:20b[19d], 11QPs^a/11Q5 xxi)[260] Angel provides the following translation: "in the moments of her exaltation, I will not let up", where the "moments of her exaltation" is a reference to orgasm.[261] In contrast Sir 51:19d in GI reads: "and lamented my ignorances of her". 51:20c(19e) in MS B ("My hand opened her gate", ידי פתחה שעריה), an allusion to sexual intercourse, has no corresponding verse in GI, nor has the reconstructed 11QPs^a/11Q5 xxi text of 51:20d(19f) ("and her secrets [lit. nakedness] I came to know", אתבונן [מערמיה]). 51:20e(20b) in MS B ("I found [her] in pureness", ובטהרה מצאתי) may convey that wisdom is ready for sex after a period of uncleanness. GI is not significantly different here. 51:21 in both Hebrew and Greek has more images of burning passion for wisdom.

In the whole of the poem, especially in 51:13-22, the author's own description of his love affair is interwoven with references to the praise of God, passages that appear to return at the closing of every major part of the poem. Remarkably, an openness on sexual issues, including sexual intercourse, female nakedness, and orgasm, is found along with lines about praising God. Eros and the sacred are not at odds. This is certainly one of the most revolutionary characteristics of Ben Sira's erotically highly-charged poem. On the other hand, the translation demonstrates a tendency to tone down the erotic. Usually it does so by replacing the erotic terminology employed by the Hebrew text, resulting in an almost neutral description of seeking and finding wisdom for the purpose of learning.

Conclusion

In certain passages the translator appears to modify his grandfather's explicit sexual references. While there are exceptions where the translation enhances such references (26:13a; 36:22), sometimes it tones down the erotic by additions or

---

[260] Sanders, "Sirach 51:13ff," 81-82, translates "and on her heights I do not waver", taking as a basis וברומיה from the text for "and in/on her heights" alluding to wisdom's heights in Prov 8:2; 9:3, 14 (מרום). Isaac Rabinowitz, "The Qumran Hebrew Original of Ben Sira's Concluding Acrostic on Wisdom," *HUCA* 42 (1971) 173-84, 175, 179, reads: "I have made myself toil over her, and on her heights I am not / at ease", understanding it without an erotic connotation. Celia Deutsch, "The Sirach 51 Acrostic: Confession and Exhortation," *ZAW* 94 (1982) 400-409, 402, reads "and on her heights I did not weary".

[261] Cf. Andrew Angel, "From Wild Men to Wise and Wicked Women: An Investigation into Male Heterosexuality in Second Temple Interpretation of the Ladies Wisdom and Folly," in *A Question of Sex: Gender and Difference in the Hebrew Bible and Beyond* (ed. Deborah W. Rooke; Sheffield: Phoenix, 2007) 145-61, 156.

substitutions. In certain cases where the sage speaks about beauty and desire as something natural and positive, or about traits such as "sensibility", the translation adds a moral evaluation. We may see this in 3:11b concerning mothers, in 25:21b probably in the context of selecting a wife, in the mutilated text of 26:16b, and perhaps in 40:23 in the context of marriage. In 7:19a "sensible wife" is translated by "a wise and *good* wife". The toning down of the erotic seems to be particularly evident in the wisdom poems (4:15b; 51:14, 15d, 16, 17, 18, 19abcd [= 19ab-20ab in 11QPs^a/11Q5 xxi] and possibly in 51:27b). Moral severity is especially harsh in depicting the dangers of daughters in 26:10-12 (G I), whereas the original may have dealt with wives and done so in milder tones.

Within the work as a whole, attitudes toward sexuality depend on a number of factors. People who can most damage one's honour and status attract the greatest anxiety. They include above all one's daughters. According to 7:24; 26:10-12 and 42:11-12 daughters have no self-control and must be controlled by their father. The sage apparently sees them primarily in terms of their sexuality and its dangers, so that just contact with a male would result in promiscuity. Controlling one's wife's sexuality may be the issue in 25:25-26 and 42:6a. Reserving the wife's sexuality solely for the husband (26:15b, possibly 26:16b, and possibly in 40:23) is also an issue of control. On the other hand, the sage admits that husbands and men in general are also capable of bringing shame on themselves by sexual wrongdoing.

The context in which the teachings on sexuality appear also plays an important role. In a good marriage, desire and sex are not negative. There are even comments which refer to enjoying a wife's sexuality without making any mention of offspring (26:13a and 36:22). There are relatively few passages where the writer openly comments on desire or sexuality in the context of a bad marital relationship or concerning a wicked woman (25:21; perhaps 25:25; 26:8-9; perhaps 42:6a), but they are uniformly negative. Instructions on both marriage and extramarital relations clearly show that for Ben Sira sex is only permitted and affirmed in the context of a licit relationship, namely, marriage. All forms of extramarital intercourse are discouraged or condemned. For Ben Sira's fear of consequences, or the fear of being controlled through sexuality play a significant role beside the call to obey "the law of the Most High" (23:23a). In 6:1-3(= 6:2-4 in GI); 18:30 – 19:3 and 23:4-6 we see that while passions are not negative in themselves, they should not control one's life. One of Ben Sira's main goals is to help the young cope with temptation. In this he stands in continuity with other wisdom writers, such as Proverbs, in assuming that men need instruction about adultery and prostitution and their dangers.

Following one's desires is not only legitimate but almost commanded in the wisdom poems, when a student is advised to pursue, find, and possess wisdom. Losing control is not a danger in these passages, which have remarkably erotic descriptions, and where the symbolism celebrates love that has no other purpose beyond itself (14:24-27 in Hebrew; possibly 15:3; 24:16-21; 51:13-21). Being in wisdom's bonds may also protect her lover from sexual immorality (6:29a, GI; 15:4; perhaps 24:22). It is obvious, however, that even the most positive descriptions of a good marriage are not as open on matters of sexuality as the wisdom poems. Openness in constructing the symbolism did not translate into a similar openness in real life.

Finally we may note some of the work's silences. It does not address same-sex relations, an important issue in engagement with Hellenistic culture. The sin of Sodom and Gomorrah in 16:8 is their people's pride (ὑπερηφανίαν), not same-sex relations. The sage says nothing about male prostitution, the sexuality of widowers, intermarriage with Gentiles, forbidden degrees of marriage in terms of kinship, and bestiality, and an allusion to rape comes at most in the reference to a eunuch wanting to violate a young woman (20:4). There are no references to purity issues such as sexual intercourse during menstruation or pregnancy, though one possible reference to the purity of personified wisdom occurs in 51:20e(20b), MS B (= 51:20b in GI).

3.2.2   Wisdom of Solomon

The Wisdom of Solomon[262] is a Jewish work[263] written in sophisticated Greek, most probably in Alexandria in the early first century C.E.,[264] perhaps even more specifically in the aftermath of the riots of 38 C.E.[265] The sense of living in a

---

[262] The Greek text used is that of Rahlfs/Hanhart ed. *Septuaginta*; cf. also Joseph Ziegler, ed., *Sapientia Salomonis* (SVTG 12.1; 2d ed.; Göttingen: Vandenhoeck & Ruprecht, 1980). The translation is from *NETS*, except where I have modified it with my own translation, indicated by an asterisk.

[263] Cf. Davila, *Provenance*, who notes that one could make a case for its being a Christian composition, and then from the 2nd half of the first century at the latest, on the basis that it appears to have been used by 1 Clement (219-25).

[264] Lester L. Grabbe, *Wisdom of Solomon* (GAP; Sheffield: Sheffield Academic Press, 1997), favours the reign of Augustus (94).

[265] So David Winston, *Wisdom of Solomon* (AB 43; Garden City: Doubleday, 1979) 24-25, who writes of the apocalyptic vision in 5:16-23, that it "could only be called forth by a desperate historical situation in which the security of the Jewish community of Alexandria (and for a short while even that of Palestine) was dangerously threatened by a power against which it was hopeless to put up any serious resistance" (23). Also favouring this setting: Samuel Cheon, *The Exodus Story in the Wisdom of Solomon: A Study in Biblical Interpretation* (JSPSup 23; Sheffield: Sheffield Academic Press, 1997) 125-49; Collins, *Between Athens and Jerusalem*, 195, 202; John J. Collins, "Apocalyptic Eschatology in Philosophical Dress in the Wisdom of Solomon," in *Shem in the Tents of Japhet: Essays on*

hostile environment in Egypt is particularly strong in the latter half of the work, which employs the story of the exodus to voice its distress that those who once welcomed Israel have become Israel's oppressors (19:13-17).[266] Allusion to revoked equal rights there suggests at least a context in the deteriorating relations between Jews and both the Greeks and locals in Egypt,[267] but before the major disturbances later in the century and early in the next of which the work shows no trace.[268] There are multiple opposites or contrasts within the work beside those of the author's Jewish community and the citizens and locals of Alexandria. The author vehemently attacks typically Egyptian idolatry, where gods are depicted as animals, but also images of distant rulers as gods, a scarcely veiled allusion to Rome's emperors,[269] and the deifying of elements of nature.

At the same time the author is well versed in Hellenistic culture, including streams of Middle Platonism and Stoicism, probably through general education rather than specialist study,[270] but to the extent that he employs both its

---

the *Encounter of Judaism and Hellenism* (ed. James L. Kugel; JSJSup 7; Leiden: Brill, 2002) 93-108, 94, 107. Grabbe, *Wisdom of Solomon*, agrees that Winston's observation (22-23) that Wisdom uses 35 words or expressions not elsewhere found before the first century C.E. is a convincing argument against an earlier date, but sees absence of reference to Caligula's plans as counting against dating it to the later setting (89).

[266] So Barclay, *Jews in the Mediterranean Diaspora*, 191.

[267] Thus Winston, *Wisdom of Solomon*, writes: "In contrast to Pseudo-Aristeas' mild criticisms of heathen cults, the author of Wisd's wrathful exhibition of the innumerable crimes and corruptions connected with pagan idolatry and his unrestrained attack on Egyptian theriolatry (worship of animals), is an unmistakable sign of the complete rupture which had in his time sundered the Jewish community from the native Egyptians and Greeks" (3). On the deteriorating relationship between Jews, on the one hand, and both local Greeks and Egyptians, on the other, since Egypt came under Roman control in 47 B.C.E. see Grabbe, *Wisdom of Solomon*, who notes the removal from Jews of exemption from poll tax in 24-23 B.C.E., and the riots against them in 38 C.E., followed by Philo's embassy in 39-40 C.E. (86).

[268] On the possibility that the tradition of persecution under Antiochus Epiphanes still informs the author's concerns, see Robert J. Miller, "Immortality and Religious Identity in Wisdom 2-5," in *Reimagining Christian Origins: A Colloquium Honoring Burton L. Mack* (ed. Elizabeth A. Castelli and H. Taussig; Valley Forge: Trinity, 1996) 199-213, 208-209; Cheon, *Exodus Story*, 145.

[269] On Augustus' decision to put Egypt under his direct rule and so become an absent ruler see Winston, *Wisdom of Solomon*, 21, 63, who notes also that Wisdom's reflection on the development of ruler worship based on such absence does not fit the earlier Ptolemaic period when treatment of rulers as gods was a commonplace (22); similarly Collins, *Between Athens and Jerusalem*, 195.

[270] So Gilbert, "Wisdom Literature,": "He shows no mastery of these philosophies. His knowledge, indirect, seems to derive only from his general education" (312).

language[271] and ideas to his own ends and appears to be among those who assumed that the best of Hellenistic culture coheres with the best of his own.[272] This is the case in particular with regard to the laws of nature and of life, and the way of wisdom and righteousness.[273] The author could assume his attack on idolatry would win approval not only from Jews but also from more sophisticated Greek and Roman critics.[274]

We meet, then, in this work an author addressing primarily his own Jewish community under stress and employing the learning at his disposal, both Jewish and non-Jewish, to encourage them to hold firm in their faith in the light of the reward of immortality which awaits the good. He does so in the face of not only diverse external threats (ideological and political), but of internal threats, not least from those who have made common cause with outsiders in rejecting the way of wisdom.[275] In one sense these are more immediately being addressed along with

---

[271] On Wisdom's Greek language and style as standing on its own and not derivative from LXX see the detailed discussion in Winston, *Wisdom of Solomon*, 14-28; and also Grabbe, *Wisdom of Solomon*, 32, 35.

[272] On the tension between universalism and particularism in Wisdom see Collins, *Between Athens and Jerusalem*, 201.

[273] On the connection between the Jewish Law and more universal law and the relation between the two see Collins, *Between Athens and Jerusalem*, 199-200; Collins, *Jewish Wisdom*, 192, 220, where he concludes that we should probably assume, that, like Philo, the author adheres to Torah. David Winston, "Wisdom in the Wisdom of Solomon," in *The Ancestral Philosophy: Hellenistic Philosophy in Second Temple Judaism: Essays of David Winston* (ed. Gregory E. Sterling; BJS 331; StudPhilMon 4; Providence: BJS, 2001) 83-98, concludes of Wisdom: "She is clearly the archetypal Torah, of which the Mosaic law is but an image" (91) and notes that the author assumes Wisdom is needed in addition to Torah for its true understanding (9:17) (91). Similarly Burkes, *God, Self, and Death*, who while noting references to the Jewish Law (1:9; 4:20; 5:7; also 2:12; 6:4; 9:9; 16:6; 18:9) portrayed as light (18:4), points out that the book is not "torah-centered" and that "the author assumes the importance of the law as a ground of knowledge, but is not attempting to expound it" (176). See also Jack T. Sanders, "When Sacred Canopies Collide: The Reception of the Torah of Moses in the Wisdom Literature of the Second-Temple Period," *JSJ* 32 (2001) 121-36, who sees the author like Ben Sira merging sapiential and Torah traditions, while maintaining the superiority of Wisdom (129).

[274] So Collins, *Between Athens and Jerusalem*, 199, 200, who uses this observation to argue against the thesis of Barclay, *Jews in the Mediterranean Diaspora*, who claims that Wisdom expresses cultural antagonism and writes: "the author of *Wisdom* employs his considerable learning not to integrate his Judaism with his environment but to construct all the more sophisticated an attack upon it!" (184). The "document drowns its integrative potential in a sea of polemic" and is "an educated and deeply Hellenized exercise in cultural aggression" (184). See also Collins, *Jewish Wisdom*, 212.

[275] Winston, *Wisdom of Solomon*, writes: "By presenting Judaism in intellectually respectable terms, he sought to shore up the faith against hostile anti-Semitic attacks from

the faithful inasmuch as to reject the author's message is to join the unfaithful and unbelieving.[276]

Within the context of these diverse tensions we also find references to sexuality. These include various forms of sexual wrongdoing which the author associates directly with idolatry, but also similar phenomena linked to the godless life generally which defies the value of ethics in what it sees as the need to make the best of one's mortal existence. The latter meet us in the opening section of the work.

Fools of Death and the Future of the Afflicted Righteous

The first major section of the work is commonly identified as consisting of the first five chapters, largely on internal grounds, not least because 6:1 appears to begin again, like 1:1, with an address to kings. Viewed as a structural pattern, however, 6:1-11 appears to correspond to 1:1-5, and the whole section 1:1 – 6:11 reflects a concentric pattern, frequently employed elsewhere by the author.[277] Then in 6:12 the author begins a new section, signalled by the closing words of 6:11, "You will be instructed", picked up again in 6:21-22: "What wisdom is and how she came into being", though one could easily hear 6:20 as summing up the message of section one: "the desire for wisdom leads to a kingdom". The author was probably familiar with categories of Hellenistic rhetoric. This first part, then, matches what was called protreptic discourse, in other words, exhortation, while the second is closer to an encomium, a speech of praise.[278]

The first discourse begins with the author in the persona of Solomon addressing the rulers of the earth, who in turn function as representative of all hearers of the work. The message is simple: "Love righteousness!" (1:1) and, as 1:12a puts it, "Do not zealously seek death by the error of your life" (μὴ ζηλοῦτε θάνατον ἐν πλάνῃ ζωῆς ὑμῶν) (1:12a). The contrast in 1:1-5 is stark. On the

---

without and gnawing doubts from within, and through a determined counterattack against the immoral pagan world which he threatened with divine retribution, he attempted to revive the flagging spirits of his hard-pressed people" (64).

[276] Thus, as John S. Kloppenborg, "Isis and Sophia in the Book of Wisdom," *HTR* 75 (1982) 57-84, observes: "Wisdom of Solomon has the character of preaching to the converted, or perhaps more accurately, of preaching to those in danger of falling away" (63).

[277] On this see Gilbert, "Wisdom Literature," 302-305; Nickelsburg, *Jewish Literature*, 205; Grabbe, *Wisdom of Solomon*, 24.

[278] Collins, *Between Athens and Jerusalem*, notes that of the rhetorical categories *logos protreptikos* fits 1-6, *encomium*, 6:22 – 9:18 and the last part is epideictic (196). On the author's use of Hellenistic rhetoric see Grabbe, *Wisdom of Solomon*, 35-38.

one hand, we have: "righteousness", "goodness", "sincerity of heart", those not testing but trusting God, the "holy and disciplined spirit", and on the other: "crooked thoughts", "the foolish", "a soul that plots evil", "body involved in sin"; "deceit"; "senseless thoughts"; "unrighteousness". Right thinking and right behaviour are essential.

In 1:6-11 the focus falls on the wrongdoers being found out and by implication being called to account. Here the emphasis is on speech and thought. The wrongdoing or wrongdoers to be found out include: "blasphemers"; "guilt of their words"; "inner feelings"; "their tongues"; "what is said"; "those who utter unrighteous things"; "the intrigues of the impious"' "their words"' "their lawless deeds"; "the noise of grumblings"; "slander"; "mouth uttering falsehood". The speech to be reported in 2:1-20 will amply illustrate the author's meaning. The assumption is that God who finds these things out will act in judgement at some time in the future. We shall return to theme of judgement in our discussion of eschatology below.

The author then speaks of death, which is set in parallel to destruction (1:12). His argument is that death/destruction is something you bring on yourselves "by the deeds of your hands" (1:12). The author reflects an understanding of creation according to which God intended that human beings not die ("God did not make death"; 1:13), but be immortal (1:13-15).[279] This intention, however, had been subverted by human beings themselves. Apparently drawing on ancient mythology which depicted Death as a personalised entity,[280] the author generalises the story of Genesis 3, which we may presume he and his readers knew well, to speak of human beings summoning, befriending, and entering a covenant with death:

ἀσεβεῖς δὲ ταῖς χερσὶν καὶ τοῖς λόγοις προσεκαλέσαντο αὐτόν,
φίλον ἡγησάμενοι αὐτὸν ἐτάκησαν καὶ συνθήκην ἔθεντο πρὸς αὐτόν,
ὅτι ἄξιοί εἰσιν τῆς ἐκείνου μερίδος εἶναι.

But the impious by their deeds and words summoned it;
considering it to be a friend, they wasted away and made a covenant with it,
because they are worthy to belong to its company. (1:16)

The author appears to be adapting Isa 28:16 LXX, addressed to Jerusalem's leaders who were confident that they would weather the storm and escape death:

ὅτι εἴπατε ἐποιήσαμεν διαθήκην μετὰ τοῦ ᾅδου καὶ μετὰ τοῦ θανάτου
συνθήκας καταιγὶς φερομένη ἐὰν παρέλθη οὐ μὴ ἔλθη ἐφ᾽ ἡμᾶς.

---

[279] Thus Burkes, *God, Self, and Death*, writes: "Everyone has the potential for immortality by virtue of being fashioned on the divine model, and only those who join death's company experience it (1:16; 2:24)" (185).

[280] On this see A. Hayman, "The Survival of Mythology in the Wisdom of Solomon," *JSJ* 30 (1999) 125-39, 130-34; Collins, *Jewish Wisdom*, 189-90.

Because you have said, "We have made a covenant with Hades and agreements with death, if a rushing storm passes through, it will not come to us".[281]

In Wisdom the meaning is quite different, where the reality of death becomes the basis for philosophy of life for the ungodly. You make a covenant with death, as 1:12 explains, "by the error of your life". Here we may note that in what appears to be a generalising of the Genesis story as in *2 Bar.* 54:19, the author makes every person the Adam of his own soul, and also removes from the Genesis story its aetiology of death as God's decree. For elsewhere it appears that physical mortality derives from the substance of the human being, made from dust and returning to it as a normal process (7:1-6).[282] Such a reading of Genesis also passes over any notion that the serpent might have seduced Eve, a reading which the author's Greek translation might have suggested. The friendship with Death does not appear to have sexual associations. It is also apparent that the author is not blind to the mortality of human beings, generally, but assumes a distinction between those whose bodies die, but do not really die, because they have immortality, and those whose death brings their existence to an end, dying in the complete sense.[283] The Genesis imagery will return in 2:23-24 below.

The exhortation about death not only reinforces the importance of the choice between righteousness and unrighteousness, but also provides a background for the speech of those who "belong to its party", that is, the party of death, in 2:1-20. Here the words of the wrongdoers, addressed in 1:6-11 as something to be exposed and brought to account, come to expression. It is one of a number of occasions where the author gives voice to its characters. The foolish who befriend death[284]

---

[281] So David Seeley, "Narrative, the Righteous Man and the Philosopher: An Analysis of the Story of the Dikaios in Wisdom 1-5," *JSP* 7 (1990) 55-78, 60.

[282] So Karina Martin Hogan, "The Exegetical Background of the 'Ambiguity of Death' in the Wisdom of Solomon, *JSJ* 30 (1999) 1-24, 16, 18; Burkes, *God, Self, and Death*, 169; Levison, *Portraits of Adam*, 55.

[283] Michael Kolarcik, *The Ambiguity of Death in the Book of Wisdom 1–6* (AnBib 127; Rome: Pontifical Institute Press, 1991), argued that the reference is not to physical death, but death as separation from God (180). See also Hogan, "Ambiguity of Death," 19. Cf. Collins, *Jewish Wisdom*, who argues it must mean both physical and spiritual death, but that the righteous only seem to die (188).

[284] On the likely employment of the motif of the lover shut out from and pining for his beloved, common in Greco-Roman literature, see J. R. Dodson, "Locked-Out Lovers: Wisdom of Solomon 1.16 in Light of the Paraclausithyron Motif," *JSP* 17 (2002) 21-35. He concludes: "An allusion to a paraclausithyron here would demonstrate the extent of their commitment to evil and assist in making their actions look ludicrous: these fools, like the locked-out lovers, with their hands and voices, begged, pined, and pleaded *not* for a maiden to love them, but for Death himself to make a covenant with them" (35).

and, like Qoheleth,[285] see no hope beyond this life, declare: "Come, therefore, let us enjoy the good things that exist, and make good use of the creation as in youth" (2:6),[286] a vulgarised stereotype of Epicureanism, typical of its opponents. [287] The exhortation continues:

> 7 οἴνου πολυτελοῦς καὶ μύρων πλησθῶμεν,
> καὶ μὴ παροδευσάτω ἡμᾶς ἄνθος ἔαρος·
> 8 στεψώμεθα ῥόδων κάλυξιν πρὶν ἢ μαρανθῆναι·
> 9 μηδεὶς ἡμῶν ἄμοιρος ἔστω τῆς ἡμετέρας ἀγερωχίας,
> πανταχῇ καταλίπωμεν σύμβολα τῆς εὐφροσύνης,
> ὅτι αὕτη ἡ μερὶς ἡμῶν καὶ ὁ κλῆρος οὗτος.
> 7 Let us take our fill of costly wine and perfumes,
> and let no flower of spring pass us by.
> 8 Let us crown ourselves with rosebuds before they are withered.[288]
> 9 Let none of us be without share in our revelry;
> everywhere let us leave signs of enjoyment,
> because this is our portion, and this our lot. (2:7-9)

Behind these revelries of youth, plucking spring flowers, one might suspect a reference to sexual wrongdoing. This is made more probable in the light of the author's elaboration of the deeds of the "ungodly" in 3:10 – 4:9. The Old Latin has *pratum*, "meadow" in 2:9a, and so appears to have used a Greek text that read

---

[285] So Winston, *Wisdom of Solomon*, pointing to the parallels between 2:1 and Eccl 2:22-23; 2:6; 9:7 (115, 118). See also V. D'Alario, "La Réflexion sur le Sens de la Vie en Sg 1 – 6: Une Réponse aux Questions de Job et de Qohélet," in *Treasures of Wisdom: Studies in Ben Sira and the Book of Wisdom: Festschrift M. Gilbert* (ed. Nuria Calduch-Benages and Jacques Vermeylen; BETL 143; Leuven: Peeters, 1999) 313-29, 324-25; Harrington, *Apocrypha*, 56.

[286] Grabbe, *Wisdom of Solomon*, writes: "The most likely audience is the educated Jewish youth of Alexandria who found the surrounding Hellenistic culture attractive, including the various cults, and might be tempted to abandon Judaism altogether" (93); similarly James M. Reese, *Hellenistic Influence on the Book of Wisdom and Its Consequences* (Rome: PBI, 1970), speaking of their attraction to the Isis cult (40). It is not clear to me why youth are singled out, especially since these speakers look back on their youth.

[287] On similarities and differences between Epicureanism and the strategy of the ungodly here see Winston, *Wisdom of Solomon*, who notes: "only a grossly distorted understanding of Epicureanism could conceivably reconcile that philosophy with the latter's crude and unprincipled brand of hedonism" (114). He notes that the accusations are similar to *1 Enoch* 102:6-11 (115). See also Grabbe, *Wisdom of Solomon*, 51; Collins, *Jewish Wisdom*, 192-94; Seeley, "Narrative, the Righteous Man and the Philosopher," who notes similar stereotypical attacks in Epictetus, Plutarch, and Dio Chrysostom (67).

[288] On linking wine and perfume with adorning oneself with roses in Horace see Winston, *Wisdom of Solomon*, 119.

λειμών "meadow" instead of the ἡμῶν, read by surviving Greek manuscripts.[289] The word was used as a euphemism for female pubic hair and would make explicit the sexual promiscuity, probably to be implied as a component of the revelry.[290] The speech then depicts the ambition of the foolish to "oppress the righteous poor man", exploit the widow, and have no regard for "the gray hairs of the aged" or the weak (2:10-11).[291] The mockery of the righteous man to which the long speech gives voice (2:12-20) includes references to wrongdoing, described as "actions" opposed by the righteous man, "sins against the law" (ἁμαρτήματα νόμου) and "sins against our training" (ἁμαρτήματα παιδείας ἡμῶν) (2:12). These make best sense as spoken by unfaithful Jews.[292]

The author then responds to their speech with a refutation, which returns to themes already enunciated just before the speech. Again the author returns to Genesis material, declaring that God intended immortality for human beings: "God created human beings for incorruption and made them in the image of his own nature (ἰδιότητος or eternity: ἀιδιότητος)" (2:23; cf. 1:13-15). The implication of having the two statements in parallel is that the author interprets human

---

[289] On this see Ziegler, *Sapientia Salomonis*, whose eclectic text accordingly reads λειμών (99).

[290] On this see José Ramón Busto Saiz, "The meaning of Wisdom 2:9a," in *VIIth Congress of the International Organization for Septuagint and Cognate Studies, Leuven 1989* (ed. Claude E. Cox; SBLSCS 31; Atlanta: Scholars, 1991) 355-59, who draws attention to Euripedes *Cyclops* 171, where λειμών "clearly has a sexual meaning" (357), speaking of the drunken man's carousing with a woman, who boasts he can "catch a handful of breast and look forward to stroking her meadow (λειμῶνος)". Accordingly 2:9a "presents the wicked man's behaviour, who professes a hedonistic and materialistic concept of life. With this in mind, it would seem very strange if we couldn't find any reference to sexual behaviour in this passage. Having accepted the euphemism, the meaning of the whole passage becomes clear" (358). See also Hans Hübner, *Wörterbuch zur Sapientia Salomonis* (Göttingen: Vandenhoeck & Ruprecht, 1985) who notes this meaning (2). Thus Armin Schmitt, "Zur dramatischen Form von Weisheit 1,1-6,21," *BZ* 37(1993) 236-58, concludes similarly, that the reference to meadowland adventure can function as a metaphor for sexual promiscuity (249).

[291] While one might expect the self-indulgence to be at the expense of others, engage in exploitation, and violently resent criticism, the connection may also reflect, as Seeley, "Narrative, the Righteous Man and the Philosopher," observes, "an apparent *topos* in Greco-Roman moral philosophy which associates the pursuit of pleasure with aggressive wrongdoing", which accounts for the unexpected shift here from self-indulgence to violence (68). He notes also that such discussion often included the notion of danger to the philosopher (70-72), and post mortem vindication (75), though not the idea of judgement as here (76).

[292] So Gilbert, "Wisdom Literature," 309; Collins, *Jewish Wisdom*, 194; Burkes, *God, Self, and Death*, 174-75.

immortality as deriving from their being made in God's image. Again, as in 1:12, 16, the author attributes death not to God but to human choice, and castigates the wrong reasoning of the speakers, whom he depicts as blinded by wickedness, ignorant of divine mysteries, and not recognising the rewards of holiness and blamelessness (2:21-22).

The explanation of death here differs from 1:12, 16, in claiming that "through the envy of the devil death entered the world, and those who belong to his party experience it" (φθόνῳ δὲ διαβόλου θάνατος εἰσῆλθεν εἰς τὸν κόσμον, πειράζουσιν δὲ αὐτὸν οἱ τῆς ἐκείνου μερίδος ὄντες) (2:24). If one takes διαβόλου in the sense of "opposer" or "adversary", one might see here a reference to Cain, who because of envy killed Abel. The suggestion receives some support from the prominence of Cain in 10:3-4, where his sin is made responsible for the flood.[293] An allusion to Cain, here, would, however, be unmediated,[294] unless we assume hearers were already familiar with this view of Cain, but it is nowhere else attested at the time. More commonly, the passage is understood as referring to the devil. This receives support from the preceding parallel in 1:16, which speaks of an alliance with Death. The author would then be drawing on tradition relating to Genesis 3 which saw the serpent acting either as (cf. 2 Enoch 31:3-6; Rev 12:9) or on behalf of the devil (Apoc. Mos. 17:4) and the devil responding to his envy of Adam and Eve, either because of their elevation to a higher status (2 Enoch 29:4-6; 31:3) or because they now have what he once had, namely a place in the garden, before he was expelled (Apoc. Mos. 16:3). We might then surmise that the author is offering an aetiology of death, relating it to the garden of Eden, or is seeing that encounter as (perhaps, in addition) representative of what happens when people choose to "belong to his party", an expression used also of belonging to Death ("belong to its party") in 1:16. In neither instance, however, do sexual motifs such as seduction play a role.

The author's counter to their speech then proceeds to extol the future of the righteous, who, he argues, only seem to die, but in reality live on in peace (3:1-3). Neither their literal dying nor their suffering is denied, but their death was not really death, because it did not bring their extinction. Their reward however is more than survival. The author draws on rich eschatological imagery to depict their day of visitation as a time when they will both shine and "judge nations and rule over peoples" (3:7-8).[295] We shall return to possible implications of this for understanding sexuality in our discussion of the author's eschatology.

---

[293] So Levison, Portraits of Adam, 51-52.

[294] So Hogan, "Ambiguity of Death," 21, but notes that nevertheless Cain is depicted as "the archetype of all evildoers" (24).

[295] Judith H. Newman, "The Democratization of Kingship in Wisdom of Solomon," in The Idea of Biblical Interpretation: Essays in Honor of James L. Kugel (ed. Hindy Najman and Judith H. Newman; JSJSup 83; Leiden: Brill, 2004) 309-28, notes that at a number of

In his explanation the author then returns to the "impious" who reasoned wrongly, "neglected the righteous person", "revolted from the Lord", disdained wisdom and instruction, whose hope is in vain, and whose labour is "unprofitable" and their "deeds useless" (3:10-11). This list of their characteristics concludes with a motif which then sets the focus for the exposition to follow: αἱ γυναῖκες αὐτῶν ἄφρονες, καὶ πονηρὰ τὰ τέκνα αὐτῶν, ἐπικατάρατος ἡ γένεσις αὐτῶν ("their wives are foolish and their children evil; their offspring are accursed") (3:12). Though in itself the foolishness of their wives could mean many things, it is likely to have a sexual reference in the light of what follows.[296] For in both 3:16-18 and again in 4:3-6 the author goes to great lengths to depict the offspring of illicit sexual relations as accursed.[297] The reference to sexual wrongdoing is quite unambiguous in 3:16, τέκνα δὲ μοιχῶν ἀτέλεστα ἔσται, καὶ ἐκ παρανόμου κοίτης σπέρμα ἀφανισθήσεται ("But the children of adulterers will not reach maturity, and the offspring of unlawful intercourse will perish"). Set in parallel to the reference to adultery (τέκνα δὲ μοιχῶν "But the children of adulterers") the reference to "unlawful intercourse" (παρανόμου κοίτης) may simply repeat the allusion to adultery. More likely it adds to adultery all kinds of other illicit sexual relations, including incest, marriage within forbidden degrees, and quite possibly also marriage to non-Jews. These are aspects of the wrongdoing addressed as belonging to the party of death and the devil in 2:7-9, where already one possible textual reconstruction would indicate sexual promiscuity.

The author develops his condemnation of such illicit sexual relations by using contrast, a common rhetorical technique in the author's repertoire. Thus in contrast to ἐπικατάρατος ἡ γένεσις αὐτῶν "their offspring are accursed" in 3:13a, we immediately find reference to those who are blessed: ὅτι μακαρία στεῖρα ἡ ἀμίαντος ἥτις οὐκ ἔγνω κοίτην ἐν παραπτώματι ἕξει καρπὸν ἐν ἐπισκοπῇ ψυχῶν ("For blessed is the barren woman who is undefiled, she who has not known intercourse that involved transgression; for she will have fruit at the visitation of souls") (3:13). As Cheon notes, the author chooses three categories of

---

places the work assumes that all were created to rule (317), and all righteous will be crowned (320), just as Wisdom is a gift offered to all human beings (311), not confined to a temple or city (327). Thus the work democratises kingship through a new image of Israel (327).

[296] So J. Reider, *The Book of Wisdom* (New York: Harper & Brothers, 1957), who, drawing attention to Prov 5:5, translates ἄφρονες as "wanton" (76); similarly Samuel Cheon, "Three Characters in the Wisdom of Solomon 3-4," *JSP* 12 (2001) 105-13, 108.

[297] Cf. Harrington, *Apocrypha*, who asserts of 3:13b-19 and what follows: "The sexual imagery in this and the following contrasts most likely refers to idolatry on the basis of the familiar biblical equation between adultery/fornication and idolatry" (61).

people traditionally seen as cursed to enhance the contrast.[298] The contrast with the barren woman finds an echo in 4:1, κρείσσων ἀτεκνία μετὰ ἀρετῆς ("Better is childlessness with virtue").[299]

The blessedness is not that, though being barren, she has not engaged in licit sexual intercourse, for instance, with her husband, on grounds such as seeing non-procreative sex as wrong, but rather that as a woman who was not able to become pregnant she did not use this as an opportunity to engage in illicit sex (οὐκ ἔγνω κοίτην ἐν παραπτώματι "she who has not known intercourse that involved transgression") (3:13). The author might have chosen as his contrast the woman who, while able to fall pregnant, remains chaste, but instead cites the more extreme case where fear of pregnancy plays no role and where she may not even be married or may no longer be married, if, for instance, barrenness had led to her divorce. Such a chaste barren woman, far from being under the shame of not being able to bear children (cf. Gen 30:23; Judg 13:2; Job 15:34; Isa. 4:1; *1 Enoch* 98:5; Luke 1:25) and so accursed,[300] a status appropriate in the author's view for children of adulterers, he declares blessed. The example and reversal will have found its inspiration in the broader context of Isaiah 52 – 53 which has already informed his portrait of the righteous man. For immediately after those chapters we read: "Sing, O barren one who did not bear; burst into song and shout, you who have not been in labor!" (Isa 54:1). There it promises her literal fruit. Here she is promised fruit "at the visitation of souls". This is probably metaphorical, although it need not be.

The author then cites another extreme case of blessedness: the eunuch, again reflecting the broader context in Isaiah upon which he has been drawing, where what was traditionally seen as an accursed state is reversed (cf. Deut. 23:1; 2 Kgs 20:18).[301] For there in 56:2-5 the eunuch is encouraged not to say, "I am just a dry tree", but to receive a promise: δώσω αὐτοῖς ἐν τῷ οἴκῳ μου καὶ ἐν τῷ τείχει μου τόπον ὀνομαστὸν κρείττω υἱῶν καὶ θυγατέρων ὄνομα αἰώνιον δώσω αὐτοῖς "I will give to them, in my house and within my wall, an esteemed place and I will give them an everlasting name better than that of sons and daughters"* (56:5).

Wisdom apparently uses the word εὐνοῦχος here to designate a man not able to engage in sexual intercourse. This explains the reference to his hand. He might

---

[298] Cheon, "Three Characters," writes: The author "has carefully selected for this rebuttal characters who traditionally have been considered images of curse and misfortune in Ancient Israel (Gen. 30.23; Deut. 23.1; Ps. 109.8)" (107).

[299] Winston, *Wisdom of Solomon*, observes that this is "a characteristically Platonic note", referring to Plato, *Symp.* 208E (133).

[300] On barrenness as shame and sometimes seen as the fruit of sin, see Winston, *Wisdom of Solomon*, 131; Cheon, "Three Characters," 109.

[301] So Winston, *Wisdom of Solomon*, 132; Cheon, "Three Characters," 109.

still have sexual responses and so use his hands to express them: καὶ εὐνοῦχος ὁ μὴ ἐργασάμενος ἐν χειρὶ ἀνόμημα μηδὲ ἐνθυμηθεὶς κατὰ τοῦ κυρίου πονηρά ("also the eunuch who has done no lawless deed with his hand, nor thought evil things against the Lord"*; 3:14). Presumably, the reference is to a eunuch who might engage in sexual relations through manual stimulation or masturbation. This makes it unlikely, therefore, that εὐνοῦχος here simply means a man who has chosen voluntary celibacy.[302] Whether the author might contemplate that a eunuch might ever engage manually in a licit sexual relationship is unclear. His point is that, like the barren woman, no fear of pregnancy or making others pregnant need restrain him from illicit relations, but his faithfulness to God does. The author includes in his reward: κλῆρος ἐν ναῷ κυρίου θυμηρέστερος ("a very delightful lot in the temple of the Lord"*) (3:14; cf. Isa 56:5), a promise which stands in some tension with the biblical statement excluding eunuchs (Deut 23:1), though the author may have envisaged a category not covered there and in any case speaks of a temple to come, probably heavenly.[303] Unlike the barren woman, he is not promised the fruit of children, but "the fruit of good labours" (3:15).

The author playfully develops the motif of fruit at the judgement (3:13b, 15) to serve his contrast with those engaging in illicit sexual relations. For in treating the latter in both 3:16-19 and 4:3-6 the author focuses more on the children than on the parents. At the judgement, "children born of unlawful unions are witnesses of evil against their parents" (ἐκ γὰρ ἀνόμων ὕπνων τέκνα γεννώμενα μάρτυρές εἰσιν πονηρίας κατὰ γονέων) (4:6).[304] Such children of illicit liaisons will either not reach maturity, or perish, or if not, will have no status and no honour in old age, or, dying young, will have no hope (3:16-19) and be useless, like seeds which fail to take root, or if they do, produce branches which will not last and be uprooted by the wind, or break off before they reach maturity, producing unripe fruit good for nothing (4:3-6).[305] Again the author appears to draw motifs from the context of Isaiah used previously, where in 57:1-4, 20, we

---

[302] Cf. Lothar Ruppert, "Gerechte und Frevler (Gottlose) in Sap 1,1 – 6,21: Zum Neuverständnis und zur Aktualisierung alttestamentlicher Traditionen in der Sapientia Salomonis," in *Die Weisheit Salomos im Horizont Biblisacher Theologie* (ed. Hans Hübner; Biblische-Theologische Studien 22; Neukirchen-Vluyn: Neukirchener Verlag, 1993) 1-54, who argues that the reference is not to a eunuch from birth or castrated male, but to someone who has chosen not to marry and have children (42-43), possibly reflecting an espousal of ascetic ideals by the author (43).

[303] So Winston, *Wisdom of Solomon*, 132; Ruppert, "Gerechte und Frevler," 43.

[304] Cf. Harrington, *Apocrypha*, who reads "children of unlawful unions as a reference not to sexual wrongdoing but to idolatry (62).

[305] Winston, *Wisdom of Solomon*, notes that the author plays with the double meaning of ἄωρος as indicating both ripeness of fruit and maturity (134).

find the contrast between the righteous taken away who will have rest, and the offspring of adulterers and prostitutes.[306] The intent here seems not to condemn the children, but to shame and condemn the parents by depicting what the author believes will be the result of their deeds. The allusion to premature death elicits a further contrast with the righteous who die prematurely, traditionally seen as accursed,[307] who will be at rest and whose wisdom and maturity consists in something other than gray hair and old age (4:7-9).

The point of this series of contrasts seems less to deal with an intellectual problem, namely disadvantage of the barren, eunuchs and those who die young, and more to use the contrasts to underline the alternative ways or righteousness and wickedness,[308] in which in at least the first two instances sexual behaviour is in focus, and is indirectly so also in the third, inasmuch as it continues to speak of the offspring of illicit sexual relations.

It is possible that the author's transition to Enoch in 4:10-15 intends to cite him as an example of someone dying prematurely, particularly given the reference to the "youth that is quickly made perfect" in 4:16, which echoes 4:13 ("being perfected in a short time"). His 365 years do after all contrast with his son's 969 years! The author's chief concern is not, however, timing, but the contrast between righteousness and wickedness, which most likely continues to envisage sexual wrongdoing.

Enoch is depicted as εὐάρεστος θεῷ γενόμενος ("one who became well-pleasing to God") (4:10a), drawing on Gen 5:24 LXX, εὐηρέστησεν δὲ Ενωχ τῷ θεῷ ("And Enoch pleased God") (also 5:22; Sir 44:16), which continues: καὶ οὐχ ηὑρίσκετο ὅτι μετέθηκεν αὐτὸν ὁ θεός ("and he was not found because God took him away" (Gen 5:24 LXX). Accordingly, the author continues: καὶ ζῶν

---

[306] On this see Pancratius C. Beentjes, "Wisdom of Solomon 3,1-4,19 and the Book of Isaiah," in *Studies in the Book of Isaiah: Festschrift Willem A. M. Beuken* (ed. Jacques T. A. G. N. van Ruiten, and Marc Vervenne; BETL 132; Louvain: Peeters, 1997) 413-20.

[307] Cheon, "Three Characters," notes: "The untimely death of a youth is dealt with in 4.7-16,21 which is considered as a curse in the wisdom tradition (Prov. 9.11; 10.27; 21.16; cf. 3.1-2,16, 18; 4.10; 5.5-6, 11; 8.35-36)" (110).

[308] So Cheon, "Three Characters," who writes: "the real targets of the antitheses are the wicked family members rather than their counterparts, the righteous figures. In other words, each contrast expresses that the wicked husbands, wives and children should be more cursed than their counter-characters who have been traditionally accursed in the Jewish religion" (112). "The three righteous figures would have been selected as a literary device to find fault with the wicked husbands, their wives and progeny, rather than to praise these three characters themselves" (112). Cf. Nickelsburg, *Jewish Literature*: "the author generalizes his discussion of right and wrong perspectives on judgement by declaring invalid certain classical examples of this-worldly reward and punishment (3:12 – 4:15)" (206); Grabbe, *Wisdom of Solomon*: "Even if the righteous are barren or eunuchs, they are blessed" (14).

μεταξὺ ἁμαρτωλῶν μετετέθη ("and, while living amongst sinners, was taken" (4:10b). He imports into the Genesis account the fact that Enoch was in the midst of sinners, going on to use this as the explanation of why God took him, an idea then repeated in 4:14, διὰ τοῦτο ἔσπευσεν ἐκ μέσου πονηρίας ("therefore he hastened [OR: hastened him] from the midst of evil"). He then uses it as a basis for addressing evil: ἡρπάγη, μὴ κακία ἀλλάξῃ σύνεσιν αὐτοῦ ἢ δόλος ἀπατήσῃ ψυχὴν αὐτοῦ ("He was seized in order that wickedness should not affect his understanding or guile deceive his soul"). There may be an allusion in these words to the serpent's deceiving or seducing Eve in Gen 3:13. The author expands his explanation in a way, that, given the preceding context, probably includes an allusion to illicit sexual desire:[309] βασκανία γὰρ φαυλότητος ἀμαυροῖ τὰ καλὰ καὶ ρεμβασμὸς ἐπιθυμίας μεταλλεύει νοῦν ἄκακον ("For the fascination of wickedness obscures the things that are good, and roving desire undermines an innocent mind") (4:12). Enoch serves as a model, both as one who pleased God by resisting such desire and as one rescued from such danger by being taken away. He is also an example of one brought to the end of his life's journey early, then to enter eternal life, in contrast to the offspring of illicit sex who die young and have no hope (3:18).

In 4:16 the author returns to the contrast between the fate of the righteous who are dead and of the wicked. In speaking of the righteous as condemning the impious who are living, the author may well reflect knowledge of traditions which give Enoch this role, but here all the righteous share it, including the youth quickly perfected who judges the aged. The focus then moves to the wicked, who scoff at the end of the righteous, but whom the author depicts as both in anguish, dry and barren, on the one hand, imagery related to the earlier contrasts, and, on the other, as facing annihilation (4:19).

This continues into chap. 5, where the author depicts the wicked as being brought to judgement, seeing the true fate of the righteous and repenting, for whom then the author has composed a speech (5:4-14). This passage, 4:20 – 5:14, like 3:1-9, uses apocalyptic tradition such as we find in Daniel 7-12; *1 Enoch* 37 – 71; 92 – 105; and *2 Baruch* 51,[310] here based on Isa 52:13 – 53:12,[311] whose

---

[309] So Ellis, *Sexual Desire*, 56.

[310] See Nickelsburg, *Jewish Literature*, 207, and his detailed treatment in George W. E. Nickelsburg, *Resurrection, Immortality, and Eternal Life in Intertestamental Judaism* (HTS 26; Cambridge MA: Harvard University Press, 1972) 82-92.

[311] So M. Jack Suggs, "Wisdom of Solomon 2:10–5:23: A Homily Based on the Fourth Servant Song," *JBL* 76 (1957) 26-33. See also Nickelsburg, *Jewish Literature*, 207-208; and his foundational study in Nickelsburg, *Resurrection*, 68-92 and that of Lothar Ruppert, *Der leidende Gerechte: Eine motivgeschichtliche Untersuchung zum Alten Testament und zwischentestamentlichen Judentum* (FB 5; Würzburg: Echter, 1972) 70-105. See also his restatement in Ruppert, "Gerechte und Frevler," 5-35. Collins, "Apocalyptic Eschatology,"

context the author has already employed in depicting the barren woman (54:1), the eunuch (56:2-5), and the righteous who died early (57:1-4, 20). When in their speech the wicked speak of being ashamed of their ways of "lawlessness ... and destruction" (ἀνομίας . . . καὶ ἀπωλείας) (5:7), we should probably understand that, in the light of what has been highlighted thus far, as including, above all, sexual wrongdoing and greedy exploitation (2:6-11; 3:12, 16-19; 4:3-6, 10-14; cf. also 5:8b). They bewail that their arrogance and wealth had dissipated into thin air, using imagery that recalls their depiction of death in their first speech (2:2-5).[312] Thus the author has them speak of their hope dissipating like wind-blown dust, light frost, smoke, and the memory of a passing guest (5:14 cf. 2:2), in contrast to the crowning of the righteous (5:15-16). The author then pictures God making "creation his weapon for vengeance on his enemies", using imagery of armour drawn again from the Isaiah chapters which lie behind this section, here Isa 59:17-19, combined with images from nature (5:17-23), using creation, as later chapters display God doing so in the exodus.[313]

The return to exhorting kings in 6:1-20 (cf. 1:1-11) repeats the warning about judgement (6:3, 5-8), based on whether they "keep the law or walk according to the counsel of God" (6:4). These warnings and the exhortation, "For they will be made holy who observe holy things in holiness" (6:10), appear to remain in the context of confronting rulers, rather than speaking to people more generally. Nothing here suggests a focus on sexual wrongdoing.

The transition to the next section is uncertain. In 6:12-20 the author begins speaking of wisdom which is the dominant theme through to the end of chap. 10. Oral presentations made it easy to slide from one section to a new one, including for one passage, such as 6:1-11 both to be the beginning of a new one and to function as a structural inclusion with a previous one. A similar phenomenon is evident in 11:1-3.

Wisdom, Partner of the Wise

This second major section contains extensive descriptions of Wisdom, portrayed as a woman, building on tradition already developed in Proverbs and expanded in Sirach 24 and Baruch 4. The first description comes in 6:12-20, followed by

---

discusses Ruppert's thesis of a source, concluding that the material is too embedded to make this possible (97).

[312] On the relationship between the two speeches of the wicked see Moira McGlynn, *Divine Judgement and Divine Benevolence in the Book of Wisdom* (WUNT 139; Tübingen: Mohr Siebeck, 2001) 77-80.

[313] So Collins, "Apocalyptic Eschatology," 101-102; Gilbert, "Wisdom Literature," 310.

Solomon's further exhortation to his fellow rulers with the announcement that he would explain to them who wisdom is (6:21-25). We then have a long autobiographical account in which Solomon underlines his shared humanity, from his birth to his adulthood (7:1-6), explains his resolve to seek wisdom (7:7-14), asks for discernment to be able to depict wisdom (7:19-23a), gives an account of wisdom (7:23b – 8:1), describes his own response to wisdom (8:2-21), finally offers his prayer for wisdom (9:1-18), and then depicts Wisdom's role in Israel's history (10:1-21).

While one might initially translate the feminine pronouns referring to wisdom as "it", when these passages are taken as a whole, it is apparent that Wisdom is here depicted as a person. This in turn colours the way we read the imagery. Thus, beginning in 6:12, to speak of wisdom as "radiant and unfading", of "those who love her" (τῶν ἀγαπώντων αὐτὴν) and "those who see her" (τῶν ζητούντων αὐτήν) and then in 6:13 of her as one who "anticipates those who set their desire on her to make herself known in advance" (φθάνει τοὺς ἐπιθυμοῦντας προγνωσθῆναι) and even more so in 6:14 of "those who rise early for her" (ὁ ὀρθρίσας πρὸς αὐτὴν) and "find her sitting at their gates" (πάρεδρον γὰρ εὑρήσει τῶν πυλῶν αὐτοῦ) (cf. Prov 1:20-21 LXX; 8:3), is to speak of her as a woman and of the relationship to her as one of love, in which erotic images are also to be expected as belonging to normal and healthy intimate relations. The imagery continues in 6:15, which speaks of fixing one's thought on her (τὸ γὰρ ἐνθυμηθῆναι περὶ αὐτῆς) and lying awake on her account (ὁ ἀγρυπνήσας δι᾿ αὐτὴν). The image of her "sitting at their gates" is more daring, following the precedent of the author of Proverbs 1 – 9, since it indicates patterns of behaviour more characteristic of the strange woman or the prostitute who might place herself in public in these ways. Such behaviour informs the description of her as going about seeking those worthy of her (τοὺς ἀξίους αὐτῆς αὐτὴ περιέρχεται ζητοῦσα), graciously appearing to them in their paths (ἐν ταῖς τρίβοις φαντάζεται αὐτοῖς εὐμενῶς) and meeting them (ὑπαντᾷ αὐτοῖς) (6:16). The author makes abundantly clear that he employs these metaphors not for any illicit purpose, but to urge observance of the Law: "love of her is keeping her laws, and paying attention to her laws is confirmation of incorruption" (ἀγάπη δὲ τήρησις νόμων αὐτῆς προσοχὴ δὲ νόμων βεβαίωσις ἀφθαρσίας) (6:18), so "the desire for wisdom leads to a kingdom" (ἐπιθυμία ἄρα σοφίας ἀνάγει ἐπὶ βασιλείαν) (6:20). In its own subtle and playful way these statements about wisdom also help us to see that the author affirms sexual response as something appropriate if in its proper place. We noted this phenomenon also in Ben Sira, though also positive use of erotic imagery does not necessarily always imply positive attitudes to erotic love in reality.

In 6:23 the author contrasts wisdom and envy in a way that may suggest a personification also of the latter: οὔτε μὴν φθόνῳ τετηκότι συνοδεύσω ὅτι οὗτος οὐ κοινωνήσει σοφίᾳ ("nor indeed will I travel in the company of consumptive envy, because this [possibly: "he"] can have no fellowship with wisdom"*). This may in turn allude to envy as the devil's companion in 2:24 through which death came: φθόνῳ δὲ διαβόλου θάνατος εἰσῆλθεν εἰς τὸν κόσμον πειράζουσιν δὲ αὐτὸν οἱ τῆς ἐκείνου μερίδος ὄντες ("but through the envy of the devil death entered the world, and those who belong to his party experience it").

The author then has Solomon underline his common humanity by depicting his origins through the normal processes of pregnancy and birth as understood at the time:

1 εἰμὶ μὲν κἀγὼ θνητὸς ἄνθρωπος ἴσος ἅπασιν καὶ γηγενοῦς ἀπόγονος πρωτοπλάστου· καὶ ἐν κοιλίᾳ μητρὸς ἐγλύφην σὰρξ 2 δεκαμηνιαίῳ χρόνῳ παγεὶς ἐν αἵματι ἐκ σπέρματος ἀνδρὸς καὶ ἡδονῆς ὕπνῳ συνελθούσης.
1 I also am mortal, like everyone else, a descendant of the first-formed individual born on earth, and in the womb of a mother I was molded into flesh, 2 within the period of ten months being compacted with blood, from the seed of man and the pleasure that accompanies intercourse. (7:1-2)

Allusion to creation of the first human being from earth reappears in 15:8, 11 in the context of ridiculing clay idols (cf. also 10:1, πρωτόπλαστον πατέρα κόσμου "first-formed father of the world"). The passage reflects ancient understandings of the processes of procreation: the male sperm understood as seed joins with the woman's blood, is moulded into flesh and over ten months (by inclusive reckoning) produces a child.[314] Sexual intercourse is clearly seen as something

---

[314] See Winston, *Wisdom of Solomon*, 163-64 on 10 months in literature of the time. With regard to being compacted with blood he notes *1 Enoch* 15:4 and writes that "We have here a commonplace of Greek science" (164), referring to Aristotle *Gen. An.*19-20, according to which females do not produce semen as some had thought but only males, a view already articulated by Hippocrates *Genitalia*, according to which semen provides form, and the rest comes from the mother (similarly Philo *Opif.* 132). Aristotle writes that semen acts on women's secretion like rennet on milk (739b21), an understanding also expressed in Indian sources. According to Aristotle pleasure occurs because not only semen but also pneuma is emitted 728a10 (165). "Our own author is characteristically unable to resist the urge to supply some of the physiological details of the formation of the embryo in accord with the latest findings of the science of his day", for which Alexandria was a leading centre (165). See also Pieter W. van der Horst, "Sarah's Seminal Emission: Hebrews 11:11 in the Light of Ancient Embryology," in *Greeks, Romans and Christians: Essays in Honour of Abraham J. Malherbe* (ed. David L. Balch, Everett Ferguson, and Wayne A. Meeks; Minneapolis: Fortress, 1990) 287-302, 298. See also the general

positive, but the expression, ἡδονῆς ὕπνῳ συνελθούσης (lit. "by the sleep of pleasure coming together") may reflect the belief that conception is directly related to the level of pleasure in sexual intercourse, as quite dramatically depicted in the *Genesis Apocryphon* where Bitenosh refutes Lamech's fear that she may have become pregnant and given birth to the wondrous baby, Noah, as the result of a liaison with a Watcher, by recalling to him the height of their pleasure in the occasion of their (presumably, previous) intercourse (2.9-10). The positive approach to sexual pleasure in the appropriate context coheres with our observations above about the author's employment of erotic imagery in his picture of Wisdom.

When Solomon then returns to speak of wisdom, the metaphor is sustained. He loved her (7:10). She is "mother" of good things (7:12). She taught Solomon (7:22) the knowledge which God gave him about the science of the universe, including herbal medicine using plants and roots (7:17-22a; cf. 1 Kgs 4:33).[315] Solomon's neatly composed description of wisdom in 21 epithets (7:22b-23)[316] and exposition (7:24 – 8:1) remains abstract, only occasionally returning to the personal metaphor. The statement that "nothing defiled gains entrance into her" (οὐδὲν μεμιαμμένον εἰς αὐτὴν παρεμπίπτει) (7:25b) appears not to be understood as a sexual metaphor, any more than that "she penetrates all things" (7:24).

On the other hand, when Solomon returns to recount his experiences with Wisdom, erotic allusions abound. Thus he begins: "Her I loved and sought out from my youth; I sought to take her as my bride, and became enamored of her beauty" (ταύτην ἐφίλησα καὶ ἐξεζήτησα ἐκ νεότητός μου καὶ ἐζήτησα νύμφην ἀγαγέσθαι ἐμαυτῷ καὶ ἐραστὴς ἐγενόμην τοῦ κάλλους αὐτῆς) (8:2; cf. Prov 7:4; Sir 15:2).[317] A little later, having extolled her roles, again rather more in abstract terms drawing on his exposition in 7:23b – 8:1, he writes: "I determined then to take her to live with me, knowing that she would be a good counsellor for me, and a comfort in cares and grief" (ἔκρινα τοίνυν ταύτην ἀγαγέσθαι πρὸς

---

discussion in Marilyn B. Skinner, *Sexuality in Greek and Roman Culture* (Oxford: Blackwell, 2005) 151-54.

[315] Winston, *Wisdom of Solomon*, notes that according to *1 Enoch* 8:3 this is forbidden knowledge, but points to its importance to the Essenes according to Josephus *B.J.* 2.136 on Essenes and to the depiction of Solomon's medical knowledge in Josephus *A.J.* 8.45-49 (176).

[316] On this see Winston, *Wisdom of Solomon*, who describes the list as "borrowed largely from Greek philosophy" (178).

[317] Winston, *Wisdom of Solomon*, notes Philo's allegorical treatment of Abraham, Sarah, and Hagar, in Philo *Congr.* 74, drawing on an old Greek allegory of Bion of Borysthenes cited in Plutarch (192-93).

συμβίωσιν εἰδὼς ὅτι ἔσται μοι σύμβουλος ἀγαθῶν καὶ παραίνεσις φροντίδων καὶ λύπης) (8:9), images of the good wife. Marital imagery returns again in 8:16, "When I enter my house, I shall find rest with her; for companionship (OR: intercourse) with her has no bitterness, and life with her has no pain, but gladness and joy" (εἰσελθὼν εἰς τὸν οἶκόν μου προσαναπαύσομαι αὐτῇ οὐ γὰρ ἔχει πικρίαν ἡ συναναστροφὴ αὐτῆς οὐδὲ ὀδύνην ἡ συμβίωσις αὐτῆς ἀλλὰ εὐφροσύνην καὶ χαράν) (cf. Sir 6:28). Winston draws attention to συναναστροφη, a word used for sexual intercourse (cf. 3 Macc 2:31-33; 3:5; Let. Arist. 169), which may be its meaning here.[318] His prayer continues her image as a female figure, indeed, as seated by God's throne (9:4), but does not employ sexually related imagery, though 8:3 could in more general terms affirm: "the Lord of all loves her"* (ὁ πάντων δεσπότης ἠγάπησεν αὐτήν).

The prayer concludes with the words, "And thus the ways of those on earth were set right, and human beings were taught what is pleasing to you, and were saved by wisdom" (καὶ οὕτως διωρθώθησαν αἱ τρίβοι τῶν ἐπὶ γῆς καὶ τὰ ἀρεστά σου ἐδιδάχθησαν ἄνθρωποι καὶ τῇ σοφίᾳ ἐσώθησαν) (9:18). This then sets the scene for the presentation of Wisdom's engagement in Israel's history, a series of seven contrasts between righteous and wicked.[319] In this depiction of Wisdom's role no sexually related motifs feature.

The brief depiction of Adam, unnamed,[320] appears primarily positive, with the emphasis on his formation, deliverance from "his transgression"[321] (παραπτώματος ἰδίου),[322] and authority to rule (10:1-2), in contrast to Cain, who

---

[318] Winston, Wisdom of Solomon, 196.

[319] On this see Winston, Wisdom of Solomon, noting the pairs are incomplete (211).

[320] On the role of anonymity in the work, which also includes Solomon, see the discussion in Samuel Cheon, "Anonymity in the Wisdom of Solomon," JSP 18 (1998) 111-19, who concludes that it is a literary technique which "functions in two different ways. One is for the intended audience within his community, and the other is for the outsiders, the aggressors" (118). For the former: "the anonymity makes them both generalize their ancestors' history and identify it with their own situation, defining both themselves and their antagonists" (118) and for the latter it obfuscates identification in a time of political instability (117).

[321] Cf. Levison, Portraits of Adam, who argues that the author intends the meaning that Wisdom kept Adam from transgressing (60). I consider it unlikely that the author would be suggesting something to his hearers so contrary to known tradition.

[322] Cf. Alviero Niccacci, "Wisdom as Woman, Wisdom and Man, Wisdom and God," in Treasures of Wisdom: Studies in Ben Sira and the Book of Wisdom: Festschrift M. Gilbert (ed. Nuria Calduch-Benages and Jacques Vermeylen; BETL 143; Leuven: Peeters, 1999) 369-85, who argues that in αὕτη πρωτόπλαστον πατέρα κόσμου μόνον κτισθέντα διεφύλαξεν ("She carefully guarded the first-formed father of the world, when he alone was created" 10:1) μόνον "alone" refers not to Adam, but to both Adam and Eve

not only abandoned Wisdom (10:3), but is depicted as the cause of the flood (10:4a), from which Wisdom then saved Noah (10:4b). There follows the contrast between the wicked nations at Babel (10:5) and Abraham, apparently, as in *LAB* 6, associated with the Babel episode, but also depicted in relation to the sacrifice of Isaac (10:5). So far, sexual wrongdoing plays no role in what is described and no reference is made, for instance, to the angels and the women, Noah's nakedness, or Abraham and Sarah's encounter with Pharaoh, though the author knows a version of the story of the Watchers, where unlike in the Book of the Watchers of *1 Enoch* the giants do not self-destruct, but are drowned in the flood (14:6).[323] Lot is depicted as another "righteous man" in contrast to his wife, "an unbelieving soul", but nothing is said about the sins of the "Five Cities" (10:6) except at the level of generalities: "wickedness", "folly", and "failure" (10:6-8). A later reference to where the occasion is employed as an analogy to Egypt's eventual hostility, focuses only on failure of hospitality (19:13-17). Nothing indicates the nature of their inhospitable behaviour, though we may assume hearers would be familiar with the attempted male rape. We hear nothing of Lot and his daughters. Jacob is portrayed only in positive colours as guided and instructed by Wisdom, in contrast to his angry brother and other enemies (10:9-12). The attempted seduction of Joseph features only in the summary of Wisdom's work, who "delivered him from sin" (10:13). Wisdom is next depicted rescuing "a holy people and blameless race" from "a nation of oppressors" through Moses (10:15-21).

Various strands of influence flow into the author's depiction of Wisdom, including the image of Woman Wisdom from Proverbs, reflected even more dramatically in Ben Sira. The erotic dimensions are at home here, though more restrained.[324] These may also reflect resonance with Isis traditions[325] which the

---

and so "his transgression" refers to both (369-72), and speculates that it assumes acceptance of marriage as normal (374).

[323] The author does appear to know the Book of the Watchers, since he cites *1 Enoch* 5:7 in 3:9. Shannon Burkes, "Wisdom and Apocalypticism in the Wisdom of Solomon," *HTR* 95 (2002) 21-44, suggests that 7:20-21 could refer to the spirits of Enoch mythology (36). On 14:6a see also Hayman, "Survival of Mythology," 136.

[324] Cf. Webster, "Sophia," who denies them altogether: "this personification is elusive as light, and definitely not erotic" (76). She argues that Wisdom is degendered and made like the barren woman and the eunuch (77). While I believe we have shown that the erotic is not absent, one can agree with Webster that it is different from what we find in Proverbs and Ben Sira and it is true that here Wisdom "is seen but not heard (6.16), present but not touched (9.10), given but not grasped (8.21)" (75). See also Claudia V. Camp, "The Female Sage in Ancient Israel and in the Biblical Wisdom Literature," in *The Sage in Israel and the Ancient Near East* (ed. John G. Gammie and Leo G. Perdie; Winona Lake: Eisenbrauns, 1990) 185-203, who comments: "The fundamental metaphor for Wisdom is no longer the wise woman of the house and street, as it is in Proverbs, but rather the sublime 'throne

author appears to have adapted for his depiction.[326] On the one hand, it helps explain how the author can speak of both God and the king loving Wisdom,[327] while at the same time resisting any notion that Wisdom is the king's mother or not subordinate to God.[328] Erotic imagery was also known in Greco-Roman images of the pursuit of knowledge,[329] but it is interesting that where streams of Stoic and Middle Platonic influence[330] appear strongest, such as in 7:22b – 8:1, erotic or marital imagery is minimal.[331] While the use of erotic and marital imagery may occur in contexts where sex and marriage rate lowly, in this work it is probably correct to see them as reflecting positive appreciation.[332] The author's

---

partner' of the king (Wis 6:14), who is God's 'throne partner' (Wis 9:4) as well" (202). Silvia Schroer, "The Book of Sophia," in *Searching the Scriptures: Volume Two: A Feminist Commentary* (London: SCM, 1995) 17-38 also notes that "it is Sophia's omniscience, not her beauty, that is the motive for the sage to marry her" (24); similarly p. 25.

[325] On the significance of the parallels with the Isis traditions see especially Kloppenborg, "Isis and Sophia," who critically reviews the earlier discussion of parallels in Reese, *Hellenistic Influence*, 45-48. Kloppenborg concludes from his own analysis: "What is distinctive in the Wisdom of Solomon is (1) the saving role of Sophia, corresponding to Isis's major function; (2) the selection of events which the author used as examples of this role; and (3) the allusive retelling of these events in such a way that they resonate with the mythic pattern characteristic of the Isis-Horus cycle" (72).

[326] As Winston, *Wisdom of Solomon*, observes, the Wisdom figure "was the perfect bridge between the exclusive nationalist tradition of Israel and the universalist philosophical tradition which appealed so strongly to the Jewish youth of Roman Alexandria" (37).

[327] Kloppenborg, "Isis and Sophia," 76-77.

[328] Kloppenborg, "Isis and Sophia," 78.

[329] David Winston, "The Sage as Mystic in the Wisdom of Solomon," in *The Ancestral Philosophy: Hellenistic Philosophy in Second Temple Judaism: Essays of David Winston* (ed. Gregory E. Sterling; BJS 331; StudPhilMon 4; Providence: BJS, 2001) 99-113, notes that there are "Greek models for the personification of Virtue/Wisdom as a beautiful maiden. In the famous parable known as the 'Choice of Heracles' and later adapted by Philo (*Sacr.* 21-29), the Sophist Prodicus of Ceos had personified virtue as a fair maiden of high bearing who invited Heracles to choose her (Xenophon *Mem.* 2:1:21-33)" (105) and points also to a eulogy of Aristotle (105). On Philo's use of erotic imagery in speaking of the relation between the sage and Wisdom he draws attention to *Congr.* 74; *Contempl.* 68; *Spec.* 4.14 (102, 106).

[330] On the influence of Isis tradition and also Middle Platonic and Stoic thought see Collins, *Between Athens and Jerusalem*, 196; Collins, *Jewish Wisdom*, 197-99 (Stoicism); 200-202 (Middle Platonism); 203-204 (Isis).

[331] See also Kloppenborg, "Isis and Sophia," who notes that despite stoicising, the personal element of the Isis figure is retained (70).

[332] Camp, "The Female Sage", contends that "Real women are mentioned only in the eschatological adulation of those who remain childless rather than transgressing the

silence about women among the righteous in the account of Wisdom's engagement with history, where one might easily have heard of Eve, Sarah, and Rachel, is indicative of disinterest, quite in contrast to *LAB* or *Jubilees*. It does not, however, imply idealisation of female celibacy or denigration of sexual relations, which must be affirmed to make the author's imagery of Wisdom work, but this is male-oriented reflection to which female imagery and interests are subordinated.

God's Engagements and the Idolaters' Sins

The third major section of the work begins in 11:1, but is not clearly marked off from what precedes. Indeed, it begins still speaking of Wisdom, but thereafter Wisdom fails to appear. Instead we find an extended contrast between elements of creation used by God, on the one hand, to bless Israel and, on the other, to plague the Egyptians, interrupted by two excursuses, one in defence of God's goodness (11:15 – 12:27) and the other an attack on worship of elements, idols, and animals gods (13 – 15).

There is little pertaining to sexuality in the contrasts. The first excursus includes a depiction of the Canaanites as people whom God hated "for their detestable practices" (12:4). It then expounds these as "works of sorcery and unholy rites, their merciless slaughter of children, and their sacrificial feasting on human flesh and blood" (12:4-5). They are accordingly an "accursed race", of evil origin, "their wickedness inborn" (12:10-11), but nothing is said of sexual malpractice.

In the second excursus, described by Barclay as "one of the most sustained attacks on Gentile religiosity which we have from the pen of a Diaspora Jew",[333] the author begins by claiming that "all human beings who were ignorant of God were foolish by nature" (μάταιοι μὲν γὰρ πάντες ἄνθρωποι φύσει οἷς παρῆν θεοῦ ἀγνωσία), since "from the good things that are seen they were unable to know the one who is, nor, though paying attention to his works, did they recognize the craftsman" (ἐκ τῶν ὁρωμένων ἀγαθῶν οὐκ ἴσχυσαν εἰδέναι τὸν ὄντα

---

marriage bed (Wis 3:13; cf. Sir 23:22-26). In sum, then, the long and richly textured intertwining of wisdom thought with the real life of men and women in society is abandoned by this writer in favor of mystical speculation" (202); similarly Niccacci, "Wisdom as Woman," who speculates that seeing the sage's relation to Wisdom as like God's (Prov 4:7; Sir 36:29/24; Prov 8:22) would lead to supplanting marriage and supporting celibacy (383-84).

[333] Barclay, *Jews in the Mediterranean World*, 81, who notes that its "closest parallel" is to be found in Philo *Decal.* 52-81, perhaps reflecting a common source or tradition (186).

οὔτε τοῖς ἔργοις προσέχοντες ἐπέγνωσαν τὸν τεχνίτην) (13:1).[334] Paul is beholden to this analysis when he writes: "For what can be known about God is plain to them, because God has shown it to them. Ever since the creation of the world his eternal power and divine nature, invisible though they are, have been understood and seen through the things he has made" (Rom 1:19-20).[335] Unlike Paul, who goes to attack people's foolishness for denying their own nature and engaging in same-sex relations, the author proceeds to attack belief that natural elements (fire, air, stars, water, moon, and sun) are gods (13:2-3). The author then ridicules the creation of idols, including prayer to them for money, travel, aid, life, and also marriage and children (13:17-19; cf. Isa 44:9-20; Jer 10:1-16; Let Jer).

Only after this exposition on idolatry does the author make the connection to sexual wrongdoing, such as we find in Paul. Thus at the beginning of 14:11-31, which forms the centre of the concentric structure which patterns the excursus, 13 – 15,[336] the author declares: ἀρχὴ γὰρ πορνείας ἐπίνοια εἰδώλων εὕρεσις δὲ αὐτῶν φθορὰ ζωῆς ("For the invention of idols was the beginning of sexual wrongdoing, and the discovery of them the corruption of life"*) (14:12). The link with sexual wrongdoing receives no further elucidation until after another theory on the origins of idols, namely their derivation from the grief of the untimely death of children, whose image of remembrance evolves into a god[337] and sets a pattern which rulers then follow, enhanced by the artistry and skill of the artisan (14:15-21). Next the author links ignorance of God to ignorance in calling strife and great evils peace (14:22).[338] Accordingly, the author explains:

23 ἢ γὰρ τεκνοφόνους τελετὰς ἢ κρύφια μυστήρια ἢ ἐμμανεῖς ἐξάλλων
θεσμῶν κώμους ἄγοντες 24 οὔτε βίους οὔτε γάμους καθαροὺς ἔτι
φυλάσσουσιν, ἕτερος δ᾽ ἕτερον ἢ λοχῶν ἀναιρεῖ ἢ νοθεύων ὀδυνᾷ. 25 πάντα
δ᾽ ἐπιμὶξ ἔχει αἷμα καὶ φόνος, κλοπὴ καὶ δόλος, φθορά, ἀπιστία, τάραχος,
ἐπιορκία, 26 θόρυβος ἀγαθῶν, χάριτος ἀμνηστία, ψυχῶν μιασμός, γενέσεως
ἐναλλαγή, γάμων ἀταξία, μοιχεία καὶ ἀσέλγεια.

23 For whether performing ritual murders of children or secret mysteries, or holding frenzied revels with strange laws, 24 they no longer keep either their lives or their marriages pure, but they either kill one another by treachery or grieve one another by adultery. 25 And all things are an overwhelming confusion of blood and murder, theft

---

[334] See also Winston, *Wisdom of Solomon*, who suggests Wisdom and Paul may be drawing on "common Jewish-Hellenistic apologetic tradition" used also by Philo (248).

[335] See also Collins, *Between Athens and Jerusalem*, 200.

[336] On this see Nickelsburg, *Jewish Literature*, 211.

[337] On the background of this theory known as Euhemerist see Winston, *Wisdom of Solomon*, 270, who points to its appearance also in *Let. Aris.* 134-37 and *Sib. Or.* 3:108-113 (270-71).

[338] Winston, *Wisdom of Solomon*, observes: "This theme of war-in-peace was common in Cynic-Stoic diatribe literature of the first century CE" (279).

and deceit, corruption, unfaithfulness, tumult, perjury, 26 turmoil of those who are good, forgetfulness of favours, defilement of souls, sexual perversion, disorder in marriages, adultery, and debauchery.* (14:23-26)

The primary focus in this depiction of sin[339] is sexual wrongdoing: "they no longer keep either their lives or their marriages pure" (οὔτε βίους οὔτε γάμους καθαροὺς ἔτι φυλάσσουσιν). The words νοθεύων ὀδυνᾷ translated, "grieve one another by adultery," mean literally: "corrupting a marriage he causes grief", which could include adultery, but could carry wider connotations, including, for instance, engagement in male same-sex relations. The juxtaposition of "sexual perversion, disorder in marriages, adultery, and debauchery" (γενέσεως ἐναλλαγή γάμων ἀταξία μοιχεία καὶ ἀσέλγεια) gives them prominence, as does their placement to conclude the list and to form an inclusion with the references to sexual wrongdoing with which the depiction begins in 14:24. The author apparently envisages a wide range of activities. The words γενέσεως ἐναλλαγή ("sexual perversion") may well refer to same-sex relations.[340] ἐναλλαγή means "change" or "inversion". γενέσεως in this combination appears to address change which in some way has an impact on reproduction. Reese renders: ἐναλλαγὴ γενέσεως "perversion of procreation".[341] That would include, as Countryman notes, much more than same-sex relations.[342] It is noteworthy that the author gives significantly less prominence to same-sex relations than we find in *Sibylline Oracles*, *Pseudo-Aristeas*, Philo, and Paul. There is also no explicit reference to sexual exploitation of minors, servants, or victims of war, and condemnation of prostitution is present only by implication.

In the context γάμων ἀταξία could refer to incestuous marriage.[343] In a Jewish context one might think of marriage to non-Jews, but here the focus is behaviour among idolaters. μοιχεία is a common word for adultery and probably means that here. ἀσέλγεια is probably intended to encompass everything else by way of sexual wrongdoing. As Nickelsburg notes, "In combining a polemic against idolatry with an attack against sexual immorality, the author parallels book 3 of the Sibylline Oracles and Aristeas".[344] Like Paul, the author deems such

---

[339] Winston, *Wisdom of Solomon*, notes similar lists of wrongdoing in Philo *Gig.* 51; *Conf.* 46 (279).

[340] Winston, *Wisdom of Solomon*, draws attention to the expression φύσεως ἔργων ἐναλλαγή in Philo *Cher.* 92 and ἐνήλλαξε τάξιν φύσεως αὐτῆς in *T. Naph* 3:4 (280).

[341] Reese, *Hellenistic Influence*, 20.

[342] L. William Countryman, *Dirt, Greed, and Sex: Sexual Ethics in the New Testament and Their Implications for Today* (2d. ed., Minneapolis: Fortress, 2007) 62.

[343] Winston, *Wisdom of Solomon*, notes that ἀταξία can mean sensual excess but also what is irregular and inordinate (Plato *Leg.* 840E) (280).

[344] Nickelsburg, *Jewish Literature*, 211.

behaviour and idolatry as without excuse and worthy of just penalty (τὰ δίκαια 14:30; ἡ τῶν ἁμαρτανόντων δίκη 14:31; cf. τὴν ἀντιμισθίαν ἣν ἔδει τῆς πλάνης αὐτῶν ἐν ἑαυτοῖς ἀπολαμβάνοντες Rom 1:27).

The remaining chapters return to the contrasts with which 11:4-14 began. In none of them do we find sexual themes. The reference to "secret sins" in 17:3 need not imply these. As Barclay notes, "the author holds firmly to 'the light of the law' (18.4) in a world darkened by impiety".[345] The author depicts the Egyptians' "bitter hatred of strangers", making slaves of those once their benefactors, and "who had already shared the same rights", a thinly veiled allusion to his own situation, as far worse than what happened at Sodom (19:13-17), but here, too, there are no sexual allusions.

The work ends with a reflection on the way creation may be played as an instrument to serve various divine purposes (19:18-21). While it is a reflection on the contrasts developed in the second half of the work, it raises some issues pertinent to sexuality, especially in relation to eschatology.[346]

Eschatology and Sexuality?

One could conclude from the account of Wisdom's engagement and of God's actions through creation in relation to the exodus that there is a process at work in the universe which punishes the wicked and rewards or delivers the righteous. Such an understanding could find further support from the middle section which not only ends by reporting Wisdom's interventions, but also explains its omnipresence.[347] In tension with this is the depiction of the suffering of the righteous man in the opening section, where there is no indication that his espousal of Wisdom guarantees any such deliverance or protection during this life. Rather, unlike Ben Sira, the author opts for the apocalyptic solution to human suffering, which guarantees life beyond this life and that physical death is not annihilation.[348]

---

[345] Barclay, *Jews in the Mediterranean World*, 191.

[346] Gilbert, Wisdom Literature," writes: "The last verse of the book (19:22) is there to say that what has happened will always be happening again, no matter where and no matter how. The events of the exodus confirm the author's hope and view of the last things. As they also strengthen the wish for wisdom he evokes in his readers" (310).

[347] On this see Burkes, *God, Self, and Death*, 163-64.

[348] So Burkes, *God, Self, and Death*, 187-88, who notes that the author assumes God acted in the past and will in the future (165) and writes: "Despite his grounding in a philosophical sapiential mode, the author accepts an apocalyptic option for explaining why God does not rescue the innocent in this life" (168). She concludes: "Since God is not obvious in the present world and must be inferred from the divine works, the book adopts the familiar intermediary of Wisdom personified, which takes on Stoic elements and is elevated to the creating and protecting office of deity itself" (189).

It goes, indeed, further than that in relation to both the righteous and the wicked. For the warnings about the wicked, including the exhortations to rulers, point them forward to future judgement (1:6-11; 3:10; 4:6; 6:3-8) and the scene showing the blessedness of the righteous depicts the wicked as being brought to see that blessedness and their own wretchedness (5:1-14). This means that the author envisages some limited post mortal existence also for the wicked, enough for them to be brought face to face with their wickedness before, apparently, they are annihilated (4:19).[349] The image of God the warrior appears designed to show that act of destruction and judgement (5:17-23). In the case of the righteous they are not only at rest in the hands of God. The author depicts them as shining and ruling over nations.

κοὶ ἐν καιρῷ ἐπισκοπῆς αὐτῶν ἀναλάμψουσιν καὶ ὡς σπινθῆρες ἐν καλάμῃ διαδραμοῦνται· κρινοῦσιν ἔθνη καὶ κρατήσουσιν λαῶν, καὶ βασιλεύσει αὐτῶν κύριος εἰς τοὺς αἰῶνας.

In the time of their visitation they will shine out, and as sparks through the stubble, they will run about. They will judge nations and rule over peoples, and the Lord will be king over them forever. (3:7-8; cf. also 5:6)

As Burkes notes, "this sounds like a collective action on a worldwide scale".[350] The light imagery to depict future embodied existence is widespread, reaching back to Dan 12:3 (cf. also *1 Enoch* 104:2; 38:4; 39:76; 4 Ezra 7:97; *2 Bar.* 51:10; 4 Macc 17:5; *2 Enoch* 66:7; Matt 13:43).[351] It also has resonance with Greco-Roman notions about the soul.[352] The traditional motif about ruling nations and peoples could be dismissed here as mere symbolism without substance,[353] but it is hard to

---

[349] So Burkes, *God, Self, and Death*, who similarly concludes that the ungodly vanish after death but live long enough to see their wrong (184). Cf. Hogan, "Ambiguity of Death," 15; and Nickelsburg, *Jewish Literature*, who writes: "Death and immortality are states in which the ungodly and the unrighteous participate here and now and which continue unbroken in spite of biological death" (205).

[350] Burkes, *God, Self, and Death*, 185.

[351] Winston, *Wisdom of Solomon*, 128.

[352] So John J. Collins, "The Mysteries of God: Creation and Eschatology in 4QInstruction and the Wisdom of Solomon," in *Wisdom and Apocalypticism in the Dead Sea Scrolls and in the Biblical Tradition* (ed. F. García Martínez; BETL 168; Leuven: Peeters, 2003) 287-305, who writes that the "idea of astral immortality was widespread in the Hellenistic world, as a form of immortality of the soul" (292).

[353] Cf. Collins, "Apocalyptic Eschatology," who sees the judgement scene in chap. 5 functioning as a myth, not to be taken literally, but there to facilitate discussion (100) and speaks similarly of the devil (101). Referring to Philo's appropriation of messianic ideas and of the hope of the ingathering of the exiles, Collins surmises: "It may be that the author of Wisdom also affirmed them, insofar as they were found in the torah, but he makes no mention of them in his book" (105), going on to argue that in Wisdom "the cosmos is

see why this should be so.[354] If it reflects a belief in a world order which includes nations and peoples, these are presumably the righteous, not the wicked, who would have been exterminated. The author assumes Gentile rulers can, indeed, do God's will.[355] Accordingly the author may be embracing the prophetic notion of Israel (or, at least, faithful Israel) ruling over the nations (that is, the faithful and righteous nations) (cf. from among the cluster of Isaiah chapters: 51:5; 55:4-5; 60:2-3).[356] This implies some kind of embodiment, whatever form that might take, possibly understood not as earthly bodies transformed and transfigured, but heavenly bodies.[357] The hint of a future temple, referred to in relation to the faithful eunuch, may envisage a temple in a transformed world. If there is something like this, then we might wonder what place sexual relations might have in such a world. If the barren woman is literally to bear children (3:13), they must be presupposed. A default answer is that it would be a world fully conforming to God's will and Law, which also has space for normal family relations, including marriage and sexual relations, but this must remain at the level of speculation,

---

programmed to deal with unrighteousness when it arises, but the only definitive resolution of the problem is found in the respective fates of righteous and wicked after death" (105). Cf. also Nickelsburg, *Resurrection*, who notes the tension in the author's statements about judgement between those which assume judgement at death (3:13, 18; 4:6) and those, like 5:17-23, which speak of a day of visitation, but resolves the tension in favour of identifying death as the day of visitation (89).

[354] Burkes, *God, Self, and Death*, notes the language of revelation, mysteries, foreknowledge and secrets (8:8; 7:20-21) (177) and rightly observes: "The result is that the sapiential approach occasionally shades into the apocalyptic sphere" (178).

[355] So Grabbe, *Wisdom of Solomon*, 60-61.

[356] Collins, *Jewish Wisdom*, notes that "In the case of Wis. Sol., however, there is no overt messianic eschatology. The hope of national restoration might be inferred from the pattern of the exodus, but the book never addresses the question of a final resolution of history" (217). It comes closest to this, however, in 3:7-8 and is evoked through the account of Israel. So Alexander Di Lella, "Conservative and Progressive Theology: Sirach and Wisdom," *CBQ* 28 (1966) 139-54, 154, and Michael Kolarcik, "Creation and Salvation in the Book of Wisdom," in *Creation in the Biblical Traditions* (ed. Richard J. Clifford and John J. Collins; CBQMS 24; Washington: CBA, 1992) 97-107, 104-107, who writes: "This interpretation of the exodus reaffirms the feasibility of postulating the ultimate judgment and serves as the paradigm of salvation – God's recreation of the world in favour of the just" (104). "In recounting the plagues, the author appeals to the same principle used for the ultimate judgment of Wisdom 5. God employs the forces of the cosmos to save the just and to destroy the wicked" (106).

[357] On whether Wisdom assumes resurrection see the discussion in Burkes, *God, Self, and Death*, 172-73. Cf. Collins, *Jewish Wisdom*: "There is never any suggestion of resurrection of the body, nor indeed of resurrection of the spirit" (186).

since the author nowhere addresses it. The same is true of any notion of a return to Eden, as paradise, which would have been equally possible.

Conclusion

In two different contexts the author addresses sexual wrongdoing. It is prominent among the sins of those renegade Jews and others who make an alliance with death and the devil and despise and attack the righteous. The promiscuity perhaps alluded to already in 2:9 in the context of reference to their indulgent revelry comes to direct expression in the related section 3:12 – 4:6, which attacks both adultery and probably illicit sexual intercourse in general, possibly in the case of Jews, intermarriage, and where sexual wrongdoing is set in contrast to the barren woman and the eunuch who resist such temptations. Enoch's elevation is probably to be seen also in the context of being delivered from the dangers which sexual wrongdoing posed in his world.

The second major context is among idolaters, which includes a range of religious practices from worship of Egyptian gods to emperor worship. Here, too, sexual wrongdoing receives foremost attention. Indeed such idolatry is seen as its root. Its manifestations include adultery, but also illicit sexual relations, probably including male same-sex relations and incest, but these are not specified as such. Given the political allusions to Rome and its emperors ruling Egypt directly in absentia and both the development of the imperial cult and the notorious marital infidelities associated with their rule, one might see the author here including an allusion to their practices. Neither context gives prominence to male same-sex relations, surprisingly, given its place in contemporary Jewish literature from the area, such as *Pseudo-Aristeas*, *Sibylline Oracles* 3, and Philo.[358] With prostitution it is probably implied. Nothing is said of various forms of sexual abuse and exploitation of the young and vulnerable, but this is also probably implied in the general categories. The major focus appears to be sexual wrongdoing in the context of drunken partying and similar activity in the public sphere.

Otherwise sexual wrongdoing is not prominent. It fails to appear in the account of Wisdom's engagement with human history, where one could easily have found it in relation to the watchers, the rescue of Abraham and Sarah (or Isaac and Rebecca) from Pharaoh's (or Abimelech's) wants, the nakedness of Noah and the curse of Canaan, the incest of Lot's daughters, the planned assault of the men of Sodom and Gomorrah – much for Wisdom to do! It is somewhat surprising that the author never has Solomon address his own sin, not least, his mixed marriages. His account of Wisdom's engagement with Israel's past

---

[358] On this see Collins, *Between Athens and Jerusalem*, 199; Collins, *Jewish Wisdom*, 192.

similarly presents the unnamed righteous as ideals,[359] sanitised of failure, including Jacob, Lot, and even Adam whose transgression receives mention only as something from which Wisdom delivered him, but also Israel in the wilderness.[360] The righteous are apparently blameless.

On the positive side, inspired both by his own Jewish tradition and competing Isis tradition, the author employs the image of Wisdom as a woman, to whom the wise man relates as a lover, and potential spouse, though the erotic is quite constrained compared with Proverbs and Ben Sira. Collins observes that "No positive value is attached to children and families, and the author certainly does not acknowledge a commandment to increase and multiply. It is not difficult to see how such a perspective on life could encourage asceticism or even celibacy".[361] On the other hand, the author's stance seems not to be negative towards sexuality. There is nothing negative implied in Solomon's depiction of his conception and birth, as made possible through the pleasure of sexual intercourse. Similarly the image of the chaste barren woman and eunuch serve not to promote celibacy but to set their chastity in contrast to the profligacy of the wicked. The use of such imagery to depict Wisdom and her relation to the wise also appears to assume the appropriateness of erotic love and marriage in their proper context. It would hardly achieve the author's purpose if his assumption were that such behaviour is unworthy in its proper context. The author's somewhat inconsistent images of the future allow for the possibility that he might see a form of future existence for both faithful Jews and faithful Gentiles where it would make sense to envisage human community and some kind of normal human life, including sexual relations, but he never takes us that far nor says anything to exclude it.

3.2.3   Pseudo-Aristeas

This writing[362] purports to be written by Aristeas, whom, it claims, Ptolemy II Philadelphus (283-246 B.C.E.) sent along with Andreas, to Eleazar, the high priest

---

[359] So Collins, *Between Athens and Jerusalem*, who notes that correspondingly "the author has nothing good to say about the ancient Canaanites and Egyptians" (202).

[360] Grabbe, *Wisdom of Solomon*, 42.

[361] Collins, *Jewish Wisdom*, 191.

[362] The following discussion is based on the Greek text edition reproduced in David M. Miller and Ian W. Scott, ed. "'Letter of Aristeas': Edition 1.0," in *The Online Critical Pseudepigrapha* (ed. Ken M. Penner, David M. Miller, and Ian W. Scott; Atlanta: SBL, 2006) no pages; online: http://www.purl.org/net/ocp/LetAris.html, based on that of H. St. J. Thackeray, "Appendix: The Letter of Aristeas," in *An Introduction to the Old Testament in Greek* (ed. H. B. Swete; Cambridge: Cambridge University Press, 1914) 531-606. The

of Jerusalem, who in turn describes them both as "highly esteemed" by Ptolemy, "gentlemen of integrity, outstanding in education, worthy in every respect" of the king's "conduct and justice" (43). Its author is more likely to have written in the latter third of the second century B.C.E., adopting the persona of Aristeas[363] to achieve his ends.[364] Apart from such self-congratulation, the author's praise of the alleged addressee, Philocrates, as committed to learning, whether through "the accounts (of others) or by actual experience", as the path to true piety (2), also reflects the values he espouses. The same is true of his idealised description of those sent from Jerusalem to translate the Law: "men of the highest merit and of excellent education due to the distinction of their parentage; they had not only mastered the Jewish literature, but had made a serious study of that of the Greeks as well" (121).[365]

The work presents itself as a report (διήγησις) (8) of an initiative of Demetrius of Phaleron to have the laws of the Jews translated and incorporated into the king's library as part of its planned expansion from 200,000 to 500,000 volumes (10). In the persona of Aristeas the author claims to have used the occasion to raise the issue of Jewish prisoners with the king, whom his father had taken captive during his campaigns in Palestine, and to have argued that the God who prospers his reign is none other than the God of the Jews, known elsewhere as Zeus and Jove (17). Accordingly the king decrees liberation for Jewish slaves, including those transported under the Persians, and compensation for their captors (19-27). The report then returns to the theme of the translation, citing a supposed letter from Demetrius requesting the translation as a replacement for earlier inadequate transcriptions of the Hebrew text (29-32), the king's response by way

---

English translation is that of R. J. H. Shutt, "Letter of Aristeas," *OTP*, 2.7-34, except where I have provided my own, indicated by an asterisk.

[363] On this see Oswyn Murray, "Aristeas and Ptolemaic Kingship," *JTS* 18 (1967) 337-71, who notes with regard to the author's strategy that the "elaborate machinery which Aristeas employed is evidence only of the seriousness with which he regarded his task" (343).

[364] For recent discussion of date see Collins, *Between Athens and Jerusalem*, 98-101, who after reviewing the alternatives of an early or late second century B.C.E. date, favours the proposal of E. J. Bickerman, "Zur Datierung des Pseudo-Aristeas," in E. J. Bickerman, *Studies in Jewish and Christian History* (3 vols; AGJU 9; Leiden: Brill, 1976-86) 1.108-36, who, on the basis of salutations, language, and geography, argued that the work was produced in the period 145-125 B.C.E., during the reign of Ptolemy VIII Euergetes II (Physcon).

[365] On the author's emphasis on education see Barclay, *Jews in the Mediterranean Diaspora*, 140. "On the basis of their common *paideia*, Jews and Greeks alike prize rational thought above bodily desires (5-8, 130, 140-41, 321), and together extol moderation and self-control (122, 222-23, 237, 256)" (141).

of a letter to Eleazar, which both reports the liberation and requests translators, six from each tribe (35-40), and then Eleazar's letter of acceptance (41-51). This fictional account serves to assert both that Jews should have a proper place in Ptolemaic Egypt, having suffered injustice in the past, and that their Law has not only divine sanction but can also claim royal patronage. The author's self-projection is clearly designed to enhance the profile of the Jewish people and its sacred law within Ptolemaic society and at the same time have them remain loyal to both.[366]

Already from its opening 51 paragraphs it is clear that the work aims at much more than a report of the translation of the Law. It is making a case both specifically for the quality and authority of this translation, and also for the excellence of the Law itself, and, by implication, the wisdom and respectability of those who base their lives on it. Thus while the account of the completion of the translation must wait until 301, the intervening material, far from being a set of extraneous digressions, builds this case. The work's ring composition reflects the education which the author values, including skills in creating his argument using common literary forms: a list of gifts, a travel account,[367] Eleazar's speech, and a symposium.[368] As Honigman notes, "While the main narrative in B.Ar. focuses on a narrow, albeit central, topic – the translation of the Jewish Law into Greek – the digressions allowed the author to broaden the scope of his work to include a comprehensive presentation of this Law, as well as of the people abiding by it".[369]

The author's seemingly self-conscious indulgence (cf. 83) in describing the artistry and orderliness of the king's gifts (51b-82) both underlines the latter's

---

[366] Barclay, *Jews in the Mediterranean Diaspora*, observes: "Through all this, the Jewish author is doing his utmost to glorify the Ptolemaic regime: he makes notable efforts to exonerate Ptolemy I Soter for his enslavement of the Jews (14, 23) and paints Philadelphus in the most glowing colours as a paragon of virtue (15-15, 26-28 etc.)" (142).

[367] Moses Hadas, *Aristeas to Philocrates* (JAL; New York: Harper, 1951) notes the popularity of travel accounts from the Odyssey onwards, but especially since Alexander's conquests which brought "greatly enlarged geographical horizons" (49).

[368] Sylvie Honigman, *The Septuagint and Homeric Scholarship in Alexandria: A Study in the Letter of Aristeas* (New York: Routledge, 2003) 15-18. Similarly Barclay, *Jews in the Mediterranean Diaspora*, writes of the author possessing "rhetorical training of some sophistication" (140).

[369] Honigman, *Septuagint*, 19. She writes that the author "aimed at endowing the LXX with a charter myth about its origins, with the purpose of giving the LXX the status of a sacred text" (8); cf. Hadas, *Aristeas*: "The analogy of the structure of other books, indeed, might suggest that the theme of the translation is designed as a 'historical' framework to serve as a vehicle for other matter" (59); Barclay, *Jews in the Mediterranean Diaspora*, 139; Gottfried Schimanowski, "Der *Aristeasbrief* zwischen Abgrenzung und Selbstdarstellung," in *Persuasion and Dissuasion in Early Christianity, Ancient Judaism, and Hellenism* (ed. Pieter van der Horstet al.; CBET 33; Leuven: Peeters, 2003) 45-64, 46.

respect for the Jewish cult and generally commends orderliness and beauty as fundamental values which will continue through the writing. The idealisation then extends to the author's account of Jerusalem, its temple, altar, services, surroundings, and the abundant fertility of the land (83-120),[370] the emphasis falling on orderliness, beauty, and sufficiency at each point, designed, again, to evoke awe and pride in Israel's cult.[371] Within this account the author further reflects his rhetorical training in developing a contrast (*synkrisis*),[372] comparing the balance of land and city in relation to Jerusalem with that of other large cities (109 indicates that Alexandria is in mind), where "everyone is bent on cultural delights, and the whole population in its philosophy is inclined to pleasure" (πάντων ἐπὶ τὸ κατὰ ψυχὴν ἱλαροῦσθαι νενευκότων, καὶ τῇ κατασκευῇ πάντας ἀνθρώπους ἐπὶ τὰς ἡδονὰς εὐκαταφόρους εἶναι) (108). This probably includes sexual pleasures of which the author disapproves, but this is not said. From his comments elsewhere it is clear that "all" here means most, since the author has already recognised that there are certainly some, such as the king and those like himself, who do not fall under this generalisation.

The author next announces a return to the account of the translation (121), but goes no further than praising the translators who "not only mastered the Jewish literature, but had made a serious study of that of the Greeks" (121). They "had a tremendous facility for the negotiations and questions arising from the Law, with the middle way as their commendable ideal" (122) and emulated faithfully the excellence of Eleazar the high priest (122), who espoused the good life as achieved by "observing the laws" and "by hearing much more than reading" (127).

The author then effectively illustrates the qualities he has just praised in the way he addresses a matter of contention about which "mankind as a whole shows a certain amount of concern", namely those parts of Jewish Law concerned with "meats and drinks and beasts considered to be unclean" (128), allegedly reporting Eleazar's explanation.[373] Far from being distractions from the theme of the Law's translation, these are key issues which might threaten to undermine its status and

---

[370] As Hadas, *Aristeas*, notes, the description is based not on reality, but on the LXX (64). Similarly Collins, *Between Athens and Jerusalem*, notes that the state envisaged is not the Hasmonean realm (103).

[371] Collins, *Between Athens and Jerusalem*, rightly notes that "no mention is made of the efficacy of the sacrifices or their effect on the relations between human beings and God. The liturgy is considered as *spectacle* and is admired for its emotional effect on onlookers" (195).

[372] "A fixed element in the rhetoricians' *progymnasmata*". So Hadas, *Aristeas*, 50.

[373] Davila, *Provenance*, notes that Josephus in his summarising of Aristeas makes no reference either to the journey to Jerusalem or the high priest's speech and contemplates that it may have been added secondarily (123-24). If so, they have captured well the subtle emphases of the rest of the work.

the peaceful co-existence of Jews with the respected authorities of Ptolemaic society. The explanation begins with an assertion of "the important matter of modes of life and relationships, inasmuch as through bad relationships men become perverted, and miserable their whole life long" (τὰς ἀναστροφὰς καὶ τὰς ὁμιλίας, οἷον ἐνεργάζονται πρᾶγμα, διότι κακοῖς ὁμιλήσαντες διαστροφὰς ἐπιλαμβάνουσιν ἄνθρωποι, καὶ ταλαίπωροι δι᾽ὅλου τοῦ ζῆν εἰσιν) (130). Such perversion will include same-sex relations understood as sexual perversion, though this is evident only later in the work (152).

The author can assume that in being concerned about corruption through wrong relationships he stands on common ground with the best of Jewish and Greek tradition.[374] Indeed, this is true of much of what follows in the high priest's speech. This includes the affirmation in 132 of monotheism, and of God's omnipotence and omniscience.[375] Monotheism was a respected philosophical position and is assumed already in the claim that Zeus and Jove are names for Israel's God (16).[376] Slightly more controversial is the statement in 134 where the author reports the high priest as showing "that all the rest of mankind ('except ourselves', as he said) believe that there are many gods", but, again, we should note the exceptions to "all the rest of mankind", namely the monotheists and these may include Aristeas and his companion if they are to be included in the words, "except ourselves" (παρ᾽ ἡμᾶς), as Beavis suggests.[377] Certainly the Euhemeristic stance of the dismissal of idolatry in 135-137 would have found common ground with many Greeks, perhaps even the claim that "those who have invented these

---

[374] So Reinhard Weber, *Das Gesetz im hellenistischen Judentum: Studien zum Verständnis und zur Funktion der Thora von Demetrios bis Pseudo-Phokylides* (ARGU 10; Frankfurt: Peter Lang, 2000), 134. On the common pattern in Hellenistic philosophy of differentiating oneself from what the masses believe see Reinhard Feldmeier, "Weise hinter 'eisernen Mauern': Tora und jüdisches Selbstverständnis zwischen Akkulturation und Absonderung im Aristeasbrief," in *Die Septuaginta zwischen Judentum und Christentum* (ed. Martin Hengel and Anna Maria Schwemer; WUNT 1.72; Tübingen: Mohr Siebeck, 1994) 20-37, 30-31, who cites Panaetius, Poseidonius, and Cleanthes. He notes that when the author claims that Jews place no great value on food, drink, and clothing in themselves (141), but rather see their entire lives as under God's rule, he is setting up the kind of ideal for which Cynic-Stoic diatribe also strove (32).

[375] So Weber, *Gesetz im hellenistischen Judentum*, 129.

[376] This is far from syncretism. It is a Gentile saying that Greeks refer to Israel's God by these names, not a Jew doing the reverse. On this see Barclay, *Jews in the Mediterranean Diaspora*, who points out that the author does not have the high priest reciprocate Ptolemy's generosity by sending gifts to Egyptian temples (143). Similarly Mary Ann L. Beavis, "Anti-Egyptian Polemic in the Letter of Aristeas 130-165 (the High Priest's Discourse)," *JSJ* 18 (1987) 145-51, 147.

[377] Beavis, "Anti-Egyptian Polemic," 147.

fabrications and myths are usually ranked to be the wisest of the Greeks" (137).[378] Such critiques belonged to the licence of makers of *chreia*.[379] As Hadas notes, "if the High Priest speaks scornfully of unenlightened pagans, enlightened pagans would have done the same. In deriding Euhemerism he was not alone in his own day, nor was he alone in speaking against theriolatry and other superstitions".[380] Disparagement of Egyptian religion for its worship of animals (138) was commonplace.[381] At the same time the author reports that the wisest among the Egyptians, their "leading priests", declared the Jews "men of God" as true worshippers of God (140), a further claim to validation and indication that the author's disparagements have their limits.[382]

At this point the author rationalises the "strict observances connected with meat and drink and touch and hearing and sight" (142) as surrounding Jews

ἀδιακόποις χάραξι καὶ σιδηροῖς τείχεσιν, ὅπως μηθενὶ τῶν ἄλλων ἐθνῶν
ἐπιμισγώμεθα κατὰ μηδέν, ἀγνοὶ καθεστῶτες κατὰ σῶμα καὶ κατὰ ψυχήν,
ἀπολελυμένοι ματαίων δοξῶν, τὸν μόνον θεὸν καὶ δυνατὸν σεβόμενοι
παρ'ὅλην τὴν πᾶσαν κτίσιν.

with unbroken palisades and iron walls to prevent our mixing with any of the other peoples in any matter, being thus kept pure in body and soul, preserved from false beliefs, and worshipping the only God omnipotent over all creation. (139)

While the primary focus here is protection against idolatry, the notion of being prevented from "mixing with other peoples in any matter" suggests wider concerns. In 142 we see that these include "being perverted by contact with others or by mixing with bad influences" (ὅπως οὖν μηθενὶ συναλισγούμενοι μηδ' ὁμιλοῦντες φαύλοις διαστροφὰς λαμβάνωμεν) (142). As already in 130 this probably includes sexual perversion (cf. 152). The separation will doubtless

---

[378] There is no need to dismiss this and see the speech as attacking only Egyptian religion with Beavis, "Anti-Egyptian Polemic," 148.

[379] Hadas, *Aristeas*, 51.

[380] Hadas, *Aristeas*, 62; similarly Collins, *Between Athens and Jerusalem*, 193.

[381] See Honigman, *Septuagint*, who observes that the criticism of polytheism in statements about the Greeks and Egyptians follows the conventional pattern of elaborating *chreia* by stating opposite before moving on to positive argument (20). "The Apology for the Law is so inconspicuous in its religious boldness that it is misleading to assume, as has been done on occasion, that it contains some violent polemics against Greeks stemming from a Jewish monotheistic point of view" (21). Similarly Schimanowski, *Aristeasbrief*, 53.

[382] Schimanowski, *Aristeasbrief*, notes the appeal to the wisdom of Egyptian priests already since Herodotus (54). As Donaldson, *Judaism and the Gentiles*, notes, this also implies that at the very least the priests, themselves, also fall within the category of being "people of God" (111, 113) and goes on to show how the author clearly assumes other exceptions, including the king (*Let. Arist.* 233, 276, 280) and good philosophers (111-16).

include prohibition of intermarriage, though not articulated here and perhaps allowing exemptions in relation to wise and learned Greeks.[383]

The author then has the high priest engage in a creative process of rationalisation via allegory[384] which in effect turns the unrest about Jewish concerns with prohibiting certain foods on its head. Thus, far from promoting alleged hostility towards other peoples, the rules forbidding people to eat birds of prey symbolise rejection of violence and injustice (143-148) and those enjoining the eating of animals with cloven hoof and which chew the cud symbolise the importance of discernment and memory, directed towards pursing what is good and just (149-161), in other words, values which the best of the Greeks also affirm.[385] Within this context the author elaborates further on the need for separation, now explicating what in all probability was implied in his earlier comments about perversion (130, 142):

οἱ γὰρ πλείονες τῶν λοιπῶν ἀνθρώπων ἑαυτοὺς μολύνουσιν ἐπιμισγόμενοι, συντελοῦντες μεγάλην ἀδικίαν, καὶ χῶραι καὶ πόλεις ὅλαι σεμνύνονται ἐπὶ τούτοις. οὐ μόνον γὰρ {προάγουσι} τοὺς ἄρσενας, ἀλλὰ καὶ τεκούσας ἔτι δὲ θυγατέρας μολύνουσιν. ἡμεῖς δὲ ἀπὸ τούτων διεστάλμεθα.

The majority of other men defile themselves in their relationships, thereby committing a serious offense, and lands and whole cities take pride in it: they not only procure the males, they also defile mothers and daughters. We are quite separated from these practices. (152)

---

[383] Collins, *Between Athens and Jerusalem*, writes: "What the Jews really refuse to mingle with are 'vain opinions,' not other nations as such. Enlightened pagans, such as the Egyptian priests, can appreciate the Jewish position. The significant distinction is not between Jews and Gentiles, but between 'men of God, a title applicable to none others but only to him who reveres the true God' and 'men of food and drink and raiment' (140)" (193). This somewhat overstates the author's position, who does after all speak of "mixing with any of the other peoples in any matter", so that we should probably see this as the standard to which there were some exceptions. Donaldson, *Judaism and the Gentiles*, is, however, correct in observing that the separation is directed not to be "from Gentiles per se, but from polytheistic worship" (113) – better: polytheistic worshippers. Donaldson notes that the author assumes philosophy is also a way to Israel's God, though an inferior one (116)

[384] On the use of allegory in interpreting Homer see Feldmeier, "Weise hinter 'eisernen Mauern'," 25.

[385] Honigman, *Septuagint*, notes that such allegorical interpretation of dietary taboos is found in Pythagorean tradition (21). "In fact, the arguments found in *B.Ar.* do not go far beyond conventional clichés, and in this sense the Apology for the Law does not display any more philosophical originality than the 72 sayings of the Symposium (chs. 187-300)" (21).

This attack gives particular profile to two kinds of sexual wrongdoing. It does so by citing them as the way that most of the rest of humanity defile themselves and then by making them an alleged focus of pride in lands and cities. The focus here will be moral defilement. The first is the procurement of males. The target here is the engaging of male prostitutes, rather than male same-sex relations in general. The second is incest with mothers and daughters. While these were abhorrent to Jews, many Greek writers attacked male same-sex relations, and incest with mothers or daughters was also widely condemned. Honigman suggests that the real target in the second instance is not actual practices in Alexandria or Egypt, but the early Stoic claim of Chrysippus, according to Plutarch, "that sexual intercourse with mothers or daughters or sisters, eating certain food, and proceeding straight from childbed or deathbed to a temple have been discredited without reason" (Plutarch *Stoic. rep.* 1044F).[386] Honigman notes that the author may well have omitted "sisters" out of respect for the brother-sister marriages of the Ptolemies.[387] She also considers the possibility that the author may be responsible for the link with male same-sex relations as a further instance of early Stoic permissiveness, but this is uncertain. She notes that "it would not be impossible to imagine condemnations of pederasty in the Alexandrian Hellenistic literature", though no traces survive.[388]

Mice and weasels symbolise mischievousness, defilement, and, the weasel, uniquely, malicious speech, since according to our author's quaint understanding it conceives through its ears and gives birth through its mouth (163-168),[389] which the author uses to attack malicious informers, probably with people in mind who maligned Jews to the authorities.[390] The author then has Eleazar summarise his argument: "In the matter of meats, the unclean reptiles, the beasts, the whole underlying rationale is directed toward righteousness and righteous human relationships" (169). This is an argument for upholding such laws, not abandoning them as only symbolic.[391] Here right relations are informed not only by biblical laws, but by the sense of orderliness which marked the earlier account of the king's gifts and the temple in its surrounds: περὶ βρωτῶν οὖν καὶ τῶν

---

[386] Cited by Honigman, *Septuagint*, in her discussion (22). She observes that the attacks are "no different in essence nor more violent in tone than those launched by other Greek philosophers of anti-Stoic affiliation" (22).

[387] Honigman, *Septuagint*, 22.

[388] Honigman, *Septuagint*, 22.

[389] This strange piece of zoology probably derives from careless observance of mating in which many species bite ears in the process and of birth where the mother licks the newborn.

[390] Collins, *Between Athens and Jerusalem*, notes that this detail would fit the reign of Physcon (100).

[391] So rightly Feldmeier, "Weise hinter 'eisernen Mauern'," 24.

ἀκαθάρτων ἑρπετῶν καὶ κνωδάλων καὶ πᾶς λόγος ἀνατείνει πρὸς δικαιοσύνην καὶ τὴν τῶν ἀνθρώπων συναναστροφήν δικαίαν ("The fact is that everything has been solemnly set in order for unblemished investigation and amendment of life for the sake of righteousness") (144). Following the brief summary the author notes how the legislation espouses moderation by its exclusion of wild animals among those to be sacrificed, "to prevent those who offer sacrifices being conscious in themselves of any excess (ὅπως οἱ προσφέροντες τὰς θυσίας μηθὲν ὑπερήφανον ἑαυτοις συνιστορῶσι)... Thus the man who offers the sacrifice makes an offering of every facet of his being" (170).

The high priest's exposition might convince an educated Greek in Ptolemaic Alexandria that the apparently divisive Jewish food laws promote the opposite, namely right relations, and protect the people from perverted ideas and behaviours.[392] They would surely all the more enhance the pride of Jews that their faith could hold its head high in the world of Greek rationality[393] and might on the one hand dissuade some who saw such engagement as requiring them to abandon such observances[394] and on the other, encourage others to set aside their fears that such engagement, including translation of their sacred scriptures into Greek,[395]

---

[392] So Barclay, *Jews in the Mediterranean Diaspora*, who writes of the account of the high priest's speech that in it the author "seeks understanding and tolerance from interested Gentiles" (149). Beavis, "Anti-Egyptian Polemic," speculates that opponents may have associated concern about animals with Egyptian abstinence from eating sacred animals and suggests that the counter to this must envisage potential opponents as readers (150-51). Feldmeier, "Weise hinter 'eisernen Mauern'," still contemplates the possibility of two fronts, but affirms that the first hearers and recipients of this work are more likely to be found among the Jewish than the Greek population of Alexandria (34). Hadas, *Aristeas*, finds the idea of envisaging Gentile readers as incredible: "Surely a pagan reader would penetrate Aristeas' pagan mask at once" (65-66). We should, then, he argues, see such matters as the sabbath, circumcision, abstinence from eating pork addressed (66). Similarly Victor A. Tcherikover, "The Ideology of the Letter of Aristeas," *HTR* 51 (1958) 59–85, 62; Schimanowski, *Aristeasbrief*, 61.

[393] So Tcherikover, "Ideology," who writes: "He never preached assimilation among the Greeks. On the contrary, the whole Letter is nothing if not a eulogy to Judaism. Not assimilation among the Gentiles is Aristeas' aspiration, but the opening of the world of culture before Jews and Judaism. He would like to enter this world with his head held high, like a man who has mighty cultural values in his possession, open to everyone, Jews and Gentiles alike. But these values are inseparably connected with the Torah" (79).

[394] So Tcherikover, "Ideology," 84.

[395] Collins, *Between Athens and Jerusalem*, sees the author as "proclaiming the adequacy of the Septuagint over against the Hebrew" (103); Tcherikover, "Ideology," writes that from the author's perspective: "from now on the Jews would not need the Hebrew language any more, even in their religious service; Greek, the language of the King

might compromise their faith.[396] The latter would certainly be on side with the attack on sexual perversion, while the former would recognise it as consistent with the enlightened philosophy they admired. The author opens to us a window on what might well have been the stance of many educated Jews living in Alexandria. As Hadas writes:

> Aristeas' views of Jews and Judaism cannot have been his own but must reflect the unique social, intellectual, and spiritual climate of the Egyptian Jews in the second century BCE, when their numbers and prestige had made them a considerable element in the population and before anti-Semitism had raised its head.[397]

After a transition in which the author reports the departure of the delegation from Eleazar and its special welcome by the king, marked to be a day of celebration coinciding with the celebration of a sea victory over Antigonus, the author describes preparations for a banquet, in which Jewish scruples about food are carefully respected and the usual pagan religious rites replaced by a prayer led by

---

and the State, would serve for all their spiritual needs, and there would be no language barrier between the Jews and the Greeks" (76).

[396] Tcherikover, "Ideology," speaks of "those Jews who have not yet freed themselves from the 'lack of education and stubbornness' of their Palestinian brethren. Those were people who continued to use the Hebrew Torah in spite of the fact that it was preserved in Alexandria only in bad copies (30), and who commented on the Torah in a rational way and not in the fashion of allegorical interpretation (144)" (83). "Very cautiously he tries to impress upon his readers the idea that no abyss separates Judaism from Hellenism. With some good will on both sides, it would be easy to bridge the two worlds" (69). Similarly Schimanowski, *Aristeasbrief*, 62; Gruen, *Heritage and Hellenism*, who writes that the synthesis which the writer seeks to achieve is not between Judaism and Hellenism, but "between Diaspora Jews and the center in Jerusalem" (221). Collins, *Between Athens and Jerusalem*, summarises the author's view: "The Torah, to be properly appreciated, must be complemented by Greek culture" (194). See also Noah Hacham, "The Letter of Aristeas: A New Exodus story?" *JSJ* 36 (2005) 1-20, who writes: "The ideology of *Aristeas* is thus expressed clearly: a total commitment to the Torah and its sanctity on the one hand, and a Greek casting for the Egyptian Jews on the other. In other words, the Torah is accepted into the Hellenistic world with no reservations whatsoever" (4). He argues that the author adapts the exodus story to create a new foundation story which explains how Jews in Egypt live in very different circumstances and why to remain there is appropriate. "Therefore, leaving Egypt is unfitting as it is where a new world is created regarding Jews, a world of mutual appreciation and foreign participation in the Jewish religion" (15).

[397] Hadas, *Aristeas*, 63. Similarly Tcherikover, "Ideology," 85; Gruen, *Heritage and Hellenism*, who writes: "The treatise plainly portrays cultivated Jews as comfortable in a Hellenic setting, attuned to Greek customs and modes of thought, and content under the protection of a Hellenistic monarch" (215).

the eldest priest among the delegates (182-186). The emphasis on the Jewish food laws and customs here matches the concern about separateness, probably serving as a model of what the author deemed as appropriate where commensality occurred, in which the king and his entourage conform to Jewish standards: "'Everything of which you partake,' he said, 'will be served in compliance with your habits; it will be served to me as well as to you'" (πάντα {δι' ὑμῖν}, εἶπε, παρέσται καθηκόντως, οἷς συγχρήσησθε, κ'ἀμοὶ μεθ' ὑμῶν) (181).[398]

There follows an extensive section in which the king poses a question related to kingship to each of the 72 guests in 5 groups of 10 and 2 of 11 (187-294).[399] There is nothing particularly Jewish in the sages' replies, aside from the sometimes artificial references to God.[400] The elaborate account serves to prove the superiority of Jewish wisdom,[401] but does so in terms reflecting common values about governance. As Barclay notes, "here the most brilliant of all the Ptolemaic kings, the patron of the greatest centre of Hellenistic culture, stands in awe of Judaism, whose representatives astound him with their wisdom (200-1, 293-94, 312)".[402] The responses emphasise divine control, not least in affirming existing orders, including the king's authority, as determined by God. They also espouse a sense of one's honour: "Always have an eye to your glory and prominence, so that you may say and think what is consistent with it" (218). The "highest form of glory" is "honouring God. This is not done with gifts or sacrifices, but with purity of heart and of devout disposition" (234). This is a

---

[398] Barclay, *Jews in the Mediterranean Diaspora*, observes that the work "enables us to see with peculiar clarity how certain Jews wished themselves to be perceived by non-Jews and on what basis they wished their relationships to be conducted" (139). Similarly Hacham, "Aristeas," who writes: "The Jews did not refrain from reclining in the banquet with the foreign king, obviously because of his positive traits, and because such a person will not affect the Jews dining with him in any negative way" (17).

[399] Hadas, *Aristeas*, notes in relation to teaching about governance that "the tradition was at its strongest and freshest early in the Hellenistic period when the problem of kingship was new and pressing" (42) and finds similar values reflected in Hecataeus (45). See also Murray, "Aristeas and Ptolemaic Kingship," 337-38. On the awkwardness of having 7 days instead of 6 times 12, he suggests that this may reflect a model where Alexander faced 10 questions each day (348). He also notes absence of any comment about the significance of the sabbath in this context (348).

[400] So Collins, *Between Athens and Jerusalem*, 194; similar Gruen, *Heritage and Hellenism*, who writes: "The dragging of God into every response, even when patently artificial or altogether immaterial, might well have coaxed a smile from the *Letter*'s readers" (219).

[401] Gruen, *Heritage and Hellenism*, who writes: "Jews have not only digested Hellenic culture, they have also surmounted it. The *Letter* plainly addresses itself, first and foremost, at Jews" (221).

[402] Barclay, *Jews in the Mediterranean Diaspora*, 142.

widely attested relative contrast which sets priorities of the one above the other, not a rejection of cult, which would not fit the value which the author has given to it earlier in the work. Generosity and clemency are also strongly espoused, including towards opponents (227).

Particular attention is given to moderation (209), and self-control. Thus in response to the question, "What must be one's conduct in relaxation and leisure?" we hear: Θεωρεῖν ὅσα {παίζεται} μετὰ περιστολῆς καὶ πρὸ ὀφθαλμῶν τιθέναι τὰ τοῦ βίου μετ' εὐσχημοσύνης καὶ καταστολῆς γινόμενα {βίῳ συμφέρον καὶ καθῆκον}. ἔνεστι γὰρ καὶ ἐν τούτοις ἐπισκευή τις ("Be a spectator of entertainments which exercise restraint and keep before your eyes things in life done with decency and moderation – that is suitable and appropriate to life") (284; cf. also 246). Among what might be considered indecent and immoderate acts of entertainment will also be those of a sexual nature. The same is true of the advice about banquets, where, however, only positive advice is proffered, hailing the kind of intellectual entertainment which this banquet, itself, exemplifies (286-287). The author assumes his Jewish hearers attend both theatre and banquets.

The concern with excess and self-control recurs frequently. What matters is "real self-mastery, not being carried away by wealth and glamour, nor having, as a result overweening or unworthy ambitions (τὸ καλῶς ἄρχειν ἑαυτοῦ, καὶ μὴ τῷ πλούτῳ καὶ τῇ δόξῃ φερόμενον ὑπερήφανον καὶ ἄσχημόν τι ἐπιθυμῆσαι) ... do not desire overmuch (μὴ πολλῶν ὀρέγου)" (211); "control of oneself , and not being carried away by one's impulses ... the majority are likely to incline toward things to eat and drink and pleasure (τὸ κρατεῖν ἑαυτοῦ καὶ μὴ συγκαταφέρεσθαι ταῖς ὁρμαῖς. πᾶσι γὰρ ἀνθρώποις φυσικὸν εἶναι τὸ πρός τι τὴν διάνοιαν ῥέπειν)" (222-223, similarly 237). According to 256 "philosophy" is to have "a well-reasoned assessment of each occurrence ... and not to be carried away by impulses but to study carefully the harmful consequences of the passions" (τὸ καλῶς διαλογίζεσθαι πρὸς ἕκαστον τῶν συμβαινόντων ... καὶ μὴ ἐκφέρεσθαι ταῖς ὁρμαῖς, ἀλλὰ τὰς βλάβας καταμελετᾶν τὰς ἐκ τῶν ἐπιθυμιῶν ἐκβαινούσας). Another response declares

277 ὅτι φυσικῶς ἅπαντες, εἶπεν, ἀκρατεῖς καὶ ἐπὶ τὰς ἡδονὰς τρεπόμενοι γεγόνασιν· ὧν χάριν ἀδικία πέφυκε καὶ τὸ τῆς πλεονεξίας χύμα. 278 τὸ δὲ τῆς ἀρετῆς κατάστημα κωλύει τοὺς ἐπιφερομένους ἐπὶ τὴν ἡδονοκρασίαν, ἐγκράτειαν δὲ κελεύει καὶ δικαιοσύνην προτιμᾶν. ὁ δὲ θεὸς πάντων ἡγεῖται τούτων.

277 that all men have become naturally intemperate and inclined to pleasures, as a result of which injustice came about and the mass of greed. 278 The virtuous disposition, on the other hand, restrains those who are attracted to the rule of pleasure, and commands them to respect self-control and justice more highly. God directs all these matters. (277-78)

Taken together these statements espouse moderation and control of the passions and impulses, among which we may assume are sexual desires. These are probably in view in the question about women: πῶς {ἂν} ἁρμόσαι γυναικί; "How can one reach agreement with a woman?" (250) The answer is revealing:

> 250 {γινώσκων} ὅτι μὲν θρασύ ἐστιν, ἔφη, τὸ θῆλυ γένος, καὶ δραστικὸν ἐφ' ὃ βούλεται πρᾶγμα, καὶ μεταπίπτον εὐκόπως διὰ παραλογισμοῦ, καὶ τῇ φύσει κατασκεύασται ἀσθενές· δέον δ'ἐστι κατὰ τὸ ὑγιὲς χρῆσθαι, καὶ μὴ πρὸς ἔριν ἀντιπράσσειν. 251 κατορθοῦται γὰρ βίος, ὅταν ὁ κυβερνῶν εἰδῇ, πρὸς τίνα σκοπὸν δεῖ τὴν διέξοδον ποιεῖσθαι. Θεοῦ δ'ἐπικλήσει καὶ βίος κυβερνᾶται κατὰ πάντα.
>
> 250 "By recognizing," he replied, "that the female sex is bold, positively active for something which it desires, easily liable to change its mind because of poor reasoning powers, and of naturally weak constitution. It is necessary to have dealings with them in a sound way, avoiding provocation which may lead to a quarrel. 251 Life prospers when the helmsman knows the goal to which he must take the passage. Life is completely steered by invocation of God". (250-251)

This passage assumes not only that women have inferior minds and weaker constitutions, a standard element in Peripatetic philosophy,[403] but that their desires are excessive and difficult to control. While not specifying sexual desire, this will doubtless be included in what the author had in mind. Accordingly males must control women, including their sexuality. It is interesting that while family is valued as support (241-242) and neglect of children eschewed (248; cf. also the concern for women and children transported by Ptolemy I, in 14), nothing is said of marriage.[404]

The author returns to his direct address to Polycrates claiming that "all who will inherit this narrative will, I think, find it incredible" (297) and asserting its integrity and inerrancy. He then finally reports the undertaking of the translation which he claims was achieved on the basis of agreement after comparing versions (302), miraculously within 72 days (307), was received with acclamation (308-310) and sealed with a curse against all who might alter it (311). The author then explains absence of references to the Jewish Law in previous Greek literature on the basis that those who intended to use it had suffered afflictions (312-316). This is a more conservative stance than those of Aristobulus and Philo who claimed that the great Greek philosophers learned their wisdom from the Law of Moses.[405] The

---

[403] So Hadas, *Aristeas*, 198.

[404] Murray, "Aristeas and Ptolemaic Kingship," suggests that "the question about how to get on with one's wife and its answer (250) might recall the struggles of Physcon and Cleopatra II; the general condemnation of women would be appropriate after the death of Cleopatra III" (370).

[405] So Collins, *Between Athens and Jerusalem*, 191.

work ends with an account of the king sending the delegation back to Jerusalem but with the assurance of a welcome should ever any of them return (317-321). Nothing in this final section pertains to sexuality.

Conclusion

Pseudo-Aristeas has one single explicit sexual reference in which it condemns male homosexual prostitution and incest with mothers and daughters (152). Beside that it mentions a number of contexts where sexual issues might have arisen, including large cities, public entertainment and banquets, and says much about controlling passions, among which sexual passions were doubtless included, not least in its image of women's desires which need men's control, but in all of these the allusion is by implication only. While the author has obviously imbibed typically Stoic values of moderation and self-control, especially of the passions, including by implication sexual desire, and is concerned to argue the reasonableness of those elements in his religion which might seem odd, not least, regarding foods and unclean animals, he also shows himself as in many respects conservative. He does not espouse the view that Greek culture is beholden to the teachings of Moses. He insists on observance of the food laws he is happy to allegorise. He envisages commensality but only on Jewish conditions. While his disparaging remarks about the idolatry and wickedness of other peoples would have sat comfortably with popular philosophers of his day, his insistence on separation, and on measures to ensure it, is noteworthy, despite the defence that the ultimate goals coincide with popular Hellenistic ideals. It is likely in this regard that he would have generally disapproved of intermarriage, but allowed for exceptions providing comparable piety was evident.

On matters of sexual wrongdoing the author assumes he is making common cause with the best of Greek thought, though his examples of convergence are rather limited (using male prostitutes) and extreme (incest with mothers and daughters). Aside from sharing the typically negative view of women derived from Peripatetic influence, and possibly a particular reading of Genesis 2 – 3,[406] to which, however, he makes no direct reference, the author has nothing to say about a wide range of areas pertaining to family and sexual relations which featured in Jewish or Greek literature or both, including marriage, sexual intimacy, procreation, abortion, contraception, adultery, divorce, polygyny, rape, abduction, divorce, same-sex relations male and female other than prostitution, pederasty, and incest beyond the instances mentioned. Important texts on marriage and sexuality such as Genesis 1 – 3 leave no trace. Instead we find two fairly extreme examples of wrongdoing, and warnings about passions and self-control, which have their

---

[406] See Loader, *Septuagint*, 58.

home in popular philosophy. The author gives no indication that his Jewish tradition has anything particularly commendable or worth mentioning in the sexual realm which he might commend as enhancing pride in the Law.

3.2.4   4 Maccabees

This work is written in sophisticated Greek[407] in florid Asian style[408] by an author well versed in Greek rhetorical skills and popular philosophy,[409] but totally committed to observance of Torah as a way of life. It was probably composed some time in the mid to late first century C.E. in the region between Syrian Antioch and Asia Minor.[410] It addresses Jews who would have appreciated engagement with the Greco-Roman culture of their neighbours while maintaining adherence to their own law and able to catch the author's allusions to the biblical heritage.[411] In form it presents itself as philosophical discourse (cf. φιλοσοφώτατον λόγον ἐπιδείκνυσθαι μέλλων, "I am about to discuss an eminently philosophical subject"; 1:1), while also incorporating praise

---

[407] The text edition used in this chapter is that of Rahlfs/Hanhart, *Septuaginta*, and the English translation that of *NETS*, unless I have provided my own (indicated by an asterisk). I also take into account the Sinaiticus text and its discussion in David A. deSilva, *4 Maccabees: Introduction and Commentary on the Greek Text in Codex Sinaiticus* (SCS; Leiden: Brill, 2006).

[408] E. Norden, *Die antike Kunstprosa vom VI. Jahrhundert v. Chr. bis in die Zeit der Renaissance* (2 vols; 7th ed.; Darmstadt: Wissenschaftliche Buchgesellschaft, 1974) 1.416-20; Hans-Josef Klauck, *4. Makkabäerbuch* (JSHRZ 3.6; Gütersloh: Mohn, 1989) 665.

[409] On this see deSilva, *4 Maccabees*, xii-xiii. Barclay, *Jews in the Mediterranean Diaspora*, comments: "his engagement with Hellenism has touched only the surface of his faith; it has not brought about any fundamental reconceptualization of Judaism" (374). Referring to his language and style Klauck, *4. Makkabäerbuch*, observes that it only makes sense on the basis that the author must have had a rhetorical education (665). He notes that his use of philosophical material is eclectic, based on what he had imbibed in his schooling, and shows no particular interest in differentiating its diverse sources (666).

[410] So deSilva, *4 Maccabees*, xiv-xx. He sees "the least assailable case" (xvi) for dating as indicated through 4:2 which has changed the description of Apollonius' jurisdiction in 2 Macc 3:5 to "Syria, Phoenicia, and Cilicia", which were under a single administration 19 – 72 C.E. (xv-xvi), but as Klauck, *4. Makkabäerbuch*, notes, this does no more than establish the *post quem* date (668-69). Klauck argues for the last decade of the century. Similarly Collins, *Between Athens and Jerusalem*, 203-204; J. W. van Henten, "Datierung und Herkunft des Vierten Makkabäerbuches," in *Tradition and Re-interpretation in Jewish and Early Christian Literature: Essays in Honour of Jurgen C. H. Lebram* (ed. J. W. van Henten, H. J. de Jonge, et. al.; SPB; JSJSup 36; Leiden: Brill, 1986) 136-49, 145.

[411] So deSilva, *4 Maccabees*, xix-xx.

(encomium) of martyrs, who exemplify its argument.[412] As deSilva puts it, "the fundamental purpose of 4 Maccabees is to stimulate commitment to the Jewish way of life, especially the covenant stipulations of Torah (18:1-2)".[413] That includes such matters as refusing to eat pork, about which the author shows no signs of the allegorising tendencies of *Pseudo-Aristeas* and Philo by which they seek to make sense of these requirements.[414]

The Passions

Most of this work, all but the first three of eighteen chapters, is taken up with an account of the bravery of an elderly priest, Eleazar, and then of seven brothers and their mother, who underwent a cruel death at the hands of Antiochus because they refused to abandon the Law by eating pork. This account does more than impress listeners with models of Torah faithfulness. For the author it also demonstrates a proof for his thesis, enunciated in his opening sentence, that "pious reason is absolute master of the passions" (αὐτοδέσποτός ἐστιν τῶν παθῶν ὁ εὐσεβὴς λογισμός),[415] a theme constantly repeated throughout both the narrative of martyrdom (5:23; 6:31, 33, 35; 7:16, 18, 23; 13:1, 3-5, 16; 14:1; 15:1; 16:1; 18:2) and all the more intensively in the opening chapters which provide a systematic exposition of its parts (1:1, 3-5, 7, 9, 13-14, 19, 29-31, 33; 2:6, 7, 9, 18, 24; 3:17-

---

[412] On the combination of both philosophical discourse and encomium see deSilva, *4 Maccabees*, xxi-xxiii. See also the extensive discussion in David A. deSilva, *4 Maccabees* (GAP; Sheffield: Sheffield Academic Press, 1998) 51-126.

[413] deSilva, *4 Maccabees*, xxvi. He also reviews the various proposals about the possible setting for which it was composed, including the anniversary of the martyrdoms, Hanukkah, celebrating the purification of the temple, or another festival focused on the Law (xxiii-xxv). The primary focus, however, is not martyrdoms or liberation but living according to Torah, which was a relevant theme in many settings. So also Klauck, *4. Makkabäerbuch*, 664. See also deSilva, *4 Maccabees* (GAP), 21-25. The work does not function as paraenesis by promoting particular ethical behaviours. See the discussion in Stephen Westerholm, "Four Maccabees: A Paraenetic Address?" in *Early Christian Paraenesis in Context* (ed. James Starr and Troels Engberg-Pedersen; BZNW 125; Berlin: de Gruyter, 2004) 191-216.

[414] So deSilva, *4 Maccabees*, xvii; Collins, *Between Athens and Jerusalem*, 206; Klauck, *4. Makkabäerbuch*, though he notes some allegorisation in 5:26 and observes in addition that the work lacks any personification of wisdom reflected in the Alexandrian works (667).

[415] The thesis gave the work the title preserved in Eusebius and Jerome: Περὶ αὐτοκράτορος λογισμοῦ. On this see Klauck, *4. Makkabäerbuch*, 647; deSilva, *4 Maccabees*, xiv.

18).[416] In the expression ὁ εὐσεβὴς λογισμός the word εὐσεβής is of crucial significance, because it preserves the author's emphasis that not just reason or reasoning (λογισμός), but reasoning informed by Torah is the secret to controlling the dangers which the passions pose.[417] While the martyrdom stories depict mastery of the passions of fear and pain, the exposition in the first three chapters deals with a range of passions, including sexual desire.

The initial systematic treatment deals with passions under two categories, pleasure and pain, understood as belonging in two different sequences: desire-pleasure-delight and fear-pain-sorrow (1:20-22). Earlier the author distinguishes between control of gluttony and lust and control of passions which impede justice, such as malice, and those impeding courage, such as anger, fear and pain (1:3-4). Neither pleasure nor pain is something evil in itself. Both are like plants within us which need tending. "By weeding, pruning, tying up, watering and in every way irrigating each of these, reason, the master cultivator, tames the jungles of habits and passions" (1:29).[418]

Illustrating desire, the author first focuses on control of appetite, particularly for forbidden food (1:32-35), the aspect later elaborately illustrated through the bravery of the martyrs and, along with sexual relations, a major issue in social

---

[416] On the integration between the philosophical discourse and the martyrdom narratives as demonstration, supporting the philosophical argument, see Klauck, *4. Makkabäerbuch*, 649-50; deSilva, *4 Maccabees*, xxvi-xxviii.

[417] deSilva, *4 Maccabees*, writes: "This single adjective will come to encompass reasoning and walking in conformity with the religious and ethical heritage of the Jewish people as expressed in the Jewish Scriptures (and particularly in the way of life defined by observance of the Torah)" (68; similarly 70). See also his discussion of the role of piety in philosophical ethics (70). "Even though the author claims that his speech has as its purpose the demonstration of a proposition, an impression promoted through the frequent return to this proposition throughout the speech as a refrain, it quickly becomes clear that the author's principal interest is in promoting the world view and way of life that he regards as the superlative means by which his hearers can advance reason's mastery over the passions and maintain an honorable life of virtue" (68). Similarly Weber, *Gesetz im hellenistischen Judentum*, 215. Cf. Mary Rose D'Angelo, "Εὐσεβεία: Roman Imperial Family Values and the Sexual Politics of 4 Maccabees and the Pastorals," *BibInt* 11 (2003) 139-65, who claims that in 4 Maccabees "εὐσεβεία appears to carry the implications of *pietas*, the Roman and imperial virtue that best approximates 'family values' combined with religious observance. Εὐσεβεία is thus manifested in appropriate familial relations" (131, 150). These are certainly present in 18:7-10, but they are part of a broader understanding which is fundamentally Torah faithfulness and goes beyond family values to include such matters as observance of food laws, so central to the work's main exemplars.

[418] Similarly Ellis, *Sexual Desire*, 68.

relations of Jews with outsiders.[419] Then in 2:2-3 he turns to sexual desire, citing the example of Joseph:

2 διανοίᾳ περιεκράτησεν τῆς ἡδυπαθείας. 3 νέος γὰρ ὢν καὶ ἀκμάζων πρὸς συνουσιασμὸν ἠκύρωσε τῷ λογισμῷ τὸν τῶν παθῶν οἶστρον.

2 by his faculty of thinking he gained control over the urge for gratification. 3 For when he was a young man and in his prime for intercourse, by his reason he rendered powerless the frenzied desire of his passions. (2:2-3)

The author assumes that his hearers are familiar with the account in Gen 39:7-12 of Joseph's resisting the attempted seduction by Potiphar's wife. As to be expected it was widely used as an example of rejecting sexual wrongdoing, both as adultery and as pre-marital chastity,[420] such as in *Jub.* 39:5-11; Wis 10:13; *T. Jos.* 3 – 9; and *Asen.* 4:7; 7:3, 5,[421] where it is also closely associated with issues of food (19:11), as also in the Additions to Esther C 26, 28 and Jdt 10:3-5.[422] deSilva notes that by emphasising that Joseph was "young" (νέος), the author shows that "Joseph's display of self-control was all the more admirable", citing Aristotle on the potency of such desire in the young (*Rhet.* 2.12.3).[423] The author then explains:

4 καὶ οὐ μόνον δὲ τὴν τῆς ἡδυπαθείας οἰστρηλασίαν ὁ λογισμὸς ἐπικρατεῖν φαίνεται, ἀλλὰ καὶ πάσης ἐπιθυμίας. 5 λέγει γοῦν ὁ νόμος Οὐκ ἐπιθυμήσεις τὴν γυναῖκα τοῦ πλησίον σου οὐδὲ ὅσα τῷ πλησίον σού ἐστιν. 6 καίτοι ὅτε μὴ ἐπιθυμεῖν εἴρηκεν ἡμᾶς ὁ νόμος, πολὺ πλέον πείσαιμ' ἂν ὑμᾶς ὅτι τῶν ἐπιθυμιῶν κρατεῖν δύναται ὁ λογισμός.

---

[419] On this see Petra von Gemünden, "Der Affekt der ἐπιθυμία und der νόμος: Affektkontrolle und soziale Identitätsbildung im 4. Makkabäerbuch mit einem Ausblick auf den Römerbrief," in *Das Gesetz im frühen Judentum und im Neuen Testament: Festschrift für Christoph Burchard zum 75. Geburtstag* (ed. Dieter Sänger and Matthias Konradt; NTOA 57; Göttingen: Vandenhoeck & Ruprecht; Fribourg: Academic Press, 2006) 55-74, 53, 66. She notes 1:30 – 2:6a deals with two important issues of social significance: sexual intercourse with outsiders (2:1-3) and the much more critical problem of eating food forbidden in Torah (1:33-35) (68).

[420] von Gemünden, "Affekt," observes that Joseph is widely used as a model of pre-marital chastity (σωφροσύνη) (65).

[421] von Gemünden, "Affekt," 64.

[422] von Gemünden, "Affekt," 65-66. Klauck, *4. Makkabäerbuch*, draws attention to Stoic-Cynic accounts of Heracles as model of resisting sexual wrongdoing through philosophy (695).

[423] deSilva, *4 Maccabees*, 94. He sees this reflected in the author's use of "the colorful image of the gadfly that continually stings and drives its host mad" (94). On the young resisting sexual wrongdoing in Roman literature, Klauck, *4. Makkabäerbuch*, draws attention to Xenophon of Ephesus 2.5.1-7; Heliodorus 1.9.3 – 10.4; 11.9.1 (695).

4 It is apparent that reason prevails not only over the frenzied urge for gratification but also over every desire. 5 For the law says, "You shall not covet your neighbor's wife or anything that is your neighbor's". 6 In fact, since the law has told us not to covet, I could persuade you all the more that reason is able to overcome the desires. (2:4-6)

Thus the author cites only the last of the ten commandments,[424] but thereby gives it particular prominence.[425] He cites it in the form in which it appears in the LXX, where in Deut 5:21 it is singled out as a prohibition on its own and in Exod 20:17 it has been made the first item in the list of what should not be coveted, compared with the Hebrew in both instances which begins with the neighbour's household.[426] The author has chosen to cite only the initial prohibition, directly related to Joseph's situation, and its generalising conclusion (οὐδὲ ὅσα τῷ πλησίον σού ἐστιν, "or anything that is your neighbour's"), which enables him to apply it more broadly to show that the Law addresses wrongly-directed desire of any kind, not only adulterous desire. This probably reflects the understanding that this commandment could summarise all the commandments of the second table (cf. also Rom 7:7).[427]

The passage illustrates by citing the commandment, what the author understands to be the basis for controlling the passions, namely a mind informed and made wise by knowing and upholding the Law, in this instance, the prohibition of coveting. In treating other passions we find a similar appeal to the biblical law and to examples from biblical history. These include Jacob's disapproval of the anger of Levi and Simeon which led to the slaughter of the Shechemites (2:19, citing Gen 49:7 LXX), a deed celebrated elsewhere as heroic (*ALD* 78; Jdt 9:2-4; *Asen.* 23:14 ; *Theod.* frag. 7-8) and made the focus of instruction about sexual wrongdoing and prohibiting intermarriage with Gentiles (*Jub.* 30:1-23; cf. also *ALD* 3a / 4QLevi[b] ar/4Q213a 3-4), but not here.[428]

Understood in its context, the author's statement, μὴ ἐπιθυμεῖν εἴρηκεν ἡμᾶς ὁ νόμος ("the law has told us not to covet") (2:6), is not an instruction to root out desire, including sexual desire and pleasure, as something evil, but rather

---

[424] Unlike *Jub.* 39:6; and *T. Jos.* 3:3, the author sees no need to address the anachronism that the commandments were given after the time of Joseph. Cf. Gruen, *Heritage and Hellenism*, 79-80.

[425] So deSilva, *4 Maccabees*, 95.

[426] On this see Loader, *Septuagint*, 8-9.

[427] Klauck, *4. Makkabäerbuch*, 695; von Gemünden, "Affekt," 67.

[428] deSilva, *4 Maccabees*, suggests that the author's critical stance may reflect the situation of being a minority where xenophobic behaviour was to be avoided as much as possible (103). "The author is intent on showing that 'zeal for the law' does not necessarily lead to acts of aggression that would render the body politic unstable" (103). Interestingly the author cites Phinehas' zeal in 18:16 as something positive, but offers no detail.

to control it.[429] As Ellis notes, "presumably, the author of *4 Maccabees* knows that Joseph engaged in sexual intercourse in the context of marriage".[430] When the author writes in 2:1 αἱ τῆς ψυχῆς ἐπιθυμίαι πρὸς τὴν τοῦ κάλλους μετουσίαν ἀκυροῦνται ("the desires of the soul for enjoyment of beauty are rendered powerless"), neither desire nor beauty is being outlawed. They are part of God's creation. The issue is control. Accordingly, the author explains:

21 ὁπηνίκα γὰρ ὁ θεὸς τὸν ἄνθρωπον κατεσκεύασεν, τὰ πάθη αὐτοῦ καὶ τὰ ἤθη περιεφύτευσεν. 22 ἡνίκα δὲ ἐπὶ πάντων τὸν ἱερὸν ἡγεμόνα νοῦν διὰ τῶν αἰσθητηρίων ἐνεθρόνισεν, 23 καὶ τούτῳ νόμον ἔδωκεν, καθ' ὃν πολιτευόμενος βασιλεύσει βασιλείαν σώφρονά τε καὶ δικαίαν καὶ ἀγαθὴν καὶ ἀνδρείαν.

21 Now when God fashioned human beings, he planted in them their passions and habits, 22 but at the same time he enthroned the mind among the senses as a sacred governor over them all. 23 And to this mind he gave the law. The one who adopts a way of life in accordance with it will rule a kingdom that is temperate, just, good and courageous. (2:21-23)

Like Philo he employs the garden as an image to represent the planting of faculties within the human being (*Leg.* 1.43-55).[431] And like Philo (*Leg.* 3.118; *Opif.* 30) and, before him, Zeno, and Plato with his famed image in the *Phaedrus* of the charioteer, he understands the mind as governor of the passions, but here, a mind shaped by Torah,[432] so that the mind to the passions is like Torah to nature/creation.[433] On the other hand, as Aune notes, in contrast to Philo the author rejects the Platonic tripartite division of the soul: "therefore, since passions are not part of a lower, 'lustful' portion of the human soul, he cannot conceive of them as being completely removed from the soul".[434] Within this framework sexual desire is therefore not something to be denied or denigrated but something positive, but

---

[429] So rightly Ellis, *Sexual Desire*, 67.

[430] Ellis, *Sexual Desire*, 71.

[431] So deSilva, *4 Maccabees*, 103; Klauck, *4. Makkabäerbuch*, 699.

[432] Collins, *Between Athens and Jerusalem*, 207. deSilva, *4 Maccabees*, notes that in *Gorgias* 504D Plato depicts the function of the "law" as helping to provide such governance (104): "And the regular and orderly states of the soul are called lawfulness and law, whereby men are similarly made law-abiding and orderly; and these states are justice and temperance."

[433] So Weber, *Gesetz im hellenistischen Judentum*, 220-21.

[434] David E. Aune, "Mastery of the Passions: Philo, 4 Maccabees and Earliest Christianity," in *Hellenization Revisited: Shaping a Christian Response within the Greco-Roman World* (ed. Wendy E. Helleman; Lanham: University Press of America, 1994) 125-58, 136, and on Philo, p. 139. Cf. also Weber, *Gesetz im hellenistischen Judentum*, 241-48.

needing discipline and direction, in accordance with biblical law.[435] The author makes this very clear: οἷον ἐπιθυμίαν τις οὐ δύναται ἐκκόψαι ἡμῶν ἀλλὰ μὴ δουλωθῆναι τῇ ἐπιθυμίᾳ δύναται ὁ λογισμὸς παρασχέσθαι ("No one of us can eradicate such desire, but reason can provide a way for us not to be enslaved by it") (3:2). As deSilva argues, "from 2:21-22 it is clear why the author would disagree with the majority Stoic view that the πάθη are bad in themselves ..., being created and pronounced 'good' by God",[436] pointing to the affinity of the author's stance to "Plato (Phaedo 93-94), Poseidonius and the Peripatetics that the passions were to be controlled, or moderated (metriopathein), and not destroyed (cf. Plutarch, On Moral Virtue 3 [Moralia 442A-443D)"[437] and even more so to Pseudo-Aristeas (211, 222, 237, 256).[438]

The Human Family

The other references to sexuality in the broadest sense are to be found within the narratives of martyrdom. Confronted with the demand that they eat pork, Eleazar responds to the king, reaffirming the author's theme that the Law teaches the self-control that enables people to overcome all pleasures and desires and to withstand the kind of pain which his refusal will bring (5:23).[439] Beside the generalisations about control (e.g. 5:34-37; 6:31-33; 7:16-23), specific references relate to enduring the pain in prospect. The same is true in the accounts of the seven young men (e.g. 8:27-29; 13:1-4). At the conclusion of those accounts the author emphasises the bonds of brotherhood in the first of a number of references to pregnancy, childbirth, and mothering. The purpose is to show that the brothers' reason, their adherence to Torah, enabled them even "to overcome the passions of brotherly love"* (τῶν τῆς φιλαδελφίας παθῶν κρατῆσαι) (14:1).

---

[435] So Aune, "Mastery of the Passions," who writes: "the author of 4 Macc, while not using the term *apatheia* or describing the passions as being entirely rooted out, suggests that complete mastery over the passions is possible for anyone who is willing to obey the Law" (139).

[436] deSilva, *4 Maccabees*, 103; so also Klauck, *4. Makkabäerbuch*, 666; similarly deSilva, *4 Maccabees* (GAP), 53-54. He also notes that the author does not espouse the idea of the "evil inclination" of Jewish anthropology, but rather sees inclinations and passions as something which "can be cultivated for good or perverted for evil depending on the possessor's cultivation of the same" (103).

[437] deSilva, *4 Maccabees* (GAP), 53. See also Aune, "Mastery of the Passions," 136.

[438] See deSilva, *4 Maccabees*, 67.

[439] Klauck, *4. Makkabäerbuch*, notes that that Stoics, Seneca, especially, often used stories of Stoic martyrs to reinforce the correctness of their teaching (662).

19 οὐκ ἀγνοεῖτε δὲ τὰ τῆς ἀδελφότητος φίλτρα, ἅπερ ἡ θεία καὶ πάνσοφος πρόνοια διὰ πατέρων τοῖς γεννωμένοις ἐμέρισεν καὶ διὰ τῆς μητρῴας φυτεύσασα γαστρός, 20 ἐν ᾗ τὸν ἴσον ἀδελφοὶ κατοικήσαντες χρόνον καὶ ἐν τῷ αὐτῷ χρόνῳ πλασθέντες καὶ ἀπὸ τοῦ αὐτοῦ αἵματος αὐξηθέντες καὶ διὰ τῆς αὐτῆς ψυχῆς τελεσφορηθέντες 21 καὶ διὰ τῶν ἴσων ἀποτεχθέντες χρόνων καὶ ἀπὸ τῶν αὐτῶν γαλακτοποτοῦντες πηγῶν, ἀφ' ὧν συντρέφονται[440] ἐναγκαλισμάτων φιλάδελφοι ψυχαί· 22 καὶ αὔξονται σφοδρότερον διὰ συντροφίας καὶ τῆς καθ' ἡμέραν συνηθείας καὶ τῆς ἄλλης παιδείας καὶ τῆς ἡμετέρας ἐν νόμῳ θεοῦ ἀσκήσεως.

19 You are not ignorant of the bonds of brotherhood, which the divine and all-wise Providence has allotted through fathers to their descendants, implanting them through their mother's womb. 20 In that womb brothers dwell an equal length of time and are shaped for the same time. They grow from the same blood, and from the same lifespring they are brought to mature birth. 21 Born after an equal time of gestation, they drink milk from the same fountains by whose embraces minds filled with brotherly love are nourished together. 22 They grow robust through common nurture, daily companionship, other education and our discipline in divine law. (13:19-22)

Brotherly affection (φιλαδελφία) was a well known theme in Greco-Roman literature.[441] Citing Plutarch's treatise, [*On Brotherly Love*] *De fraterno amore* (*Mor.* 478A-492D) and Aristotle's discussion in *Eth. nic.* 8.12.3-4 (1161b30-1162a2); 8.12.6 (1162a9-15), deSilva observes that "nearly every detail of the discussion of 'the affection of brotherhood' in 4 Macc 13:19 – 14:1 is represented also in these and other non-Jewish texts".[442] When 13:19 speaks of the bonds of brotherhood being implanted through the wombs of mothers, this may simply refer to the whole process of being born through the same mother, but it could be more specific and reflect the view that the father implants seed in the mother who

---

[440] deSilva, *4 Maccabees*, notes that the reading in Sinaiticus, συνστρέφονται ("are compacted together"), seems "much more appropriate to the topics of fraternal unity, harmony, and solidarity that will be invoked so heavily by the author than the more neutral 'they were nursed together' favored in Rahlfs's critical text" (211).

[441] On the theme in 4 Maccabees compared with Plutarch see Hans-Josef Klauck, "Brotherly Love in Plutarch and in 4 Maccabees," in *Greeks, Romans and Christians: Essays in Honour of Abraham J. Malherbe* (ed. David L. Balch; Everett Ferguson; Wayne A. Meeks; Minneapolis: Fortress, 1990) 144-56, who sees the author writing at about the same time as Plutarch but with the claim for internal Jewish consumption that its brotherly love is superior (155). See also Klauck, *4. Makkabäerbuch*, 738-39.

[442] deSilva, *4 Maccabees*, 210. He notes that already Xenophon described the basis of the bonds of sibling affection as the father's seed and mother's nurture: "those who are sprung from the same seed, nursed by the same mother, reared in the same home, loved by the same parents, and who address the same persons as father and mother, how are they not the closest of all?" (Xenophon *Cyr.* 8.7.14) (210-11). See also Klauck, *4. Makkabäerbuch*, 739.

incubates it, as is assumed in one of the two main theories of conception in the ancient world.[443] While 15:6 simply refers to her seven pregnancies, and 16:7 identifies the pregnancy by its length of ten months (ἑπτὰ κυοφορίαι καὶ ἀνόνητοι ἑπτὰ δεκάμηνοι), 13:20-21 enters into more detail, referring to pregnancy as the time during which children are residing (κατοικήσαντες) and being formed (πλασθέντες) in their mother's womb, growing (αὐξηθέντες) through her blood (ἀπὸ τοῦ ... αἵματος),[444] and being brought to maturity (τελεσφορηθέντες) through her life (διὰ τῆς ... ψυχῆς), ready to be born (ἀποτεχθέντες). This reflects an understanding at least of the mother's blood supply as crucial in the process. Common nurture and upbringing also features in such discussions in the parallels, but, significantly, here that upbringing is strongly focused on instruction in Torah.

The author returns to the motif in his encomium on the mother. It begins by stating:

κaὶ μὴ θαυμαστὸν ἡγεῖσθε εἰ ὁ λογισμὸς περιεκράτησε τῶν ἀνδρῶν ἐκείνων ἐν ταῖς βασάνοις ὅπου γε καὶ γυναικὸς νοῦς πολυτροπωτέρων ὑπερεφρόνησεν ἀλγηδόνων.

Do not think it remarkable if reason had full control of those men in the midst of tortures, when even the mind of a woman disdained agonies still more intense. (14:11)

The argument reflects the widespread view that women's reasoning was inferior, such as found in *Let. Arist.* 251 and with roots in part in Aristotle *Pol.* 1.13 (1260a12-14; cf. also Seneca *Marc.* 7.2; Philo *Leg.* 2.44-50), and is making the case that if reason informed by Torah could enable even a woman to resist, then the superiority of this way is surely proved.[445] In 15:30 the author even employs a play on words between "men" and "manliness, courage" when he attributes the latter to the mother: ὦ ἀρρένων πρὸς καρτερίαν γενναιοτέρα καὶ ἀνδρῶν πρὸς ὑπομονὴν ἀνδρειοτέρα ("More noble than males in perseverance, more manly than men in endurance"; cf. 2 Macc 7:21 τὸν θῆλυν λογισμὸν ἄρσενι θυμῷ διεγείρασα "she reinforced her woman's reasoning with a man's

---

[443] On this see Plutarch *Am. prol.* 3 (*Mor.* 495E-496B), and the discussion in Skinner, *Sexuality in Greek and Roman Culture*, 151-54 and van der Horst, "Sarah's Seminal Emission," 290-96.

[444] Cf. Wis 7:2, δεκαμηνιαίῳ χρόνῳ παγεὶς ἐν αἵματι ἐκ σπέρματος ἀνδρὸς καὶ ἡδονῆς ὕπνῳ συνελθούσης ("within the period of ten months being compacted of blood, from the seed of man and the pleasure of that accompanies intercourse").

[445] See deSilva, *4 Maccabees*, 217-18; David A. deSilva, "The Perfection of 'Love for Offspring': Greek Representations of Maternal Affection and the Achievement of the Heroine of 4 Maccabees," *NTS* 52 (2006) 251-68, 254.

courage").[446] As deSilva notes in relation to the virtues listed in 1:3-4, "ἀνδρεία, 'manliness,' as its very name implies, is a 'gendered' virtue. If submissiveness and passivity are feminine virtues in the cultures of the first-century Mediterranean, 'manliness' refers to 'rising' to the occasion and 'standing up' to any challenge rather than being overcome by it".[447] Accordingly, in 16:14 "she is given explicitly masculine titles to match the ἀνδρεία of her soul: ὦ μῆτερ δι'εὐσέβειαν θεοῦ στρατιῶτι πρεσβῦτι καὶ γύναι – 'Mother, through piety [you are at the same time] soldier, elder [a religious title; here perhaps signifying an official of the synagogue) and woman".[448] As Moore and Anderson note , "the prime exemplar of masculinity in 4 Maccabees is a woman".[449] Antiochus, by contrast, who gives way to his passions of anger, is a failed man, "feminized" and emerges as a servant of the passions and their seductiveness.[450] In the struggle he thus becomes like a woman, a cause of greatest shame for a man.[451]

To enhance his argument the author then follows the pattern used in relation to the brotherly bond, but now applied to the even greater emotional bond of mothers and children: that even she was able to resist. Thus he writes: "Consider how complex is the affection of a mother's love for her children, channelling all her feeling into a sympathy rooted deep within" (14:13), further illustrating the same bond from birds, animals, and bees (14:14-20). As Young notes, "maternal love (στοργή) was of a lower order; it was complex (πολύπλοκος) and connected to the bowels (πρὸς τῶν σπλάγχνων συμπάθειαν, 14:13); the author uses this to contrast it to the mother's λογισμός, trained in the law, which overcomes her natural love".[452] Again, the topic of mothers' affection for their offspring was a common theme (cf. Plutarch *Am. prol.* 1 – 3 [*Mor.* 493B-496A]; Aristotle *Eth.*

---

[446] Stephen D. Moore and Janice Capel Anderson, "Taking it like a Man: Masculinity in 4 Maccabees," *JBL* 117 (1998) 249-73, see the author "embroidering 2 Macc. 7:21" throughout (266).

[447] deSilva, *4 Maccabees*, 74; see also deSilva, "Love for Offspring," 254; Moore and Capel Anderson, "Taking it like a Man," 253.

[448] Robin Darling Young, "The 'Woman With the Soul of Abraham': Traditions about the Mother of the Maccabean Martyrs," in *"Women Like This": New Perspectives on Jewish Women in the Greco-Roman World* (ed. A. J. Levine; EJL 1; Atlanta: Scholars, 1991) 67-81, 78.

[449] Moore and Capel Anderson, "Taking it like a Man," 252.

[450] Moore and Capel Anderson, "Taking it like a Man," 255, 257.

[451] On this see Moore and Capel Anderson, "Taking it like a Man," 259-64, who cite the similar humiliations in Judg 4:9; 9:54; Jdt 9:10; 13:15, 17; 14:8; 16:5-6 (262). See also *LAB* 31:17, 9.

[452] Young, "Woman With the Soul of Abraham," 76.

nic. 8.12.2-3 [1161b17-29]), including illustrations from nature.[453] That theme continues in the following chapter:

4 ὦ τίνα τρόπον ἠθολογήσαιμι φιλότεκνα γονέων πάθη, ψυχῆς τε καὶ μορφῆς ὁμοιότητα εἰς μικρὸν παιδὸς χαρακτῆρα θαυμάσιον ἐναποσφραγίζομεν, μάλιστα διὰ τὸ τῶν παθῶν τοῖς γεννηθεῖσιν τὰς μητέρας τῶν πατέρων καθεστάναι συμπαθεστέρας. 5 ὅσῳ γὰρ καὶ ἀσθενόψυχοι καὶ πολυγονώτεραι ὑπάρχουσιν αἱ μητέρες, τοσούτῳ μᾶλλόν εἰσιν φιλοτεκνότεραι. 6 πασῶν δὲ τῶν μητέρων ἐγένετο ἡ τῶν ἑπτὰ παίδων μήτηρ φιλοτεκνοτέρα ἥτις ἑπτὰ κυοφορίαις τὴν πρὸς αὐτοὺς ἐπιφυτευομένη φιλοστοργίαν 7 καὶ διὰ πολλὰς τὰς καθ᾽ ἕκαστον αὐτῶν ὠδῖνας ἠναγκασμένη τὴν εἰς αὐτοὺς ἔχειν συμπάθειαν.

4 How can I characterize the passions involved in the love of parents for their children? We impress upon the tender nature of a child a remarkable likeness both of soul and of form, especially is this true of mothers, because they are more sympathetic in their feelings toward their offspring than fathers. 5 For to the extent that mothers are of tender spirit and bear more children, so much the more attached are they to their children.[454] 6 But more than all other mothers, the mother of the seven boys was attached to her children. Through seven pregnancies she had implanted in herself tender love toward them, 7 and though, because of the many birth pangs she suffered with each of them, she was bound to feel sympathy for them. (15:4-7)

Similar emphasis on pregnancy, the pain of giving birth, and breastfeeding as the basis for the mother-child bond are found in the account in Plutarch (*Am. prol. 3* [*Mor.* 495D-496C]; *Lib. ed. 5* [*Mor.* 3D]).[455] The notion of likeness also has parallels: "the author echoes the Stoic observation that children resemble their parents not only physically, but morally and psychologically as well".[456] In his emphasis on the bond between mother and child the author not only mentions tenderness, but also differentiates the impact of father and mother on grounds of his construction of gender: "We impress upon the tender nature of a child a remarkable likeness both of soul and of form, especially is this true of mothers, because they are more sympathetic in their feelings toward their offspring than fathers" (15:4). This view is similarly reflected in Greco-Roman sources (Aristotle

---

[453] See deSilva, *4 Maccabees*, 218-19; and the more detailed discussion in deSilva, "Love for Offspring," 254-61.

[454] deSilva, *4 Maccabees*, also supports this reading (222), rather than treating the clause as concessive: "Considering that mothers are the weaker sex and give birth to many" (*NRSV*).

[455] So deSilva, *4 Maccabees*, 219; deSilva, "Love for Offspring," who notes that Plutarch sees "the rerouting of the flow of the mother's blood from monthly evacuation to the nurturing of the foetus, thence to the production of milk after the child's birth", citing *Am. prol. 3* (*Mor.* 495E-496B) (257).

[456] deSilva, *4 Maccabees*, 219; Klauck, *4. Makkabäerbuch*, 743.

Eth. nic. 8.12.3 [1161b20-28]; Xenophon *Oec.* 7.24; Plutarch *Am. prol.* 3 [*Mor.* 496A]). deSilva notes that the author makes no mention of breastfeeding here, usually also cited in this context (cf. Plutarch *Am. prol.* 3 [*Mor.* 496C]; *Lib. ed.* 5 [*Mor.* 3D]), who contrasts its intimacy with suckling in the animal kingdom), though he mentions it in 16:7.[457] The author appears to espouse a theory in addition that the more pregnancies a woman has had, the more attached she becomes, when he writes: "For to the extent that mothers are of tender spirit and bear more children, so much the more attached are they to their children" (15:5), then arguing that this would apply to the mother of seven (15:6). deSilva sees this as an innovation of the author.[458] The author's further innovations are to present the mother as also suffering pains to bring rebirth, both for her slain children to a life in eternity with God,[459] but also for the nation (16:13; 15:29).[460]

The author emphasises the bond to underline the mother's courage in not pleading for her sons' release or dissuading them from their defiance. "Thus I have demonstrated that not only men overcame their passions, but also (even*) a woman disdained the greatest tortures" (16:2). The key is reason informed by Torah: "By the reason that is rooted in piety, the mother quenched passions so many and so great" (16:4).[461] The author then returns again to the theme of childbirth in a hypothetical account of how the mother might have spoken:

6 ὦ μελέα ἔγωγε καὶ πολλάκις τρισαθλία, ἥτις ἑπτὰ παῖδας τεκοῦσα
οὐδενὸς μήτηρ γεγένημαι. 7 ὦ μάταιοι ἑπτὰ κυοφορίαι καὶ ἀνόνητοι ἑπτὰ
δεκάμηνοι καὶ ἄκαρποι τιθηνίαι καὶ ταλαίπωροι γαλακτοτροφίαι. 8 μάτην
δὲ ἐφ᾽ ὑμῖν, ὦ παῖδες, πολλὰς ὑπέμεινα ὠδῖνας καὶ χαλεπωτέρας
φροντίδας ἀνατροφῆς. 9 ὦ τῶν ἐμῶν παίδων οἱ μὲν ἄγαμοι, οἱ δὲ γήμαντες
ἀνόνητοι· οὐκ ὄψομαι ὑμῶν τέκνα οὐδὲ μάμμη κληθεῖσα μακαρισθήσομαι.
10 ὦ ἡ πολύπαις καὶ καλλίπαις ἐγὼ γυνὴ χήρα καὶ μόνη πολύθρηνος· 11
οὐδ᾽ ἂν ἀποθάνω, θάπτοντα τῶν υἱῶν ἔξω τινά.

---

[457] deSilva, *4 Maccabees*, 222-23; deSilva, "Love for Offspring," 257.

[458] deSilva, "Love for Offspring," 258.

[459] Collins, *Between Athens and Jerusalem*, notes that the author omits all references to resurrection, so prominent in his source 2 Maccabees 7, instead espousing post mortem survival of the soul (206).

[460] deSilva, "Love for Offspring," 260.

[461] On Hellenistic parallels hailing the bravery of women, especially Plutarch *Mulier. virt.* (*Mor.* 240C-263C), see deSilva, *4 Maccabees*, 232-33, who notes that "the mother, then, ... in no way falls short of the Greek culture's bravest female heroes" (233); deSilva, "Love for Offspring," 263; and Moore and Capel Anderson, "Taking it like a Man," citing Xenophon, *Oec.* 10.1, where Socrates hails a woman as having man's intelligence (267). They rightly observe that such claims reinforce a value system which sees women as inferior and only able to rise above their status by becoming like men (269).

6 O how wretched I am, thrice unhappy time and again; though I bore seven boys, I have become mother of none. 7 In vain, my seven pregnancies, useless, my seven (ten month periods*) periods of gestation, unfruitful my nursings, wretched the nourishings at my breast. 8 In vain, my boys, did I endure many birth pangs for you and the still more trying anxieties of your upbringing. 9 Alas for my boys, some unmarried, others married to no purpose. 10 I shall not see your children or have the happiness of being called grandmother. I, a woman with many and fair children, am a widow, alone, with much to lament. 11 Nor, when I die will I have any of my sons to bury me. (16:6-11)

On this deSilva observes: "The fictive lament again shows how deeply immersed in classical literature the author was", pointing to parallels in Euripides, *Troiades*: the speech of Andromache, 758-760; Cassandra's lament, 380-381; and Hecuba's lament, 473-488, 503-505.[462] Like Wisd 7:4, the author uses the standard Greco-Roman reckoning of the length of pregnancy as 10 months (δεκάμηνοι), counting months as 28 days (Virgil *Ecl.* 4.61), changing the original 9 months in his source (cf. 2 Macc 7:27).[463] Both 15:7 and 16:8 refer to the pain involved in the process of giving birth. As in 13:21, in 16:7 we find reference to nourishment through breast feeding. Her complaint bemoans that she has in vain had to put up with what she describes as "the still more trying anxieties of your upbringing" (16:7). In 16:9 she laments about her sons that some are "unmarried, others married to no purpose". This reflects the assumption that not to marry is a loss and then not to have children is a curse, a value also expressed in her authentic speech (cf. 18:9 below). In 16:10 she laments that she would fail to become a grandmother[464] and now be left a widow and without the security of sons to bury her. The issue is less burial than care in old age.

Then finally the author gives us her actual words to her sons, in which issues of sexuality are prominent. The speech sits awkwardly and somewhat unmediated in the work, leading some to speculate that it is an interpolation, but consistency of style makes that unlikely.[465] It serves to articulate values which are important in the author's overall theme of control of the passions.

---

[462] deSilva, *4 Maccabees*, 230-31. Klauck, *4. Makkabäerbuch*, points also to Menander 419.25-30 (747). See also deSilva, "Love for Offspring," 262-63. He notes that unlike those women this mother faces not despair but hope based on her faith that she would again see her sons in the realm of eternity (17:5-6) (266-67). He notes also that the author does not depict her as not having feeling (cf. 15:11, 16; 16:3-4) though she does not weep. Not weeping is part of her control so as not to undermine her sons' resolve (264-65).

[463] Klauck, *4. Makkabäerbuch*, 747; deSilva, *4 Maccabees*, 231.

[464] Klauck, *4. Makkabäerbuch*, cites the consolation of the prospect of grandchildren in Seneca *Marc.*16.7-9 (748).

[465] See the discussion in Hugh Anderson, "4 Maccabees," *OTP*, 2.531-64, 532; Klauck, *4. Makkabäerbuch*, who writes that the final section is somewhat of a collection of leftovers

7 ὅτι ἐγὼ ἐγενήθην παρθένος ἁγνὴ οὐδὲ ὑπερέβην πατρικὸν οἶκον,
ἐφύλασσον δὲ τὴν ᾠκοδομημένην πλευράν. 8 οὐδὲ ἔφθειρέν με λυμεὼν
ἐρημίας φθορεὺς ἐν πεδίῳ, οὐδὲ ἐλυμήνατό μου τὰ ἁγνὰ τῆς παρθενίας
λυμεὼν ἀπάτης ὄφις. 9 ἔμεινα δὲ χρόνον ἀκμῆς σὺν ἀνδρί· τούτων δὲ
ἐνηλίκων γενομένων ἐτελεύτησεν ὁ πατὴρ αὐτῶν, μακάριος μὲν ἐκεῖνος, τὸν
γὰρ τῆς εὐτεκνίας βίον ἐπιζήσας τὸν τῆς ἀτεκνίας οὐκ ὠδυνήθη καιρόν. 10
ὃς ἐδίδασκεν ὑμᾶς ἔτι ὢν σὺν ὑμῖν τὸν νόμον καὶ τοὺς προφήτας.

7 I was a pure virgin and did not step outside my father's house, but I kept watch over
the built rib. 8 No seducer or corrupter on a desert plain corrupted me, nor did the
seducer, the snake of deceit, defile the purity of my virginity. 9 At the time of my
maturity I remained with my husband; when these sons came of age, their father died.
Blessed was he, for he lived a life marked by the blessing of children and did not suffer
the grief of the time of childlessness. 10 While he was still with you, he taught you the
law and the prophets. (18:7-10)

It features what must have been the author's ideal of young womanhood.
Accordingly the mother had been a chaste virgin. She had achieved this by not
stepping outside her father's house. In this she upheld traditional virtues, common
both to Judaism and to Hellenistic ideals. Thus deSilva notes that Euripides
presents Andromache as remaining under Hector's roof, avoiding the bad
reputation of those who did not (*Tro.* 645-653). D'Angelo cites the *Laudatio
Turiae* 1.10 about an unnamed Roman matron concerned to protect her chastity
and Ovid's couplet, "let the bride fear her husband, let the guard of the bride be
sure/ this is right, this the laws and the leader (Augustus) and modesty command"
(*Ars* 3.613-615).[466] Similar values inform the instruction of Ben Sira that
daughters should be kept at home (7:24-25; 42:9-14; 26:10-12; similarly *Ps.-Phoc.*
215-216). Bader raises the possibility that the author may be contrasting the
mother with Dinah, especially if the author shares the view that she would never
have been abducted had she not left her father's house in the first place (cf. *Gen.
Rab.* 80:1-2).[467]

The author then tells us that she eschewed adultery and remained married
during her fertile years, as the Augustan laws required, and so was also observant
of the biblical prohibition of adultery and the command to multiply. As D'Angelo
observes,

---

for which the author has found no place in the account thus far (658). Young, "Woman
With the Soul of Abraham," suggests that "perhaps this text is an attempt to connect her
death in 17:1 with her own prior training in virtue" (79). The hearer is at least spared the
prospect of physical, perhaps even sexual, violence done to the mother by her suicide.
Similarly Bader, *Tracing the Evidence*, who sees a possible contrast here with Dinah (141).

[466] D'Angelo, "Εὐσεβεία," 155.

[467] Bader, *Tracing the Evidence*, 140.

The centrality of εὐσεβεία and its association with familial duty, the concern with the mother's freedom from *stuprum* and adultery, her marriage for the duration of her fertility, her submission to the teaching of her husband: all these suggest that both the Augustan social legislation and the imperial propaganda that accompanied it have had a hand in the revisions of this narrative, for all are concerns that make no appearance at all in 2 Maccabees 6–7.[468]

The Jewish background is strongly evident in the allusions to the Genesis creation story. The words, ἐφύλασσον δὲ τὴν ᾠκοδομημένην[469] πλευράν ("I kept watch over the built rib"; cf. *LAB* 32:15) allude to the creation of woman, but do so in a way that τὴν ᾠκοδομημένην πλευράν must refer to herself not just as a woman, but as the female partner for a husband, reading the Genesis narrative as an aetiology of marriage. In the words, οὐδὲ ἔφθειρέν με λυμεὼν ἐρημίας φθορεὺς ἐν πεδίῳ οὐδὲ ἐλυμήνατό μου τὰ ἁγνὰ τῆς παρθενίας λυμεὼν ἀπάτης ὄφις ("No seducer or corrupter on a desert plain corrupted me, nor did the seducer, the snake of deceit, defile the purity of my virginity"), we can recognise an allusion to the snake of Genesis 3, which most probably assumes the LXX translation of 3:13, where the Hebrew הִשִּׁיאַנִי is rendered ἠπάτησέν με, which unlike the Hebrew can bear the meaning "sexually seduced me" (cf. here: ἀπάτης ὄφις). The reference to the destroyer and corrupter on the plain (λυμεὼν ἐρημίας φθορεὺς ἐν πεδίῳ) appears not to derive from the Genesis creation account, but from Deut 22:25-27, which speaks of rape in a deserted place (ἐν πεδίῳ). In the related account in Exod 22:15 we find the verb ἀπατήσῃ used of seduction. Possibly all three texts, Gen 3:13; Deut 22:25-27, and Exod 22:15, lie behind the formulations here. Klauck suggests that the myth of the Watchers may also play a role.[470] The end-effect of this part of the speech is to depict being sexually seduced and losing one's virginity as a, if not the, primal sin to which Eve

---

[468] D'Angelo, "Εὐσεβεία," 157, referring to the Julian laws on "*stuprum* (*lex iulia de adulteriis*) and the requirement of marriage and remarriage for those of an age to produce children (*lex iulia de maritandis ordinibus*)" (156). She concludes: "The Maccabean mother fulfills these expectations, and surpasses them, by also realizing the Roman ideal of the *univira*"(156). On the Augustan laws see also Eva Marie Lassen, "The Roman Family: Ideal and Metaphor," in *Constructing Early Christian Families: Family as Social reality and Metaphor* (ed. Halvor Moxnes; London: Routledge, 1997)103-20, 107-108.

[469] deSilva, *4 Maccabees*, notes that Sinaiticus reads, οἰκοδουμένην ("that was being built up"), which he argues "conveys more of a dynamic sense that, as the young woman was growing to maturity, she was 'becoming' more and more that helpmate for which God first removed the rib from Adam's side" (258).

[470] Klauck, *4. Makkabäerbuch*, 755. D'Angelo, "Εὐσεβεία," notes that early interpreters who equated the serpent and devil (as in Wis 2:24) linked Eve's seduction with Gen 4:1 (קָנִיתִי אִישׁ אֶת יהוה) to suggest that Cain was fathered by the devil, citing *Pirqe R. E.* 21, *Tg. Ps.-J.* on Gen. 4:1; John 8:44; 1 John 3:12 (155).

fell and which each young woman faces anew – also an issue of self-control, which the mother had exercised.

The mother then declares of her husband who died: "Blessed was he, for he lived a life marked by the blessing of children and did not suffer the grief of the time of childlessness" (18:9). As in the hypothetical speech, here too we find the assumption that a marriage with children is a blessing and without them is a matter of grief (and has no purpose according to 16:9). As noted above this fits Augustan laws and matches Gen 1:28. It appears to leave no place for marriage which might be only for companionship and intimacy. The author most likely espoused the view that sexual relations had their warrant only in the intent to procreate, though this may give too much weight to these statements.

The father's role is particularly noted in relation to teaching according to 18:10 where the mother declares: "While he was still with you, he taught you the law and the prophets". The speech continues with detail about what this entailed, listing a range of biblical figures who faced adversity: Abel murdered by Cain; Isaac, who features a number of times because of his willingness to obey in face of danger; Joseph in prison; Phinehas; Hananias, Azarias, and Misael; Daniel; Isaiah; David the psalmist; Solomon; and Ezekiel.

D'Angelo argues that "the husband's sudden appearance in 18:9 demotes the mother from teacher of her sons to student of her husband".[471] Similarly Moore and Capel Anderson comment that while earlier generations deemed the speech a depiction of ideal domestic piety,[472] "it is hard to avoid the suspicion that we are witnessing not just a domestic scene but also a scene of domestication, that the martyr is being tamed and herded into the patriarchal fold".[473] "The 'manly' woman is effectively, if clumsily 'feminized'".[474] It is likely however that contrary to our contemporary perspectives, and despite her heroic behaviour, the author and his hearers will have all along assumed a patriarchal framework, as is also the case in the story of Judith, and not have seen any need to correct what had been written. Indeed, all along her heroic stance has been interpreted within a patriarchal framework, as we have seen. In a crisis she has acquitted herself – with the virtues of a man.

---

[471] D'Angelo, "Εὐσεβεία," 156.

[472] So Moses Hadas, *The Third and Fourth Books of Maccabees* (JAL; New York: Harper, 1953) 239; similarly André Dupont-Sommer, *Le Quatrième Livre des Machabées: Introduction, Traduction et Notes* (Paris: Champion, 1939) 154.

[473] Moore and Capel Anderson, "Taking it like a Man," 270.

[474] Moore and Capel Anderson, "Taking it like a Man," 272. "The tacked-on speech of 18:6-19 returns the woman to her proper place on the continuum in relation to her husband" (273). Similarly Young, "Woman With the Soul of Abraham," who writes: "The speech may be, then, the author's attempt to justify the mother by including her in a pious, domestic setting" (79).

Conclusion

In addressing the passions the author of 4 Maccabees is concerned to promote to his Jewish hearers the power of the mind informed by Torah to control them. While the exemplars which take up the greatest portion of the work depict the overcoming of fear, brotherly and maternal bonds, and the lure of forbidden foods, the opening chapters include a wide survey, in which sexual desire also features. Like the other passions, sexual desire is not denigrated, maligned or signalled out for extirpation. For like them it is part of God's creation. The issue is control. That control is effectively the discipline of conforming one's responses to sexual desire to what Torah teaches, which happens also to coincide in some respects with what Augustan law required, namely chastity before and in marriage and engagement in marriage for the purpose of having children. This desired outcome and conformity finds expression in both the hypothetical and the actual speech of the mother with which the work concludes. Conformity to both biblical and Greco-Roman expectations in such matters is a mark of the work. This is achieved by ignoring many issues which might have been just as relevant for dealing with the passions, such as prostitution, male and female, pederasty, bestiality, and much more. In other words, the author has gone for coherence and chosen not to include other major sexual issues of his day.

The work is also remarkable for its interest in the processes of giving birth and appears here to be dependent on similar interests in the Greco-Roman world. While they serve to enhance the significance and potency of feelings which both the brothers and the mother had to overcome, they are not presented negatively. In the process the author touches on details of conception (probably understood as implantation of seed in the woman), shaping of the foetus, its nourishment in the womb (including from blood), the pain of contractions and giving birth, breast feeding, and even the sometimes very tiring and challenging tasks of bringing up little children. One might extend the interest in families with reference to fathers' instructing their boys (and girls?) in the biblical heritage, and, returning to the moral values: keeping daughters chaste, getting and remaining married for the purpose of bearing children. This domestic pattern with its patriarchal structure served not only as an ideal, which the author is by no means springing on his hearers as a surprise in the final speech, but also as the evaluative register by which the author hails the mother's supreme sacrifice as being so praiseworthy because in her mastery of the passions she has gone beyond herself and expectations of her gender in behaving like a man and then even superseded that.

3.2.5 Pseudo-Phocylides

Until recent centuries believed to be the work[475] of the 6th or 7th century[476] B.C.E. Miletian philosopher, Phocylides, famed for his wise instruction,[477] this work of 231 hexameter lines is now recognised as pseudonymous. It is the work of a Jewish author emulating ancient Ionic dialect, but also using vocabulary and style belonging to the turn of the era,[478] and probably to be dated somewhere between the mid first century B.C.E. and the mid first century C.E.[479] It survives in 157 manuscripts of which five are important witnesses to the Greek text, dating from the 10th to the 13th century.[480] Its combination of Jewish wisdom and Hellenistic gnomic poetry reflects both the Septuagint[481] and non-Jewish sources.[482] The

---

[475] The Greek text which forms the basis of this chapter is that of Pascale Derron, *Pseudo-Phocylide: Sentences* (Budé; Paris: Société d'Édition "Les Belles Lettres", 1986). The translation is that of Walter T. Wilson, *The Sentences of Pseudo-Phocylides* (CEJL; Berlin: de Gruyter, 2005), unless otherwise indicated by an asterisk where I have provided my own translation.

[476] Fragment 4 of the little that survives of the historical Phocylides apparently refers to the destruction of Nineveh in 612 B.C.E.

[477] See the extensive review of research, including the popularity of the work during the middle ages, in Pieter W. van der Horst, *The Sentences of Pseudo-Phocylides: With Introduction and Commentary* (SVTP 4; Leiden: Brill, 1978) 3-54; supplemented in Pieter W. van der Horst, "Pseudo-Phocylides Revisited," *JSP* 3 (1988) 3-30, 3-14. See also the review in Weber, *Gesetz im hellenistischen Judentum*, 278-80.

[478] On language, metre, and style see especially Derron, *Pseudo-Phocylide*, lxvi-lxxxii; van der Horst, *Pseudo-Phocylides*, 55-58.

[479] So van der Horst, "Pseudo-Phocylides Revisited," 15; Gerbern S. Oegema, *Poetische Schriften*, who proposes the period from the early first century B.C.E. to early first century C.E. (67). If written in Alexandria it would have to be some time before the tensions which began in the time of Caligula. So Weber, *Gesetz im hellenistischen Judentum*, 281.

[480] See the collation in Pascale Derron, "Inventaire des Manuscrit du Pseudo-Phocylide," *Revue d'Histoire des Textes* 10 (1980) 237-47; and the discussion in Derron, *Pseudo-Phocylide*, lxxxiii-cxvi. In addition most of lines 5-79, with some modifications, are found interpolated by a Christian into *Sibylline Oracles* 2 (55-149). On this see van der Horst, *Pseudo-Phocylides*, 84-85.

[481] On its use of LXX see Max Küchler, *Frühjüdische Weisheitstraditionen: Zum Fortgang weisheitlichen Denkens im Bereich des frühjüdischen Jahweglaubens* (OBO 26; Fribourg: Universitätsverlag; Göttingen: Vandenhoeck & Ruprecht, 1979) 280-81.

[482] So most recently Wilson, *Sentences*, 7. See his discussion of literary genres where he concludes: "it is probably most accurate to refer to the *Sentences* as a *gnomic poem*, a designation that offers certain advantages over other recent proposals for its genre" (10), among which he discusses wisdom poem, didactic poem, wisdom instruction, and gnomologia (10-11).

author is frequently located in Alexandrian Judaism on the basis of a probable allusion in 102 to human dissection, known to have been practised there, but might belong elsewhere among the many diaspora communities of which our knowledge is minimal.[483] Important for our purposes is that the work reflects the values of a sophisticated Greek-speaking Jew, writing within a Hellenistic environment, probably to reinforce among his fellow Jews a sense that as they embrace wider Hellenistic culture they should recognise that its wisest had affirmed what Jewish faith had always known and taught through Torah, so providing all the more reason for them to remain faithful,[484] and among other things to teach accordingly in their schools.[485] In this sense it belongs broadly among those works which argue dependence of Greek culture on Moses. At the same time the work belongs to the classicising of the period which characterised Greco-Roman writers, who not only cited ancient authors, but also summarised and reworked them in an effort to communicate what they thought they meant – or should have meant.[486]

True to his fictional strategy of presenting the words of a 6/7th century Phocylides, whose primary concern had apparently been day to day living and ethics, the author focuses on instructions for daily living. It doing so he both camouflages his Jewish sources[487] and passes over distinctively Jewish concerns with cult and ritual, including prohibition of idolatry.[488] At the same time the focus on right relations, suggested by the author's designating his theme as "the

---

[483] So Wilson, *Sentences*, 12-13.

[484] So Wilson, *Sentences*, who writes: "Demonstrating the indebtedness of the founders of Greek culture to Mosaic wisdom in this way would have facilitated for Jews the task of reconciling their pride in Judaism with their engagement in Hellenistic civilization" (4). Similarly Oegema, *Poetische Schriften*, 68; Weber, *Gesetz im hellenistischen Judentum*, 290. See also van der Horst, "Pseudo-Phocylides Revisited," 15-16, who writes: "the hypothesis that Ps-Phoc addressed himself to a pagan audience in order to win them over to a kind of 'ethical monotheism' (and that this was the function of his pseudonym) is a theory that has now definitely to be laid *ad acta*" (16). Cf. Johannes Thomas, *Der jüdische Phokylides: Formgeschichtliche Zugänge zu Pseudo-Phokylides und Vergleich mit der neutestamentlichen Paränese* (Fribourg: Universitätsverlag; Göttingen: Vandenhoeck & Ruprecht, 1992), who wonders why an author would emphasise sexual ethics if Jews are his real audience (358) and suggests that the author is perhaps just engaged in exploration with no purpose beyond expressing his thoughts (360-61), but the former surely fits the strategy of assuring them that the best Greek authors agreed with Jewish laws and the latter makes little sense of the use of a pseudonym.

[485] So Wilson, *Sentences*, 11-12; Weber, *Gesetz im hellenistischen Judentum*, 292.

[486] So Wilson, *Sentences*, 5, 32.

[487] On these see Wilson, *Sentences*, 17-22.

[488] So Wilson, *Sentences*, 6; Thomas, *Phokylides*, 291.

mysteries of righteousness" (229), coheres well with a major emphasis in Torah.[489] Non-Jewish sources are also evident[490] but similarly woven into a fictional fabric, and probably belonging to a body of material which had already merged Jewish and popular Hellenistic philosophical tradition in a manner which renders derivations mostly very difficult to discern.[491] The product of the author's strategy is a work without an evident theological rationale[492] and without traces, except to the discerning eye, of particular Jewish influence. History shows that the author largely succeeded in his ploy of passing off his work as that of the ancient Phocylides, at least from medieval times onward. The work served then widely as a school text book on moral instruction, perhaps one of its original functions.[493] At the same time, its addressees are assumed to be elite males who own households (or will do so) and who are sufficiently well educated to appreciate the sophistication of its archaising style.[494] The author might appear to be at his most daring when in the persona of Phocylides he speaks of people becoming gods at their death (103-104), grounds for some in the past to deny the author was a Jew or to propose emendation,[495] but even here such language would probably have been

---

[489] So Thomas, *Phokylides*, 55; Barclay, *Jews in the Mediterranean Diaspora*, 343, who writes of the author: "He encourages them to be proud of behaving in accordance with the 'mysteries of righteousness' (v. 229) *because Phocylides taught them*, quite beside the fact that they are mostly drawn from the Jewish law" (346).

[490] On these see Wilson, *Sentences*, 14-17, and the table in Derron, *Pseudo-Phocylide*, setting out an extensive list of parallels from both Jewish/Christian and Greco-Roman sources (35-54).

[491] On this see Niebuhr, *Gesetz und Paränese*, 8. He points out that the author appears to draw on source material in which commandments and prohibitions have been extracted from the Pentateuch and reordered (20). Similarly Weber, *Gesetz im hellenistischen Judentum*, who notes that the source was probably not in a defined or fixed form, but probably material with loose boundaries and somewhat fluctuating content, used eclectically depending on the different situations being addressed (286-87).

[492] As Gilbert, "Wisdom Literature," notes: "Though the first groups of sayings are inspired by the Decalogue and Leviticus 19, the strictly religious significance of the latter has almost disappeared in the *Sentences*" (316). "There is a constant invitation to practise the fundamental virtues, but without a similarly constant appeal to religious motives" (316).

[493] Thomas, *Phokylides*, doubts this on grounds that its themes are too limited (360).

[494] So Wilson, *Sentences*, who notes the elite status of the supposed hearer (32-33), so that all instructions assume this status and the work enjoins actions that contribute to stability as what is fitting, including such things as concern for the unfortunate, reconciliation with enemies, and harmonious households (38-39).

[495] On this see van der Horst, *Pseudo-Phocylides*, 6; and also John J. Collins, "Life After Death in Pseudo-Phocylides," in *Jerusalem, Alexandria, Rome: Studies in Ancient Cultural Interaction in Honour of A. Hilhorst* (ed. Florentino García Martínez and Gerard P. Luttikhuizen; Leiden: Brill, 2003) 75-86, pointing to the parallel in *2 Bar.* 50:2-4 (80-81); and Pieter W. van der Horst, "Pseudo-Phocylides on the Afterlife: A Rejoinder to John J.

understood not as embracing polytheism but as belonging within Jewish expectation of post-mortal life as being at least like the angels.[496]

The sayings are loosely connected, as is common in such collections, but there are some minimal signs of structure, not least in the opening and closing lines (1-2, 228-30) which bracket the whole. Within the work most sayings are clustered according to theme,[497] all related as in similar literature to "cultivating personal qualities and relationships, especially as they concern the following subjects: wealth, virtue, speech, wisdom, self-control, women, marriage, parents, friends, fate, and death"[498] and take the form of imperatives with some exceptions where there are explanations (e.g. 103-115). A further structural element is to be found in 3-8, where we find what appears to be a summary based in part on the Decalogue, which signals many of the themes to follow. As Wilson notes "it is also possible to think of vv. 3-8 as providing a summary introduction or preview of the poem itself",[499] noting that it would then correspond to the *propositio* of an oration, so that 9-22 would then represent the *probatio*, which "expands upon and explains the proposition, showing its implications for the audience".[500]

Sexuality in the Opening Summary and in Scattered Allusions

Matters pertaining to sexuality occur mainly within the cluster of sayings related broadly to the household in 175-227, but brief references of possible relevance occur in 59, 67, and 76, and not least in the summary in 3-8.

Collins," *JSJ* 35 (2004) 70-75, who disputes elements on Collins's view, but not the understanding of "gods" here. Nothing indicates how the author might have viewed sexual life in the resurrected state.

[496] So van der Horst, *Pseudo-Phocylides*, 185-88; Wilson, *Sentences*, 145-46.

[497] On this see Wilson, *Sentences*, 22-30, who notes the influence of Plato's tetrad of virtues, wisdom, justice, moderation and courage as having shaped the first major section in 9-131 (24-28), with 132-227 reflecting "different kinds of social relationships or referent" (29): relations with "outsiders" (132-152), work (153-174) and household (175-227) (28-29).

[498] So Wilson, *Sentences*, 12, summarizing the observations of Teresa Morgan, *Literate Education in the Hellenistic and Roman Worlds* (Cambridge: Cambridge University Press, 1998) on gnomic school texts (125-44). Wilson notes, however, that the work reflects distinctively Jewish emphases in its stress on caring about the less powerful ("the poor, children, slaves, and animals") (12). See also van der Horst, *Pseudo-Phocylides*, 65.

[499] Wilson, *Sentences*, 76.

[500] Wilson, *Sentences*, 77. See also Küchler, *Frühjüdische Weisheitstraditionen*, who argues that the work should be seen as a composition in itself (274).

3 Neither commit adultery nor rouse homosexual passion
(μήτε γαμοκλοπέειν μήτ᾽ ἄρσενα Κύπριν ὀρίνειν).
4 Neither devise treachery nor stain your hands with blood.
5 Do not become rich unjustly, but live from honourable means.
6 Be content with what you have and abstain from what is another's.
7 Do not tell lies, but always speak the truth
8 Honor God foremost, and afterwards your parents. (3-8)

It is an expansion and reformulation[501] of the prohibitions of the Decalogue (Exod 20:3-17; Deut 5:7-21), but apart from the first line also significantly influenced by Leviticus 19.[502] To adultery is added homosexual passion; to murder, devising treachery, staining one's hands with blood; to theft, becoming rich unjustly, rather than living from honourable means, being content with what one has and abstaining from what belongs to another; to bearing false witness, not telling lies, but speaking the truth. The final line picks up themes of the first table: honouring God and parents, but characteristically omitting prohibition of idolatry, taking God's name in vain (but cf. 16-17), and observing the sabbath.[503] Here no grounds are given for the prohibitions. They are assumed to carry their own authority.[504]

The order, adultery, murder, theft, follows the most likely order in the LXX of Deuteronomy, as preserved in Codex Vaticanus, and is attested elsewhere, not least in Philo who argues that having the prohibition of adultery as the first of the second table gives it major significance (*Decal.* 121).[505] Like Philo, this author associates the prohibition of adultery with other sexual prohibitions. The association is evident also in the lists in Mark 7:21-22 and 1 Cor 6:9, which follow the same order (cf. Matt 15:13). Here the link is with homosexual passion, based on Lev 18:22; 20:13. The formulation, μήτε γαμοκλοπέειν, typically obscures the source. Κύπρις, in μήτ᾽ ἄρσενα Κύπριν ὀρίνειν, was a designation of Aphrodite, and was used commonly to refer to sexual passion (as also 67, 190).[506] We met it in this sense in *Sib. Or.* 5:429-430, also in association with the related noun γαμοκλοπίη. As Wilson notes, the association of adultery and homoerotic behaviour is found also in *Sib. Or.* 3:595-596, 374; 4:33-34; 5:166; Philo, *Hypoth.*

---

[501] Thomas, *Phokylides*, notes that only two words connect it to the language of the Decalogue: ψεύδεα and τιμᾶν, which is, even then, used of God (98).

[502] So Niebuhr, *Gesetz und Paränese*, who cautions that descriptions which depict 3-8 as a summary of the Decalogue define its sources too narrowly (20).

[503] Wilson, *Sentences*, notes that Did. 2:2-3, which also gives a summary of the Decalogue at the beginning of its instructions, similarly "omits references to peculiarly Jewish practices, while incorporating prohibitions from outside the Decalogue" (75).

[504] So Thomas, *Phokylides*, 97.

[505] On this see Loader, *Septuagint*, 12.

[506] See van der Horst, *Pseudo-Phocylides*, 111; Wilson, *Sentences*, 79. It occurs regularly, for instance, in Euripides.

7.1; Josephus *Ap.* 2.199, 215, as well as in non-Jewish sources such as in Musonius Rufus frag. 12.86.8-10.[507]

Sexual wrongdoing becomes a major theme in the cluster of sayings in 175-217, to which we return below. Sexual themes may be part of the concern with moderation of the passions in 55-69B, including the instruction, "Let emotions be moderate (Ἔστω κοινὰ πάθη), neither great not excessive" (59). Here not emotion itself but its excess is the target of the author's concerns. In 67 we then read: "Love of virtue is revered, but love of passion earns shame (σεμνὸς ἔρως ἀρετῆς ὁ δὲ Κύπριδος αἶσχος ὀφέλλει)". "Love" (ἔρως) is neutral; its object makes it good or bad. Here, too, we are probably to think of excess, however, so that Κύπρις is being used to denote sexual passion: it becomes problematic when it becomes the object of love or obsession. As van der Horst puts it, "This line again warns against excesses: sexual excesses bring shame upon a man".[508] The following lines broaden the perspective, but cohere with these concerns in not scolding desire for food and drink in banqueting but eating and drinking in excess. Wilson draws attention to the similar emphasis both in Sir 31:12 – 32:13, of which he considers these lines might easily serve as a summary, but also in the Egyptian Pap. Insinger 6.8-19.[509] In 76, "Practice moderation, and refrain from shameful deeds (Σωφροσύνην ἀσκεῖν, αἰσχρῶν δ' ἔργων ἀπέχεσθαι)" probably has broader application than deeds of sexual wrongdoing which bring shame, though van der Horst notes: "In view of the common meaning of σωφροσύνη the αἰσχρὰ ἔργα possibly are sexual sins".[510]

Sexuality as Major Theme

The major treatment of sexual wrongdoing as a theme, foreshadowed in the summary, 3-8, occurs in 175-194, and material of relevance also follows in 195-227. The whole section reflects as its substructure the household code concerned with parents, children, and slaves.[511] Thomas speaks of it as an elaboration of the Hellenistic Jewish household pattern through relating it to Torah, in particular,

---

[507] Wilson, *Sentences*, 79-81.

[508] van der Horst, *Pseudo-Phocylides*, 159.

[509] Wilson, *Sentences*, 123-24.

[510] van der Horst, *Pseudo-Phocylides*, 166.

[511] On household codes see the review of research in David L. Balch, "Household Codes," in *Greco-Roman Literature and the New Testament: Selected Forms and Genres* (ed. David E. Aune; SBLSBS 21; Atlanta: Scholars, 1988) 25-50; and earlier James E. Crouch, *The Origin and Intention of the Colossian Haustafel* (FRLANT 109; Göttingen: Vandenhoeck & Ruprecht, 1972) on Stoic lists (37-73), their use in Hellenistic Judaism (74-101), Colossians (103-145), and *Pseudo-Phocylides* (76).

Leviticus 18.[512] He notes that whereas the prohibitions derive from Leviticus 18, the grounds given for the prohibitions show no connection with Leviticus 18, none bringing specifically Israelite arguments, but rather reflecting the kind of reasoning present in wisdom literature.[513] Thus he points to Stoic arguments from nature in 176, 190, 191; popular philosophical discussion about Eros in 194; literary dependence on Homer in 195b-197, and Theognis in 201-204, though he notes that few such grounds are offered in 181-189.[514]

The similarity of this material to the summaries of the law found in Philo *Hypothetica* and Josephus *Contra Apionem* make it probable that all three share some kind of common source material.[515] We shall discuss this further in the next volume after all three authors have been discussed. The treatment which follows considers the statements in *Pseudo-Phocylides* as they stand.

> 175 remain not unmarried (Μὴ μείνῃς ἄγαμος), lest you perish nameless,
> 176 And give something to nature yourself (δός τι φύσει καὐτός):
> beget in turn as you were begotten (τέκε δ' ἔμπαλιν, ὡς ἐλοχεύθης). (175-176)

According to Wilson vv. 175-176 announce not only the section's major theme but also its fundamental criterion, φύσις.[516] Thomas also sees it as setting a positive tone for all that follows, integrating it within the tradition of the household which undergirds the passage, and showing that the positive aspect influences the author more than the prohibitions.[517] The motivation, here, lies not in obedience to a divine command to multiply, as in Gen 1:28; 9:1, but in concern about perpetuating one's name through producing (male) offspring. This is, as Wilson notes, a common concern already in biblical sources (Gen 48:16; Deut 25:5-10; Ruth 4:5, 10; Sir 40:19).[518] The assumption is that marriage exists at least for that purpose. The appeal to nature may include reference to natural sexual desire, but the focus is primarily on order and making one's proper contribution to nature by producing children. So this comes as a second element of motivation beside

---

[512] Thomas, *Phokylides*, 59. See also his discussion of the influence of Leviticus 18 here, which he sees the author reworking in terms of affirming its content while removing direct verbal links (64-71).

[513] Thomas, *Phokylides*, 87.

[514] Thomas, *Phokylides*, 87.

[515] On this see Niebuhr, *Gesetz und Paränese*, who, noting the parallels to 184-185, 186, 187, 188, and 190 in Philo *Hypoth.* 7, and Josephus *Ap.* 2.190-219, concludes that behind these lies a tradition of formulating the demands of Torah, which takes its starting point from Leviticus 18 and 20 (31).

[516] Wilson, *Sentences*, 189.

[517] Thomas, *Phokylides*, 78.

[518] Wilson, *Sentences*, 189.

perpetuating one's name. The emphasis on marriage as according to nature on the basis that it provides for procreation was a widely held view among Stoics.[519] The author probably shares their view also that engaging in sexual intercourse for reasons other than for procreation is inappropriate. Van der Horst notes that some have seen in this exhortation an attempt to counter the diminishing interest in marriage to which Augustus gave attention in promulgating the Julian laws,[520] but it is more probably to be seen, along with the following exhortations, as belonging to general instruction rather than addressing a particular situation.

177 Do not prostitute your wife, defiling your children
(Μὴ προαγωγεύσῃς ἄλοχον σέο τέκνα μιαίνων).
178 For an adulterous bed does not produce similar offspring.
(οὐ γὰρ τίκτει παῖδας ὁμοίους μοιχικὰ λέκτρα). (177-178)

While having one's wife work as a prostitute seems an unconnected theme, its connection with what precedes lies in the concern with offspring and again there are two kinds of concern. On the one hand, doing so defiles one's own children. Here the concern is not any kind of ritual defilement, but the contamination of a household brought about by the possibility that some siblings may not be children of the father. The motif of defilement may well echo Lev 19:29 which forbids prostituting one's daughter as defiling her in a ritual and probably moral sense.[521] The author typically transforms the meaning into something else. The second concern is that the offspring will be different. The issue here is not aesthetics but disharmony and shame brought upon the husband. While the second line appears to change the focus to adultery, it, too, belongs closely with the first and is probably best understood as spelling out one of the implications of having one's wife function as a prostitute: she thereby commits adultery. Wilson draws attention to the effects of adulterous relations on offspring depicted in Sir 23:22-27, "Her children will not take root, and her branches will not bear fruit. She will leave behind an accursed memory and her disgrace will never be blotted out". Similar motifs occur in Wis 3:16-18; 4:3-6, which speak of the offspring of adulterers as either dying young or having no honour in old age. The focus in 177-178 appears to be different. Wilson notes that "complaints about the prevalence (especially among elites) of married women prostituting themselves, conniving husbands, and illegitimate children were a stock-in-trade of contemporary moralists and

---

[519] So van der Horst, *Pseudo-Phocylides*, 226-27; and see the extensive discussions in Will Deming, *Paul on Marriage and Celibacy: The Hellenistic Background of 1 Corinthians 7* (2d ed.; Grand Rapids: Eerdmans, 2004) 47-104; and Ellis, *Sexual Desire*, 104-45.

[520] Van der Horst, *Pseudo-Phocylides*, 227.

[521] So Thomas, *Phokylides*, 69.

satirists".[522] The possibility that a wife might engage in prostitution is envisaged in Proverbs LXX, which depicts Woman Folly as both an adulteress and a prostitute through its rewriting and expansion of 9:12-18. Philo includes it as a prohibition in *Spec.* 3.31

The next five lines deal with incest on the basis of the prohibitions in Lev 18:6-18, but for the author typically selective, reformulated, and refocussed.

179 μητρυιῆς μὴ ψαῦε τὰ δεύτερα λέκτρα γονῆος·
180 μητέρα δ' ὥς τίμα τὴν μητέρος ἴχνια βᾶσαν.
181 μηδέ τι παλλακίσιν πατρὸς λεχέεσσι μιγείης.
182 μηδὲ κασιγνήτης ἐς ἀπότροπον ἐλθέμεν εὐνήν.
183 μηδὲ κασιγνήτων ἀλόχων ἐπὶ δέμνια βαίνειν.[523]

179 Touch not your stepmother, since she is your father's second wife;[524]
180 but honor as mother the one following your mother's footsteps.
181 Have no sort of sexual relations with your father's mistresses (lit. concubines).
182 Approach not your sister's bed, (which is) abhorrent.
183 Do not go to bed with your brothers' wives. (179-183)

The instructions assume the addressee is male and of an age where he might have a father who is alive and still sexually active and might have married brothers. This in part accounts for their being no reference to prohibition of sexual relations with one's daughter-in-law (cf. Lev 18:15) or granddaughters (cf. Lev 18:10). Prohibition of incest with one's mother is assumed (Lev 18:7),[525] as reflected in the prohibition of having sexual relations with one's stepmother as one's father's second wife (179-180; as Lev 18:8; cf. also 20:11; Deut 23:1; 27:20). Nothing is said of sexual relations with one's aunt (cf. Lev 18:12-14), let alone one's niece which some saw as a corollary and which became a matter of dispute reflected in CD 5.7-11. Prohibiting sex with sisters or sisters-in-law (182-183) matches Lev 18:9, 11, 16 (cf. also Mark 6:18).

---

[522] Wilson, *Sentences*, 191. See also van der Horst, *Pseudo-Phocylides*, 228.

[523] On the placement of this line here as conjectured by Jacob Bernays rather than between 194 and 195 as in all but one manuscript, see van der Horst, *Pseudo-Phocylides*, 232; van der Horst, "Pseudo-Phocylides Revisited," 26.

[524] On the problems of translation, including the use of λέκτρα apparently to mean wife and the nominative τὰ δεύτερα λέκτρα in apposition to the genitive μητρυιῆς, see van der Horst, *Pseudo-Phocylides*, 229-30.

[525] As Thomas, *Phokylides*, notes, its absence here is not unexpected given that sexual relations with one's own mother were abhorrent also in Hellenistic culture (65).

The expansion of the prohibition of touching (ψαύω here means to have sexual relations with)[526] the wife of one's father in Lev 18:8 to include concubines (181), while not made explicit in the biblical text, is doubtless implied. Wilson notes the close connection achieved by the author through the first word of each line: μητρυιῆς (179) μητέρα (180), pointing to a similar parallelism in 181-182: μηδὲ κασιγνήτης and μηδὲ κασιγνήτων.[527] Reuben's intercourse with Bilhah (Gen 35:22; 49:4) was an infamous instance and in *Jubilees* became the platform for the angel's discourse about incest where it is seen as grounded in Lev 18:8 (33:1-20). The fact that men usually married around age 30 and women in their late teens could easily lead to situations where a young man born of the first wife would be close in age to the father's second wife and the proximity of age and place might easily lead to sexual engagement. The same would apply where Roman Law made it possible that a widower choose to take a concubine rather than remarry.

Given the focus on such a young man, the provisions of Leviticus 18 are well covered. The author goes beyond the latter in grounding the prohibition of sexual relations with a stepmother not in infringement of the rights of one's father, a stance also represented in Greek literature in Phoenix being cursed by his father for engaging in sex with his concubine (Homer *Il.* 9), but in honouring her as one honoured one's mother, an extension of the command to honour parents found also in Philo *Virt.* 225. Similarly the prohibition of sexual relations with sisters-in-law is depicted not as infringing the rights of one's brother as Lev 18:16, but simply as "abhorrent" ἀπότροπον. This is closer to the declarations in Leviticus 20 that certain sexual infringements are simply a "disgrace" (ὄνειδός) (20:17) or an "abomination" (βδέλυγμα) (20:13; cf. also 20:12, 14). As Wilson notes, however, the formulation of 183 is much closer to Hesiod *Op.* 328-329 (ὅς τε κασιγνήτοιο ἑοῦ ἀνὰ δέμνια βαίνῃ κρυπταδίης εὐνῆς ἀλόχου "goes to the bed of his own brother for clandestine sexual relations with his wife") and the prohibition was consistent also with values of the Greco-Roman world.[528]

184 A woman should not destroy an unborn babe in the womb,
185 nor after bearing it should she cast it out as prey for dogs and vultures.

---

[526] ψαύω like its synonym ἅπτομαι, both meaning "to touch", is used as a euphemism for sexual intercourse. For the latter, cf. Gen 20:6; Prov 6:29; 1 Cor 7:1; Philo *Leg.* 3.32; Josephus *A.J* 1.163; 2.57. See also Wilson, *Sentences*, 191 n. 23.

[527] Wilson, *Sentences*, 191.

[528] Wilson, *Sentences*, 192. He draws attention to Plato *Leg.* 838A-B; Euripides *Andr.* 173-175; Plutarch *Cic.* 29.4-5; Cicero *Pis.* 28; *Mil.* 73, while noting Philo's claim that Greeks and Egyptians tolerated marriage to sisters or half sisters (*Spec.* 3.22-25), supported at least with regard to half sisters by evidence from the Greek world (192 n. 28, 29) and with regard to sisters, as a characteristic of the Ptolemaic dynasty.

186 Lay not a hand on your wife while she is pregnant (μηδ' ἐπὶ σῇ ἀλόχῳ ἐγκύμονι χεῖρα βάληαι). (184-186)

The prohibition of induced abortion, exposure of infants, and doing violence to a pregnant wife, either deliberately to effect abortion or to do so incidentally by engaging in sexual intercourse with her (184-186), addresses abuses frequently attacked by Jews in the Greco-Roman world (e.g. Philo *Hypoth.* 7.7; Josephus *Ap.* 2.202), and are the obverse of 175-176, the injunction to give birth to children. Line 186 appears to derive from a reading of Exod 21:22-23, which treats it harm to the wife not as incidental or accidental as there, but as something deliberate.[529] That harm is therefore probably violence.[530] This is more likely than that it refers to sexual intercourse during pregnancy,[531] which some in ancient times saw as doing harm to the foetus (as in the *Damascus Document* 4QD^e/4Q270 2 ii.15-16; 6QD/6Q15 5 2-3; and 4QD^b/4Q267 9 vi.4-5),[532] especially if it is expounding Exod 21:22-23.

Concern about neglect of marriage and procreation caused Augustus to introduce his measures, and male worries about women showing disinterest in producing offspring featured regularly in moral discourse.[533] One element of concern was the indulgence in sexual pleasure for its own sake, which resulted in various practices of contraception, abortion, and exposure. Wilson cites Plutarch's disapproval of "licentious women who employ drugs and instruments to produce abortions for the sake of the enjoyment of conceiving again" (*Tu. san.* 134F).[534]

187 μηδ' αὖ παιδογόνον τέμνειν φύσιν ἄρσενα κούρου.
187 Do not cut the male procreative faculty of a youth.*

---

[529] Thomas, *Phokylides*, observes that the author would probably not have expected fights among his more sophisticated hearers in which wives might suffer incidental harm (72).

[530] Van der Horst, *Pseudo-Phocylides*, who writes: "Very probably the verse simply means: treat a pregnant woman gently, do not beat her (so as to prevent a miscarriage?)" (235). Similarly Wilson, *Sentences*, 194; Thomas, *Phokylides*, 71.

[531] So Crouch, *Origin*, 85; cf. also Niebuhr, *Gesetz und Paränese*, 29.

[532] On this see Loader, *Dead Sea Scrolls on Sexuality*, 139-40. Cf. also 1QapGen/1Q20 2.9-10, 13b-14a and Josephus *B.J.* 2.161.

[533] So Catharine Edwards, *The Politics of Immorality in Ancient Rome* (Cambridge: Cambridge University Press, 1993), who draws attention to Plato *Theaet.* 149D; Ps.-Heraclitus *Ep.* 7.5; Cicero *Clu.* 32-34; Seneca *Helv.* 16:3-4 (84). See also Wilson, *Sentences*, who points to a tolerance on the one hand of abortion and exposure, but also voices raised in protest at the practice (193).

[534] Wilson, *Sentences*, 193.

The injunction against castration connects well with what proceeds, namely the concern about preventing or subverting the processes of producing children, and so also with 175-176. The occurrence of the word φύσιν here (as in 176) also reflects the underlying axiom that anything which is unnatural is to be avoided, and here, certainly not to be thwarted. We find castration condemned also in Josephus (A.J. 4.290-291; Ap. 2.270-271) and Philo (Hypoth. 7.7), who connects it to Deut 23:2, which excludes those with crushed testicles from the assembly of the people. Eunuchs were not uncommon in the world of the time and generally accepted as part of life, though we occasionally hear voices raised against the practice of castration before it was finally forbidden by imperial edict under Domitian Lex Cornelia de sicariis et veneficis (Suetonius Dom. 7.1).

Whereas 184-187 are concerned with acts which are contrary to nature because they prevent the production of offspring, the following instructions in 188-194 address the appropriate direction of sexual desire and its moderation.

188 μηδ' ἀλόγοις ζώοισι βατήριον ἐς λέχος ἐλθεῖν.
188 Do not engage in sexual relations with irrational animals*

The prohibition of sexual relations with animals has its biblical roots in Lev 18:23 (cf. also 20:15-16; Exod 22:18), where it is applied to both men, as defiling to oneself (ἐκμιανθῆναι), and women, as "abominable" (μυσερόν). Here in 188 the focus is men. The word ἀλόγοις probably implies the argument that it is particularly inappropriate for beings who have reason (λόγος) to do so (similarly Philo Spec. 3.43-50), though it is a standard description of animals. The focus is apparently not concern for animals, but about action contrary to one's own nature as a rational being. Abuse of animals, possibly including in a sexual sense, appears also in 2 Enoch 59:5 (cf. 58:6). For condemnation of bestiality see also Sib. Or. 5.393.

189 μηδ' ὕβριζε γυναῖκα ἐπ' αἰσχυντοῖς λεχέεσσιν.
189 Do not outrage a woman by shameful acts of sex.

The focus of concern in this prohibition is the woman, matching the concern in 180 which enjoins honouring of one's stepmother. Here dishonouring, represented by ὕβριζε, envisages an act which humiliates or violates the dignity of a woman, whether one's wife or any other woman. The αἰσχυντοῖς λεχέεσσιν ("shameful acts") most likely refer to sexual acts which the author deems abusive, but what precisely these are is difficult to determine. The focus could be sexual assault, for which ὑβρίζω is attested,[535] but given the emphasis in 166-194 the focus is more

---

[535] Wilson, Sentences, 195.

likely to be particular acts driven by excessive sexual desire. Possibly the author has in mind ways of engaging in sexual intercourse which the author considers shameful and so bringing shame on the woman, including such practices as *fellatio, cunnilingus,*[536] and anal intercourse, or alternatively, sexual intercourse during menstruation (cf. Lev 15:24; Lev 18:19; 20:18; CD 5.6-7; 4QD^a/4Q266 6 ii.1-2), although one would have to assume that listeners would think of the latter. It is at least an element in Leviticus 18 on which the author has been drawing (18:19; cf. 20:18) and on this ground is probably to be preferred.[537] Thomas notes that the author makes the husband responsible for breach of such taboos.[538] The assumption is that intercourse during menstruation reflects failure of men to moderate their passions. That theme is generalised in 193-194. Here in 189 specific abuses appear to be in mind. The concern with behaviours resulting from immoderate and ill-directed passion continues in the following lines.

190 μὴ παραβῇς εὐνὰς φύσεως ἐς Κύπριν ἄθεσμον.
191 οὐδ' αὐτοῖς θήρεσσι συνεύαδον ἄρσενες εὐναί.
192 μηδέ τι θηλύτεραι λέχος ἀνδρῶν μιμήσαιντο.
190 Go not beyond natural sexual unions for illicit passion;
191 unions between males are not pleasing even to beasts.
192 And let women not mimic the sexual role of men at all. (190-192)

The statement in 190 could summarise the import of the preceding lines, which are also concerned with actions deemed contrary to nature, whether in castrating a young male or involvement in bestiality or engagement in sexual activity which shames a woman.[539] Κύπριν here, as in 3 and 67, designates sexual passion, qualified negatively here by the word ἄθεσμον. Line 190, however, also belongs closely together with 191-192, which further illustrate sexual relations deemed contrary to nature, namely male and female same-sex relations, and so probably 190 is already directed to that theme, echoing the opening statement associated with the prohibition of adultery in 3 (μήτ' ἄρσενα Κύπριν ὀρίνειν; similarly *Sib. Or.* 5:430, παίδων Κύπρις ἄθεσμος).[540] The condemnation of same-sex

---

[536] Van der Horst, *Pseudo-Phocylides*, points to the reading, χείλεσσι, in MS P, which would imply oral sex (237). Among other options he mentions variations in sexual intercourse, adultery, and intercourse during menstruation.

[537] So van der Horst, *Pseudo-Phocylides*, 237; Thomas, *Phokylides*, 66; Wilson, *Sentences*, 195.

[538] Thomas, *Phokylides*, 67.

[539] Wilson, *Sentences*, 196. He notes that Philo's list of unnatural sexual acts includes intercourse during menstruation (*Spec.* 3.32); with a sterile woman (36); bestiality (48), prostitution (51), as well as adultery (52).

[540] So van der Horst, *Pseudo-Phocylides*, 238.

relations derives from Lev 18:22 (cf. 20:13), where, as here (188), it is juxtaposed to bestiality. The theme is taken up also by Philo (*Hypoth.* 7.1 and Josephus (*Ap.* 2.199). The argument that homosexual relations do not occur in the animal kingdom, further reinforcing that it is contrary to nature, is to be found also among Hellenistic authors (e.g. Plutarch *Brut. an.* 990D and Ovid *Metam.* 9.733-734 on relations among females; earlier Plato *Leg.* 836C).[541] The concern about women mimicking men's roles reflects the concern in same-sex relations between women, where one takes the active male role, a concern implicit in Rom 1:26-27. Females usurping male roles, just as males taking an inferior female role, was offensive in the Greco-Roman world.[542]

193 μηδ' ἐς ἔρωτα γυναικὸς ἅπας ῥεύσῃς ἀκάθεκτον·
194 οὐ γὰρ ἔρως θεός ἐστι, πάθος δ' ἀίδηλον ἁπάντων.
193 Be not inclined to utterly unrestrained lust for a woman.
194 For *Erōs* is no god, but a passion destructive of all. (193-194)

In question is not ἔρως, here "sexual desire", in itself, but making a god of it (194) and not bridling it (ἀκάθεκτον). γυναικός means any woman, including one's own wife. Here the focus has moved from behaviour to attitude in a manner typical of Hellenistic moral philosophy.[543] Here it is appropriate to cite Philo's disapproval of men who are inordinately lustful towards their wives (Philo *Spec.* 3.9; cf. 3.79, 113), and Seneca's disdain for those who treat their wives as though they are their mistresses (*Matr.* 85).[544] Control and moderation apply as much to the sexual realm as they do to all the rest of life and are a fundamental value espoused by the author (cf. 59-69). Failure to exercise restrain leads to chaos and destruction. Especially a man in authority should show he can control his sexual appetite.[545] Fear of Eros was a commonplace, while embracing also its appeal.[546] This may have been further reinforced by the view that excessive sexual indulgence weakened men, their ejaculations signifying a loss of life.[547] While the appeal not to make a god of Eros might appear to cohere well with the author's

---

[541] See van der Horst, *Pseudo-Phocylides*, 239; Wilson, *Sentences*, 197.

[542] Wilson, *Sentences*, 198.

[543] On this see Martha C. Nussbaum, *The Therapy of Desire: Theory and Practice in Hellenistic Ethics* (Princeton: Princeton University Press, 1994), 485; also Thomas, *Phokylides*, who observes that this exhortation goes beyond the previous warnings to address what underlies them and operates in typical Hellenistic fashion in highlighting the psychological dimension which calls for discipline in handling sexual relations (81).

[544] Cf. Wilson, *Sentences*, who cites them already in relation to 189 (195).

[545] See Wilson, *Sentences*, 198.

[546] See Wilson, *Sentences*, 199.

[547] See Michel Foucault, *The Use of Pleasure: Volume 2 of the History of Sexuality* (New York: Vintage, 1990) 130-33, referring to Hippocrates, Plato, and Aristotle.

Jewish background, representing a faint hint of prohibition of idolatry otherwise absent in the work, the value system reflected in these lines is beholden to Hellenistic values.[548]

195 Στέργε τεὴν ἄλοχον· τί γὰρ ἡδύτερον καὶ ἄρειον,
196 ἢ ὅταν ἀνδρὶ γυνὴ φρονέῃ φίλα γήραος ἄχρις
197 καὶ πόσις ᾖ ἀλόχῳ, μηδ᾽ ἐμπέσῃ ἄνδιχα νεῖκος;
195 Love your wife: for what is sweeter and better
196 than when a wife is lovingly disposed to her husband into old age
197 and husband to his wife, and strife does not split them asunder? (195-197)

These words echo the positive statement with which this section began in 175, which affirms marriage. While the word, ἔρως does not occur, the theme connects closely with what precedes, since it now depicts appropriate affection between husband and wife. It may well envisage sexual union, including procreation (as in 175-176), but its focus lies elsewhere, in particular on loving attitude (φρονέῃ φίλα). The shift from behaviour to attitude has occurred already in the transition from 192 to 193. While loving one's wife makes for good order, indeed, harmony, it is also something much more, and so is expressed in the engaged language of "sweetness" (ἡδύτερον). Here we find an ideal based on some level of mutuality of affection, not just hierarchy and control. It coheres with the respect for women already noted in 179-180 and 189. This idea has firm roots in Hellenistic tradition, for which Homer *Od.* 6.182-184, adapted here, was an inspiration: "For nothing is greater and better than when husband and wife dwell in a home in one accord".[549] Wilson observes that "Pseudo-Phocylides' adaptation of the Homeric passage emphasizes both the presence of mutual and abiding love in marriage and the absence of strife this fosters".[550] Marital harmony is a common theme, both in Jewish (e.g. Sir 25:1; 26:1-2) and Greco-Roman literature.[551]

The lines also mark a transition to a focus on the household, both its beginnings and the maintenance and protection of its members.

198 μή δέ τις ἀμνήστευτα βίῃ κούρῃσι μιγείη.
198 Let no one have sex with maidens forcibly (or) without honourable wooing.

This topic fits appropriately at the beginning of what might lead to marriage and household. It addresses the issue of rape in relation to girls (κούρῃσι) and appears to derive from Exod 22:16 (15 LXX), which provides for the situation where a

---

[548] So Wilson, *Sentences*, 199.
[549] Van der Horst, *Pseudo-Phocylides*, 241-42; Wilson, *Sentences*, 202.
[550] Wilson, *Sentences*, 202.
[551] See Wilson, *Sentences*, 202-203.

man seduces a girl not yet betrothed (παρθένον ἀμνήστευτον) and what he must subsequently do, namely pay a bride price and marry her. Here in 198 the rare word ἀμνήστευτα appears to be adverbial, meaning something like "without honourable wooing" or perhaps something like outside the context of a betrothal situation, as the context of Exod 22:16 suggests.[552] It is a straightforward prohibition with explicit reference to force (βίη), which may show influence from Deut 22:28-29. This is no way to start a household (similarly Philo *Spec.* 3.65-71). The author may well have the consequences delineated in Exod 22:16 and Deut 22:28-29 in mind. He then proceeds to another instance of a bad beginning.

> 199 Bring not into your house an evil, wealthy woman;
> 200 you will be your wife's hireling, all for a wretched dowry.
> 201 We seek well-bred horses and ploughers of earth –
> 202 strong-necked bulls – and of dogs the best of all.
> 203 But foolishly we do not contend to marry a good woman;
> 204 nor does a woman reject a wicked man if he is wealthy. (199-204)

The second bad beginning is to marry a bad and wealthy woman, because you will be bound to her on account of the size of her dowry and need to pay it back if the marriage dissolves. While it was not uncommon to urge that the size of dowry not be a factor in choosing a wife, there was awareness of the problem which a woman with a large dowry might pose, to the extent that it became a topos in comedy, the poor man as servant of his wife.[553] The author is drawing here not on biblical resources but the wisdom of the Hellenistic world. This appears also to be the case in 201-204 where he has reworked Theognis *El.* 183-188.[554]

The next two lines consider new beginnings, warning against many marriages.

> 205 Do not add marriage to marriage, calamity to calamity (πήματα πῆμα).
> 206 Nor permit yourself strife with your kinsfolk about possessions. (205-206)

---

[552] Thomas, *Phokylides*, notes that by transferring to the man (ἀμνήστυετα) what originally referred to the woman (ἀμνήστευτον) the author typically reinforces the importance seen throughout the work of the need for men to act responsibly (74).

[553] On this see Wilson, *Sentences*, 204.

[554] So van der Horst, *Pseudo-Phocylides*, 243; Wilson, *Sentences*, 204. Thomas, *Phokylides*, suggests that the loose citation, compared to the more exact quotation of Homer a few lines earlier, is because in contrast to the citation from Homer, the author is concerned not to have Phocylides directly cite someone who is to be seen not as his forerunner but as his contemporary (82).

Though it could apply to polygyny, it more probably applies to remarriage.[555] The connection between marriage, property and inheritance explains the link between the two lines, because new marriages produce new wealth and new heirs, and so inevitable disputes in dealing with the complications of inheritance which result. With the common expression calamity to calamity (πήματα πῆμα) (Herodotus *Hist.* 1.67-68; Sophocles *Ant.* 595) the author indulges in cynicism, somewhat in tension with his earlier ideal of marriage, but probably in the sense that the starting point was already something disastrous. Many inscriptions reflect an ideal of being married once and not remarrying after death of a spouse,[556] a value also evident in Luke's image of Anna (2:36).

Attention next turns to the children of the household.

> 207 Do not be severe with your children, but be gentle.
> 208 If a child sins against you, let the mother judge her son,
> 209 or else the elders of the family or the chiefs of the people.
> 210 Do not grow locks in the hair of a male child.
> 211 Braid not his crown or the cross-knots on the top of his head.
> 212 For men to wear long hair is not seemly, just for sensual women.
> 213 Protect the youthful beauty of a handsome boy;
> 214 for many rage with lust for sex with a male (πολλοὶ γὰρ λυσσῶσι πρὸς ἄρσενα μεῖξιν ἔρωτος). (207-214)

It is noteworthy that in 208-209 the author removes the father from a situation where as the one wronged he might act inappropriately and instead recommends that others exercise the necessary discipline (cf. also Sir 3:2 on the maternal role in relations to sons).[557] The primary concern in 210-214 is protection of a boy from homosexual predators. That includes making sure he does not have long hair and braiding, which, we may assume, would make him more attractive to them, probably more effeminate in appearance. The notion that long hair was unbecoming of a male was a widely-held view in the Greco-Roman world (including Paul, 1 Cor 11:14-15) with some exceptions (Sparta, Cynics, Jewish Nazirites). Wilson notes that vase paintings depicting homoerotic scenes regularly portray the passive partner as having long hair.[558] Pederasty, tolerated between male citizens and their inferiors, youth, non-citizens and slaves, in Greek society, met with disapproval in Roman society and was seen by Jews as a sign of

---

[555] Thomas, *Phokylides*, sees here the author's espousal of monogyny and of remaining unmarried after the death of a spouse (63, 83). See also Wilson, *Sentences*, 205.

[556] See Wilson, *Sentences*, 206.

[557] Wilson, *Sentences*, notes similar advice in Cicero and similar emphasis on gentleness, especially towards one's own children, in contrast to slaves (207).

[558] Wilson, *Sentences*, 208.

decadence. The prominence of the warning here reflects that the author sees his society as one in which the danger was a present reality.

> 215 Guard a virgin in closely shut chambers,
> 216 and let her not be seen before the house until her wedding day.*
> 217 The beauty of children is hard for parents to protect. (215-217)

This advice mirrors the concerns of Ben Sira (42:9-11; cf. also 4 Macc 18:7), but probably not his degree of pessimism (cf. 26:10-12), and reflects the social pattern according to which a father was held responsible for his daughter until she passed to control of the one who should succeed him, namely her husband, and that her value and status as a virgin was of paramount importance. It is noteworthy that 217 depicts this role as a shared responsibility. Thomas notes the absence of common Jewish concerns with female cosmetics and ornaments.[559]

The remaining pieces of advice address other aspects of the household, including kin, the aged, and slaves, with a strongly positive attitude towards each, but not addressing aspects of sexuality. These would have been relevant in relation to sexual engagement with slaves. Presumably the silence reflects that the author saw nothing problematic in what was the common practice in both Jewish and non-Jewish circles, according to which sexual access to slaves was assumed.

The work concludes with an enigmatic saying about purity.

> 228 ἁγνείη ψυχῆς, οὐ σώματός εἰσι καθαρμοί.
> 228 Let there be purity of the soul where there are purifications of the body.

Wilson's translation here reflects one of many interpretations and is to be compared with that of van der Horst: "Purifications are for the purity of the soul, not of the body".[560] The statement has been taken as indicating a dismissive attitude towards ritual purification.[561] Wilson sees in the statement "a certain

---

[559] Thomas, *Phokylides*, 84.

[560] See also Nikolaus Walter, *Pseudepigraphische jüdisch-hellenistische Dichtung: Pseudo-Phokylides, Pseudo-Orpheus, Gefälschte Verse auf Namen griechischer Dichter* (JSHRZ 4.3; Gütersloh: Gütersloher Verlagshaus, 1983), who translates: "(Rituelle) Reinigungen bedeuten Heiligung der Seele, nicht des Körpers" (216).

[561] Klaus Berger, *Die Gesetzesauslegung Jesu: Ihr historischer Hintergrund im Judentum und im Alten Testament: Teil I: Markus und Parallelen* (WMANT 40; Neukirchen–Vluyn: Neukirchener Verlag, 1972) 467; similarly Roger P. Booth, *Jesus and the Laws of Purity: Tradition History and Legal History in Mark 7* (JSNTS 13; Sheffield: JSOT, 1986) 85-87; and see the critique of Pieter W. van der Horst, "Pseudo-Phocylides and the New Testament," *ZNW* 69 (1978) 187-202. In van der Horst, "Pseudo-Phocylides Revisited," 27-28, he notes the suggestion that ἁγνείη be read as "fasting". Heikki Räisänen, *Paul and the Law* (Philadelphia: Fortress, 1986) 36-38, argues that the verse

'moralization' of purificatory rituals and their rationale", such as we find in Sir 34:18 – 35:10, *Pseudo-Aristeas*, Philo and Josephus.[562] He adds: "It should be emphasized that Pseudo-Phocylides does not abrogate the actual performance of such rites, and he appears to take for granted the validity of their purity rules in the somatic, as well as in the moral, domain".[563] This would be confirmed if 189 includes concern about impurity contracted by sexual intercourse during menstruation. The focus on moral purity coheres with the absence of many specifically Jewish concerns about purity which the author could not credibly include as instructions of Phocylides, including after seminal emission, during menstruation, and after childbirth.

Conclusion

Pseudo-Phocylides enables us to see the sexual mores which its author upheld in the context of his strategy of having the ancient Phocylides mouth Jewish values and so reinforce them for his fellow Jews. To include distinctively Jewish laws pertaining to sexuality, such as in relation to menstruation, seminal emissions, and childbirth, would have blown his cover. The same would have applied to sabbath, which was relevant for some on sexual issues. Divorce and polygyny are addressed only indirectly, in the instruction not to multiply marriages. Debauchery linked with banquets may be implied, but is not expressed. Nothing is said about masturbation, about cosmetics, about prostitution except against having one's wife ply the trade, nor about the desirable quality of daughters as potential spouses, though it warns against the wicked rich woman.

Despite their terseness, this set of instructions reflects some underlying values. They include that sexual desire, like other human desires, such as hunger, may be both misdirected and be excessive and is frequently both. The emphasis on excess matches the emphases of popular Stoic philosophy. The concern with direction is informed more specifically by Jewish values, some of which, like the prohibitions of adultery, incest, and bestiality, would also have been widely shared in the Greco-Roman world and others, less widely, such as the concern about same-sex relations by both men and women and with pederastic predation. Some elements remain unclear, for instance, whether the warning against acts which bring shame on one's wife include disapproved modes of intercourse. Another underlying value deeply rooted in popular Stoic philosophy and framing the

---

takes for granted the existence of purification laws and intends rather "to point out that the real meaning of external rites, a meaning that is spiritual and internalised", and in relation to such law implies "no demonstrable *reduction* of it to a moral law" (38).

[562] Wilson, *Sentences*, 71-72.

[563] Wilson, *Sentences*, 71.

author's concerns is that of order, in particular of the household, with which the author can identify the righteousness of Torah. This sense of order also relates to what is deemed to be according to nature. Here the emphasis falls in particular on affirming the value of procreation within the institution of marriage and prohibiting whatever does not serve it, to the degree of apparently sharing the disapproval of some later Stoics of sexual intercourse simply for pleasure or to express intimate love independent of procreational purpose. This would be implied in possible references to forbidding sexual intercourse during pregnancy and during menstruation, though it is far from certain that the text indicates this.

3.3   *Fragmentary Judeo-Hellenistic Works*

3.3.1   **Theodotus**

In *Praep. ev.* 9.22.1-11 Eusebius includes 8 fragments containing 47 lines which contain excerpts and summaries of the epic poet Theodotus[564] about Jacob, embedded in the work of Alexander Polyhistor, who wrote in the mid first century B.C.E.[565] and on the basis of other evidence is considered a faithful reproducer of his sources.[566] There has been considerable debate about whether Theodotus was a Jew or a Samaritan. The former seems more likely, given that the author's sympathies are clearly on the side of Jacob and his sons, not the people of Shechem,[567] though others still argue that a Samaritan might easily have identified himself as a Jew and spoken negatively of Shechemites as pagans.[568] The poem's

---

[564] The following discussion is based on the text edition and translation of Carl R. Holladay, "Theodotus," in Carl R. Holladay, *Fragments from Hellenistic Jewish Authors: Volume 2: Poets: The Epic Poets Theodotus and Philo and Ezekiel the Tragedian* (SBLTT 30; PS 12; Atlanta: Scholars, 1989) 51-204, except where I have offered my own translation of a word or citation, indicated by an asterisk. Citation is by fragment and line.

[565] The words περὶ Ἰουδαίων in fr. 1 are probably not the title of *Theodotus'* work, but "Polyhistor's general designation of the work". So Holladay, "Theodotus," 58, and see his discussion, pp. 53-58.

[566] So F. Fallon, "Theodotus," *OTP*, 2.785-93, 785. See also John Strugnell, "Introduction: General Introduction, with a Note on Alexander Polyhistor," *OTP*, 2.777-79.

[567] On these issues see Holladay, "Theodotus," 53-58, 58-68; and the discussion of the major proponent of the Samaritan hypothesis, J. Freudenthal, *Hellenistische Studien: Heft 1 und 2: Alexander Polyhistor und die von ihm erhaltenen Reste judäischer und samaritanischer Geschichtswerke* (Breslau: Skutsch, 1875) in John J. Collins, "The Epic of Theodotus and the Hellenism of the Hasmoneans," *HTR* 73 (1980) 91-104; Collins, *Between Athens and Jerusalem*, 58.

[568] So Louis H. Feldman, "Philo, Pseudo-Philo, Josephus, and Theodotus on the Rape of Dinah," *JQR* 94 (2004) 253-77, 275; D. Mendels, *The Land of Israel as Political*

description of Shechem in fragment 1, apparently based on first-hand knowledge, favours a date for its origin before the mid 2nd century B.C.E.,[569] though its focus on the wickedness of the Shechemites might also fit John Hyrcanus' conquests in the latter part of that century.[570] The work is extraordinary for its thoroughly Hellenised form, emulating Homeric style, while espousing a strongly separatist ideology,[571] and could be at home anywhere in the Greco-Roman Jewish diaspora, though the author's apparently first-hand knowledge of Shechem may indicate the Palestine Syria region.[572]

Concept in Hasmonean Literature: Recourse to History in Second Century BCE: Claims to the Holy Land (Tübingen: Mohr Siebeck, 1987) 110-16; Pieter W. van der Horst, "The Interpretation of the Bible by the Minor Hellenistic Jewish Authors," in Pieter van der Horst, *Essays on the Jewish World of Early Christianity* (NTOA 14; Fribourg: Universitätsverlag; Göttingen: Vandenhoeck & Ruprecht, 1990) 187-219, 194-95; Michael B. Daise, "Samaritans, Seleucids, and the Epic of Theodotus," *JSP* 17 (1998) 25-51, who argues that the work is a late third or early second century B.C.E. "expression of Samaritan intent to regain Shechem from Seleucid control" (31). The reconstruction does not adequately account for the issue of intermarriage in the text.

[569] So Fallon, "Theodotus," 788, who writes: "Since Theodotus describes Shechem as having a 'smooth wall' and since this phrase is not a customary epic description, then he must have observed the city prior to the middle of the second century B.C." (789), by which time it no longer stood. For the archaeological evidence and its significance see Robert J. Bull, "Note on Theodotus' Description of Shechem," *HTR* 60 (1967) 221-27. He concludes: "The archaeological evidence thus indicates that there was a strong defense enclosure about the city of Shechem from the time of its Hellenistic reoccupation ca. 331 until the first half of the second century B.C., at which time the defense wall fell into disuse" (227).

[570] So Collins, *Between Athens and Jerusalem*, 58; Collins, "Epic," who questions dependence on the author's comments about the wall (101); Oegema, *Poetische Schriften*, 54, 57, 59; H. G. Kippenberg, *Garazim und Synagoge: Traditionsgeschichtliche Untersuchungen zur samaritanischen Religion der aramäischen Periode* (Berlin: de Gruyter, 1971) 83-90; 112. See the discussion in Holladay, "Theodotus," 68-70; Fallon, "Theodotus," 786. Cf. Gruen, *Heritage and Hellenism*, who argues that the focus is not to be found in support for Hyrcanus nor in a pro- or anti-Samaritan but in the concern to cast the patriarchs in a better light : "Theodotus' verse rendition smoothed out some rough spots in the Genesis narrative" (124). This does not adequately take into account the apparent interest in forcing the circumcision issue.

[571] Collins, *Between Athens and Jerusalem*, writes: "it is striking that Jewish nationalism is comfortably clad in such an obviously Hellenistic dress. If this poem was written in support of John Hyrcanus, it offers a remarkable illustration of the Hasmonean blend of nationalism and Hellenization" (60). See also the discussion in Carl R. Holladay, "Hellenism in the Fragmentary Hellenistic Jewish Authors: Resonance and Resistance," in *Shem in the Tents of Japhet: Essays on the Encounter of Judaism and Hellenism* (ed. James L. Kugel; JSJSup 74; Leiden: Brill, 2002) 65-91, 82-90.

[572] Holladay, "Theodotus," leaves the issue open (72).

Fragment 3 mentions Laban's promise to Jacob that he marry his daughter, Rachel, and the deception which led to Jacob first marrying Leah. Its few lines clearly paint Laban as a villain, who "wound a skein of wile", offering no justification as in Gen 29:26 that custom required that the eldest daughter had priority, and depicting Jacob as particularly savvy about what was going on. As in Genesis nothing is said of the problem that by marrying both Jacob contravened the laws of incest.

Fragments 4 – 8 are taken up with the account of the rape of Dinah, based on Gen 34:1-31. The story is foreshadowed already to some degree in Fragment 2 which depicts Hamor and his son Shechem as "a very stubborn pair" (μάλ' ἀτειρέε φῶτε), casting them in a negative light, and her brothers as "exceedingly wise in understanding" (νόῳ πεπνυμένοι αἰνῶς) (3 17), and in fragment 3 18-19 which describes Dinah as "having a very beautiful appearance, a stunning figure and a noble heart too"* (περικαλλὲς ἔχουσα εἶδος, ἐπίστρεπτον δὲ δέμας καὶ ἀμύμονα θυμόν), language reminiscent of the description of Rachel in LXX Gen 29:17: Ραχηλ δὲ καλὴ τῷ εἴδει καὶ ὡραία τῇ ὄψει ("but Rachel was shapely in figure and lovely in appearance"). [573]

Fragment 4, mainly Polyhistor's summary of Theodotus,[574] then describes Dinah and Jacob's wives as working with wool, a non-biblical detail, but a reasonable deduction given her brothers were shepherds (cf. Gen 33:13). More significant is the description of Dinah's visit to Shechem. Where the Genesis account simply reports that she "went out to visit the women of the region" (34:1), Theodotus states that "Dinah, while still a virgin, came to Shechem when there was a great festival because she wanted to see the city" (καὶ τὴν Δείναν παρθένον οὖσαν εἰς τὰ Σίκιμα ἐλθεῖν πανηγύρεως οὔσης βουλομένην θεάσασθαι τὴν πόλιν) (4 7-9).[575] The author does not indicate how he viewed this endeavour.[576] In *Genesis Rabbah* it is viewed negatively (80:1-2).[577] It may

---

[573] Holladay, "Theodotus," 171.

[574] Holladay, "Theodotus," 52.

[575] Josephus also mentions the festival (*A.J.* 1.337), perhaps in dependence on *Theodotus* (so Kippenberg, *Garizim* 56 n. 123).

[576] Bader, *Tracing the Evidence*, speculates "that she had an element of either curiosity (wishing to see the city) or even business savvy" (104), adding "that possibly a fairly innocent 'wool-working woman' may not know the dangers or perils that might lie in a more urban area at the time of a festival' (105). Angela Standhartinger, "'Um zu sehen die Töchter des Landes': Die Perspektive Dinas in der jüdisch-hellenistischen Diskussion um Gen 34," in *Religious Propaganda and Missionary Competition in the New Testament World* (ed. Lukas Bormann, Kelly del Tredici, and Angela Standhartinger; Leiden: Brill, 1994) 89-116, sees it as likely to have been an approved exception that a daughter or wife of a household be permitted to leave the preserve of the home for special events such as festivals (94-95).

also be that *ALD* sees her as blameworthy, if we read it as declaring that she defiled her family. [578]

The description of Shechem's deed matches the account in Genesis: Συχὲμ δὲ τὸν τοῦ Ἐμμὼρ υἱὸν ἰδόντα ἐρασθῆναι αὐτῆς καὶ ἁρπάσαντα ὡς ἑαυτὸν διακομίσαι καὶ φθεῖραι αὐτήν ("When Shechem, the son of Hamor, saw her, he loved her; and, seizing her as his own, he carried her away and raped her") (4 9-11; cf. καὶ εἶδεν αὐτὴν Συχεμ ὁ υἱὸς Εμμωρ ὁ Χορραῖος ὁ ἄρχων τῆς γῆς καὶ λαβὼν αὐτὴν ἐκοιμήθη μετ' αὐτῆς καὶ ἐταπείνωσεν αὐτήν. "And Sychem the son of Hemmor the Chorrite, the ruler of the land, saw her, and seizing her he lay with her and humbled her") (Gen 34:2). The reference to Shechem's love (ἐρασθῆναι always used of sexual passion in Homer)[579] derives from Gen 34:3 (ἠγάπησεν τὴν παρθένον "he loved the maiden"). Apart from that the mildly positive description of Shechem in Gen 34:3 (καὶ προσέσχεν τῇ ψυχῇ Δινας τῆς θυγατρὸς Ιακωβ καὶ ἠγάπησεν τὴν παρθένον καὶ ἐλάλησεν κατὰ τὴν διάνοιαν τῆς παρθένου αὐτῇ) leaves no trace. The use of φθείρω "destroy"[580] is stronger than ταπεινόω "humiliate".[581]

The account reports Shechem's approach to Jacob with his father, summarising Gen 34:4-12, but nothing of his amorous words to Dinah. "Instead," as Holladay observes, "according to Theodotus, Shechem raped her, then immediately asked his father to get her as his wife."[582] References in Genesis to defilement (ἐμίανεν 34:5, 13), and later to "treating our sister as a whore" (ὡσεὶ πόρνῃ χρήσωνται τῇ ἀδελφῇ ἡμῶν 34:31) do not appear. Instead of reporting the brothers' expressing outrage and deceitfully demanding that the Shechemites be circumcised, Theodotus has Jacob himself declare that he would not give her away in marriage until all the Shechemites were circumcised (τὸν δὲ οὐ φάναι δώσειν, πρὶν ἂν ἢ πάντας τοὺς οἰκοῦντας τὰ Ζίκιμα περιτεμνομένους Ἰουδαῖσαι) (4 13-15) and without any apparent hint of deceit, but as Theodotus

---

[577] It also sees Dinah as having to be forcibly removed from her new husband.

[578] See Loader, *Enoch, Levi, and Jubilees*, 88-89.

[579] Holladay, "Theodotus," 175.

[580] For the use of φθείρω in this sense (though not in Homer) see Holladay, "Theodotus," 175. It is hard to see how Bader, *Tracing the Evidence*, can write of this fragment of "a point of ambiguity" whether this was done against Dinah's will (104), not clarified till fragment 6 (105).

[581] As Holladay, "Theodotus," notes, use of similar language by Josephus *A.J.* 1.337 (θεασάμενος δ' αὐτὴν Συχέμμης [ὁ] Ἐμμώρου τοῦ βασιλέως υἱὸς φθείρει δι' ἁρπαγῆς καὶ διατεθεὶς ἐρωτικῶς) may indicate dependence or at least a common source (175). See also Holladay, "Resonance and Resistance," where he notes "how thoroughly the language of the LXX has been recast" in Theodotus' account (84).

[582] Holladay, "Resonance and Resistance," 84.

explains: οὐ γὰρ δὴ θεμιτόν γε τόδ' Ἑβραίοισι τέτυκται, γαμβροὺς ἄλλοθεν εἴς γε νυούς τ' ἀγέμεν ποτὶ δῶμα, ἀλλ' ὅστις γενεῆς ἐξεύχεται εἶναι ὁμοίης ("For, indeed, this very thing is not allowed for Hebrews to bring home sons-in-law and daughters-in-law from another place but only one who boasts of being of the same race") (4 19-21).

This statement about the prohibition of intermarriage might appear slightly ambiguous, since its final statement appears to rule out intermarriage with anyone not of Jewish race (γενεῆς), but this does not fit the context, where intermarriage with a Shechemite, a person of another race, is contemplated. Polyhistor's summary of Theodotus' description of Jacob's demand, before apparently citing him directly, indicates something amounting to the incorporation of all Shechemites into the "race" of the Jews, using the word Ἰουδαΐζω / Ἰουδαϊσμός. This word appears to have been formed in opposition to Ἑλληνίζω, Ἑλληνισμος possibly in the early second century B.C.E., and to mean: "to live as a Jew" (2 Macc 2:21; 8:1; 14:38; 4 Macc 4:26; Esth 8:17; Gal 2:14; cf. 2 Macc 4:13). Thus what in Genesis was a ruse has become virtually a serious demand for mass conversion of a people, to be incorporated into Israel, providing the only basis for legitimate marriage. It is in this sense that the work would seem very appropriate to the reign of Hyrcanus with his policy of forced Judaising,[583] rather than just a requirement of individuals. On the other hand, it is not advocating forced conversion here, but stipulating a way in which someone may become part of the community of the circumcised, the people of the covenant.[584] Having Jacob genuinely express openness to intermarriage on the basis of circumcision is important evidence for the flexible approach to intermarriage such as we see in *Aseneth*.[585]

After fragment 5 brings further detail about circumcision, reporting its divine mandate to Abraham, fragment 6 returns to the story of Dinah, reporting that while Hamor "was encouraging his subjects to be circumcised, one of the sons of Jacob named Simeon decided to kill both Hamor and Shechem since he was unwilling to endure civilly the outrage to his sister" (καὶ τοὺς ὑποτασσομένους

[583] So Collins, *Between Athens and Jerusalem*, 59, who notes that "after the death of Antiochus VII Sidetes in 129 B.C.E., John Hyrcanus began a campaign against the neighbors of the Jews. He compelled the Idumeans to be circumcised and accept the laws of the Jews. He ravaged Shechem, destroyed the temple of Mt. Gerizim, and later, about 107 B.C.E. besieged and destroyed Samaria. The poem of Theodotus could easily be read as a paradigmatic justification for the actions and policies of Hyrcanus" (59). Similarly Oegema, *Poetische Schriften*, 57.

[584] So Donaldson, *Judaism and the Gentiles*, 102. He writes: "Further, this transition is not simply ethnic and cultural, but is one with religious and ethical dimensions as well ... Gentiles who become circumcised are becoming part of a covenant community" (103).

[585] So Kugel, "Rape of Dinah," 78.

παρακαλοῦντος περιτέμνεσθαι, ἕνα τῶν ᾿Ιακὼβ υἱῶν τὸ ὄνομα Συμεῶνα διαγνῶναι τόν τε ᾿Εμμὼρ καὶ τὸν Συχὲμ ἀνελεῖν, τὴν ὕβριν τῆς ἀδελφῆς μὴ βουληθέντα πολιτικῶς ἐνεγκεῖν) (6 2-6). As in Jdt 9:2, Theodotus has Simeon taking the initiative, so differing from the Genesis account, which attributed it to both "Simeon and Levi" (Gen 34:25).[586] The reference to τὴν ὕβριν τῆς ἀδελφῆς ("the outrage to his sister") echoes ἄσχημον ("unseemly thing") of Gen 34:7. The explanation μὴ βουληθέντα πολιτικῶς ἐνεγκεῖν ("since he was unwilling to endure civilly")[587] preserves something of the critical stance of Genesis which has Jacob rebuke Simeon and Levi for their deed (34:30) and later curse their anger (49:5-7).

In this account Simeon communicates with Levi, seeking his assent, possibly a reflection of the latter's special status,[588] and citing to him an oracle which declared that God would give ten nations to Abraham's sons (9). None of this is to be found in Genesis, though the alleged oracle may well refer to Gen 15:18-21, which lists ten nations, including the Canaanites and Perizzites who appear in Gen 34:30 in the context of Jacob's complaint.[589] The author has a reworked tradition which now, far from depicting Jacob's concern, rather seeks to justify the brothers' deed by giving it divine sanction and seeing it as implied in the promise of the land. The deed might then be seen as a variant on the slaughters mandated in the conquest according to the Book of Joshua.[590]

Divine sanction for the brothers' action, contrary to the account in Genesis, is assumed in *ALD*, where Levi apparently consults his brother and father about acting in accordance with the Law (1:1-3 / 1c2) and hails his action as destroying the works of violence (12:6 / 78).[591] Levi receives similar prominence in *Jubilees*

---

[586] Holladay, "Theodotus," notes that Simeon is mentioned first as the elder of the two in Gen 34:25, although both act (183).

[587] Holladay, "Theodotus," notes the derivation of πολιτικως from πολιτικος, meaning "'befitting a citizen' 'civic,' 'civil' hence adverbially 'civilly,' 'courteously,'" citing its use in Polybius 18.48.7; 23.5.7 (184 n. 108). Nothing indicates that it carries anything other than positive connotations.

[588] Cf. Holladay, "Theodotus," who sees Simeon's prominence as reflecting a "lack of sympathy for priestly or Levitical groups" in contrast to the prominence of Levi in *Jub.* 30:4-6,13-23 and *T. Levi* 5:3-4; 6:1-8 (183); similarly Fallon, "Theodotus," 792-93.

[589] So Fallon, "Theodotus," 793; Holladay, "Theodotus," 188. Collins, "Epic," suggests it also reflects the time of Hyrcanus' expansionary policies (100).

[590] It is interesting that an account of circumcising the Israelites occurs immediately before the first of these slaughters at Jericho in Josh 5:2-7; 6:1-21.

[591] The later *T. Levi* has an angel commission Levi's vengeance on Shechem (5:3, 5). It then reports his forlorn attempt to stop the circumcision, his deed of execution, and his father's rebuke that they had killed circumcised men (6:3-7). Nothing in the context suggests the theme of intermarriage, though it features as a theme elsewhere (*T. Jud.* 13:7; cf. 14:6; *T. Reub.* 3:8; *T. Dan.* 5:5; *T. Naph.* 1:10-11).

which makes a special point of heightening the severity of the offence ("she was only a small girl, twelve years of age" 30:2) and then, after describing the deed done by "Simeon and Levi" (30:4) as one based on deception ("They spoke deceptively and acted in a crafty way toward them, and deceived them" 30:3) , but without mention of circumcision (though they killed everyone "in a painful way" (30:4, 17), speaks of their action as "a punishment on all Shechemites" (30:4), and as the basis for affirming God's choice and blessing of the Levites to exercise vengeance (30:17-19). Indeed his deed warrants Levi being "recorded on heavenly tablets as a friend and just man" (30:20) and the brothers also as "friends" (30:21) and as having done "what was right, justice, and revenge against sinners" (30:23). Both *ALD* and *Jubilees* relate the deed to the theme of intermarriage,[592] as here in Theodotus.[593] It plays a similar role, ironically, in *Aseneth,* as noted above.

Fragment 7 then reinforces this perspective when apparently Polyhistor summarising Theodotus declares that "God implanted this notion in their mind" (7 1),[594] adding "because the Shechemites were godless", and following it by Theodotus' own words: "God disabled the inhabitants of Shechem, for they did not honor whoever came to them, the low, not even the noble; neither did they dispense justice nor enforce laws throughout their city. Their deadly deeds were their chief concern".[595] What the description of Hamor and Shechem in fragment 2 as "a very stubborn pair" foreshadowed is now explicit. These are wicked people who deserved to be slaughtered. Their sin, in particular, was failure of hospitality. Nothing suggests lack of hospitality in a general sense in the Genesis story. In fact, as Gruen notes, Theodotus has Hamor act very hospitably and courteously towards Jacob.[596] There may however be an allusion to the notorious lack of hospitality at Sodom and Gomorrah, particularly because here, as there, this was expressed

---

[592] On this see Loader, *Enoch, Levi, and Jubilees*, 88-94, 165-75.

[593] Judith also declares divine warrant of Simeon's act, to whom God "gave a sword" (9:2), but makes no link with the theme of intermarriage; similarly Philo *Migr.* 225. The accounts in Josephus, *A.J.* 1.337-340 and *Gen. Rab.* 80 lack this and also the reference to a divine mandate, though both consider the deed fully justified. In addition, like *Jubilees*, Josephus makes no reference to their being circumcised and then sore, though he notes Jacob's disapproval (340-41).

[594] This goes far beyond the biblical account. On this see Holladay, "Theodotus," 189; Collins, "Epic," 95.

[595] On this see also Reinhard Pummer and Michel Roussel, "A Note on Theodotus and Homer," *JSJ* 13 (1982) 177-82.

[596] Gruen, *Heritage and Hellenism*, who writes: "In the poem Hamor receives Jacob in welcoming fashion and provides him with land – thus going one better than the biblical version which has Jacob purchase the lot" (124). This could on the other hand be wishful thinking in a context of justifying taking Samaritan land.

through an act of sexual violence.[597] They are also condemned for lawlessness in general. Fragment 8 then depicts the slaughter itself carried out by Simeon and Levi. Nothing is said of its occurring during the time when the men were still feeling the soreness of their circumcision (cf. Gen 34:25).[598] Indeed, nothing indicates that they were circumcised,[599] but only that Hamor had been encouraging them in this direction (6 1-3). Their brothers then join them for pillage (as also Gen 34:27). Only then do we hear of the rescue of Dinah: "After they had rescued their sister, they carried her with the captives to their father's house" (8 20-21). In Genesis the rescue occurs before the plundering (34:26).

Conclusion

Despite the one trace of disapproval the account of the rape of Dinah and its revenge seems focused primarily on justification of the act and setting it in the context of concern about intermarriage, its context also in *Jubilees* and *Aramaic Levi Document*. It depicts the Shechemites as wicked, apparently treating Shechem's rape as typical of the people's breach of hospitality and putting them in the same category as Sodom and Gomorrah, whose breach of hospitality was also expressed in an act of sexual violence. Marriage for Jews can only be with those prepared to become Jews and join their nation, which for males includes circumcision. Apparently Theodotus represents the stance that intermarriage was acceptable where the Gentile partner underwent circumcision. As Holladay puts it, "Hamor's family will have to be circumcised – no debate. By extension, there can be no intermarriage between Jews and non-Jews".[600] This is probably more likely

---

[597] Feldman, "Rape of Dinah," notes the comparable lack of hospitality, but without making the specific connection with the sexual theme. Thus he writes: "For Theodotus, the Hivvites (like the Sodomites), did not show hospitality to strangers" (273) and speaks of *Theodotus* "describing them in tones reminiscent of Homer's Cyclops (*Od.* 9.215) and of the biblical Sodomites (Gn 18:20)" (275). Standhartinger, "Um zu sehen die Töchter des Landes," argues that the rape of Dinah was simply the trigger for punishment that was due to them anyway ("lediglich Auslöser einer verdienten Bestrafung" (97). This needs modifying however in the light of the significant link here between sexual violation and inhospitality.

[598] According to Josephus, the brothers attacked the Shechemites "during a feast when they were engaged in indulgence and festivity" (*A.J.* 1.337-40).

[599] Fallon, "Theodotus," comments: "The absence in Theodotus of the account of the circumcision and of the motif of the pain may be due to the summation and omission by Alexander Polyhistor, but it is also possible that Theodotus omitted the circumcision because he shared the same concern as Jubilees and the Testament of Levi" (786), namely, that the brothers might have slain people already circumcised (cf. *T. Lev.* 6:6). This is not, however, clear in *Jubilees* (cf. 30:17).

[600] Holladay, "Resonance and Resistance," 90.

than that it promotes the kind of incorporation into Israel of peoples through the forced Judaising of neighbours undertaken by John Hyrcanus. The obverse to contemplating such mass Judaising as a basis for intermarriage is to see it as forbidden altogether, not only on grounds of people not belonging and not being circumcised, but also because they are typically (stereotypically) perpetrators of sexual wrongdoing, a stance already present in *Jubilees*, where even marriage to converted Gentile partners is a pollution. This does not appear to be the stance of Theodotus, who has Jacob make a genuine offer of a basis for intermarriage.

3.3.2   Ezekiel the Tragedian

Ezekiel the Tragedian, a Jewish work probably of second century B.C.E., depicting the story of Moses, and displaying familiarity with the works of classical Greek tragic poets, has little of relevance. Eusebius cites Polyhistor's summary of the work which includes the information that at a certain point it deals with Moses' marriage to Zipporah, "introducing Chum and Zipporah speaking in dialogue:

> 5 5 ΧΟΥΣ· ὅμως κατειπεῖν χρή σε, Σεπφώρα, τάδε.
> 5 6 ΣΕΠΦ· ξένῳ πατήρ με τῷδ' ἔδωκεν εὐνέτιν.
> (Chum): Zipporah, it is necessary for you to tell me this.
> (Zipporah): My father gave me to this stranger as a wife.
> (Eusebius *Praep.ev.* 9.28.4c)

This identifies Moses' marriage to a non-Israelite. Holladay notes that since Zipporah's statement, based on Exod 2:21b, "is crafted as a response to Chum's inquiry, the line may be intended to respond to the charge that Moses married a foreigner".[601] Apart from this nothing in the context addresses intermarriage as an issue. Why Chum insists that he be told is unsure, as is his identity. He could be a brother or another suitor.[602] The preceding two fragments had mentioned Raguel's seven daughters, and has Zipporah address Moses as the stranger, informing him of the peoples of the region and the role of her father as priest, ruler and judge.

---

[601] Carl R. Holladay, "Ezekiel the Tragedian," in Carl R. Holladay, *Fragments from Hellenistic Jewish Authors: Volume II: Poets* (TT 30; Pseud. Ser. 12; Atlanta: Scholars, 1989) 301-529, 436 n. 69.

[602] On this see Holladay, "Ezekiel the Tragedian," 435-36 n. 66.

3.3.3 Pseudo-Eupolemus

Two fragments, probably of Samaritan authors, are also brought to us by Eusebius *Praep. ev.* 9.17.1-9) from Polyhistor (mid first century B.C.E.),[603] one as anonymous, the longer one as by Eupolemus, but now widely recognised as incompatible with the other Eupolemus fragments.[604] They probably emanate from the first half of the second century B.C.E., or at least before the time of John Hyrcanus.[605] Both refer to giants. The second reports that they lived in Babylonia and were destroyed because of their wickedness, an apparent allusion to the flood, but that at least one, Belus, survived who built a tower, and that Abraham "traced his family to the giants". The first fragment mentions the flood and its survivors, who included giants who built Babylon and its tower, but were then "scattered throughout the whole earth" (2-3). These are interesting connections with Enoch tradition[606] and the myth of the Watchers and their sexual wrongdoing, but neither the Watchers nor their deed receives mention in what has survived.

More directly relevant to issues of sexuality is the brief retelling of the stay of Abraham and Sarah in Egypt (6-7; cf. Gen 12:10-20).[607] The account adds that he went there "with all his house" (πανοικίᾳ), and goes on directly to report that "the king of the Egyptians took his wife in marriage" (τήν τε γυναῖκα αὐτοῦ τὸν βασιλέα τῶν Αἰγυπτίων γῆμαι). The Genesis account does not speak at this point of marriage, but of Sarah being taken into Pharaoh's house (12:15), but in 12:19 has Pharaoh complain that he had taken her as his wife. The report of Abraham's plot with Sarah (12:11-13) becomes simply: "because Abraham had said that she was his sister" (φάντος αὐτοῦ ἀδελφὴν εἶναι). The account then passes over Abraham's benefits (Gen 12:16) and then supplements the description of the woes that befell Pharaoh and his household ("it happened that his people and his household were perishing"; cf. Gen 12:17, "the LORD afflicted Pharaoh

---

[603] The text and translation are from Carl R. Holladay, "Pseudo-Eupolemus," in Carl R. Holladay, *Fragments from Hellenistic Jewish Authors: Volume 1: Historians* (TT 20; Pseud. Ser. 10; Chico: Scholars, 1983) 157-87.

[604] See the discussion of the issues of Samaritan authorship in Collins, *Between Athens and Jerusalem*, 47-49.

[605] Collins, *Between Athens and Jerusalem*, 48.

[606] According to the longer fragment Enoch was the source of Abraham's knowledge of astrology, which he taught the Egyptians (8), was himself taught by the angels of God (9), and is equated with Atlas (9).

[607] The account is dependent on the Septuagint version, to be assumed on the basis of the evidence that the author elsewhere uses its form for names. So Hengel, *Judaism and Hellenism*, 1.89. See also Collins, *Between Athens and Jerusalem*, who notes that this could have been possible not only in Egypt, but also in Palestine (48-49). He notes also the influence of Berossus and of Enoch tradition (49).

and his house with great plagues because of Sarai, Abram's wife"), with the information "that the king was unable to have intercourse with her" (ὅτι οὐκ ἠδύνατο αὐτῇ συγγενέσθαι), something Polyhistor notes as remarkable (περισσότερον δ' ἱστόρησεν "he also reported rather remarkably"). This additional detail ensures that Sarah was not rendered thereby unclean for Abraham, as Bilhah would later be for Jacob because of Reuben's sleeping with her (*Jub.* 33:9; cf. Gen 35:22). The same detail occurs, doubtless for the same reason, in the much more elaborate account of 1QapGen ar/1Q20 19.13 – 20.33,[608] where Pharaoh was impotent for two years (19.17-18), a result of Abraham's prayers that Sarah not be defiled (15). Both *Genesis Apocryphon* and *Jubilees* mention that Sarah was taken "by force" (1QapGen ar/1Q20 19.11, 14; *Jub.* 13:11, but clearly this did not mean rape in the former and the same is to be assumed for the latter.[609] The further additional detail of the king consulting his diviners has a parallel in the former, though there they fail and Hyrcanus learns the truth from Lot (19-26). It bridges the gap in the Genesis narrative where the hearer is left wondering how Pharaoh came to make the connection between his ills and Sarah's status. Interestingly, they assure the king that she is not a widow (χήραν). This may well reflect the following assumptions about the king's understanding: Sarah was Abraham's sister, but of such an age that she would have to have been married, because everyone married, so, if now unmarried, must accordingly be widowed. The account ends abruptly with the king returning Sarah to her husband, Abraham, but without any words of recrimination, perhaps because the account in Genesis could read as though she had been defiled ("'What is this you have done to me? Why did you not tell me that she was your wife? 19 Why did you say, "She is my sister," so that I took her for my wife?'" (12:18-19).

The fragments illustrate that in the mid to early second century a Samaritan author also assumed the value system according to which sexual intercourse with someone other than one's husband rendered a woman unclean for her husband, reflected in the instruction about divorce in Deut 24:1-4 and probably in Gen 35:22 (cf. *Jub.* 33:9).

---

[608] On this see Loader, *Dead Sea Scrolls on Sexuality*, 294-96. Similar assurance is to be found in the account in Philo, *Abr.* 96-98; and Josephus *A.J.* 1.162-165.

[609] On this see Loader, *Enoch, Levi, and Jubilees*, 151.

3.3.4 Other Fragmentary Remains

3.3.4.1 Demetrius

The fragments of the late third century Demetrius, who wrote in Egypt, are also preserved in Polyhistor and cited in Eusebius (*Praep. ev.* 9.19.4; 9.21.1; 9.29.1-3, 15, 16) and one in Clement of Alexandria (*Strom.* 1.21.141.1-2).[610] Amid his concerns to explain chronological and other anomalies, some of Demetrius' explanations touch on matters broadly pertaining to sexuality. Thus fragment 2 deals at length with Jacob's being sent by his parents to obtain a wife in Haran (1; cf. Gen 27:41 – 28:5), and his marrying "Leah and Rachel, the two daughters of his maternal uncle" . Aside from his showing that it was quite feasible that "in seven years spent with Laban twelve children were born" (5), and providing detail and dates for each birth (3-5),[611] Demetrius may reflect sensitivity to issues of appropriate spouses, when he mentions that the daughters were from his maternal uncle, though, like other authors and the biblical text itself, he makes no comment on the marriages contravening the incest prohibitions. He also makes no mention of Laban's deceit in making Jacob first marry Leah (Gen 28:15-25, nor of his justification in terms of custom (cf. Gen 28:26-28). This fragment also briefly mentions the rape (φθαρῆναι φθοράν)[612] of Dinah, who, Demetrius calculates, to have been "sixteen years and four months old" (9)[613] and her brothers, Simeon and Levi, who avenged her on "Hamor and his son Shechem, and all their menfolk because of Dinah's rape" as being respectively twenty-one years and four months and twenty years and six months old. He offers, however, no further reflection and makes no mention of their trick about circumcision nor of Jacob's disapproval.

A similar concern with appropriate spouses may also be present in Fragment 3 in the account of Moses' marriage to Zipporah (1-2). At one level Demetrius is keen to explain that the two could be contemporaries, though they belonged to different generations: "Therefore, there is nothing contradictory in saying that

---

[610] The text and translation used here are those of Carl R. Holladay, "Demetrius," in Carl R. Holladay, *Fragments from Hellenistic Jewish Authors: Volume 1: Historians* (TT 20; Pseud. Ser. 10; Chico: Scholars, 1983) 51-91.

[611] Zilpah is wrongly described as handmaid of Rachel (3), probably an error which came into the text secondarily. On this see Holladay, "Demetrius," 81 n. 7.

[612] Bader, *Tracing the Evidence*, makes much of the term "defile" used in the translation of *OTP*, but the word does not mean that (111).

[613] On the complications of determining Dinah's age here and in *Jubilees* and *T. Levi* see T. Baarda, "The Shechem Episode in the Testament of Levi: A Comparison with Other Traditions," in *Sacred History and Sacred Texts in Early Judaism: A Symposium in Honour of A. S. van der Woude* (CBET 5; ed., J. N. Bremmer and F. García Martínez; Kampen: Pharos, 1992) 11-73, 16-17.

Moses and Zipporah lived at the same time" (3). He does this by extrapolating from the Septuagint version of Gen 25:1-3. Equally important, however, is the affirmation she was a descendant of Abraham through Keturah, and on the basis of Gen 25:6 that Abraham sent his concubines to the east, warding off any misunderstanding which might flow from Aaron and Miriam's statement "that Moses had married an Ethiopian woman" (3; cf. Num 12:1; Jos *A.J.* 2 250-252). Here we may detect a concern about intermarriage with Gentiles.[614]

3.3.4.2 Pseudo-Sophocles

A fragment of iambic poetry attributed probably pseudonymously to Sophocles, probably emanating from a collection of such excerpts from the late third or early second century B.C.E., and preserved in Clement of Alexandria (*Strom.* 5.14.111,4-6), cited in Eusebius, *Praep. ev.* 13.13.38,[615] speaks of Zeus' sexual promiscuity:

> For Zeus wed the mother of this man,
> not in golden form, not clothed
> with feathers of a swan, as he made pregnant
> the maid of Pleuron, but completely as a man.

Clement then notes that it continues:

> Swiftly the adulterer stood upon the steps
> of the bride.

and then, commenting on its immorality, cites more:

> And he, without touching table or basin,
> rushed to bed with heart aflame
> and through that whole night he kept mounting her.

3.3.4.3   Pseudo-Menander / Pseudo-Philemon

A fragment attributed by Clement of Alexandria (*Strom.* 5.14.119.2) and Eusebius *Praep. ev.* 13.13.45-6 to Menander, but by Pseudo-Justin *De Monarchia* 4, to Philemon, and similarly deriving from the same collection, emphasises the vanity

---

[614] So Collins, *Between Athens and Jerusalem*, 35.

[615] See H. Attridge, "Fragments of Pseudo-Greek Poets," *OTP*, 2.821-30, 826-27; also the introduction in Oegema, *Poetische Schriften*, 86-93, who dates the collection to between mid second century to mid first century B.C.E. (88).

of performing sacrifices without living honourably and to illustrate the latter includes the words:

> For man must honorable be
> And must not seduce women, nor commit adultery
> Nor steal nor slay for sake of gain,
> Nor look to others' property, nor covet
> Either wealthy woman or house
> Or goods or even slave or servant lass
> Or horses, cattle or any beast at all. What then?
> Covet not, O friend, even a needle's thread.
> For God is nearby and is watching you.

The words, "And must not seduce women, nor commit adultery, nor steal nor slay for sake of gain" are preserved in both sources, but only *Pseudo-Justin* has the following four lines. The text alludes to the Decalogue, following the order in Exod 20:13-15 LXX (οὐ μοιχεύσεις, οὐ κλέψεις, οὐ φονεύσεις) and typically expands the first of these. The four lines present only in Pseudo-Justin, "Nor look to others' property, nor covet either wealthy woman or house or goods or even slave or servant lass or horses, cattle or any beast at all. What then?" expand the final prohibition of the Decalogue, again following the LXX sequence of placing the coveting of neighbour's wife first, here narrowed to the "wealthy woman", which shifts the focus from sexual desire to greed for wealth. The penultimate line which both share, cites the prohibition itself: "Covet not, O friend, even a needle's thread". Perhaps the intervening lines were added as explanation.

Conclusion

The material considered in this volume is extensive and diverse. It includes writings ranging over three centuries and from different settings. In many cases date and location are in dispute and in a number what survives comes to us not in the language of composition. All this makes an integrative assessment difficult, if not questionable. The matter is further complicated by the fact that these writings will mostly reflect the views of the educated male, a fact not without relevance for considering the topic at hand. Notwithstanding these limitations the following remarks will endeavour to give a brief outline of the main themes of relevance to understanding attitudes towards sexuality. It will not repeat the detailed discussion of texts, which rightly belongs within the consideration of each writing as a whole. The assessment will also be partial, since a comprehensive assessment needs to take into account both the findings of the previous volumes dealing with *1 Enoch*, *Aramaic Levi Document*, *Jubilees*, and with the collection, known as the Dead Sea Scrolls, but also those of volumes to come, on Josephus, Philo, the *Testaments of the Twelve Patriarchs*, and the New Testament. What is offered here is comment on the material discussed in this volume.

Intermarriage

The issue of intermarriage between Jews and Gentiles, attested in Numbers, Deuteronomy, Ezra, Nehemiah, *Jubilees*, *Aramaic Levi Document*, *4QMMT* and elsewhere among documents found at Qumran, comes to expression in a number of writings considered in this volume. Most dramatically it forms the background for the piece of entertainment with intent, *Aseneth*, which cleverly exploits the exception which Joseph's marriage provided, to defend marriage to women who convert, in the process subverting Levi, its traditional arch-opponent, into defender and champion of Aseneth, and making her its symbolic patroness. *2 Baruch* also assumes marriage to proselytes (42:45). Esther LXX with its Additions takes an opposite ploy, portraying Esther's royal marriage not as something to admire, but as something forced on her, which she bemoans, and perhaps even suggesting, like *Jubilees*, that marrying not only any uncircumcised man but also any foreigner, even a proselyte, is abhorrent (C 26-28 / 14:15-17). *LAB* clearly makes prohibition of intermarriage a theme, first modelled by "our mother Tamar", who even preferred incest to intermarriage (9:5), but then repeated in what follows, sometimes connected with fear of idolatry (already 9:2; but also 21:1; 30:1; 44:7), sometimes for its own sake (18:13-14). Phinehas' zeal in Numbers 25 is the inspiration (cf. 18:13-14; 30:1; 47:1). Abhorrence of such relations with Gentiles has the author even deem the concubine's rape as deserved (45:3; 47:8) and may account for his passing over the experiences of Abraham and Sarah with Pharaoh and Abimelech, and Isaac and Rebecca with the latter, and the stories of seeking wives in Aram, in silence. Yet marriage to Ruth appears unproblematic, though it puts David and Goliath, described as Orpah's son, in opposite camps (61:6).

The issue surfaces also in *2 Baruch*, where the concern appears to be the people's integrity as a nation (42:4-5; 48:22-24; 60:1-2, probably alluding to Judg 3:5-6); and in Job's final instructions in *T. Job*. 45:3. Intermarriage is probably included in the closer relations with Gentiles allegedly proposed by some citizens according to 1 Macc 1:11-15. The report probably alludes to Num 25:3 and belongs within a broader context which hails Phinehas the champion against intermarriage(2:53-54), and includes mention of attempts to change the Law (1:49), associated elsewhere with laxity in relation to intermarriage. It is perhaps alluded to under the similar theme of mixing in 2 Macc 14:37-38; 14:3. It may form part of *Aristeas'* concerns with mixing (139, 142) and be presupposed where eschatological visions presume the absence of Gentiles from the land (*Pss. Sol.* 17:28; *Sib. Or.* 5:264). A comparable prohibition is present in Ornias' boast in the *Testament of Solomon* about strangling those under the star sign of Aquarius who are passionate about women under the sign of Virgo (2:2). In most instances marriage to proselytes rarely comes to expression (possibly assumed in *2 Bar.* 42:4-5), but is probably deemed acceptable (as with Ruth in *LAB* 61:6), though assumed to be exceptional. Theodotus, who claims that intermarriage with someone from another place or not boasting of belonging to the same race is forbidden (4 18-21), apparently assumes such belonging would be made possible by circumcision. Interestingly, Sirach never addresses the issue of intermarriage with Gentiles, not even Solomon's, though it appears to assume only marriage among fellow Jews throughout (cf. *4QMMT* C 18, 25). One, but not the only, source of foreign wives was military conquest, where women were spared death, only to be taken away as captives or slaves (cf. 11QT^a/11Q19 63.10-15). Thus *LAB* reports Sisera's desire to present his mother with Jael (31:1, 7). The accounts in 1 and 2 Maccabees make regular mention of such outcomes of battle and conquest (see also *Sib. Or.* 3:265-270, 525-527; *T. Mos.* 4:3; 8:3). Its horror informs the fears of conquest in Judith (4:12; 7:14; 16:4) and for her own plight. Aseneth at first despises Joseph as such a prisoner (*Asen.* 4:9-10).

Tobit draws the boundaries of acceptable marriage even more tightly, not only eschewing intermarriage with Gentiles, but also with those outside one's own clan, on pain of death, alleging this is divine Law (4:12-13; 1:9; 3:15; 6:12-13, 18; 7:10, 11), with the patriarchs as models (4:12). Judith's ideal marriage reflects a similar stance, at least in modelling a similar endogamy (8:1; similarly *LAB* 9:9; cf. also Esther C16/14:15, where she emphasises the tribe of her family of origin). The concern in both is more clearly inheritance (4:13b; 6:12; cf. 8:21; 10:10; 14:13). Its strictness goes even beyond *Jubilees*.

Marriage and Household

Tobit depicts what must have been an ideal, indeed, the norm for many, allowing us to see the concerns of the patriarchal household, including: providing for parents in old age (4:3-4); a father's initiative to find an appropriate partner (4:12; similarly *Asen.* 4:7; Sir 7:23, 25; 26:19-21; cf. also 4QD^f/4Q271 3 8-16); engagement of another to negotiate with the future bride's father (5:3-4, 10; 6:13); agreements, preparations, enactment of marriage (7:11-16); consummation (8:1-8a); feasting (8:19-20; cf. also 1 Macc 9:37-42); the new set of relations created by the marriage which include honouring one's parents-in-law as much as one's own and reciprocal recognition of a new son or daughter (8:21; 10:12); and the giving of a dowry (8:21; 10:10; cf. 2 Macc 1:14). In its message of imploring greater faith in God in the midst of adversity, it incidentally portrays two marital partnerships, one, stable, with male authority unquestioned, the other, refreshingly rocky with failures on both sides, but all within the dominant ideal of the household ruled by a man with loyal and submissive support from his wife.

These values inform the image of Judith, portrayed as an exception in two respects: because of her husband's untimely death and because she heroically used her sexual attractiveness to defeat Holofernes. Her act of leadership was one-off; she returned to her household leadership, which was also exceptional, but remained within the overall framework of patriarchal society (cf. also 2 Macc 3:10 which assumes some widows and orphans inherited wealth). The shorter text of *Aseneth* even has God addressed as like a mother (Ph 12:8). The heroic mother in 4 Maccabees is hailed as having shown manly courage (14:11). *LAB* gives particular prominence to women in its rewriting of biblical stories. It has Amram cite Tamar as a model, "our mother" (9:5), depicts Jephthah's daughter, Seila, as a new Isaac (32:5; though passing over *Jubilees'* hero, Rebecca, unnamed) and celebrates Deborah as a "mother from Israel" (33:6) and Jael, but then had also declared Deborah's rule as Israel's punishment to be ruled by a woman (30:2). To have a woman in control, it is assumed, shames men, because she usurps what is understood as a male role. Thus to die at the hands of a woman, whether Judith (Jdt 9:10; 13:15; 16:6) or Jael (*LAB* 31:1, 9; Judg 4:9), or like a woman (*Asen.* 25:7), is particularly shaming. Women play a prominent role in the *Testament of Job*, though interpreters frequently read Sitidos more harshly than I suspect the author intended, and the three daughters more positively.

The framework of an ordered society in which proper status is honourable and loss of status, shameful, provides the setting for some very positive depictions of marital partnership. Beyond those noted in Tobit and from the same era, we have positive comments in Sirach. Having a devoted wife is worth more than all other possessions including friendships (40:19, 23), whose beauty he can even describe using temple imagery as sacred space (26:16-18). The ideal future is sometimes pictured as family life (so *Sib. Or.* 3:594, 767-795; similarly *T. Abr.* A10:3), and grief, as the absence of the joy of bride and bridegroom (Bar 2:23; *2 Bar.* 10:13-16; 1 Macc 1:27). *Pseudo-Phocylides* urges men to marry and uses Homer to hail the blessings of lasting marital harmony (195-197). A positive stance toward marriage is reflected in *LAB*'s accounts of arranging husbands for Kenaz's daughters (29:2) and having the Danites find themselves wives (48:3). *Aseneth* celebrates romance in its playful account of Aseneth falling in love, Joseph's joy, their sustained kissing and embracing (19:11; 20:1), and the imagery of a new creation (11:1). *LAB* uses language and imagery of classical tragedy to have Seila voice her grief at not fulfilling what it sees as the young woman's dream: the joy and celebration of entering the bridal chamber (40:6). Tobit shares the romantic spirit in having Raphael declare Sarah foreordained for Tobias (6:18; 7:11). For all its "boy's humour" the *Tale of the Three Youths* recognises romantic love in lifelong marital partnership (1 Esdr 4:25; echoing Gen 2:24). 2 Maccabees even appears positive about Nicanor's advice to Judas Maccabeus that he settle down and get married (14:23).

Sirach appears to insist not only on a wife maintaining sexual fidelity to her husband, her mouth/vagina sealed (26:15b MS C), a "sensible" wife (25:8), or "wife with (her) husband" (40:23), but also that he, too, keep himself exclusively for her (36:24-27; cf. also 25:1 which may originally be about sexual compatibility), a less common stance, at least with the exception of adultery. He can even depict a man's adultery as offence not just against another man by stealing his property, as it were, but against his wife, against his own bed (23:18). Also 26:19-21 implies that men are instructed to keep themselves "intact" exclusively for their wives but here the emphasis is on having legitimate heirs and probably not on marital fidelity. Exclusion of premarital sex is assumed in Sirach, for both women, where one confronted the prospect of pregnancy and the shame it brought on the household and its head (similarly Tob 3:14-15; cf. *Sib. Or.* 2:280-

281), and damaged the prospects of carrying value and trust into a marriage, but apparently also for men; hence his concern that they marry young (7:23). The author of *Aseneth* makes a special point of Joseph and Aseneth's abstaining from sexual intercourse before marriage (21:1; Ph 20:8).

Such partnerships are, however, far from equal. Tobit was always wiser than Anna, though he was not always right (2:14-15). Similarly Job is always wiser than Sitidos, who still warranted sympathy from hearers. Sirach is particularly concerned about the evil wife, who is loud and garrulous instead of submissive and silent (26:23-27; 25:25-26), shames a man's honour by being richer or more resourceful than he, setting him in dependence on her (25:22), or engages in wickedness bringing further shame on him and his children (possibly 3:11b; 23:22-26; 26:7-9). Sitidos' compassionate support of Job ran into the same danger (23:7-9).

Sirach also lays bare some of the problems faced in a polygynous marriage, such as disputes among rival wives (26:5-6; 28:15; 37:11). *LAB* does similarly in highlighting the ridicule faced by Hannah from a fellow wife because of her sterility (50:1). Manoah's solution in face of Eluma's sterility according to *LAB* was that he (not divorce her but) take an additional wife, leading to charge and countercharge about who was really at fault (42:1-3): ultimately it was God, because God made her sterile (42:4). Sterility was also Sothonim's problem, the wife of Nir (*2 Enoch* 71:1-2). In each case, as for their biblical forebears, the outcome was a special birth: Samson, Samuel, and Melchizedek. We find no trace of the disapproval of polygyny expressed in CD 4:20-21.

Processes of Conception, Pregnancy, and Childbirth

Some authors show or reflect a particular interest in the processes of conception, pregnancy, and childbirth. Picturing pain as like the pain of childbirth is a common place, but sometimes elaborated as in *1 Enoch* 62:4, which speaks of "a woman in labor, when the child enters the mouth of the womb, and she has difficulty in giving birth". Sirach urges his hearers to remember their mother's pain (7:27-28; similarly Tob 4:3). In 4 Ezra, however, in the course of discussion of issues of theodicy and incidental to them, we find extensive engagement of issues of childbirth and pregnancy, the foetus, nine months of fashioning with fire and water, contractions, the belief that children born later are weaker and smaller, and breast feeding (4:40-42; 5:46-52; 8:9-11). It also includes images of a sterile woman, who later gave birth to a son who died on his wedding night (9:38 – 10:4); of the land's giving birth (10:14; 6:53, 54, 7:62, 116), and of menstruating women bearing monsters (5:8) and premature prodigies (6:21). Detailed attention to these processes occurs also in 4 Maccabees in arguing connections between brothers and between mothers and children: a ten month pregnancy, with formation through the mother's blood, giving birth, breastfeeding and nurture (13:19-22; 15:4-7; 16:6-11; cf. also 2 Macc 7:27; *LAB* 51:2-3), including the claim that the more children a woman bears the more she is attached to them (15:5). Wisdom also employs the Hellenistic inclusive measure of 10 months, having Solomon report his formation in his mother's womb through blood, having been conceived "from the seed of a man and the pleasure that accompanies intercourse" (7:1-2). *LAB* also reflects interest in stories of sterility and childbirth (23:4, 7), often adds women and children to general references to numbers (5:4-7), describes the baby Isaac as given by God to Sarah and then birth as being summoned back by God, in his case in the 7th month, and goes on to declare those who bear children in the 7th month as blessed (23:8). It also uses the invisibility of pregnancy in the first three months (9:5), depicts Moses as like a woman in the pain of labour when he saw Israel's sin with the golden calf at Sinai (12:5), notes failed pregnancies and child deaths among the Philistines (55:4, 6, 10), and employs images of breastfeeding in relation to Hannah (51:3), and Jonathan and David's intimacy (62:10). It even has Deborah celebrate that earth produced the rib from which Israel was born, an extraordinary bypassing of the first man, emphasising women's role as life-givers (32:15; cf. also Jdt 16:14, which may also allude to Gen 2:22; cf. Ps 104:30).

Sexual Attractiveness and Sexual Pleasure

Most writings we considered see physical attractiveness as something positive, especially the beauty of women, and so thereby at some level affirm sexual response. The issue is usually how that response is handled. Sirach is happy to hail a wife's beauty (26:13a, 16-18; 36:22 [27]), comparing it with sacred space (26:17-18), but also warns against: choosing a wife just on the basis of beauty; responding to the beautiful woman who is wicked (25:21); seductiveness (26:9); and the beauty of another man's wife (9:8). Daughters are not to parade their beauty before men (42:12). He even cautions against succumbing to the impact of the beauty of one's own wife if she is evil (25:21).

Beauty, including sexual attractiveness, plays a key role in the *Tale of the Three Youths*, Tobit, Judith, Susanna, Theodotus (of Dinah; frag. 2 18-19), *Aseneth*, and *LAB*'s depiction of Jael, in each case as something that is good. Registering and affirming a woman's sexual beauty is sexual response and in this sense such depictions affirm sexual response. The ethical issue is how or whether a man (since these are all couched as male discourse) chooses to act on that sexual response. According to the *Tale of the Three Youths* men can make fools of themselves in doing so, even king Darius with his concubine (1 Esdr 4:31; cf. also Antiochus' lavish gift of cities to his concubine in 2 Macc 4:30). According to Judith, Susanna, and *LAB*'s depiction of Jael, they can engage in sexual violence or seek to. All these accounts also assume that sexual response may lead to appropriate sexual engagement in the context of marriage. None of these instances suggests lack of emotional involvement in such engagement. Sirach is probably expressing that degree of emotional engagement when he speaks of the severity of wounds of the heart (25:13).

The joy of sex, understood as the joy of bride and bridegroom, is strong enough to keep appearing as a metaphor of pleasure and delight. The erotic plays a significant role in *Aseneth*, such as when it describes Aseneth's breasts as standing upright like apples when Joseph placed his hands between them (8:8), pictures her and her beautiful appearance in 18:9, and richly employs images of fruit and harvest. The erotic may possibly have formed an element in the entertainment which *Pseudo-Aristeas* assumes, as long as it is "done with decency and moderation" (284-287). Wis 7:1-2 makes a special point of explaining conception as the result of the seed of a man and the pleasure of sexual intercourse (cf. also *LAB* 40:6). Heightened pleasure is linked in *Genesis Apocryphon* to belief that it creates a greater chance of conception (2:9-10).[1] Possibly the author of Tobit is being playful in having the model wife of Raguel called Edna, a word which can mean "sexual pleasure", as in Gen 18:12. Against taunts from her rival wife, Penninah, about her sterility *LAB* has Hannah declare that wealth consists not in the number of offspring but in abounding in God's will, which for her included sexual relations with Elkanah, even though she was sterile (50:1-5). While the assumption may be that sterile women should keep trying just in case, there also appears to be an acceptance of the role of sexual intercourse as of value in itself, so not something from which sterile wives should abstain, Rachel as Jacob's preferred lover though sterile, perhaps illustrating the point (Gen 29:30 – 30:24).

In our world of effective contraception we can more easily differentiate sexual intercourse for pleasure and intimacy from sexual intercourse also for procreation; in theirs such distinctions were necessarily blurred. Wisdom assumes that a sterile women might be tempted to engage in illicit sexual relations, when it pronounces those who do not as not only honourable but also blessed (3:13). Oftentimes the goal of procreation is explicit, such as in the angel's instruction in *LAB* to Manoah to go and have sexual intercourse with Eluma (42:7), enabling her to give birth to Samson; ceding Agag the opportunity of one last night of intercourse with his wife before his execution, from which Saul's executioner was born; and in the exhortation in *Pseudo-Phocylides* to marry and so pay nature back for its generosity with offspring (175-176). Other times procreation is not immediately in focus, such as in Tobias and Sarah's wedding night, where the emphasis lies in the oneness depicted in Gen 2:24 (8:6-8), similarly in Joseph and Aseneth's coming together as two people in love (20:4). The erotic is particularly notable in the depictions of wisdom as a woman in Sirach, but is sustained also in the Book of

---

[1] On this see Loader, *Dead Sea Scrolls*, 289-90.

Wisdom (cf. also *1 Enoch* 42:1-3; Bar 3:9-37; 4:1), though symbolic appropriation of the erotic need not imply that it was highly valued in real life. This is all the more so where, as in Proverbs 1 – 9, the erotic imagery for wisdom has its origins partly in an inversion of the figure of the street woman.

Sex and Danger

Many of the documents considered show also great concern about the dangers entailed in what men do with their sexual response to women and women's beauty, and vary both in the severity of their warnings and in their understanding of what is involved. Sirach warns not only of the dangers of passion, often depicted as a consuming fire (6:1-3; 9:8; 23:16; cf. Prov 6:27), in relation to other men's wives or prostitutes (9:3, 4, 6-7, 8-9; and 23:16-21), but also to one's own wife (9:2). Possibly influenced by Stoic thought, he strongly espouses moderation and control. Not to maintain control and express one's sexual response appropriately leads not only to transgression of the commandments, but also to the shame of being dominated by a woman, Solomon's failing (47:19-21). It can also lead to impotence, becoming a "dry tree" through loss of seed (6:2). Shame motivates many of his exhortations, including shame before one's parents of sexual wrongdoing (41:17), and in public through exposure of one's own deeds and especially of the deeds of unrestrained daughters (42:9-14, esp. 42:11). Sirach warns against being obsessed with sexual intercourse (23:4-6). Desire in excess, like wine in excess (26:8-9; 32:5-6; cf. 31:27-28), and, especially when both are combined (18:30 – 19:3), is dangerous (6:1-2; 23:4-6), but, appropriately controlled and directed, is something positive, though the author's grandson appears more reluctant to embrace the erotic, just as he glosses his grandfather's comments about beautiful women, by ensuring we know they are not just that but also morally good (26:16b). Sirach's fear of mishandling sexual responses also slips over into blaming women for presenting men with such temptations, so declaring Eve, or perhaps wicked women or wives in general, as the source of sin (25:24).

In 4 Maccabees control of passion is a major theme and while its primary focus is not sexual passion, it clearly takes the stance that sexual desire is not evil in itself, but belongs, as it puts it, to the garden of plants which we are to control (1:29), not eradicate (2:21-23; 3:2), citing Joseph as a prime example (2:2-3; similarly *LAB* 43:5; 1 Macc 2:53-54). *Pseudo-Phocylides* similarly warns against excess (59, 76), not against sexual desire, itself, though clearly deploring love of passion for its own sake (67) and unrestrained desire for women (193-194). The theme of control of passions is fundamental also in the expositions of *Pseudo-Aristeas* (177, 227, 237, 256, 277-278). Many of the tales and legends exploit, sometimes with humour and ridicule, men's failure to exercise such control, from the light-hearted speech about women in the *Tale of the Three Youths* about silly men who enslave themselves to women (4:18-19; cf. *T. Jud.* 15:5-6), to the depiction in Judith of the besottedness of Holofernes, mixed with wine, and of his soldiers; Sisera's similar stupidity (*LAB* 31:3-7); Samson's obsession with Delilah (*LAB* 43:5); and the criminal sexual exploitation of the judges in Susanna, who are both secretive and sick with desire, echoed in the account of the corrupt judge in *Psalms of Solomon* 4 with his lustful eyes (4:11-12). In none of these is registering sexual attractiveness and so having sexual response, thus, sexual desire or passion, evil in itself. The issue is always how this is handled, averting the danger that "roving desire undermines an innocent mind" (Wis 4:12). Passion misdirected and passion enacted in wrongdoing is sin. This is also true of Tobit which celebrates Sarah's beauty. When it has Tobias declare on his wedding night that he is taking Sarah not for πορνεία (8:7), it is not suggesting sex without passion, but affirming the legitimacy of the relationship (cf. 4:12-13) in which, as the allusion to Genesis evokes, they are to become one flesh.

There are, however, traces of a much more negative stance. While 4 Ezra does not appear to make any connection between the fruit of Adam's fall, the burden of "an evil heart", the "weak nature" of mortality, and sexuality (3:4-7, 20-22), *2 Baruch* suggests that the primal sin resulted in many woes, which included beside untimely death, mourning, affliction, illness, labour, pride, and bloodshed, also "conception of children, and the passion of parents" (56:6), or at least sexual desire. Its vision of the future envisages the disappearance of untimely death and adversity, and the uprooting of what is clearly evil, including "condemnations, contentions, revenges, blood, zeal, hate" along with "passions" (73:4). The latter, apparently identified as seizing desires and desire of lust, will be terminated (83:14). If sexual desire is in view, the focus is probably its excess, since elsewhere the work assumes sexual relations and presumably legitimate desire expressed in them in the interim. The assumption here is that sexual desire came into existence along with human mortality because human beings would no longer be immortal and so need to reproduce, and sexual desire serves that end. This assumes also that sexual intercourse has no point if not for procreation, and so would have no point in any return to immortality. *2 Baruch* assumes, however, that in the age to come procreation will continue, since it speaks of childbirth now without pain (73:7), despite its understanding that people will not grow old (51:16) and will be like angels (51:9-10). Childbirth without pain does not necessarily imply conception without passion. The concern is probably therefore only with excessive and immoderate passion.

The *Apocalypse of Abraham* includes a symbolic reading of the Genesis story in which Eve represents desire or, perhaps, mind/intent (23:10-11), and expounds desire as the head of all lawlessness (24:9), yet has apparently no qualms about having Adam and Eve entwine, so that the issue there is probably also excess and misdirection. In its depiction of Eden, *2 Enoch* omits references to human beings as male and female, to their coming together, at most retains reference to the consequence of pain in childbirth as a result of Eve's sin, described as ignorance, and as the deed by which death came (30:17), but makes no connection between sin and sexuality, nor to any cursing of humanity or the land, so that sending Adam out into the world appears part of the original plan, not as punishment, and procreation a consequence of the need to survive (30:16-17; 32:1). By contrast, *Sibylline Oracles* 1-2 seems to picture Eden as sexless, identifying Adam's desire as only for conversation and depicting Adam and Eve as naked but without sexual desire, apparently being described as ἀκρασία ("licentiousness"), until Eve sinned. Accordingly, as in *2 Baruch* and *2 Enoch*, they then moved to mortal space, to work the land, which is not cursed but declared good and fruitful (1:54; cf. also the absence of the land's curse in 4 Ezra 3:7; 7:12), and only then received the command to multiply (1:57-58, 65-66). Sex for procreation is accordingly not an evil, but a necessity for survival, but consistent with its image of the garden, and differently from *2 Baruch*, the current text declares that the age to come will have no commerce and no marriage (2:238). On the other hand, the *Apocalypse of Moses* is much more negative, identifying the poison sprinkled by the serpent on the fruit which Eve consumes as sexual passion (19:3; 25:3-4). Thus unlike in Gen 3:16 it comes not from God but from the devil. She is condemned to return to the sin of the flesh, identified as intercourse with her husband (25:4). The negative attitude towards sexuality is reflected also in the strict separation of male and female in different parts of the garden (15:2-3). At most it allows sexual intercourse without passion, with hope of return to a paradise (28:4) in the third heaven (37:5) to be clothed again with a garment of glory and be in a state where sex has no place. This is still some way, however, from the clear declarations in the *Testament of Solomon* which depict sexual desire as demonic.

It was possible to interpret God's judgement on Adam and Eve as introducing both sex and death, especially since the words to Eve portrayed her as from then on to be constantly returning with sexual desire to her husband and bearing the sequences, painful pregnancy (Gen 3:16). To read that as the introduction of sexual desire and sexual response altogether, stands in tension with Gen 2:20-25 and its image of intimacy, which is also sexual. It was understandable to make a link between mortality and the need to procreate and thus to subordinate sexual desire to that end. The link is certainly there in Gen 1:27-28. What we see in some documents, therefore, is the reduction of sexual desire and sexual intercourse to a necessary evil for survival of humankind. That, at least, gives it a place in the interim, yet never for pleasure or intimacy alone, although one sees in the *Apocalypse of Moses* something which comes close to the espousal of celibacy. Interestingly, similar forces are at work in that other later writing, *Zosimus*, where a compromise is reached of sexual intercourse to produce two children and then abstinence. *2 Enoch* 71:1-2 has Nir as an old man become celibate on his appointment as priest, exposing the huge problem when his wife Sothonim is found pregnant, not knowing, herself, how she could be carrying what she calls this "indecency" (71:6), but then miraculously giving birth to Melchizedek. Nothing, however, suggests his celibacy was following a standard rule for priests. It may simply serve the account of the miracle. *LAB* may have Amram oppose trends to celibacy when he confronts those contemplating it in face of the Egyptian menace. 4 Maccabees has the woman martyr declare that only procreation makes sense of marriage (16:9, 18:9; and bemoan she will not be a grandmother, 16:10) and, reflecting a positive appropriation of Augustan marriage laws, has her declare that to serve that end she ensured she was married during her fertile years (18:9). The mandate to multiply features regularly (e.g. *1 Enoch* 67:13; 65:12; *2 Enoch* 42:11; 71:37; *Sib. Or.* 1:65; *LAB* 3:11 – to do so like schools of spawning fish; 13:10), though, as noted above, its particular placement reflects various understandings of the Genesis creation stories.

At the other end of human story, eschatology, we see similar potential for different stances towards sexuality. Some continue to see future hope as earth-, or better, land-based community around the temple and holy city, with defined holy spaces and place also for normal family relations, including sexual relations. The vision of an endless day (inspired by Isa 60:19-20 and present in *1 Enoch* 58:3, 5-6; *2 Enoch* 65:7-11; 4 Ezra 7:39-42; *LAB* 19:10; 26:13; cf. also Rev 21:22-25; 22:5), probably assumed by many to be an eternal Sabbath, need have no negative implications for normal sexual relations, unless one espoused the view of *Jubilees* which forbade sex on the sabbath (50:8; cf. also CD 11.5; possibly 12:4; 4QD^e/4Q270 2 i.18-19; *4QHalakhah A*/4Q251). Where hope envisaged very long life or immortality, some might call into question the need for sexual intercourse for procreation and, where that was seen as its main or sole function, envisage a future without sexual relations (as did Luke in 20:34-36). Where it was seen as more than that, nothing need have changed. Where people saw the future as a return in some form to a paradise which was non-sexual, then one would expect, similarly, to find a future paradise as non-sexual (cf. *Apoc. Mos.* 28:4; 37:5). Where in addition, as in *Jubilees*, one understood paradise as a most holy place (3:12; 4:26; 8:19), then sexual relations would be inappropriate anyway. It seems that *LAB*, which otherwise affirms sexual relations in this life, saw the future abode of the righteous as a "place of sanctification" (19:12-13; 26:13; 33:5); and so would probably have seen it as an abode of people living in celibacy (similarly *Sib. Or.* 2:328 which foresees there "no marriage, no death, no sales, no purchases"). For many this meant a future forever in the land assuming normal family life and sexual relations, including Bar 2:34; Tobit (13:5, 11, 13-17); and *Parables of Enoch* (*1 Enoch* 39:10; 43:4; 45:5-6; 51:1-5, including the garden of paradise: 60:8, 23; 61:12; similarly 4 Ezra 7:119-126), *Sib. Or.* 3:767-795; 4:45;

5:420-421; 4 Ezra 9:8; *2 Bar.* 51:9-10, 16; and apparently Wis 3:7-8; cf. also 3:13, which reports that the barren woman will bear children. Sometimes this is viewed as an endless day without night (*1 Enoch* 58:3, 5-6; *2 Enoch* 65:7-11; *4 Ezra* 7:39-42; *2 Bar.* 28:2; *Sib. Or.* 2:327). By contrast the *Testament of Job* looks to a heavenly hope (*T. Job.* 33:3-9), as does the *Testament of Solomon*; and probably *LAB* (11:15; 13:8-9; 19:10) and *Aseneth*. In the latter Aseneth's ascent, which has her appear male (15:1; Ph 15:1), is best understood not as denying her sexuality nor as her returning to an androgynous state, but as a way of affirming her as having reached equal status in the heavenly world to men.

Purity Issues

In comparison with the collection found at Qumran, the writings we have considered rarely address *purity issues* in relation to sexuality. Priestly impurity is under fire in the *Psalms of Solomon*, among other things, because of neglect of menstrual impurity (8:12; possibly the target of *Ps.-Phoc.* 189; and a major issue in CD 5.6b-7a). The Letter of Jeremiah ridicules pagan priests who function in sexual impurity (29). 1 Macc 1:48-49 may target such impurity and 14:36 speaks of the defilement of the temple. In 3:57 it notes observance of the provision in Deut 20:7 about sending the newly-married back from the battlefront. *LAB* has Amram put incest ahead of fear of defilement by intermarriage of offspring with Egyptians, and reports the required abstention from intercourse before the revelation at Sinai (11:2; cf. Exod 19:15), but earlier depicts the defilement of adultery in Lamech's time (2:8). Morning ritual washings in *Sib. Or.* 3:591-593 may include dealing with seminal impurity; in Judith, however, washings seem related to purification before eating (12:7-9).

Rape and Sexual Violence

Concern with lack of control of sexual passion finds expression in a range of ways. A number of writings make mention of *rape or attempted rape and sexual violence*: 4 Ezra 10:22; *2 Bar.* 27:11; 44:2; *T. Job* 39:1-2; Judith, both in relation to herself (cf. 12:11-12) and also pointing to Dinah (9:2; alluded to also in Theod. 4.11; *Asen.* 23:14; *Demetrius* 9); Susanna; *Ps.-Phoc.* 198; and the grotesque accounts in *T. Sol.* 14:4, which include pederastic rape and the story of Eros as the offspring of anal rape. Holofernes' eunuch reduces Judith to being a "pretty girl", an object for his (or their) exploitation (12:13), as also at another level Esther portrays Ahasuerus as wanting to show off Vashti's beauty (as a sex object?) (1:11), which she refused. Not to rape Judith would apparently bring shame on Holofernes (Jdt 11:11-12). *LAB* 45:1-6 recounts the rape of the Levite's concubine, linking it with the violence threatened against Lot's visitors, but then alleges that she deserved what was coming to her because of former sexual relations with Amalekites and declares that the people took the matter too seriously (47:8). LXX Esther with its Additions now portrays Esther's story as forced abduction from her husband Mordecai and conscription against her will to serve in the king's harem and then to be his consort. Many of the references to women taken in war will imply sexual violence. Sirach addresses sexual exploitation of slaves, apparently exceeding the norm in ruling against sex even with one's own maidservant (41:22/24). He warns against seducing virgins, but there the appeal is self-interest: the likely fine her father might impose (9:5).

Concern with Women's Sexuality

Sirach's extreme statements about daughters reflect the assumption that they are scarcely able to control their sexual desires and, left to their own devices, would be likely to engage in sex indiscriminately (42:9-14; 26:10-12, perhaps originally of wives; cf. also 26:7-9; 25:25-26). Clearly he assumes that some women do not do so, but they are married and submissive (emphasised especially in the Greek translation) to their husbands. Daughters are therefore a constant worry: defilement by seduction (cf. 4QD^e/4Q270 2 i.16-17a), pregnancy outside marriage, infidelity in marriage, even being divorced/"hated" (42:9), all bring shame on a father, one of the author's main concerns. He even portrays daughters as crudely going about with their quiver open looking for arrows (26:12). Accordingly daughters are to be closely guarded, kept indoors and out of view (42:11-12a), not allowed to mix with married women because the latter would inevitably corrupt them (42:12b-13). His portrait of the potential infidelity of wives reflects a similarly low view of women's capacity for control and so, consequently, the need for men to control women. He can declare a wicked man as still preferable to a good woman, though he may have also added that a godfearing daughter is better than a shameless son (42:14). He recommends a seal on a wicked wife (42:6), speaks of the evil wife as a shaking yoke, who may also be adulterous (26:7), contravening divine law, shaming her husband, producing offspring which threaten the household's future (23:22-26) and much more. She is like water which flows without control (25:25-26). Sirach's negative stance may derive from reading Gen 3:16 as implying an uncontrolled sexuality. If 25:24 is about Eve, then she is the beginning not only of sin, but of what he sees as the huge problem of women's sexuality.

Later *Pseudo-Aristeas* draws on Aristotle's assessment to make the similar claim that women need male control because they have inferior reasoning power (250-51; cf. 4 Macc 14:11 and the mother's exceptional *manly* qualities in 15:30). Keeping daughters indoors and under control is reflected also in 2 Macc 3:19-20 (similarly 3 Macc 1:18); *Ps.-Phoc.* 215; 4 Macc 18:7; and not least in the fabulous tower of Aseneth, where she dwelt untouched and unseen with her seven assistant fellow virgins. Concern with wicked women appears in *Pss. Sol.* 16:7-8 as a prayer to be kept from seduction by attractive women. Both the heroic woman of 4 Maccabees and Susanna provide models of young women who resisted seduction, unlike Eve, understood as having been seduced by the serpent (cf. also *LAB* 13:8; 4 Macc 18:7-10; cf. also Deut 22:25-27; Exod 22:15), an interpretation made possible by Genesis LXX, and possibly behind the depiction of Enoch in Wis 4:14.

Adultery

The command not to commit *adultery* is widely informative of the ethical stance of these writings, though other factors such as shame, and danger to the household's future, also play a significant role. Sirach deplores both the adulterer's secret liaisons (23:18-21; secrecy noted also of the adulterous predators in *Pss. Sol.* 4 and Susanna) and those of the adulteress (23:22-26). She flouts the Law of the Most High, wrongs her husband, and produces illegitimate offspring (23:23). Sirach's reference to wounds of the heart may well include personal hurt caused through an adulterous wife (25:13). He can also contemplate that men might hurt their wives and so speaks of adultery as wronging them (23:18). This goes beyond the usual notion that adultery is chiefly a matter of stealing another man's property. Wisdom emphasises the impact on households of adultery, declaring the offspring of adulterous relations cursed (3:12, 16-18; 4:3-6; similarly Sir 23:24-26; *Sib. Or.* 2:257-258), who will also be called to bear witness against their parents at the judgement (4:6). The shame of being illegitimate offspring, still reflected today in the abusive appellation, "bastard!", was widely recognised, including as an allegation against Alexander (*Sib. Or.* 3:381-387) and then against John Hyrcanus (*T. Mos.* 5:4; cf. Jos *A.J.* 13.292). *Psalms of Solomon* 4 depicts the adulterous sexual predator as a destroyer of households (4:20; similarly 15:11). He is aligned to the serpent understood as the seducer (4:9-10). Susanna cites prophetic witness in introducing its instance of what it saw as an ongoing abuse (5). It assumes the death penalty (22) as in Deut 22:21-24; Lev 20:10 (cf. also Sir 9:9), but this may reflect more the world of the narrative than reality.

Specific reference to the commandment not to commit adultery comes in *LAB* 11:10 (with an added reason, appealing to the Egyptians' restraint) and in 44:6-7, 10, where it is linked, as in 4 Macc 2:4-6, to the prohibition of coveting, applied in relation to sexual lust after a neighbour's wife (helped by the LXX use of the broader term, ἐπιθυμήσεις) a connection also present in *Pseudo-Philemon*. *Pseudo-Phocylides* also cites the Decalogue prohibition of adultery, following the LXX order (3; as also *LAB* 11:10), as does the *Testament of Abraham* in its account of the overzealous "friend of God", Abraham, behaving, it seems, like Phinehas (A10:8-9; B12:2-4; cf. also B10:13; 1 Macc 2:54). *LAB* gives adultery prominence by introducing it as the first major sin by which the people defiled themselves (2:8-10), similarly alleged probably of priests in *Pss. Sol.* 8:10, has the worshippers of the golden calf treated like adulterers (12:7), and depicts it as Gad's defilement (25:10). Wisdom makes it a chief characteristic of the sin of idolaters (14:24-26). It features also in the charges of the Sibyl in *Sib. Or.* 3:594-595, 764, of adulterous idol-worshippers in 3:36-38, and again in *Sib. Or.* 4:31-34 and *Sib. Or.* 5:430; similarly *Sib. Or.* 1:178. Poor Sitidos who sold her hair to support Job, went to excess according to the *Testament of Job* and showed both lack of faith and lack of sensitivity to the shame brought by her deed on Job by thereby allowing herself to be treated as an adulteress, though she remained chaste throughout (23:7-9). As already noted Joseph is the model of resistance against adultery (Wis 10:13; 4 Macc 2:2-3). *Aseneth* takes that one step further in its playful story, in having him resist the women of Egypt who were all intent on sleeping with him (7:23)! Sirach is particularly harsh about old men who engage in adulterous liaisons (25:2; 42:8); and warns against those remaining unmarried, who too easily become wandering raiders on others' plots (36:30-31).

Divorce

Sirach commends divorcing the recalcitrant wife (25:26), and cautions against marrying a woman with a rich dowry, where divorce could mean substantial loss (cf. 25:21; similarly: *Ps.-Phoc.* 199-200). A divorcee, a technically "hated" woman, is to be treated always with suspicion (7:26). A daughter's divorce, if that is the reference of "hated" in 42:9, brings shame on a father. The warning against multiple marriages in *Ps.-Phoc.* 205-206 probably refers to divorce and remarriage (cf. also the critique of Cleopatra in *Sib. Or.* 3:357-358). Tobit's ideal of marriage sees marital partners determined by heaven, and, by implication, marriage without any prospect of divorce (6:18; 7:11 GI; 6:13; 7:11; 8:21 GII), but such affirmations have cohabited well with divorce over time and probably did then. *Pseudo-Eupolemus* reflects the assumption of Deut 24:1-4; *Jub.* 33:9 (cf. Gen 35:22) that had Pharaoh had sex with Sarah she would have become unclean for Abraham and so, like *Genesis Apocryphon*, rewrites the story to avert that possibility.

Prostitution

In most instances the sin of adultery sits beside similar charges, including against *prostitution* and same-sex relations. Both the Hebrew זנות and the Greek πορνεία, though originally indicating prostitution, carry the much broader meaning of any illicit sexual activity in writings we have considered in this period (e.g. Tob 4:12, used of intermarriage). Nevertheless prostitution, itself, remains an issue. Sirach, taking its cue from indications already in Proverbs and more strongly in its LXX version, identifies the strange woman as a prostitute, seen clearly in 9:3 (read in the context of 9:3-4, 6-7) and 41:20. Warnings against female musicians (9:4; music an accompaniment of immoral behaviour also according to *LAB* 2:7-8) and about consorting with other men's wives over wine and feasting (9:8-9) belong here, indicative of a common context where Sirach assumes that sexual wrongdoing takes place. Within 18:30 – 19:3 the Greek specifies the dangerous women in 19:2 as prostitutes. Like the author of Proverbs Sirach sees adultery as something much more serious than prostitution (prostitutes cost little and are just "spittle"; 26:22; Prov 6:26), but similarly appears to assume that the two might coincide where the woman engaging in prostitution is someone else's wife. The adulterer's finding forbidden bread sweet (23:17) recalls the sweet bread of Woman Folly in Prov 9:12-18 LXX, who as a wife plies prostitution. This practice is explicitly identified in *Ps.-Phoc.* 177-178, which notes that it makes wives not only prostitutes but also adulteresses.

Whereas the *Letter of Jeremiah* appears to address prostitution related to foreign cults (42-43), the attacks in 2 Macc 6:3-6 on prostitution in the temple precincts, in *Pss. Sol.* 2:11-13, where men apparently set up their daughters as prostitutes, and those in *T. Mos.* 8:3, where wives are apparently engaging in prostitution with foreigners at the same time that men try to disguise their circumcision, are all probably dealing with prostitution in the context of foreign cultural influences (cf. also 1 Macc 1:15; 2:46; 2 Macc 6:10; *Jub.* 15:33-34). In the Gentile world, *Sib. Or.* 3:43-44 bemoans widows who do not maintain fidelity but engage in secret prostitution (cf. 4QD^e/4Q270 2 i.17). This may reflect a value found elsewhere that sees it as a virtue that widows not remarry, exemplified by Judith (8:1-3; 16:22; cf. also Luke 2:36-37) and perhaps reflected in the disparagement of having many marriages in *Sib. Or.* 3:359-362, a scarcely veiled reference to Cleopatra, and in the reference to multiple marriages in *Ps.-Phoc.* 205-206, though that appears more likely to refer to divorce and remarriage.

Sib. Or. 5:388 charges Rome with making prostitutes of its vestal virgins. In its extensive account *LAB* has Amram completely exonerate Tamar for her acted prostitution (and incest) with Judah, on grounds that she thereby avoided having sex with Gentiles (9:5). Its account of Jephthah makes (39:1-11) no mention of his being born of a prostitute and therefore sent away by his brothers (Judg 11:1). On the other hand in its compression of Samson's story it makes Delilah a prostitute (43:5), conflating Judg 16:1 and 4. This helps round out her character as seducer, and Samson's folly as the one seduced by her wiles through his eyes (43:5).

Same-Sex Relations

Concern with *same-sex* acts occurs in writings which address the evils of Gentile culture. Thus typically it features in the *Sibylline Oracles*, *Pseudo-Aristeas* and

Pseudo-Phocylides. In its attack on the Romans the earliest stratum of *Sibylline Oracles* addresses three aspects: male to male intercourse, pederasty, and male prostitution of boys, probably seen as aspects of a single activity rather than as three separate activities (*Sib. Or.* 3:185-187). Then in 3:596-599 it lays the charge of "impious intercourse with male children" against a wide range of nations. The prohibition, linked closely in 3:764 with adultery and infanticide, rests on what the author sees as universal law which will one day rule (3:758). *Sib. Or.* 4:33-34 similarly links adultery and "hateful and repulsive abuse of a male", targeting pederastic exploitation as characteristic of the shamelessness of the Gentile world. *Sib. Or.* 5:166-168 similarly attacks Rome for its "adulteries and illicit intercourse with boys" as an "effeminate and unjust, evil city" and "unclean" and in 5:387 for "pederasty", beside incest, prostitution of its virgins, probably *fellatio*, and bestiality. It looks to a future without "adulteries and illicit love of boys" (5:430).

MS P of *2 Enoch*, which arguably preserves the uncensored text, is very specific, speaking of judgement for "sin which is against nature, which is child corruption in the anus in the manner of Sodom" (10:2) and the wickedness of those sowing worthless seed, including "abominable fornications, that is, friend with friend in the anus, and every other kind of wicked uncleanness which it is disgusting to report" (34:1-2), here apparently addressing both pederasty and adult to adult consensual male same-sex relations. *LAB* may have Lamech confessing homosexual exploitation (2:10) and clearly makes a connection between the rape of the Levite's concubine at Nob and the violent lack of hospitality at Sodom, on the basis of the sexual violence in both (45:1-6). Sexual violence as an expression of inhospitality also accounts for the connection made in Theodotus between the Shechemites' treatment of Dinah and the response to Lot's guests by the men of Sodom (7; cf. also *T. Levi* 6:8-11). Wisdom, like Sir 16:8, emphasises the people of Sodom's lack of hospitality without specifying its sexual reference (10:6-8; 19:13-17; cf. also 4 Ezra 7:110-115), which its hearers, however, would have known well. *2 Baruch* may know tradition depicting Manasseh's Jerusalem as Sodom (*Lives Proph* 3:6-9), and so connect their sexual violence with his against women (64:2). A clearer depiction appears in *Apoc. Abr.* 24:8, which describes what is apparently adult to adult male consensual same-sex relations, not in anal intercourse, but where naked men stand forehead to forehead. Wis 14:26 probably alludes to male same-sex relations as perversion, matching the perversion by idolaters of the true nature of God, though the target may be even broader.

Pseudo-Aristeas depicts what it alleges is the practice of most of humankind, and in which their cities have great pride, namely "procuring males", i.e. male prostitution, as perversion beside incest (152; cf. also 108; 130). *Pseudo-Phocylides* appends arousing homosexual passion to its citing of the decalogue's prohibition of adultery (3), and depicts same-sex relations as going beyond what it sees as natural sexual relations, something it believes not even animals do (Plato's argument in *Laws* 836C), and similarly deplores women mimicking men's roles, a rare allusion to female same-sex relations (190-192). In addition it cautions parents about boys and their vulnerability to homosexual predators, advising against long or braided hair, lest boys look effeminate (210-14).

The *Testament of Solomon* presents male same-sex relations as a grotesque phenomenon of the demonic, depicting Ornias as raping boys, and Onoskelis as perverting men from their true natures, probably with reference both to male same-sex relations and bestiality, each of which it features. Beelzeboul includes spreading sodomy in his repertoire. The generic attack on the lustful behaviour of kings in the *Parables of Enoch*, probably implied in allusion to banquets (46:4-5; 62 – 63), and in the apparent allusion to Herod's bathing at Callirhoe (67:8-10), is too broad to identify specific acts, though Josephus accused Herod of lust, including same-sex relations (*A.J.* 16.229-231). The same is true of the generic references to sexual wrongdoing as harvesting meadows or plucking spring flowers (Wisd 2:7-9) and sowing seed other than in one's own field (Sir 26:19-21).

Bestiality, Incest, and Other Sexual and Related Sins

Other deplored practices include *bestiality*, among many sexual abuses alleged against the Romans in *Sib. Or.* 5:387-396; and cited also in *Ps.-Phoc.* 188. According to the *Testament of Solomon* it explains the origin of the demon Onoskelis, the offspring of liaison with a donkey (4:1-2) and may be addressed as abuse of animals in *2 Enoch* 59:5; 58:6. *Incest* between parents and children is another of the allegations against Rome in *Sib. Or.* 5:387-396 (cf. also 7:42-45 where it is alleged of the Parthians). Such attacks, also in *Pseudo-Aristeas* where incest between parents and children features beside male prostitution (152), can safely assume widespread agreement also from Gentiles, but in *Pss. Sol.* 8:9 this it is alleged also of Jerusalem's inhabitants (cf. also 4QApocrJer A/4Q383 fr. A; CD 6.14 – 7.4b; 4Q477 2 ii.8; 4QApocJer C^b/4Q387 fr. A; 4QInstr^d/4Q418 101 ii. 5). *Pseudo-Phocylides* broaches the wider issue of incestuous marriages, reworking Leviticus 18, and attacks incest with not only one's mother and stepmother, but also father's concubine, and sister-in-law (179-183). Wis 14:26 may also allude to such concerns and the reference to offspring of unlawful intercourse in 3:16 might envisage a range of possibilities beside adultery, including incest. *T. Abr.* B10:13 assails a woman for adultery with her son-in-law. While *LAB* defends Tamar as rightly preferring incest to intermarriage (9:5), its concern with incest may explain its difference from *Jubilees* in not, for instance, depicting Cain as marrying his sister, but Themech (2:1), namesake, fatefully, of Sisera's mother (31:8). Like most other writings, however, it mentions Amram's marriage to his aunt, Jochabed (9:9, 12), without comment. We find nothing to reflect the concern of the

Damascus Document with marrying nieces (cf. 4QD^e/4Q270 2 ii.16; CD 5.7b-11a; *4QHalakhah A*/4Q251 17).

More distinctively Jewish is the attack on *infanticide*, such as we find in *Sib. Or.* 3:765-766; 5:145-146; and *Ps.-Phoc.* 184-186, which also addresses attempts to *abort* pregnancies by either the mother or husband through violence (cf. also *Sib. Or.* 2:282, but this is late and recycling the *Apocalypse of Peter*). Anal intercourse belongs to the demonic according to *T. Sol.* 14:3-4, but such practices may be envisaged in the warning in *Pseudo- Phocylides* about shameful acts of sex with a woman (189), though an allusion to menstrual sex (cf. Lev 18:19; 20:18) is more likely. *Coitus interruptus* is perhaps implied in *LAB* 9:4. Possibly the allusion to kings' burning mouths in a sexual context in *Sib. Or.* 5:392, alludes to *fellatio*, but this is uncertain. *Pseudo-Phocylides* opposes castration (187) and Wisdom declares the eunuch potentially blessed when he remains chaste and does not give manual expression to his sexuality (3:14-15). Such eunuchs, who cannot engage in intercourse, but still have sexual drive, are assumed in Sirach's comment about a eunuch wanting to violate a young woman (20:4) and perhaps in embracing a virgin and groaning (30:20), and probably in the eunuch who managed Esther's harem, in contrast to others who were assumed to have no sexual *libido* at all.

To some aspects of potential relevance we find little or no reference. There is very little attention given to matters of ritual purity in relation to sexual matters or sacred space and time, probably nothing about masturbation, widowers, little about divorce and remarriage, sacral prostitution, celibacy or sexual asceticism, slaves and sexual exploitation.

Sexual Mythology

The *myth of the Watchers* continues to exercise influence, as reflected in some writings. As expected, we see this especially in the *Parables of Enoch* and *2 Enoch*. While the former reports their sexual liaison with women in 39:1, the major focus throughout most of the work is on their teaching metallurgy and the secrets of sorcery under the leadership of Azazel, a renaming of Asael. The former leads to warfare, but, unlike in the *Book of the Watchers*, not to creation of women's cosmetics or jewellery. The fate of the Watchers in the end, after their period of internment in chains, is held up as an example to kings, who are similarly to face fiery judgement. There may be allusions to the Watchers' wives and children in 60:24-25. Only in the listing of angels in 69:2-12 within the Noah material does the theme of sexual wrongdoing appear, where we read of Shemihazah, called Yeqon, but also of Asbe'el as leading their fellows into sexual defilement with women. Eve's being led astray by another angel, Gadre'el, is an admixture to the myth, but probably not sexual in focus. The rest returns to the themes of sorcery and forbidden secrets, perhaps suggestive of false teaching, but not about sexual wrongdoing. We find condemned angels, including the 200 Grigori (Watchers), in *2 Enoch*, mention of their defiling sexual wrongdoing leading to the birth of giants *2 Enoch* (18:4), but nothing about their teaching. The figure Satanail, a rebel cast from heaven, assumes greater importance. At most the Grigori's sin is a warning against all sin, not against sexual sin in particular. *2 Baruch* notes that evil women may endanger angels (56:10-11). Judith alludes to Titans and giants (16:6; cf. also *Sib. Or.* 3: 110-155).

Sometimes reference to giants appears unconnected with the myth and is a way of speaking of mighty warriors, as in Bar 3:26-28 and 1 Macc 3:3. Some retellings of Genesis pass over them without or with little mention, such as 4 Ezra 3; *LAB*, and Wisdom, though it knows a tradition according to which the giants were drowned in the flood (14:6), unlike in *1 Enoch* and *Jubilees*, but present in *Pseudo-Eupolemus*. *LAB* appears to transfer some of the Watchers' traits to Lamech, such as the teaching of metallurgy and also the defilement of adultery (2:10), but knows of the angels who taught magic before they succumbed to sin (34:1-5), a version of the myth closer to *Jubilees*. *2 Baruch* mentions their sin of mingling with human women, using the same language in its condemnation of Jews mingling with Gentiles in intermarriage (56:12), and knows of their binding in chains (56:13). The *Apocalypse of Abraham* alludes to their defilement through sexual wrongdoing (24:6), perhaps reflected also in speaking of Azazel's being enamoured with the earth (13:6) and in its use of star imagery to speak of the nations and their angelic representatives (14:6).

For the *Testament of Solomon* the myth is foundational, with demons declaring their descent from the Watchers (2:4; 5:3; 5:8); Beelzeboul claiming to be their sole survivor (6:1), who excites lust for sexual wrongdoing among priests (6:4); Lix Tetrax, specialising in rendering households dysfunctional (probably through sexual wrongdoing) (7:5); the "Worst" who corrupted Solomon (8:11); Obyzouth, who strangles newborns (13:3); and the winged dragon's anal rape of women, producing Eros as offspring (14:1-4). At the same time this composite work reflects diverse streams of influence independent of the myth, including the distinctive tradition of 36 demons in chap. 18, which includes one who separates man and wife, perhaps through marriage breakdown or perhaps literally in space and time. The work also knows Asmodeus who meets us in Tobit as the demon which causes men to die in the bridal chamber before consummating the marriage. Its binding by Raphael in Tobit 8:3 recalls the binding of the Watchers. By contrast *Sib. Or.* 1 – 2, which also knows the myth, converts the Watchers into the watchful and inventive, euhemeristically (cf. also *Sib. Or.* 3:110-155), but still retains traces of the myth in reporting their punishment, without giving grounds for it, and speaking of the giants. Other ancient mythical material of special note, beside that of the Watchers and the many grotesque instances in the *Testament of*

Solomon, includes the male-female mythology which appears in the *Parables of Enoch*, probably derived from the myth of separating earth and sky (*1 Enoch* 54:8; 60:7-8, 16).

Biblical Stories

Some biblical stories are a regular source of reflection on sexual behaviour. Joseph is the model of chastity par excellence (1 Macc 2:53-54; 4 Macc 2:4-6; *LAB* 43:5; Susanna 13; Wis 10:13), not least in *Aseneth* where he is confronted with a whole nation of women wanting to behave like Potiphar's wife. His marriage to the Egyptian woman Aseneth provided an important instance for reflection among those advocating intermarriage with proselyte converts. That issue had been addressed more exclusively in *Jubilees* and, apparently, the *Aramaic Levi Document*, using the story of Dinah's abduction, so that the portrayal of Levi as Aseneth's champion represents strongly subversive irony. Mostly Levi and Simeon's revenge for Dinah inspires zealous adherence to Torah (but cf. the only brief mention in *Demetrius* 9 and *LAB* 8:6, 8, 11, where she is reported as becoming Job's wife, as in *T. Job* 1:5). In Judith and Theodotus it is Simeon's initiative (Jdt 9:2-4; *Theod.* 6); elsewhere, that of both (*Asen.* 23:24; cf. *T. Levi* 5:3-4; 6:3, where the initiative is Levi's, and *Jub.* 30:18, where he gets the main credit). The excesses and Jacob's disapproval are mainly ignored (cf. 4 Macc 2:19-20, a notable exception). Theodotus has Jacob genuinely offer circumcision as a basis for intermarriage, though reporting the brothers' decision otherwise. There may be a hint of blame on Dinah in Theodotus for not staying home (as later in *Genesis Rabbah*; cf. also 4 Macc 18:7-10), but that is uncertain (cf. also *ALD* 1c). Closely associated with Levi's priestly zeal is that of Phinehas, whose exploits to destroy those engaged in intermarriage in Numbers (25:6-13; cf. Ps 106:31) inspire a number episodes in *LAB*, though it has him and his people far too upset about what happened to the concubine compared with her sin of having sex with Gentiles. His zeal, apparently alluded to also in *4QMMT* in the context of intermarriage (C 31-32), may include such concerns also in the context of Mattathias, whose deed it inspired (1 Macc 2:24-26). This is especially so in his speech in 1 Macc 2:54, where it comes immediately after reference to Joseph's chastity and in a context where intermarriage is likely to have been an element of what some envisaged as entailed in closer relations with Gentiles (1:11-14; cf. also 4 Macc 18:12). On the other hand, a critical reading of Phinehas may have inspired the author of the *Testament of Abraham* to depict Abraham's overzealousness.

Solomon is another figure who inevitably attracted attention as a negative model, but this comes in only a few writings. In Sirach the issue is not intermarriage with Gentiles but the shame of falling under women's power by failing to control his passions (47:19-21). His *Testament* notes his fall to sexual desire at the hands of the seventh and worst demon (8:11; cf. also the later 26:1-5). The later *Lives of the Prophets* has Abijah warn Solomon that "his wives would change him" (18:4). The image of Zerubbabel in the *Tale of the Three Youths* in 1 Esdras appears to be patterned on Solomon, but positively, including on women. The mother in 4 Maccabees includes Solomon in the list of those about whom her husband taught their children, presumably positively. In his *Psalms* we find nothing addressing the topic of Solomon and his sexual behaviour, nor in his *Wisdom* do we find such references, despite issues of sexuality including sexual wrongdoing occurring in both, and erotic images of his devotion to Wisdom in the latter. The Canticles or Song of Solomon are a rich source for erotic imagery, both literal, as in *Aseneth*, and metaphorical, as in depictions of Wisdom as lover in Sirach (cf. also Bar 3:24-28).

Other figures who might have featured in a sexual context, such as Noah and Ham; Lot and his daughters; Abraham and Sarah, Isaac and Rebecca with Gentile rulers; Reuben; Judah and Tamar; David and Bathsheba (cf. Susanna TH 15-18); play a minimal role or none at all. *LAB* elevates Tamar and engages sexual issues in a number of its rewritten stories (e.g. Lamech), but is silent on the others listed. The story of David and Bathsheba will have influenced the retelling of Susanna's story in TH and receives brief attention in the *Lives of the Prophets*, in the report on Nathan, who foresees it. The discussion, above, of same-sex relations notes ways in which the story of Sodom features, which can exemplify failure of hospitality (probably with the threats of sexual violence assumed), sexual violence broadly or as male homosexual rape, or male same-sex relations as perverse. Similarly we have noted above the major role which the Genesis creation stories play in the material. Within the material we also find influence from Tobit's image of Tobit and Anna on the depiction of Job and Sitidos in the *Testament of Job* and from Judith and Holofernes on the accounts of Deborah, Seila, and Sisera in *LAB*.

Grounds for Sexual Ethics

Beyond mere motifs *the grounds or motives for constructing sexual ethics* in these writings are diverse but generally cohesive. While adherence to Torah is a regular element, including at times reference or allusion to specific commands and prohibitions, sometimes it is generalised to keeping what is also depicted as universal law, conforming to what is established order, displayed in creation and its presumed regular orderly patterns, and sometimes expressed as what is assumed therein to be natural order. Such more universal perspectives will have been at home in contexts where Jews were engaged with wider culture (already in apocalyptic literature reflecting encounter with eastern cultures, but especially in encountering Hellenistic thought) or were concerned to assert the value of their own traditions within it, such as in the pseudonymous writings in the name of a

Gentile author (like Aristeas, Phocylides, the Sibyl). But even these can at the same time cite specific provisions of Torah, such as *Pseudo-Phocylides'* use of the decalogue and of Leviticus 18. At another level we find the universalising ethical perspectives of *2 Enoch* and the *Testament of Abraham*, with the former reinforcing law by its image of order in the heavenly world, not unlike the appeal to divine order in *1 Enoch* 1 – 5. The statements abhorring male same-sex relations and bestiality sometimes appeal to what is natural and unnatural, as in *2 Enoch* 10:3 MS P or the argument in *Pseudo-Phocylides* that animals do not engage in same-sex copulation.

In other contexts appeal is made to consequences, such as the intrusion of unknown or bastard offspring into a household threatening its future stability. Household stability was paramount and informs concern about adultery, the behaviour of daughters (more than that of sons, who obviously cannot fall pregnant), rivalry among wives, and household control, usually in the hands of the male head. Beside such social and economic considerations (which also include incurring a fine for seducing someone's virgin and facing disaster in divorcing a wife with a rich dowry) were concerns about honour and shame, which, in turn depended on an underlying set of values about what was and what was not deemed to be shameful. The latter included for a man lack of control, becoming dependent, especially on an inferior, like a woman or a slave, and so also by implication becoming or acting like a woman or slave (another ground for disapproving same-sex relations, at least among males). To do deliberate harm to a person could therefore be much more than doing physical injury, which may not necessarily bring dishonour, but could include lowering someone's status by rendering them no longer able to exercise control. A woman's shame was correspondingly not to be able to perform what society expected of a woman, namely bearing children (e.g. Tob 3:9) and providing internal support for a household. Bearing someone else's children, or bearing none, and being seen to be non-submissive, was womanly shame.

Sometimes ethics appears motivated by regard for the other person, though this is surprisingly rare. It doubtless informs concerns with pederasty and male prostitution, which is also exploiting the young, and sexual violation, including rape. Self-interest, as preservation from harm or danger, such as in the control of passions, avoidance of being shamed, preservation of inheritance, perhaps also losing one's seed and therefore vigour, is more dominant. This informs attitudes towards what sexual behaviour is appropriate. At times however self-interest merges with interest in another's well-being. This appears to be the case in some statements and stories about marriage, marital relations, and children. Then we move beyond a perspective of ethics as prevention of wrong to one of expressing love, intimacy, and positive engagement, including in a sexual sense, which despite Sirach, is mostly not limited to metaphor (as in his erotic imagery of

Woman Wisdom), but affirmed in real life in an idealism which was shared across many cultures, including the ideal of a lasting supportive marriage which *Pseudo-Phocylides* cites from Homer and is celebrated in Hellenistic romances. It can also be reflected in concern for the nation, heroically so, for instance, in the case of Judith. Concern for nation plays a key role in treatments of intermarriage, including maintaining its ethnic, religious, and moral purity. This is so also where admission is by proselyte conversion and even when rules are bent in Judith to welcome Achior, the Ammonite (cf. Deut 23:2). It is also one of the contexts of concern about procreation and the fear of wasting one's seed (cf. *LAB* 9:4 in allusion to Onan's wasted seed).

Generally the material considered offers a fascinating glimpse into what happens at the interface of engagement of a strongly ethnic religious and cultural tradition with broader currents within the amalgam know as Hellenistic culture. In many aspects there is a convergence, including appreciation of sexual attraction, hopes, expectations, and ground rules of marriage and household, including its hierarchy of normally male headship, women's household management, the place of children, slaves and extended family, on the one hand, and the centrality of procreation and marital fidelity, on the other, reinforced by legislation. The Jewish side would meet challenges to its acceptance of polygyny and find the integrity of its belief in creation threatened by pessimistic approaches to sexuality, but would find reinforcement for its sense of divine law, embodied in Torah and discerned in the orders of creation, through Stoic notions of world order and the best of Hellenistic ideals of domestic order. It would find its allies in those who saw male same-sex relations as disorder, bolstering its prohibitions with a sense of the natural law of God's creation, including notions of sin and shame where this is reversed or perverted. Sexual passion, which belonged to the created order, and only in a few instances is depicted as an appended punishment for sin, is to be controlled and directed in line with the Decalogue, not least its final provision, which in turn informs why lack of control becomes shameful and sinful, but this harmonised well with popular Hellenistic emphases on moderation.

Even where we find the fiercest generalisations about Gentile culture and its sexual depravity, such as on the lips of the Sibyl, or in *Pseudo-Aristeas* and *Pseudo-Phocylides*, we find at the same time an embracing of shared values and, by the ploy of pseudonymity, a strategy of identity with selective demarcation. Yet in that process we can detect the ongoing "control" of core theological values. These include the positive value of creation as God's despite its failures, in contrast to a dualism which disowns it or parts of it, and a firm sense of divine commandments. These can be supplemented by rational argument and the strong ideological underpinning of universalist perspectives on good order, but are largely fixed and non-negotiable or their authority is unchallenged, even though on that account their interpretation may be debated all the more fiercely.

Bibliography

Alexander, Philip S. "Contextualizing the Demonology of the Testament of Solomon," in *Die Dämonen: Die Dämonologie der israelitisch-jüdischen und frühchristlichen Literatur im Kontext ihrer Umwelt – Demons: The Demonology of Israelite-Jewish and Early Christian Literature in Context of their Environment* (ed. Armin Lange, Hermann Lichtenberger, K. F. Diethard Römheld;Tübingen: Mohr Siebeck, 2003) 613-35

Alexiou, M. and P. Dronke, "The Lament of Jephtha's Daughter: Themes, Traditions, Originality," *Studi medievali* ser. 3, 12 (1971) 825-51

Allison, Dale C. *Testament of Abraham* (CEJL; Berlin: de Gruyter, 2003)

Alonso-Schöckel, Luis. "Narrative Structures in the Book of Judith," in *Protocol of the Colloquy of the Center for Hermeneutical Studies in Hellenistic and Modern Culture* 11 (Berkeley: Graduate Theological Union, 1975) 1-20

Andersen, Francis I. "2 (Slavonic Apocalypse of) Enoch," *OTP*, 1.91-221

Anderson, Hugh. "4 Maccabees," *OTP*, 2.531-64

Angel, Andrew. "From Wild Men to Wise and Wicked Women: An Investigation into Male Heterosexuality in Second Temple Interpretation of the Ladies Wisdom and Folly," in *A Question of Sex: Gender and Difference in the Hebrew Bible and Beyond* (ed. Deborah W. Rooke; Sheffield: Phoenix, 2007) 145-61

Aptowitzer, Victor. "Asenath, the Wife of Joseph: A Haggadic Literary-historical Study," *HUCA* 1 (1924) 239-306.

Arcari, Luca. "A Symbolic Transfiguration of a Historical Event: The Parthian Invasion in Josephus and the Parables of Enoch," in *Enoch and the Messiah Son of Man: Revisiting the Book of Parables* (ed. Gabriele Boccaccini; Grand Rapids: Eerdmans, 2007) 478-86

Archer, Léonie J. *Her Price is Beyond Rubies: The Jewish Woman in Greco-Roman Palestine* (JSOTSup 60; Sheffield: JSOT, 1990)

Atkinson, Kenneth R. "4QMMT and Psalm of Solomon 8: Two Anti-Sadducean Documents," *Qumran Chronicle* 11 (2003) 57-77

Atkinson, Kenneth R. *An Intertextual Study of the Psalms of Solomon: Pseudepigrapha.* (Studies in the Bible and Early Christianity; Lewiston: Mellen, 2001)

Atkinson, Kenneth R. "Herod the Great, Sosius, and the Siege of Jerusalem (37 B.C.E.) in Psalm of Solomon 17," *NovT* 38 (1996) 313-22

Atkinson, Kenneth R. *I Cried to the Lord: A Study of the Psalms of Solomon's Historical Background and Social Setting* (JSJSup 84; Leiden: Brill, 2004)

Atkinson, Kenneth R. "On the Use of Scripture in the Development of Militant Davidic Messianism at Qumran: New Light from *Psalm of Solomon* 17," in *Interpretation of Scripture in Early Judaism and Christianity: Studies in Language and Tradition* (ed. Craig A. Evans; JSPSup 33; Sheffield: Sheffield Academic Press, 2000) 106-23

Atkinson, Kenneth R. "Psalms of Salomon," *NETS*, 763-76

Atkinson, Kenneth R. "Taxo's Martyrdom and the Role of the *Nuntius* in the *Testament of Moses*: Implications for Understanding the Role of Other Intermediary Figures," *JBL* 125 (2006) 453-76

Atkinson, Kenneth R. "Towards a Redating of the Psalms of Solomon: Implications for Understanding the *Sitz im Leben* of an Unknown Jewish Sect," *JSP* 17 (1998) 95-112

Attridge, Harold. "Fragments of Pseudo-Greek Poets," *OTP*, 2.821-30

Auerbach, M. "The Historical Allusions of Chapters IV, XI, and XIII of the Psalms of Solomon," *JQR* 41 (1951) 379-91

Aune, David E. "Mastery of the Passions: Philo, 4 Maccabees and Earliest Christianity," in *Hellenization Revisited: Shaping a Christian Response within the Greco-Roman World* (ed. Wendy E. Helleman; Lanham: University Press of America, 1994) 125-58

Baab, O. J. "Adultery," *IDB* (New York: Abingdon, 1962) 1.51

Baab, O. J. "Prostitution," *IDB* (New York: Abingdon, 1962) 3.931-34

Baarda, T. "The Shechem Episode in the Testament of Levi: A Comparison with Other Traditions," in *Sacred History and Sacred Texts in Early Judaism: A Symposium in Honour of A. S. van der Woude* (ed. J. N. Bremmer and F. García Martínez; CBET 5; Kampen: Pharos, 1992) 11-73

Bach, Alice. *Women, Seduction, and Betrayal in Biblical Narrative* (Cambridge: Cambridge University Press, 1997)

Bader, Mary Anna. *Tracing the Evidence: Dinah in Post-Hebrew Bible Literature* (Studies in Biblical Literature 102; New York: Peter Lang, 2008)

Baker, Cynthia. "Pseudo-Philo and the Transformation of Jephthah's Daughter," in *Anti-Covenant: Counter-Reading Women's Lives in the Hebrew Bible* (ed. Mieke Bal; Bible and Literature Series 22; Sheffield: Almond, 1989) 175-209

Bal, Mieke. "The Elders and Susanna," *BibInt* 1 (1993) 1-19

Balch, David L. "Household Codes," in *Greco-Roman Literature and the New Testament: Selected Forms and Genres* (ed. David E. Aune; SBLSBS 21; Atlanta: Scholars, 1988) 25-50

Ball, Charles J. "Epistle of Jeremy," *APOT*, 1.596-611

Bampfylde, Gillian. "The Similitudes of Enoch: Historical Allusions," *JSJ* 15 (1984) 9-31

Barclay, John M. G. *Jews in the Mediterranean Diaspora: From Alexander to Trajan (323 BCE - 117 CE)* (Edinburgh, T&T Clark, 1996)

Bartlett, John R. *1 Maccabees* (GAP; Sheffield: Sheffield Academic Press, 1998)

Baslez, Marie-Françoise. "Polémologie et histoire dans le livre de Judith," *RB* 111 (2004) 362-76

Battifol, P. *Le livre de la prière d'Aseneth* (Studi Patristica: Études d'ancienne littérature chrétienne, 1-2; Paris: Lerous, 1889-90)

Bauckham, Richard. "The Liber Antiquitatum Biblicarum of Pseudo-Philo and the Gospels as 'Midrash'," in *Gospel Perspectives Vol 3: Studies in Midrash and Historiography* (Sheffield: JSOT, 1983) 33-76

Bauckham, Richard. "Tobit as a Parable of the Exiles of Northern Israel," in *Studies in the Book of Tobit* (ed. Mark Bredin; London: T&T Clark, 2006) 140-64

Beavis, Mary Ann L. "Anti-Egyptian Polemic in the Letter of Aristeas 130-165 (the High Priest's Discourse)," *JSJ* 18 (1987) 145-51

Beentjes, Pancratius C. "Prophets and Prophecy in the Book of Ben Sira," in *"Happy the One who Meditates on Wisdom" (Sir. 14,20): Collected Essays on the Book of Ben Sira* (ed. Pancratius C. Beentjes; CBET 43; Leuven: Peeters, 2006) 207-29

Beentjes, Pancratius C. *The Book of Ben Sira in Hebrew: A Text Edition of All Extant Hebrew Manuscripts and A Synopsis of All Parallel Hebrew Ben Sira Texts* (VTSup 68; Leiden: Brill, 1997)

Beentjes, Pancratius C. "Wisdom of Solomon 3,1-4,19 and the Book of Isaiah," in *Studies in the Book of Isaiah: Festschrift Willem A.M. Beuken* (ed. Jacques T. A. G. N. van Ruiten, and Marc Vervenne; BETL 132; Louvain: Peeters, 1997) 413-20

Begg, Christopher T. "The Golden Calf Episode according to Pseudo-Philo," in *Studies in the Book of Exodus: Redaction, Reception, Interpretation* (ed. M. Vervenne; BETL 126; Leuven: Peeters, 1996) 577-94

Ben-Dov, Jonathan "Exegetical Notes on Cosmology in the Parables of Enoch," in *Enoch and the Messiah Son of Man: Revisiting the Book of Parables* (ed. Gabriele Boccaccini; Grand Rapids: Eerdmans, 2007) 143-49

Berger, Klaus. *Die Gesetzesauslegung Jesu: Ihr historischer Hintergrund im Judentum und im Alten Testament: Teil I: Markus und Parallelen* (WMANT 40; Neukirchen-Vluyn: Neukirchener Verlag, 1972)

Berquist, Jon L. *Controlling Corporeality: The Body and the Household in Ancient Israel* (New Brunswick: Rutgers University Press, 2002)

Berquist, Jon L. "Controlling Daughters' Bodies in Sirach," in *Parchments of Gender: Deciphering the Bodies of Antiquity* (ed. M. Wyke; Oxford: Clarendon, 1998) 95-120

Berrin, Shani. *"Pesher Nahum, Psalms of Solomon* and Pompey," in *Reworking the Bible: Apocryphal and Related Texts at Qumran: Proceedings of a Joint Symposium by the Orion Center for the Study of the Dead Sea Scrolls and Associated Literature and the Hebrew University Institute for Advanced Studies Research Group on Qumran, 15-17 January, 2002* (ed. Esther G. Chazon, Devorah Dimant, and Ruth A. Clements; STDJ 58; Leiden: Brill, 2005) 65-84

Berthelot, Katell. "The Biblical Conquest of the Promised Land and the Hasmonean Wars according to 1 and 2 Maccabees," in *The Books of the Maccabees: History, Theology, Ideology: Papers of the Second International Conference on the Deuterocanonical Books, Pápa, Hungary, 9-11 June, 2005* (ed. Géza G. Xeravits and József Zsengellér; JSJSup 118; Leiden: Brill, 2007) 45-60

Bickerman, Elias J. *The God of the Maccabees: Studies in the Origin and Meaning of the Maccabean Revolt* (Leiden: Brill, 1979)

Bickerman, Elias J. "Zur Datierung des Pseudo-Aristeas," in E. J. Bickerman, *Studies in Jewish and Christian History* (3 vols; AGJU 9; Leiden: Brill, 1976-86) 1.108-36

Bird, Phyllis A. "Prostitution in the Social World and Religious Rhetoric of Ancient Israel," in *Prostitutes and Courtesans in the Ancient World* (ed. Christopher A. Faraone and Laura K. McClure; Wisconsin: University of Wisconsin Press, 2006) 40-58

Black, Matthew. *The Book of Enoch or 1 Enoch: A New English Edition* (SVTP 7; Leiden: Brill, 1985)

Blessing, K. "Desolate Jerusalem and Barren Matriarch: Two Distinct Figures in the Pseudepigrapha," *JSP* 18 (1998) 47-69

Boccaccini, Gabriele. "The Enoch Seminar at Camaldoli", in *Enoch and the Messiah Son of Man: Revisiting the Book of Parables* (ed. Gabriele Boccaccini; Grand Rapids: Eerdmans, 2007) 3-16

Bogaert, Pierre-Maurice. *Apocalypse de Baruch: Introduction, Traduction du Syriaque et Commentaire* (2 vols SC 144-45: Paris: Cerf, 1969)

Bohak, Gideon. *Joseph and Aseneth and the Jewish Temple in Heliopolis* (SBLEJL 10; Atlanta: Scholars, 1996)

Bohn, B. "Rape and the Gendered Gaze: Susanna and the Elders in Early Modern Bologna," *BibInt* 9 (2001) 259-86

Bolyki, János. "'As soon as the signal was given' (2 Macc 4:14): Gymnasia in the Service of Hellenism," in *The Books of the Maccabees: History, Theology,*

*Ideology: Papers of the Second International Conference on the
Deuterocanonical Books, Pápa, Hungary, 9-11 June, 2005* (ed. Géza G.
Xeravits and József Zsengellér; JSJSup 118; Leiden: Brill, 2007) 131-39

Bolyki, János. "'Never Repay Evil with Evil': Ethical Interaction between the
Joseph Story, the Novel Joseph and Aseneth, the New Testament and the
Apocryphal Acts," in *Jerusalem, Alexandria, Rome: Studies in Ancient
Cultural Interaction in Honour of A. Hilhorst* (ed. Florentino García Martínez
and Gerard P. Luttikhuizen; JSJSup 82; Leiden: Brill, 2003) 41-53

Booth, Roger P. *Jesus and the Laws of Purity: Tradition History and Legal
History in Mark 7* (JSNTS 13; Sheffield: JSOT, 1986)

Böttrich, Christfried. *Adam als Mikrokosmos: Eine Untersuchung zum slavische
Henochbuch* (Frankfurt: Peter Lang, 1995)

Böttrich, Christfried. *Das slavische Henochbuch* (JSHRZ 5.7; Gütersloh:
Gütersloher Verlagshaus, 1995)

Böttrich, Christfried. *Weltweisheit-Menschheitsethik-Urkult: Studien zum
slavischen Henochbuch* (WUNT 2.50; Tübingen: Mohr Siebeck, 1992)

Bow, Beverly, and George W. E. Nickelsburg, "Patriarchy with a Twist: Men and
Women in Tobit," in *"Women Like This": New Perspectives on Jewish Women
in the Greco-Roman World* (ed. Amy-Jill Levine; SBLEJL 1; Atlanta,
Scholars, 1991) 127-43

Box, G. H. *The Apocalypse of Abraham* (London: SPCK, 1919)

Bremmer, Jan N. "Remember the Titans!" in *The Fall of the Angels* (ed. Christoph
Auffarth, Loren T. Stuckenbruck; Themes in Biblical Narrative: Jewish and
Christian Traditions 6; Leiden: Brill, 2004) 35-61

Brooke, George J. "Men and Women as Angels in *Joseph and Aseneth*," *JSP* 14
(2005) 159-77

Brooke, George J. "Susanna and Paradise Regained," in *Women in the Biblical
Tradition* (ed. George J. Brooke; Lewiston: Edwin Mellen, 1992) 92-111

Brown, Cheryl A. *No Longer Be Silent: First Century Jewish Portraits of Biblical
Women* (Louisville: Westminster John Knox, 1992)

Brüll, Nehemiah. "Das apokryphische Susanna Buch," *Jahrbuch für jüdische
Geschichte und Literatur* 3 (1877) 1-69

Budin, Stephanie Lynn. *The Myth of Sacred Prostitution in Antiquity* (Cambridge:
Cambridge University Press, 2008)

Buitenwerf, Rieuwerd. *Book III of the Sibylline Oracles and its Social Setting:
With an Introduction, Translation, and Commentary* (SVTP 17; Leiden: Brill,
2003)

Bull, Robert J. "Note on Theodotus' Description of Shechem," *HTR* 60 (1967)
221-27

Burchard, Christoph, with Carsten Burfeind and Uta Barbara Fink, *Joseph und
Aseneth* (PVTG 5; Leiden: Brill, 2003)

Burchard, Christoph. "Joseph und Aseneth: Eine jüdisch-hellenistische Erzählung von Liebe, Bekehrung und vereitelter Entführung," *TZ* 61 (2005) 65-77

Burchard, Christoph. "Joseph and Aseneth," *OTP*, 2.177-247

Burchard, Christoph. "The Text of *Joseph and Aseneth* Reconsidered," *JSP* 14 (2005) 83-96

Burchard, Christoph. *Untersuchungen zu Joseph und Aseneth* (WUNT 8; Tübingen: Mohr, 1965).

Burke, David G. *The Poetry of Baruch: A Reconstruction and Analysis of the Original Hebrew Text of Baruch 3:9–5:9* (SBLSCS 10; Chico: Scholars, 1982)

Burkes, Shannon. *God, Self, and Death: The Shape of Religious Transformation in the Second Temple Period* (JSJSup 79; Leiden: Brill, 2003)

Burkes, Shannon. "'Life' Redefined: Wisdom and Law in Fourth Ezra and Second Baruch," *CBQ* 63 (2001) 55-71

Burkes, Shannon. "Wisdom and Apocalypticism in the Wisdom of Solomon," *HTR* 95 (2002) 21-44

Burnette-Bletsch, Rhonda. "At the Hands of a Woman: Rewriting Jael in Pseudo-Philo," *JSP* 17 (1998) 53-64

Busch, Peter. *Das Testament Salomos: Die älteste, christliche Dämonologie, kommentiert und in deutscher Erstübersetzung* (TUGAL 153; Berlin: de Gruyter, 2006)

Busto Saiz, José Ramón. "The Meaning of Wisdom 2:9a," in *VIIth Congress of the International Organization for Septuagint and Cognate Studies, Leuven 1989* (ed. Claude E. Cox; SBLSCS 31; Atlanta: Scholars, 1991) 355-59

Camp, Claudia V. "The Female Sage in Ancient Israel and in the Biblical Wisdom Literature," in *The Sage in Israel and the Ancient Near East* (ed. John G. Gammie and Leo G. Perdie; Winona Lake: Eisenbrauns, 1990) 185-203

Camp, Claudia V. "Wife," in *Women in Scripture: A Dictionary of Named and Unnamed Women in the Hebrew Bible, the Apocryphal/Deuterocanonical Books, and the New Testament* (ed. Carol Meyers; Grand Rapids: Eerdmans, 2001) 372-73

Caquot, A. and P. Geoltrain, "Notes sur le texte éthiopien des 'Paraboles' d'Hénoch," *Sem* 13 (1963) 39-54

Carr, David. "Gender and the Shaping of Desire in the Song of Songs and Its Interpretation," *JBL* 119 (2000) 233-48

Charles, R. H. "II Baruch," *APOT*, 2.470–526

Charles, R. H. "Book of Enoch," *APOT*, 2.163-281

Charles, R. H. rev. J. P. M. Sweet, "The Assumption of Moses,"*AOT*, 601-16

Charles, R. H. rev. L. H. Brockington, "The Syrian Apocalypse of Baruch," *AOT*, 835–95

Charlesworth, James H. "Can We Discern the Composition Date of the Parables of Enoch?" in *Enoch and the Messiah Son of Man: Revisiting the Book of Parables* (ed. Gabriele Boccaccini; Grand Rapids: Eerdmans, 2007) 450-68

Charlesworth, James H. "History of the Rechabites," *OTP*, 2.443-61

Cheon, Samuel. "Anonymity in the Wisdom of Solomon," *JSP* 18 (1998) 111-19

Cheon, Samuel. *The Exodus Story in the Wisdom of Solomon: A Study in Biblical Interpretation* (JSPSup 23; Sheffield: Sheffield Academic Press, 1997)

Cheon, Samuel. "Three characters in the Wisdom of Solomon 3-4," *JSP* 12 (2001) 105-13

Chesnutt, Randall D. *From Death to Life: Conversion in Joseph and Aseneth* (JSPSup 16; Sheffield: Sheffield Academic Press, 1995).

Chesnutt, Randall D. "Revelatory Experiences Attributed to Biblical Women in Early Jewish Literature," in *"Women Like This": New Perspectives on Jewish Women in the Greco-Roman World* (ed. Amy-Jill Levine; SBLEJL 1; Atlanta: Scholars, 1991) 107-25

Chesnutt, Randall D. "The Dead Sea Scrolls and the Meal Formula in *Joseph and Aseneth*: From Qumran Fever to Qumran Light," in *The Bible and the Dead Sea Scrolls: The Princeton Symposium on the Dead Sea Scrolls: Volume 2: The Dead Sea Scrolls and the Qumran Community* (ed. James H. Charlesworth; Waco: Baylor University Press, 2006) 397-425

Christian, Mark A. "Reading Tobit Backwards and Forwards: In Search of 'Lost Halakhah'," *Henoch* 28 (2006) 63-95

Clanton, Jr., Dan W. "(Re)Dating the Story of Susanna: A Proposal," *JSJ* 34 (2003) 121-40

Coblentz Bautch, Kelley. "Adamic Traditions in the Parables? A Query on 1 Enoch 69:6," in *Enoch and the Messiah Son of Man: Revisiting the Book of Parables* (ed. Gabriele Boccaccini; Grand Rapids: Eerdmans, 2007) 352-60

Coggins, Richard J. *Sirach* (GAP; Sheffield: Sheffield Academic Press, 1998)

Cohen, Shaye J. D. "Ioudaios: 'Judaean' and 'Jew' in Susanna, First Maccabees, and Second Maccabees," in *Geschichte-Tradition-Reflexion: Festschrift für Martin Hengel zum 70. Geburtstag: Bd 1: Judentum* (ed. Hubert Cancik, Hermann Lichtenberger, and Peter Schafer; Tübingen: Mohr Siebeck, 1996) 211-20

Collins, John J. "Apocalyptic Eschatology in Philosophical Dress in the Wisdom of Solomon," in *Shem in the Tents of Japhet: Essays on the Encounter of Judaism and Hellenism* (ed. James L. Kugel; JSJSup 7; Leiden: Brill, 2002) 93-108

Collins, John J. *Between Athens and Jerusalem: Jewish Identity in the Hellenistic Diaspora* (2d ed; Grand Rapids: Eerdmans, 2000)

Collins, John J. "Cult and Culture: The Limits of Hellenization in Judea," in *Hellenism in the Land of Israel* (ed. John J. Collins and Gregory E. Sterling;

Christianity and Judaism in Antiquity 13; Notre Dame: University of Notre
Dame Press, 2001) 38-61

Collins, John J. *Daniel: A Commentary on the Book of Daniel* (Hermeneia;
Minneapolis: Fortress, 1993)

Collins, John J. *Jewish Wisdom in the Hellenistic Age* (Louisville: Westminster
John Knox, 1997)

Collins, John J. "*Joseph and Aseneth*: Jewish or Christian?" *JSP* 14 (2005) 97-112

Collins, John J. "Life After Death in Pseudo-Phocylides," in *Jerusalem,
Alexandria, Rome: Studies in Ancient Cultural Interaction in Honour of A.
Hilhorst* (ed. Florentino García Martínez and Gerard P. Luttikhuizen; Leiden:
Brill, 2003) 75-86

Collins, John J. "Marriage, Divorce, and Family in Second Temple Judaism," in
Families in Ancient Israel (ed. Leo G. Perdue, Joseph Blenkinsopp, John J.
Collins and Carol Meyers; Louisville: Westminster John Knox, 1997) 104-62

Collins, John J. "Sibylline Oracles," *ABD*, 6.2–6

Collins, John J. "Sibylline Oracles," *OTP*, 1.362–472

Collins, John J. "Some Remaining Traditio-Historical Problems in the Testament
of Moses," in *Studies on the Testament of Moses* (ed. George W. E.
Nickelsburg; SBLSCS 4; Cambridge: SBL, 1973) 38-43

Collins, John J. *The Apocalyptic Imagination: An Introduction to Jewish
Apocalyptic Literature* (2d ed.; Grand Rapids: Eerdmans, 1998) 243-47

Collins, John J. "The Date and Provenance of the Testament of Moses," in *Studies
on the Testament of Moses* (ed. George W. E. Nickelsburg; SBLSCS 4;
Cambridge: SBL, 1973) 15-37

Collins, John J. "The Judaism of the Book of Tobit," in *The Book of Tobit: Text,
Tradition, Theology: Papers of the First International Conference on the
Deuterocanonical Books, Pápa, Hungary, 20-21 May, 2004* (ed. Géza G.
Xeravits and József Zsengellér; JSJSup 98; Leiden: Brill, 2005) 23-40

Collins, John J. "The Mysteries of God: Creation and Eschatology in
4QInstruction and the Wisdom of Solomon," in *Wisdom and Apocalypticism in
the Dead Sea Scrolls and in the Biblical Tradition* (ed. F. García Martínez;
BETL 168; Leuven: Peeters, 2003) 287-305

Collins, John J. *The Sibylline Oracles of Egyptian Judaism* (SBLDS 13; Missoula:
Scholars, 1974)

Collins, John J. "The Third Sibyl Revisited," in *Things Revealed: Studies in Honor
of Michael E. Stone* (ed. Esther Chazon and David Satran; Leiden: Brill, 2004)
3–19

Cook, Joan E. "Creation in 4 Ezra: the Biblical Theme in Support of Theodicy," in
Creation in the Biblical Traditions (ed. Richard J. Clifford and John J. Collins;
CBQMS 24; Washington: CBA, 1992) 129-39

Cook, Joan E. "Pseudo-Philo's Song of Hannah: Treatment of a Mother in Israel," *JSP* 9 (1991) 103-14

Cooper, Kate. *The Virgin and the Bride: Idealized Womanhood in Late Antiquity* (Cambridge: Harvard University Press, 1996)

Countryman, L. William. *Dirt, Greed, and Sex: Sexual Ethics in the New Testament and Their Implications for Today* (2d ed., Minneapolis: Fortress, 2007)

Cousland, J. R. C. "Tobit: A Comedy in Error?" *CBQ* 65 (2003) 535-53

Craghan, John. *Esther, Judith, Tobit, Jonah, Ruth* (OT Message 16; Wilmington: Glazier, 1982)

Craven, Toni. *Artistry and Faith in the Book of Judith* (Chico: Scholars, 1983)

Craven, Toni. "The Book of Judith in the Context of Twentieth Century Studies of the Apocryphal/Deuterocanonical Books," *CurBR* 12 (2003) 187-229

Craven, Toni. "Women Who Lied for the Faith," in *Justice and the Holy* (ed. D. A. Knight and P. J. Paris; Atlanta: Scholars, 1989) 35-49

Crenshaw, James L. *Defending God: Biblical Responses to the Problem of Evil* (Oxford: Oxford University Press, 2005)

Crenshaw, James L. "The Contest of Darius' Guards," in *Images of Man and God: Old Testament Stories in Literary Focus* (ed. Burke O. Long; Sheffield: Almond, 1980) 74-88

Crouch, James E. *The Origin and Intention of the Colossian Haustafel* (FRLANT 109; Göttingen: Vandenhoeck & Ruprecht, 1972)

D'Alario, V. "La Réflexion sur le Sens de la Vie en Sg 1 – 6: Une Réponse aux Questions de Job et de Qohélet," in *Treasures of Wisdom. Studies in Ben Sira and the Book of Wisdom. Festschrift M. Gilbert* (ed. Nuria Calduch-Benages and Jacques Vermeylen; BETL 143; Leuven: Peeters, 1999) 313-29

D'Angelo, Mary Rose. "Εὐσεβεία: Roman Imperial Family Values and the Sexual Politics of 4 Maccabees and the Pastorals," *BibInt* 11 (2003) 139-65

Daise, Michael B. "Samaritans, Seleucids, and the Epic of Theodotus," *JSP* 17 (1998) 25-51

Davila, James R. *The Provenance of the Pseudepigrapha* (JSJSup 105; Leiden: Brill, 2005)

Day, L. "Faith, Character and Perspective in Judith," *JSOT* 95 (2001) 71-93

de Jonge, Marinus. "The Christian Origin of the Greek life of Adam and Eve," in *Pseudepigrapha of the Old Testament as Part of Christian Literature: The Case of the Testaments of the Twelve Patriarchs and the Greek Life of Adam and Eve* (ed. Marinus de Jonge; Leiden: Brill, 2003) 181-200

de Jonge, Marinus, and Johannes Tromp, *The Life of Adam and Eve and Related Literature* (GAP; Sheffield: Sheffield Academic Press, 1997)

De Troyer, Kristin. "An Oriental Beauty Parlour: An Analysis of Esther 2.8-18 in the Hebrew, the Septuagint and the Second Greek Text," in *A Feminist*

Companion to Esther, Judith and Susanna (ed. Athalya Brenner; Sheffield: Sheffield Academic Press, 1995) 47-70

De Troyer, Kristin. "Der lukianische Text: Mit einer Diskussion des A-Textes des Estherbuches," in *Im Brennpunkt: Die Septuaginta: Studien zur Entstehung und Bedeutung der Griechischen Bibel: Band 2* (ed. Siegfried, Kreuzer and Jürgen Peter Lesch; BWANT 161; Stuttgart: Kohlhammer, 2004) 229-46

De Troyer, Kristin. "Esther in Text- and Literary-Critical Paradise," in *The Book of Esther in Modern Research* (ed. Sidnie White Crawford, Leonard J. Greenspoon; JSOTSup 380; London: T&T Clark, 2003) 31-49

De Troyer, Kristin. *Rewriting the Sacred Text: What the Old Greek Texts Tell us about the Literary Growth of the Bible* (SBLTCS 4; Atlanta: SBL, 2003)

De Troyer, Kristin. "Zerubbabel and Ezra: A Revived and Revised Solomon and Josiah? A Survey of Current 1 Esdras Research," *CurBR* 1 (2002) 30-60

De Villiers, Pieter G. R. "Understanding the Way of God: Form, Function and Message of the Historical Review in 4 Ezra 3:4-27," *SBLSP* 20 1981 (ed. Kent Harold Richards; Chico: Scholars, 1981) 357-78

Delling, Gerhard. "Einwirkungen der Sprache der Septuaginta in 'Joseph und Aseneth'," *JSJ* (1978) 29-56

Deming, Will. *Paul on Marriage and Celibacy: The Hellenistic Background of 1 Corinthians 7* (2d ed.; Grand Rapids: Eerdmans, 2004)

Derron, Pascale. "Inventaire des Manuscrit du Pseudo-Phocylide," *Revue d'Histoire des Textes* 10 (1980) 237-47

Derron, Pascale. *Pseudo-Phocylide: Sentences* (Budé; Paris: Société d'Édition "Les Belles Lettres", 1986)

Descamp, Mary Therese. *Metaphor and Ideology: Liber Antiquitatum Biblicarum and Literary Methods through a Cognitive Lens* (BIS 87; Leiden: Brill, 2007)

Descamp, Mary Therese. "Why Are These Women Here? An Examination of the Sociological Setting of Pseudo-Philo through Comparative Reading," *JSP* 16 (1997) 53-80

Deselaers, Paul. *Das Buch Tobit: Studien zu seiner Entstehung, Komposition und Theologie* (NTAO; Göttingen: Vandenhoeck & Ruprecht, 1982)

deSilva, David A. *4 Maccabees* (GAP; Sheffield: Sheffield Academic Press, 1998)

deSilva, David A. *4 Maccabees: Introduction And Commentary on the Greek Text in Codex Sinaiticus* (SCS; Leiden: Brill, 2006)

deSilva, David A. "Judith the Heroine? Lies, Seduction, and Murder in Cultural Perspective," *BTB* 36 (2006) 55-61

deSilva, David A. "The Perfection of 'Love for Offspring': Greek Representations of Maternal Affection and the Achievement of the Heroine of 4 Maccabees," *NTS* 52 (2006) 251-68

Desjardins, Michael. "Law in 2 Baruch and 4 Ezra," *ScRel/StRel* 14 (1985) 25-37

Deutsch, Celia. "The Sirach 51 Acrostic: Confession and Exhortation," *ZAW* 94 (1982) 400-409

Di Lella, Alexander. "Conservative and Progressive Theology: Sirach and Wisdom," *CBQ* 28 (1966) 139-54

Di Lella, Alexander. "Women in the Wisdom of Ben Sira and the Book of Judith," in *Congress Volume: Paris 1962* (ed. J.A. Emerton; Leiden: Brill, 1991) 39-52

Dietzfelbinger, Christian. *Pseudo-Philo: Antiquitates Biblicae (Liber Antiquitatum Biblicarum)* (JSHRZ 2.2; Gütersloh, Gütersloher Verlagshaus, 1979)

Dillmann, Gustav. *Das Buch Henoch* (Leipzig: F.C.W. Vogel, 1853)

Dimant, Devorah. "A Cultic Term in the Psalms of Solomon in the Light of the Septuagint," *Textus* 9 (1981) 28-51

DiTommaso, Lorenzo. *The Book of Daniel and the Apocryphal Daniel Literature.* (SVTP 20; Leiden: Brill, 2005)

Docherty, Susan. "*Joseph and Aseneth*: Rewritten Bible or Narrative Expansion?" *JSJ* 35 (2004) 27-48

Dochhorn, Jan. "Die Verschonung des samaritanischen Dorfes (Lk 9.54–55): Eine kritische Reflexion von Elia-Überlieferung im Lukasevangelium und eine frühjüdische Parallele im *Testament Abrahams*," *NTS* 53 (2007) 359-78

Dochhorn, Jan. "Warum der Dämon Eva verführte: Über eine Variante in Apc Mos 26,2 – mit einem Seitenblick auf Narr Zos (gr) 18-23," in *Jüdische Schriften in ihrem antik-jüdischen und urchristlichen Kontext* (ed. Hermann Lichtenberger and Gerbern S. Oegema; SJSHRZ 1; Gütersloh: Gütersloher Verlagshaus, 2002) 347-64

Dochhorn, Jan. *Die Apokalypse des Mose: Text, Übersetzung, Kommentar* (Tübingen: Mohr Siebeck, 2005)

Dodson, J. R. "Locked-Out Lovers: Wisdom of Solomon 1.16 in Light of the Paraclausithyron Motif," *JSP* 17 (2002) 21-35

Doering, Lutz. "Jeremiah and the 'Diaspora Letters' in Ancient Judaism: Epistolary Communication with the Golah as Medium for Dealing with the Present," in *Reading the Present in the Qumran Library: The Perception of the Contemporary by Means of Scriptural Interpretation*s (ed. Kristin de Troyer and Armin Lange; SBLSym 30; Atlanta: SBL, 2005) 43-72

Donaldson, Terence L. *Judaism and the Gentiles: Jewish Patterns of Universalism (to 135 CE)* (Waco: Baylor University Press, 2007)

Doran, Robert. "Jason's Gymnasium," in *Of Scribes and Scrolls: Studies on the Hebrew Bible, Intertestamental Judaism and Christian Origins* (ed. H. W. Attridge, J. J. Collins and T. H. Tobin; Lanham: University Press of America, 1990) 99-109

Doran, Robert. "Serious George, or the Wise Apocalypticist – Response to 'Tobit and Enoch: Distant Cousins with a Recognizable Resemblance,' and 'The Search for Tobit's Mixed Ancestry: A Historical and Hermeneutical Odyssey'," in *George W. E. Nickelsburg in Perspective: An Ongoing Dialogue of Learning* (ed. Jacob Neusner and Alan J. Avery-Peck; Leiden: Brill, 2003) 254-62

Doran, Robert "The High Cost of a Good Education," in *Hellenism in the Land of Israel* (ed. John J. Collins and Gregory E. Sterling; Christianity and Judaism in Antiquity 13; Notre Dame: University of Notre Dame Press, 2001) 94-115

Douglas, Rees Conrad. "Liminality and Conversion in Joseph and Aseneth," *JSP* 3 (1988) 31-48

Dschlunigg, Peter. "Überlegungen zum Hintergrund der Mahlformel in JosAs: Ein Versuch," *ZNW* 80 (1989) 272-75

Duling, Dennis C. "Testament of Solomon," *OTP*, 1.935-87

Dundes, Alan. "Response [to Alonso-Schöckel]" in *Protocol of the Colloquy of the Center for Hermeneutical Studies in Hellenistic and Modern Culture* 11 (Berkeley: Graduate Theological Union, 1975) 27-29

Dupont-Sommer, André. *Le Quatrième Livre des Machabées: Introduction, Traduction et Notes* (Paris: Champion, 1939)

Edwards, Catharine. *The Politics of Immorality in Ancient Rome* (Cambridge: Cambridge University Press, 1993)

Ego, Beate, "Das Buch Tobit," in *Einführung zu den Jüdischen Schriften aus hellenistisch-römischer Zeit: Unterweisung in erzählender Form* (ed. Gerbern S. Oegema, JSHRZ 6.1.2; Gütersloh, Gütersloher Verlagshaus, 2005) 115-50

Ego, Beate. "'Denn er liebt sie' (Tob 6,15 Ms. 319): Zur Rolle des Dämons Asmodäus in der Tobit-Erzählung," in *Die Dämonen: Die Dämonologie der israelitisch-jüdischen und frühchristlichen Literatur im Kontext ihrer Umwelt - Demons: The Demonology of Israelite-Jewish and Early Christian Literature in Context of their Environment* (ed. Armin Lange, Hermann Lichtenberger, K. F. Diethard; Tübingen: Mohr Siebeck, 2003) 309-17

Ego, Beate. "The Book of Tobit and the Diaspora," in *The Book of Tobit: Text, Tradition, Theology: Papers of the First International Conference on the Deuterocanonical Books, Pápa, Hungary, 20-21 May, 2004* (ed. Géza G. Xeravits and József Zsengellér; JSJSup 98; Leiden: Brill, 2005) 41-54

Elder, Linda Bennett. "Judith," in *Searching the Scriptures: Volume Two: A Feminist Commentary* (ed. Elisabeth Schüssler Fiorenza; London: SCM, 1995) 455-69

Eldridge, Michael D. *Dying Adam with his Multiethnic Family: Understanding the Greek Life of Adam and Eve* (SVTP 16; Leiden: Brill, 2002)

Ellis, J. Edward. *Paul and Ancient View of Sexual Desire: Paul's Sexual Ethics in 1 Thessalonians 4, 1 Corinthians 7 and Romans 1* (LNTS 354; London: T&T Clark, 2007)

Embry, Bradley. "The Psalms of Solomon and the New Testament: Intertextuality and the Need for a Re-evaluation," *JSP* 13 (2002) 99-136

Endres, John C. *Biblical Interpretation in the Book of Jubilees* (CBQMS 18; Washington: CBA, 1987)

Engel, Helmut. *Die Susanna-Erzählung: Einleitung, Übersetzung und Kommentar zum Septuaginta-Text und zur Theodotion-Bearbeitung* (OBO 61; Fribourg: Universitätsverlag; Göttingen: Vandenhoeck & Ruprecht, 1985)

Eron, Lewis John. "'That Women Have Mastery Over Both King and Beggar,'(*TJud.* 15.5) – The Relationship of the Fear of Sexuality to the Status of Women in Apocrypha and Pseudepigrapha: 1 Esdras (*3 Ezra*) 3-4, Ben Sira and *the Testament of Judah*," *JSP* 9 (1991) 43-66

Eshel, Hanan. "An Allusion in the Parables of Enoch to the Acts of Matthias Antigonus in 40 B.C.E.?" in *Enoch and the Messiah Son of Man: Revisiting the Book of Parables* (ed. Gabriele Boccaccini; Grand Rapids: Eerdmans, 2007) 487-91

Esler, Philip Francis. "Ludic History in the Book of Judith: The Reinvention of Israelite Identity?" *BibInt* 10 (2002) 107-43

Esler, Philip Francis. "The Social Function of *4 Ezra*," *JSNT* 53 (1994) 99-123

Fallon, F. "Theodotus," *OTP*, 2.785-93

Fassbeck, Gabriele. "Tobit's Religious Universe Between Kinship Loyalty and the Law of Moses," *JSJ* 36 (2005) 173-96

Felder, Stephen. "What is the Fifth Sibylline Oracle?" *JSJ* 33 (2002) 363-85

Feldman, Louis H. "Josephus' Jewish Antiquities and Pseudo-Philo's Biblical Antiquities," in *Josephus, the Bible, and History* (ed. Louis H. Feldman and Gohei Hata; Leiden: Brill, 1989) 59-80

Feldman, Louis H. "Philo, Pseudo-Philo, Josephus, and Theodotus on the Rape of Dinah," *JQR* 94 (2004) 253-77

Feldman, Louis H. "Prolegomenon," in M. R. James, *The Biblical Antiquities of Philo* (New York: KTAV, 1971) i-clxix

Feldman, Louis H. "Questions about the Great Flood, as Viewed by Philo, Pseudo-Philo, Josephus, and the Rabbis," *ZAW* 115 (2003) 401-22

Feldman, Louis H. *"Remember Amalek!": Vengeance, Zealotry, and Group Destruction in the Bible according to Philo, Pseudo-Philo, and Josephus* (Cincinnati: Hebrew Union College Press, 2004)

Feldmeier, Reinhard. "Weise hinter 'eisernen Mauern': Tora und jüdisches Selbstverständnis zwischen Akkulturation und Absonderung im Aristeasbrief," in *Die Septuaginta zwischen Judentum und Christentum* (ed. Martin Hengel and Anna Maria Schwemer; WUNT 1.72; Tübingen: Mohr Siebeck, 1994) 20-37

Fink, Uta Barbara. *Joseph and Aseneth: Revision des griechischen Textes und Edition der zweiten lateinischen Übersetzung* (FSBP 5; Berlin: de Gruyter, 2008)

Fisk, Bruce N. *Do You Not Remember? Scripture, Story and Exegesis in the Rewritten Bible of Pseudo-Philo* (JSPSup 37; Sheffield: Sheffield Academic Press, 2001)

Fitzmyer, Joseph A. "Tobit," in *Qumran Cave 4: Parabiblical Texts, Part 2* (ed. M. Broshi et al.; DJD 19; Oxford: Clarendon, 1995) 1-79

Fitzmyer, Joseph A. *Tobit* (CEJL Berlin: de Gruyter, 2003)

Foucault, Michel. *The Use of Pleasure: Volume 2 of the History of Sexuality* (New York: Vintage, 1990)

Fox, Michael V. "Three Esthers," in *The Book of Esther in Modern Research* (ed. Sidnie White Crawford and Leonard J. Greenspoon; JSOTSup 380; London: T&T Clark, 2003) 50-60

Freedman D. N. and B. E. Willoughby, "נָאַף," *TDOT* (ed. Johannes Botterweck and Helmer Ringgren; Grand Rapids: Eerdmans, 1999) 9.113-18

Freudenthal, J. *Hellenistische Studien: Heft 1 und 2: Alexander Polyhistor und die von ihm erhaltenen Reste judäischer und samaritanischer Geschichtswerke* (Breslau: Skutsch, 1875)

Fröhlich, Ida. "Historiographie et Aggada dans le Liber Antiquitatum Biblicarum du Pseudo-Philon," *Acta Antiqua Academiae Scientarum Hungaricae* 28 (1980) 353-409

Fröhlich, Ida. "The Parables of Enoch and Qumran Literature," in *Enoch and the Messiah Son of Man: Revisiting the Book of Parables* (ed. Gabriele Boccaccini; Grand Rapids: Eerdmans, 2007) 343-51

Fröhlich, Ida. *"Time and Times and Half a Time": Historical Consciousness in the Jewish Literature of the Persian and Hellenistic Eras* (JSPSup19; Sheffield: Sheffield Academic Press, 1996)

Fröhlich, Ida. "Tobit against the Background of the Dead Sea Scrolls," in *The Book of Tobit: Text, Tradition, Theology: Papers of the First International Conference on the Deuterocanonical Books, Pápa, Hungary, 20-21 May, 2004* (ed. Géza G. Xeravits and József Zsengellér; JSJSup 98; Leiden: Brill, 2005) 55-70

Garrett, Susan R. "The 'Weaker Sex' in the *Testament of Job*," *JBL* 112 (1993) 55-70

Gaster, Moses. "The Logos Ebraikos in the Magical Papyrus of Paris, and the Book of Enoch," *JRAS*, 3d series, 33 [1901] 109-17

Gauger, Jörg-Dieter. *Sybillinische Weissagungen: Griechisch Deutsch: Auf der Grundlage der Ausgabe von Alfons Kurfeiss* (2d ed.; Düsseldorf: Artemis & Winkler, 2002)

Geffcken, J. *Die Oracula Sibyllina* (GCS 8; Leipzig: Hinrichs, 1902)

Geffcken, J. *Komposition und Entstehungszeit der Oracula Sibyllina* (TU 23, N.F. 8.1; Leipzig: Hinrichs, 1902)

Gerber, Christine. "Das zweite Makkabäerbuch: Was die Geschichte lehrt," in *Kompendium Feministische Bibelauslegung* (ed. Luise Schottroff, Marie-Theres Wacker, Claudia Janssen, and Beate Wehn; Gütersloh: Gütersloher Verlagshaus, 2007) 392-400

Gieschen, Charles A. "The Different Functions of a Similar Melchizedek Tradition in 2 Enoch and the Epistle to the Hebrews," in *Early Christian Interpretation of the Scriptures of Israel: Investigations and Proposals* (ed. Craig A. Evans and James A. Sanders; Sheffield: Sheffield Academic Press, 1997) 364-79

Gieschen, Charles A. "The Name of the Son of Man in the Parables of Enoch," in *Enoch and the Messiah Son of Man: Revisiting the Book of Parables* (ed. Gabriele Boccaccini; Grand Rapids: Eerdmans, 2007) 238-49

Gilbert, Maurice. "Wisdom Literature," in *Jewish Writings of the Second Temple Period* (ed. Michael E. Stone; CRINT 2.2; Assen: Van Gorcum; Philadelphia: Fortress, 1984) 283-324

Glancy, Jennifer A. "The Accused: Susanna and her Readers," in *A Feminist Companion to Esther, Judith and Susanna* (ed. Athalya Brenner; Sheffield: Sheffield Academic Press, 1995) 288-302

Glancy, Jennifer A. "The Mistress-Slave Dialectic: Paradoxes of Slavery in Three LXX Narratives," *JSOT* 72 (1996) 71-87

Goldstein, Jonathan A. *1 Maccabees* (AB 41; Garden City: Doubleday, 1976)

Goldstein, Jonathan A. *2 Maccabees* (AB 41a; Garden City: Doubleday, 1983)

Goldstein, Jonathan A. "The Apocryphal Book of 1 Baruch," *PAAJR* 46-47 (1979-1980) 179-99

Goodfriend, Elaine Adler. "Adultery," *ABD* (New York: Doubleday, 1992) 1.82-86

Goodfriend, Elaine Adler. "Prostitution," *ABD* (New York: Doubleday, 1992) 5.505-10

Grabbe, Lester L. "The Parables of Enoch in Second Temple Jewish Society," in *Enoch and the Messiah Son of Man: Revisiting the Book of Parables* (ed. Gabriele Boccaccini; Grand Rapids: Eerdmans, 2007) 386-402

Grabbe, Lester L. *Wisdom of Solomon* (GAP; Sheffield, Sheffield Academic Press, 1997)

Gray, Patrick. "Points and Lines: Thematic Parallelism in the Letter of James and the *Testament of Job*," *NTS* 50 (2004) 406-24

Green, Peter. *The Year of Salamis, 480–479 B.C.* (London: Weidenfeld & Nicolson, 1970)

Greenfield, Jonas C. and Michael E. Stone, "The Enochic Pentateuch and the Date of the Similitudes," *HTR* 71 (1977) 51-65

Gruen, Erich S. *Diaspora: Jews amidst Greeks and Romans* (Cambridge: Harvard University Press, 2002)

Gruen, Erich S. *Heritage and Hellenism: The Reinvention of Jewish Tradition* (Berkeley: University of California Press, 1998)

Gunkel, Hermann. *Genesis* (HAT 1/1; Göttingen: Vandenhoeck & Ruprecht, 1917)

Gurtner, Daniel M. with David M. Miller and Ian W. Scott, ed. "'2 Baruch': Edition 2.0," in *The Online Critical Pseudepigrapha* (ed. Ken M. Penner, David M. Miller, and Ian W. Scott; Atlanta: SBL, 2007) no pages; online: http://www.purl.org/net/ocp/2Bar.html

Hacham, Noah. "The Letter of Aristeas: A New Exodus story?" *JSJ* 36 (2005) 1-20

Hadas, Moses. *Aristeas to Philocrates* (JAL; New York: Harper, 1951)

Hadas, Moses. *The Third and Fourth Books of Maccabees* (JAL; New York: Harper, 1953)

Hall, Robert G. "Epispasm and the Dating of Ancient Jewish Writings," *JSP* 2 (1988) 71-86

Hall, Robert G. "The 'Christian interpolation' in the Apocalypse of Abraham," *JBL* 107 (1988) 107-110

Halpern-Amaru, Betsy. "Portraits of Women in Pseudo-Philo's *Biblical Antiquities*," in *"Women Like This": New Perspectives on Jewish Women in the Greco-Roman World* (ed. Amy-Jill Levine; SBLEJL 1; Atlanta: Scholars, 1991) 83-106

Halpern-Amaru, Betsy. *The Empowerment of Women in the Book of Jubilees* (JSJSup 60; Leiden: Brill, 1999)

Hanhart, Robert, ed. *Esdrae liber I* (SVTG 8.1; Göttingen: Vandenhoeck & Ruprecht, 1974)

Hanhart, Robert, ed. *Esther* (SVTG 8.3; Göttingen: Vandenhoeck & Ruprecht, 1983)

Hanhart, Robert, ed. *Iudith* (SVTG 8.4; Göttingen: Vandenhoeck & Ruprecht, 1978),

Hanhart, Robert, ed. *Tobit* (SVTG 8.5; Göttingen: Vandenhoeck & Ruprecht, 1983)

Hannah, Darrell D. "The Book of Noah, the Death of Herod the Great, and the Date of the Parables of Enoch," in *Enoch and the Messiah Son of Man: Revisiting the Book of Parables* (ed. Gabriele Boccaccini; Grand Rapids: Eerdmans, 2007) 469-77

Harrington, Daniel J. *Invitation to the Apocrypha* (Grand Rapids: Eerdmans, 1999)

Harrington, Daniel J. "Pseudo-Philo," *OTP*, 2.297-377

Harrington, Daniel J. "The 'Holy Land' in Pseudo-Philo, 4 Ezra, and 2 Baruch," in *Emanuel: Studies in Hebrew Bible, Septuagint, and Dead Sea Scrolls in Honor of Emanuel Tov* (ed. Shalom M. Paul, Robert A. Kraft, Lawrence H. Schiffman, and Weston W. Fields, with the assistance of Eva Ben-David; VTSup 94; Leiden: Brill, 2003) 661-72

Harrington, Daniel J. "The Original language of Pseudo-Philo's 'Liber Antiquitatum Biblicarum'," *HTR* 63 (1970) 503-14

Harrington, Daniel J. "Wisdom and Apocalyptic in 4QInstruction and 4 Ezra," in *Wisdom and Apocalypticism in the Dead Sea Scrolls and in the Biblical Tradition* (ed. Florentino García Martínez; BETL163; Leuven: Peeters, 2003) 343-55

Harrington, Daniel J., Jacques Cazeaux, Charles Perrot, and Pierre Maurice Bogaert, *Pseudo-Philon: Les Antiquités Bibliques* (2 vols; SC 229-30; Paris: Cerf, 1976)

Hayes, Christine E. *Gentile Impurities and Jewish Identities: Intermarriage and Conversion from the Bible to the Talmud* (Oxford: Oxford University Press, 2002)

Hayman, A. "The Survival of Mythology in the Wisdom of Solomon," *JSJ* 30 (1999) 125-39

Hayward, Robert. "The Figure of Adam in Pseudo-Philo's Biblical Antiquities," *JSJ* 23 (1992) 1-20

Heijerman, Mieke. "Who Would Blame Her? The 'Strange' Woman of Proverbs 7," in *A Feminist Companion to Wisdom Literature* (ed. Athalya Brenner; Sheffield: Sheffield Academic Press, 1995) 100-109

Hellmann, Monika. *Judit – eine Frau im Spannungsfeld von Autonomie und göttlicher Führung: Studie über eine Frauengestalt des Alten Testaments* (Europäische Hochschulschriften. Reihe XXIII. Theologie 444; Frankfurt: Peter Lang, 1992)

Hengel, Martin. *Judaism and Hellenism: Studies in their Encounter in Palestine during the Early Hellenistic Period* (2 vols; London: SCM, 1974)

Hester, J. David. "Eunuchs and the Postgender Jesus: Matthew 19.12 and Transgressive Sexualities," *JSNT* 28 (2005) 13-40

Hieke, Thomas. "Endogamy in the Book of Tobit, Genesis, and Ezra-Nehemiah," in *The Book of Tobit: Text, Tradition, Theology: Papers of the First International Conference on the Deuterocanonical Books, Pápa, Hungary, 20-21 May, 2004* (ed. Géza G. Xeravits and József Zsengellér; JSJSup 98; Leiden: Brill, 2005) 103-20

Himbaza, Innocent. "Israël et les nations dans les relectures de Juges 19,22-25: débats sur l'homosexualité," *BibNot* 131 (2006) 5-16

Himmelfarb, Martha. "Levi, Phinehas, and the Problem of Intermarriage at the Time of the Maccabean Revolt," *JSQ* 6 (1999) 1-24

Hobbins, John F. "The Summing up of History in 2 Baruch," *JQR* 89 (1998) 45-79

Hofmann, Norbert Johannes. *Die Assumptio Mosis: Studien zur Rezeption massgültiger Überlieferung* (JSJSup 67; Leiden: Brill, 2000)

Hogan, Karina Martin. "The Exegetical Background of the 'Ambiguity of Death' in the Wisdom of Solomon, *JSJ* 30 (1999) 1-24

Holladay, Carl R. "Hellenism in the Fragmentary Hellenistic Jewish Authors: Resonance and Resistance," in *Shem in the Tents of Japhet: Essays on the Encounter of Judaism and Hellenism* (ed. James L. Kugel; JSJSup 74; Leiden: Brill, 2002) 65-91

Holladay, Carl R. *Fragments from Hellenistic Jewish Authors: Volume 2: Poets: The Epic Poets Theodotus and Philo and Ezekiel the Tragedian* (SBLTT 30; PS 12; Atlanta: Scholars, 1989)

Holladay, Carl R. *Fragments from Hellenistic Jewish Authors: Volume 1: Historians* (SBL TT 20; PS 10; Chico: Scholars, 1983)

Holm-Nielsen, Svend. *Die Psalmen Salomos* (JSHRZ 4.2; Gütersloh: Mohn, 1977)

Holm-Nielsen, Svend. "Erwägungen zu dem Verhältnis zwischen den Hodajot und den Psalmen Salomos," in *Bibel und Qumran: Beiträge zur Erforschung der Beziehungen zwischen Bibel- und Qumranwissenschaft* (ed. Hans Bardtke; Berlin: Evangelische Haupt-Bibelgesellschaft, 1968) 112-31

Honigman, Sylvie. *The Septuagint and Homeric Scholarship in Alexandria: A Study in the Letter of Aristeas* (New York: Routledge, 2003)

Hubbard, M. "Honey for Aseneth: Interpreting a Religious Symbol," *JSP* 16 (1997) 97-110

Hübner, Hans. *Wörterbuch zur Sapientia Salomonis* (Göttingen: Vandenhoeck & Ruprecht, 1985)

Humphrey, Edith M. *Joseph and Aseneth* (GAP; Sheffield: Sheffield Academic Press, 2000)

Humphrey, Edith M. "On Bees and Best Guesses: The Problem of *Sitz im Leben* from Internal Evidence as Illustrated by *Joseph and Aseneth*," *CurBS* 7 (1999) 223-36

Humphrey, Edith M. *The Ladies and the Cities: Transformation and Apocalyptic Identity in Joseph and Aseneth, 4 Ezra, the Apocalypse and the Shepherd of Hermas* (JSPSup 17; Sheffield: Sheffield Academic Press, 1995)

Ilan, Tal. "'And Who knows Whether You have not Come for a Time Like this?' (Esther 4:14): Esther, Judith and Susanna as Propaganda for Shelamzion's Queenship" in Tal Ilan, *Integrating Women into Second Temple History* (TSAJ 76; Tübingen: Mohr Siebeck, 1999) 127-53

Ilan, Tal. *Jewish Women in Greco-Roman Palestine* (TSAJ 44; Tübingen: Mohr Siebeck, 1995)

Instone-Brewer, David. *Divorce and Remarriage in the Bible: The Social and Literary Context* (Grand Rapids: Eerdmans, 2002)

Jacobson, Howard A. "The *Liber Antiquitatum Biblicarum* and Tammuz," *JSP* 8 (1991) 63-65

Jacobson, Howard A. *A Commentary on Pseudo-Philo's Liber Antiquitatum Biblicarum with Latin Text and English Translation* (2 vols.; AGAJU 31; Leiden: Brill, 1996)

James, M. R. *The Biblical Antiquities of Philo* (London: SPCK, 1917; Eugene: Wipf and Stock, 2006)

Jensen, Joseph. "Does Porneia mean Fornication?" *NovT* 20 (1978) 161-84

Jobes, Karen H. "Esther: To the Reader," in *NETS*, 424-25

Kaiser, Otto. "Beobachtungen zur Komposition und Redaktion der Psalmen Salomos," in *Das Manna fällt auch heute noch: Beiträge zur Geschichte und Theologie des Alten, Ersten Testaments: Festschrift für Erich Zenger* (ed. Frank-Lothar Hossfeld and Ludger Schwienhorst-Schönberger; HBS 44; Freiburg: Herder, 2004) 362-78

Kampen, John. "The Books of the Maccabees and Sectarianism in Second Temple Judaism," in *The Books of the Maccabees: History, Theology, Ideology: Papers of the Second International Conference on the Deuterocanonical Books, Pápa, Hungary, 9-11 June, 2005* (ed. Géza G. Xeravits and József Zsengellér; JSJSup 118; Leiden: Brill, 2007) 11-30

Kappler, Werner, and Robert Hanhart, ed. *Maccabaeorum liber I* (SVTG 9.1; Göttingen: Vandenhoeck & Ruprecht, 1990)

Kappler, Werner, and Robert Hanhart, ed. *Maccabaeorum liber II* (SVTG 9.1; Göttingen: Vandenhoeck & Ruprecht, 1976).

Kedar-Kopfstein, B. "סָרִיס," *TDOT* (ed. Johannes Botterweck and Helmer Ringgren; Grand Rapids: Eerdmans, 1999) 10.345-50

Kippenberg, H. G. *Garazim und Synagoge: Traditionsgeschichtliche Untersuchungen zur samaritanischen Religion der aramäischen Periode* (Berlin: de Gruyter, 1971)

Klauck, Hans-Josef. "Brotherly Love in Plutarch and in 4 Maccabees," in *Greeks, Romans and Christians: Essays in Honour of Abraham J. Malherbe* (ed. David L. Balch, Everett Ferguson, and Wayne A. Meeks; Minneapolis: Fortress, 1990) 144-56

Klauck, Hans-Josef. *4. Makkabäerbuch* (JSHRZ 3.6; Gütersloh: Mohn, 1989)

Klijn, A. F. J. "2 (Syriac Apocalypse of) Baruch," *OTP*, 1.615-52

Klijn, A. F. J. "Der syrische Baruch-Apokalypse," in *Apokalypsen* (JSHRZ 5.2; Gütersloh: Gütersloher Verlagshaus,1976) 103-84

Klijn, A. F. J. "Recent Developments in the Study of the Syriac Apocalypse of Baruch," *JSP* 4 (1989) 3-17

Kloppenborg, John S. "Isis and Sophia in the Book of Wisdom," *HTR* 75 (1982) 57-84

Klutz, Todd E. "The Archer and the Cross: Chorographic Astrology and Literary Design in the *Testament of Solomon*," in *Magic in the Biblical World: From the Rod of Aaron to the Ring of Solomon* (ed. Todd E. Klutz; JSNTSup 245; London: T&T Clark, 2003) 219-44

Klutz, Todd E. *Rewriting the Testament of Solomon: Tradition, Conflict and Identity in a Late Antique Pseudepigraphon* (LSTS 53; London: T&T Clark, 2005)

Knibb, Michael A. "The Book of Enoch or Books of Enoch? The Textual Evidence for 1 Enoch," in *The Early Enoch Literature* (ed. Gabriele Boccaccini and John J. Collins; JSJSup 121; Leiden: Brill, 2007) 21-40.

Knibb, Michael A. *The Ethiopic Book of Enoch: A New Edition in the Light of the Aramaic Dead Sea Fragments* (2 vols; Oxford: Clarendon, 1978)

Knibb, Michael A. "The Structure and Composition of the Parables of Enoch," in *Enoch and the Messiah Son of Man: Revisiting the Book of Parables* (ed. Gabriele Boccaccini; Grand Rapids: Eerdmans, 2007) 48-64

Knight, Jonathan. *The Ascension of Isaiah* (Sheffield: Sheffield Academic Press, 1995)

Knights, Chris H. "A Century of Research into the Story/Apocalypse of Zosimus and/or the History of the Rechabites," *JSJ* 15 (1997) 53-66

Knights, Chris H. "The *Abode of the Blessed*: A Source of the *Story of Zosimus?*" *JSP* 17 (1998) 79-93

Knittel, Thomas. *Das griechische 'Leben Adams und Evas': Studien zu einer narrativen Anthropologie im frühen Judentum* (TSAJ 88; Tübingen: Mohr Siebeck, 2002)

Koehler, Ludwig, and Walter Baumgartner, ed. *Lexicon in Veteris Testamenti Libros* (Leiden: Brill, 1958)

Kolarcik, Michael. "Creation and Salvation in the Book of Wisdom," in *Creation in the Biblical Traditions* (ed. Richard J. Clifford and John J. Collins; CBQMS 24; Washington: CBA, 1992) 97-107

Kolarcik, Michael. *The Ambiguity of Death in the Book of Wisdom 1–6* (AnBib 127; Rome: Pontifical Institute Press, 1991)

Kollmann, Bernd. "Göttliche Offenbarung magisch-pharmakologischer Heilkunst im Buch Tobit," *ZAW* 106 (1994) 289-99

Kraeling, Emil. *The Brooklyn Museum Aramaic Papyri: New Documents of the Fifth Century B.C. from the Jewish Colony at Elephantine* (New Haven: Yale University Press, 1953)

Kraemer, Ross S. "When Aseneth Met Joseph: A Postscript," in *For a Later Generation: The Transformation of Tradition in Israel, Early Judaism, and Early Christianity* (ed. Randal A. Argall, Beverly A. Bow, and Rodney Alan Werline; Harrisburg: Trinity, 2000) 128-35

Kraemer, Ross S. *When Joseph Met Aseneth: A Late Antique Tale of the Biblical Patriarch and His Egyptian Wife, Reconsidered* (New York: Oxford University Press, 1998)

Kratz, Reinhard G. "Die Rezeption von Jer 10 und 29 im pseudepigraphischen Brief des Jeremia," in *Das Judentum im Zeitalter des Zweiten Tempels* (FAT 42; Tübingen: Mohr Siebeck, 2004) 316-39

Küchler, Max. *Frühjüdische Weisheitstraditionen: Zum Fortgang weisheitlichen Denkens im Bereich des frühjüdischen Jahweglaubens* (OBO 26; Fribourg: Universitätsverlag; Göttingen: Vandenhoeck & Ruprecht, 1979)

Kugel, James L. "The Rape of Dinah, and Simeon and Levi's Revenge," in James L. Kugel, *The Ladder of Jacob: Ancient Interpretations of the Biblical Story of Jacob and his Children* (Princeton: Princeton University Press, 2006) 36-80, 231-39

Kugler, Robert A. and Richard L. Rohrbaugh, "On Women and Honor in the Testament of Job," *JSP* 14 (2004) 43-62

Kulik, Alexander. *Retroverting Slavonic Pseudepigrapha: Toward the Original of the Apocalypse of Abraham* (SBLTCS 3; Leiden: Brill, 2005)

Kurfess, A. "Oracula Sibyllina I/II," *ZNW* 40 (1941) 151-65

Lambert, W. G. *Babylonian Wisdom Literature* (Oxford: Oxford University Press, 1960)

Lassen, Eva Marie. "The Roman Family: Ideal and Metaphor," in *Constructing Early Christian Families: Family as Social Reality and Metaphor* (ed. Halvor Moxnes; London: Routledge, 1997) 103-20

Lebram, J. C. H. "Jerusalem, Wohnsitz der Weisheit," in *Studies in Hellenistic Religions* (ed. M. J. Vermaseren; Leiden: Brill, 1979) 103-28

Leemhuis, Fred. "The Arabic Version of the Apocalypse of Baruch: A Christian Text?" *JSP* 4 (1989) 19-26

Lesses, Rebecca. "The Daughters of Job," in *Searching the Scriptures: A Feminist Commentary* (ed. Elisabeth Schüssler Fiorenza; London: SCM, 1994) 139-49

Leuenberger, Martin. "Ort und Funktion der Wolkenvision und ihrer Deutung in der syrischen Baruchapokalypse: Eine These zu deren thematischer Entfaltung," *JSJ* 36 (2005) 206-46

Lévi, Israel. *The Hebrew Text of the Book of Ecclesiasticus* (SSS 3; Leiden: Brill, 1904)

Levine, Amy-Jill, "Diaspora as Metaphor: Bodies and Boundaries in the Book of Tobit," in *Diaspora Jews and Judaism: Essays in Honor of, and in Dialogue with, A. Thomas Kraabel* (ed. J. Andrew Overman and Robert S. MacLennan; SFSHJ 41; Atlanta: Scholars, 1992) 107-17

Levine, Amy-Jill. "'Hemmed in on Every Side': Jews and Women in the book of Susanna," in *A Feminist Companion to Esther, Judith and Susanna* (ed. Athalya Brenner; Sheffield: Sheffield Academic Press, 1995) 303-23

Levine, Amy-Jill. "Sacrifice and Salvation: Otherness and Domestication in the Book of Judith," in *A Feminist Companion to Esther, Judith and Susanna* (ed. Athalya Brenner; Sheffield: Sheffield Academic Press, 1995) 208-23

Levine, Amy-Jill. "The Sibylline Oracles," in *Searching the Scriptures: Volume Two: A Feminist Commentary*, (ed. Elisabeth Schüssler Fiorenza; London: SCM, 1995) 99-108

Levison, John R. "Is Eve to Blame? A Contextual Analysis of Sirach 25:24," *CBQ* 47 (1985) 617-23

Levison, John R. "Judith 16:14 and the Creation of Woman," *JBL* 114 (1995) 467-69

Levison, John R. *Portraits of Adam in Early Judaism: From Sirach to 2 Baruch* (JSPSup 1; Sheffield: JSOT, 1988)

Lieber, Andrea. "I Set a Table before You: The Jewish Eschatological Character of Aseneth's Conversion Meal," *JSP* 14 (2004) 63-77

Lightfoot, Jane Lucy. *The Sibylline Oracles: With Introduction, Translation and Commentary on the First and Second Books* (Oxford: Oxford University Press, 2007)

Lipiński, E. "מֹהַר," *TDOT* (ed. G. Johannes Botterweck and Helmer Ringgren; Grand Rapids: Eerdmans, 1997) 8:142-49

Lipka, Hilary B. *Sexual Transgression in the Hebrew Bible* (HBM 7; Sheffield: Phoenix, 2006)

Littman, Robert J. *Tobit: The Book of Tobit in Codex Sinaiticus* (SCS; Leiden: Brill, 2008)

Loader, William. "Attitudes towards Sexuality in Qumran and Related Literature – and the New Testament," *NTS* 54 (2008) 338-54

Loader, William. *Enoch, Levi, and Jubilees on Sexuality: Attitudes towards Sexuality in the Early Enoch Literature, the Aramaic Levi Document, and the Book of Jubilees* (Grand Rapids: Eerdmans, 2007)

Loader, William. "Sexuality and Ptolemy's Greek Bible: Genesis 1-3 in Translation: '... Things Which They Altered For King Ptolemy' (Genesis Rabbah 8.11)," in *Ptolemy II Philadelphus and his World* (ed. Paul McKechnie and Philippe Guillaume; MnemSupp 300; Leiden: Brill, 2008) 207-32

Loader, William. *Sexuality and the Jesus Tradition* (Grand Rapids: Eerdmans, 2005)

Loader, William. "The Beginnings of Sexuality in Genesis LXX and Jubilees," in *Die Septuaginta – Texte, Kontexte, Lebenswelten* (ed. Martin Karrer and Wolfgang Kraus; Tübingen: Mohr Siebeck, 2008) 300-12

Loader, William. *The Dead Sea Scrolls on Sexuality: Attitudes towards Sexuality in Sectarian and Related Literature at Qumran* (Grand Rapids: Eerdmans, 2009)

Loader, William. *The Septuagint, Sexuality and the New Testament: Case Studies on the Impact of the LXX in Philo and the New Testament* (Grand Rapids: Eerdmans, 2004)

Loader, William. "The Strange Woman in Proverbs, LXX Proverbs and *Aseneth*" in *Septuagint and Reception: Essays Prepared for the Association for the Study of the Septuagint in South Africa* (ed. Johann Cook; VTSup 127; Leiden: Brill, 2009) 97-115

Loewenstamm, Samuel E. "The Testament of Abraham and the Texts concerning the Death of Moses," in *Studies on the Testament of Abraham* (ed. George W. E. Nickelsburg; Missoula: Scholars, 1976) 219-25

Longenecker, Bruce. *2 Esdras* (GAP; Sheffield: Sheffield Academic Press, 1995)

Longenecker, Bruce. W. *Eschatology and the Covenant: A Comparison of 4 Ezra and Romans 1–11* (JSNTSup 57; Sheffield: JSOT, 1991)

Ludlow, Jared W. *Abraham Meets Death: Narrative Humor in the Testament of Abraham* (JSPSup 41; Sheffield: Sheffield Academic Press, 2002)

MacDonald, Dennis Ronald. "Tobit and the *Odyssey*," in *Mimesis and Intertextuality in Antiquity and Christianity* (ed. Dennis Ronald MacDonald; Studies in Antiquity and Christianity; Harrisburg: Trinity, 2001) 11-40

Marshall, Mary J. *Jesus and the Banquets: An Investigation of the Early Christian Tradition concerning Jesus' Presence at Banquets with Toll Collectors and Sinners* (PhD Thesis; Murdoch University, 2002) (http://wwwlib.murdoch.edu.au/adt/browse/view/adt-MU20051110.163641)

McCracken, David. "Narration and Comedy in the Book of Tobit," *JBL* 114 (1995) 401-18

McGlynn, Moira. *Divine Judgement and Divine Benevolence in the Book of Wisdom* (WUNT 139; Tübingen: Mohr Siebeck, 2001)

McKinlay, Judith E. *Gendering Wisdom the Host: Biblical Invitations to Eat and Drink* (JSOTSup 216; Sheffield: Sheffield Academic Press, 1996)

McLay, R. Timothy. "Sousanna: To the Reader," *NETS*, 986-87

McLay, R. Timothy. *The OG and Th Versions of Daniel* (SBLSCS 43; Atlanta: Scholars, 1996)

McNeil, Brian. "Narration of Zosimus," *JSJ* 9 (1978) 68-82

Mendels, D. *The Land of Israel as Political Concept in Hasmonean Literature: Recourse to History in Second Century BCE: Claims to the Holy Land* (Tübingen: Mohr Siebeck, 1987)

Meredith, Betsy. "Desire and Danger: The Drama of Betrayal in Judges and Judith," in *Anti-Covenant: Counter-Reading Women's Lives in the Hebrew Bible* (ed. Mieke Bal; Bible and Literature Series 22; Sheffield: Almond, 1989) 63-78

Merk, Otto, and Martin Meiser, "Das Leben Adams und Evas (JSHRZ II/5)," in *Einführung zu den Jüdischen Schriften aus hellenistisch-römischer Zeit: Unterweisung in erzählender Form* (ed. Gerbern S.Oegema; JSHRZ 6.1.2; Gütersloh: Gütersloher Verlagshaus, 2005) 151-94

Merkel, Helmut. *Sibyllinen* (JSHRZ 5.8; Gütersloh: Gütersloher Verlagshaus, 1998)

Miles, Margaret M. *Carnal Knowing: Female Nakedness and Religious Meaning in the Christian West* (Boston: Beacon, 1989)

Milik, J. T. "La Patrie de Tobie," *RB* 73 (1966) 522-30

Milik, J. T. "Problèmes de la littérature Hénochique à la lumière des fragments araméens de Qumrân, *HTR* 64 (1971) 333-78

Milik, J. T. *The Books of Enoch: Aramaic Fragments of Qumran Cave 4* (Oxford: Clarendon, 1976)

Miller, David M. ed. "'Assumption of Moses': Edition 1.0," in *The Online Critical Pseudepigrapha* (ed. Ken M. Penner, David M. Miller, and Ian W. Scott; Atlanta: SBL, 2007) no pages; online: http://www.purl.org/net/ocp/Mois.html

Miller, David M. ed. "'The History of the Rechabites': Edition 1.0," in *The Online Critical Pseudepigrapha* (ed. Ken M. Penner, David M. Miller, and Ian W. Scott; Atlanta: SBL, 2006) no pages; online: http://www.purl.org/net/ocp/HistRech.html

Miller, David M. and Ian W. Scott, ed. "'Letter of Aristeas': Edition 1.0," in *The Online Critical Pseudepigrapha* (ed. Ken M. Penner, David M. Miller, and Ian W. Scott; Atlanta: SBL, 2006) no pages; online: http://www.purl.org/net/ocp/LetAris.html

Miller, David M. and Ken M. Penner, ed. "'Testament of Solomon': Edition 1.0," in *The Online Critical Pseudepigrapha* (ed. Ken M. Penner, David M. Miller, and Ian W. Scott; Atlanta: SBL, 2006) no pages; online: http://www.purl.org/net/ocp/TSol.html

Miller, Robert J. "Immortality and Religious Identity in Wisdom 2-5," in *Reimagining Christian Origins: A Colloquium Honoring Burton L. Mack* (ed. Elizabeth A. Castelli and H. Taussig; Valley Forge: Trinity, 1996) 199-213

Milne, Pamela J. "What Shall We Do With Judith? A Feminist Reassessment of a Biblical 'Heroine'," *Semeia* 62 (1993) 37-58

Mittmann-Richert, Ulrike. *Einführung zu den Jüdischen Schriften aus hellenistisch-römischer Zeit: Historische und legendarische Erzählungen* (JSHRZ 6.1.1; Gütersloh: Gütersloher Verlagshaus, 2000)

Moore, Carey A. *Daniel, Esther and Jeremiah: The Additions* (AB 44; Garden City: Doubleday, 1977)

Moore, Carey A. *Judith* (AB 40; Garden City: Doubleday, 1985)

Moore, Carey A. *Tobit* (AB 40A; Garden City: Doubleday, 1996)

Moore, Stephen D., and Janice Capel Anderson, "Taking it like a Man: Masculinity in 4 Maccabees," *JBL* 117 (1998) 249-73

Morgan, Teresa. *Literate Education in the Hellenistic and Roman Worlds* (Cambridge: Cambridge University Press, 1998)

Morgenstern, Matthew. "Language and Literature in the Second Temple Period," *JJS* 48 (1997) 139-40

Mukenge, André Kabaselle. *L'unité littéraire du livre de Baruch* (EBib 38; Paris: Gabalda, 1998)

Munnich, Olivier, ed. *Susanna – Daniel – Bel et Draco* (SVTG XVI.2; 2d ed.; Göttingen: Vandenhoeck & Ruprecht, 1999)

Munoa, Phillip B. III, *Four Powers in Heaven: The Interpretation of Daniel 7 in the Testament of Abraham* (JSPSup 28; Sheffield: Sheffield Academic Press, 1998)

Murphy, Frederick J. "2 Baruch and the Romans," *JBL* 104 (1985) 663-69

Murphy, Frederick J. *Pseudo-Philo: Rewriting the Bible* (New York: Oxford University Press, 1993)

Murphy, Frederick J. *The Structure and Meaning of Second Baruch* (SBLDS 78; Atlanta: Scholars, 1985)

Murray, Oswyn. "Aristeas and Ptolemaic Kingship," *JTS* 18 (1967) 337-71

Myers, Jacob. *I and II Esdras* (AB 42; Garden City: Doubleday, 1974)

Naumann, Weigand. *Untersuchungen über den apokryphen Jeremiasbrief* (BZAW 25; Giessen: Töpelmann, 1913) 1-53.

Neubauer, Adolf. *The Book of Tobit: The Text in Aramaic, Hebrew and Old Latin with English Translations* (Ancient Texts and Translations; Eugene: Wipf & Stock, 2005; originally Oxford: Clarendon, 1878)

Newman, Judith H. "The Democratization of Kingship in Wisdom of Solomon," in *The Idea of Biblical Interpretation: Essays in Honor of James L. Kugel* (ed. Hindy Najman and Judith H. Newman; JSJSup83; Leiden: Brill, 2004) 309-28

Niccacci, Alviero. "Wisdom as Woman, Wisdom and Man, Wisdom and God," in *Treasures of Wisdom: Studies in Ben Sira and the Book of Wisdom: Festschrift M. Gilbert* (ed. Nuria Calduch-Benages and Jacques Vermeylen; BETL 143; Leuven: Peeters, 1999) 369-85

Nickelsburg, George W. E. "An Antiochan Date for the Testament of Moses," in *Studies on the Testament of Moses* (ed. George W. E. Nickelsburg; SBLSCS 4; Cambridge: SBL, 1973) 33-37

Nickelsburg, George W. E. "Discerning the Structure(s) of the Enochic Book of Parables," in *Enoch and the Messiah Son of Man: Revisiting the Book of Parables* (ed. Gabriele Boccaccini; Grand Rapids: Eerdmans, 2007) 23-47

Nickelsburg, George W. E. *Jewish Literature Between the Bible and the Mishnah: A Literary and Historical Introduction* (2d ed.; Minneapolis: Fortress, 2005)

Nickelsburg, George W. E. "Response to Robert Doran," in *George W. E. Nickelsburg in Perspective: An Ongoing Dialogue of Learning* (ed. Jacob Neusner and Alan J. Avery-Peck; Leiden: Brill, 2003) 263-66

Nickelsburg, George W. E. *Resurrection, Immortality, and Eternal Life in Intertestamental Judaism* (HTS 26; Cambridge: Harvard University Press, 1972)

Nickelsburg, George W. E. "The Bible Rewritten and Expanded," in *Jewish Writings of the Second Temple Period: Apocrypha, Pseudepigrapha, Qumran Sectarian Writings, Philo, Josephus* (ed. Michael E. Stone; CRINT 2; Philadelphia: Fortress, 1984) 89-156

Nickelsburg, George W. E. "The Search for Tobit's Mixed Ancestry: A Historical and Hermeneutical Odyssey," in *George W. E. Nickelsburg in Perspective: An Ongoing Dialogue of Learning* (ed. Jacob Neusner and Alan J. Avery-Peck; Leiden: Brill, 2003) 241-53

Nickelsburg, George W. E. "Tobit and Enoch: Distant Cousins with a Recognizable Resemblance," in *George W. E. Nickelsburg in Perspective: An Ongoing Dialogue of Learning* (ed. Jacob Neusner and Alan J. Avery-Peck; Leiden: Brill, 2003) 1.217-39

Nickelsburg, George W. E. "Tobit, Genesis and the *Odyssey*: A Complex Web of Intertextuality," in *Mimesis and Intertextuality in Antiquity and Christianity* (ed. Dennis Ronald MacDonald; Studies in Antiquity and Christianity; Harrisburg: Trinity, 2001) 41-55

Nickelsburg, George W. E. "Where is the Place of Eschatological Blessing?" in *Things Revealed: Studies in Early Jewish and Christian Literature in Honor of Michael E. Stone* (ed. Esther G. Chazon, David Satran, and Ruth A. Clements; JSJSup 89; Leiden: Brill, 2004) 53–71

Nickelsburg, George W. E. "Torah and the Deuteronomic Scheme in the Apocrypha and Pseudepigrapha: Variations on a Theme and Some Noteworthy Examples of its Absence," in *Das Gesetz im frühen Judentum und im Neuen Testament: Festschrift für Christoph Burchard zum 75. Geburtstag* (ed. Dieter Sänger, Matthias Konradt; NTOA 57; Göttingen: Vandenhoeck & Ruprecht; Fribourg: Academic Press, 2006) 222-35

Nickelsburg, George W. E. and James C. VanderKam, *1 Enoch: A New Translation* (Minneapolis: Fortress, 2004)

Nicklas, Tobias. "Marriage in the Book of Tobit: A Synoptic Approach," in *The Book of Tobit: Text, Tradition, Theology: Papers of the First International Conference on the Deuterocanonical Books, Pápa, Hungary, 20-21 May, 2004* (ed. Géza G. Xeravits and József Zsengellér; JSJSup 98; Leiden: Brill, 2005) 139-54

Niebuhr, Karl-Wilhelm. *Gesetz und Paraäse: Katechismusartige Weisungsreihen in der frühjüdischen Literatur* (WUNT 2.28; Tübingen: Mohr Siebeck, 1987)

Nikiprowetzky, Valentin. *La Troisième Sibylle* (Ètudes Juives 9; Paris: Mouton, 1970)

Nikolsky, Ronit. "The History of the Rechabites and the Jeremiah literature," *JSP* 13 (2002) 185-207

Nir, Rivka. *The Destruction of Jerusalem and the Idea of Redemption in the Syriac Apocalypse of Baruch* (SBLEJL 20; Leiden: Brill, 2003)

Norden, E. *Die antike Kunstprosa vom VI. Jahrhundert v. Chr. bis in die Zeit der Renaissance* (2 vols; 7th ed.; Darmstadt: Wissenschaftliche Buchgesellschaft, 1974)

Nowell, Irene. "The Book of Tobit: An Ancestral Story," in *Intertextual Studies in Ben Sira and Tobit: Essays in Honor of Alexander A. Di Lella* (ed. Jeremy Corley and Vincent T.M. Skemp; CBQMS 38; Washington: CBA, 2005) 3-13

Nowell, Irene. "The Book of Tobit," in *The New Interpreter's Bible: A Commentary in Twelve Volumes: Volume Three: The First and Second Books of Kings; The First and Second Books of Chronicles; The Book of Ezra; The Book of Nehemiah; The Book of Esther; The Book of Tobit; The Book of Judith* (Nashville: Abingdon, 1999) 975-1071

Nussbaum, Martha C. *The Therapy of Desire: Theory and Practice in Hellenistic Ethics* (Princeton: Princeton University Press, 1994)

Oegema, Gerbern S. "Aristeasbrief (JSHRZ II/1)," in *Einführung zu den Jüdischen Schriften aus hellenistisch-römischer Zeit: Unterweisung in erzählender Form* (ed. Gerbern S. Oegema; JSHRZ 6.1.2; Gütersloh: Gütersloher Verlagshaus, 2005) 49-65

Oegema, Gerbern S. *Einführung zu den Jüdischen Schriften aus hellenistisch-römischer Zeit: Apokalypsen* (JSHRZ 6.1.5; Gütersloh: Gütersloher Verlagshaus, 2001)

Oegema, Gerbern S. *Einführung zu den Jüdischen Schriften aus hellenistisch-römischer Zeit: Poetische Schriften* (JSHRZ 6.1.4; Gütersloh: Gütersloher Verlagshaus, 2002)

Oegema, Gerbern S. "Joseph und Aseneth (JSHRZ II/4)," in *Einführung zu den Jüdischen Schriften aus hellenistisch-römischer Zeit: Unterweisung in erzählender Form* (ed. Gerbern S. Oegema; JSHRZ 6.1.2; Gütersloh: Gütersloher Verlagshaus, 2005) 97-114

Oegema, Gerbern S. "Portrayals of Women in 1 and 2 Maccabees," in *Transformative Encounters: Jesus and Women Re-viewed* (ed. Ingrid Rosa Kitzberger; BIS 43; Leiden: Brill, 2000) 244-64

Oegema, Gerbern S. "Pseudo-Philo: Antiquitates Biblicae (JSHRZ II/2)," in *Einführung zu den Jüdischen Schriften aus hellenistisch-römischer Zeit: Unterweisung in erzählender Form* (ed. Gerbern S. Oegema; JSHRZ 6.1.2; Gütersloh: Gütersloher Verlagshaus, 2005) 66-77

Olson, Daniel C. in consultation with Melkesedek Workeneh, *Enoch: A New Translation; The Ethiopic Book of Enoch, or 1 Enoch, Translated with Annotations and Cross-References* (North Richland Hills: BIBAL, 2004)

Olyan, Saul M. "The Israelites Debate their Options at the Sea of Reeds: *LAB* 10:3, its Parallels, and Pseudo-Philo's Ideology and Background," *JBL* 110 (1991) 75-91

Orlov, Andrei A. "'Noah's Younger Brother': Anti-Noachic Polemics in 2 Enoch," *Henoch* 22 (2003) 259-73

Orlov, Andrei A. "Noah's Younger Brother Revisited: Anti-Noachic Polemics and the Date of 2 (Slavonic) Enoch," *Henoch* 26 (2004) 172-87

Orlov, Andrei A. "On the Polemical Nature of 2 (Slavonic) Enoch: A Reply to C. Böttrich," *JSJ* 34 (2003) 274-303

Orlov, Andrei A. *The Enoch-Metatron Tradition* (TSAJ 107; Tübingen: Mohr Siebeck, 2005)

Otzen, Benedikt. *Tobit and Judith* (GAP; Sheffield: Sheffield Academic Press, 2002)

Pearce, Sarah. "Echoes of Eden in the Old Greek of Susanna," *Feminist Theology* 11 (1996) 10-31

Penn, Michael. "Identity Transformation and Authorial Identification in *Joseph and Aseneth*," *JSP* 13 (2002) 171-83

Pennington, A. "The Apocalypse of Abraham," *AOT*, 363–91

Pervo, Richard I. "Aseneth and Her Sisters: Women in Jewish Narrative and in the Greek Novels," in *"Women Like This": New Perspectives on Jewish Women in the Greco-Roman World* (ed. A. J. Levine; Atlanta: Scholars, 1991) 145-60

Pesch, Wilhelm. "Die Abhängigkeit des 11 salomonischen Psalms vom letzten Kapitel des Buches Baruch," *ZAW* 67 (1955) 251-63

Pietersma, Albert and Benjamin G. Wright, ed. *A New English Translation of the Septuagint (NETS)* (Oxford: Oxford University Press, 2007)

Phillips, Anthony. "Another Look at Adultery," in Anthony Phillips, *Essays on Biblical Law* (JSOTSup 344; London: Sheffield Academic Press, 2002) 74-95

Philonenko, Marc. *"Joseph et Aséneth": Introduction, texte critique, traduction et notes* (SPB 13; Leiden: Brill, 1968)

Philonenko, Marc. "Le Testament de Job et les Therapeutes," *Sem* 8 (1958) 41-53

Philonenko-Sayar, Belkis and Marc Philonenko, *Die Apokalypse Abrahams* (JSHRZ 5.5; Gütersloh: Gütersloher Verlagshaus, 1982)

Pietersma, Albert, and Benjamin G. Wright, ed. *A New English Translation of the Septuagint* (Oxford: Oxford University Press, 2007)

Piovanelli, Pierluigi. "'A Testimony for the Kings and the Mighty Who Possess the Earth': The Thirst for Justice and Peace in the Parables of Enoch," in *Enoch and the Messiah Son of Man: Revisiting the Book of Parables* (ed. Gabriele Boccaccini; Grand Rapids: Eerdmans, 2007) 363-79

Piovanelli, Pierluigi. "A Theology of the Supernatural in the Book of Watchers? An African Perspective," in *The Origins of Enochic Judaism: Proceedings of the First Enoch Seminar, University of Michigan, Sesto Fiorentino, Italy, June*

19-23, 2001 (ed. G. Boccaccini; Torino: Silvio Zamorani Editore, 2002) = *Henoch 24* (2002) 87-98

Pitkänen, P. "Family Life and Ethnicity in Early Israel and in Tobit," in *Studies in the Book of Tobit* (ed. Mark Bredin; London: T&T Clark, 2006) 104-17

Polaski, Donald. C. "On Taming Tamar: Amran's Rhetoric and Women's Roles in Pseudo-Philo's *Liber Antiquitatum Biblicarum* 9," *JSP* 13 (1995) 79-99

Portier-Young, Anathea. E. "Alleviation of Suffering in the Book of Tobit: Comedy, Community, and Happy Endings," *CBQ* 63 (2001) 35-54

Portier-Young, Anathea E. "Sweet Mercy Metropolis: Interpreting Aseneth's Honeycomb," *JSP* 14 (2005) 133-57

Priest, John. "Testament of Moses," *OTP*, 1.919–34

Pummer, Reinhard and Michel Roussel, "A Note on Theodotus and Homer," *JSJ* 13 (1982) 177-82

Rabinowitz, Isaac. "The Qumran Hebrew Original of Ben Sira's Concluding Acrostic on Wisdom," *HUCA* 42 (1971) 173-84

Rahlfs, Alfred, and Robert Hanhart, ed. *Septuaginta: Id est Vetus Testamentum graece iuxta LXX interpretes* (2d ed.; Stuttgart: Deutsche Bibelgesellschaft, 2006)

Räisänen, Heikki. *Paul and the Law* (Philadelphia: Fortress, 1986)

Rakel, Claudia. "Das Buch Judit: Über eine Schönheit, die nicht ist, was sie zu sein vorgibt," in *Kompendium Feministische Bibelauslegung* (ed. Luise Schottroff, Marie-Theres Wacker, Claudia Janssen, and Beate Wehn; Gütersloh: Gütersloher Verlagshaus, 1999) 410-21

Rakel, Claudia. "Das erste Makkabäerbuch: Frauenexistenz an den Rändern des Textes," in *Kompendium Feministische Bibelauslegung* (ed. Luise Schottroff, Marie-Theres Wacker, Claudia Janssen, Beate Wehn; Gütersloh: Gütersloher Verlagshaus, 2007) 384-91

Rakel, Claudia. *Judit über Schönheit, Macht und Widerstand im Krieg: Eine Feministisch-Intertextuelle Lektüre* (BZAW 334; Berlin: de Gruyter, 2003)

Reed, Annette Yoshiko. *Fallen Angels and the History of Judaism and Christianity: The Reception of Enochic Literature* (New York: Cambridge University Press, 2005)

Reese, James M. *Hellenistic Influence on the Book of Wisdom and Its Consequences* (Rome: PBI, 1970)

Regev, Eyal. "Pure Individualism: The Idea of Non-Priestly Purity in Ancient Judaism," *JSJ* 31 (2000) 176-202

Regev, Eyal. "The Two Sins of Nob: Biblical Interpretation, an Anti-priestly Polemic and a Geographical Error in *Liber Antiquitatum Biblicarum*," *JSP* 12 (2001) 85-104

Reider, J. *The Book of Wisdom* (New York: Harper, 1957)

Reinhartz, Adele. "Better Homes and Gardens: Women and Domestic Space in the Books of Judith and Susanna," in *Text and Artifact in the Religions of Mediterranean Antiquity: Essays in Honour of Peter Richardson* (ed. Stephen G. Wilson and Michael Desjardins; SCJ 9; Waterloo: Wilfred Laurier University Press, 2000) 325-39

Reiterer, Friedrich V. "Die Vergangenheit als Basis für die Zukunft Mattathias' Lehre für seine Söhne aus der Geschichte in 1 Makk 2:52-60," in *The Books of the Maccabees: History, Theology, Ideology: Papers of the Second International Conference on the Deuterocanonical Books, Pápa, Hungary, 9-11 June, 2005* (ed. Géza G. Xeravits and József Zsengellér; JSJSup 118; Leiden: Brill, 2007) 75-100

Reiterer, Friedrich V. "Review of Recent Research on the Book of Ben Sira," in *The Book of Ben Sira in Modern Research* (ed. Pancratius C. Beentjes; BZAW 255; Berlin: de Gruyter, 1997) 23-60

Rogers, Jessie. "'As Ploughing and Reaping Draw Near to Her': A Reading of Sirach 6:18-37," *Old Testament Essays* 13 (2000) 364-79

Rubinkiewicz, Richard. "Apocalypse of Abraham," *OTP*, 1.681-705

Ruppert, Lothar. *Der leidende Gerechte: Eine motivgeschichtliche Untersuchung zum Alten Testament und zwischentestamentlichen Judentum* (FB 5; Würzburg: Echter, 1972)

Ruppert, Lothar. "Gerechte und Frevler (Gottlose) in Sap 1,1 – 6,21: Zum Neuverständnis und zur Aktualisierung alttestamentlicher Traditionen in der Sapientia Salomonis," in *Die Weisheit Salomos im Horizont Biblisacher Theologie* (ed. Hans Hübner; Biblische-Theologische Studien 22; Neukirchen-Vluyn: Neukirchener Verlag, 1993) 1-54

Ruppert, Lothar. "Liebe und Bekehrung: Zur Typologie des hellenistisch-judischen Romans Joseph und Asenet," in *Paradeigmata: Literarische Typologie des Alten Testaments: I. Teil: Von den Anfängen bis zum 19. Jahrhundert* (ed. F. Link; Berlin: Duncker & Humblot, 1989) 33-42

Sacchi, Paolo. *Jewish Apocalyptic and its History* (JSPSup 20; Sheffield: Sheffield Academic Press, 1990) 231-49

Sacchi, Paolo. "The 2005 Camaldoli Seminar on the Parables of Enoch: Summary and Prospects for Future Research," in *Enoch and the Messiah Son of Man: Revisiting the Book of Parables* (ed. Gabriele Boccaccini; Grand Rapids: Eerdmans, 2007) 499-512

Sanders, E. P. "Testament of Abraham," *OTP*, 1.871–902

Sanders, J. A. "Sirach 51:13ff," in *The Psalms Scroll of Qumran Cave 11 (11QPS^a)* (DJD 4; Oxford: Clarendon, 1965) 79-85

Sanders, Jack T. "When Sacred Canopies Collide: The Reception of the Torah of Moses in the Wisdom Literature of the Second-Temple Period," *JSJ* 32 (2001) 121-36

Sänger, Dieter. *Antikes Judentum und die Mysterien: Religionsgeschichtliche Untersuchungen zu Joseph und Aseneth* (WUNT 2.5; Tübingen: Mohr Siebeck, 1980)

Sänger, Dieter. "Erwägungen zur historischen Einordnung und zur Datierung von 'Joseph und Aseneth'," *ZNW* 76 (1985) 86-106

Satlow, Michael L. *Jewish Marriage in Antiquity* (Princeton: Princeton University Press, 2001)

Satran, David. *Biblical Prophets in Byzantine Palestine: Reassessing the Lives of the Prophets* (Leiden: Brill, 1995)

Sawyer, Deborah F. "Gender Strategies in Antiquity: Judith's Performance," *Feminist Theology* 28 (2001) 9-26

Sayler, Gwendolyn B. *Have the Promises Failed? A Literary Analysis of 2 Baruch* (SBLDS 72; Atlanta: Scholars, 1984)

Schaller, Berndt. "Zur Komposition und Konzeption des Testaments Hiobs," in *Studies on the Testament of Job* (ed. Michael A. Knibb and Pieter W. van der Horst; SNTSMS 66; Cambridge: Cambridge University Press, 1989) 46-92

Schimanowski, Gottfried. "Der *Aristeasbrief* zwischen Abgrenzung und Selbstdarstellung," in *Persuasion and Dissuasion in Early Christianity, Ancient Judaism, and Hellenism* (ed. Pieter van der Horst et al.; CBET 33; Leuven: Peeters, 2003) 45-64

Schmitt, Armin. "Zur dramatischen Form von Weisheit 1,1-6,21," *BZ* 37 (1993) 236-58

Schodde, G. H. *The Book of Enoch* (Andover: Draper, 1882)

Schroer, Silvia. "The Book of Sophia," in *Searching the Scriptures: Volume Two: A Feminist Commentary* (London: SCM, 1995) 17-38

Schüngel-Straumann, Helen. *Tobit* (HTKAT; Freiburg: Herder, 2000)

Schüpphaus, Joachim. *Die Psalmen Salomos: Ein Zeugnis Jerusalemer Theologie und Frömmigkeit in der Mitte des vorchristlichen Jahrhunderts* (ALGHJ 7; Leiden: Brill, 1977)

Schürer, Emil. *The History of the Jewish People in the Age of Jesus Christ (175 B.C. – A.D. 135): Vol. III.1* (3 vols; ed. Geza Vermes; Fergus Millar, and Martin Goodman; Edinburgh: T&T Clark, 1986)

Schwarz, Sarah. "Reconsidering the Testament of Solomon," *JSP* 16 (2007) 203-37

Scott, Ian W., ed. "'Testament of Job': Edition 1.0," in *The Online Critical Pseudepigrapha* (ed. Ken M. Penner, David M. Miller, and Ian W. Scott; Atlanta: SBL, 2006) no pages; online: http://www.purl.org/net/ocp/TJob.html

Seeley, David. "Narrative, the Righteous Man and the Philosopher: An Analysis of the Story of the Dikaios in Wisdom 1-5," *JSP* 7 (1990) 55-78

Shutt, R. J. H. "Letter of Aristeas," *OTP*, 2.7-34

Skehan, Patrick W. "The Hand of Judith," *CBQ* 25 (1963) 94-109

Skehan, Patrick W. *The Wisdom of Ben Sira: A New Translation with Notes,
Introduction and Commentary by Alexander A. Di Lella* (AB 39; Garden City:
Doubleday, 1987)

Skehan, Patrick W. "Tower of Death or Deadly Snare? (Sir 26:22)," *CBQ* 16
(1954) 154

Skinner, Marilyn B. *Sexuality in Greek and Roman Culture* (Oxford: Blackwell,
2005)

Smith, J. Payne. *A Compendious Syriac Dictionary* (Eugene: Wipf and Stock,
1999)

Soll, William Michael. "The Family as Scriptural and Social Construct in Tobit,"
in *The Function of Scripture in Early Jewish and Christian Tradition* (ed.
Craig A. Evans, and James A. Sanders; JSNTSup 154; Sheffield: Sheffield
Academic Press, 1998) 166-75

Spittler, Russell P. "Testament of Job," *OTP*, 1.829-68

Standhartinger, Angela. *Das Frauenbild im Judentum der Hellenistischen Zeit:
Ein Beitrag anhand von 'Joseph und Aseneth'* (Leiden: Brill, 1995)

Standhartinger, Angela. "Joseph und Aseneth: Vollkommene Braut oder
himmlische Prophetin," in *Kompendium Feministische Bibelauslegung* (ed.
Luise Schottroff, Marie-Theres Wacker, Claudia Janssen, and Beate Wehn;
Gütersloh: Gütersloher Verlagshaus, 1999) 459-64

Standhartinger, Angela. "'Um zu sehen die Töchter des Landes': Die Perspektive
Dinas in der jüdisch-hellenistischen Diskussion um Gen 34," in *Religious
Propaganda and Missionary Competition in the New Testament World* (ed.
Lukas Bormann, Kelly del Tredici, and Angela Standhartinger; Leiden: Brill,
1994) 89-116

Standhartinger, Angela. "Weisheit in *Joseph und Aseneth* und den paulinischen
Briefen," *NTS* 47 (2001) 482-501

Starr Sered, Susan, and Samuel Cooper, "Sexuality and Social Control:
Anthropological Reflections on the Book of Susanna," in *The Judgment of
Susanna: Authority and Witness.* (ed. E. Spolsky; EJL 11; Atlanta: Scholars,
1996) 43-55

Steck, Odil Hannes. *Das apokryphe Baruchbuch: Studien zu Rezeption und
Konzentration "kanonischer" Überlieferung* (FRLANT 160; Göttingen:
Vandenhoeck & Ruprecht, 1993)

Steussy, Marti J. *Gardens in Babylon: Narrative and Faith in the Greek Legends
of Daniel* (SBLDS 141; Atlanta: Scholars, 1993)

Stocker, Margarita M. *Judith: Sexual Warrior: Women and Power in Western
Culture* (New Haven: Yale University Press, 1998)

Stone, Ken. *Practicing Safer Texts: Food, Sex and Bible in Queer Perspective*
(London: T. & T. Clark, 2005)

Stone, Michael Edward. *4 Ezra: A Commentary on the Book of Fourth Ezra* (Hermeneia; Minneapolis: Augsburg Fortress, 1990)

Stone, Michael Edward. "Enoch's Date in Limbo: or, Some Considerations on David Suter's Analysis of the Book of the Parables," in *Enoch and the Messiah Son of Man: Revisiting the Book of Parables* (ed. Gabriele Boccaccini; Grand Rapids: Eerdmans, 2007) 444-49

Stone, N. "Judith and Holofernes: Some Observations on the Development of the Scene in Art," in *"No One Spoke Ill of Her": Essays on Judith* (ed. James C. VanderKam; SBLEJL 2; Atlanta: Scholars, 1992) 73-93

Streete, Gail Corrington. *The Strange Woman: Power and Sex in the Bible* (Louisville: Westminster John Knox, 1997)

Strugnell, John. "Introduction: General Introduction, with a Note on Alexander Polyhistor," *OTP*, 2.777-79

Strugnell, John. "Notes and Queries on 'The Ben Sira Scroll from Masada'," *ErIsr* 9 (1969) 109-19

Stuckenbruck, Loren T. "The Parables of Enoch according to George Nickelsburg and Michael Knibb: A Summary and Discussion of Some Remaining Questions," in *Enoch and the Messiah Son of Man: Revisiting the Book of Parables* (ed. Gabriele Boccaccini; Grand Rapids: Eerdmans, 2007) 65-71

Suggs, M. Jack. "Wisdom of Solomon 2:10-5:23: A Homily Based on the Fourth Servant Song," *JBL* 76 (1957) 26-33

Suter, David W. "Enoch in Sheol: Updating the Dating of the Book of Parables," in *Enoch and the Messiah Son of Man: Revisiting the Book of Parables* (ed. Gabriele Boccaccini; Grand Rapids: Eerdmans, 2007) 415-43

Suter, David W. *Tradition and Composition in the Parables of Enoch* (SBLDS 47; Missoula: Scholars, 1979)

Sutter Rehmann, Luzia. "Das Testament Hiobs: Hiob, Dina und ihre Töchter," in *Kompendium Feministische Bibelauslegung* (ed. Luise Schottroff, Marie-Theres Wacker, Claudia Janssen, and Beate Wehn; Gütersloh: Gütersloher Verlagshaus, 1999) 465-73

Sutter Rehmann, Luzia. "Das vierte Esrabuch: Vom Ringen um neues Leben, von der sich erfüllenden Zeit und der Verwandlung der Erde," in *Kompendium Feministische Bibelauslegung* (ed. Luise Schottroff, Marie-Theres Wacker, Claudia Janssen, and Beate Wehn; Gütersloh: Gütersloher Verlagshaus, 1999) 450-58

Talshir, Zipora (with David Talshir). *1 Esdras: A Text Critical Commentary* (SBLSCS 50; Atlanta: SBL, 2001)

Talshir, Zipora (with David Talshir). *1 Esdras: From Origin to Translation* (SBLSCS 47; Atlanta: SBL, 1999)

Tcherikover, Victor A. *Hellenistic Civilization and the Jews* (Peabody: Hendrickson, 1999)

Tcherikover, Victor A. "The Ideology of the Letter of Aristeas," *HTR* 51 (1958) 59–85

Thackeray, H. St. J. "Appendix: The Letter of Aristeas," in *An Introduction to the Old Testament in Greek* (ed. H. B. Swete; Cambridge: Cambridge University Press, 1914) 531-606

Thomas, Johannes. *Der jüdische Phokylides: Formgeschichtliche Zugänge zu Pseudo-Phokylides und Vergleich mit der neutestamentlichen Paränese* (Fribourg: Universitätsverlag; Göttingen: Vandenhoeck & Ruprecht, 1992)

Tigchelaar, Eibert I. C. "Remarks on Transmission and Traditions in the Parables of Enoch: Response to James VanderKam," in *Enoch and the Messiah Son of Man: Revisiting the Book of Parables* (ed. Gabriele Boccaccini; Grand Rapids: Eerdmans, 2007) 100-109

Tilly, Michael. "Die Sünden Israels und der Heiden: Beobachtungen zu *L.A.B.* 25:9-13," *JSJ* 37 (2006) 192-211

Torrey, Charles C. *The Apocryphal Literature* (New Haven: Yale University Press, 1945)

Tov, Emanuel. *The Septuagint Translation of Jeremiah and Baruch* (HSM 8; Missoula: Scholars, 1976)

Trafton, Joseph L. "The Bible, the *Psalms of Solomon*, and Qumran," in *The Bible and the Dead Sea Scrolls: The Princeton Symposium on the Dead Sea Scrolls: Volume 2: The Dead Sea Scrolls and the Qumran Community* (ed. James H. Charlesworth; Waco: Baylor University Press, 2006) 427-46

Trafton, Joseph L. "The Psalms of Solomon in Recent Research," *JSP* 12 (1994) 3-19.

Trafton, Joseph L. "The Psalms of Solomon: New Light from the Syriac Version?" *JBL* 105 (1986) 227-37

Trafton, Joseph L. *The Syriac Version of the Psalms of Solomon* (SOCS 11; Atlanta: Scholars, 1985)

Trenchard, Warren C. *Ben Sira's View of Women: A Literary Analysis* (BJS 38; Chicago: Scholars, 1982)

Tromp, Johannes. *The Assumption of Moses: A Critical Edition with Commentary* (SVTP 10; Leiden: Brill, 1993)

Tromp, Johannes. *The Life of Adam and Eve in Greek: A Critical Edition* (PVTG 6; Leiden: Brill, 2005)

van den Eynde, Sabine. "Crying to God: Prayer and Plot in the Book of Judith," *Bib* 85 (2004) 217-31

van den Eynde, Sabine. "One Journey and One Journey Makes Three: The Impact of the Readers' Knowledge in the Book of Tobit," *ZAW* 117 (2005) 273-80

van der Horst, Pieter W. "Deborah and Seila in Ps-Philo's Liber Antiquitatum Biblicarum," in *Messiah and Christos: Studies in the Jewish Origins of*

Christianity Presented to David Flusser (ed. I. Gruenwald, S. Shaked, and G.
   Stroumsa; Tübingen: Mohr Siebeck, 1992) 111-17

van der Horst, Pieter W. "Images of Women in the Testament of Job," in *Studies
   on the Testament of Job* (ed. Michael Knibb and Pieter W. van der Horst;
   SNTSMS 66; Cambridge: Cambridge University Press, 1989) 93-116

van der Horst, Pieter W. "Pseudo-Phocylides and the New Testament," *ZNW* 69
   (1978) 187-202

van der Horst, Pieter W. "Pseudo-Phocylides on the Afterlife: A Rejoinder to John
   J. Collins," *JSJ* 35 (2004) 70-75

van der Horst, Pieter W. "Pseudo-Phocylides Revisited," *JSP* 3 (1988) 3-30

van der Horst, Pieter W. "Sarah's Seminal Emission: Hebrews 11:11 in the Light
   of Ancient Embryology," in *Greeks, Romans and Christians: Essays in
   Honour of Abraham J. Malherbe* (ed. David L. Balch, Everett Ferguson, and
   Wayne A. Meeks; Minneapolis: Fortress, 1990) 287-302

van der Horst, Pieter W. "Seven Months' Children in Jewish and Christian
   Literature from Antiquity," *ETL* 54 (1978) 346-60

van der Horst, Pieter W. "Tamar in Pseudo-Philo's Biblical History" in *A Feminist
   Companion to Genesis* (ed. Athalya Brenner; Sheffield: Sheffield Academic
   Press, 1993) 300-304

van der Horst, Pieter W. "The Interpretation of the Bible by the Minor Hellenistic
   Jewish Authors," in Pieter van der Horst, *Essays on the Jewish World of Early
   Christianity* (NTOA 14; Fribourg: Universitätsverlag; Göttingen: Vandenhoeck
   & Ruprecht, 1990) 187-219

van der Horst, Pieter W. *The Sentences of Pseudo-Phocylides: With Introduction
   and Commentary* (SVTP 4; Leiden: Brill, 1978)

van Henten, Jan W. "Datierung und Herkunft des Vierten Makkabäerbuches," in
   *Tradition and Re-interpretation in Jewish and Early Christian Literature:
   Essays in Honour of Jurgen C. H. Lebram* (ed. J. W. van Henten, H. J. de
   Jonge, et. al.; SPB; JSJSup 36; Leiden: Brill, 1986) 136-49

van Henten, Jan W. "Judith as Alternative Leader: A Rereading of Judith 7-13," in
   A Feminist Companion to Esther, Judith and Susanna (ed. Athalya Brenner;
   Sheffield: Sheffield Academic Press, 1995) 224-52

van Henten, Jan W. "Nero Redivivus Demolished: The Coherence of the Nero
   Traditions in the Sibylline Oracles," *JSP* 21 (2000) 3-17

VanderKam, James C. "The Book of Parables within the Enoch Tradition," in
   Enoch and the Messiah Son of Man: Revisiting the Book of Parables (ed.
   Gabriele Boccaccini; Grand Rapids: Eerdmans, 2007) 81-99

von Gemünden, Petra. "Der Affekt der ἐπιθυμία und der νόμος: Affektkontrolle
   und soziale Identitätsbildung im 4. Makkabäerbuch mit einem Ausblick auf
   den Römerbrief," in *Das Gesetz im frühen Judentum und im Neuen Testament:
   Festschrift für Christoph Burchard zum 75. Geburtstag* (ed. Dieter Sänger and

Matthias Konradt; NTOA 57; Göttingen: Vandenhoeck & Ruprecht; Fribourg: Academic Press, 2006) 55-74

von Loewenclau, Ilse. "Das Buch Daniel: Frauen und Kinder nicht gerechnet" in *Kompendium Feministische Bibelauslegung* (ed. Luise Schottroff, Marie-Theres Wacker, Claudia Janssen, and Beate Wehn; Gütersloh: Gütersloher Verlagshaus, 1999) 291-98

Wagner, Christian J. *Polyglotte Tobit-Synopse: Griechisch – Lateinisch – Syrisch – Hebräisch – Aramaisch* (Abhandlungen der Akademie der Wissenschaften in Göttingen; Philologisch-Historische Klasse Dritte Folge, Band 258; Göttingen: Vandenhoeck & Ruprecht, 2003)

Walsh, Carey Ellen. *Exquisite Desire: Religion, the Erotic, and the Song of Songs* (Philadelphia: Fortress, 2000)

Walter, Nikolaus. *Pseudepigraphische jüdisch-hellenistische Dichtung: Pseudo-Phokylides, Pseudo-Orpheus, Gefälschte Verse auf Namen griechischer Dichter* (JSHRZ 4.3; Gütersloh: Gütersloher Verlagshaus, 1983)

Weber, Reinhard, *Das Gesetz im hellenistischen Judentum: Studien zum Verständnis und zur Funktion der Thora von Demetrios bis Pseudo-Phokylides* (ARGU 10; Frankfurt: Peter Lang, 2000)

Webster, Jane S. "Sophia: Engendering Wisdom in Proverbs, Ben Sira and the Wisdom of Solomon," *JSOT* 78 (1998) 63-79

Weeks, Stuart, Simon Gathercole, and Loren Stuckenbruck, *The Book of Tobit: Texts from the Principal Ancient and Medieval Traditions: With Synopsis, Concordances, and Annotated Texts in Aramaic, Hebrew, Greek, Latin, and Syriac* (FSBP 3; Berlin: de Gruyter, 2004)

Wellhausen, Julius. *Die Pharisäer und die Sadducäer: Eine Untersuchung zur inneren Geschichte* (Greifswald: Bamberg, 1874)

Werline, Rodney Alan. *Penitential Prayer in Second Temple Judaism: The Development of a Religious Institution* (SBLEJL 13; Atlanta: Scholars, 1997)

Westerholm, Stephen. "Four Maccabees: A Paraenetic Address?" in *Early Christian Paraenesis in Context* (ed. James Starr and Troels Engberg-Pedersen; BZNW 125; Berlin: de Gruyter, 2004) 191-216

White Crawford, Sidnie. "Esther and Judith: Contrasts in Character," in *The Book of Esther in Modern Research* (ed. Sidnie White Crawford, Leonard J. Greenspoon; JSOTSup 380; London: T&T Clark, 2003) 61-76

Whitters, Mark F. "Testament and Canon in the Letter of Second Baruch (2 Baruch 78-87)," *JSP* 12 (2001) 149-63

Williams, David S. "A Literary Encircling Pattern in 1 Maccabees 1," *JBL* 120 (2001) 140-42

Williams, David S. "Recent Research in 2 Maccabees," CurBR 2 (2003) 69-83

Williamson, G. A. ed. *Josephus: The Jewish War* (London: Penguin, rev., 1981)

Wills, Lawrence M. "Ascetic Theology Before Asceticism? Jewish Narratives and the Decentering of the Self," *JAAR* 74 (2006) 902-25

Wills, Lawrence M. *The Jewish Novel in the Ancient World* (Ithaca: Cornell University Press, 1995)

Wilson, Walter T. *The Sentences of Pseudo-Phocylides* (CEJL; Berlin: de Gruyter, 2005)

Winninge, Mikael. *Sinners and the Righteous: A Comparative Study of the Psalms of Solomon and Paul's letters* (Stockholm: Almqvist & Wiksell, 1995)

Winston, David. "The Sage as Mystic in the Wisdom of Solomon," in *The Ancestral Philosophy: Hellenistic Philosophy in Second Temple Judaism: Essays of David Winston* (ed. Gregory E. Sterling; BJS 331; StudPhilMon 4; Providence: BJS, 2001) 99-113

Winston, David. "Wisdom in the Wisdom of Solomon," in *The Ancestral Philosophy: Hellenistic Philosophy in Second Temple Judaism: Essays of David Winston* (ed. Gregory E. Sterling; BJS 331; StudPhilMon 4; Providence: BJS, 2001) 83-98

Winston, David. *Wisdom of Solomon* (AB 43; Garden City: Doubleday, 1979)

Wright, Benjamin G. "Sirach: Introduction and Translation," *NETS*, 715-62

Wright, Benjamin G. "The Structure of the Parables of Enoch: A Response to George Nickelsburg and Michael Knibb," in *Enoch and the Messiah Son of Man: Revisiting the Book of Parables* (ed. Gabriele Boccaccini; Grand Rapids: Eerdmans, 2007) 72-78

Wright, Robert B. "Psalms of Solomon," *OTP*, 2.639–70

Wright, Robert B. *The Psalms of Solomon: A Critical Edition of the Greek Text* (JCTCRS 1; London: T&T Clark, 2007)

Yee, Gale A. *Poor Banished Children of Eve: Woman as Evil in the Hebrew Bible* (Minneapolis: Fortress, 2003)

Young, Robin Darling. "The 'Woman With the Soul of Abraham': Traditions about the Mother of the Maccabean Martyrs," in *"Women Like This": New Perspectives on Jewish Women in the Greco-Roman World* (ed. A. J. Levine; EJL 1; Atlanta: Scholars, 1991) 67-81

Zacharias, H. Daniel ed. "'Psalms of Solomon': Edition 2.0," in *The Online Critical Pseudepigrapha* (ed. Ken M. Penner, David M. Miller, and Ian W. Scott; Atlanta: SBL, 2007) no pages; online: http://www.purl.org/net/ocp/PssSol.html

Zenger, Erich. *Historische und legendarische Erzählungen: Das Buch Judit* (JSHRZ 1.6; Gütersloh: Gütersloher Verlagshaus, 1981)

Ziegler, Joseph, ed. *Sapientia Salomonis* (SVTG 12.1; 2d. ed.; Göttingen: Vandenhoeck & Ruprecht, 1980)

Ziegler, Joseph, ed. *Sapientia Iesu Filii Sirach* (SVTG 12.2; Göttingen: Vandenhoeck & Ruprecht, 1965)

Zimmermann, Frank. "Aids for the Recovery of the Hebrew Original of Judith," *JBL* 57 (1938) 67-74

Zimmermann, Frank. "The Story of Susanna and Its Original Language," *JQR* 48 (1957-58), 236-41

Zimmermann, Frank. *The Book of Tobit* (JAL; New York: Harper, 1958)

Index of Modern Authors

Alexander   138, 141
Alexiou and Dronke   283
Allison   133, 135
Alonso-Schöckel   213
Andersen   37, 38, 40, 42, 44, 46, 51
Anderson   449, 451, 452, 455
Angel   396
Aptowitzer   302
Arcari   6
Archer   249, 253, 370, 383
Atkinson   112, 113, 114, 342, 343, 344
          345, 346, 347, 348, 349, 350, 351
          352, 353, 355, 356, 357, 358, 359
                                    360
Attridge   488
Auerbach   356
Aune   445, 446
Baab   385, 388
Baarda   487
Bach   222, 228, 231, 234, 240, 301
Bader   195, 203, 264, 324, 453, 478
                             481, 487
Baker   281, 282, 283
Bal   233
Balch   462
Ball   79
Bampfylde   24
Barclay   61, 301, 330, 399, 400, 419
          422, 427, 428, 430, 434, 436

                             440, 459
Bartlett   244
Baslez   189
Battifol   302
Bauckham   167, 267
Baumgartner   383, 386, 388
Beavis   430, 431, 433
Beentjes   362, 363, 377, 410
Begg   271
Ben-Dov   29
Berger   474
Berquist   364, 371, 373, 389, 394
Berrin   346
Berthelot   244
Bickerman   247, 249, 431
Bird   388
Black   8, 15, 16, 22, 23, 24, 26, 29, 30
Blessing   50, 98
Boccaccini   5
Bogaert   100, 105
Bohak   301, 318
Bohn   233
Bolyki   246, 247, 326
Booth   477
Böttrich   37, 38, 39, 40, 41, 43, 44, 45
          46, 47, 49, 50, 51, 52, 54
Bow   151, 153, 156, 158, 159, 160
          163, 165, 174, 180, 183
Box   107

Bremmer 57
Brockington 99
Brooke 231, 232, 328
Brown 269, 278, 279, 280, 281, 282
284, 291
Brüll 215
Budin 80, 81
Buitenwerf 56, 57, 58, 59, 60, 61, 62
63, 64
Bull 477
Burchard 150, 300, 301, 304, 306
308, 317
Burke 82
Burkes 92, 400, 402, 403, 405, 417
422, 423, 424
Burnette-Bletsch 279
Busch 136, 137, 138, 139
Busto Saiz 405
Camp 383, 417, 418
Caquot 29
Carr 394
Cazenaux 258, 261
Charles 15, 17, 20, 23, 29, 99, 100, 102
Charlesworth 3, 6, 335
Cheon 398, 399, 407, 409, 410, 416
Chesnutt 119, 124, 128, 301, 310
311, 317, 318, 322, 324, 327, 328
330, 333
Christian 156
Clanton 215, 229
Coblentz Bautch 27
Coggins 362
Cohen 227
Collins 47, 52, 56, 57, 58, 61, 62, 63
64, 65, 66, 68, 73, 76, 78, 85, 87
94, 98, 106, 110, 111, 112, 113
115, 116, 127, 129, 133, 147, 148
149, 150, 155, 156, 173, 214, 215
221, 225, 228, 231, 232, 246, 249
254, 301, 308, 311, 315, 250, 318
323, 324, 329, 330, 317, 362, 365
371, 377, 398, 399, 400, 401, 402
403, 404, 405, 411, 412, 419, 420
423, 424, 425, 426, 427, 429, 431
432, 433, 434, 435, 436, 438, 440
441, 445, 451, 459, 476, 477, 480

481, 482, 485, 487
Cook, J. 89, 291
Cooper, K. 332
Cooper, S. 224, 229
Countryman 424
Cousland 150, 151, 159, 173
Craghan 187, 193, 200, 201
Craven 186, 187, 189, 199
Crenshaw 144, 146, 392
Crouch 462, 467
D'Alario 404
D'Angelo 442, 453, 454, 455
Daise 477
Davila 5, 10, 11, 98, 112, 133
300, 334, 335, 336, 398, 429
Day 191, 195, 196, 197, 199, 201, 205
de Jonge 337
De Troyer 142, 143, 236, 237, 238, 242
De Villiers 86
Delling 315
Deming 464
Derron 462, 459
Descamp 263, 265, 266, 267, 268
280, 282, 291, 297
Deselaers 170
deSilva 199, 206, 440, 441, 442, 443
444, 445, 446, 447, 448, 449, 450
451, 452, 454
Desjardins 87
Deutsch 396
Di Lella 152, 192, 209, 362, 424
Dietzfelbinger 270
Dillmann 15
Dimant 344, 346
DiTommaso 215
Docherty 327
Dochhorn 135, 337, 338, 339, 340
Dodson 403
Doering 79
Donaldson 207, 239, 329, 431, 432
480
Doran 175, 181, 246, 248, 249
Douglas 319
Dschlunigg 328
Duling 136, 137, 138
Dundes 213

Dupont-Sommer 455
Edwards 467
Ego 147, 150, 151, 152, 155, 169
Elder 192, 193, 198, 199, 206, 212
Eldridge 337, 340
Ellis 71, 72, 104, 152, 171, 172, 178
179, 224, 225, 308, 330, 354, 414
442, 445, 464
Embry 361
Endres 153
Engel 218, 219, 222, 223, 236
Eron 144, 145, 147, 389
Eshel 6
Esler 92, 97, 186, 187, 193, 194, 205
210, 212
Fallon 476, 477, 478, 483
Fassbeck 153, 157, 162, 168, 177, 184
185
Felder 65, 66, 67
Feldman 259, 262, 264, 266, 268, 276
287, 288, 289, 292, 476, 483
Feldmeier 430, 432, 433, 434
Fink 300
Fisk 259, 271, 274, 275, 282
Fitzmyer 147, 148, 149, 150, 152, 156
157, 158, 160, 170, 171, 175, 176
179, 182, 183
Foucault 470
Fox 240
Freedman 388
Freudenthal 476
Fröhlich 12, 34, 35, 149, 158, 167, 168
185, 186, 187, 188, 190, 196, 205
261, 283
Garrett 116, 117, 118, 120, 124, 125
126, 130, 131
Gaster 30
Gathercole 176, 179
Gauger 63
Geffcken 59, 76
Geoltrain 29
Gerber 253
Gieschen 31, 45
Gilbert 362, 399, 401, 403, 405, 412
422, 459
Glancy 167, 188, 209, 221, 224, 227

229, 233, 234
Goldstein 82, 244, 245, 246, 251, 252
253, 255, 256, 257
Goodfriend 385, 387, 388, 389
Grabbe 6, 34, 398, 399, 400, 401
404, 410, 424, 426
Gray 130
Green 88
Greenfield 24
Gruen 57, 61, 62, 149, 150, 151, 158
160, 161, 167, 168, 173, 179, 187
189, 192, 193, 199, 200, 201, 204
207, 215, 229, 233, 234, 247, 301
306, 435, 436, 444, 477, 482
Gunkel 159
Gurtner 98
Hacham 435, 436
Hadas 428, 429, 431, 434, 435, 436
438, 455
Hall 110, 247
Halpern-Amaru 167, 259, 260, 263
264, 274, 275, 286, 287, 291, 297
Hanhart 143, 148, 185, 237, 244, 363
398, 440
Hannah 6, 24, 25
Harrington 79, 81, 84, 95, 97, 143
258, 259, 261, 269, 270, 287, 362
404, 407, 409
Hayes 241
Hayman 402, 417
Hayward 262, 272
Heijerman 386
Hellmann 193, 205
Hengel 249, 485
Hester 203, 391
Hieke 151, 152, 155, 156, 157
Himbaza 288
Himmelfarb 247, 249, 254
Hobbins 100, 106
Hofmann 112
Hogan 403, 406, 423
Holladay 476, 477, 478, 479, 481, 482
483, 484, 485, 487
Holm-Nielsen 342, 345, 346, 351, 352
360, 361
Honigman 429, 431, 432, 433

Hubbard 317
Hübner 405
Humphrey 93, 94, 300, 301, 302, 303
306, 308, 310, 311, 312, 315, 317
318, 319, 320, 324, 325, 326, 328
329, 331, 333
Ilan 191, 215, 224, 229, 230, 251, 253
Instone-Brewer 174
Jacobson 258, 259, 260, 261, 262
264, 265, 266, 267, 269, 270, 272
274, 275, 276, 277, 278, 279, 280
283, 284, 285, 286, 287, 288, 289
291, 292
James 261, 266
Jensen 370
Jobes 236, 237
Kaiser 343, 353
Kampen 254
Kappler 244
Kedar-Kopfstein 391
Kippenberg 477, 478
Klauck 440, 441, 442, 443, 444, 445
446, 447, 450, 452, 454
Klijn 98, 99, 100, 104
Kloppenborg 408, 421
Klutz 143, 144, 145, 146, 147, 148
Knibb 4, 5, 6, 7, 13, 15, 17, 18, 20, 23
28, 29, 90, 92, 115, 129
Knight 334
Knights 334, 335
Knittel 348
Koehler 381, 385, 387
Kolarcik 403, 424
Kollmann 184
Kraeling 175
Kraemer 302, 306, 313, 314, 316, 317
318, 320, 329, 331, 332, 333
Kratz 79
Küchler 457, 460
Kugel 196, 248, 398, 406, 477, 480
Kugler 117, 118, 120, 123, 124, 127
128, 132
Kulik 106, 17, 109, 110
Kurfess 76
Lambert 88
Lassen 454

Lebram 394
Leemhuis 98
Lesses 130
Leuenberger 101
Lévi 363, 366, 367, 374, 377, 379
384, 385, 386, 391, 393
Levine 56, 57, 61, 72, 149, 151, 153
157, 159, 161, 165, 166, 176, 183
192, 194, 199, 209, 211, 212, 213
214, 223, 224, 229, 230, 232, 233
234
Levison 86, 87, 89, 90, 91, 102, 208
340, 381, 403, 406, 416
Lieber 303
Lightfoot 56, 68, 69, 70, 71, 72, 73, 74
75, 76
Lipiński 365
Lipka 387, 389
Littman 147, 148, 152, 167, 168, 170
173, 175, 179
Loader 1, 27, 166, 178, 183, 196, 232
248, 257, 268, 270, 275, 287, 288
295, 302, 304, 309, 313, 336, 340
351, 348, 349, 350, 374, 387, 388
439, 444, 461, 467, 479, 482, 486
Loewenstamm 133
Longenecker 85, 93, 94
Ludlow 134
Lunt 106, 108, 109, 110
MacDonald 148
Marshall 75
McCracken 150, 151, 160, 173, 181
McGlynn 411
McKinlay 393
McLay 214, 215
McNeil 334, 335
Meiser 337
Mendels 476
Meredith 212
Merk 338
Merkel 68
Miles 233
Milik 4, 151
Miller, D, 111, 136, 426
Miller, R. 399
Milne 188, 189, 211, 212

Mittmann-Richert   142, 143, 186, 187
     188, 190, 191, 206, 210, 215, 220
          221, 230, 237, 243, 244
Moore, C.   79, 80, 81, 82, 83, 84, 85
     148, 149, 150, 152, 153, 157, 159
     160, 161, 165, 166, 167, 168, 169
     170, 171, 172; 173, 174, 175, 176
     179, 180, 182, 183, 184, 185, 186
     188, 189, 192, 194, 196, 198, 199
     200, 201, 202, 203, 204, 205, 208
     214, 215, 216, 217, 219, 220, 221
     223, 227, 228, 229, 230, 231, 235
     236, 237, 238, 239, 240, 241, 243
Moore, S.   449, 455
Morgan   460
Morgenstern   147
Mukenge   82
Munnich   214
Munoa   134
Murphy   105, 106, 268, 273, 285, 288
Murray   427, 436, 438
Myers   88, 89
Naumann   80
Neuberger   176
Newman   406
Niccacci   416, 419
Nickelsburg   4, 5, 7, 9, 10, 13, 18, 19
     20, 24, 26, 37, 47, 52, 56, 79, 81, 82
     83, 85, 98, 106, 111, 112, 115, 129
     133, 143, 146, 148, 150, 151, 153
     155, 158, 159, 160, 161, 162, 165
     174, 180, 181, 183, 184, 187, 187
     191, 195, 206, 209, 210, 211, 231
     239, 327, 337, 342, 401, 410, 411
          420, 421, 423, 424
Nicklas   151, 155, 156, 157, 172, 174
Niebuhr   39, 46, 52, 360, 462, 464
          463, 467
Nikiprowetzky   57
Nikolsky   335
Nir   98, 99
Norden   440
Nowell   152, 159, 166, 170, 172, 177
Nussbaum   470
Oegema   56, 64, 85, 98, 106, 111, 147
     250, 256, 259, 300, 301, 337, 338

          342, 457, 458, 477, 480, 488
Olson   8, 15, 16, 17, 22, 23, 28, 29, 30
Olyan   265
Orlov   37, 38, 41, 42, 48, 51
Otzen   147, 148, 156, 171, 178, 182
     186, 195, 200, 205, 207, 218, 214
Pearce   226, 228, 231, 232, 239, 234
                                 235
Penn   322
Penner   136
Pennington   110
Perrot   258, 261
Pervo   233, 310, 311, 333
Pesch   85, 352
Phillips   389
Philonenko   110, 129, 300
Philonenko-Sayar   110
Pietersma   3
Piovanelli   6, 21
Pitkänen   152
Polaski   266, 267, 268
Portier-Young   160, 162, 303, 315
                            317, 318
Priest   111, 112, 113
Pummer   482
Rabinowitz   396
Rahlfs   363, 398, 440, 447
Räisänen   474
Rakel   186, 187, 188, 189, 200, 202
          205, 207, 210, 212, 251
Reed   33
Reese   404, 418, 421
Regev   149, 203, 299
Reider   407
Reinhartz   236
Reiterer   252, 252, 254, 362
Rogers   392
Rohrbaugh   117, 118, 120, 121, 123
          124, 125, 126, 127, 132
Roussel   482
Rubinkiewicz   106, 108
Ruppert   332, 409, 411, 412
Sacchi   24, 44, 45, 47, 53
Sanders, E,   133, 135
Sanders, J. A.   395, 396
Sanders, J. T.   400

Sänger   150, 300, 301, 319, 322, 323
               327, 328
Satlow   169, 170, 174, 175, 248, 253
               377
Satran   334
Sawyer   211, 212
Sayler   100, 104
Schaller   129
Schimanowski 428, 431, 434, 435
Schmitt   405
Schodde   15, 17
Schroer   421
Schüngel-Straumann   151, 158, 159
        160, 161, 167, 169, 174, 178, 182
Schüpphaus   346, 355, 356, 360
Schürer   68
Schwarz   136
Scott   98, 115
Seeley   403, 404, 405
Shutt   427
Skehan   197, 362, 363, 364, 366, 367
        368, 372, 373, 375, 376, 379
        380, 381, 384, 385, 386, 387, 389
               390, 391, 392, 395
Skinner   415, 48
Smith   99
Soll   153, 155, 156, 179, 181
Spittler   115, 118, 129
Standhartinger 302, 312, 315, 318, 320
        331, 332, 333, 478, 482
Starr Sered   224, 229
Steck   82
Steussy   225, 237, 242
Stocker   191, 209, 215, 218
Stone, K   393
Stone, M.   5, 24, 41, 86, 87, 88, 89, 91
               92, 93, 94, 96
Stone, N.   187
Streete   224, 228
Strugnell   367, 476
Stuckenbruck 7, 176, 179
Suggs   414
Suter   5, 12, 14, 15, 17, 22, 23, 29, 30
Sutter Rehmann   96, 121
Talshir   142, 143, 144, 145, 146
Tcherikover   249, 437

Thackeray   426
Thomas   462, 463, 464, 465, 467, 469
               470, 472, 473, 474
Tigchelaar   5, 8, 13, 28
Tilly   276
Torrey   79
Tov   82
Trafton   342, 343, 351
Trenchard   362, 363, 366, 368,
        371, 372, 373, 374, 375, 376, 377
        378, 380, 381, 382, 385, 386, 387
Tromp   112, 113, 114, 337, 339
van den Eynde   155, 161, 189, 198
van der Horst   115, 116, 119, 121, 124
        125, 126, 128, 129, 130, 267, 268
        276, 278, 281, 282, 283, 414, 448
        457, 458, 459, 460, 461, 462, 464
        465, 467, 469, 470, 471, 472, 474
               477
van Henten 66, 191, 192, 194, 210, 443
VanderKam   4, 5, 8, 9, 13, 14, 20, 28
von Gemünden   443, 444
von Loewenclau   218, 219, 228, 230
               231, 233, 234
Wagner   148
Walsh   394
Walter   383, 457, 474
Weber   430, 442, 445, 457, 458, 469
Webster   392, 393, 417
Weeks   176, 179, 181
Wellhausen   356
Werline   81
Westerholm   441
White Crawford   192, 200, 210, 211
               213
Whitters   106
Williams   245, 253
Williamson   24
Willoughby   388
Wills   150, 151, 173, 179, 205, 210
        211, 212, 213, 214, 215, 219, 228
               229, 230, 233, 234
Wilson   457, 458, 459, 460, 461, 462
        463, 464, 465, 466, 467, 468, 469
               470, 471, 472, 473
Winninge   343, 345, 352, 358

Winston   398, 399, 400, 404, 408, 409
           414, 415, 416, 418, 420, 421, 423
Wright, B.   3, 7, 10, 363, 370
Wright, R.   342, 349, 360
Yee   388
Young   449, 453, 455
Zacharias   342
Zenger   185, 186, 190, 199, 205
Ziegler   363, 309, 405
Zimmermann   148, 185, 226, 228

Index of Ancient Sources

(References to individual chapters and verses within the sections dealing with each writing are not included)*

OLD TESTAMENT

Genesis

1:26-27	70, 92
1:27	42, 54, 70, 177
	313, 499
1:28	54, 70, 177, 262
	266, 455, 463, 499
2:4-8	86
2:7	70, 177
2:8	44
2:13-14	71
2:15	70
2:18, 20	177, 383, 384
2:20-25	42, 70, 177, 499
2:22	208, 495
2:24	144, 145, 147
	172, 174, 322
	330, 493, 496
3:1-15	381
3:7	338
3:8	232
3:13	43, 232, 338
	357, 411, 454
3:14-19	86
3:16-20	44, 72, 77, 90
	102
3:16	104, 339, 340
	499, 502
3:19	273
3:24	232
4:1	455
4:10	35

4:21	260
4:23-24	261, 295
5:24	410
6:1-4	103, 183
6:1	260, 261
6:2	8, 178
6:3	269
6:4	84, 252
6:5-12	102
6:5	87
6:12	275
9:1-7	74
9:1	262, 266
9:22-27	223, 262
11:19	275
11:30	93
12:10-20	263, 485
12:11	193
13:13	263
14:18.	50
15:6	134
15:9-11	107, 275
15:18-21	481
16:1-5	167, 284
16:10	290
16:11	284
18:3	103
18:12	166, 496
18:16-23	103
19:1-29	263
19:10-11	289
19:30-38	263
20:1-18	263

20:6	466
22:17	272
24:1-67	263
24:14	157
24:15	172
24:44	157, 171
25:1-3	488
25:6	488
25:20, 26	280
26:1-16	263
27:40	247
27:41 – 48:5	487
27:46 – 29:30	263
28:15-25	487
28:26-28	487
29:9	172
29:17	193, 294, 478
29:26	478
29:27	179
29:30 – 30:24	496
30:23	167, 408
33:13	478
34:1-31	478
34:2, 3	479
34:4-12	479
34:7	236, 479
34:12	365
34:13	195
34:25-29	189, 482, 484
	486
34:30	326, 484
35:22	264, 466, 486, 504
38:1-30	264

38:8-10	390
38:9	46
38:11	167
38:17	159
38:24	267
39:1-20	264
39:7	373, 378, 444
39:7-12	443
39:9	221, 231
39:10	204
41:46-50	301
41:53-54	301
46:5-7	301
48:16	463
49:4	270, 463
49:5-7	196
49:17, 19	326
49:32	306
50:3	281
50:20	327

Exodus

2:1	269
2:2	267
2:21	484
6:20	269
14:16	248
14:17-18	23
15:13	196
15:17	364
15:25	270
16:31	317
19:15	269, 501
20:3-17	461
20:13, 14, 15	133, 287
	489
20:17	225, 270, 287
21:7	174
21:22-23	467
22:15	170, 365, 454
	471, 472, 504
22:16	174, 366
	444
22:18	469
23:9	270
23:20-22	31
23:26	262, 273
24:10	383
25:9	271
32:6	271
32:20	271, 310

33:12-16	271
34:15-16	245, 275
34:16	296

Leviticus

5:4-6	298
5:11	247
15:19-24	241
15:24-31	349
15:24	348, 349, 469
15:31	348
16:8, 21	107
18	59, 463, 466, 469
18:6-18	390, 465, 466
18:6	390
18:12	269
18:19	348, 349, 469, 511
18:20	267
18:21	156
18:22	461, 470
18:23	468
19	461
19:8	344
19:29	255, 464
19:35-36	247
20	59, 467
20:2	156
20:10	221, 235, 506
20:11-12, 14, 17, 19-21	390
20:12	267
20:13	461, 470
20:15-16	448
20:18	348, 349, 469, 508
21:9	156, 255
21:15	286
22:4-7	347
25:9-10	352
25:49	390
26:13	247

Numbers

5:11-31	271
5:13, 16-28	228
5:18	228
11:9 LXX	318
11:15	160
12:1	488
15:37-40	273
15:39	373
16:1-35	273
19:2	247

19:11-12	149
25:1-5	248, 273, 278, 491
25:1	274
25:6-8	134, 248, 273, 278
25:6-13	107, 325
25:6-18	289
27:1-11	156
30:13-15	298, 314
31:16	274
36:8-9	156, 174, 177

Deuteronomy

5:7-21	461
5:16	363
5:17-19	133, 287
5:20-21	270, 339, 444
7	304
7:2-4	241, 245, 296
7:13	272
13:7-8, 13	244
13:18	245
15:12	209
19:18-21	229
19:19	217, 234
20:7	252, 365, 501
21:3	247
21:10-14	257
22:16-17	175
22:21-24	221, 235, 503
22:25-28	227, 454, 503
22:28-29	365, 472
23:1	409, 465
23:2	206, 207, 469, 513
23:7-18	80
24:1-4	174, 260, 295
	486, 504
24:1	235
24:14	228
25:5-10	156, 463
26:6	270
27:20	465
30:4	17
31 – 34	112
31:16, 29	112, 278
31:16-17	244, 245, 275
32:10-13	317
32:34-43	114
33:1	280

Joshua

5:2-7; 6:1-21	481

Judges
3:5-6	103, 276, 491
3:13-31	205
4:9	449, 493
4:21	205
5:7	280
5:27	279
5:30	279
8:24-27, 31	281
9:53	281
9:54	198, 49
11:1	281, 505
11:29	281
11:34, 37	282
12:12	235
13:1-23	284, 285
13:17-18	315
13:2	93, 411
14:1-10	285
14:12, 17	179, 323
16:1, 4	285, 505
16:4-22	285
17:1 – 18:31	286
19:1-30	287-289
20:1-20	289
21:17-18	290
21:23	290, 293

Ruth
2:12	99
4:5, 10	463
4:18-20	267

1 Samuel
1:16	93
6:7, 10	248
11:1-5	371
13:10-15	227
17:51	205
18:6-7	207
18:25, 27	365

2 Samuel
7:10	364
11:1-5	371
20:3	378
20:8	248

1 Kings
4:32	361
4:33	415

16:31	223

2 Kings
5:18, 22	208
9:30	377
18 – 20	190
19:3	271
20:18	408

2 Chronicles
10:4. 9, 10, 11, 14	247
20:1-30	205
21:6	223
22:10-12	223
32:1-23	205

Ezra
9:1-2	100, 153, 245
9:1-15; 10:9-44	143
10:2	153, 241
10:11	245

Nehemiah
9:2; 10:31; 13:1-3	245
13:23-27	241
13:27	153

Esther* | **237-43** |
1:11	501
2:7	193
7:8 LXX	227
8:17	480

Job
2:8-9	120-21
2:10	123
4:9	47
10:10-11	92
15:34	409
19:6	387
24:3-4, 9-10	115
28:12-27	83
29:12-13	115
31:1	373
31:16-22	115
31:31	129
38:3; 40:1	127
42:13-15	119
42:15	130, 132
42:17	129

Psalms
1:1	352
18:6 LXX	324
24:3	274
36:8	99
44:3	364
50:16-17	352
57:2	99
61:10	247
77:25 LXX	317
91:5-6	28
97:5	13
104:30	208, 495
106:28	248
106:30-31	107, 134, 325
	513
116:3	387
128:3 LXX	290, 389
130:2 LXX	311
144:12	290, 389

Proverbs
1:20-21 LXX	413
2:16	357, 384
3:16	394
3:18	394
4:7	419
5:3	357, 384
5:5	407
5:20	153
6:24	153, 357, 361, 384
6:25	373, 377
6:26	505
6:27	23, 497
6:27-29	389
6:29	137, 466
6:33-35	387, 397
7:4-5	315, 384, 394, 415
7:13	373
7:17	394
7:21	384, 395
8:2	396
8:10-11, 18-19, 21	394
8:22	419
8:36	395
9:1-6	83
9:3, 14	396
9:12-18	505
9:17	373, 388
11:1	247
11:18	47

12:12	387	44:9-20	420	34:12-22	209
16:11	247	46:1	80	50:2; 51:44	80
18:10	31	47:8-9	64	50:12	93
19:14	380	49:14-23	85		
20:22	327	50:1	93	**Lamentations**	
20:23	247	51:5	424	3:27	247
21:19	373	52:1	85, 274	5:2	250
22:8	47	52:1-2	200		
27:8	383	52:7	352	**Ezekiel**	
31:10-31	146	52:13 – 53:12	409, 411	3:1-3	318
		54:1-13	85	5:11	344
Ecclesiastes		54:1	409	12:13	388
2:6, 22-23	404	54:15 LXX	315	13:17 LXX	39
7:20	147	55:4-5	424	16:17	271
7:26	387, 389	55:5-7	315	16:25	373
8:10	274	56:3	207, 290, 291, 389	16:37-39	228, 271
9:7	404	56:5	409	19:8	388
9:12	387	57:1-4, 20	409	23:38	344
		59:17-19	412	23:40	377
Canticles		60:1	60	25:3	344
1:12-14	394	60:2-3	424	28:13	233, 277
2:3-5	393	60:4-9	85	36:26-27	92
4:1-2	276	60:4	84	41:26	248
4:6, 10, 13-14	394	60:13	274		
4:9-10, 12; 5:1-2	173, 303	60:19-20	90, 500	**Daniel**	
4:11; 5:1	317	61:10	85	2:31-45	13
4:16	394	62:4	315	2:44	60, 252
5:1, 5, 13	394	65:17	11	4:35 LXX	137
		65:25	60	5:12; 6:4	218
Isaiah				7:27	60
2:3	60	**Jeremiah**		9	81
3:16	373	1:9	318	9:24, 26	90
6:6-7	318	2:13	83	11:31	255
9:3; 10:27	247	2:20	247	12:1-3	106, 280
11:6-8	60	3:8	174	12:2	28
12:6	60	4:30	377	12:3	91, 423
14:12-14	12, 41, 344	5:5	247, 420		
23:15-16	385	7:34	82	**Hosea**	
24:17-23	22	10:1-16	79	2:3, 10	228
24:21-22	14, 15, 22	10:2-25	79	2:4; 4:5	93
26:13	30	10:5	79	2:19-20; 3:2	365
28:16	402	11;10	112	4:15	221
29:13	352	12:2	364	7:4	23
30:1	174	16:9	82	10:12	47
30:10	384	23:14-15	220	14:6	230
30:27	31	25:20, 24	100		
36 – 38	190	29:1-23	79	**Joel**	
37:3	271	29:22-23 (36:22-23 LXX)		2:16	250
40 – 55	84		220, 222		
40:15-17	89	33:10-11	82	**Amos**	
43:5	84	33:20, 25	30	2:7-8	255

Jonah
3:8-9   189

Micah
1:4   13

Nahum
1:5   13

Habakkuk
1:1-4   220

Zephaniah
3:9   247

Zechariah
2:10   60
2:15 LXX   315
5:5-10   220
8:7-8   84
14:6   60

Malachi
2:11   344
2:16   382

**OLD TESTAMENT
APOCRYPHA AND
PSEUDEPIGRAPHA**
(see also sections on each
work)

Additions to Esther*
    236-43
C 26, 28   446
D 6   329

Apocalypse of Abraham*
    106-11
10:3, 8   31
13:3-8   158
13:6   509
14:6   509
22:25 – 23:12   27
23:10-11   27, 339, 498
24:6   509
24:8   506
24:9   498

Apocalypse of Moses*
    336-41
15:2-3   498
16:3   406
17:4   408
19:3   499
25:3-4   499
28:4   499, 500
29   118
37:5   499, 500
39   44

Apocalypse of Zephaniah
2:1-5   134

Aramaic Levi Document
    100, 184, 243, 304, 324
    483, 490, 510
1c   510
1c 2   196, 481
1c-3a   325
3a   309
78-81   196, 444, 480

Aseneth (Joseph and)*
    300-34
4:7   443, 492
4:9-10   492
6:1-4   193
7:3   443
7:23   504
11:1   493
12:8   492
12:15   193
19:11; 20:1   493
21:1   494
23:14   196, 444, 499
23:24   510
24:5   193
25:7   493

Baruch*
    81-85
2:23   493
2:34   500
3:9-37; 4:1   496
3:26-28   509, 511
4   10, 35, 412
4:16, 19-23, 36-37   93
5:1   200
5:5-6   93

2 Baruch*   **98-106**
3:1-9   271
4:4   108
4:5   272
14:1-19   271
27:11   501
28:2   90, 500
41:3-4; 42:4   243
42:45   491
44:2   501
48:15   91
48:22-24   243
50:2-4   459
51   411
51:9, 10, 16   498, 500
51:10   423
54:19   91, 403
56:6   340, 498
56:10-13   509
64:2   506
73:4, 7   498
83:14   498

Ben Sira / Sirach*
    362-398
1:1-10   394
1:1, 5   83
3:2   473
3:9, 11   363-64, 494, 502
4:11-19   394-95
6:1-3   392, 497
6:2   497
6:18-31   83, 395
6:28   416
7:19   146, 381
7:23-25   365-66, 453, 492
7:27-28   161, 494
9:1-9   146
9:3-4, 9   261, 385-89
    504-505
9:5   505
9:8   495, 497
9:9   502
14:20 – 15:10   93, 396-97
15:2   415
16:1-4   291
16:7   84
16:8   506
18:30 – 19:3   261, 497, 505
19:12   143
20:4   393

22:3-5	193, 367, 375
23:4-6	497
23:7-9	494
23:8	59
23:16-21	389-91
23:16	497, 507
23:17	23, 505
23:18	289, 493
23:18-21	504
23:22-27	364, 391, 464
	419, 494, 502
24	35, 412
24:1-34	83
24:1-22	397-98
24:8-27	272
24:25-31	11
25:1	471, 493
25:2	364, 391, 504
25:8	493
25:13	496, 503
25:21-22	159, 193, 378
	494, 495, 502, 504
25:24	42, 72, 497
25:25-26	382, 494, 502
	504
26:1-4, 16-18	146
26:1-2	471
26:5-6	494
26:7	248, 502
26:7-9	378, 391, 494
	495, 497, 502
26:10-12	373-75, 453
	474, 502
26:13, 16-18	375, 495
26:14	331
26:15	379-80, 493
26:16-18	376-78, 495
26:16	497
26:19-21	493, 507
26:22	505
26:23-27	494
28:15	494
28:19-20	247
30:19-20	393-94
31:12 – 32:13	261, 462
31:27-28	497
32:5-6	497
34:18 – 35:10	475
36:21	375
36:22-25	146, 376, 422
	498

36:24-27	383-85, 493
36:30-31	504
37:11	494
38:1-15	184
40:19, 23	380-81, 463, 493
41:17	365, 497
41:20	388, 504
41:22/24	502
42:6	382, 502
42:8	391, 504
42:9-14	367-73, 382, 453
	474, 497, 502
42:11	253
42:12	495
44:16	410
44:20	252
47:19-21	497, 510
51:6	247
51:13-30	83, 398-99

Demetrius*	**487-88**
9	501, 510
11:8-12	252

1 Enoch*	
37 – 71	**4-37**
1 – 5	10, 360, 512
1 – 36	37
5:7	419
6 – 8	33, 183
6 – 11	26, 32, 84, 103
6 – 16	8, 53, 103
6:1 – 7:6	40
6:1	373
6:2	8, 33
6:3	26, 33
6:7-8	26
7:1-5	53
7:1	20, 21, 27
7:2-5	74, 252
7:3	29
8:1	12, 19, 26, 21, 27, 33
8:1-2	13, 73, 249
8:3	20, 21, 26, 27, 418
9:2-3	12, 21, 35
9:8	27, 109
10:1-15	21
10:1-3	14, 21
10:4-8, 11-15	14, 181
10:4	35, 175
10:5	13

10:9-10	21, 35
10:9	14
10:12-14	8, 109
10:12	14, 15, 16, 35, 40
10:13	38
12 – 16	19, 26, 32, 34, 40
12:1	9
12:6	14, 35
13	31
13:4-7	38, 40
14:6	15
15:4	414
15:5-7	17, 36, 76, 359
15:8-12	108
15:9	181
18:6-9	12, 35, 40
21 – 22	38, 41
24:2-4	12, 35
25:2-6	360
32:2	19
32:6	27
38:4	423
39:7	423
39:10	500
42:1-3	83, 496
43:4; 45:5-6	500
51:1-5	500
54:8	510
58:3	48
58:3, 5-6	90, 359, 500
60:7-8, 16	510
60:8, 23; 61:12	500
60:24-25	508
62:4	494
65:12	500
67:13	500
69:2-12	508
86:1-3	108
89:56	345
92 – 105	411
93:1-10; 91:11-17	69
94:5	83
94:6-8; 95:5-7; 96:4-8	52
94:8; 95:5	47
97:8-10	52
98:5	408
102:6-11	404
103:2	325
104:2-6	280
104:2	423
106 – 107	20, 35, 48, 89

106:3	49
106:19	325

2 Enoch* **37-56**

8:1	19
10:3	512
18:4	509
29:1	292
29:4-6	406
30 – 32	72
30:16, 17	72, 498
31:3-6	406
31:7	72, 86
32:1	499
32:2	19
42:3	19
42:11	500
58:6	468, 507
59:5	462, 504
65:7-11	17, 90, 359, 500
	501
66:7	423
71:1-2	494
71:37	500

1 Esdras 3 – 4* **142-47**

3 – 4	213
4:13-22	233, 235
4:20	172
4:25	493
4:31	495

Ezekiel the Tragedian*
484-85

4 Ezra* **85-98**

3	509
3:4-7, 20-22	498
3:7	499
3:13-14	108
3:20-36	271
4:22-25	271
5:21-30	271
7:12	499
7:39-42	500, 501
7:97	423
7:110-115	506
7:119-126	500
9 – 10	121
9:8	500
14:47	83

History of the Rechabites
(Zosimus)* **334-36**

Jubilees

1:8-14	239
1:26	44
2:19-20	239
3	44
3:3	41
3:8-14	86
4:7	102
4:15	73
4:33	153
5:2, 3, 10, 17	275
5:6	73
7:21	73
7:34-35	359
8:19	272
10:5-11	108
10:10-12	184
11:7-8, 14-17	248
11:19-22	107
12:9	275
12:12-15	117
13:11	486
14:5-7	95
14:12	158
15:33-34	113, 505
16:15-19	295
19:9	134
20:4	373
21:23-24	359
22:16-17	248
23:13-14, 22-23	239
23:21	256, 345, 350
23:25	88, 89
25:3, 12, 18	295
25:4	323
25:7, 10	275
27:13-18	161
30:1-26	196, 325, 444, 481
30:4-6, 13-23	481
30:7	100
30:7-10	156
30:15-16	295, 345
30:17	483
30:18	309
30:20	107, 134
31:3-9	161
32:21	325
33:1-20	466

33:2-9	224
33:9-20	372
33:9	486, 505
33:20	295
36:7	31
39:5-11	443
39:6	444
39:7	306
41:23-26	372
50:8	76, 500

Judith* **185-214**

4:12	94
8:1-3	505
8:2	239, 269
8:9-27	278
9:2	481, 482
9:2-4	441, 506
9:5	284
9:10	449
10:3 Vg	279
10:13	443
11:11-12	501
12:7	60
12:13	501
12:15; 13:4-5	279
13:15, 17; 14:8	449
16:5-6	449, 509
16:22	505

Letter of Jeremiah* **79-81**

Liber Antiquitatum LAB
(Pseudo-Philo)* **258-300**

1:31-34	86
2:1	507
2:7-8	505
2:8	347, 501, 503
2:10	506, 509
3:11	500
5:4-7	495
6	417
8:6, 8, 11	510
8:7-8	119
9:2, 5	491, 492, 495
	505, 507
9:4	508, 513
9:9, 12	492, 507
11:2	501
11:10	503
11:15	501

12:5	495
13:8-9	501, 503
13:10	500
18:13-14	491
19:10	359, 500, 501
21:1	491
23:4, 7. 8	495
26:13	359, 500
29:2	403
30:1	491
30:2	492
31:1, 7	491, 498
31:1, 9	493
31:8	507
31:9, 17	449
32:5	492
32:15	454, 495
33:6	492
34:1-5	509
39:1-11	505
40:6	493, 496
42:1-4	494
42:7	496
43:5	497, 505, 510
44:6-7, 10	503
44:7	491
45:1-6	501, 506
45:3; 47:1	491
47:8	491, 501
48:3	493
50:1-5	496
50:1	389, 494
51:2-3	494, 495
55:4, 6, 10	495
61:6	491
62:10	495

Life of Adam and Eve*

336-41

6-11	118
12-14	41
47	44

Lives of the Prophets* 334

3:6-9	506
18:4	511

1 Maccabees*   244-53

1:11-15	254, 257, 491
1:14-15	113, 505
1:16	113

1:22, 23	376
1:27	493
1:41-64	255
1:41-43	254
1:44-49	255, 501
1:60-61	256
2:24-26	195, 510
2:29-38	114
2:46	505
2:52	251
2:53-54	499, 503, 510
3:3	509
4:49-50	376
7:26-49	186
7:33-50	191, 206
9:37-42	492
15:13	188

2 Maccabees*   253-58

1:14	492
2:1-3	79
2:21	480
3:5	440
3:10	492
3:19-20	502
4:9	246
4:13	480
4:18-22	247
4:30	495
5:24	94
6:3-6	505
6:10	505
6:11	114
7:21	448
7:27	452, 494
8:1	480
9:15	148
14:3	491
14:38	480, 491
15:1-37	186
15:36	243

3 Maccabees

1:18	502

4 Maccabees*   440-57

2:2-3	504
2:4-6	503, 510
2:19-20	510
4:26	480
13:19-22	256

14:11	502
15:4-7	256
16:7-8	256
17:5	423
18:7	477, 505
18:7-10	503, 510
18:12	513

**Martyrdom and
Ascension of Isaiah**

3:6-10	103-104
4:16	107

Psalms of Solomon*

342-62

2:11-13	505
4	235, 498, 503
4:9-13, 20	75
6:4	59
8:9	67, 507
8:10	59, 78, 503
8:12	501
11	82
11:3-8	85
16:7-8	502
17:28	68, 491

Pseudo-Aristeas*   426-40

108, 130	506
152	506, 507
169	416
177	497
211, 222, 237, 256	446
227, 237, 256, 277-78	497
251	448, 502
284-287	496
304-306	60

Pseudo-Eupolemus*

485-87, 504, 509

Pseudo-Phocylides*

69, **457-76**

3	503
59, 67, 76	499
175-217	59
175-205	60
175-176	496
177-178	389, 505
178-183	507
184-186, 187	508

188	507	264	491	14:4	501, 508	
189	501, 508	387-396	507			
193-194	497	387	506	**Testaments of the Twelve**		
195-197	144, 493	388	79, 505	**Patriarchs**		
198	501	392	508	*Testament of Reuben*		
199-200	377, 504	393	471	3:8	484	
205-206	504, 505	420-421	503	*Testament of Simeon*		
213	39	429-430	461	5:3	110	
215-217	253, 453	430	39, 461, 469, 504, 506	*Testament of Levi*		
215	502	*Books 7, 11*	**78-79**	5:1-2	325	
		7:42-45	507	5:3, 5	196, 481	
Sibylline Oracles*		11:243-246, 272-314	64	5:3-4; 6:1-8	481	
Book 1-2	**68-78**			6:6	483	
1.42-45	42	**Susanna***	**214-36**	8:1-19	325	
1:54	86	5-25	371	9:10	100, 309	
1:57-58	102	5	503	17:11	39	
1:65	500	8, 32	373	18:9-10	93	
1:178	504	12, 52-53, 57	353	*Testament of Judah*		
2.155	90	13	510	13:7; 14:6	481	
2:257-258	503	15-18	511	15:5-6	146, 497	
2:280-281	493	20-21	204	*Testament of Dan*		
2:282	505	22	503	5:5	481	
2:327	501			*Testament of Naphtali*		
2:328	500	**Testament of Abraham***		1:10-11	481	
Book 3	**56-64**		**133-36**	3:4	421	
36-38	504	A 4:9	107	*Testament of Joseph*		
43-44	506	A10:3	493	3 – 9	443	
108-113	420	A10:8-9	503	3:3	444	
110-155	509	B10:13; 12:2-4	503, 508	13:1	39	
185-187	79, 506					
265-270	492	**Testament of Job***		**Theodotus***	**476-84**	
357-358	504		**115-33**, 160	2 18-19	495	
359-362	505	1:5	264, 510	4 11	501	
374	461	23:7-9	494, 504	4 18-21	491	
381-387	503	33:3-9; 39:1-2	501	6	195, 510	
525-527	492	45:3	243, 491	7	506	
591-593	504	46-52	193	7-8	444	
594	493, 504					
595-596	461, 504	**Testament of Moses***		**Tobit***	**147-85**	
596-599, 758	506		**111-15**	1:9	239, 296, 492	
764	504, 506	4:3	492	2:11-14	120	
765-766	508	5:4	503	2:14-15	494	
767-795	496, 503	8:3	243, 492, 505	3:8, 16-17	137	
Book 4	**64**			3:8-9	204, 213, 513	
31-34	504	**Testament of Solomon***		3:14-15	492, 493	
33-34	461, 506		**136-141**	4:3-4	492, 494	
45	500	2:2	491	4:12-13	239, 269, 296	
Book 5	**65-68**	2:4; 5:3; 5:8	509		492, 498, 504	
145-146	508	4:1-2	507	6:12	137, 492	
166	39	6:1, 4; 8:11; 13:3	509	6:13	504	
166-168	506	14:1-4	509	6:18	323, 492, 493, 504	

7:10-11	93, 492, 493, 504
7:15	283
8:2-3	137, 512
8:6-8	496, 498
8:10	93
8:21	504
11:19	207
13:5, 11, 13-17	500

Wisdom of Solomon*

	398-26
2:7-9	507
2:13, 16, 18	323
2:24	454
3:7-8	500
3:12	503
3:13-14	291, 496, 500
3:14-15	508
3:16-19	75, 356, 464, 503
	507
4:1	291
4:3-5	75, 356, 464
4:12	498
4:14	5-6
5:5	323
7:1-2	92, 448, 495, 496
7:4	452
8:1-9, 16-18	83
10:6-8	506
10:13	443, 504, 510
13 – 15	61, 79, 81
14:6	85, 509
14:22-31	39
14:24, 26	59, 504, 506
	507
15:10-11	86
16:28-29	60
18:14-16	31
19:13-17	506

DEAD SEA SCROLLS

CD (Damascus Document)

1.7	359
2.16-17	374
3.18 – 4.12	288
4.15-18	349, 388
4.20-21	494
5.6-7	472, 504

5.6b-11	349, 465, 508
6.14 – 7.4	372, 507
7.1; 8.6-7	390
11.5	500
11.21 – 12.1	60
12.1-2	255
12.4	500
13.16-18	76
4QDᵃ/4Q266 6 ii.1-2	
	349, 469
4QDᵇ/4Q267 9 vi.4-5	467
4QDᵉ/4Q270 2 i.18-19	500
4QDᵉ/4Q270 2 ii.15-16	
	469, 508
4QDᶠ/4Q271 3 8	173
4QDᶠ /4Q271 3 9	374
6QD/6Q15 5 2-3	467

1QpHab(Pesher Habakkuk)

9 4-6	345

1Q19 (Book of Noah) 48

1Q20 (Genesis Apocryphon) 20, 35, 49

	415, 504
2.9, 13	173, 470, 496
5.3-13	50
19.11, 14	486
19.13 – 20.33	486
20.6-7	171

1Q28 (Rule of the Community)

5.8	280
8.1-11	272

1Q28b (Rule of Benedictions)

4.24-26	329

1QHᵃ (Hodayotᵃ)

ix.28	351
xii.8-9	351
xiii.7	351
xvi.4-20	272
xvi.5-6	351, 359

4Q76 (Minor Prophetsᵃ)

	380

*4Q169 (Pesher Nahum)*346

3-4 i.4-6	240
3-4 iv.1-8	345

4Q171 (Pesher Psalmsᵃ)

1-10 iii.1-2, 10-11	360

4Q184 (Wiles of the Wicked Woman) 251

1.7-8	280

4Q196 (4QpapTobᵃ ar)

	153, 168, 183

4Q197 (4QpapTobᵇ ar)

	168, 170-72, 182, 183

4Q213a (Aramaic Leviᵇ)

3-4	443

4Q249e (Serekh ha-'Edahᵉ) 336

4Q251 (Halakhah A) 500

17	508

4Q383 (Apocryphon of Jeremiah A) frag. A 507

4Q387 (Apocryphon of Jeremiah Cᵇ) frag. A 507

4QMMT (Halakhic Letter) 100, 101, 105

	184, 243, 304, 349, 490
B 75-82	295
C 4-9	348
C 6-7	257
C 18, 25	491
C 31-32	107, 325, 510

4Q415 (Instructionᵃ)

9	284

4Q417 (Instructionᶜ)

1 i.16b-18a	108

4Q418 (Instructionᵈ)

101 ii.2-5	507

4Q423 (Instructionᵍ)

3a	284

4QPolemical Text/4Q471a

	345

4Q477 (Rebukes Reported by the Overseer)
2 ii. 8 — 507

4Q491 (War Scroll^a)
11 — 329

Q541 (4QApocryphon of Levi^a)
9.i.2-5 — 329

11Q5 (Psalms^a)
xxi — 362, 395-397

11Q19 (Temple Scroll^a)
45.11 — 255
63.10-15 — 257, 491

NEW TESTAMENT

Matthew
1:18 — 338
5:28 — 287
13:43 — 423
14:21; 15:38 — 263
15:13 — 461
24:19 — 88
25:1-12 — 174

Mark
1:10 — 312
1:11; 9:7 — 15
4:15 — 158
6:18 — 465
6:24 — 175
7:1-5 — 203
7:4 — 60
7:21-22 — 461
7:24-30 — 310
12:25 — 36, 76, 275
13 — 112
13:17 — 88

Luke
1:25 — 408
2:36 — 209, 473, 505
9:54-55 — 135
11:38 — 203
20:34-36 — 76, 359, 500

John
1:9-11 — 10-11
2:6 — 203
8:4-5 — 221, 235
8:44 — 454
12:23; 17:6a, 11b-12a — 31

Romans
1:18-27 — 39, 61
1:19-20 — 420
1:26-27 — 422, 470
2:22 — 59
3:10 — 147
7:7 — 444

1 Corinthians
6:9 — 462
7:1 — 137, 466
7:2-4 — 383
7:2 — 152
7:9 — 23
11:12 — 143
11:14-15 — 473

2 Corinthians
6:14 — 248
11:3 — 232
11:14 — 338

Galatians
2:14 — 480
5:19 — 152
6:7 — 47

Philippians
2:2-10 — 31

Hebrews
13:4 — 59

2 Peter
1:17 — 15

1 John
3:12 — 454

Revelation
4:6-11 — 9
12:9 — 406
19:11-16 — 31
20:10 — 23
21:22-25; 22:5 — 359, 500

21:22-27 — 275

OTHER WRITINGS

Apuleius
Metamorphoses
4:28 – 6:24 — 139, 301

Aristotle
De generatione animalium
717b24;717a5 — 176
19-20 — 414
Ethica nichomachea
8.12.2-3 (1161b17-29) — 450
8.12.3 (1161b20-28) — 451
8.12.3-4 (1161b30-1162a2); — 447
8.12.6 (1162a9-15) — 447
Politica
1.13 (1260a12-14) — 448
8.12.2-3 [1161b17-29] — 450
8.12.3 [1161b20-28] — 451
Rhetorica
2.12.3 — 443

Cicero
In Pisonem
28 — 466
Pro Cluentio
32-34 — 467
Pro Milone
73 — 466

Clement of Alexandria
Excerpta ex Theodoto
67.2 — 75
Protrepticus
6.70 — 59
Stromata
3.6.45.3; 3.9.64.1 — 75
1.21.141.1-2 — 487
5.14.111,4-6 — 488
5.14.119.2 — 488

Euripides
Andromache
173-175 — 466
Troiades
380-381, 473-488, 503-505, 758-60 — 452

645-653	453
Eusebius	
Praeparatio evangelica	
9.17.1-9	485
9.19.4; 9.21.1	487
9.22.1-11	476
9.28.4c	483
9.29.1-3, 15, 16	487
13.13.38	488
13.13.45-6	488
Heliodorus	
1.9.3 – 10.4; 11.9.1	443
Herodotus	
Histories	
1.67-68	473
1.199	80
Hesiod	
Opera et dies 328-329	466
Homer	463
Ilias 9	466
Odyssea	
6.182-184	471
9.215	483
Protoevangelium of James	
10:1	99
13:1	232, 338
Josephus	
Jewish Antiquities	
1.162-165	486
1.337-340	482, 483
1.337	478, 479
2.250-252	488
4.126-130	274
4.212	60
4.290-291	468
5.306	285
8.45-49	415
12.106	60
12.138-146	245
12.241	247
13.291-292	112, 503
14.258	60
15.319-322	25

17.169-172	6, 24
Jewish War	
1.477	25
1.656-58	6
2.128	60
2.136	415
2.161	467
Against Apion	463
2.190-219	156, 463
2.199-202	60, 470
2.199, 215	462
2.201, 205	59
2.202	467
2.270-271	468
Laudatio Turiae	
1.10	453
Musonius Rufus	
Frag. 12	61, 462
Ovid	
Ars Amatoria	
3.613-615	453
Metamorphoses	
9.733-734	470
Pap. Insinger	
6.8-19	462
Philo	
De Abrahamo	
96-98	486
De Cherubim	
14-17	232
92	421
De Confusione Linguarum	
46	421
De Congressu	
74	415, 418
De Decalogo	
52-81	419
121	461
De Gigantibus	
51	421
De Opificio	
30	445
132	414
134-135	86
De Sacrificiis	
21-26	418

De Specialibus Legibus	
3.9, 79, 113	470
3.13	78
3.22-25	466
3.29	100
3.31	465
3.32	469
3.43-50	468
3.65-71	472
3.110-119	60
4:14	418
De Virtutibus	
225	466
De Vita Contemplativa	
27, 89	60
68	418
De Vita Mosis	
1.294-299	274
Hypothetica	463
7.1-9	156, 464
7.1	59, 462, 470
7.7	60, 467, 468
Legum Allegoriae	
1.43-55	445
2.44-50	448, 468
3.32	466
3.118	445
Migratione Abrahami	
225	482
Plato	
Gorgias 504D	445
Leges	
636C	61
836C	470, 506
838A-B	466
840E	421
Symposium 208E	408
Theaetetus 149D	467
Timaeus 69c-72d, 86c	176
Plutarch	
Bruta animalia	
990D-F	61, 470
Cicero 29.4-5	466
De amore prolis	
1 – 3 (*Mor.* 493B-496A)	
	449
3 (*Mor.* 495D-496C)	450
3 (*Mor.* 495E-496B)	448
	450

3 (*Mor.* 496A, C) 451
De liberis educandis
5 [*Mor.* 3D] 450, 451
Mulierum virtutes
Mor. 240C-263C 451
De Stoicorum repugnantiis
1044F 433
De tuenda sanitate
134F 467

Pseudo-Justin
De Monarchia 4 488

Pseudo-Heraclitus
Epistolae 7.5 467

Seneca
Ad Helviam 16:3-4 467
Ad Marciam
7.2 448
16.7-9 452
De Matrimonio 85 61, 470

Sophocles
Antigone 595 472

Strabo
Geographica 16.1 81

Suetonius
Domitianus 7.1 468

Theognis
Elegiae 183-188 472

Gospel of Thomas
114 313

Virgil
Eclogae 4.61 452

Xenophon
Oeconomicus
7.24 451
10.1 451
Cyropaedia 8.7.14 447

Xenophon of Ephesus
2.5.1-7 443

RABBINIC LITERATURE

Mishnah
Makkot 1.6 229
Sotah 1.5 228
Tamid 1.1 347

Tosefta
Sotah 15.10 265

Babylonian Talmud
Baba Batra 60b 265
Rosh ha-Shanah 11a 276
Shabbat 39a 22
Sotah 12a 269

Midrash Rabbah
Genesis Rabbah
17:5 70
20:7 340
23:2 261
57:4; 76:9 119
80:1-2 453, 478, 482, 510
Exodus Rabbah
1:24 269

Targum Ps.-Jonathan
Gen. 4:1 454
Job 2:9. 110, 119

Pirqe de-Rabbi Eliezer
21 454

Zohar
Shemoth 9a-9b 30